TOWARD A PENTECOSTAL THEOLOGY
OF PROPHETIC LEGITIMACY

Toward a Pentecostal Theology of Prophetic Legitimacy

Mark J. Chironna

CPT Press
Cleveland, Tennessee

Toward a Pentecostal Theology of Prophetic Legitimacy

Published by CPT Press
900 Walker ST NE
Cleveland, TN 37311
USA
email: cptpress@pentecostaltheology.org
website: www.cptpress.com

ISBN: 978-1-953358-43-1

Copyright © 2024 CPT Press

All rights reserved. No part of this book may be reproduced or translated in any form, by print, photoprint, microfilm, microfiche, electronic database, internet database, or any other means without written permission from the publisher.

This work is dedicated to my father,
Frank Chironna (1921–2003),
whose influence has left an indelible imprint on my
consciousness and perception from a perspective of the
prophetic, the scholarly, and the love of study.

Contents

List of Figures	ix
Acknowledgments	x
Abbreviations	xi

Introduction — 1

Chapter 1
Popular Function in Independent Pentecostalism — 4
- 1.2 Popular Prophetic Praxis in Pentecostalism — 6
- 1.3 Methodology — 25
- 1.4 Conclusion — 69

Chapter 2
Old Testament Prophetic Legitimacy — 71
- 2.1 Introduction — 71
- 2.2 Moses: Primary Prototype and Paradigmatic Prophet — 73
- 2.3 Samuel: Transitional and Archetypal Prophet — 88
- 2.4 Elijah and Elisha: Prefiguring John the Baptist and Jesus — 99
- 2.5 Conclusion — 131

Chapter 3
New Testament Prophetic Legitimacy — 133
- 3.1 Introduction — 133
- 3.2 John the Baptist — 138
- 3.3 Agabus — 149
- 3.4 Paul — 160
- 3.5 Jesus as Prophet — 179

Chapter 4
Latter Rain Participant Violet Kiteley as Exemplar of Prophetic Legitimacy — 193
- 4.1 Introduction — 193
- 4.2 Introducing Violet Kiteley to the Latter Rain Story — 196
- 4.3 Latter Rain Restorationism — 205

4.4 Framing the Prophetic Presbytery — 218
4.5 Kiteley's Hermeneutic as a Latter Rain Pentecostal — 230
4.6 Risks within the Schema of Latter Rain Restorationism — 232
4.7 Violet Kiteley and Prophetic Legitimacy — 245

Chapter 5
Constructing a Pentecostal Theology of Prophetic Legitimacy — 249
5.1 Introduction — 249
5.2 Advancing Themes of Prophetic Legitimacy — 258
5.3 Summary Remarks — 311

Appendix: Cited Violet Kiteley Papers — 313

Bibliography — 366
Index of Biblical (and Other Ancient) References — 390
Index of Authors — 398

LIST OF FIGURES

Figure 1: The Divine Nature   214
Figure 2: Summary of Spiritual Senses   215
Figure 3: The Hand Ministry   216
Figure 4: The Prophetic Ethic   309

Acknowledgements

This work was copy edited for conventions of language, spelling, and grammar by Donna Scuderi.

ABBREVIATIONS

BAGD	Walter Bauer, William F. Arndt, F. William Gingrich, and Frederick W. Danker, *A Greek–English Lexicon of the New Testament and Other Early Christian Literature* (Chicago: University of Chicago Press, 2nd edn, 1958).
BDB	Francis Brown, Samuel Rolles Driver, and Charles Augustus Briggs (eds.), *Enhanced Brown-Driver-Briggs Hebrew and English Lexicon* (Oxford: Clarendon Press, 1977).
GEL	Johannes P. Louw and Eugene Albert Nida, (eds.), *Greek-English Lexicon of the New Testament Based on Semantic Domains* (New York: United Bible Societies, 1996).
JPTSup	Journal of Pentecostal Theology Supplement Series
JSOTSup	Journal of Study of Old Testament Supplement Series
LXX	The Septuagint Version (Rahlfs)
NASB	New American Standard Bible
NIDPCM	Burgess, S.M., *et al.* (eds.), *The New International Dictionary of Pentecostal and Charismatic Movements* (Grand Rapids, MI: Zondervan, rev edn, 2002).
NKJV	New King James Version
NRSV	New Revised Standard Version
Pneuma	*Pneuma: The Journal of the Society for Pentecostal Studies*
TDOT	G.J. Botterweck and H. Ringgren (eds.), *Theological Dictionary of the Old Testament* (15 vols.; Grand Rapids, MI: Baker, 1974-2004).
TWOT	R. Laird Harris, Gleason L. Archer Jr., and Bruce K. Waltke (eds.), *Theological Wordbook of the Old Testament* (2 vols.; Chicago, IL: Moody Press, 1999).

INTRODUCTION

There is a crisis of prophetic function in Independent Pentecostalism; it has therefore become necessary to construct a Pentecostal theology of prophetic legitimacy, one which is biblically, theologically, and psychologically/phenomenologically grounded.[1] The goal of this work is not merely to highlight the crisis in prophetic legitimacy but to propose practical recommendations favorable to a more catholic, robust, accountable, and authentic Pentecostal theology of prophetic legitimacy.

To that end, the first chapter of this work begins with a description and analysis of common questionable prophetic practices in Independent Pentecostalism, then enumerates five functional issues that detrimentally impact prophetic function and expression, arguing that these corrosive conditions damage the integrity and witness of the prophetic movement and compromise its ability to contribute positively to the church and her mission.

The second chapter considers four salient OT figures who circumscribe an understanding of prophetic legitimacy: Moses, whose call encounter with the divine presence at the burning bush provides a foundational framework from which to consider the capacity for divine revelation within human nature; Samuel, in whom the prophet and seer coalesce, and whose call encounter marks an archetypal shift in the relations among prophets, priests, and kings and their ministries;[2] Elijah, whose temperament impacts his prophetic function;

---

[1] Because these various disciplines are essential to this work, I will interact with an array of Pentecostal scholars and theologians, as well as theologians from other Christian traditions, and with scholars in cognitive, analytic, and transpersonal psychology and hermeneutic phenomenology.

[2] Samuel is considered precisely because of the coalescing of *prophet* and *seer* at this point in Israelite history. The significance of this, while underplayed by some scholars as a mere editorial insert, will be argued as an important interrelation

and Elisha, who by virtue of what he experiences points the way toward a mature way of perceiving. The stories of these definitive prophets will be examined theologically, psychologically, and phenomenologically to construct a further argument favoring a Pentecostal theology of prophetic legitimacy. As such, the issues of prophetic consciousness, perception, and enactment will be considered paramount.

The third chapter engages prophetic function in light of key NT figures including Zechariah, John the Baptist, Agabus, Paul, and Jesus. The prophetic and teaching presbytery Luke mentions in Acts 13, which includes Saul of Tarsus, will also be noted, as will the four daughters of Philip.

The fourth chapter introduces Violet Kiteley, a seminal figure in the Pentecostal tradition and an eyewitness from the beginning of the Latter Rain movement in North Battleford, Saskatchewan. While Peter Althouse, William Faupel, and others do not mention Kiteley in their works, she was indeed a key figure in Latter Rain history. Her notes, journals, teachings, and courses have been collected and digitally assembled. I will use them to argue for the construction of a Pentecostal theology of prophetic legitimacy rooted in prophetic consciousness, perception, and enactment. Kiteley's understanding of the Lukan narrative is foundational to her part in this conversation. Due to her historical context and approach to a movement widely considered to be controversial, she can serve as an exemplar of prophetic legitimacy.

In the final chapter, I will offer a pathway to the construction of a Pentecostal theology of prophetic legitimacy that minds issues of prophetic consciousness, perception, and enactment from a multidisciplinary perspective, integrating theological, psychological, and

---

between the functions of consciousness, perception, and enactment that are involved both at a communal level (between the prophetic agent and the community) and a personal level (between the prophetic agent and supplicants who seek out the prophetic agent's assistance). This too becomes significant considering the gathering of prophetic types in guilds known as the 'sons of the prophets' (1 Sam. 10.5, 10; 19.18-24; 2 Kgs 2.1-7, 15). This idea finds its initial expression in the Samuel texts where he creates a center at Ramah for their training, instruction, and support. Such prophetic guilds prefigure the disciples and the church as the fulfillment of Peter's allegorical usage of the term 'sons of the prophets' post Pentecost (Acts 3.25 NASB). These considerations will pave the way for the NT consideration of Christ as the fulfillment of the prophet, priest, and king of the new Israel's story.

phenomenological insights into a holistic vision of prophetic ministry. The intersection between the divine Spirit and human interiority demands deeper exploration. Within this construct, I will argue for a reforming of prophetic function in light of the Triune Life and what Paul refers to as 'the fellowship of his Son' (1 Cor. 1.9).

1

POPULAR PROPHETIC FUNCTION IN INDEPENDENT PENTECOSTALISM

Prophetic function and expression hold a prominent place in Pentecostalism's emphasis on spiritual gifts and direct interaction between God and his people. The sense of immediacy attending this interaction is an earmark of Pentecostal life and praxis. However, because it is mediated through the flaws and biases of human subjectivity, the understanding and interpretation of this immediacy can be easily distorted.

Within Independent Pentecostalism, the focus on direct encounter has led to a proliferation of individuals with self-authenticated ('God told me') prophetic claims and utterances. This has yielded a wholesale collapse into subjectivity and a gap between faithful prophetic consciousness and internal perception. Behind this gap are deep theological weaknesses, psychological distortions, and phenomenological occurrences, all of which reinforce the subjective bent in personal intentionality. What is highly questionable can no longer be questioned because there is no distance between self-authentication and divine sanction.

It therefore becomes imperative to explore the theological, psychological, and phenomenological foundations of prophetic legitimacy to include a more profound understanding of prophetic consciousness. This requires both a Christology and a pneumatology that issue from sound Trinitarian doctrine and a Pentecostal hermeneutic upholding the indivisible connectedness of Christ, the Spirit, and the Scriptures. Without this, there can be no prophetic legitimacy.

Regarding prophetic legitimacy, this chapter will examine the lack of answerability and accountability within Independent Pentecostalism and demonstrate the impact on orthodoxy, orthopraxy, and orthopathy of (1) a deficient methodology for scriptural interpretation, and (2) an inadequate comprehension of the Triune God. I will also illuminate certain pitfalls that constrain authentic prophetic function and expression.

In the current climate of prophetic exuberance and enthusiasm, and due to a number of questionable realities inherent in the post-denominational environment, many prophetic agents consider their words to be above question, albeit without the benefit of scrutiny, evaluation, and critique.[1] Individual claims of divine authority reveal conflicting norms and values. These inconsistencies contradict the ethics of Jesus and the principles upheld by ancient orthodoxy, orthopraxy, and orthopathy. They also mark prophetic expression with personal cognitive biases, the cognitive dissonance of conspiratorial thinking, and the privatization of prophetic utterances on social media that disregard scriptural injunctions for the giving and receiving of utterances within the context of a local church and legitimate eldership.

The chapter begins with a description and analysis of common questionable prophetic practices in Independent Pentecostalism, and it enumerates five functional issues that detrimentally impact prophetic function and expression: the projection of presumption (biases); the presumption of unmediated prophetic utterances; ambiguous community responsibility to the truth; the erosion of personal answerability among claimants of prophetic authority; and a diminished sense of keeping covenant. These corrosive conditions weaken the integrity of the prophetic movement and compromise its ability to contribute positively to the community.

As to methodology, the literary critical approach is rooted within a Pentecostal hermeneutic and a canonical approach, which underpin the methodologies employed. I intentionally emphasize the

---

[1] Rhetorical ploys serve to discredit in advance any disconfirmation of failed prophetic utterances. Statements by prophetic agents such as 'I am just observing, not making a judgment' or 'Notice this [or that diagnosis]' lay blame on the larger church's failure to believe what is prophesied, thus transferring attention and correction from the enactment's fundamental flaws to the hearers' deficient reception. Objectively and scientifically, this is demagoguery.

Pentecostal hermeneutic, which is essential to the interplay between the Holy Spirit and the text, the mind of the interpreter and the text, and the greater community and the text. Thus, the work addresses Pentecostal notions of revelation and authority, measuring specific teachings and practices against Pentecostal scholarship.

Within the domains of psychology and the text, I will examine prophetic enthusiasm and the role of technology, the concept of 'activation', and enactments within prophetic ministry that threaten legitimacy. Phenomenological concerns involving personal, intrapersonal, interpersonal, and transpersonal prophetic interactions will shed light on experiential dimensions of prophetic legitimacy.

The goal of this work is not merely to highlight the crisis in prophetic legitimacy but to propose practical recommendations favorable to a more catholic, robust, accountable, and authentic Pentecostal theology of prophetic legitimacy. Therefore, this chapter will propose a threefold Pentecostal theology of prophetic legitimacy, clarify terminology, and examine prophetic consciousness. To provide a theological framework for evaluating prophetic function, I will introduce three dyads – love of God and love of neighbor, truth and falsehood, and the apprehension and acceptance of prophetic intimations – that are integrally related to prophetic legitimacy and the complex dynamics in play.

1.2 Popular Prophetic Praxis in Independent Pentecostalism

Typical prophetic practices within Independent Pentecostalism raise a variety of theological, pastoral, and ethical concerns. The same is true of the functional approaches that shape and decide those practices. Responding wisely and effectively to these concerns requires critical and constructive theological reflection on the following matters in particular:
- expression of unconscious bias, also known as 'implicit or cognitive bias';[2]

---

[2] Pamela Fuller, Mark Murphy, and Anne Chow, *The Leader's Guide to Unconscious Bias: How to Reframe Bias, Cultivate Connection, and Create High-Performing Teams* (New York: Simon & Schuster, 2020), p. 5. 'We have unconscious biases around gender, race, job function, personality, age/generation, socioeconomic status, sexual

- presentation of 'stream of consciousness' rhetoric;[3]
- the rhetorical praxis of demagoguery;[4]
- conflation of Christian nationalism or some other specific political perspective with the gospel;[5]
- dissemination of false, disputed, or unverifiable truth claims;
- use of esoteric language known only to in-group initiates;
- reliance on proof-texting and other exegetical fallacies.[6]

---

orientation, gender identity, family status, nationality, language ability, veteran status, culture, weight, height, physical ability, attractiveness, political affiliation, virtual/remote working, hair color – even the messiness of someone's desk or their posture'. Fuller, Murphy, and Chow, *Leader's Guide*, p. 5. Such biases are influential and can have a 'positive, benign, or negative impact' (p. 5). Considering human subjectivity, the presence of unconscious bias in prophetic expression needs to be discerned, acknowledged, and disowned. These biases can suppress tolerance for people and groups and can result in some people being 'ignored ... slighted, even harassed or abused' (p. 9).

[3] William James, 'The Stream of Consciousness', *Classics in the History of Psychology*, https://psychclassics.yorku.ca/James/jimmy11.htm.

[4] Patricia Roberts-Miller *Rhetoric and Demagoguery* (Carbondale, IL: Southern Illinois University Press, 2019), p. 1, challenges the notion that 'demagoguery is conventionally thought of as a separate category from normal political discourse, and as something a certain kind of person does'. The challenge is not necessarily related to the issues of 'vehemence, nastiness, populism, and bad motives', though these expressions can be present in the speech and thinking of individuals. She argues that demagoguery needs to be 'thought of as a way of participating in public discourse', which therefore is larger than the presence of an individual or leader at the helm of a movement. Rather, it is 'a way that can become the norm in a culture that is profoundly identity-driven' (pp. 1-2). The endgame of this dynamic leads to reductionism in the exchange of thoughts and ideas, producing 'an in-group (good) and out-group (bad)' perspective (p. 2). For that reason, Roberts-Miller concludes, 'demagoguery is a continuum, and neither an identity nor a discrete category' (p. 2). In relation to the Pentecostal culture where politically partisan prophetic utterances are rife, demagoguery is alive and well. The danger is evident in its claims of divine authority. This is especially worrying in respect to the purpose of prophetic function within the context of the Christian Tradition.

[5] Christian nationalism and its variant, Christian Americanism, are gaining influence in Pentecostal and other churches. Often the focus on political interests is presumed to arise from the gospel message, being both presented and embraced as (pseudo-)doctrinal mandates. In this context, the profession of political views is often demagogic and compelling, shifting the community's primary allegiance from Christ and his kingdom to temporal 'kings' and countries.

[6] Among the exegetical fallacies in evidence are: 'Semantic Anachronism – Reading a more recent meaning of a word back into earlier literature ... Appeal to Unknown or Unlikely Meanings – Appealing to a word meaning in order to suit a theological perspective for which there is little or no lexical/semantic substance to support the meaning ... Verbal Parallelomania – Claiming verbal or conceptual

In what follows, I will seek to diagnose these problems through an ongoing process of biblical, theological, and psychological reflection, and then offer an alternative view of prophetic consciousness, agency, and function. This will be done through careful exegesis of Scripture in conversation with the wisdom of the broad Christian dogmatic and spiritual Tradition, as well as the wisdom gleaned from the fields of transpersonal psychology and phenomenology. These three domains will be considered in an interrelated way.

1.2.1 Five Functional Issues

1.2.1.1 The Projection of Presumption

1.2.1.1.1 Theological Reflections
The danger attending the projection of presumption lies in the often-unspoken agreement to accept and endorse prophetic speech acts, not through an accountability process, but through an unchallenged presumption of legitimacy. Although the projection of presumption is a largely psychological feature, its theological implications can suggest a lack or underdevelopment of what Amos Yong calls a 'coherent theology of the Spirit'.[7] Also possibly lacking is a pneuma-

---

links and even dependency of meaning based on parallels alone, being selective in using certain parallels to establish meaning, or seeing parallels in every occurrence of a word … Selective and Prejudicial Use of Evidence – Appealing to certain evidence in a selective way that justifies a particular view while ignoring or dismissing all other evidence … False Disjunctions – Permitting the acceptance of only an either/or position on an idea so as to make the various sides of an argument mutually exclusive when such a logical constraint need not be imposed on them … Over-simplified Logic Ruling – Assuming the validity of a proposition simply on account of an explanation that is merely deemed to be 'logical'. What is claimed to be 'logical' may or may not be actually logically true'. Jerry Wierwille, 'An Overview of Exegetical Fallacies', *Study Driven Faith* (December 15, 2016), http://studydrivenfaith.org/2016/12/an-overview-of-exegetical-fallacies/.

Observing the content of these 'prophetic' declarations and the Independent tribes generating them, there is a sense of diminished institutional structure. This seems evident in the lack of theological and philosophical structure in the prophesying itself. There does not seem to be a clear understanding of how to read the Scriptures. I recognize that this critique of the movement assumes a framework that many in the movement seem not to assume. Concerns with exegetical fallacies seem nonsensical in Third Wave (or wave/type) churches precisely because a proper and/or informed methodology for interpreting the text is wanting. Therefore, the misreading of Scripture leads to erroneous applications and conclusions.

[7] Amos Yong, 'What Spirit(s), Which Public(s)?: The Pneumatologies of Global Pentecostal-Charismatic Christianity', *International Journal of Public Theology* 7.3 (January 2013), p. 242.

tological understanding of discernment within the human experience.[8] These deficiencies remove the grounds by which speech acts are vetted.

1.2.1.1.2 Psychological and Phenomenological Reflections
The primary concern raised by typical Independent Pentecostal prophetic praxis is the projected presumption that (1) the agent is speaking on behalf of the divine Spirit, and (2) the agent's speech is therefore exempt from being questioned or critiqued. Personal subjectivity (a psychological acknowledgment of unconscious bias) may also be lacking.[9]

Although these tendencies can coexist with sincerity and good intentions, they are not exempt from correction and guidance. To be fair, projections of presumption can be inadvertent, as all people tend to operate in whatever has formed them, whether didactically or in praxis. (This suggests that during their training and formation agents never questioned what they learned but only ratified it, cementing their formation in misunderstanding or error). It is also possible that in the exuberance of prophetic utterance, agents inadvertently ignore appropriate constraints.

Intentional projections of presumption are equally possible and can erode the distinctions between genuine prophetic function and uninspired streams of consciousness. Equally concerning are the influence that agents exert and the power differentials that claims of divine unction create. Supporters can become enamored of those in authority. Therefore, unquestioned reliance on prophetic speech can cause damaging repercussions for the prophetic agent, her/his community, and others outside the community.[10]

Because those who receive prophetic messages are the endpoint of such communication, we cannot discount their experiences. The

---

[8] This characteristic is not strictly confined to the Independent Pentecostalism being discussed, but has been attributed to a previous wave, according to Peter Hocken, 'Charismatic Movement', *NIDPCM*, p. 517. He notes,

> [the Charismatic Movement] has always been strong on faith-affirmation and short on critical reflection … While the need for discernment is widely recognized, charismatic discernment is mostly intuitive and generally lacks an adequate underlying theology, particularly of the relationship between the working of the Holy Spirit and the functioning of the various layers of the human spirit.

[9] The issue here is *humility*, a good theological term, as is the term *sobriety* (i.e. regarding prophetic consciousness).

[10] These repercussions can be direct and indirect in the short and long term.

projection of presumption, whether it functions as a conscious or unconscious Gestalt, is embodied by both messenger and recipient. Therefore, the attitude of presumption becomes engrained in the community.[11]

1.2.1.2 The Presumption That Prophetic Utterance is Unmediated

A second presumption suggested by common practices in the post-denominational world of Independent Pentecostalism is both theological and philosophical and flows from the first presumption. It is the notion that an agent's impressions, intuitions, and 'words' are 'downloaded' from the Spirit in pristine condition. That is, they are received without any of the mediation that is inherent in the human experience of unconscious or implicit bias, personal history, cognitive function (including memory, reflection, reasoning, intuition, and imagination), the will, or the somatic realities of embodiment – all of which are involved from a psychological perspective.[12] This view of how the Spirit conveys insight suggests a divisible mind-body connection, as though certain human impressions and intuitions pass through a dedicated revelatory pathway that is segregated from the recipient's embodied humanity. I would argue that such a notion defies the human condition.

---

[11] 'Projection', *APA Dictionary of Psychology*, https://dictionary.apa.org/ projection:

> In psychoanalytic and psychodynamic theories, [is] the process by which one attributes one's own individual positive or negative characteristics, affects, and impulses to another person or group. This is often a defense mechanism in which unpleasant or unacceptable impulses, stressors, ideas, affects, or responsibilities are attributed to others ... In classical psychoanalytic theory, projection permits the individual to avoid seeing his or her own faults, but modern usage has largely abandoned the requirement that the projected trait remain unknown in the self.

'Transference', *APA Dictionary of Psychology*, https://dictionary.apa.org/ transference:

> In psychoanalysis, [transference is] a patient's displacement or projection onto the analyst of those unconscious feelings and wishes originally directed toward important individuals, such as parents, in the patient's childhood. It is posited that this process brings repressed material to the surface where it can be reexperienced, studied, and worked through ... The term's broader meaning – an unconscious repetition of earlier behaviors and their projection onto new subjects – is acknowledged as applying to all human interactions.

[12] 'Download' is a popularly-used term signifying the receipt of divine intimations, by Christians generally and by prophetic agents specifically.

How can one reconcile this presumption with the reality of personal subjectivity and with Paul's admonition that 'the spirits of prophets are *subject* to the prophets?' (1 Cor. 14.32, emphasis added).[13] The problem seems to be both psychological and theological. I would suggest that both disciplines be considered when coming to terms with prophetic expression in global Pentecostalism.

1.2.1.2.1 Biblical Reflections
If the Corinth community's unrestrained prophetic expression was linked to privilege or status, might building a following in current church culture be similarly connected? Further, how would privilege or status conflict with Thiselton's main concern 'that prophetic speech, like speaking in tongues, *remains subject to the ethics of controlled speech,* even if it necessitates a critical awareness of what one is doing?'[14] Thiselton's statement suggests that danger exists when these ethics are violated by overly enthusiastic prophetic types who lack the self-reflective awareness (SRA) to distinguish their subjectivity from the Spirit's authentic workings through a self-regulatory process of human agency.[15] This challenge has existed throughout church history. In dealing with 1 Cor. 14.32, Wesley expresses his concern over the failure to heed Paul's admonition:

> *For the spirits of the prophets are subject to the prophets* – But what enthusiast considers this? The impulses of the Holy Spirit, even in men really inspired, so suit themselves to their rational faculties, as not to divest them of the government of themselves, like the heathen priests under their diabolical possession. Evil spirits threw their prophets into such ungovernable ecstasies, as forced

---

[13] To be *subject to* is 'to submit to the orders or directives of someone – "to obey, to submit to, obedience, submission"' (*GEL*). Such submission is a conscious and voluntary act.

[14] Anthony C. Thiselton, *The First Epistle to the Corinthians: A Commentary on the Greek Text* (New International Greek Testament Commentary; Grand Rapids, MI: Eerdmans, 2000), p. 1143.

[15] 'SRA is a "meta-cognitive" ability, meaning that it involves thinking about and reflecting on one's own mental processes. Someone with good SRA is able to generate a narrative of self that is complex, clear, and multifaceted and is able to communicate that narrative in a way that allows others a much better understanding of where one is coming from.' Gregg Henriques, 'Self-Reflective Awareness: A Crucial Life Skill', *Psychology Today* (September 10, 2016), https://www.psychologytoday.com/us/blog/theory-knowledge/201609/self-reflective-awareness-crucial-life-skill. See 1.1.2.2.2.3.

them to speak and act like madmen. But the Spirit of God left his prophets the clear use of their judgment, when, and how long, it was fit for them to speak, and never hurried them into any improprieties either as to the matter, manner, or time of their speaking.[16]

Wesley's eighteenth-century insights concur with contemporary psychological research on intention and motivation in relation to self-regulation. Thus, his concern over the 'enthusiast's' failure to self-regulate remains valid.[17]

In contemporary praxis, the greater challenge might be in recognizing Paul's audience, specifically, believers in particular ecclesial households. Leaders charged with overseeing prospective prophetic agents can observe and safeguard appropriate boundaries and parameters. However, in the social media environment, the boundaries of functional ecclesial households are nonexistent. Therefore, restraint collapses and is unenforced in relation to SRA. With expression of the so-called prophetic exempt from oversight, the lure of a larger following can generate cognitive distortions (i.e. 'faulty or inaccurate thinking, perception[s], or belief[s]')[18] that impact motivations and dilute (or pollute) the integrity of prophetic expression.

1.2.1.2.2 Theological Reflections

From a Christological perspective, the theological significance of what Abraham Maslow termed 'full-humanness' is noteworthy.[19] Theologically, to be fully human is impossible apart from the cruciform process of transformation in one's interiority through the work of the Spirit. By it, the Spirit brings regenerated partakers of the divine nature into the 'maturity' Paul describes as 'the measure of the full stature of Christ' (Eph. 4.13). Paul suggests that this transformation is a co-crucifixion of the individual with Christ through the Christ-event, which keeps intact the sense of 'I' but bonds the ἐγώ,

---

[16] John Wesley, *Explanatory Notes upon the New Testament* (New York: J. Soule and T. Mason, 4th edn, 1818), p. 454.

[17] John Wesley, *The Works of John Wesley* (London: Wesleyan Methodist Book Room, 3rd edn, 1872), IV, pp. 469-70.

[18] 'Cognitive Distortion', *APA Dictionary of Psychology*, https://dictionary.apa.org/cognitive-distortion.

[19] Abraham H. Maslow, *Toward a Psychology of Being* (Floyd, VA: Sublime Books, 2014), p. 5.

ἐμοῦ to Christ.[20] The ἐγώ, ἐμοῦ is not dissolved but transformed, which seems congruent with the notion that 'the testimony [μαρτυρία] of Jesus is the spirit of prophecy' (Rev. 19.10).[21]

Regarding the disconnect between the reality of personal subjectivity and claims of unmediated prophetic utterance, how might one reconcile the limitations of human knowing with divine truth and mystery? Paul's writing seems to indicate that our knowing involves experiential learning.[22] Yet, Paul deems such learning (ἐκ μέρους) to be partial and incomplete.[23] As such, prophesying reveals its own limitations, and even divinely inspired speech is incomplete and subject to judgment (ἀνακρίνω) that demands ongoing 'learning and understanding'.[24] The continuing course correction that the fully accomplished τέλειος implies is an eschatological hope.[25] This 'fullness of time' and gathering of all things in Christ is held in the dialectical tension between the *now* and the *not yet* (Eph. 1.10). Until then, imperfections involving prophetic function (and all of life) remain.

1.2.1.2.3 Psychological (and Ethical) Reflections

For Thiselton, Paul's admonition is an ethical one. For those who argue as to whether all are capable of prophesying, Thiselton's approach is distinct:

> The dispute here is not whether all or some may prophesy; it is whether **everyone** who has the gift of using prophetic speech also

---

[20] As in Gal. 2:20, 'I' is ἐγώ, 'a reference to the speaker (with an added feature of emphasis in the form ἐγώ) – "I, I indeed"', *GEL*, p. 813.

[21] *GEL*, p. 418: the Greek μαρτυρία is a derivative of μαρτυρέω 'to witness' referring to 'the content of what is witnessed or said – "testimony, witness"', 'μαρτυρία'. The tenor of the text seems to imply that the μαρτυρία is cruciform.

[22] *GEL*, p. 382: from γινώσκω, meaning 'to come to an understanding as the result of ability to experience and learn – "to come to understand, to perceive, to comprehend"'.

[23] Paul's intent is conveyed by ἐκ μέρους, an idiom that 'literally [means] "from a part") the state of being part of something – "being part of, as a part of, in part, partially ... [as in] ... "you are the body of Christ and each member is a part of it" or " ... and each one is a part of the body" 1 Cor 12:27', 'ἐκ μέρους', *GEL*, p. 615.

[24] 'The meanings of κρίνω (30.108), ἀνακρίνω and διακρίνω (30.109) are all closely related to the process of learning and of understanding, and in some contexts the meanings shade one into the other'. *GEL*, pp. 363-64.

[25] *GEL*, p. 746: the Greek τέλειος, 'pertaining to that which is fully accomplished or finished – "complete, finished" [as in] ἡ δὲ ὑπομονὴ ἔργον τέλειον ἐχέτω "but be sure that patience completes its work" Jas 1:4'.

has the reflective and critical self-awareness and control to begin and especially **to stop** (v. 30) when the circumstances which are going on outside the speaker's immediate prophetic awareness warrant it.[26]

Notice that Thiselton sees personal subjectivity as inseparable from 'reflective and critical self-awareness'.[27] Within the field of psychology, the domain of self-reflective awareness is related to cognitive processes intricately involved with self-regulation. Contemporary SRA research now considers 'the ways in which people manage their motivational states in the service of achieving valued goals'.[28] Ridley confirms this and characterizes 'a new conceptual model of self-regulation, *reflective intentionality*, in which motivation to act is based heavily on one's conception of self'.[29] This involves 'higher order processes – specifically reflective self-awareness, emotion, and volition'.[30]

Thiselton's observations of the Pauline passage concur with contemporary psychological research in that the prophet governs her/his spirit and can cease prophesying at the appropriate moment(s). For Thiselton, one of those moments comes 'when the circumstances which are going on *outside* the speaker's *immediate prophetic awareness* warrant it'.[31] Recent findings within psychology and SRA (self-reflective awareness) suggest a relationship between reflective awareness and the motivation behind the intent to prophesy. Ridley clearly states, 'Motivation is not viewed as something that operates independent of the self, but instead is seen as one dimension of the self-regulatory process'.[32]

How might this apply to the liberties some enthusiastic agents take? Have some been driven by the feeling Thiselton describes:

> that they were so privileged by their own status as to be *either consciously unwilling or allegedly unable* to stop, on the ground that God

---

[26] Thiselton, *First Epistle*, p. 1143.
[27] Thiselton, *First Epistle*, p. 1143.
[28] Abigail A. Scholer, *et al.*, 'New Directions in Self-Regulation: The Role of Metamotivational Beliefs', *Current Directions in Psychological Science* 27.6 (2018), p. 437.
[29] D. Scott Ridley, 'Reflective Self-Awareness: A Basic Motivational Process', *Journal of Experimental Education* 60.1 (Fall 1991), p. 31 (emphasis added).
[30] Ridley, 'Reflective Self-Awareness', p. 31.
[31] Thiselton, *First Epistle*, p. 1143 (emphasis added).
[32] Ridley, 'Reflective Self-Awareness', p. 31.

had seized and overwhelmed them by his Spirit, and the Spirit must not be hindered?[33]

From a psychological perspective, the relationship between SRA and motive can be connected to other important dynamics, including the social container that shapes the collective psyche. In his seminal work on narcissism in the American culture,[34] Christopher Lasch offers profound insight into the collective psyche. He addresses 'the therapeutic sensibility',[35] stating, 'the contemporary climate is therapeutic, not religious'.[36] He further explains, 'people today hunger not for personal salvation, let alone for the restoration of an earlier golden age, but for the feeling, the momentary illusion, of personal well-being, health, and psychic security'.[37] Lasch says this in light of the 'radicalism of the sixties',[38] which many 'embraced … not as a substitute religion but as a form of therapy'.[39]

Following this radicalism, 'new therapies [were] spawned by the human potential movement',[40] possibly influenced by Carl Rogers, Rollo May, Henry Murray, Sydney Jouard, Clark Moustakas, and most influentially, Abraham Maslow. Maslow, who was 'discontented with behaviorism's view of human nature and method, drew on a long tradition linking psychology with humanities'.[41] His controversial interest in 'self actualization' emerged within the humanistic approach to psychology.[42] Maslow seems to attribute the controversy to the term's inclusion of the word 'self', which 'seems to put people off',[43] thanks to the 'linguistic habit of identifying "self" with being

---

[33] Thiselton, *First Epistle*, p. 1143.
[34] Christopher Lasch, *The Culture of Narcissism: American Life in an Age of Diminishing Expectations* (New York: W.W. Norton, 1979).
[35] Lasch, *Culture of Narcissism*, p. 4.
[36] Lasch, *Culture of Narcissism*, p. 4.
[37] Lasch, *Culture of Narcissism*, p. 4.
[38] Lasch, *Culture of Narcissism*, p. 4.
[39] Lasch, *Culture of Narcissism*, p. 4. From a theological perspective, this could perhaps be seen as a loss of the sense of the transcendent, which can have profound consequences for the psyche.
[40] Lasch, *Culture of Narcissism*, p. 4.
[41] Roy José DeCarvalho, 'A History of the "Third Force" in Psychology', *Journal of Humanistic Psychology* 30.4 (Fall 1990), pp. 22-23. These individuals 'regarded themselves as a "third force"' within psychology, seeing themselves as 'an alternative to the dominant behaviorist and psychoanalytical orientation' (p. 23).
[42] Maslow, *Psychology of Being*, p. 5.
[43] Maslow, *Psychology of Being*, p. 5.

"selfish" and with pure autonomy'.⁴⁴ Maslow defends his approach by stating, 'self-actualizing people are altruistic, dedicated, self-transcending, social, etc'.⁴⁵ Nevertheless, to 'avoid some of these misunderstandings',⁴⁶ Maslow used the term 'full-humanness' instead.⁴⁷

Regarding the self, Gal. 2.20 challenges contemporary psychological thought. Specifically, the modern notion of ἐγώ, ἐμοῦ needs to be considered in two ways. It is unlikely that the first understanding would capture Paul's sense of the *ego*, which, for the American Psychological Association (APA), is 'the self, particularly the conscious sense of self (Latin, "I")'.⁴⁸ The APA adds, 'in its popular and quasi-technical sense, ego refers to all the psychological phenomena and processes relating to the self and comprising the individual's attitudes, values, and concerns'.⁴⁹

Given that the contemporary understanding of the conscious *self* (or ego) would not include the totality of the 'self', a literary-critical perspective would suggest that Paul's use of ἐγώ, ἐμοῦ likely refers to the *self* within the framework of contemporary psychology, meaning 'the totality of the individual, consisting of all characteristic attributes, conscious and unconscious, mental and physical'.⁵⁰

There remains consideration of the second, more multifaceted implication of *self* and *ego* from a psychological perspective. It seems appropriate in arguing this point to observe the Independent Pentecostal praxis of prophetic exuberance in tandem with the attendant psychological dynamics. Those dynamics and their phenomenological realities need to be discerned in prophetic expressions (specific prophetic utterances) and in the impressions and behaviors associated with what Luke Timothy Johnson calls 'prophetic enactment'.⁵¹

---

⁴⁴ Maslow, *Psychology of Being*, p. 5.
⁴⁵ Maslow, *Psychology of Being*, p. 5. Nevertheless, those 'intelligent and capable psychologists' who opposed Maslow treated his 'empirical description of the characteristics of self-actualizing people' in a manner that conveyed to the larger social-science community that he had (according to his own words) 'arbitrarily invented these characteristics instead of discovering them' (p. 5).
⁴⁶ Maslow, *Psychology of Being*, p. 5.
⁴⁷ Maslow, *Psychology of Being*, p. 5.
⁴⁸ *APA Dictionary of Psychology*, 'Ego', https://dictionary.apa.org/ego.
⁴⁹ *APA Dictionary of Psychology*, 'Ego', https://dictionary.apa.org/ego.
⁵⁰ *APA Dictionary of Psychology*, 'Self', https://dictionary.apa.org/self.
⁵¹ Luke Timothy Johnson, *Prophetic Jesus, Prophetic Church: The Challenge of Luke-Acts to Contemporary Christians* (Grand Rapids, MI: Eerdmans, 2011), pp. 130-65.

All of this can be viewed within the broader, more comprehensive psychological definition of the *self*.[52]

Regarding the term *self*, the American Psychological Association explains,

> apart from its basic reference to personal identity, being, and experience, the term's use in psychology is wide-ranging. According to William James, self can refer either to the person as the target of appraisal (i.e., one introspectively evaluates how one is doing) or to the person as the source of agency (i.e., one attributes the source of regulation of perception, thought, and behavior to one's body or mind).[53]

Approaching the *self* as James did, I will examine prophetic agents' subjectivity in terms of their critical awareness of how they are doing what they are doing, both in the act of prophesying and in preparation for it. I will also consider the source of regulation as it relates to the realities of prophetic consciousness, prophetic perception, and prophetic enactment, all of which are embodied aspects of the prophetic agent's humanness. In addition, I will explore 'the process of individuation' as an aspect of growth in prophetic consciousness, prophetic perception, and prophetic enactment.[54]

---

[52] Although it is possible to consider the secondary definition of *ego* from a psychoanalytic perspective and the work of Freud that generated it, Freudian psychology has its controversies and opponents. As Stephen P. Thornton states regarding Freudian psychoanalytic theory, 'The question of the therapeutic effectiveness of psychoanalysis remains an open and controversial one', Stephen P. Thornton, 'Sigmund Freud (1856–1939)', in James Fieser and Bradley Dowden (eds.), *Internet Encyclopedia of Philosophy*, https://iep.utm.edu/freud/#SH7d. For the reason just stated, a Freudian approach in this work will not be taken; rather, among other approaches, a Jungian approach will be considered in relation to the unconscious and analytical psychology.

[53] *APA Dictionary of Psychology*, 'Self', https://dictionary.apa.org/self.

[54] *APA Dictionary of Psychology*, 'Self', https://dictionary.apa.org/self:

> Jung maintained that the self gradually develops by a process of individuation, which is not complete until late maturity. Alfred Adler identified the self with the individual's lifestyle, the manner in which he or she seeks fulfillment. Karen D. Horney held that one's real self, as opposed to one's idealized self-image, consists of one's unique capacities for growth and development. Gordon W. Allport substituted the word proprium for self and conceived of it as the essence of the individual, consisting of a gradually developing body sense, identity, self-estimate, and set of personal values, attitudes, and intentions. Austrian-born U.S. psychoanalyst Heinz Kohut (1913–1981) used the term to denote the

Also worthy of consideration is the collective consciousness of the culture in which Independent global Pentecostalism exists in the West, and particularly in the United States. Lasch refers to Peter Martin, critic of the narcissism of the Baby Boomer era who stated that teachers of human potential saw 'the individual will [as] all-powerful and totally [determinative of] one's fate'.[55] This modern notion runs counter to the dilatory will articulated by Paul in Romans and Luke in the Emmaus Road account (Rom. 7.19-25; Lk. 24.13-48). From a twenty-first-century perspective, Chuck DeGroat insists that the identical 'vacuousness we see beneath an individual's narcissistic grandiosity can be found at a collective level in American culture'.[56] Regarding the 'fragmentation' underlying the false notion of 'American exceptionalism',[57] DeGroat asserts that it belies the collective nature of the problem.[58] He says, 'It is an *us* problem, not a *them* problem'.[59]

It is difficult to consider examples of prophetic excess while ignoring the effect of such tendencies on our collective consciousness. The enculturation process has infused the church, coinciding with Carl Jung's notion of ego inflation,[60] 'an unconscious psychic condition' Jung saw as an 'expansion of the personality beyond its proper limits by identification with the persona or with an archetype, or in

---

sense of a coherent, stable (yet dynamic) experience of one's individuality, continuity in time and space, autonomy, efficacy, motivation, values, and desires; he believed that this sense emerges through healthy narcissistic development empathically supported by the significant figures in one's early life and that, conversely, narcissistic developmental failure leads to a fragile or incoherent sense of self.

Other psychological considerations of the concept of *self* will not be considered. However, these areas are deserving of work with dialogue partners to integrate the theological with the psychological.

[55] Lasch, *Culture of Narcissism*, p. 9.
[56] Chuck DeGroat, *When Narcissism Comes to Church: Healing Your Community from Emotional and Spiritual Abuse* (Downers Grove, IL: InterVarsity Press 2020), p. 4.
[57] DeGroat, *Narcissism Comes to Church*, p. 4.
[58] DeGroat, *Narcissism Comes to Church*, p. 4.
[59] DeGroat, *Narcissism Comes to Church*, p. 4.
[60] Leon Schlamm, 'Inflation', in David A. Leeming (ed.), *Encyclopedia of Psychology and Religion* (Boston, MA: Springer, 2014). Schlamm cites C.G. Jung, *Nietzsche's Zarathustra: Notes of the Seminar Given in 1934–9* (ed. James L. Jarrett; London: Routledge, 1989), I, pt. 2.

pathological cases with a historical religious figure'.⁶¹ Ego inflation also 'produces an exaggerated sense of one's self-importance and is usually compensated by feelings of inferiority'.⁶² These issues will be considered in various aspects by way of the prophetic figures examined in this work.

1.2.1.3 Ambiguous Community Accountability Regarding Responsibility to the Truth

1.2.1.3.1 Biblical Reflections

Problems in and abuses of prophetic function in non-denominational Pentecostalism highlight the dissolution of the accountability that was historically and ethically a matter of conscience understood 'in the context of a community'.⁶³ The 'household of God' mentioned in 1 Tim. 3.15 is the accountability safety net when exercising matters of conscience, including prophetic intimations. For Paul, the ἐκκλησία derives its existence from 'the living God', so that the church is the 'pillar' (στῦλος) and 'bulwark' or mainstay (ἑδραίωμα) of the truth (1 Tim. 3.15), much like a sea wall that offers protection

---

⁶¹ Schlamm, 'Inflation'. Schlamm also cites Jung, *Nietzsche's Zarathustra*, and C.G. Jung, *Memories, Dreams, Reflections* (ed. A. Jaffe; London: Fontana Press, 1995).

> Persona is the term Jung used to denote the outer face that is presented to the world which he appropriated from the word for the mask worn by actors in antiquity to indicate the roles they played … [For Jung] it is the archetypal core of persona that facilitates the relating that has evolved as an integral part of humans as social beings … The archetypal core gives the persona its powerful religious dimension that raises it from the banal, workaday outer vestment of an individual via its connection to the depths of the psyche.

Ann Casement, 'Persona', in David A. Leeming (ed.), *Encyclopedia of Psychology and Religion* (Boston, MA: Springer, 2014), https://doi.org/10.1007/978-1-4614-6086-2_502. 'In the analytic psychology of Carl Jung, [archetype is] any one of a set of symbols representing aspects of the psyche that derive from the accumulated experience of humankind … Examples are anima, animus, persona, shadow, supreme being, and hero', *APA Dictionary of Psychology*, 'Archetype', https://dictionary.apa.org/archetype.

⁶² Schlamm, 'Inflation'.

⁶³ Paul A. Hartog, 'Conscience', in John D. Barry, *et al.* (eds.), *The Lexham Bible Dictionary* (Bellingham, WA: Lexham Press, 2016). Conscience is 'a capacity or faculty of moral intuition, consciousness, or reflection. A person's internal awareness or sense of abiding by or transgressing moral standards. An internal witness to moral obligation based on intuition or self-assessment.'

against battering waves. The church structure thus protects the truth that the church proclaims and teaches.[64]

What consequences might be expected when presumed prophetic figures and their followers deviate from the truth? Prophetic function, as traditionally understood both broadly and narrowly, rests with 'the Spirit of truth' who leads and guides the church 'into all the truth' (Jn 16.13). The mainstay is rooted in Christ Jesus, the Person of truth who bore witness to the truth in Pilate's presence (Jn 18.37).

If God is indeed One, the Spirit does not contradict the mainstay. However, not everything the prophetic agent knows by 'Divine instinct' is 'manifested with prophetic certitude'.[65] On the road to Emmaus, Jesus said the disciples' doubts about his identity showed they were 'slow of heart to believe all that the prophets have declared' (Lk. 24.25). The Lukan account seems to show that, in Jesus' mind, the prophetic tradition is paramount in relation to the disciples' dilemma. Because belief involves the will, their slowness of heart (βραδύς, εῖα, ύ) implied a dilatory will.[66] Therefore, their slowness seems to imply their struggle to embrace a suffering Messiah who died to usher in God's kingdom.

Whatever written records from the Torah, Prophets, and Wisdom Literature were known, they were considered 'inspired' and effective 'for teaching, for reproof, for correction, and for training' (2 Tim. 3.16). The desired outcome was proficiency and competency – the state of being qualified and equipped (ἐξαρτίζω) for every good work (2 Tim. 3.17).[67] The identical Greek term appears in Eph. 4.11, speaking of the ascended Christ assigning prophets and others to bring the saints to competency for their mission as 'the body of

---

[64] Rick Brannan, *Lexical Commentary on the Pastoral Epistles: First Timothy* (Bellingham, WA: Appian Way Press, 2016), p. 137.

[65] Thomas Aquinas, *Summa Theologica* (trans. Fathers of the English Dominican Province; London: Burns Oates & Washbourne, n.d.), STh., II–II q. 171 a .5 resp.

[66] Their slowness of heart is conveyed by βραδύς, εῖα, ύ, which pertains 'to an extended period of time, with the implication of being slow to do something – "slow, dilatory". [For comparative usage] ἔστω ... βραδὺς εἰς τὸ λαλῆσαι, βραδὺς εἰς ὀργήν "be ... slow to speak and slow to become angry" Jas 1:19', *GEL*, p. 646.

[67] Being 'equipped' suggests 'to make someone completely adequate or sufficient for something – "to make adequate, to furnish completely, to cause to be fully qualified, adequacy". ἐξαρτίζω: πρὸς πᾶν ἔργον ἀγαθὸν ἐξηρτισμένος "completely qualified for every good deed" 2 Tm 3:17.' *GEL*, p. 680.

Christ' (ἐκκλησία).⁶⁸ Therefore, *every* prophetic agent is accountable to the 'pillar and bulwark [mainstay] of the truth' and answerable to authority (1 Tim. 3.15) – presumably, in Paul's view, the Christian Tradition and NT church governance, including the local church and its eldership (Tit. 1.5; Acts 14.23).

1.2.1.3.2 Theological Reflections
Aquinas makes clear that prophetic agents can deviate from the truth. He writes, 'Prophecy is by way of being something imperfect in the genus of Divine revelation: hence it is written (1 Cor. 13:8) that "prophecies shall be made void", and that "we prophesy in part", i.e. imperfectly'.⁶⁹ For Aquinas, denying prophecy's imperfection means ignoring Paul's clear counsel. This does not preclude the possibility of genuine insight from the divine Spirit. The prophet may indeed know something 'by an express revelation'.⁷⁰ Aquinas likens it to the tribunal of priests and prophets who seek Jeremiah's harm and have to listen when he proclaims, 'For in truth the LORD sent me to you to speak all these words in your ears' (Jer. 26.15). Pointing to Jeremiah's certainty, Aquinas writes,

> A sign of the prophet's certitude may be gathered from the fact that Abraham being admonished in a prophetic vision, prepared to sacrifice his only begotten son, which he nowise would have done had he not been most certain of the Divine revelation.⁷¹

Aquinas is quick to add,

> On the other hand, his position with regard to the things he knows by instinct is sometimes such that he is unable to distinguish fully whether his thoughts are conceived of Divine instinct or of his own spirit. And those things which we know by Divine instinct

---

⁶⁸ *GEL*, p. 483; Eph. 4.11; δίδωμι is

to assign a person to a task as a particular benefit to others – 'to appoint, to assign (on behalf of)'. μετὰ ταῦτα ἔδωκεν κριτάς 'after this he appointed judges (for them)' Ac 13:20. It may be possible in some languages to render δίδωμι in Ac 13:20 as 'he gave them judges', but more frequently it is necessary to use a phrase such as 'he appointed judges to rule over them'.

⁶⁹ Aquinas, *Summa Theologica*, q. 171 a. 5 resp.
⁷⁰ Aquinas, *Summa Theologica*, q. 171 a. 5 resp.
⁷¹ Aquinas, *Summa Theologica*, q. 171 a. 5 resp.

are not all manifested with prophetic certitude, for this instinct is something imperfect in the genus of prophecy.[72]

Thus, Aquinas prompts us to acknowledge that we know and prophesy in part. Regarding the prophetic agent distinguishing between truth and error, he writes,

> It is thus that we are to understand the saying of Gregory. Lest, however, this should lead to error, 'they are very soon set aright by the Holy Ghost, and from Him they hear the truth, so that they reproach themselves for having said what was untrue', as Gregory adds (*Hom.* i. *super Ezech.*).[73]

Such self-awareness seems essential and will be explored further in the later chapters.

1.2.1.4 Erosion of Personal Answerability

A fourth problem evident in independent Pentecostal circles involves the prophetic agent's obligation or personal responsibility when exercising the liberty to bring forth what the agent deems prophetic. This involves not only the stewardship of presumed intimations by the Spirit but also a willingness to explain and justify all aspects of prophetic exercise.

1.2.1.4.1 Theological (and Ecclesiological) Reflections

Such responsibility is what Rowan Williams calls 'answerability'.[74] Williams notes,

> the abbot's rule has to be characterized by accountability. Although what the abbot says must be done, without complaint … the abbot is adjured at some length to recall his answerability before God, his call to be the image of Christ in the monastery and to 'leaven' the minds of those under his care, and his duty to ignore apparent claims of status among the monks.[75]

If the abbot (as overseer) is to bear witness to the image of Christ, overseers in contemporary churches are likewise bound. Clearly, all prophetic utterance is called to be Christo-centric (Rev. 19.10).

---

[72] Aquinas, *Summa Theologica*, q. 171 a. 5 resp.
[73] Aquinas, *Summa Theologica*, q. 171 a. 5 resp.
[74] Rowan Williams, *The Way of St. Benedict* (London: Bloomsbury Continuum, 2020), p. 20.
[75] Williams, *Way of St. Benedict*, p. 20.

In writing that 'Jesus is the persona who utters the words the Christians speak',[76] Williams concurs with the writer to the Hebrews, who wrote, 'in these last days he has spoken to us by a Son' (Heb. 1.2).[77] This speaking through the Son shapes the language of prophetic utterance. Therefore, those who prophesy are answerable to (1) the One *through whom* they claim to speak, and (2) the ones *to whom* they speak. Williams says that regarding 'what is owed to human beings, you're talking about certain basic forms of social interaction that are seen as life-giving'.[78] If that which is life-giving is owed in social interaction, it is presumably owed in the highest aspects of shared life within the church. This is the notion of personal answerability, as applied in this work.

1.2.1.5 Diminished Sense of Keeping Covenant

Theological disagreement is not new to the church. Controversies have arisen since its inception. How they are addressed and whether they are resolved are matters critical to the church's sense of keeping covenant.

1.2.1.5.1 Biblical Reflections

Portions of the Lukan text speak plainly to the primitive church's active covenant keeping and highlight a waning of the same in some church circles. Pelikan reminds us that within 'the first generation of believers' there existed a semblance of 'apostolic continuity' in practices the community upheld.[79] He notes that despite the foundation of 'doctrine, fellowship, breaking of bread, [and] prayer',[80] conflict arose as the predominantly Jewish sect saw its mission divinely expanded to include the Gentiles. By the time the issue of Gentile

---

[76] Rowan Williams, *Christ the Heart of Creation* (London: Bloomsbury Continuum, 2018), p. 74.

[77] Williams could be arguing from Heb. 1.2, where the dative case *en* (in or by his Son) is used as the dative of agency. 'The true dative is used to designate the person more remotely concerned. It is the case of *personal interest*, pointing out the person *to* or *for* whom something is done.' Daniel B. Wallace, *The Basics of New Testament Syntax: An Intermediate Greek Grammar* (Grand Rapids, MI: Zondervan, 2000), p. 65.

[78] 'Interview: Rowan Williams', Goldsmiths, University of London, https://www.gold.ac.uk/faithsunit/current-projects/reimaginingreligion/landmark-interviews/rowan-williams/.

[79] Jaroslav Pelikan, *Acts* (Brazos Theological Commentary on the Bible; Grand Rapids, MI: Brazos Press, 2005), p. 170. Pelikan also notes that this 'apostolic continuity' is perhaps 'idealized'.

[80] Pelikan, *Acts*, p. 170. Pelikan cites Acts 2.42.

circumcision surfaced, a council was convened (Acts 15), and the controversy was subjected to 'theological clarification'.[81]

The Lukan text points to leaders providing oversight to address any 'theological disagreement'.[82] Pelikan rightly asserts, 'this disagreement is a measure of the seriousness with which the apostolic generation took questions of theology and principle'.[83] The text asserts that questions of Gentile circumcision stirred 'much debate' (Acts 15.7). This seminal event shows the eldership and the community mutually bearing witness to what the Spirit was saying, leading to a consensus involving the leadership and the witness of the Spirit (Acts 15.22-28).

Twice Luke's account records, 'it seemed best' (δοκεῖ, Acts 15.22, 28, LEB).[84] The first usage is in the impersonal form to imply 'to seem, to appear, to assume, to think' as it relates to the 'apostles and elders'.[85] The same term is used in the second case (Acts 15.28).[86] Whether one chooses the definition of Louw and Nida or Arndt, *et al.*, both definitions provide leeway for ongoing discernment in relation to the Spirit's work *and* the refusal to assume inarguable infallibility. Pelikan rightly avers, 'disagreement and fraternal correction' were present and active in Acts 15 and other portions of the Lukan account'.[87]

---

[81] Pelikan, *Acts*, p. 170.
[82] Pelikan, *Acts*, p. 170.
[83] Pelikan, *Acts*, p. 170.
[84] δοκεῖ, meaning 'to hold an opinion based upon appearances which may be significantly different from reality – "to seem, to appear, to assume, to think"', *GEL*, p. 370.
[85] *GEL*, p. 370.
[86] *BAGD*, p. 201 defines δοκεῖ: 'to consider as probable, *think, believe, suppose, consider*, trans., of subjective opinion (Hom.+; pap; rare LXX)'.
[87] Pelikan, *Acts*, pp. 170-71:

> The difference between the ongoing process of the church's teaching through preaching, liturgy, and catechesis on one hand and the authority of the formal and official statements and promulgations of the church on the other hand, as these are exemplified in the present chapter by the decrees of the apostolic council of Jerusalem (15:28) – and therefore the difference between (in the eventual senses of the two terms) 'apostolic tradition' and 'apostolic dogma' (16:4b) – has been formulated in the distinction between the ordinary magisterium and the extraordinary magisterium of the church That distinction is also an effort to counterbalance an exclusive emphasis, whether by its proponents or by its critics (or, for that matter, by later historians of doctrine), on the official formulations of creed (8:37) and dogma (16:4b) without paying due attention to the 'ordinary' and ongoing function of the teaching authority.

1.2.1.5.2 Theological (and Ecclesiological) Reflections
Answerability, as described by Rowan Williams, is akin to keeping covenant. The Tradition defines the community of God as being covenantal in relationship to him, the Mosaic covenant requiring the keeping of covenant with God and one another. The promised new covenant in the Messiah finds expression in the ethics Jesus revealed in the Sermon on the Mount (Jeremiah 33; Matthew 5–7). The teachings of Christ are to be understood governmentally in relationship to the covenant communities known as *churches* (Rev. 2.29, 3.22).

The testimony of Jesus is inseparable from the Spirit of Prophecy (Rev. 1.2, 1.9, 12.17, 19.10). As covenantal communities, therefore, churches are to adhere to what the Spirit is saying to them collectively. This is predominantly how the divine Spirit speaks to them. Should the Spirit of Prophecy reveal anything of a personal nature, the NT and the *Didache* call the community to guard it. Therefore, if so-called prophetic agents contradict the testimony of Jesus (Rev. 19.10), ought they not to be corrected (and in certain extreme cases silenced) by the covenanted communities they serve? The keeping of covenant requires that the prophetic agent(s) be subject to the community. Community leaders provide oversight to address issues of truth-telling, and the eldership and the community together bear witness of that which the Spirit says.

1.3 Methodology

In focusing on the canonical text and moving toward a contemporary Pentecostal theology of prophetic legitimacy, this work will consider developments in current literary theory, including the Pentecostal hermeneutic. Added to the works of Rickie D. Moore,[88] John Christopher Thomas,[89] Kenneth J. Archer,[90] and others already noted in Lee Roy Martin's compilation: Cheryl Bridges Johns, John W. McKay, Andrew Davies, and Scott A. Ellington.[91] Also important is the more

---

[88] Rickie D. Moore, *The Spirit of the Old Testament* (JPTSup 35; Blandford Forum: Deo, 2011).
[89] John Christopher Thomas, 'Pentecostal Theology in the Twenty-First Century', *Pneuma* 20.1 (Spring 1998), pp. 3-19.
[90] Kenneth J. Archer, *A Pentecostal Hermeneutic: Spirit, Scripture and Community* (Cleveland, TN: CPT Press, 2009).
[91] Lee Roy Martin (ed.), *Pentecostal Hermeneutics: A Reader* (Leiden: Brill, 2013).

recent work by Leulseged Philemon, which focuses specifically on the role of the Spirit in relation to Pentecostal hermeneutics.[92]

These voices contribute to an emphatically Pentecostal interpretation of the canonical text. Therefore, any attempt to construct a Pentecostal theology of prophetic legitimacy will build on their work. This is in keeping with literary theory, which argues, 'the meaning of the text could come from more than one source'.[93] In addition, a Pentecostal hermeneutic reaches beyond the author-text-reader-relationship and involves a community that reads the text together. Therefore, scholars have argued that within the Pentecostal tradition, the Spirit, the text, and the community engage in meaning making, which finds expression in the community's shared life.

Estes contends that the world 'behind the text' is 'author-focused';[94] the world 'at the text' is 'text-focused';[95] the world 'in front of the text' is 'reader-focused';[96] and the world 'to the side of the text' is 'context-focused'.[97] This work takes at least three of these approaches: An author-focused approach will facilitate the literary criticism perspective in relation to literary theory, incorporating both psychoanalytic and phenomenological criticism. A text-focused approach will allow examination of the biblical text from a narrative, rhetorical, and semiotic perspective. A reader-focused approach will serve in articulating reception history in relationship to Pentecostalism and its tradition within the movement.[98]

These approaches fall within specific categories of which the reader needs to be aware. First and foremost, the text's narrative reading frames the argument in terms of story. As is true of stories generally, the elements of theme, plot, and characters are present (characters in this case include God, the prophetic agent, and various aspects of the community). This implies a 'narrative criticism'

---

[92] Leulseged Philemon, *Pneumatic Hermeneutics: The Role of the Holy Spirit in the Theological Interpretation of Scripture* (Cleveland, TN: CPT Press, 2019).

[93] Douglas Estes, 'Introduction: The Literary Approach to the Bible', in Douglas Mangum and Douglas Estes (eds.), *Literary Approaches to the Bible* (Lexham Methods Series 4; Bellingham, WA: Lexham Press, 2016), p. 9.

[94] Estes, 'Literary Approach', p. 10.

[95] Estes, 'Literary Approach', p. 10.

[96] Estes, 'Literary Approach', p. 10.

[97] Estes, 'Literary Approach', p. 10.

[98] Estes, 'Literary Approach', p. 11.

approach.[99] Secondly, the text is being read as decidedly Christian Scripture. Hence 'canonical criticism' is the working approach to biblical interpretation.[100] Thirdly, given the interplay of interdisciplinary realities (theology alongside psychology and phenomenology), a 'social-scientific approach' will be employed in arguing for prophetic legitimacy.[101]

1.3.1 Literary Approach and Pentecostal Hermeneutic

The Pentecostal theology of prophetic legitimacy to be constructed here comprises the triadic relations of prophetic consciousness, perception, and enactment. Such a theology requires a particularly Pentecostal hermeneutic, of which Pentecostal scholars have developed various interpretative approaches in recent decades.

Whatever the differences among these approaches, there are also essential commonalities. In considering the broad renewal tradition within Evangelical, Charismatic Catholic, Charismatic, and Pentecostal streams, Hannah Mather recognizes the consensus, 'pneumatic interpretation of Scripture is holistic'.[102] This holism is derived from the very nature of human 'affect, ethics, and cognition',[103] with the heart as the 'locus of discernment' from which human affect flows.[104]

The assertion of holism, according to Mather, is 'further strengthened' by what she deems the essential contribution of Rickie D. Moore.[105] Mather also identifies the beginnings of the earlier Pentecostal approach that became known as a Pentecostal hermeneutic,[106] which includes the work of Roger Stronstad, Gordon Fee, William Menzies, and Howard Ervin. Mather also carefully considers the contributions of Steven Land, John Christopher Thomas, and Kenneth

---

[99] Douglas Mangum and Josh Westbury (eds.), *Linguistics and Biblical Exegesis* (Lexham Methods Series 2; Bellingham, WA: Lexham Press, 2016), Series Preface, pp. ix-x.

[100] Mangum and Westbury, *Linguistics and Biblical Exegesis*, pp. ix-x.

[101] Mangum and Westbury, *Linguistics and Biblical Exegesis*, pp. ix-x.

[102] Hannah R.K. Mather, *The Interpreting Spirit: Spirit, Scripture, and Interpretation in the Renewal Tradition* (Eugene: OR: Pickwick Publications, 2020), ch. 2.

[103] Mather, *Interpreting Spirit*, ch. 2.

[104] Mather, *Interpreting Spirit*, ch. 2. For Mather, the influence of Balthasar's pneumatology cannot be overstated. For Balthasar, understanding the Spirit's role in Scripture interpretation is impossible unless God's triune nature is understood. Mather states that the Spirit 'interprets the triune God to us'. Mather, *Interpreting Spirit*, ch. 2.

[105] Mather, *Interpreting Spirit*, ch. 4.

[106] Mather, *Interpreting Spirit*, ch. 2.

J. Archer.[107] Thomas and Archer have profoundly influenced a Pentecostal hermeneutic in terms of the role of the community in the interpretive process. Within the 'renewal tradition',[108] a priority is placed on 'personal experience' and 'communion with God',[109] as emphasized by Jackie David Johns and Cheryl Bridges Johns.[110]

Pertinent to this work is Mather's assertion, 'pneumatic interpretation cannot … be understood solely in relation to scripture because the Spirit always works through and beyond scripture'.[111] It must be noted, 'through and beyond scripture' does not imply *apart from* Scripture. The 'self-effacing' Spirit's role can only be discerned by the Spirit's movements,[112] as per Balthasar.[113] As such, the Spirit's work involves creative and redeeming dimensions within our personal lives and communicates scriptural truth in a way that impacts human affect, human ethics, and human cognition.[114] The Spirit serves us by '(self)-interpret[ing] the Father, the Son, and the Spirit to us'.[115] It is precisely in this subjective human interiority where the work of 'creating and redeeming' is made evident.[116]

Thus, the Holy Spirit's role in the heart and mind is the precise intersection of the divine Spirit's influence and the human mind's function. Of particular interest are the varieties of conscious awareness of textual nuances and their cognitive constructions, as well as perceptual frameworks that present themselves within the reading. It can be argued that such nuances, influenced and promulgated by the Holy Spirit, transcend human reasoning, even as the Spirit shapes and forms the Christological narrative within the interpreter's interiority.

These interpretive and formative processes are tied to the essential relations born of communion in the localized body where believers are called to accountability and answerability before God. As John Christopher Thomas attests, the reading of the text within such a 'hermeneutical paradigm' is modeled in the Acts 15 account of the

---

[107] Mather, *Interpreting Spirit*, ch. 3.
[108] Mather, *Interpreting Spirit*, ch. 3.
[109] Mather, *Interpreting Spirit*, ch. 3.
[110] Mather, *Interpreting Spirit*, ch. 3.
[111] Mather, *Interpreting Spirit*, ch. 3.
[112] Mather, *Interpreting Spirit*, ch. 3.
[113] Mather, *Interpreting Spirit*, ch. 2.
[114] Mather, *Interpreting Spirit*, ch. 3.
[115] Mather, *Interpreting Spirit*, ch. 3.
[116] Mather, *Interpreting Spirit*, ch. 3.

Jerusalem Council and involves 'the role of the community, the role of the Holy Spirit, and the role and place of Scripture'.[117] For a community in relationship with the Spirit, the ongoing Christological narrative is formed in corporate and informal interactions with the text, which present opportunities for 'participation in the practice of pneumatic discernment'.[118]

Considering the participation and processes here outlined, can the work of constructing a Pentecostal theology of prophetic legitimacy ignore the implications and insights of recent generations within the interdisciplinary methodologies? I suggest it cannot. Doing justice to the notions of prophetic consciousness, prophetic perception, and prophetic enactment would seem to demand that the theological dynamics be considered in conjunction with the psychological and phenomenological realities of the human psyche and the interior human experience. Although the work is rooted in a Pentecostal hermeneutic, interdisciplinary methodologies will facilitate inquiry into the profound interconnection among theology, psychology, and phenomenology in the Christological narrative.

1.3.1.1 The Spirit and the Text: Methods of Pentecostal Interpretation

John Christopher Thomas was among the first to articulate a distinctive Pentecostal hermeneutic. In his view, regarded as central to the 'Cleveland School approach',[119] the biblical narrative within the canon is foundational. It is the story, particularly the Christologically oriented story, that determines the Pentecostal hermeneutic.[120] According to Thomas, 'Pentecostals avoid a canon within the canon approach by taking seriously the theological dimension of all Scripture, especially narrative'.[121]

This view is heavily dependent on early Pentecostal approaches to Scripture, which Chris E.W. Green describes as sharing two

---

[117] John Christopher Thomas, 'Pentecostal Biblical Interpretation', in Steven L. McKenzie (ed.), *Oxford Encyclopedia of Biblical Interpretation* (Oxford: Oxford University Press, 2013), II, p. 94.
[118] Thomas, 'Pentecostal Biblical Interpretation', II, p. 94.
[119] Mather, *Interpreting Spirit*, ch. 5.
[120] Thomas, 'Pentecostal Biblical Interpretation', p. 90.
[121] Thomas, 'Pentecostal Biblical Interpretation', p. 89. See also Gerald T. Sheppard, Howard M. Ervin, Mark D. McLean, Russell P. Spittler, Rickie D. Moore, John McKay, J.C. Thomas, Larry R. McQueen, Kenneth J. Archer, Robby Waddell, Lee Roy Martin, also in McKenzie.

'interpretive habits':[122] (1) the early Pentecostals came to the Scriptures 'expecting to encounter *Christ*',[123] and (2) they came to the Scriptures 'expecting to *encounter* Christ'.[124] Kenneth J. Archer follows this line of thought, underscoring the authority of narrative and the focus on Jesus, but shifting the emphasis to the community as interpreter, arguing that Pentecostals share 'Central Narrative Convictions',[125] which guide the community's engagements with the text.

1.3.1.2 The Spirit and the Mind of the Pentecostal Interpreter

First, in the process of 'pneumatic interpretation' and as the Spirit leads toward 'the assessment of truth',[126] readers make both 'conscious and subconscious judgment[s]',[127] which influence perceptions and the entire perceptual process.[128] Such pneumatic discernment for Mather leads to 'pneumatic appropriation … an act of communication brought by the Spirit through [the reader's] engagement with scripture'.[129] However, this process is threatened (if not thwarted) by 'pneumatic hindrances' to interpretation that arise in the interpreter's lived experience.[130]

Amos Yong's seminal work considers a 'pneumatology of quest',[131] whereby an inquiry is made based on the Holy Spirit's role in the interpreter's life, not only in relation to theological reflection but also epistemologically in relation to the self and metaphysically in relation to the world at large.[132]

Finally, the work of Cheryl Bridges Johns is innovative regarding her view of what is needed: 'a new Bible, one that can speak to us as Holy Scripture and pull us outward in centripetal force into new worlds'.[133] Johns offers 'a view of the Bible as living subject whose

---

[122] Chris E.W. Green, *Sanctifying Interpretation: Vocation, Holiness, and Scripture* (Cleveland, TN: CPT Press, 2nd edn, 2020), p. 130.
[123] Green, *Sanctifying Interpretation*, p. 130.
[124] Green, *Sanctifying Interpretation*, p. 130.
[125] Archer, *Pentecostal Hermeneutic*, p. 214.
[126] Mather, *Interpreting Spirit*, ch. 1.
[127] Mather, *Interpreting Spirit*, ch. 1.
[128] Mather, *Interpreting Spirit*, ch. 1.
[129] Mather, *Interpreting Spirit*, ch. 1.
[130] Mather, *Interpreting Spirit*, ch. 1.
[131] Amos Yong, *Spirit-Word-Community: Theological Hermeneutics in Trinitarian Perspective* (Eugene, OR: Wipf & Stock, 2002), p. 8.
[132] Yong, *Spirit-Word-Community*, p. 8.
[133] Cheryl Bridges Johns, 'Grieving, Brooding, and Transforming: The Spirit, the Bible, and Gender', *Journal of Pentecostal Theology* 23.2 (2014), p. 144.

existence is grounded in the economic life of God'.[134] This aspect is an essential issue for this work, as there can be no grounds for constructing a Pentecostal theology of prophetic legitimacy without a careful consideration of both the economic and the imminent Trinity.

1.3.1.3 Method in Operation: Considering Revelation and Authority

Pastor, author, and Bible teacher David Guzik asserts that in relation to the secret things, 'God never declares *everything* to man'.[135] Instead, the text assumes the 'secrets God has and will always have'.[136] Yet Guzik notes, 'God does reveal *some* things to man'.[137] God indeed speaks and 'is not silent'.[138] Because God communicates with his creatures, it is essential to heed his speaking. The question then is, 'How does God speak?'

It is precisely here that various answers arise within Independent Pentecostal streams. Because identity is essential for communities, and because these streams have distanced themselves from their denominational relatives and in many significant ways also from the Tradition, identity would seem more significant. The community needs to define itself in a way that establishes, sanctions, and justifies its existence. In that regard, each community requires a grammar that helps to shape and support their prophetic legitimacy. However, no single grammar is shared by all, thereby fueling a crisis of prophetic legitimacy among contemporary Pentecostal communities, one resembling that experienced by the first Christian communities.

Doctrinal formulations (and especially those related to distinctive beliefs) are significant for the Independent Pentecostal movement. Arguably, 'revelation' is the most significant for some or even all in the movement. Lindbeck asserts, 'doctrines are communally authoritative'.[139] While certain doctrines might be rejected by some Independent communities, those that embrace implicit or explicit doctrinal formulations find their existence authorized through them. In Lindbeck's accurate appraisal, these communities see their

---

[134] Johns, 'Grieving, Brooding, and Transforming', p. 145.
[135] David Guzik, *Deuteronomy* (Santa Barbara, CA: David Guzik, 2004), 'Dt 29:29'.
[136] Guzik, *Deuteronomy*, 'Dt 29:29'.
[137] Guzik, *Deuteronomy*, 'Dt 29:29'.
[138] Guzik, *Deuteronomy*, 'Dt 29:29'.
[139] Lindbeck, *Nature of Doctrine*, ch. 4.

formulations as being 'essential to the identity or welfare of the group'.[140] That certainly seems true of many contemporary figures in Independent Pentecostal circles, especially those who have major platforms and globally recognized ministries. But there has not yet been an agreed-upon understanding of these core doctrines within the Independent Pentecostal movement, much less one that coheres with the teachings of the larger historical Tradition.

1.3.2 Psychological and Phenomenological Method: Concerns in the Independent Pentecostal Environment

Within the Independent Pentecostal movement, certain trends are evident or ubiquitous, reflecting tribal tendencies within the global Pentecostal community and often marrying them with characteristics from the broader culture. The separate elements include spiritual enthusiasm, technology, prophetic 'activation', and common forms of prophetic enactment.

1.3.2.1 Enthusiasm and Technology

In the past few decades, venues such as the Internet and 24/7 cable news broadcasting; the advent of social media platforms such as Facebook, Instagram, and Twitter; and the rise and spread of Third Wave spirituality, theology, and praxis have created a novel environment for the dissemination of prophetic messages. Pentecostals have always used various media platforms to communicate, arguably better than other Christian traditions. Today, social media platforms particularly afford Independent prophets huge reach, immediate response, and the ability to communicate directly with their audiences but without editorial oversight or control.[141] The evolving environment presents increasingly fluid outlets in which long-standing issues are manifested. As it does with the lack of critical scrutiny, technology amplifies the enthusiasm evidenced in unfaithful prophetic expression.

---

[140] Lindbeck, *Nature of Doctrine*, ch. 4.

[141] The lack of editorial and/or theological scrutiny applied prior to social media distribution distinguishes it from the use of legacy media. In addition, the immediacy of expression implies a different psychology of interaction. Because there is no editorial accountability, and because technology facilitates instantaneous communication, prophetic agents respond to events in real time, often without the benefit of critical reflection. Also, the only coherent vision governing what gets published is a platform's bottom line. Algorithms control publication, and controversial posts (which increase traffic) can be afforded maximum visibility. This is a form of editorial scrutiny; but it is by no means a pastoral one.

This issue was familiar to John Wesley, a forefather of modern Pentecostalism, who was himself derided as an enthusiast in his day. His reflections suggest balance by acknowledging and offering correction for presumption, a common excess of enthusiasts.

Perhaps then, enthusiasm in general can be described as a religious madness arising from some falsely imagined influence or inspiration of God – at least, from imputing something to God which ought not to be imputed to him or expecting something from God which ought not to be expected from him.[142]

Wesley adds:

[Those governed by enthusiasm] may likewise imagine themselves to be influenced or directed by the Spirit when they are not. I allow, 'if any man have not the Spirit of Christ, he is none of his'; and that if ever we either think, speak, or act aright, it is through the assistance of that blessed Spirit. But how many impute things to him, or expect things from him, without any rational or scriptural ground!'[143]

Instead of denying or excusing such excesses, Wesley addressed them. Thus, he implied the community's obligation to uncover veiled presuppositions and faulty presumptions of authority that might ensnare the well-meaning. Such faulty presumptions and unfaithful practices are not necessarily suggestive of malicious intent. The question is whether contemporary prophetic agents consider themselves to be above fallibility and reproof. If they do, how (historically and theologically) did such a posture develop? What exactly can and should be done in response, so that prophetic ministries are less prone to abuses?

It seems that the Scriptures and the Tradition agree: when presumed prophetic agents claim that 'divine authority' endorses their enactments and postulations,[144] their claims are to be vetted (1 Jn 4.1). Matters of truth and falsehood (not always easily distinguished) are to be evaluated, as are the phenomenological vagaries of supposed

---

[142] Wesley, *Works of John Wesley*, pp. 469-70.
[143] Wesley, *Works of John Wesley*, pp. 473-74.
[144] David E. Aune, *Prophecy in Early Christianity and the Ancient Mediterranean World* (Grand Rapids, MI: Eerdmans, 1991), p. 229.

prophetic experience, possible mystical states, and ecstatic phenomena.[145]

1.3.2.2 Enthusiasm and Prophetic 'Activation'

The popular notion of 'prophetic activations',[146] which refers to 'spiritual exercises that use words, actions, phrases, objects, Scripture verses, worship songs and dance, prophetic prayers, and more to *trigger* the prophetic gifts',[147] is a mode by which prophetic enthusiasm is energized. John Eckhardt, a widely read Third Wave pastor and leader recognized as a reliable popular authority on the prophetic, asserts that such activations 'are designed to break down the barriers that hinder and prevent people from operating in prophecy'.[148]

Whether these activations conform to what Amos Yong calls a 'coherent theology of the Spirit' remains in question.[149] Yong rightly states, 'developments in global Pentecostalism beg for attention'.[150] The combining of a ravenous prophetic appetite with unrestrained prophetic expression and global reach seemingly 'qualifies' any Independent voice to satisfy it. Therefore, large numbers of Independents see and dutifully embrace all forms of prophetism as spiritual nourishment. Potentially, such an emphasis can divorce prophetic function from a holistic Pentecostal church life rooted in proven disciplines and spiritual formation.

---

[145] Ancient issues of 'prophetic protocol' could serve as guidelines for contemporary praxis. Aune, *Prophecy in Early Christianity*, p. 229.

[146] John Eckhardt, *The Prophet's Manual: A Guide to Sustaining Your Prophetic Gift* (Lake Mary, FL: Charisma House, 2017), p. 278. Prophetic activation is taught by many: see BSSM School Planting, 'Activating Students in the Prophetic with Ben Armstrong', https://bssm.net/schoolplanting/2016/10/25/activating-students-in-the-prophetic-with-ben-armstrong/; Dan McCollam, *Basic Training for Prophetic Activation* (Vacaville, CA: iWar, 2012); Sean and Christa Smith Ministries, *Prophetic Activation Series*, https://seansmithministries.com/product/the-prophetic-activation-series/; Patricia King, 'Prophetic Activation: Discerning the Times', *Patricia King YouTube Channel* (February 15, 2020), https://www.youtube.com/ watch?v=37ZFm C0vMG0.

[147] Eckhardt, *Prophet's Manual*, p. 278 (emphasis added).

[148] Eckhardt, *Prophet's Manual*, p. 278.

[149] Yong, 'What Spirit(s), Which Public(s)?', p. 242. Among the questions that come to mind: Is eligibility for 'activation' universal? Are any limiting factors under discussion?

[150] Yong, 'What Spirit(s), Which Public(s)?', p. 258.

1.3.2.3 Questionable Prophetic Enactments

An additional issue in Independent tribes is the embrace of questionable prophetic enactments. These focus largely on a reimagined Jesus who bore humanity's sufferings so that we might be spared any cross-bearing. This premise shapes the exercise of faith in prophetic utterance. Having seemingly distanced themselves from the church's sharing in the sufferings of Christ, they conclude that Jesus' suffering offers us total authority and dominion over all of Creation. Fee addresses this ideology and makes clear that it is not resonant with the larger Christian Tradition.[151] Instead, it arises from a form of triumphalism that, based on the associated praxis, suggests a shift from the Tradition to a self-oriented, self-grounded, self-authenticating authority in which 'revelation' is authoritative in and of itself, requiring no other witness to its veracity.

1.3.2.4 Method in Operation: Inherent Post-Denominational Concerns

The church's post-denominational setting is marked by particular challenges. Since the Latter Rain Movement emerged in North Battleford, Saskatchewan in February of 1948, an often-misguided presumption of faithful prophetic praxis has proliferated within the Independent movement, as the following characteristics seem to confirm.

1.3.2.4.1 Loss of Accountability (Interpersonal and Institutional, Ministerial and Theological)

Within the community life of Classical Pentecostalism, denominational structure provides a form of accountability (however adequate or deficient) in relation to prophetic discernment and praxis.

---

[151] Gordon D. Fee, *God's Empowering Presence: The Holy Spirit in the Letters of Paul* (Grand Rapids, MI: Baker Academic, 2011), p. 895:

> Triumphalism was not the necessary corollary of life in the Spirit, experienced in dynamic and powerfully visible ways, as [Paul's] own life attests. Here is one who could keep the two together; the empowering Spirit, visibly manifest among them often and regularly in giftings and empowerings of an extraordinary kind; while at the same time Paul was filled with the joy of the Spirit in the midst of suffering and weaknesses of all kinds. Paul's word to the Philippians is worth our hearing and heeding today: 'Join with others in following my example, brothers and sisters, and take note of those who live according to the pattern we gave you' (3:17). In the context of Philippians that included both 'the power of Christ's resurrection and the fellowship of his sufferings'.

Likewise, the Charismatic Movement is in large part tied to enduring mainline denominational structures that govern prophetic expression within particular creedal, scriptural, historical, and traditional boundaries.

By contrast, many Independent Pentecostals have relaxed or relinquished the clear accountability that once connected prophetic activity to the historical Tradition, including its hierarchical controls. While this has produced a level of freedom, it does not necessarily portend growth. Nor is it likely to prevent the fractiousness Independents sought to avoid. It seems clear from history that abolishing an existing system forces the installation of a new one – in this case, the creation of a new systematic theology, however unsystematic its appearance might be.

1.3.2.4.2 Non-Holistic Approach to Prophetic Function
If prophetic function in Independent Pentecostalism is on the leading edge of problematic practices, its overemphasis segregates it from holistic Pentecostal spirituality and spiritual formation. With emphases thus unbalanced and the prophetic 'addiction' increasing, churches more readily accept and incorporate unfaithful and often esoteric practices. This highly productive environment suggests a growing 'cottage industry' of prophetism in which Independent churches embrace but largely fail to test potentially limitless 'menus' of activity.

1.3.2.4.3 Lack of Historical and Theological Examination
As regards prophetic praxis, the non-holistic approach exposes a lacuna in Pentecostal scholarship between the Classical Pentecostal commitment to self-examination and that seen in Independent circles. Certain concerns shared by Classical Pentecostalism and the Charismatic Renewal can be easily distinguished from the concerns of Independent Pentecostals. For example, historical and theological study are often shunned in the latter group, as are those who pursue such studies. Over time, this divide creates an echo chamber of sorts, an inbreeding of largely unchecked ideas and practices.

Are the historical and theological studies of Classical Pentecostal and Charismatic Renewal essential? Absolutely and unequivocally, yes. Issues of Spirit baptism, glossolalia, xenolalia, etc. are important realities that require further exploration and scrutiny.

1.3.2.5 Method in Operation: Phenomenological Concerns within Four Relational Categories

Because prophetic function is inherently relational, matters of human interaction contribute to its outcomes. Additionally, because relational conduct is marked by the distortions to which all humanity is prone, distortions of prophetic function are possible. All problems present in prophetic expression fall into four broad categories of experience and impact. I will now summarize them for context regarding the human experience and its role in prophetic function.

1. Personal: matters related to the subjects themselves.
2. Intrapersonal: matters related to the existential and phenomenological interior dynamics of personal subjectivity and its ramifications.
3. Interpersonal: matters related to relationality and intersubjectivity with the community.
4. Transpersonal: matters related to the transcendent and the numinous,[152] the divine influence overarching the previous categories.

1.3.2.5.1 The Personal and Intrapersonal

The personal and intrapersonal are inclusive of the inner life, meaning the interiority and spirituality of the prophetic agent. This category includes (1) the agent's psychological state of being (personal), (2) the agent's existential/phenomenological way of being (intrapersonal), and (3) the theological foundation of the agent's spiritual formation (personal).

If as Christians we 'live and move and have our being' in Christ (Acts 17.28), an ontological approach to the human *way of being* applies. One approach involves

---

[152] 'Numinous', in F.L. Cross and Elizabeth A. Livingstone (eds.), *The Oxford Dictionary of the Christian Church* (Oxford: Oxford University Press, 2005).

Numinous. A word coined by R. Otto to denote the elements of a non-rational and amoral kind in what is experienced in religion as the 'holy'. The numinous is thus held to include feelings of awe and self-abasement (at the *Mysterium Tremendum*) as well as an element of religious fascination (the *fascinans*). Otto developed his psychological analyses for the first time in *Das Heilige* (1917; Eng. tr., 1923). nun. In popular usage, a member of any Religious Institute of women. In RC canon law, however, the term is correctly used only of members of enclosed orders whose members live in houses, which outsiders are not normally permitted to enter and which the members are only rarely permitted to leave (*CIC* [1983], can. 667).

- our use of language as a means of interpretation and meaning making;
- our emotions, feelings, and moods (which provide our movement);
- and the embodied nature in which we incarnate those interpretations and movements.[153]

As embodied persons or embodied spirits,[154] our spirituality is profoundly human. Becoming more angelic is not our goal. Such an idea is rooted in gnostic dualism and provides cover for subtle deceptions. Instead, the Christian's goal is to become *more human*, with Christ as our exemplar.

The fundamental way of being human is foundational to the construction of a Pentecostal theology of prophetic consciousness, perception, and enactment. It will be argued that one's way of being leads to one's way of knowing (consciousness), which leads to one's way of seeing (perception), which results in one's way of acting (enactment).

1.3.2.5.2 The Interpersonal

If prophetic expression and utterance are the means of 'human transmission of allegedly divine messages',[155] then Nissinen correctly purports, 'the prophetic process of transmission consists of the divine sender of the message, the message itself, the human transmitter of the message and the recipient(s) of the message'.[156] Once the prophetic agent delivers inspired speech, the interrelational dynamic becomes paramount, with enactment leading to some form of reception by the larger community, whether welcoming or circumspect. In the interpersonal life of communion, the prophetic agent engages with the community at large. In this context, the agent's social awareness flows from self-awareness. The question then becomes how the prophet is held accountable for what is spoken.

---

[153] Alan Sieler, *Coaching to the Human Soul: Ontological Coaching and Deep Change*, Volume 1: *Linguistic Basics of Ontological Coaching* (Australia: Newfield, 2005), p. 8.

[154] David G. Benner, *Care of Souls: Revisioning Christian Nurture and Counsel* (Grand Rapids, MI: Baker Books 1998), p. 53. Benner uses the phrase 'embodied souls and inspirited bodies'.

[155] Martti Nissinen, *Prophets and Prophecy in the Ancient Near East* (ed. Peter Machinist; Writings from the Ancient World; Atlanta, GA: Society of Biblical Literature, 2003), p. 1.

[156] Nissinen, *Prophets and Prophecy*, p. 2.

R.R. Wilson avers that the prophet serves a mediatorial role in the community.[157] Particularly in relation to Pentecostal spirituality, shared communion requires the continued work of integrating what Steven Jack Land calls 'the language of holiness and the language of power'.[158] Classical Pentecostalism continues to embrace such a spirituality as an 'apocalyptic movement of spiritual transformation',[159] which Land says is undergirded by 'a soteriology which emphasizes salvation as participation in the divine life more than the removal of guilt'.[160]

1.3.2.5.3 The Transpersonal
Ecclesial authority and oversight are of prime significance, with the transpersonal following the previous categories and encompassing them. The transpersonal touches the transcendent (the numinous), as the Spirit is intricately and inextricably bound to the life of the church. The seemingly Silent Observer is the sovereign Spirit (2 Cor. 3.17), who is intimately involved in previous levels. However, at the level of ecclesial authority, the sovereign Spirit's role is to be firmly understood if the Spirit of Prophecy is to endorse prophetic function (Rev. 19.10).

1.3.3 Ecclesiological Method: Contextual Concerns Regarding Prophetic Legitimacy, Catholicity, and Revelation

Concerns with contemporary prophetic function arise within larger contexts involving the preservation of validity through scriptural and ecclesial authority, observance of the Tradition, and fidelity to the creeds. Also contributing to the challenges within prophetic function is the inherent tension between the suggestion of a global Pentecostal culture and the burgeoning diversity within the Independent Pentecostal movement. In this regard, a lack of catholicity and the incumbent lack of a unified grammar seem to induce an unresolved

---

[157] Robert R. Wilson, *Prophecy and Society in Ancient Israel* (Philadelphia, PA: Fortress Press, 1980), p. 22.
[158] Steven Jack Land, *Pentecostal Spirituality: A Passion for the Kingdom* (Cleveland, TN: CPT Press 2010), p. 9.
[159] Land, *Pentecostal Spirituality*, p. 9.
[160] Land, *Pentecostal Spirituality*, p. 9. Participation in the divine life also includes the ontological, existential, psychological, and phenomenological dynamics within human subjects – personally, interpersonally, interpersonally, and transpersonally.

and often unspoken confusion of terms.[161] This lack of clarity is evident in the practical matters of church life and Christian living, as well as in varying and often esoteric views of what revelation is, how it is received, and how it is evaluated.

1.3.3.1 Approach to Questions of Validity

Both the OT and NT canon (and parts of the Tradition that have addressed such expression) reveal parameters within which appropriate prophetic expression might occur.[162] Although most global Pentecostals ostensibly affirm the validity and necessity of scriptural and ecclesial authority over prophetic consciousness, agency, and function, in practice adherence is not always evident.

Although these matters invite examination, either memorializing or deconstructing prophecy altogether is insufficient. Pentecostals would agree with other Continuist Christians that extinguishing enthusiasm for the Holy Spirit's operations and ministrations is not the goal. Those who embrace the continuation of the charismatic and confess the sufficiency of Scripture, while trusting the Spirit's leading in the making of the church's theology and spirituality, would necessarily hold that the appropriate use of the prophetic gifts is found in the received Tradition.

The Oneness Pentecostal movement might disagree. In 1913, Robert Edward McAlister preached at a Pentecostal Holiness meeting in California and declared that although Jesus commanded his disciples to "'baptize [disciples] in the name of the Father and of the Son and of the Holy Spirit", the NT invariably records the apostles baptizing only "in the name of Jesus".[163] This statement created no small stir. Gill quotes Frank J. Ewart as stating, 'The gun was fired

---

[161] Diminished catholicity distorts the community's interpersonal and intrapersonal relations and the subjective, collective, and (most importantly) transpersonal realities empowered by the Spirit.

[162] Apart from what is present in the OT and NT canon, consider the admonitions to 'prophets' within the *Didache*, which dates from the early second century. See Shawn J. Wilhite, 'Thirty-Five Years Later: A Summary of *Didache* Scholarship Since 1983', *Currents in Biblical Research* 17.3 (2019), pp. 266-305. Note, however, that the *Didache* gives far more 'room' for the prophetic than the Tradition does later, after the Montanist controversies. See, too, the response to the Saint Medard prophets.

[163] Kenneth Gill, 'Dividing Over Oneness: The Oneness Movement Pushed Pentecostals to Organize', *Christianity Today* 58 (February 24, 2021), https://www.christianitytoday.com/history/issues/issue-58/dividing-over-oneness.html.

from that platform which was destined to resound throughout all Christendom'.[164]

McAlister's sermon prompted many Pentecostal adherents to be 'rebaptized to follow the ways of the apostolic church'.[165] Here there appears a way of interpreting the Pentecostal experience as being unique in church history and a call back to the primitive church, through the Spirit's workings within the movement. According to Gill, Pentecostals 'believed [that] older doctrines, long diseased by generations of unfaithfulness and the inability to heed God's Spirit, were being uncovered by this "new light" of the Holy Spirit'.[166] In believing this was 'new light', McAlister and the later Oneness movement essentially divorced themselves from the Tradition and created their own 'new light' tradition.

This seems to indicate a belief in the authority of revelation beyond the canon and the creedal confessions from which the canon was ratified. Although the Oneness issue is not part of this study, it demonstrates a perception within one group (Oneness) that other Pentecostals saw as a departure from the Tradition. Oneness believers considered former saints in other pre-Pentecostal traditions to be infected by unfaithfulness and a profound inability to heed the Spirit's work. They tied this to the formulaic approach to baptism in the name of Jesus, as the revelation of the name of God, rejecting the Tradition in relation to the triune nature of the Godself. The Assemblies of God responded with their Statement of Fundamental Truths, a 'repudiation of Oneness beliefs'.[167]

The argumentation of this work stems from the view that the canon is complete, and the creeds are essential to understanding the nature of the prophetic, the Spirit's role in the expression of prophetic function, and prophetic legitimacy. In all of this, we are to mind Paul's exhortation to 'pursue love and strive for the spiritual gifts, and especially that [we] may prophesy' (1 Cor. 14.1). The purpose then, is to serve the greater good. This includes what Daniela Augustine anticipates: the fullness of God's good creation in 'the

---

[164] Gill, 'Dividing Over Oneness'.
[165] Gill, 'Dividing Over Oneness'.
[166] Gill, 'Dividing Over Oneness'.
[167] Gill, 'Dividing Over Oneness'.

charismatic practice of *glossolalia* (and interpretation)',[168] which is 'a foretaste of the ultimate destiny of heaven and earth ... being called together into one holy *koinonia*'.[169] In other words, 'the greater good' is always understood in relation to what Scripture calls the kingdom of God, and the charismata are works of the Spirit only when used in ways appropriate to the character of God's rule.

Could one also argue, as Augustine does regarding glossolalia, that the charism of prophecy 'points to the teleological joining of the terrestrial and celestial in Christ and, therefore, in his church as the new redeemed community of the Spirit?'[170] The interpretation of tongues as a prophetic expression is, in essence, prophetic speech that partially discloses the divine mind and intent for the faith community. Therefore, prophetic utterance provides the aforementioned 'foretaste of the ultimate destiny of heaven'[171] – when it is appropriately used for 'upbuilding and encouragement and consolation' that anticipates the promise-fulfillment schema of the eschaton (1 Cor. 14.3).

1.3.3.2 The Global Context: The Independent Pentecostal Movement

The community at the center of discussion in this work is the Independent Pentecostal or Neocharismatic movement, a subset of the larger Pentecostal community, which itself is not easy to define. Building on Hollenweger, Todd M. Johnson explains Pentecostalism in terms of its more historical development in 'three waves: Pentecostals, Charismatics, and neocharismatics',[172] in that order, with the Third Wave being comprised of 'thousands of schismatic or other independent Charismatic churches [that] have come out of the Pentecostal and Charismatic movements'.[173]

---

[168] Daniela C. Augustine, *Pentecost, Hospitality, and Transfiguration: Toward a Spirit-inspired Vision of Social Transformation* (Cleveland, TN: CPT Press, 2012), p. 35.

[169] Augustine, *Pentecost, Hospitality, and Transfiguration*, p. 35.

[170] Augustine, *Pentecost, Hospitality, and Transfiguration*, p. 35.

[171] Augustine, *Pentecost, Hospitality, and Transfiguration*, p. 35; although tongues and prophecy will ultimately cease according to Paul (1 Cor. 13.8), their teleological trajectory points to 'the mutual indwelling of heaven and earth', a present sign of the church's 'ultimate Christic destiny'.

[172] Todd M. Johnson, 'The Global Demographics of the Pentecostal and Charismatic Renewal', *Society* 46.6 (November 2009), p. 479.

[173] Johnson, 'Global Demographics', p. 481. In this work, Johnson fixes the Third Wave's start in 1945. It should be noted that Johnson now prefers the term *type* to *wave* when referring to movements within Pentecostalism, with *type* allowing for overlapping movements, and *wave* suggesting successive ones.

As to terminology in this work, James K.A. Smith asserts,

some, like Douglas Jacobsen, have adopted the nomenclature of 'small-*p*' pentecostalism as a way of honoring the diversity of pentecostal/charismatic theolog*ies* while at the same time recognizing important family resemblances and shared sensibilities.[174]

Although this work recognizes Smith's distinction and is focused on the proliferation of prophetism in the Independent Pentecostal movement, it foregoes the 'small-p' notation and acknowledges the global Pentecostal community's inclusion of Classical Pentecostalism, Independent Pentecostalism, and Charismatic communities (largely within denominational churches).

Regarding Pentecostalism's 'global' designation, Wolfgang Vondey credits researchers and their determination 'to point to a certain homogeneity among Pentecostal beliefs and practices, and to allow for interpretations of the movement that are not bound to isolated phenomena'.[175] Vondey is suggesting that because of the sheer size of global Pentecostalism, researchers seek to identify a commonality across its various streams that can serve as 'a common denominator'.[176]

As to worldwide expansion, Vondey includes Classical Pentecostalism and Charismatic movements among 'Roman Catholic, Protestant, and Orthodox churches … and so-called neocharismatic groups',[177] the latter being considered a 'catch-all category that comprises 18,810 independent, indigenous, post-denominational denominations and groups'.[178] These 'form a stark ecclesiastical contrast to the rootedness of the Charismatic Movements in the established churches'.[179]

---

[174] James K.A. Smith, *Thinking in Tongues: Pentecostal Contributions to Christian Philosophy* (Grand Rapids, MI: Eerdmans, 2010), p. xvii. All italics are Smith's. In footnote 12 on p. xvii, Smith cites Douglas Jacobsen, *Thinking in the Spirit: Theologies of the Early Pentecostal Movement* (Bloomington, IN: Indiana University Press, 2003), pp. 8-12.

[175] Wolfgang Vondey, *Pentecostalism: A Guide for the Perplexed* (London: Bloomsbury T&T Clark, 2013), p. 15.

[176] Vondey, *Pentecostalism*, p. 15.

[177] Vondey, *Pentecostalism*, p. 17.

[178] Vondey, *Pentecostalism*, p. 17.

[179] Vondey, *Pentecostalism*, p. 19.

Significantly, Johnson suggests, 'independents now number more than the first two waves combined'.[180] They 'have become filled with the Spirit, or empowered or energised by the Spirit, and have experienced the Spirit's supernatural and miraculous ministry'.[181] They 'exercise gifts of the Spirit … and emphasise signs and wonders, supernatural miracles and power encounters'.[182] Johnson states, however, that they 'do not identify themselves as either Pentecostals or Charismatics',[183] having rejected the first two waves.

The drive toward Independent Pentecostalism seems to foster an intentional and consequential diversity, with an inherent contrariness. Anderson suggests diversity as the primary characteristic of Pentecostal identity.[184] Similarly, dis-identification with Classical Pentecostalism and the Charismatic Renewal has shaped Third-Wave identity and is related socially and psychologically to 'narrative identity',[185] which will be considered later in this work.

How then do Independent Pentecostal leaders identify themselves? According to Johnson, they choose descriptors such as 'Independent, Postdenominationalist, Restorationist, Radical, Neo-Apostolic or the "Third Wave" of the twentieth-century Renewal'.[186] These terms assert an unlatching from many theological, philosophical, practical, and institutional moorings that might have tethered Independents to their predecessor groups. Some within their ranks

---

[180] Johnson, 'Global Demographics', p. 481.
[181] Johnson, 'Global Demographics', p. 481.
[182] Johnson, 'Global Demographics', p. 481.
[183] Johnson, 'Global Demographics', p. 481.
[184] Allan H. Anderson, *To the Ends of the Earth: Pentecostalism and the Transformation of World Christianity* (Oxford: Oxford University Press, 2013), p. 4. Anderson aptly captures the diversity of this global movement:

> 'Pentecostalism' has been used to embrace large movements as widely diverse as the celibacy-practicing Pentecostal Mission in India; the Saturday-Sabbath keeping and 'Oneness' True Jesus Church in China, the uniform-wearing, highly ritualistic Zion Christian Church in Southern Africa, and Brazil's equally enormous, prosperity-oriented Universal Church of the Kingdom of God. These are lumped together with the Assemblies of God, the various Churches of God, the Roman Catholic Charismatic movement, 'Neocharismatic' independent church with prosperity and 'Word of Faith' theologies, the 'Third Wave' evangelical movement with their use of spiritual gifts framed within a non-subsequence theology, and many other forms of Charismatic Christianity as diverse as Christianity itself.

[185] Dan P. McAdams and Kate C. McLean, 'Narrative Identity', *Current Directions in Psychological Science* 22.3 (June 2013), pp. 233-38.
[186] Johnson, 'Global Demographics', p. 481.

seem to reject denominational and creedal structures (while others honor them).[187] Those who seem to reject these structures yet embrace (as their restorationist predecessors did, although for varying reasons) an eschatological conviction that some aspect(s) of the primitive church will be restored to original intent,[188] including a renewed view of apostolicity.

As it relates to prophetic function and expression, and for the purpose of this work, the Independent Pentecostal brand (or brands) of spirituality associated with the Third Wave seems to distinguish its (or their) prophetic praxis from that in classical Pentecostal and Charismatic communities.[189] Within the Latter Rain, for example, Violet Kiteley, whose role, views, and ministry will be examined in Chapter 4, spoke on Malachi 3 and claimed, 'God is calling for Reformation' by the 'Fire – (Holy Spirit)' where the 'prophetic un-locks … God's … Revelation'.[190] In addition, she emphasized that the Eucharist

---

[187] Jonathan Black, 'Pentecostals and the Creed', *Apostolic Theology* (November 21, 2017), https://www.apostolictheology.org/2017/11/pentecostals-and-creed.html.

> It's true that most Pentecostal denominations have not adopted the historic Creeds of the Church as statements of faith. But that does not mean they don't hold to the Creeds as statements of faith. How can that be? Well, in the Apostolic Church, for example, the three historic Creeds of the Church (the Three Ecumenical Creeds), weren't thought of as something we could adopt, because adopting them would imply that we didn't already hold to them. Rather than statements of faith which we adopt, the Creeds are deposits handed down to us. So, for the early Apostolics, to depart from the Creeds in any way was to depart from orthodox Christianity and cease to be a Christian church.

[188] Robert Cornwall, 'Primitivism and the Redefinition of Dispensationalism in the Theology of Aimee Semple McPherson', *Pneuma* 14.1 (January 1992), p. 23:

> Dispensational premillennialism, with its belief in the imminent return of Jesus Christ, combined with a distinctive form of primitivism or restorationism, to form two central elements of early pentecostal theology … According to Grant Wacker, this primitivist impulse, which Pentecostals often referred to as the 'latter rain' theory, preceded and bolstered the Pentecostal version of premillennialism. Their primitivism enabled them to redefine dispensationalism to fit the restoration of spiritual gifts, including tongues and prophecy, into their dispensational scheme.

[189] An often-practiced intentional distancing from historic Christianity has also created a gap between orthodoxy and orthopraxy within neo-Charismatic ranks.

[190] Violet Kiteley, 'Malachi 3: God Is Calling for Reformation', *Violet Kiteley Papers*, p. 1. Direct images of this cited page and all cited pages from the Violet Kiteley Papers Collection can be viewed in the Appendix.

(which she referred to as the 'Lord's Table')[191] is 'key'.[192] The teaching also addresses what she perceived as a 'door opened' to 'deception' which is 'the Problem'.[193]

1.3.3.3 The Crisis of Prophetic Legitimacy

Very often, prophetic messages are published to remote audiences via social media. While these audiences include devotees, these declarations are also consumed by uncertain numbers of people who are relatively unknown to the speakers and/or not immersed in the language of the speakers' Independent prophetic subculture. This again raises the question of what Aune calls 'prophetic legitimacy'.[194] The issue of truth versus falsehood is present whenever prophetic utterance is in question.[195] Truth is an essential divine attribute, as the Scripture records that Christ is the embodiment of truth (Jn 14.6), the Spirit is referred to as 'the Spirit of truth' (Jn 16.13), and Isaiah speaks of God as 'the God of truth' (Isa. 65.16, NASB). Therefore, our relations with the triune God are essentially relations with the truth.

God, as eternal truth, must be utterly congruent and without contradiction. Biblically and theologically, therefore, there is a plumb line for discerning and evaluating what is true. Regarding the global spread of Independent Pentecostalism, the influence and authority (or perceived authority) of self-identified prophetic figures produce significant social and cultural impacts. Their truth claims need to be evaluated in light of Scripture, theology, and philosophy. Therefore, the issue of prophetic legitimacy warrants examination.

1.3.3.3.1 The Crisis of Prophetic Legitimacy in Ancient Christianity
David Aune asserts, 'early Christianity was the heir of a great variety of traditions' from ancient Judaic prophetic practices and 'Greco-Roman paganism'.[196] Within ancient Greco-Roman culture, Aune notes, 'a general distinction between solicited and unsolicited oracles'.[197] He describes this in terms of those 'diviners or mantics who

---

[191] Kiteley, 'Calling for Reformation', p. 1.
[192] Kiteley, 'Calling for Reformation', p. 1.
[193] Kiteley, 'Calling for Reformation', p. 1.
[194] Aune, *Prophecy in Early Christianity*, p. 229.
[195] This will be shown in the introduction of three dyads related to prophetic legitimacy (see 1.3.5.2).
[196] Aune, *Prophecy in Early Christianity*, p. 229.
[197] Aune, *Prophecy in Early Christianity*, p. 229.

practiced the divinatory arts in close association with holy places and free-lance mantics whose divinatory gifts were personal'.[198] This seems to indicate that diviners who were present at the holy places operated in response to supplicants who came seeking guidance. The mantics were not affiliated with any particular holy shrine but operated independently within the culture. These ancient practices are not far removed from contemporary prophetic independent practices.

Aune enumerates varying types of prophets as the 'shamanistic prophet, the court and cult prophets, and the free prophets'.[199] Are such prophetic expressions at all reminiscent of ancient Judaic practices? Aune claims, 'early Judaism had a variety of ... prophetic types'.[200] These included 'visionaries' who composed 'apocalyptic literature',[201] presumably by virtue of their phenomenological experiences. This particular expression seems suggestive of those Independent Pentecostal prophetic agents who seem given to visionary experience.

In addition, during Second Temple Judaism, 'millennial movements' lent themselves to 'eschatological prophecy' generated by figures identified with such movements.[202] This too seems reminiscent of contemporary 'Bible prophecy' buffs who specialize in topics related to 'the last days'. In the same ancient period, some who were 'closely associated with the priesthood' articulated 'clerical prophecy'.[203] It is not uncommon within the Independent Pentecostal communities for itinerant prophets to dispense words to pastoral leaders in the various communities in which they are received.

Considering all of this, Aune's assertion that such practices were 'not simply assimilated without change, but were "Christianized"' seems a plausible reality that could potentially continue in recent times.[204] Where Aune does distinguish between early Christian and ancient Judaic prophecy, as contrasted with Greco-Roman practices

---

[198] Aune, *Prophecy in Early Christianity*, p. 229.
[199] Aune, *Prophecy in Early Christianity*, p. 229.
[200] Aune, *Prophecy in Early Christianity*, p. 230.
[201] Aune, *Prophecy in Early Christianity*, p. 230.
[202] Aune, *Prophecy in Early Christianity*, p. 230.
[203] Aune, *Prophecy in Early Christianity*, p. 230.
[204] Aune, *Prophecy in Early Christianity*, p. 230.

and in relation to prophetic legitimacy,[205] he speaks of the 'five characteristic elements of Greco-Roman prophetic inspiration'.[206] Some of the practices Aune enumerates might have been present in some Gentile Christian communities but were not considered legitimate and therefore required correction.[207]

Contrasting the Israelite-Jewish prophetic tradition with the Greco-Roman tradition can be difficult, according to Aune. He argues that despite 'many mutually distinct features, the interpretation of east and west during the Hellenistic and Roman period makes it very difficult if not impossible to untangle the blended elements'.[208] With this in mind, Aune contends, 'Christian prophecy is most adequately treated if it is regarded as a distinctively Christian institution; if so, any typology of Christian prophetism should be based primarily on internal rather than external criteria'.[209] From its inception and in relation to prophetic legitimacy, the Pentecostal movement

---

[205] Aune, *Prophecy in Early Christianity*, p. 229, does not speak to contemporary Christianity.

> In early Christianity, as in ancient Israel, a variety of criteria were employed at various times and places for the purpose of distinguishing the false prophet from the true. These criteria were no more successful than those used in ancient Israel, since they were both *ad hoc* formulations which in actuality were symptomatic of a deeper conflict. In all the passages in early Christian literature where tests for unmasking false prophets are discussed (with the notable exception of Did. 11–12), the primary purpose of these criteria was to denounce a particular false prophet (or group of false prophets) whom the author regarded as particularly threatening. Conflict among various prophets or between prophets and other types of Christian leaders in which prophetic *legitimacy* is questioned is a way of solving the problem of conflicting authority as perceived in what appear to be conflicting norms and values.

[206] Aune, *Prophecy in Early Christianity*, p. 229.

[207] Aune, *Prophecy in Early Christianity*, p. 230, cites H. Bacht's detailed research, which suggests five characteristic elements of Greco-Roman prophetic inspiration: (1) a state of divine possession, (2) mantic frenzy (madness), (3) dependence on artificial means for inducing the prophetic experience, (4) 'man' takes the initiative, frequently through the use of magic, and (5) the general lack of religious or moral value in the content of inspired speech.

[208] Aune, *Prophecy in Early Christianity*, p. 230.

[209] Aune, *Prophecy in Early Christianity*, p. 230. This is inseparable from the arguments about Hellenism and the first Christians. Was the 'Jewish' Gospel 'Hellenized', or was Hellenism (itself already affecting and being affected by Jewish tradition and experience) Christianized? 'Internal criteria' refers to examination by the community and for the community's sake. 'External criteria' are those outside the community and particularly involve criteria that the in-group has rejected from the Great Tradition and replaced with their own ideas.

understood itself as heir of the first apostles and the earliest NT communities. B.F. Lawrence makes this abundantly clear:

> The time between the beginning and the present has been sufficient to establish precedent, create habit, formulate custom. In this way they [the 'older denominations'] have become possessed of a two-fold inheritance, a two-fold guide of action, a two-fold criterion of doctrine – the New Testament and the church position. The Pentecostal Movement has no such history; it leaps the intervening years crying, *'Back to Pentecost'*. In the minds of these honest-hearted, thinking men and women, this work of God is immediately connected with the work of God in New Testament days. Built by the same hand, upon the same foundation of the apostles and prophets, after the same pattern, according to the same covenant, they too are a habitation of God through the Spirit. They do not recognize a doctrine or custom authoritative unless it can be traced to that primal source of church instruction: the Lord and His apostles.[210]

Lawrence contends for an aspect of prophetic legitimacy for the Classical Pentecostal Movement that has carried over into Independent Pentecostalism. Even Independent communities could echo his query to his detractors: 'And now perhaps you are asking, "In what particulars are you so earnestly striving to revert to primitive Christianity?" The answer is of course, "In every way"'.[211] For Lawrence, this meant more than recognizing 'the fundamentals of Christianity'.[212] Specifically, he argued that the Classical Pentecostal Movement was 'laboring to obtain that *supernatural character* of the religion which was so pre-eminently a mark of it in the old days'.[213]

Just as Aune raises these issues of prophetic legitimacy regarding the ancient world, here we see raised within the ranks and roots of Pentecostalism issues of authority and discernment in its tribes.

---

[210] B.F. Lawrence, 'Back to Pentecost', *The Weekly Evangel* (May 1916), p. 4.
[211] Lawrence, 'Back to Pentecost', p. 4.
[212] Lawrence, 'Back to Pentecost', p. 4.
[213] Lawrence, 'Back to Pentecost', p. 4 (emphasis added).

1.3.3.4 The Crisis of Catholicity and Prophetic Legitimacy in Independent Pentecostalism

Assuming Aune's distinction between internal and external criteria is accurate, how might these criteria apply to Independent communities, particularly when insiders and outsiders find communication with the Tradition difficult? Although there is little if any sense of catholicity within the Independent Pentecostal movement, some within the movement are considered authoritative insiders and have become essential to the movement's identity and welfare. Typically, these insiders speak for those in and beyond their own circles.

Regarding catholicity, Chris E.W. Green offers a 'theology of catholicity' that can be understood as 'Pentecostal and catholic, true to both Azusa Street and Nicaea'.[214] Green contends for a recovery of 'the doctrine of catholicity' in response to 'the sectarianism that haunted Pentecostalism from the beginning'.[215] He notes that since Classical Pentecostalism's inception, Pentecostals 'have given little thought to the doctrine of catholicity'.[216] The question is *why*? What underlies this dearth of thought? Anticipating the question, Green notes, 'given [Pentecostals'] restorationist concerns and ambitions, it is perhaps closer to the truth to say that they have been opposed to [catholicity]'.[217]

In speaking of the larger church and appealing for Pentecostal recognition of catholicity, Green states that catholicity is 'nothing less than a confession that the church shares in the fullness of God's nature, the fullness of which is the hope of all creation'.[218] He focuses on the Pentecostal phenomena of glossolalia, saying, 'The Pentecostal experience of speaking in tongues bears a unique witness to catholicity as communion with an infinite God'.[219] Assuming Green is correct, and given the nature of Peter's sermon on the Day of Pentecost (in which the Spirit creates a kind of prophetic umbrella under which the entire church is to function and bear witness to Christ) (Acts 2.14-21; Joel 2.28-29), could not the same appeal be made in

---

[214] Chris E.W. Green, '"We Have Come to Fullness": Toward a Pentecostal Catholicity', *Journal of Biblical and Theological Studies* 5.2 (2020), p. 357.
[215] Green, 'Toward a Pentecostal Catholicity', p. 357.
[216] Green, 'Toward a Pentecostal Catholicity', p. 357.
[217] Green, 'Toward a Pentecostal Catholicity', p. 357.
[218] Green, 'Toward a Pentecostal Catholicity', p. 357.
[219] Green, 'Toward a Pentecostal Catholicity', p. 357.

relation to Christian prophecy? One could argue that the intended focus of Christian prophecy is the Christian narrative and the Good News of the Incarnation (and all it presupposes and enacts). However, variations on that theme can be legion.

Both within and between Independent circles, a lack of clarity seems evident. I would argue that it springs from the nature of Independent Pentecostalism, whose very emergence and existence suggest a moving away from denominationalism's strictures and toward a greater openness to the Spirit's work. Like their forebears, most Independents are not creedal but averse to doctrinal statements that seem to limit or delegitimize potentially acceptable expressions of the Holy Spirit's activity. However, the creed would not limit what is faithful to the Spirit's work; the challenge arises when prophetic activity exceeds canonical bounds. Although independence is believed to provide freedom from the perceived restraints of a tradition, independent churches and movements invariably form alternative traditions.[220] This makes communication difficult, so that attempts to be ecumenical or to respect the teachings and practices of the larger Christian Tradition present a challenge.[221]

This dynamic begs certain questions within the Independent tribes, particularly regarding the definition and deployment of terms related to all things prophetic. It can be argued that word usage discloses its meaning within a given community and suggests inter-community differences. For example, does *Spirit baptism* mean the same thing in Independent Pentecostalism that it does in Classical Pentecostalism? How might these groups' usages of the term compare with usage among Anglicans or Methodists? Furthermore, how is the term being used in relation to the larger Christian Tradition? Even within Independent tribes, is there any overlap or symmetry regarding Spirit baptism and its connection to speaking in tongues?

As to the various Independent usages of terminologies, it becomes evident that, at best, the understanding of doctrinal formulations is incomplete. Because the movement and its communities are diverse, grammatical differences exist regarding what is understood

---

[220] Independent Pentecostals' lack of catholicity within the larger Pentecostal body is understandable and is largely attributable to identifying in-group uses of grammar.

[221] These teachings and practices include the canon of Scripture, creeds, liturgies of baptism and the Lord's supper, and ordination.

as prophetic. Therefore, it is common for Independent Pentecostals to seem to talk past each other, failing to acknowledge their disparate deployments of supposedly shared terminologies.

For example, in speaking of the revelatory nature of prophecy, John Eckhardt refers to the Scriptures as 'the perfect revelation of Jesus'.[222] He simultaneously asserts, 'prophecy is never a mind reflection, it is something far deeper than this'.[223] If, at that point where the Spirit interacts with the human mind, prophecy occurs outside the mind's reflective properties, what exactly is deeper? Is this an allusion to unconscious processes between the prophetic agent and the divine Spirit? What precisely is implied by the claim that divine encounters are launched by revelation? Is there a process in which aspects of revelation might be related? Different teachers give different answers. Due to variances in grammatical usage and definition, clarity seems diminished. Thus, if consistency and legitimacy are to be ratified, these matters need to be elucidated and reconciled.

1.3.3.4.1 Biblical (and Historical) Reflections
Considering the often-unacknowledged variances in language and the obfuscation they engender, how are doctrinal formulations agreed to in community life, and to what degree are they functional? Many Independent Pentecostals adhere to the belief that speaking in tongues is the 'initial evidence' of Spirit baptism; but even where this belief is not held,[224] the doctrinal formulation sometimes abides as a

---

[222] John Eckhardt, *Prophetic Activation: Break Your Limitations to Release Prophetic Influence* (Lake Mary, FL: Charisma House, 2016), intro.

[223] Eckhardt, *Prophetic Activation*, intro.

[224] Frank D. Macchia, *Baptized in the Spirit: A Global Pentecostal Theology* (Grand Rapids, MI: Zondervan, 2006), p. 35.:

> Not all Pentecostals globally hold to the doctrine of speaking in tongues as the initial evidence of Spirit baptism, however, though the experience of glossolalia is arguably still fairly widespread in the movement. And even among those who hold this initial-evidence doctrine, the relationship between tongues and Spirit baptism varies. Seymour regarded tongues as a sign of the empowerment of the church to reach out to all nations, implying a boundary-crossing experience that produces a diverse church … He later regarded love as the primary sign of Spirit baptism.

See also Andrew K. Gabriel, 'Three Ways People Misunderstand Tongues as "Initial Evidence" of Spirit Baptism', *Exploring Theology, Scripture, and Ministry*, https://www.andrewkgabriel.com/2017/01/24/misunderstanding-tongues-as-initial-evidence-of-spirit-baptism/. And Mookgo S. Kgatle, 'Spirit Baptism and the Doctrine of Initial Evidence in African Pentecostal Christianity: A Critical

support to community cohesion and identity. Until and unless a viable grammatical substitute is offered, a doctrinally untenable position can be seen as a unifying Pentecostal distinctive. Thus, Pentecostal dogma is deeply sectarian, whether that sectarianism is intended, implied, or unconsciously unintentional (owing to an incomplete understanding of catholicity). Perhaps ecumenical bridges can be built when such terminology becomes more adjectival. How that can be accomplished requires further inquiry and dialog. In the view of Lutheran theologian and ecumenicist George A. Lindbeck, grammatical shifts in the language patterns are associated with doctrinal beliefs.[225] However, grammatical variations seem compatible with the desire of some in the Independent Pentecostal movement to maintain independence from denominational affiliations.

Regarding contemporary prophetic legitimacy, what internal criteria exist within Independent streams? In mainline denominational Pentecostalism, such criteria include Bible prophecy, most often from premillennial perspectives. The exercise of the gifts in contemporary Assemblies of God, Church of God, Pentecostal Holiness, Foursquare, and other denominations would more than likely be guided by the work of the late Howard Carter.[226] The Word of Faith movement, various Charismatic communities, and Independent Pentecostals also embraced Carter's seminal work. Esteemed Pentecostal scholar Gordon Fee had been considered trustworthy within the Assemblies of God and other Pentecostal traditions in relation to the charisms.[227] However, the distrust of academic scholarship among Pentecostal denominations is evident in Fee's dismissal from involvement with the Assemblies of God, precisely because his scholarship led him to challenge a dispensational view of Christian history. Despite resistance, Pentecostal scholarship is growing. Yet its influence

---

Analysis', *HTS Theological Studies* 76.1 (March 2020), https://hts.org.za/index.php/hts/article/view/5796.

[225] 'Catholics and Protestants often interpret differently. In any case, it is not the lexicon but rather the grammar of the religion which church doctrines chiefly reflect', George A. Lindbeck, *The Nature of Doctrine: Religion and Theology in a Postliberal Age* (Louisville, KY: Westminster John Knox Press, 25th anniversary edn, 2009), ch. 4.

[226] Howard Carter, *Questions and Answers on Spiritual Gifts* (Tulsa, OK: Harrison House, 1976).

[227] Gordon D. Fee, *The First Epistle to the Corinthians* (New International Commentary on the New Testament; Grand Rapids, MI: Eerdmans, rev. edn, 2014).

within Pentecostal ranks remains marginal, with the distrust of academia firm within many communities, including Independents.

1.3.4 The Wider Theological Method

1.3.4.1 The Revelation Context

Although the diversity of grammar promotes divergent views of revelation, it can be agreed that all things prophetic are anchored in a sense of divine revelation through which God speaks and the hearer responds. As will be shown through the views of several figures, the overall experience and understanding of perceiving and receiving divine revelation have been highly individualized, even among prophetic voices who draw from shared Pentecostal roots. To be considered now is a key figure in prophetic history and two voices of Pentecostal scholarship.

1.3.4.1.1 Revelation as Understood by William Branham and the Latter Rain
The notions of 'revelational' and 'revelatory' are not new within Independent Pentecostalism. The ways in which Pentecostals use such language are shaped by major figures, including William Marrion Branham, not in relation to doctrine as it is traditionally understood, but in relation to ministerial practice and immediacy of awareness, spontaneity, and insight within the context of preaching, praying for others, and prophesying. There is a profound sense of the Spirit being present with prophetic agents in the exercise of their ministerial duties. This is far more than preaching or teaching under the inspiration of the Spirit. Instead, it is reminiscent of scriptural accounts in which prophetic expression occurs within the dynamics of real-time ministry. One such example is the coming of Agabus to Philip's house to deliver a prophetic word to Paul, who is abiding there (Acts 21.10-11).

Branham, who was known worldwide, was and remains controversial.[228] He claims to have been launched into global ministry through a message delivered by an angel sent by God. Kydd quotes the angelic message:

> Fear not. I am sent from the presence of Almighty God to tell you that your peculiar life and your misunderstood ways have been

---

[228] An example is Branham's 'serpent seed doctrine'. 'The Serpent's Seed', *Voice of God Recordings*, https://branham.org/en/biblestudy/TheSerpentSeed..

to indicate that God has sent you to take a gift of divine healing to the peoples of the world. IF YOU WILL BE SINCERE, AND CAN GET THE PEOPLE TO BELIEVE YOU, NOTHING SHALL STAND BEFORE YOUR PRAYER, NOT EVEN CANCER.[229]

Kydd categorizes aspects of Branham's ministry as being 'revelatory'.[230] This includes Branham's claim of the angel's ongoing presence with him and accompanying revelatory indicators upon which Branham relied in effectuating his work.[231] Among those named indicators were 'vibrations in his left hand',[232] which identified the 'source of an illness'.[233] The angel spoke of this as the '"first pull", as in a fish pulling on a line'.[234] Branham spoke of an additional 'pull' as the supernatural 'gift of discernment',[235] a way in which the Holy Spirit was 'able to discern diseases, and thoughts of men's hearts, and other hidden things that only God could know and then reveal' to Branham as the revelatory agent.[236]

In 1947, three notable pastors in the Vancouver, British Colombia area – Walter McAllister, Clarence Hall, and J. Ern Baxter – invited Branham to a series of revival meetings there.[237] The signs and wonders that accompanied Branham's ministry impacted and influenced brothers George and Ern Hawtin, who were involved with Sharon Bible College and would become two of the original principals of the Latter Rain in North Battleford, Saskatchewan.[238] 'The Hawtin brothers returned home [from Branham's Vancouver meetings] with renewed zeal and passion to see the Holy Spirit do the same at the Sharon School'.[239] The Hawtin brothers called the students to

---

[229] R.A.N. Kydd, 'Healing in the Christian Church', *NIDPCM*, p. 708. All emphasis is Branham's, according to Kydd.
[230] Kydd, 'Healing', p. 708.
[231] Kydd, 'Healing', pp. 708-709.
[232] Kydd, 'Healing', p. 708.
[233] Kydd, 'Healing', p. 709. In this regard, Branham believed, 'all sicknesses and accidents were caused by evil spirits'.
[234] Kydd, 'Healing', p. 708.
[235] Kydd, 'Healing', p. 709.
[236] Kydd, 'Healing', p. 709.
[237] Chet Swearingen and Phyllis Swearingen, '1948 Latter Rain Revival', Beautiful Feet, https://romans1015.com/latter-rain/.
[238] Swearingen and Swearingen, 'Latter Rain Revival', https://romans1015.com/latter-rain/.
[239] Swearingen and Swearingen, 'Latter Rain Revival', https://romans1015.com/latter-rain/.

extended seasons of fasting and prayer, 'coupled with intense study of the Scriptures'.[240] In the days leading up to February 14, 1948, there was great expectation, and 'extended chapel services' were scheduled.[241] (Chapter 4 will further explore this period in North Battleford and its relation to prophetic legitimacy. This will be done through the personal testimony of Violet Kiteley, who participated in the Latter Rain Revival).

This call to fasting and prayer came during what Violet Kiteley and others called 'a spiritual dearth'.[242] What followed was a significant display of the revelatory gifts of prophetic expression – the earmark of Latter Rain prophetism, which remains the earmark of today's Independent Pentecostal prophetism. Branham could be seen as the person who popularized the idea that personal 'revelation' is normative. Even when nuanced by appeals to the authority of Scripture, this idea became the norm for many who were unaware of its implications and/or inclined to embrace it. It is also important to understand that in the domain of Pentecostal studies, scholars have weighed in on the concept of *revelation* and the construct of *revelatory*. This too is important if a Pentecostal theology of prophetic legitimacy is to be constructed.

1.3.4.1.2 John McKay and Rickie D. Moore on Revelation and Authority in Pentecostal Experience and Theology
Groups within the global Pentecostal movement define terms such as *revelation* and *revelatory* differently. In relation to prophetic legitimacy, how do Pentecostal scholars engage the term *revelatory*? Some, such as John W. McKay, use *revelation* to describe a charismatic way of reading the canon. For McKay, the Pauline approach involves the Spirit's 'removal of the veil'.[243] He views this as a living and vital

---

[240] Swearingen and Swearingen, 'Latter Rain Revival', https://romans1015.com/latter-rain/.

[241] Swearingen and Swearingen, 'Latter Rain Revival', https://romans1015.com/latter-rain/.

[242] Violet Kiteley, 'Restoration Basics', Lecture Notes (December 3, 2009), *Violet Kiteley Papers*, p. 1; 'Latter Rain', William Branham, https://william-branham.org/site/research/topics/latter_rain.

[243] John W. McKay, 'When the Veil Is Taken Away: The Impact of Prophetic Experience on Biblical Interpretation', in Lee Roy Martin (ed.), *Pentecostal Hermeneutics: A Reader* (Leiden: Brill, 2013), p. 61 (first published in the *Journal of Pentecostal Theology* 5 (1994), pp. 17-40).

interchange between the text's reader and the Pentecostal Spirit, whom the canon indicates has inspired the text (2 Tim. 3.16-17).

McKay cites 2 Cor. 3.16-17 for Paul's understanding of how the charismatic Spirit removes what hinders the spiritual senses from perceiving and comprehending Christ when reading canonical texts.[244] For McKay, such a process, which is more than an intellectual approach, provides for the expression of 'prophetic Christianity'.[245] What the community then experiences through the reading is a sense of the narrative's real-time drama. From such an encounter with the text, the narrative can be contextualized contemporaneously, preserving its passion and intention and inspiring the community to *live into* the text.[246] This approach distinguishes between the letter that kills and the Spirit that gives life and leads to the removal of the veil (2 Cor. 3.6, 17). Such an encounter with the Spirit reveals the text's Christological implications in one's personal and communal context.

This use of the term *revelation* is somewhat similar to Rickie D. Moore's concept by which 'Pentecost is arguably the source of divine revelation that most effectively illuminates and ignites interaction with all other theological sources'.[247] From a Pentecostal framework, these illuminated sources 'include Scripture, for sure, but they even include the ultimate source of revelation, Jesus, as they surely did in the book of Acts for Jesus' disciples'.[248] Moore adds that the early Christian disciples were 'inspired, empowered, and ignited to become witnesses of Jesus to the ends of the earth'.[249] One could argue that, for Moore, the Spirit, the text, and Jesus all impact the community (disciples) of the Spirit.

Approaches to experience and the revelatory process such as McKay's and Moore's include the totality of what is embodied within our humanness, including the human psyche's cognitive, subjective, and affective faculties. This approaches the realm of the revelatory

---

[244] McKay, 'Veil Is Taken Away', p. 61.

[245] McKay, 'Veil Is Taken Away', p. 59.

[246] To *live into* the text is to embrace the proscriptions, prescriptions, and spirit of the text, allowing it to form one's perspectives, beliefs, and behaviors.

[247] Rickie D. Moore, 'Revelation: The Light and Fire of Pentecost', in Wolfgang Vondey (ed.), *The Routledge Handbook of Pentecostal Theology* (London: Routledge, 2020), ch. 5.

[248] Moore, 'Revelation', ch. 5.

[249] Moore, 'Revelation', ch. 5. Given that this is present in the Lukan narrative, the contemporary community of disciples can have encounters with the same Spirit and the same Jesus.

from the perspective of an existential human phenomenology. It also establishes parameters from which prophetic legitimacy can be affirmed canonically, communally, and personally. Therefore, such approaches seem to offer a way forward for global and Independent Pentecostal movements.

It must be noted that for scholars such as McKay and Moore, answerability and accountability are standards of their profession. As such, their premises, arguments, and insights are subject to peer scrutiny within academic and religious institutional structures. As regards prophetic legitimacy, the challenge within Independent tribes is a lack of any official or unofficial, explicit or de facto magisterium, which also makes a consistent prophetic grammar difficult. Later in this work, I will argue that early Latter Rain adherents embraced what might be considered a de facto magisterium, even within Independent circles.

1.3.4.2 Conclusory Notes Regarding Concerns

It seems necessary for humility to temper any approach to prophetic activity. Such humility cannot be understood solely in attitudinal terms. It shows itself in practice by its deference to the Tradition and its submission to the authority of Scripture given and received through the Spirit among the people of God. In addressing political tribalism, Rowan Williams urges the humility of accountability and writes, 'Modernity becomes toxic at many levels when it loses the capacity for self-critique, and when it canonizes the myth of automatic improvement through time'.[250] In the absence of self-critique, we too can sacrifice covenant answerability and presume a universality of thought in response to new contexts or methods of interaction.

New methods include evolving technologies. Because social media enable 'prophetic words' to be disseminated beyond the boundaries of the local church, they minimize accountability, liability, and answerability. One can therefore argue that the advance of social media released a floodgate of prophetic utterance, whether rightly constrained or wholly unbridled. The digital environment constitutes a largely ungoverned platform to a potentially limitless audience.

---

[250] Rowan Williams, 'Overcoming Political Tribalism', *ABC Religion and Ethics*, https://www.abc.net.au/religion/rowan-williams-overcoming-political-tribalism/11566242.

1.3.5 Research Aims and Objectives

1.3.5.1 Proposing a Threefold Pentecostal Theology of Prophetic Legitimacy

Given that I am adapting Aune's term, *prophetic legitimacy*, and relating it to a variety of issues concerning prophetic function (in particular, a modern lack of clarity and catholicity), it becomes necessary to construct a Pentecostal theology of prophetic legitimacy. With that construct in mind, I will present my argument from canonical, theological, psychological, and phenomenological perspectives. Within the construct, I also identify three domains by which prophetic agents and the communities they serve can discern and validate prophetic legitimacy. The domains are:

- Prophetic consciousness
- Prophetic perception
- Prophetic enactment

From a canonical perspective, this threefold construct circumscribes what seems evident theologically and establishes the prophetic composition and implications of the Pentecostal theology to be proposed. Additionally, I propose that the construct provides a framework for evaluating claims that the triune God has spoken. These closely related domains also form a progression: Prophetic consciousness leads to prophetic perception. Once prophetic perception is clarified, prophetic enactment becomes evident in prophetic expressions and possible dramatic acts.[251]

The domains exemplify a way of knowing (consciousness), a way of seeing (perception), and a way of acting (enactment). Thus, prophetic legitimacy involves an intersection of the theological and ontological. It is theological because the prophetic agent has been apprehended for prophetic speech and action; it is ontological because it involves human beings – embodied spirits who filter their observations through internal processes including thoughts, emotions, feelings, moods, and the physiological responses the processes entail.[252]

---

[251] With prophetic enactment comes the agent's stewardship in communicating the divine message. The term itself is derived from Johnson, 'Prophetic Enactment', pp. 130-65. Prophetic enactment becomes evident in prophetic expressions and possible dramatic acts.

[252] One can refer to embodied spirits as *embodied souls*.

I will argue that prophetic consciousness involves observing and then interpreting. Thus, perceptual realities form and are transformed, often impacting or being impacted by memory, imagination, intuition, reasoning, and volition. As a result, the prophetic agent takes action, whether through a prophetic expression or dramatic act. I will argue that the communities of faith where prophetic function is exercised are responsible for recognizing, substantiating, and validating the prophetic legitimacy of the speech and other acts they observe.

To that end, the three domains will enable the community to distinguish between legitimacy and non-legitimacy in relation to (1) the message and the manner in which it is expressed, and (2) its ultimate reception, or perhaps rejection, by the greater community. I will argue that communities can weigh legitimacy only with respect to the canon, the Great Tradition, and the community's attending to that Tradition.

From a historical and future-forward perspective, the Tradition provides the lattice and boundaries within which prophetic legitimacy can be maintained, sustained, and celebrated. Within the life and relations shared by the agent and the community, challenges such as the projection of presumption and the presumption of unmediated utterance can be sorted out, and accountability and answerability can be ensured. This is particularly pertinent within Independent Pentecostal tribes where the prevailing Western individualization has profoundly impacted social relations and produced gaps in prophetic legitimacy. Often, these gaps indicate deeper problems, which can be addressed through the same lattice and boundaries.

Within the canonical text and the community (wherein lies the communion of saints), the work of the Spirit provides essential safeguards that enable the church to maintain 'the testimony of Jesus', which is 'the spirit of prophecy' (Rev. 19.10).

1.3.5.1.1 Essential Terminology

In considering the proposed threefold construct in relation to prophetic legitimacy, defining key terms is essential and requires interplay among disciplines. For example, the term *prophetic expression(s)* will be significant throughout this study. It is used much as the term *speech-act* is used. Mangum and Widder address speech-act theory this way:

Speech-act theory is primarily concerned with how language is used to perform actions. That is, people speak to bring about various outcomes or accomplish specific purposes. At the most basic level, a speech act is any action that can be performed by someone saying they are completing the action ... In speech-act theory, any meaningful expression using language is an 'utterance', regardless of the medium of expression. An utterance may also be called a 'locution' or 'locutionary act', referring to the meaningful content of the expression. The terms 'illocutionary' and 'perlocutionary' are also common in speech-act theory. Osborne explains these as the three dimensions of communication: 'locutionary (what it says), illocutionary (what it does), and perlocutionary (what it effects)' (Osborne, *Hermeneutical Spiral*, 23). The illocutionary aspect is what the utterance accomplishes, and the perlocutionary aspect is what effect the speaker intended the act to have (Osborne, *Hermeneutical Spiral*, 502).[253]

For the purposes of this work, a *prophetic expression* is uttered by a prophetic agent in its appropriate context on behalf of God to the people of God. Mangum and Widder state,

> the power of speech-act theory goes beyond the words themselves and requires a close reading of the context, including [per John Searle] 'the intentions, attitudes, and expectations of the participants, the relationships existing between participants, conventions that are unspoken rules and conventions that are understood

---

[253] Douglas Mangum and Wendy Widder, 'Speech-Act Theory', in John D. Barry, *et al.* (eds.), *The Lexham Bible Dictionary* (Bellingham, WA: Lexham Press, 2016):
> Speech act theory is a subdiscipline of the philosophy of language and was founded by J. L. Austin and his student John Searle. Austin's central idea is that in making a statement one is performing an action. He isolated three types of linguistic actions that can occur when we communicate verbally: the locutionary act – the uttering of the words; the illocutionary act – what we do in uttering the words (understood as the meaning of the sentence); and the perlocutionary act – what we bring about by uttering the words.

Kit Barker, 'Speech Act Theory, Dual Authorship, and Canonical Hermeneutics: Making Sense of Sensus Plenior', *Journal of Theological Interpretation* 3.1-2 (2009), p. 231. Barker noted, 'Austin, *How to Do Things with Words*, chs. 8–10. Though these distinctions are sometimes contested, most scholars are willing to speak in terms of these three components: locution, illocution, and perlocution' (p. 231 n. 12).

to be in play when an utterance is made or received' (Pratt, Toward a Speech Theory, 86).[254]

The 'intentions, attitudes, and expectations of the participants' are tied to how the prophetic agent and the community being addressed apprehend the prophetic word.

Also key to this research is the term *consciousness*, which defies philosophical definition. Therefore, to begin with the philosophy of consciousness is to recognize the struggle. In fact, Thomas Nagel decries as 'reductionist euphoria' the excitement over 'analyses of mental phenomena and mental concepts' that were intended to aid the understanding of consciousness.[255] From a philosophical perspective, mind-brain relations are difficult to articulate (as are relations between mind and body), making the concept of consciousness 'notoriously ambiguous'.[256] Gennaro notes that claims of consciousness being 'synonymous with, say, "awareness" or "experience" or "attention" … [are] not generally accepted today'.[257] He is pointing to research regarding the 'unconscious experiences' he sees as possible examples of 'subliminal perception',[258] the psychological possibility of which remains debatable.[259] This work will explore the unconscious domain in relation to the mystical state, particularly in light of the psychology of William James, the work of Carl Gustav Jung, and possible applications within the theological conversation.

Any meaningful conversation about mind-brain and mind-body relations will require some sort of working concept. This research

---

[254] Mangum and Widder, 'Speech-Act Theory'.
[255] Thomas Nagel, 'What Is It Like to Be a Bat?', *Philosophical Review* 83.4 (Oct. 1974), p. 435.
[256] Rocco J. Gennaro, 'Consciousness', in James Fieser and Bradley Dowden (eds.), *Internet Encyclopedia of Philosophy*, https://iep.utm.edu/freud/#SH7d, https://iep.utm.edu/consciou/#H1.
[257] Gennaro, 'Consciousness', https://iep.utm.edu/consciou/#H1.
[258] Gennaro, 'Consciousness', https://iep.utm.edu/consciou/#H1.
[259] *Subliminal perception* ['Subliminal Perception', *APA Dictionary of Psychology*, https://dictionary.apa.org/subliminal-perception] can be defined as

> the registration of stimuli below the level of awareness, particularly stimuli that are too weak (or too rapid) for an individual to consciously perceive them. There has been much debate about whether responses to subliminal stimuli actually occur and whether it is possible for subliminal commands or advertising messages to influence behavior. Experimental evidence indicates that subliminal commands may not directly affect behavior but may prime later responses.

will not focus on solving elusive philosophical debates about consciousness; however, it will argue the definitions of conscious experience and phenomena from a psychological perspective. The ubiquity of conscious experience across many species does not ensure our ability to grasp those experiences. Giraffes, dogs, cats, and aardvarks experience consciousness. As humans, however, we cannot intuit or approximate an animal's perspective of its phenomenological experiences. Yet within human phenomenology, we can attempt to explain what consciousness is like.[260]

From a foundational psychological perspective, one can say that *consciousness* is simply 'the state of being conscious',[261] as the etymology suggests. The term *conscious* (and, by extension, the noun *consciousness*) is derived from the Latin *conscius*, which means 'knowing, aware'.[262] It is derived from *conscire*, which means to 'be (mutually) aware'.[263] Ultimately, the term *conscious* evolved to carry the sense of 'knowing or perceiving within oneself, [as in being] sensible inwardly, aware'.[264]

Consciousness is 'an organism's awareness of something either internal or external to itself'.[265] This prompts us to ask, 'What is awareness?' Simply defined, *awareness* is the 'perception or knowledge of something' that requires 'accurate reportability of something perceived or known'.[266] Within the discipline of psychology, accurate reportability 'is widely used as a behavioral index of conscious awareness'.[267] For example, when God calls Jeremiah to prophetic function, God asks, 'What do you see?' (Jer. 1.11). Being focused on a specific feature of a certain almond tree in early bloom, Jeremiah reports, 'I see a branch of an almond tree' (Jer. 1.11). The text conveys the

---

[260] Nagel, 'What Is It Like', p. 435.
[261] 'Consciousness', *APA Dictionary of Psychology*, https://dictionary.apa.org/consciousness.
[262] 'Conscious', *Online Etymology Dictionary*, https://www.etymonline.com/search?q=conscious.
[263] 'Conscious', *Online Etymology Dictionary*, https://www.etymonline.com/search?q=conscious.
[264] 'Conscious', *Online Etymology Dictionary*, https://www.etymonline.com/search?q=conscious.
[265] 'Consciousness', *APA Dictionary of Psychology*, https://dictionary.apa.org/consciousness.
[266] 'Consciousness', *APA Dictionary of Psychology*, https://dictionary.apa.org/consciousness.
[267] 'Consciousness', *APA Dictionary of Psychology*, https://dictionary.apa.org/consciousness.

divine affirmation that Jeremiah has 'seen well' (Jer. 1.12).[268] Hence, from a psychological perspective, Jeremiah is consciously aware of what he is seeing. Although the visual field of humans is typically limited and 'blindsight' is possible,[269] the almond branch was within Jeremiah's perceptual field, and he was aware of it. (He could not be aware of what he could not perceive).

Consciousness is a 'person's subjective, firsthand experience of reality and one's own thoughts'.[270] That subjective, firsthand experience is *awareness*, which is variable. The degree to which one is wakeful is the degree to which one is aware,[271] because 'wakefulness and awareness – are the basic properties of consciousness'.[272] For the purposes of this work, awareness encompasses (1) that which is external and part of the human agent's overall environment, and (2) that which is internal to the agent.

---

[268] Given that this work presents consciousness from a theological, psychological, and phenomenological perspective, Husserl's work on the phenomenology of consciousness is noteworthy. Jeremiah's vision of the almond tree (Jer. 1.11-13) can be read in Husserlian terms. Moran and Cohen remind us that for Husserl, 'perceptual experience ... forms the basis of all consciousness'. Dermot Moran and Joseph Cohen, 'Perception', *The Husserl Dictionary* (London: Continuum, 2012). If this is accurate, one cannot divorce consciousness from perception. Based on what seems a reasonable supposition, this work argues that perception rises from consciousness, including that particular form of consciousness referred to as *prophetic consciousness*. With respect to Husserl, Moran and Cohen, 'Perception', *Husserl Dictionary*, add, 'Perception moreover offers a paradigm of a *kind of consciousness* where intention finds fulfillment, where the activity of perceiving receives immediate and constant confirmation and collaboration' (emphasis added). Regarding perception, fulfillment seems to be in accurately recognizing that of which one is conscious, as Jeremiah was conscious of the almond branch.

[269] 'Blindsight', *APA Dictionary of Psychology*, https://dictionary.apa.org/blindsight. Blindsight is:

> the capacity of some individuals with damage to the striate cortex (primary visual cortex or area V1) to detect and even localize visual stimuli presented to the blind portion of the visual field. Discrimination of movement, flicker, wavelength, and orientation may also be present. However, these visual capacities are not accompanied by conscious awareness.

[270] Paul Moes and Donald J. Tellinghuisen, *Exploring Psychology and Christian Faith: An Introductory Guide* (Grand Rapids, MI: Baker Academic, 2014), p. 64.

[271] Moes and Tellinghuisen, *Psychology and Christian Faith*, pp. 64-65:

> Our own experiences, like differences in how we feel from one day to another when waking up in the morning, show us that wakefulness and awareness fluctuate. Neuropsychological research confirms these variations. If both wakefulness and awareness are very low, a person would experience a coma; if both are high, the experience is conscious wakefulness.

[272] Moes and Tellinghuisen, *Psychology and Christian Faith*, p. 64.

James claims that within human consciousness there is a 'sense of reality',[273] 'a feeling of objective presence'.[274] This can occur in the realm of feeling what is within the human domain; it can also occur in the domain of religious experience. When tied to religious experience, this involves 'religious conceptions'.[275] James argues that, because of our sense of reality, such conceptions present as 'appearing real'.[276] Why state it as 'appearing real?' Conceptions are formed from perceptions. How is it that they appear real? If one is aware of what one sees/perceives (as Jeremiah was aware), it is indeed real (as was the branch of the almond tree). What one conceives internally based on recognition is the internal representation of what is presented objectively and externally. What one conceives is formed from what one perceives. If perception is skewed, conception will be likewise. This implies the possibility of not perceiving well, and therefore not conceiving well. In Jeremiah's case, he needed a corresponding external confirmation: 'You have seen well' (Jer. 1.12). What he sees becomes a religious conception when God interprets his perception and transposes its meaning to speak beyond its significance as something concretely real. James speaks of what is perceived as concretely real when he states,

> the whole universe of concrete objects, as we know them, swims … in a wider and higher universe of abstract ideas, that lend it its significance. As time, space, and the ether soak through all things so (we feel) do abstract and essential goodness, beauty, strength, significance, justice, soak through all things good, strong, significant, and just.[277]

Notice that James keys in on 'a wider and higher universe of abstract ideas'.[278] He sees ideas as abstractions that provide 'the background for all our facts' and are 'the fountain-head of all the

---

[273] James, *Varieties of Religious Experience*, p. 58. 'Psychologists such as Abraham Maslow and Viktor Frankl' pioneered the term *transpersonal psychology* in the 1960s. Kendra Cherry, 'The Practice of Transpersonal Psychology: History, Popularity, and Research Areas', https://www.verywellmind.com/what-is-transpersonal-psychology-2795971.
[274] James, *Varieties of Religious Experience*, p. 58.
[275] James, *Varieties of Religious Experience*, p. 58.
[276] James, *Varieties of Religious Experience*, p. 58.
[277] James, *Varieties of Religious Experience*, p. 56.
[278] James, *Varieties of Religious Experience*, p. 56.

possibilities we conceive of'.²⁷⁹ Therefore, what is seen is the activity of perception, which leads to what is *conceived*. Perception occurs relative to awareness. What is conceived is formed in the mind that is rooted in understanding.²⁸⁰

Sufficient for argumentation here is the basic implication of consciousness as a form of awareness that includes both internal and external realities. As the work progresses, this awareness will include aspects of the unconscious that relate to genuinely mystical states. However, once the term *prophetic* prefaces terms such as *consciousness* and *perception*, a theological concept is constructed and particularized. In other words, prophetic consciousness and prophetic perception speak of aspects of consciousness that are designated specifically in relationship to prophetic function and are therefore to be evaluated as to prophetic legitimacy.

1.3.5.1.2 A Particular Look at Prophetic Consciousness

Allusions to prophetic consciousness are not novel. Brueggemann states, 'the task of prophetic ministry is to nurture, nourish, and evoke a consciousness and perception alternative to the consciousness and perception of the dominant culture around us'.²⁸¹ Notice that Brueggemann mentions both consciousness and perception in relation to prophetic function. His emphasis of these words comports with his argument against what he calls a 'royal

---

²⁷⁹ James, *Varieties of Religious Experience*, p. 56.

²⁸⁰ Consciousness and perception are interrelated. Humans experience them subjectively, in the liminal intersection of the mind and the brain.

²⁸¹ Walter Brueggemann, *The Prophetic Imagination* (Minneapolis, MN: Fortress Press, 2001), p. 3. The construct of 'prophetic consciousness' was not new when Brueggemann used the term. Abraham Joshua Heschel used the term in *The Prophets* (Peabody, MA: Hendrickson, 2010), p. xi, which was originally published in 1962. Heschel approaches the idea from a phenomenological perspective. In 1974, Rotenstreich used the term in a way reminiscent of Heschel's usage. Rotenstreich traced it to the 1920s and 'mainly to phenomenology as conceived by Husserl'. Nathan Rotenstreich, 'On Prophetic Consciousness', *Journal of Religion* 54.3 (July 1974), p. 186. More recent works also use the term. In 1986, Schneiders addressed the issue in Sandra Marie Schneiders, 'Prophetic Consciousness: Obedience and Dissent in the Religious Life', which was included in her book, *New Wineskins: Re-Imagining Religious Life Today* (New York: Paulist Press, 1986), pp. 266-84. In addition, Ashbrook's research on biogenetic structural theory addresses the issue of prophetic consciousness and the symbolic processes that occur in relation to the brain and contemplative practice. See James B. Ashbrook, 'From Biogenetic Structuralism to Mature Contemplation to Prophetic Consciousness', *Zygon: Journal of Religion & Science* 28.2 (June 1993), pp. 231-50.

consciousness',[282] which is built on power differentials and produces oppression.[283] For Brueggemann, consciousness and perception produce the imagining of an alternative community where power differentials are devoid of oppression and tyranny. Brueggemann juxtaposes the relations between Moses as prophetic agent and Pharaoh as an oppressor of God's people. From Brueggemann's standpoint, the prophetic agent exists to critique and perhaps serve in the process of critiquing, in order to dismantle a royal consciousness that controls the oppressed through power differentials.

Brueggemann's alternative community foreshadows the ideal in which justice and righteousness flourish in relation to the love for God and neighbor. Although binary, the love of God and the love of neighbor are not opposing ideas but complementary ones that will be shown essential to prophetic legitimacy. Nevertheless, I propose that prophetic consciousness, perception, and enactment require more than understanding an alternative community with an alternative imagination. Therefore, in constructing a Pentecostal theology of prophetic legitimacy, the concern will be the personal and interpersonal realities bearing on the experiences (both subjective and social) of psychology and phenomenology, within a theological construct of prophetic function and expression.

1.3.5.2 Three Dyads Related to Prophetic Legitimacy

In relation to prophetic legitimacy, the concern of this work involves the aforementioned three dyads, which will be discussed more fully in Chapter 5. They are not necessarily presented in order of importance; however, all three are interrelated and essential:

1. love of God and love of neighbor;
2. truth and falsehood;
3. apprehension and acceptance (of prophetic intimations).

Foundational to all prophetic integrity and legitimacy is love of God and love of neighbor. Secondly, to speak truth requires discerning truth by virtue of the assistance of the Spirit of truth (Jn 16.13). Finally, the prophet is both to apprehend the message and to accept it from within her own interiority so that it can be assimilated and then delivered. At that point the message is apprehended by the

---

[282] Brueggemann, *Prophetic Imagination*, pp. 21-38.
[283] Pharaoh serves as an example.

community, discerned for truth or falsehood, and (if true) is to be accepted and lived out. This process is always and necessarily personal, interpersonal, intrapersonal, and transpersonal, as well as biblical-theological, psychological, and phenomenological.

Grasping these dynamics in anything like their fullness requires a multidisciplinary approach that includes biblical, theological, psychological, and phenomenological perspectives. Any attempt to construct a Pentecostal theology of prophetic legitimacy outside the context of these domains would seem destined to fall short in evaluating, discerning, and validating genuine communication from the divine Spirit.

As for the construct under discussion, because the dyads will also be considered in relation to their interpersonal and intrapersonal inclinations, they involve matters of subjectivity and objectivity. Note that my argument presupposes the human ability to apprehend objective truth; otherwise, it would be impossible to relate and interact with the One whom the canon refers to as the 'God of truth' (the faithful God noted in Deut. 32.4; Ps. 31.5; Isa. 65.16; Jn 14.17; 15.26; 16.13 [Spirit of truth]).

1.3.5.3 The Hope of This 'Conversation'

The matters under discussion here can be understood from multiple perspectives, including theology and psychology, particularly as their interplay is essential to this work. Because these disciplines remain works in progress and process, placing them in conversation is not an exact science but an attempt to find in the text a window into the world of the text. The hope is that this viewing point will produce an expanded awareness of what the narrative reveals in, about, and through the narrative's participants.

Although a canonical approach is essential to the method being used to present this argument, it is insufficient. Absent a literary-critical approach, theological and psychological perspectives of the text are similarly insufficient. Therefore, the literary-critical approach will place psychological commentary in dialogue with the theological dimensions of the considered narratives. All of this will be held in tension with the overarching canonical perspective of the meta-narrative from Genesis to Revelation.

It is important to note the impossibility of psychoanalyzing characters from the scriptural narratives. Because they cannot be interviewed, their psychological states cannot be fully known. However, within what is known of the human psyche through contemporary research in psychology and transpersonal psychology, certain phenomenological realities are implicit. Being ubiquitous to the human condition, they can be recognized and annotated wherever past human experience is documented, or present reality is observed. Therefore, a bridge can be built between the text's revealed human responses and contemporary scientific observations within the social sciences.

Likewise, phenomenological research can supplement an understanding of human experience as revealed or suggested within the canonical narrative.[284] Again, these are approximal ways of identifying human experience, as neither theology, psychology, nor phenomenology are perfect. However, they can provide a handle with which to grasp the realities presented within the literature. They can also facilitate conversation about the prophetic legitimacy that supports fruitful prophetic consciousness, perception, and enactment.

In establishing a conversation inclusive of Scripture, theology, psychology, and phenomenology, I am attempting at best to provide ways of understanding subjective human experience as it occurs in the presence of the scriptural God of truth. Clearly, the relations between subjectivity and objectivity are critical in this and other contexts.

1.4 Conclusion

Having explored concerns raised by contemporary prophetic function among independent Pentecostals, this chapter has sought to capture elements of the current prophetic landscape and facilitate a viable discussion of its relationship to the tradition of legitimacy and accountability that have governed prophetic function since the inception of the church. In terms relevant to the current environment, I also laid the overall argument's groundwork and methodology, seeking to integrate the theological and psychological/phenomenological domains, which are inherently synthesized in the life of the prophetic

---

[284] For the purposes of this research, the overlap between psychology and phenomenology should be noted.

agent. In addition, I introduced the construct for prophetic legitimacy that will be fully presented in Chapter 5.

Chapter 2 will now begin my tracing of the tradition of prophetic legitimacy through the OT examples of Moses, Samuel, Elijah, and Elisha. Subsequent chapters will add to the record citing NT examples and the more contemporary case of the late Violet Kiteley, an exemplar within the Independent Pentecostal movement.

2

OLD TESTAMENT PROPHETIC LEGITIMACY

2.1 Introduction

Brueggemann describes prophets as mediatorial figures who seem to emerge from hiddenness claiming their prophetic expressions are divine revelations.[1] Some hearers accept their claims, but others reject them.[2] However, these figures speak for God in an intervening reconciliatory role.[3] Within the OT canon, a 'cadre of individual persons and their remembered, transmitted words (and actions)'[4] speak for God and call his people into their relationship with him and one another.

In this chapter, I seek to illumine the path to prophetic legitimacy using a theological, psychological, and phenomenological methodological approach to the canonical texts involving four pivotal OT figures: Moses, Samuel, Elijah, and Elisha. These prophetic agents serve as touchstones for this investigation, as they embody the ideals of prophetic consciousness, perception, and enactment. In addition, their narratives provide historical and theological foundations that bridge two gaps: first, between ancient Israel's OT and NT periods;

---

[1] Walter Brueggemann, *Theology of the Old Testament: Testimony, Dispute, Advocacy* (Minneapolis, MN: Fortress Press, 2005), p. 622. See 'prophetic expressions' as described in 1.3.5.1.1.
[2] Brueggemann, *Theology of Old Testament*, p. 622.
[3] D. Miall Edwards, 'Mediation, Mediator', in ed. James Orr, *et al.* (eds.), *The International Standard Bible Encyclopaedia* (Chicago, IL: Howard-Severance, 1915), p. 2018.
[4] Brueggemann, *Theology of Old Testament*, p. 622.

and second, between the contemporary Independent Pentecostal movement and its yearning to return to the primitive church.

The aim is to discern the qualities that make these figures indispensable to the understanding and advancement of prophetic legitimacy within the contemporary Independent Pentecostal movement and Global Pentecostalism generally. In this regard, Moses stands out as the paradigmatic prophet who declares his own prefiguring of the eschatological Prophet, Christ (Deut. 18.15; Acts 3.22). Moses therefore shapes the prophetic order, both in the text and in Israel's consciousness and memory. His mediatorial role as prophet and Torah-giver is foundationally essential to prophetic consciousness, perception, and enactment. Therefore, I will explore the theological, psychological, and phenomenological dimensions of his prophetic legitimacy in relation to the prophetic consciousness, perception, and enactment that result from his encounter with the numinous in the Exodus narrative.

I will explore Samuel as the transitional, archetypal prophetic figure, the last of the judges and a prophet in whom classical prophetic function and visionary seership converge (1 Sam. 9.9). In this way, he marks a significant juncture in Israel's history and paves the way for the anointing of kings. By anointing Saul and David, Samuel foreshadows the era of the Messiah who embodies prophetic, priestly, and kingly attributes. Moreover, in establishing prophetic guilds, Samuel demonstrates his commitment to crucial elements of prophetic legitimacy that ensure the perdurance and replication of prophetic legitimacy, namely, answerability, accountability, and the formation of prophetic agents.

The nuances of prophetic formation represented in the Moses and Samuel narratives provide a framework for comprehending the continuity of prophetic legitimacy through the lives of Elijah and Elisha. These preexilic prophets prefigure John the Baptist and Jesus, respectively. They continue the prophetic guilds and charismatic activity, with dramatic prophetic expressions that reveal the dynamic interplay between prophetic consciousness, perception, and enactment and create expectations for Israel's future (Mal. 4.5-6). They also embody the canonical OT prophetic figure, and their powerful demonstrations of the Spirit's confirmation validate their prophetic offices.

2.2 Moses: Primary Prototype and Paradigmatic Prophet

2.2.1 Moses from a Biblical/Theological Perspective

When Moses the Levite is born to Amram and Jochebed (Exod. 2.1; 1 Chron. 23.12-14; Exod. 6.20; Num. 26.59), a pharaoh who 'did not know Joseph' or Joseph's God orders the killing of male babies (Exod. 1.22).[5] Moses is spared due to his parents' faith, the assistance of Shiphrah and Puah (Exod. 1.15), and his mother's determination to protect him (Exod. 2.2).[6]

Exodus 2.2 intimates that Jochebed perceives the child's significance and prepares an ark to preserve him from 'the politics of genocide'.[7] Zornberg argues, in such contexts, 'possibilities of memory,

---

[5] The tyrant's fear of the Israelites' soaring population prompts the infanticide. It is difficult to conceive of a king in the most advanced civilization of the then known world not knowing his nation's history, the significance of Joseph, and the reason for the Hebrews' presence. Fearing that the Israelites' fruitfulness would lead to insurrection, the tyrant enslaves them. Terence E. Fretheim, *Exodus* (Interpretation: A Bible Commentary for Teaching and Preaching; Louisville, KY: John Knox Press, 1991), p. 24, observes: 'five verbs are used to stress *an extraordinary increase in numbers* (one verb is used for the plague of frogs, 8:3!). This language connects with the promise of fruitfulness to Israel's ancestors (cf. Gen. 17:2–6; 48:4), the fulfillment of which is anticipated in Gen. 47:27.'

[6] Scrutiny of the narrative reveals profound but hidden female influences on the prophet-to-be's formation. Donald E. Gowan, *Theology in Exodus: Biblical Theology in the Form of a Commentary* (Louisville, KY: Westminster John Knox Press, 1994), p. 2, asserts that God's 'direct participation … in human affairs is not described'. Even so, the text affords no room to doubt God's activity. The necessary feminine intervention in the persons of Shiphrah, Puah, Moses' mother, Moses' sister, and Pharaoh's daughter reveals the hidden hand of God's Spirit in ensuring Moses' prophetic purpose by sparing him from infanticide. The necessary feminine influence will recur thematically in the prophetic significance of Hannah, Elizabeth, and Jesus' mother, Mary.

[7] Eugene Carpenter, 'Exodus', in *Evangelical Exegetical Commentary* (ed. H. Wayne House and William D. Barrick; Bellingham, WA: Lexham Press, 2012), p. 127:

> Josephus, *Ant.* 2.10.3-7, gives an account about Moses that augments his 'divine-like' features, his beauty, his size, and the special grace that attended his birth. In his report Amram, the father, is presented as the protector of the child and his mother, differing greatly from the mt. Nachmanides (Ramban), *Commentary on the Torah*, trans. C.B. Chavel (New York: Shilo, 1973), 14, observes that 'she saw in him some unique quality which, in her opinion, foreshadowed that a miracle would happen to him and he would be saved'. Therefore she acted on this observation. Cf. Cassuto, 18, who agrees, and Hertz, *Pentateuch and Haftorahs*, 14–15, who disagrees.

Avivah Gottlieb Zornberg, *Moses: A Human Life* (New Haven, CT: Yale University Press, 2016), ch. 1: 'The construction [of Exod. 2:2] places emphasis on the

communication, and understanding are narrowed'.[8] Nevertheless, Moses' prophetic formation moves toward a way of remembering, communicating, and understanding. Brueggemann argues that, in nurturing an alternative consciousness, Moses' prophetic agency would dismantle Pharaoh's and Egypt's lack of ethical consciousness.[9] This dismantling requires legitimate, authorized, and empowered prophetic function and awaits Israel's 'capacity to grieve',[10] which comes when Israel cries out for help (Exod. 2.23-25).[11] This groaning is a legal, ethical, moral, and spiritual complaint with the sense of engaging in battle. God is present yet hidden in the people's trauma and in the sparing and raising up of Moses.

Moses' spiritual and prophetic formation unfolds in a natural way from his infancy and establishes God's ways of working in human affairs. At a basic level, the prophetic is critique to what miscarries God's intention. Brueggemann asserts that this 'criticism begins in the capacity to grieve', which is 'the most visceral announcement that things are not right'.[12] From this 'not right' place, God's hidden ways come into the open. The prophetic is uttered when the time arrives for God to break his silence, so that the hiddenness of his power transitions to inspired speech (Hab. 3.4). Arguably, God's voice is heard in Moses' first cry from the womb. After all, infancy narratives are inseparable from the roles of prophets who follow in Moses'

---

last word in the clause, he. The כִּי clause explains what she observed about the child, namely, that God's favor rested on Moses.'

[8] Zornberg, *Moses*, ch. 1.
[9] Brueggemann, *Prophetic Imagination*, p. 3.
[10] Brueggemann, *Prophetic Imagination*, p. 11.
[11] G. Hasel, 'זעק', *TDOT*, IV, pp. 112-13.

zāʿaq; זָעֲקָה zǎʿāqāh; צָעַק tsāʿaq; צְעָקָה tsʿāqāh Ancient Near East: 1. Egyptian; 2. Akkadian; 3. West Semitic. II ... 1. Lament; 2. Prayer. **I. Ancient Near East** 1. *Egyptian*. The Egyptian verb *dʾk* is attested in the New Kingdom (20th dynasty) with the meaning 'cry, shout'. The crying can be directed 'to (*r*) the heavens' as a cry for help ... There is no known term in Akkadian that is cognate with the Hebrew root. The verb *ragāmu(m)* is used primarily for legal complaint in the sense 'lodge a complaint against, accuse', etc., and thus exhibits a similarity to one of the Hebrew usages. There is an even broader semantic correspondence in the use of the noun *rigmu(m)*, 'shout, cry, voice'. The phrase *rigmu(m) šakānu(m)*, 'lift the voice, cry', appears frequently with human subjects in reference to a dirge, bewailing a defeat, lamentation, cries of anguish uttered by a sick man, and the disturbing noise of human beings, which rises to the gods.

[12] Brueggemann, *Prophetic Imagination*, p. 11.

footsteps, and there is a setting apart even from the womb (Jer. 1.5; Gal. 1.15).[13]

With a sense of immediacy, the text moves from Moses' infancy to adulthood and indicates that what he sees challenges his consciousness and perception,[14] which are already 'going out' to his brothers.[15] This intimates exodus in Moses' inclinations and action, with the passage speaking beyond his physical exit from the palace to the brickyard. It is also his initial attempt as deliverer – an indication of the ethical, moral, legal, and spiritual conflict fomenting in his psyche, which he seems unable to reconcile and integrate.[16]

The consequences of striking down the Egyptian by looking 'this way and that' require consideration. Fretheim suggests, 'Moses made sure he was not being observed, an action that establishes premeditation and the absence of impulsiveness (hiding the body shows a concern for secrecy)'.[17] However, might this be a different kind of trepidation, with Moses interring the Egyptian to bury his mistake? 'In the OT, *tāman* means to "hide by burying"'.[18] Given what follows, the conjecture seems plausible. Yet, burying his mistake in judgment

---

[13] Moses' mother, in preparing an ark, sets it in the reeds of the Nile, thus allowing the hidden yet present Miriam to observe what unfolds. Pharaoh's daughter will become Moses' intercessor before her father. As a virgin, she cannot lactate. Moses' sister overhears the conversation between Pharaoh's daughter and her maids regarding the child's nursing. Miriam then intercedes, resulting in Moses' being nursed and weaned by his birth mother. This is significant, as the narrative indicates that God's Spirit involves feminine nurturance in the process of human and prophetic formation.

[14] John I. Durham, *Exodus* (Word Biblical Commentary 3; Dallas, TX: Word, 1987), p. 18: 'The writer jumps without a single comment from Moses' infancy and his escape from death in the river Nile to his headlong and impulsive involvement in the plight of his people. We are brought from the first appearance of the deliverer, at his birth, to his espousal in adulthood of his people's agony.'

[15] According to Horst Dietrich Preuss, 'יָצָא', *TDOT*, IV, p. 225-26, the idea in the Hebrew is

yāṣā'; מוֹצָא *môṣā'*; תּוֹצָאוֹת *tôṣā'ôt* ... The Semitic root *yṣ'* is used primarily to refer to various forms of going out or in (qal) or leading out or in (hiphil). The root appears also in Akkadian as (*w*)*aṣû* (cf. Ezr. 6:15), in Ugaritic, in Phoenician and Punic, and in Aramaic (although the more common Aramaic word for 'go out' is *npq*, with 11 occurrences in Biblical Aramaic). In Arabic, *hrg'* is more common. The name 'I-ṣa-Yà has been found at Ebla.

[16] I would argue a connection with his days of being nursed at his mother's breast and the shaping of his awareness, consciousness, and perception from what his mother shared. This would frame his development in Pharaoh's household.

[17] Fretheim, *Exodus*, p. 42.

[18] Diether Kellermann, 'טָמַן', *TDOT*, V, p. 342.

is an insufficient ruse, as his adoptive father finds him out and places a bounty on his head.

Moses' actions lead to unanticipated consequences, including his flight from Egypt into an extended period of liminality in the desert, which is prerequisite for his prophetic formation. Moses fully identifies with the Hebrews' brickyard experience. Therefore, an exodus precedes his returning in the power of the Spirit with full prophetic legitimacy to dismantle, disarm, and publicly disgrace the powers and power differentials shaping Egyptian societal systems (Lk. 4.14; Col. 2.15). Fulfilling this mission confirms Moses' prophetic legitimacy.

Brueggemann speaks of the 'anxiety about survival' caused by Pharaoh's 'oppressive social policy',[19] which includes 'the practice of forced labor'.[20] Such injustice is not within Moses' lived experience but that of his Hebrew brothers and sisters. Thus far, Pharaoh's prophetic expressions had the assumed backing and authorization of Egyptian gods and were uncontested. Now, his adopted son's killing of the Egyptian challenges them. As Ashby bluntly notes, the person who is later entrusted with the Decalogue is 'taking the law into his own hands'.[21] His attempt the next day to reconcile two of his Hebrew brothers foreshadows his prophetic mediatorial role, yet his 'motives are understandably misunderstood by another Hebrew'.[22] Thus, Moses is accused of an ulterior motive, becomes subject to 'furtive fear',[23] and makes 'an ignominious flight out of Egypt'.[24] It is difficult to surmise whether Moses' sense of justice was formed strictly through his connection to the Hebrew slaves or was also affected by his Egyptian upbringing (Egypt's oppressive ways notwithstanding). Fretheim postulates the latter.[25] What can be noted is that Moses' action is motivated from a deep place of conviction, which indicates that prophetic formation is transpiring.

---

[19] Brueggemann, *Prophetic Imagination*, pp. 26-27.
[20] Brueggemann, *Prophetic Imagination*, p. 27.
[21] G.W. Ashby, *Go out and Meet God: A Commentary on the Book of Exodus* (International Theological Commentary; Grand Rapids, MI: Eerdmans, 1998), p. 15.
[22] Ashby, *Meet God*, p. 15.
[23] Ashby, *Meet God*, p. 15.
[24] Ashby, *Meet God*, p. 15.
[25] Fretheim, *Exodus*, p. 45, 'Moses' sense of justice has been learned, not from his Hebrew heritage, but from his *Egyptian upbringing* (cf. Acts 7:22!). This is a significant testimony to God's work in creation among those outside the community of faith.'

Forty years of desert liminality becomes the setting of Moses' prophetic formation and the time span necessary to remove the threat posed by his adoptive father.[26] Having fled, Moses settles at a well in Midianite territory (Exod. 2.15), where he acts as deliverer for seven daughters of a Midianite priest, intervening when shepherds abuse their father's water rights (Exod. 2.16-17).[27] Notably, the daughters identify Moses as 'an Egyptian' (Exod. 2.19). The text seemingly implies not only Moses' appearance, which reflects Egyptian culture, but also his inability to escape being identified as an Egyptian.

Having already shifted from his Hebrew identity to that of an Egyptian and then a Midianite, Moses will become the Hebrews' leader. The encounter at Horeb, which is pivotal in establishing his prophetic call, involves a theophany. As to the landscape, 'the sole geographic reference ... is that the mountain was beyond the customary Midianite grazing area'.[28] The text mentions a particular 'mountain of God' (Exod. 3.1). Whether this is a theological reference to Sinai or suggests 'a religious center for the seminomadic tribes of the wilderness' can only be conjectured.[29] The text makes certain, however, that the Horeb encounter bore witness to its own purpose. What transpired would be emblazoned in Moses' psyche and become the foundation for all he thought and said as spokesperson for the divine. It is an originating and 'energizing memor[y]'.[30]

---

[26] A. Scott Moreau, Harold Netland, and Charles van Engen (eds.), *Evangelical Dictionary of World Missions* (Baker Reference Library; Grand Rapids, MI: Baker Books, 2000), p. 579:

> Liminality. Derived from the Latin word *limen,* liminality suggests a threshold, chasm, or margin. Anthropologists utilize the term to refer to an ambiguous phase that is uncharacteristic of the past and future states; it is a state of 'in-betweenness', a transitional stage of life in which one is torn away from familiarity. The liminal state has been likened to invisibility, ambiguity, darkness, death, limbo, and being in the womb. French folklorist and ethnographer Arnold van Gennep speaks of three different stages of passage in the life cycle: preliminal rites of separation, liminal rites of transition, and postliminal rites of incorporation.

[27] The text names the father as Reuel, yet he is also known as Jethro, Jether, and Hobab (Exod. 3.1; 4.18; Num. 10.29; Judg. 4.11).

[28] Durham, *Exodus*, p. 30.

[29] Nahum M. Sarna, *Exodus* (JPS Torah Commentary; Philadelphia, PA: Jewish Publication Society, 1991), p. 14.

[30] Brueggemann, *Prophetic Imagination*, p. 1.

What occurs first with Moses at Horeb will occur later with the children of Israel and will underpin the transmission of prophetic revelation. Moses' experience at the bush will be their experience over Mount Sinai (Exod. 3.12). For prophetic consciousness to be as intended, it is necessary for that critical memory to be embedded in the collective psyche of the community, bearing prophetic witness to God's intent. Childs argues that while the patriarchs were given theophanic encounters, they were not mandated to transmit what they received to others.[31] However, Moses' call is a 'deep disruptive seizure' for which he claims himself unprepared yet called to share with his people (Exod. 3.13).[32] His recalcitrance evokes a remonstrance and the addition of Aaron as a support (Exod. 4.14). The text assumes some communication between the two, although Aaron has been in Egypt for the duration. How this transpires is unknown. However, Moses clearly arrives at the edge of his liminal space (wilderness) and enters the territory of mystery, though 'not seeking such an experience'.[33] The initiative for prophetic legitimacy is solely in God's hands, requiring the One whose essence is shrouded in mystery to disclose himself.[34]

Moses' response, 'Here I am',[35] marks the beginning of his conversance with God. His encounter with the holy initiates the bringing of his identity struggles to light and speech. Experientially, he does not know the God of his father. Neither is there any record that Moses had a relationship with his own father. Given the likelihood of

---

[31] Brevard S. Childs, *The Book of Exodus: A Critical, Theological Commentary* (Old Testament Library; Louisville, KY: Westminster John Knox Press, 2004), p. 56.

[32] Childs, *Book of Exodus*, p. 56.

[33] Durham, *Exodus*, p. 30.

[34] Childs, *Book of Exodus*, p. 56, claims, 'the series of questions raised by Moses in objection to being sent echo the inner and outer struggles of the prophets of Israel'. Although some truth might attend this claim, Childs seems to seek the verification of an organizing and governing pattern within the response to the call. Other scholars engage in this, including 'Zimmerli, Habel, and Richter'. Durham, *Exodus*, p. 29. Durham claims that for Zimmerli, the response to the theophany plays itself out in two distinct but related ways: 'a Jeremiah-Moses type, involving divine manifestation to the person called, the reluctance of that person, and an answer to the reluctance in promises and signs; and a Micaiah-Isaiah type involving a vision of God enthroned and announcing his word to his heavenly council' (p. 29). Jeremiah alludes to the requirement of standing in the heavenly council to both see and hear the word, contrasting such prophetic validation with its lack among false prophets who experienced no genuine divine manifestation (Jer. 23.18-20).

[35] The response is elicited by the One who twice calls him by name (Exod. 3.4).

his being weaned and separated from his birth family by the age of three, any relational memories would be scant. Yet the inception of what one could call a theology of prayer is being established in his life. Hiller reminds us, 'theological speech about God and humans finds its beginning *in the act* of speaking between God and humans'.[36] Cocksworth correctly asserts, 'it is in the crucible of prayer that the mind is formed towards its proper end: knowing and loving God'.[37] Prevot notes various theologians' work on prayer and their concern for the contemporary collapse caused by the uncoupling of prayer and theology.[38] He states, 'a total divorce of prayer from theology would be unthinkable. It would entail the radical negation of both conversations and, therefore, the erasure of the entire problematic.'[39] This uncoupling is also unimaginable for one called to faithful speech on God's behalf.

As Moses is transparent with God (in prayer), he is concerned about his own credibility and asks what God's name is. God answers, 'I am who I am' (Exod. 3.14). What are we to make of this? Soulen offers, 'I am' is a 'nameless name', a sign of the incomprehensible mystery of God'.[40] This perhaps defines the Tetragrammaton,[41] but God's nature remains incomprehensible and undefinable, defying explanation and enshrouded in mystery.[42] God instructs Moses,

> Thus you shall say to the Israelites, 'I am has sent me to you. … The Lord, the God of your ancestors, the God of Abraham, the

---

[36] Doris Hiller, 'Faith, Experience and the Concept of Prayer: Some Reflections on Theological Epistemology', *Neue Zeitschrift für Systematische Theologie und Religionsphilosophie* 42.3 (Jan 1, 2000), p. 317 (emphasis added).

[37] Ashley Cocksworth, *Karl Barth on Prayer* (eds. John Webster, Ian A. McFarland, and Ivor Davidson; T&T Clark Studies in Systematic Theology 26; London: Bloomsbury T&T Clark, 2015), p. 171.

[38] Andrew Prevot, 'Reversèd Thunder: The Significance of Prayer for Political Theology', *The Other Journal: An Intersection of Theology and Culture* 21 (September 17, 2012), https://theotherjournal.com/2012/09/17/reversed-thunder-the-significance-of-prayer-for-political-theology/.

[39] Prevot, 'Reversèd Thunder'.

[40] R. Kendall Soulen, *Distinguishing the Voices, Volume 1: The Divine Name(s) and the Holy Trinity* (Louisville, KY: Westminster John Knox Press, 2011), p. 10.

[41] John D. Barry, 'Tetragrammaton', in John D. Barry, *et al.* (eds.), *The Lexham Bible Dictionary* (Bellingham, WA: Lexham Press, 2016): 'Tetragrammaton. A term for the four letters of the personal name of Israel's God, derived from the Greek for "four" and "letter". In Hebrew, the name consists of four consonants, יהוה (*yhwh*).'

[42] Soulen, *Distinguishing the Voices*, p. 10.

God of Isaac, and the God of Jacob, has sent me to you': This is my name forever, and this is my title for all generations (Exod. 3.14-15).

Moses' questioning conveys a 'fuller divine revelation'.[43] The invitation, by way of questions in the divine mystery, enlarges prophetic consciousness and perception. Fretheim insightfully says, 'God's revelation is thereby tied directly to the human situation'.[44] God condescends to answer, to the extent that the God-self can be grasped. For the prophetic agent to speak of God, this is essential. Only then can the spokesperson bring to speech things about the God who is enshrouded in mystery. Moses' communication makes it clear, therefore, that 'the more one understands God, the more mysterious God becomes'.[45] This deficiency is prerequisite to prophetic expressions, as the paltriness of the human condition and ability to know the unknowable God can foster intellectual honesty and humility in one who speaks on God's behalf.

Moses' maturation process is essential to the formative encounters ahead, including the events at Mount Sinai. Durham sees what occurs in Exod. 19.1–20.20 and 24.1-11 as 'the climactic narrative of the entire OT'.[46] It all stems from Moses' seminal experience at Horeb and the theophany-call sequence God initiated via a common bramble (Exod. 3.1–4.17). In Durham's choice of language, 'this pattern is the *shaping-factor*'.[47] For Wenk, it is the OT 'identity-forming narrative'.[48]

---

[43] Fretheim, *Exodus*, p. 62.

[44] Fretheim, *Exodus*, p. 62.

[45] Fretheim, *Exodus*, p. 63. This God is 'the God of truth' (Isa. 65.16 NASB), and the more one hears and knows about this God, the clearer one's paucity of knowledge becomes. Only in this God's presence can truth and grace help men and women own unwanted and unwelcomed truths (Isa. 65.16; Jn 1.17).

[46] Durham, *Exodus*, p. 30.

[47] Durham, *Exodus*, p. 30 (emphasis added).

[48] Matthias Wenk, 'What is Prophetic about Prophecies: Inspiration or Critical Memory?: A Fresh Look at Prophets and Prophecy in the New Testament and Contemporary Pentecostalism', *Journal of Pentecostal Theology* 26.2 (September 2017), p. 181. The essential idea is Moses' call as a call to prophetic legitimacy sanctioned only by God's apprehending him to lead an exodus – a departure from one way of being into another, from slavery in Egypt to sonship in the land of promise, via the Red Sea and the wilderness. This prefigures an exodus via Christ's Passion, through suffering, death, burial, and resurrection. This identity-forming narrative

2.2.2 Moses from a Psychological Perspective

In Moses' flight to liminal space, the psychological processes required for individuation and wholeness unfold,[49] bringing him to the maturity that prophetic legitimacy requires. Being situated within a 'biological and cultural context' supportive of internal conflict,[50] Moses exhibits aggression against the Egyptian culture by killing the taskmaster who strikes a Hebrew.[51] The mention of both ethnic terms – *Hebrew* and *Egyptian* – indicates significance. This is not only about conflict between slave and taskmaster but is also between Moses' shifting identities in his formerly less heightened consciousness. This awareness is now fully expressed, but not only to Pharaoh. Moses makes it known to himself in a definitive and life-altering way. The result is Moses' attempt to bury the event in the sand.

In approaching the text psychologically, the burying of the dead Egyptian can offer insight into the budding prophet's internal conflicts and can aid our grasp of what prophetic formation can entail. If we think of burying the Egyptian as a 'conceptual metaphor',[52] we can see how the text structures the reader's thinking and perception of reality, both in relation to this narrative and the perception with which Moses wrestled. To argue further, in Job, the myth of the phoenix is related to length of days and multitudinous grains of sand (Job 29.18). Moses will spend forty years (14,600 days) walking the desert sands after attempting to bury his disowned way of being. Throughout that time, the memory of a hidden, 'dead' Egyptian laid

---

is what Wenk terms 'critical memory' (p. 181). Not only is Moses subject to the identity-forming narrative; the ancient Israelite nation collectively carries a social responsibility to bear witness to it.

[49] By individuation, I imply the forming of a 'stable personality'. Rebecca Fraser-Thill, 'What Is Individuation?', https://www.verywellmind.com/individuation-3288007.

[50] Dan P. McAdams, *The Person: An Introduction to the Science of Personality Psychology* (Hoboken, NJ: John Wiley & Sons, 5th edn, 2009), p. 3.

[51] 'Aggression', *APA Dictionary of Psychology*, https://dictionary.apa.org/aggression. *Aggression* is:

> behavior aimed at harming others physically or psychologically. It can be distinguished from anger in that anger is oriented at overcoming the target but not necessarily through harm or destruction. When such behavior is purposively performed with the primary goal of intentional injury or destruction, it is termed hostile aggression.

[52] Sarah J. Dille, *Mixing Metaphors: God as Mother and Father in Deutero-Isaiah* (London: T&T Clark, 2004), pp. 10-11.

under his feet can represent the 'Egyptian part' of Moses that remains unreconciled within his interiority.

Psychologically speaking, we can infer from the text that Moses' internal struggle involves his sense of Hebrew identity, his adoption and rearing as an Egyptian, and his desire to identify with his own people. Regarding individuation (the stabilizing of personality),[53] Moses – a biological Hebrew raised in a culturally Egyptian household (no less, the royal household)[54] – is both similar and different from those around him. In his 'biological and cultural context',[55] his aggression against another Egyptian can indicate that he finds it somewhat 'impossible to establish normal rapport'.[56] While he may have expressed attachment to Pharaoh's daughter for a season, he refuses to be called her son (Heb. 11.24). Although this is a faith decision, it involves emotional conflict and a level of rejection. How can one reject the person who spared his life?

Moses has begun his individuation and is moving toward full ownership of his identity as a son of Abraham. This movement involves psychological trauma, but where does the trauma lie? Moses cannot be a prophet unless he is from among his brothers (Deut. 18.15). He is a Hebrew; yet an element of faith needs to be actuated, psychologically, for Moses to become fully like his brethren (Heb. 2.17). Transformation requires more than embracing his ethnic heritage. He needs to experience his brethren's pain and 'sympathize with [their]

---

[53] Leon Schlamm, 'Individuation', in David A. Leeming (ed.), *Encyclopedia of Psychology and Religion* (Boston, MA: Springer, 2014):

> Jung defined individuation, the therapeutic goal of analytical psychology belonging to the second half of life, as the process by which a person becomes a psychological individual, a separate indivisible unity or whole, recognizing his innermost uniqueness, and he identified this process with becoming one's own *self* or *self*-realization, which he distinguished from 'ego-centeredness' and individualism. The self, the totality of personality and archetype of order, is superordinate to the ego, embracing consciousness and the unconscious; as the center and circumference of the whole psyche, the self is our life's goal, the most complete expression of individuality (Jung 1916/1928, 1939a, 1944, 1947/1954, 1963). The aim of individuation, equated with the extension of consciousness and the development of personality, is to divest the self of its false wrappings of the persona, the mask the personality uses to confront the world.

[54] McAdams, *The Person*, p. 3.
[55] McAdams, *The Person*, p. 3.
[56] Conrad W. Baars and Anna A. Terruwe, *Healing the Unaffirmed: Recognizing Emotional Deprivation Disorder* (Staten Island, NY: Society of St. Paul, 2002), ch. 2.

weaknesses' (Heb. 4.15), especially if he will claim to speak on behalf of their God.

As the text moves toward the sympathetic suffering Moses embraces as an adult,[57] what he sees challenges the consciousness and perception that are rooted in what he feels (Exod. 2.11). His refusal to be known as the adoptive son of Pharaoh's daughter involves a psychological disowning with several implications (Heb. 11.24).[58] Psychologically, the contrast between his Hebrew heritage and his Egyptian enculturation become difficult to balance. Any resulting internal incongruence would then undermine the essential coherence between prophetic expressions and pure, heart-empowered motivations.

The late Conraad Baars diagnosed such issues as 'frustration neurosis and/or deprivation neurosis',[59] a maladjustment resulting from the withholding of affirmation. Moses certainly experiences cognitive dissonance.[60] He is not an Egyptian, yet he disowns affirmation from his Egyptian upbringing, which fosters his adoptive father's ultimate rejection. At the same time, Moses' Hebrew brothers fail to affirm the Hebrew identity he willingly embraces. This rejection is fundamental to his existential crisis on the path to individuation.

Moses vocalizes his existential crisis in prayer when God summons him as his prophet. Moses' negation is pregnant with emotional deprivation as he cries out, *'Who am I* that I should go to Pharaoh?'

---

[57] Durham, *Exodus*, p. 18.

[58] 'ἀρνέομαι', *BAGD*, p. 107, this refusal is 'ἀρνέομαι … [meaning] to refuse consent to someth., *refuse, disdain* … ἠρνήσατο λέγεσθαι υἱός *he refused to be known as the son* Hb 11:24 (JFeather, ET 43, '32, 423–25)'.

[59] Baars and Terruwe, *Healing the Unaffirmed,* author's preface:

> Persons with emotional deprivation disorder are absolutely incapable of establishing … spontaneous contact. They can only establish emotional rapport with others when and to the extent that others direct themselves to them, precisely as parents orient themselves to their children. As long as somebody does this, individuals with emotional deprivation disorder feel at ease, safe, and happy; but in every other kind of contact they feel strange and uncertain.

[60] 'Cognitive Dissonance', *APA Dictionary of Psychology*, https://dictionary.apa.org/cognitive-dissonance:

> an unpleasant psychological state resulting from inconsistency between two or more elements in a cognitive system. It is presumed to involve a state of heightened arousal and to have characteristics similar to physiological drives (e.g., hunger). Thus, cognitive dissonance creates a motivational drive in an individual to reduce the dissonance.

(Exod. 3.11, emphasis added). Zornberg addresses the inner conflict Moses suffers when God self-identifies as the God of Moses' father (Exod. 3.6). Zornberg asks, 'Which father? How well does Moses know his birth father's voice?'[61] The text evokes an identity crisis and asks who affirms Moses' sonship: is it the adoptive father who now seeks his death or the birth father with whom the text reveals little (if any) childhood involvement? Zornberg aptly notes, 'For Moses the issue of identity is fraught with ambiguity from the beginning'.[62]

We can only conjecture as to how Moses' contemporaries would have understood such psychological issues. However, the ambiguity Zornberg mentions seems aligned with Baars and Terruwe's assessment that some form of emotional deprivation engenders the frustration in Moses' adulthood. The text symbolically evokes this struggle by representing a theophany occurring on a thorn bush. Considering that 'linguistic expressions are containers' for meaning,[63] life for Moses and his people is likewise thorny.[64] The negation of the thorn bush that burns with theophanic fire but is not consumed can only be reconciled by the presence of the purifying Spirit-fire. This revelation is not only for and of Israel; it can also reveal a self-awareness in Moses' psyche that exposes his struggle with the 'thorny complexity of human pain'.[65]

The fact that Pharaoh's daughter named Moses after Jochebed fully relinquished him implies that his mother may have given him a different name at birth. It might equally suggest the need for Jochebed to trust that Pharaoh's daughter (for 'all intents and purposes' his acting mother) was entrusted with the sacred act.[66] Yet from the fiery thorn bush, the name he is twice called is the name by which the divine presence knows him.[67]

---

[61] Zornberg, *Moses*, ch. 1.
[62] Zornberg, *Moses*, ch. 1.
[63] George Lakoff and Mark Johnson, *Metaphors We Live By* (Chicago, IL: University of Chicago Press, 1980), p. 10. Aspects of the challenging human condition can be depicted linguistically as the way of thorns and thistles (Gen. 3.18).
[64] In the existential realities of our broken places, a costly prickliness infuses our ontological way of being. The cursed ground is a negation to be reckoned with psychologically (Gen. 3.17).
[65] Zornberg, *Moses*, ch. 1.
[66] Zornberg, *Moses*, ch. 1.
[67] Who then gave him his name? (See Eph. 3.15.) Can the double enunciation be a psychological affirmation of his dual identity as Hebrew and Egyptian? Is the

Moses' premature attempt to mediate and deliver by going out to his brothers perhaps equally involves going out from the seemingly irreconcilable part of himself (Exod. 2.11). As such, the attempt stems from a profound lack of self-awareness that leads to self-rejection and the inability to integrate the parts of himself that he preferred to erase. His Hebrew brothers do not know him as he seems to know himself. From their perspective, his failure to see how others perceive him is a hindrance to congruent actions and motives. They have no knowledge of Moses' 'evolving life story'.[68] His sense of self has no bearing on the Hebrew slaves; thus, it indicates an underdeveloped emotional intelligence.[69] Therefore, his *going out* is as much for him as for his brothers. It indicates (1) the conflict fomenting deep within his psyche, and (2) his inability to integrate and reconcile his current self with the narrative identity that developed during his nursing period.[70]

Moses' internal and existential conflict is tied to who he is, from whence he has come, and to where he is going. Therefore, his individuation process is inseparable from the transcendent-yet-hidden influence of the God who called him to prophetic agency.

2.2.3 Moses from a Phenomenological Perspective

The Moses account presents a pattern of awakening experienced by God's prophetic agents. Moses sees an anomaly and questions his conscious observation. Interestingly, the text places this example of religious phenomenology at Horeb, 'the mountain of God' (Exod.

---

calling of his name twice essential to his prophetic legitimacy at this point in his individuation? Does it signify the reconciling of his internal conflict? Is all of this taking place in the presence of the theophanic glory?

[68] McAdams and McLean, *Narrative Identity*, p. 233.

[69] 'Emotional Intelligence', *APA Dictionary of Psychology*, https://dictionary.apa.org/emotional-intelligence:

> a type of intelligence that involves the ability to process emotional information and use it in reasoning and other cognitive activities, proposed by U.S. psychologists Peter Salovey (1958–) and John D. Mayer (1953–) … It comprises four abilities: to perceive and appraise emotions accurately; to access and evoke emotions when they facilitate cognition; to comprehend emotional language and make use of emotional information; and to regulate one's own and others' emotions to promote growth and well-being.

[70] Recent studies indicate that such early memories are possible. See Taylor and Francis Group, 'Earliest Memories Can Start from the Age of Two-and-a-Half: New Study and a Review of Decades of Data Pushes the Memory Clock Back Over a Year, but the Study Confirms Everyone Is Different', *ScienceDaily* (June 14, 2021), www.sciencedaily.com/releases/2021/06/210614110824.htm.

3.1), a 'place of revelation' that Fretheim notes to be 'far removed from the sights and sounds of the religious community'.⁷¹ Although the reader understands that Moses sees the angel of the Lord, Moses is not yet aware of God's inbreaking into the realm of Creation.

How Moses comes to recognize this is inseparable from his way of perceiving all that unfolds. The word translated 'looked' is רָאָה (*rā'â*), the metaphorical sense of which includes the notion of 'perceive'.⁷² While God's intervention initiates Moses' perceptual process, the man exercises his 'perceptual intentions' in relation to 'an ordinary material object'.⁷³ As such, the world Moses occupies at Horeb 'remains as' what Robert Sokolowski terms 'the believed-in' world.⁷⁴ Phenomenologically, however, the place the burning-yet-not-consumed bramble bush occupies differs from his everyday expectations, displacing him into what he likely perceived as an 'imaginary world' marked by a 'kind of suspension of belief, a turn into the mode of "as if"'.⁷⁵

Thus, Moses makes a mental shift away from memory and into the imaginal realm,⁷⁶ an interior shift to what Sokolowski would argue is a 'kind of nowhere and "no-when"',⁷⁷ a perceptual place removed from the 'here and now'.⁷⁸ 'The Lord saw' Moses' interior shift and the 'curiosity' that induced it,⁷⁹ drawing him into the sphere where invisible mysteries coalesce with visible realities. Such coalescence would not only have challenged Moses' habitual perceptions; it would also make room for a new, unforeseen awareness.

Phenomenologically, within the theophanic encounter, Moses comes to terms with two memories: the buried Egyptian soldier and the latent fear of Pharaoh's face and cobra-ornamented crown. These are far from Brueggemann's notion of 'energizing memories and …

---

⁷¹ Fretheim, *Exodus*, pp. 53-54.
⁷² Robert D. Culver, '2095 רָאָה', in *TWOT*, II, p. 823, 'The extended and metaphorical senses in the Qal include to regard, perceive, feel, understand, learn, enjoy'.
⁷³ Robert Sokolowski, *Introduction to Phenomenology* (Cambridge: Cambridge University Press, 2000), p. 12.
⁷⁴ Sokolowski, *Introduction to Phenomenology*, p. 72.
⁷⁵ Sokolowski, *Introduction to Phenomenology*, p. 71.
⁷⁶ Memory and imagination are 'structurally very similar'; therefore, 'the same sort of displacement of the ego or self' would be taking place. Sokolowski, *Introduction to Phenomenology*, p. 71.
⁷⁷ Sokolowski, *Introduction to Phenomenology*, p. 71.
⁷⁸ Sokolowski, *Introduction to Phenomenology*, p. 71.
⁷⁹ Fretheim, *Exodus*, p. 54.

radical hopes'.[80] Could such memories be psychologically debilitating and, therefore, a phenomenological hindrance? The question in Exod. 4.1, 'But suppose they do not believe me or listen to me' comes from a phenomenological perspective in the atmosphere of a *saturated phenomenon*,[81] the experience of a transcendent excess that is consuming yet not consuming, overwhelming yet not overwhelming. The saturated phenomenon preserves and does not destroy Moses' intuitive processes. Instead, it expands them, a paradox akin to the burning but unconsumed shrub.

Another sign, that of the leprous hand being transformed, offers a similar shift in consciousness and perception in relation to an altogether different fear (Exod. 4.6-7). Ceremonially and communally, skin disorders rendered sufferers and anyone and anything they touched ritually, ceremonially, and socially unclean (Lev. 13.45). The judgment was to dwell in isolation, alienated from the community (Lev. 13.46). That Moses' hand alternated easily between health and disease revealed a God who can reverse that which invalidates his people. These two signs impact Moses' consciousness and perception of God's transcendence and imminence in a way that establishes his confidence to stand before Pharaoh (Egypt) and his brethren (Israel), affirming by his very ontology the embodiment of prophetic credibility and legitimacy.

The third sign, the turning of the Nile's waters into blood, differs from the first two and begins the plagues that dismantle the mythos of Pharaoh's enthronement. Therefore, theologically, psychologically,

---

[80] Brueggemann, *Prophetic Imagination*, p. 1.
[81] Alexei V. Nesteruk, *The Sense of the Universe: Philosophical Explication of Theological Commitment in Modern Cosmology* (Minneapolis, MN: Fortress Press, 2015), p. 519:

> Saturated Phenomena – Stand for the group of phenomena which cannot be represented in the phenomenality of objects, that is in rubrics of: quantity, quality, relation and modality. The issue of the saturated phenomenon concerns the possibility that certain phenomena do not manifest themselves in the mode of objects and yet still do manifest themselves. These phenomena undergo saturation by the excess of intuition over the concept or signification in them; the saturated phenomena cannot be constituted because they are saturated. Here such a definition of experience is implied that it cannot be determined by a transcendental subject. On the contrary, it is to the extent that *ego* cannot comprehend the phenomenon that this *ego* is constituted by it. The examples of the saturated phenomena can be found in various fields of the human activity: painting, revelation of the Divine, the givenness of truth, events of life etc. Theory of the saturated phenomena was advanced by J. L. Marion.

and phenomenologically, Moses has reached the place of prophetic legitimacy.

2.3 Samuel: Transitional and Archetypal Prophet

2.3.1 Introduction

As this section will show, Samuel is pivotal in prophetic history. Both his role and ways of prophetic functioning bear upon prophetic figures from his day until ours. Therefore, his essential example will help guide the discussion of prophetic legitimacy and its cultivation in praxis.

Ira M. Price states, 'The prophetic order of the Old Testament is generally regarded as founded upon the authority of the utterances in Deut. 18:15, 18'.[82] Peter attests to Christ's fulfillment of this text and offers this theological assertion: 'All the prophets, as many as have spoken, *from Samuel and those after him*, also predicted these days' (Acts 3.24, emphasis added).[83] In omitting the prophetic figures between Moses and Samuel, Peter suggests an interregnum and alludes to a teleological economy that is (1) affirmed, acknowledged, and referenced by Moses (the prototype), and (2) further formed, advanced, and structured by Samuel, its new archetype in relation to the kingdom.[84]

Echoing Peter's assertion in Acts 3.24, Price describes the period between Moses and Samuel as 'the middle ages of [Israel's] history' and sees Samuel as a 'reformer' who influences 'political and

---

[82] Ira M. Price, 'The Schools of the Sons of the Prophets', *Old Testament Student* 8.7 (March 1889), p. 244.

[83] See also Acts 3.17-26.

[84] Samuel A. Meier, *Themes and Transformations in Old Testament Prophecy* (Downers Grove, IL: IVP Academic, 2009), p. 129:

> It is precisely Samuel's role as kingmaker that he recollects in order to motivate Saul to do what the prophet asks: 'Yahweh sent me to anoint you as king (limšāḥŏkā lĕmelek) over His people, over Israel; now therefore listen to the words of Yahweh' (1 Sam 15:1). Kings listen to prophets not only because kings, like everyone else, are awed before a voice that claims to be speaking divine words. A prophet has a further unique claim upon a king: without the prophet, the king would not be sitting in his regal position. Even more sobering is the fact that a prophet has the authority to remove a king should the king fail to cooperate and fulfill his part of the bargain in submitting to prophetic authority.

religious' spheres.⁸⁵ The Book of Judges' stark final statement says, '*In those days* there was no king in Israel; all the people did what was right in their own eyes' (Judg. 21.25, emphasis added). This emphasizes Samuel's emergence during a disordered era, with his providential elevation therefore representing movement toward its resolution.

Israel long desired a king, but such governance required a mediatorial priesthood in keeping with the Mosaic edict (Deut. 17.14-20).⁸⁶ Samuel embodied both the revelatory prophetic and mediatorial priestly functions. Therefore, he is archetypal and transitional. In him the priestcraft is temporarily recovered, the prophetic order is established, and the judge/prophet era ends.⁸⁷ Samuel was also a prophet and seer,⁸⁸ a relevant fact when constructing a Pentecostal theology of prophetic legitimacy.⁸⁹ Robert Kirkpatrick avers that Aubrey R.

---

⁸⁵ Price, 'Sons of the Prophets', p. 244.

⁸⁶ Samuel would model the prophetic agent working in concert with a priestly delegate for the sake of a sound monarchy. Nathan continued this model in 2 Samuel 12, as did others.

⁸⁷ This movement toward monarchy required the repurposing of the priestly tribe and the priestcraft that was corrupted and judged in Eli (1 Sam. 2.12-17, 22-25, 27-34). Prophetic schools would complement the priests' functions.

⁸⁸ 'Seer', in David Noel Freedman, Allen C. Myers, and Astrid B. Beck (eds.), *Eerdmans Dictionary of the Bible* (Grand Rapids, MI: Eerdmans, 2000), p. 1179, a seer is 'one who experiences and reports or interprets a dream or vision (e.g., 1 Sam. 9.9; Amos 7:12; 2 Chr. 9:29). Such figures (Heb. *Rē'eh, hōzeh*) are frequently associated with ecstatic states (cf. 2 Chr. 29:25, 30). Visionaries may have been associated with the royal court (e.g., 2 Sam. 24:11; 1 Chr. 25:5).' *Prophet* and *seer* indicate various aspects of prophetic function, including forthtelling, foretelling, and the visionary dynamics associated with prophetic operations and ways of seeing. The dimension of the clairvoyant evident in Samuel continues with the sons of the prophets in the days of Elijah and Elisha (1 Sam. 9.16 and 10.2-7; 2 Kgs 2.1-18). The consciousness of prophets moving in signs and wonders (as seen with Moses, Samuel, Elijah, and Elisha) paved the way for the Luke-Acts narrative and the Lukan view of Jesus as charismatic, prophetic Messiah.

⁸⁹ This work considers Samuel's archetypal transitional role essential in understanding prophetic consciousness and perception. From a prophetic perspective, he was essential to the discerning of what was to emerge in Israel's future. An insertion in 1 Sam. 9.9 includes the terms *nabi* and *ro'eh*, which are treated as synonymous. Ontologically, these functionalities can be described as *ways of knowing* (prophet) and *ways of observing or seeing* (seer). Joyce G. Baldwin, *1 and 2 Samuel: An Introduction and Commentary* (Tyndale Old Testament Commentaries 8; Downers Grove, IL: InterVarsity Press, 1988), p. 95, makes room theologically for considering the terms not merely synonymously but functionally:

> In a modern book this verse would be a footnote. It points out how the story of Saul's encounter with Samuel fits into Samuel's story thus far. He had been referred to as the 'prophet' (Heb. *nābî'*) in 1 Samuel 3:20, and the narrator

Johnson 'makes too much of the distinction of "seer" and "prophet" in 1 Samuel 9:9'.[90] However, Wilson notes that Johnson 'recognized the complexities of prophetic phenomena'. Neither excludes the ecstatic states revealed in 1 Sam. 10.9-13, however controversial they may be.

2.3.2 The Call of Samuel

2.3.2.1 The Call of Samuel from a Biblical-Theological Perspective

Despite his youth, Samuel occupied the sacred space near the ark of the covenant, which was strictly reserved for the priestly line. He served under the tutelage of the aged and almost sightless high priest, Eli, Aaron's descendant. Although Samuel was not from the Aaronic line, he was in the Levitical tribe (1 Chron. 6.22-30). Leithart argues that Samuel's function 'was limited to that of a Levite'.[91] Nevertheless, Leithart describes the ephod as 'the garb of priests' and sees the early Samuel narrative as addressing 'the custom of priests'.[92]

The text states, 'the word of the Lord was rare in those days; visions were not widespread' (1 Sam. 3.1).[93] This prophetic dearth

---

considered this to be the appropriate word to describe Samuel, but Saul and his servant were wanting him to do them a favour by discerning where the lost asses were; this was the role of a diviner or 'seer' (from Heb. *rō'eh*, 'to see'). Later the two words were used interchangeably, for in 1 Chronicles Samuel is called a *rō'eh* without any sense of incongruity (1 Chr. 9:22; 26:28; 29:29).

It is noteworthy that the term 'man of God' commonly described prophets in ancient Israel (1 Sam. 9.8). Within the Pentecostal tradition, the appellations 'man of God' and 'woman of God' are derived from that ancient notion and are applied to prophetic functionaries. Samuel was recognized as prophet in chapter 3 and exhibits elements of clairvoyance in chapter 9, inviting us to acknowledge 'the complexities of prophetic phenomena'. Wilson, *Prophecy and Society*, p. 9. Further consideration will be given to the constructs of *nabi* and *ro'eh* from a phenomenological perspective.

[90] Robert W. Kirkpatrick, *The Creative Delivery of Sermons* (New York: Mac Millan, 1944), pp. xxii, 235.

[91] Peter J. Leithart, *A Son to Me: An Exposition of 1 and 2 Samuel* (Moscow, ID: Canon Press, 2003), p. 46.

[92] Leithart, *Son to Me*, pp. 46, 44-45.

[93] Denoting rarity is

905a יָקָר (*yāqār*) *precious*. 905b יְקָר (*yĕqar*) *preciousness, honor, splendor, pomp* 905c יַקִּיר (*yaqqîr*) *very precious, honor*. The root and its derivatives are employed 65 times. It comes from a Semitic root which conveys the idea of 'heavy', 'honor', 'dignity'. An object is considered precious or valuable either because of its intrinsic worth or its rarity.

suggests judgment on Eli's house for his failure to discipline his derelict sons (1 Sam. 2.12-17). First Samuel 2 notes an 'environment of corruption' and the absence of God's word through Eli.[94] The book's third chapter traces Samuel from his call as a youth to his adult maturation. It also discloses Eli's waning eyesight, indicating physical blindness and the metaphorical loss of spiritual vision (1 Sam. 3.2).[95]

The text's physical setting emphasizes such contrasts as Israel enters its leadership transition. Juxtaposed with Eli's compromised sight, the dimming menorah, the rarity of words and visions from God is the young priest in a posture of evening repose before the ark of God (1 Sam. 3.3), stewarding the sacred space entrusted to him.[96] Noteworthy is the profound 'lack of word/vision, of God's presence, in this place, where of all places the presence of God should be most powerfully present'.[97] Precisely, literally, and metaphorically, these details point to Samuel's unfolding story of stewarding the word of the Lord.[98]

2.3.2.1.1 Samuel's Relation to the House of Eli

Samuel's placement in Eli's house contributed to his legitimate prophetic development, both through Eli's beneficial instructions and the negative examples he and his sons presented. Eli's eventual recognition of God's voice and his lucid instructions to Samuel awakened the boy's prophetic perception (1 Sam. 3.9). Such awakening is God's exclusive domain and cannot be actuated through Eli's volition. Yet Eli's history of divine encounters within the priesthood presumably honed his perception. He could therefore prepare Samuel, saying, 'Go, lie down; and if he calls you, you shall say, "Speak, Lord, for your servant is listening"' (1 Sam. 3.9). Eli additionally advised

---

John E. Hartley, '905 יָקָר', in *TWOT*, I, p. 398. While *rare* indicates divine revelation as being honorable and precious, it wasn't readily present. Neither were visionary experiences (both prophetic words and prophetic seeing are evident in this text).

[94] Johanna W.H. van Wijk-Bos, *Reading Samuel: A Literary and Theological Commentary* (Reading the Old Testament; Macon, GA: Smyth & Helwys, 2011), p. 43.

[95] Later, the narrative affirms Eli's dullness in perceiving the promptings of God to Samuel (1 Sam. 3.5-7). Yet, in spite of Eli's dullness due to failure to discipline his sons, metaphorically speaking, 'the lamp of God had not yet gone out' (1 Sam. 3.3).

[96] Within the Samuel narrative, 'this is the first mention of the Ark', van Wijk-Bos, *Reading Samuel*, pp. 43-44.

[97] van Wijk-Bos, *Reading Samuel*, pp. 43-44.

[98] The same details intimate the ultimate import of Samuel's stewardship for Israel.

Samuel to assume the restful posture of a listening servant.[99] Unlike Hophni and Phineas, who disobey their father's instruction, Samuel proves to be an obedient 'son'. He 'went and lay down in his place', ready to respond should God call him again.

Eli's mentoring of Samuel at this critical juncture facilitated Samuel's initiation into prophetic perception (1 Sam. 3.9). Three sequential summonses from God and three sequential responses to Eli transpired before Eli realized that God was summoning the boy (1 Sam. 3.4-9). With the fourth summons, the narrative subtly shifts: 'The Lord *came and stood there,* calling as before' (1 Sam. 3.10, emphasis added). Some manifestation of the Lord's form enabled Samuel to link both form and voice, and he obediently responded as Eli instructed.

Samuel's growth is evident in the contrast between this initial experience and his later ability to perceive 'the word of the Lord' (1 Sam. 3.21). This maturing of prophetic proclivity would seem significant, as God reportedly 'let none of his words fall to the ground' (1 Sam. 3.19).[100] The process of Samuel's 'becoming God's "true prophet" to "all Israel"' implied progress for the nation.[101] Instead of the Lord's word being rare (1 Sam. 3.1), 'the Lord revealed himself to Samuel at Shiloh' and sustained this recovery through Samuel's agency (1 Sam. 3.21). God's self-revelation at Shiloh, 'the sanctuary … once filled with corruption and scorn for God and God's people' marks a confluence with Samuel's maturation and Israel's movement from degradation toward the divine intent.[102] It also effectuates the national recovery so that 'sight and sound [were] once again potent vehicles of God's presence'.[103]

---

[99] The listening posture is seen in Eugene Peterson's assertion (*Working the Angles: The Shape of Pastoral Integrity* [Grand Rapids, MI: Eerdmans, 1987], p. 45), 'prayer is never the first word. It is always the second word. God has the first word. Prayer is answering speech; it is not primarily "address" but "response". Essential to the practice of prayer is to fully realize this secondary quality.' Eli's instruction to Samuel seems compatible with Peterson's view.

[100] The text may allude to the relational vulnerabilities between an infallible God and a fallible prophetic agent who, in his humanity, finds God faithfully supporting that which he utters within his calling.

[101] van Wijk-Bos, *Reading Samuel*, p. 44.

[102] van Wijk-Bos, *Reading Samuel*, p. 44.

[103] van Wijk-Bos, *Reading Samuel*, p. 44. The self-revealing of God to Samuel is his *dābār* (דָּבָר), God's '*word, speaking, speech, thing, anything, everything*'. Earl S. Kalland, '399 דָּבַר', in *TWOT*, I, p. 180.

2.3.2.1.2 Samuel, the Schools, and the Prophetic Order

Price sees Samuel as a reformer and 'reorganizer',[104] a role uniquely germane to this study's interest in the perpetuation of prophetic legitimacy and the current popularity of prophetic schools. Price notes, 'during [Samuel's] life' there arise 'collections or schools of sons of the prophets ... attributed to Samuel as their founder'.[105] Although Price avows that the guilds' 'continuous existence can be traced down through Old Testament history and literature',[106] they singularly 'form the beginnings of the prophetic order'.[107] Price also considers the text's mention of the groups' characteristics: '1) as collected in bands or schools; 2) in particular localities; 3) under different teachers; 4) with specified instruction; [and] 5) with an occupation; as to their means of subsistence'.[108] At Samuel's Naioth headquarters in Ramah, the company of prophets is active 'with Samuel standing in charge of them' (1 Sam. 19.20), a hierarchy suggesting some sort of training and education.

If Samuel concerned himself with the community's generational maintenance, his priestly training would reinforce, from the Torah's perspective, the community's sense of identity as Abraham's people. Once established in Canaan, Israel's foundational confession decreed their beginnings and the Exodus event,[109] a narrative that would be uttered when presenting the tithes and first fruits.[110] Samuel's schooling as a Levitical priest is inseparable from the Exodus narrative.[111] Brueggemann explains that the Levitical priest 'is charged to tell the truth ... spot the dangers and ... locate the edges of safe and viable conduct and imagination in the community'.[112] So, even as Torah

---

[104] Price, 'Sons of the Prophets', p. 244. Price bases his claim on Samuel's record as 'priest, prophet, and judge'.

[105] Price, 'Sons of the Prophets', p. 244. The specific text from which Price cites 'schools' of prophetic agents is 1 Sam. 19.18-24.

[106] Price, 'Sons of the Prophets', p. 244.

[107] Price, 'Sons of the Prophets', p. 244.

[108] Price, 'Sons of the Prophets', p. 244. 'The earliest mention of these bands is found in 1 Sam. 10:2-5'.

[109] See Deut. 26.1-11.

[110] In addition, prophetic function would address any false narratives, to dismantle and delegitimize them before the community.

[111] Walter Brueggemann, *The Creative Word: Canon as a Model for Biblical Education* (Philadelphia, PA: Fortress Press, 1982), p. 39, emphasizes that Torah 'provides the grounds for solidarity and consensus in the community'. This, in his view, is a 'subversive consensus' (p. 28).

[112] Brueggemann, *Creative Word*, p. 40.

provides a 'core of memory ... to organize all of experience',[113] the 'word from the prophet' is 'something immediate, intrusive ... surprising' and 'not known in advance'.[114] Samuel's 'presiding over' the company speaks to the experiential authority by which he assesses what is unknown until God discloses it (1 Sam. 19.20). If Samuel's primacy in the prophetic order is as Price believes, the content of prophetic messages would derive from Torah.[115]

2.3.2.2 The Call of Samuel from a Psychological Perspective

Within adoptive systems there exists a 'complex interplay',[116] which Samuel would have experienced in the house of Eli. Psychologically, this interplay would impact the development of Samuel's consciousness and perception, and his formational journey to prophethood.[117] Contemporary approaches to such considerations can provide insight into prophetic function. Samuel's ontogeny matters to his prophetic maturation and can illuminate the tension of his subjectivity, psychological narrative identity, and the identity-forming narrative the canon reveals.

Samuel's origin from a barren womb is significant primarily because the journey from barrenness to birth shaped Hannah's consciousness and perception, which then shaped Samuel's. Hannah's inability to conceive deeply provoked her (1 Sam. 1.6-11). Her weeping before the spiritually dull Eli prompted him to rebuke her (1 Sam. 1.12-14). Therefore, Hannah confessed her vexation, causing Eli's change of heart and his priestly pronouncement and blessing (1 Sam.

---

[113] Brueggemann, *Creative Word*, p. 41.

[114] Brueggemann, *Creative Word*, pp. 40, 41. It should be added that although the prophetic word is not known to the nation or the prophetic agent until God discloses it (Amos 3.7), the prophetic agent is somewhat prepared by virtue of previous encounters with the divine Spirit. It is the characteristic of the 'word's' immediacy that is intrusive and surprising.

[115] It is important to note that tradition-critical and redaction-critical methodologies would dispute this claim. However, for the purpose of this argument and in dealing with the text's social-literary context, such arguments are not germane.

[116] Sharon K. Roszia and Allison D. Maxon, *Seven Core Issues in Adoption and Permanency: A Comprehensive Guide to Promoting Understanding and Healing in Adoption, Foster Care, Kinship Families and Third Party Reproduction* (London: Jessica Kingsley, 2019), p. 15, illustrate the interplay in a triangular fashion involving the adopted person, the birth parents, and the adoptive parent(s).

[117] Roszia and Maxon, *Adoption and Permanency*, p. 15.

1.17),[118] which may be the text's indication that divine grace was actualized through human agency. Following the priestly blessing, Hannah in fact conceived and named the child *Samuel* (1 Sam. 1.20).[119] This is Hannah's basis for dedicating him from the womb to be a *nazir*.[120] It also suggests profound implications for the psychological shaping of Samuel's consciousness and perception, being a source from which he would derive his sense of identity and behavior.[121]

---

[118] Hannah vowed that if she was granted a firstborn son, he would be a Nazirite according to Numbers 6, dedicated to the service of the Lord from birth (1 Sam. 1.10-11). Did the priestly blessing in 1 Sam. 1.17 open her womb because of her vow?

[119] Robert D. Bergen, *1, 2 Samuel* (New American Commentary 7; Nashville, TN: Broadman & Holman, 1996), p. 71.

> That name – Samuel – has also created an etymological and interpretive puzzle for generations of European and American scholars. The majority of interpreters have rejected the etymological link suggested in the text (vv. 17, 20, 27-28; 2:20) between the name *šĕmû'ēl* and the verb 'ask' *(šā'al)*.
>
> Suggested meanings for Samuel's name include 'His Name Is El,' 'Name of El/God,' 'Heard of God,' 'Asked of God,' 'He Who Is from God,' 'Offspring of God,' and 'El Is Exalted.' Cf. Klein, *1 Samuel*, 9–10; R. Gordon, *I and II Samuel* (Grand Rapids: Zondervan, 1988), 76; McCarter, *I Samuel*, 62; and Driver, *Notes*, 19 (p. 71 n. 24).

The text shows this act of naming to be intentional and specific. Bergen asserts, 'metathesizing (i.e., reversing) the first two letters of Samuel's name (= *měšû'al*) creates a word meaning "He who was asked for"; acrostically, the name may be derived from the Hebrew phrase meaning 'asked from God' (= *šā'ûl min 'ēl*)' (p. 71).

[120] R.K. Harrison, 'Nazirite', in Geoffrey W. Bromiley (ed.), *International Standard Bible Encyclopedia* (Grand Rapids, MI: Eerdmans, rev. edn, 1988), p. 501:

> Nazirite naz'ə-rīt [Heb *nāzîr* – 'consecrated one', < *nāzar*, 'to consecrate'; cf. also *nādar* – 'to vow'; Gk *nazeiraíos*, plus various words indicating 'holiness' or 'devotion'. In Nu. 6:21b, c the RSV supplies 'Nazirite' (cf. AV, NEB)]; AV NAZARITE. The basic meaning of the different Hebrew and Greek terms is that of 'one consecrated, a devotee' … The role of Nazirite was that of a votary, a sacred person who was consecrated to divine service for a specific period of time as the result of a vow and as an expression of special commitment to God … A Nazirite could be one whose vow was made for him without his knowledge or approval, as with Samuel, who was offered to God in a vow made by his mother (1 S. 1:11). It is conceivable that Hannah herself was a Nazirite, since she was familiar with the general prescriptions.

[121] Based on contemporary research, being raised in a priestly setting introduces a cadre of factors that may have contributed to the challenges Eli's sons *and* Samuel's sons faced (1 Sam. 2.12-17, 8.1-6). Anthony Isacco, *et al.*, 'How Religious Beliefs and Practices Influence the Psychological Health of Catholic Priests', *American Journal of Men's Health* 10.4 (July 2016), p. 325,

From a literary-critical perspective, Hannah appears to be dominant in Samuel's formation,[122] with her influence continuing after she entrusts him to Eli. The text states that she 'used to make for him a little robe and take it to him each year' (1 Sam. 2.19).[123] This suggests her ongoing psychological nurturance, which would likely influence his interpretation of God's call. Her ritual pilgrimages to Shiloh would presumably include interaction with her son and likely some impartation of her wisdom and concern. Samuel's later choice to settle in Ramah suggests his deep psychic bond to his origins (1 Sam. 8.4, 19.18-22).

After weaning Samuel, Hannah entrusted him to Eli, with whom the text intimates he formed a bond. This influence upon the boy's psychological and spiritual consciousness and perception would have positive and negative ramifications. Samuel seems psychologically conscious that Eli's instruction regarding the Lord's call is valid, and he perceives that obeying him is wise.

2.3.2.3 The Call of Samuel from a Phenomenological Perspective

Aune's insights into the seer's prophetic makeup suggest phenomenological distinctions in relation to Samuel's call. It must be noted

---

Priests are often expected to take on more responsibilities and live alone as a result of the dwindling numbers. Basic workplace research has consistently indicated that increased workloads and decreased supports are correlated with negative psychological outcomes such as burnout (Maslach, Schaufeli, & Leiter, 2001).

The fact that Samuel failed much the way Eli did yet didn't receive reproof from Yahweh suggests many complex theological and psychological questions.

[122] The text suggests that while Samuel was in the couple's care, Hannah alone named the child and was his primary influence (1 Sam. 1.20-28). Leithart, *Son to Me*, p. 41, notes, 'Weaning was sometimes elaborately celebrated in the ancient world, since it marked his transfer from his mother's care to his father's (Gen. 21:8)'. Leithart here uses Isaac's weaning as prototypical example. If the custom was widely practiced in Israel, one could reasonably assume that Hannah and Elkanah followed suit. As such, it would be a significant rite of passage, thereby impacting Samuel's consciousness and perception.

[123] The Hebrew word for this liturgical robe is *mĕ'îl* (מְעִיל), which also denotes 'part of the priestly vestments worn by the high priest to cover the ephod', Victor P. Hamilton, '1230 מְעִיל', in *TWOT*, I, p. 520. Leithart, *Son to Me*, p. 46, states, 'the robes of the high priest and other dignitaries' become a 'motif' in the overall narrative (Exod. 28.4; 1 Sam. 15.27). For Leithart, this motif marks the text's movement toward Samuel's call as prophet. The garment is 'also associated with oracles', which supports Leithart's view of 'Samuel [as] a seer and prophet' (p. 46).

that regarding the synonymity of the terms *prophet* and *seer*, Aune carefully distinguishes each word's implied meaning:

> The oldest Hebrew terms for inspired individuals who mediate divine communications are 'seer' (*hozeh, ro'eh*), i.e. one who 'sees' what is hidden to others, 'man of God', and 'man of the Spirit'. The most common term for 'prophet' is *nabi'*, a word which etymologically means 'one who is called', but which came to mean 'speaker, spokesman (of God)', ... or 'proclaimer'.[124]

Theologically, the outcomes of prophetic function are seen as identical, which seems permissive of the terms' synonymity. From a phenomenological perspective, however, one who sees what is hidden from others may not be phenomenologically equivalent to a speaker, spokesperson, or proclaimer. Assuming that ancient prophets were 'inspired individuals' endued by the Spirit to 'mediate divine communication',[125] precisely how was the communication mediated? Was the mediation visionary? If so, the prophet's message conveyance as a spokesperson is phenomenologically distinct; the medium of visionary trance differs phenomenologically from an audition by the Spirit. The phenomenological aspect of the speaker/spokesperson implies a way of speaking that is unique to the speaker. The phenomenological aspect of 'one who sees what is hidden to others' is of another intentionality altogether.

Johnson's observation of what Wilson paraphrases as 'the complexities of prophetic phenomena' intimates aspects of consciousness that produce phenomenological differences.[126] Prophetic agents present in their own words and prophetic expressions what they consciously perceive. Moses does not speak as Isaiah does. Ezekiel does not replicate Daniel's speech. What results as 'the *word* that Isaiah the son of Amoz *saw*' indicates Isaiah's adept articulation (Isa. 2.1, emphasis added). He clothes in his own words that which is shown to him. However, Jeremiah responds to his experience by simply stating what is apparent within his perceptual field and listening as God conveys its meaning (Jer. 1.11-12).

These phenomenological distinctions clarify the differences between the *nabi'* and *ro'eh* functions Samuel expressed. It can be

---

[124] Aune, *Prophecy in Early Christianity*, p. 83.
[125] Aune, *Prophecy in Early Christianity*, p. 83.
[126] Wilson, *Prophecy and Society*, p. 9.

assumed that the prophetic guilds he oversaw operated in both functions, as he did, the dual emphasis being perhaps insinuated where the notions of the 'word of the Lord' and 'visions' are juxtaposed (1 Sam. 3.1). Tsumara enunciates the connection, writing, 'The term *vision* (*ḥāzôn*) denotes God's revelation, which is the equivalent of *the word of the Lord* (v. 1)'.[127]

In 1 Samuel 10, the prophet anoints Saul as king, thereby authorizing, empowering, and legitimizing him.[128] Saul is confirmed with these signs following (1 Sam. 10.2-8):

1. The reiterated prophetic word about the return of the donkeys that Saul was sent to retrieve, to be confirmed by two men at Rachel's tomb (1 Sam. 10.2).
2. The encounter at the Oak of Tabor with three individuals ascending to offer sacrifice to God at Bethel (1 Sam. 10.3-4).
3. The encounter with the band of prophets at Gibeath-elohim, where Saul is caught up in prophetic frenzy with the prophets (1 Sam. 10.5-6, 10).

---

[127] David Toshio Tsumura, *The First Book of Samuel* (New International Commentary on the Old Testament; Grand Rapids, MI: Eerdmans, 2007), p. 174 (emphasis added). Whether or not this text implies synonymity and equivalence in every case is a matter of debate. I would argue that this is not the case. However, Tsumura cites examples for it. Tsumura, *First Book of Samuel*, p. 174:

> The term *vision* (*ḥāzôn*) denotes God's revelation, which is the equivalent of *the word of the Lord* (v. 1). It should be noted that the prophetic 'vision' is used for the divine message communicated to the prophets, and the message was usually to be delivered to the prophet's audience orally in words. But sometimes the *vision* was directed to be 'written down' (Hab. 2:2). In Amos 1:1; Mic. 1:1; Isa. 2:1; etc., the 'vision' is recorded in words. Thus, in the biblical prophecy the 'vision' was something to be explained or expressed in words, and its message is more important than the visionary experience of the prophet itself. The rarity of *the word of the Lord* might be construed as a sign of divine disfavor (see Ps. 74:9; Lam. 2:9; Amos 8:11; Mic. 3:6f.) (emphasis added).

It seems possible however, that certain communications from the divine presence are intuitive auditions apart from anything visual (consider 1 Kgs 18.41). This suggests distinctions between the 'word of the Lord' and 'visions' in the same text. In 1 Samuel 10, there is no indication that Samuel conveyed something he saw regarding the lost donkeys. Instead, he seemed to *know* this intuitively. Likewise, in the Pentecostal and Latter Rain tradition, when prophets speak of the '[w]ord of the Lord', they are not speaking about visionary experience but about what I call a *way of knowing* by the Spirit. Violet Kiteley, '(Untitled) Violet Kiteley Personal and Latter Rain Account', *Violet Kiteley Papers*, p. 3. The closest vocabulary to approximate this way of knowing is tied to intuition, which will be developed further in Chapter 5.

[128] Walter Brueggemann, *First and Second Samuel* (Interpretation: A Bible Commentary for Teaching and Preaching; Louisville, KY: John Knox Press, 1990), p. 74.

Each of these signs would have prophetic significance; here it suffices to say that Samuel operated in a way of knowing what had and had not occurred. Regarding the latter, he anticipated the future before it arrived. This involves ways of knowing *intuitively* by the Spirit, which vary phenomenologically according to individual temperament, cognition, and perception.

What is the signs' purpose, and why is the prophet required to verbalize them? For Gordon, 'signs' are 'intended to bring about knowledge of God (e.g., Ex. 7:3; Dt. 4:34)'.[129] Phenomenologically, they are to make an impression on the recipient's psyche, producing a greater awareness of the recipient's relationship with God. Regarding that which legitimizes the Spirit's integral work among his people, Samuel shares (1) in close camaraderie with the prophetic guilds in Ramah and (2) mediatorially with the nation. Thus, he moves the people toward their intended purpose and destiny.

2.4 Elijah and Elisha: Prefiguring John the Baptist and Jesus

With respect to prophetic history and prophetic legitimacy, the roles and acts of Elijah and Elisha are indispensable. In addition to their foreshadowing of John the Baptist and Jesus, they model an alternative identity, vision, and vocation for Israel,[130] as Moses did. Brueggemann considers Elijah and Elisha's presence in OT history as 'the prophetic counterforce' that intrudes into the royal, elitist consciousness of corrupt kings in unexpected and unconventional ways,[131] revealing an existing tension between Yahweh and Baal. The Elijah and Elisha narratives are 'anti-Baalistic',[132] showing that 'God is about the business of bringing his purposes to fruition'.[133] This cannot occur apart from his agents' participation, as they deal with

---

[129] V.R. Gordon, 'Sign', in Geoffrey W. Bromiley (ed.), *International Standard Bible Encyclopedia* (Grand Rapids, MI: Eerdmans, rev. edn, 1988), p. 506.

[130] Walter Brueggemann, *Testimony to Otherwise: The Witness of Elijah and Elisha* (St. Louis, MO: Chalice Press 2001), p. 5.

[131] Walter Brueggemann, *1 and 2 Kings* (Smyth and Helwys Bible Commentary; Macon, GA: Smyth & Helwys, 2000), p. 207.

[132] Ian J. Hauser, 'Yahweh Versus Death – The Real Struggle in 1 Kings 17–19', in Alan J. Hauser and Russell Gregory, *From Carmel to Horeb: Elijah in Crisis* (Sheffield: Almond Press, 1990), p. 11.

[133] August H. Konkel, *1 and 2 Kings* (NIV Application Commentary; Grand Rapids, MI: Zondervan, 2006), p. 277.

the 'continued frustration of covenant relationship' in the northern and southern kingdoms.[134]

2.4.1 Elijah Is Indeed a Prophet

2.4.1.1 Elijah from a Biblical/Theological Perspective

Within the context of Ahab's immersion in idolatrous practices and the consequences that followed (1 Kgs 16.31-33), Fretheim notes Elijah's 'abrupt appearance' in the king's court (1 Kgs 17.1).[135] Sirach 48.1 states, Elijah's word 'burn[s] like a torch' (Sir. 48.1); Slager adds that he bursts 'on the scene like a sudden leap of flame'.[136] The sudden ignition of Elijah's appearance is crucial. From the outset he is depicted as being zealous for God. In opposing Ahab's royal court, Elijah declares himself emissary of Yahweh's heavenly council (1 Kgs 17.1; Jer. 23.18). In a confrontation reminiscent of Moses' approach to Pharaoh in Exod. 5.1, Elijah announces that the weather is under his oversight, and no rain will fall until he declares it (1 Kgs 17.1-2). Well-versed in Torah's prohibitions (Deut. 6.14), Elijah 'understands God's curses',[137] as Ahab and many other attendees do. Brueggemann notes, 'drought [was] widely understood ... as a divine curse'.[138] Thus, Elijah voices the divine displeasure and prays until the 'rain is withheld' (Jas 5.17).[139] God hides him for three and a half years, during which 'the drought and consequent famine ... reached disastrous proportions'.[140] Elijah alone can reverse these consequences. After his hidden years, he reappears before Ahab (1 Kgs 18.15-17), who disavows his own iniquity and assigns all blame to Elijah, Israel's 'troubler' (1 Kgs 18.17). Refusing to cower or accept the accusation, Elijah places the responsibility on Ahab (1 Kgs 18.18),[141] 'shift[ing]

---

[134] Konkel, *1 and 2 Kings*, p. 277.

[135] Terence E. Fretheim, *First and Second Kings* (Westminster Bible Companion; Louisville, KY: Westminster John Knox Press, 1999), p. 96.

[136] Donald Slager, Preface to Roger A. Bullard and Howard A. Hatton, *A Handbook on Sirach* (United Bible Societies' Handbooks; New York: United Bible Societies, 2008), p. 959.

[137] Peter J. Leithart, *1 and 2 Kings* (Brazos Theological Commentary on the Bible; Grand Rapids, MI: Brazos Press, 2006), p. 129.

[138] Brueggemann, *1 and 2 Kings*, p. 207.

[139] Brueggemann, *1 and 2 Kings*, p. 207.

[140] Jerome T. Walsh, *1 Kings* (Berit Olam Studies in Hebrew Narrative and Poetry; Collegeville, MN: Liturgical Press, 1996), p. 237.

[141] Walsh, *1 Kings*, pp. 243-44:

the focus from Ahab's fury over the drought to his own struggle against apostasy', the drought's 'real cause'.[142] Elijah is clear: the apostasy has consequences, and the people recognize crop-producing rain as 'the measure of an effective king'.[143]

Shown unable to deliver his people,[144] Ahab concedes to a contest on Carmel. If Baal is seen as a 'god of the storm and fertility, who brings rains' and 'ensures the growth of new crops',[145] then Baal must prove responsive to the liturgical protocols of his worship. Israel has forgotten the promise that *their* God sends the early and the latter rains and has marginalized the God who established them in the land (Deut. 11.14).[146] However, on Carmel, Elijah is established as the legitimate prophetic mediator for Israel's God, who responds when Elijah calls.

The Carmel face-off establishes the tension among Ahab, Jezebel, and the 450 prophets of Baal (1 Kgs 18.22), with Elijah as the seeming lone voice speaking on God's behalf. For him, confronting the false prophets is a 'life-or-death occasion' that must dismantle the radical Baalist narrative.[147] Israel is compromised, hobbling back and forth between Yahweh and Baal (1 Kgs 18.21), and its impaired consciousness and perception need to be exposed.[148] By God's wisdom

---

Elijah accuses Ahab and the whole house of Omri of disobedience to Yahweh. To this sin he attributes the 'troubling' of Israel, that is, the drought. But Ahab himself is guilty of an even greater sin. He has not only disobeyed Yahweh; he has also taken up with Baal. These claims are in harmony with the information in 16:25-33, which decried Omri's evil as following Jeroboam's calf-idols (16:25-26) and identified Ahab's greater evil as Baal worship (16:31-33).

[142] Robert L. Cohn, 'The Literary Logic of 1 Kings 17–19', *Journal of Biblical Literature* 101.3 (1982), p. 340.

[143] Brueggemann, *1 and 2 Kings*, p. 209.

[144] Under Ahab's oversight, a marriage to 'Sidonian Princess Jezebel bat Ethbaal' was arranged. Marvin A. Sweeney, *Jewish Mysticism: From Ancient Times through Today* (Grand Rapids, MI: Eerdmans, 2020), p. 120. For the Omride Dynasty, the union 'secure[d] a Phoenician ally' and provided access to beneficial trade routes and military support against Ahab's Aramean enemies. Such a marriage was forbidden, according to Deut. 7.1-7. Despite the alliance, Ahab's economic policies failed miserably, being tied to false ideologies and idolatry.

[145] Sweeney, *Jewish Mysticism*, p. 28.

[146] The 'semi-nomadic desert dwellers' attracted to the Fertile Crescent [seem] forgetful of the God whose eyes are always on the land (Deut. 11:12). Sweeney, *Jewish Mysticism*, p. 28.

[147] Brueggemann, *1 and 2 Kings*, p. 226.

[148] Konkel, *1 and 2 Kings*, pp. 299-300:

and knowledge, Elijah will remove every façade of the Baalist narrative and the Omride dynasty's alliances with Ethbaal.

Elijah understood the deconstructing and disillusioning effects that the court's public humiliation would produce, provided it touched the collective consciousness *prior* to any demonstration of the Spirit and power. Therefore, he allowed the Baal prophets to go first (1 Kgs 18.25). Everything Elijah did on the mount was intentional and comprehensive in relation to prophetic enactment, including his:

- addressing of the people for their idolatry and compromise;
- allowing the false prophets to go first and publicly display their ineffective prophetic frenzy as they cry out, scream, jump about, mutilate their own flesh, and shed blood, to no avail;
- mocking and taunting of the prophets and Baal while inciting them to intensify their futile efforts;
- final taunt to awaken Baal, who was incapable of being awakened from 'sleep'.[149]

Elijah reproves the people for 'limping with two different opinions' (1 Kgs 18.21).[150] This word of judgment is tied to divine disfavor and metaphorically notes a disqualifying disfigurement for one 'functioning as a priest' (Lev. 21.18).[151] Because of the prevailing

---

The contest at Mount Carmel shows that the Lord of Israel will tolerate no compromise; Elijah challenges the people to 'stop hopping between two boughs'. The word for 'bough' (s^e '*ippîm*) is also used to refer to thoughts (e.g., Job 4:13). Just as boughs branch off from trees, so thoughts and opinions can branch off in more than one direction. This wordplay describes the prevarication of the people in their professed worship; prayers and homage at the bull shrine can have nothing to do with Yahweh. The silence of the people is a concession to the truth of Elijah's words.

[149] James Swanson, יָשֵׁן, *Dictionary of Biblical Languages with Semantic Domains: Hebrew (Old Testament)* (Oak Harbor: Logos Research Systems, 1997); *Sleep* is denoted by

3825 III. יָשֵׁן (*yā·šēn*): adj ... sleeping, i.e., pertaining to being in an altered state of awareness that is not being awake (1Sa 26:7, 12; 1Ki 3:20; 18:27; SS 5:2; Da 12:2+), note: for cj in Hos 7:6, see 3822; note: for MT text in SS 7:10[EB 9], see 3825; **2.** LN 74 asleep, i.e., pertaining to not taking action, as a figurative extension of being in a state of rest and so not able to take action (Ps 78:65+).

[150] Elijah offers a picture of 'hobbling along on two uneven crutches', Walsh, *1 Kings*, p. 245.

[151] Walsh, *1 Kings*, p. 245.

syncretism,[152] disengaging and distancing Baalism from Yahweh worship requires the deconstruction of Baal's truth claims, even as Elijah's prophetic wisdom is revealed by his words and enactments.

In what transpires, Elijah seeks to remind those present that unlike surrounding nations that can worship many gods, the Shema states. 'the Lord is one' (Deut. 6.4 NASB). The God who 'is on the side of exclusivism' lays exclusive claim on Israel,[153] opposing the people's seeming desire. Their refusal to answer is problematic (1 Kgs 18.21),[154] and Elijah's prophetic legitimacy is at stake.

Elijah then establishes the core issue, contrasting his minority position with the majority's view: 'I, even I only am left a prophet of the Lord; but Baal's prophets number four hundred fifty' (1 Kgs 18.22). Are Baal and Yahweh equal in the people's minds? For Elijah, only 'the God who answers by fire' and consumes one of the sacrifices can respond and prove himself God (1 Kgs 18.24). The people accept this challenge, and Elijah displays full confidence that God will answer his prayer. This is not unlike Moses' confidence when using his staff in Pharaoh's presence; he fully expects it to perform as God promised.

The key in the Carmel narrative lies in (1) seeing who is in charge, and (2) realizing that Elijah's opposers resist none of his instruction. When Elijah directs the Baalist prophets and the people to invoke Baal's name, they do so from morning until noon. 'But there was no

---

[152] Clinton E. Arnold, 'Syncretism', in Ralph P. Martin and Peter H. Davids (eds.), *Dictionary of the Later New Testament and Its Developments* (Downers Grove, IL: InterVarsity Press, 1997), p. 1146; *Syncretism*, a term used

> by anthropologists and historians to refer to the blending of religious beliefs. This typically occurs when the social circumstances of one group bring them into contact with another. As the two groups interact, members of one group may begin to assimilate aspects of the religious beliefs of the other, resulting in a transformation of the traditional religion. For Christians throughout history, the notion of syncretism has had largely negative connotations and is sometimes associated with heresy. This is due to the fact that assimilation is often perceived as a departure from the purity of the original. Many modern-day missiologists thus distinguish syncretism from contextualization, with the latter understood as an appropriate expression of the gospel in culturally relevant forms.

[153] Walsh, *1 Kings*, pp. 245-46.

[154] This reminds us of the syncretism and cultural accommodation present in today's church and prophetic circles, as reflected in the problem statement in Chapter 1.

voice, and no answer' (1 Kgs 18.26). This is a profound negation of Baal,[155] who is no god and is now fully delegitimized.

The tension increases, and Elijah's mocking provokes the Baalist prophets and others to continue their invocations past noon. The Baalist prophets are now dysfunctional, *limping* around the altar (the same Hebrew word that Elijah used about limping on two crutches). If this is their ritual dance, it exposes both their false worship and their now invalidated truth claims. The embodied enactments of the Baal prophets is as malformed as their god.

Walsh suggests, '"limping with two different opinions" is in effect a Baalist stance'.[156] Their redoubled efforts only exacerbate their folly. Elijah intensifies his ridicule and suggests that Baal is perhaps on a journey or sleeping the sleep of death.[157] His taunts drive further Baalist invocations and, frenzied, they shed their own blood. Sweeney argues, 'the self-gashing and blood are meant to represent the reversal of creation in which blood is shed and [it] calls to the gods for action to restore creation to its natural order'.[158] This reversal is the anti-narrative to the truth of God's sacrificial love and redemption of Creation by blood (Jn 3.16; Heb. 9.12).

The Baalist prophets and their followers continue, entering trance-like, ecstatic prophetic states (they 'raved on') by sheer force of human will[159] – an indication that, however real certain ecstatic approaches might seem to those who experience them, they do not

---

[155] Walsh asserts that the phrasing, '*There was no*', is significant, the words *there was* being impersonal. 'Rather than presence, the narrator hints at Baal's nonentity', Walsh, *1 Kings*, p. 248. In Hebrew, the English clause is contained in one word: אֵין, אַיִן (*'ayin* /ah·yin/), which is present tense. See Ludwig Koehler, Walter Baumgartner, and Johann Jakob Stamm, 'אַיִן', *The Hebrew and Aramaic Lexicon of the Old Testament* (Leiden: Brill, 2000). Therefore, the proper English translation would be 'There *is* no'. Walsh emphatically states that this 'suggests an absolute judgment of nonexistence', Walsh, *1 Kings*, p. 248. According to Walsh, there is no entity, no present tense, and no answer because there is no voice available to answer. Baal is no god and is fully delegitimized at this point in the narrative.

[156] Walsh, *1 Kings*, p. 248.

[157] Walsh, *1 Kings*, p. 249, 'The references to Baal's being on a journey and being asleep may allude to commonly known mythological stories of the god, including his temporary imprisonment in the underworld by the god Death'.

[158] Sweeney, *Jewish Mysticism*, pp. 121-22.

[159] BDB, '[נָבָא] S5012 TWOT1277 GK5547] vb. denom. prophesy (in oldest forms, of religious ecstasy with or without song and music; later, essentially religious instruction, with occasional predictions … **1.** *prophesy* under influence of divine spirit: a. in the ecstatic state, with song 1 S 10:11; 19:20 and music 1 Ch 25:1, 2, 3.'

indicate prophetic legitimacy.[160] The narrative details the grotesque display that reveals the corruption of idolatry and the power of deception to diminish humanness.

At the time of the evening oblation, Elijah repairs the altar. All that has transpired has set the stage, and his prophetic enactments now favor an affirming response from Israel's God. The Levitical repairing of the altar of sacrifice places Elijah in a dual role like that of the transitional priest/prophet-seer, Samuel. The altar's twelve stones evoke the energizing memory of Gilgal (Josh. 4.2-3). Elijah makes a trench, which for Sweeney marks 'the holy boundaries of the altar and catch[es] the blood of animal sacrifice to ensure its proper entry into the ground'.[161] This seems to reference indirectly the blood poured out at the altar's base, per Torah's guidelines (Lev. 4.7). Elijah instructs Baal's prophets to douse the sacrifice with copious amounts of water (a drastic measure during drought). The Baal sacrifice had not been doused, yet Baal failed to answer, a fact that challenges the Baal narrative. Elijah's dousing and abstention from using man-made fire seems illogical. However, the water is a drink offering to Yahweh that, for Sweeney, is 'characteristic of the temple observance of Tabernacles'.[162] Significantly, such a drink offering 'marks the end of the fruit harvest and the onset of the rainy season in the fall'.[163] Hence, Elijah is prophetically enacting the imminence of rain.

When the time of the evening sacrifice arrives, Elijah offers a simple prayer to the God of the patriarchs (1 Kgs 18.36-37), reminding him that Elijah has acted on God's instruction. Elijah states his desire for the people to know Yahweh as the true God and Elijah as his legitimate prophet.[164] The moment his prayer ends, 'the fire of the Lord' falls, consuming both the sacrifice and sacrificial structure. The people then fall on their faces, confessing that Yahweh is God.

God and his spokesperson are vindicated. Elijah's prophetic message reiterates Moses' prophetic message to Pharaoh that the Lord alone is God (Exod. 7.5). Elijah's prayer acknowledges the continuity of the grand narrative by addressing the God of Israel's fathers, who

---

[160] Self-willed experiences stand in contradistinction to the sovereign Spirit's work.
[161] Sweeney, *Jewish Mysticism*, p. 122.
[162] Sweeney, *Jewish Mysticism*, p. 122.
[163] Sweeney, *Jewish Mysticism*, p. 122.
[164] Ultimately, Elijah wants the people's hearts turned back to the God who is rich in mercy and forgiveness.

will turn the people's 'hearts back' (1 Kgs 18.37). This prophetic enactment manifests God's mercy and makes the opportunity for repentance known.[165] Elijah intends for God's people to realize with all his prophets that God 'forgives Israel, restores it, brings it back to the land for the sake of his own name'.[166]

The text depicts Elijah's fiery intensity, which is fueled by an ultimacy expressed in embodied, prophetic zeal. The narrative perhaps invites us to expect God to answer as Elijah has asked. For Brueggemann, then, this is a decisive moment of congruence when God answers by fire (lightning).[167] Thus, God's name is cleared, and Elijah's trustworthiness and legitimacy are validated.[168]

2.4.1.2 Elijah from a Psychological Perspective

Following Elijah's slaughter of the Baalist prophets,[169] he becomes a fugitive, fleeing Jezebel's threat on his life (1 Kgs 19.1-2). This flight is psychologically consequential, his fear driving him 'further south into the wilderness (19:4-10)'.[170] There he will first stop at Beersheba, leave his servant, and in a state of major depressive disorder,[171] unwisely move into personal isolation and exhaustion in the desert.

As Walsh keenly observes, 'Without as within, Elijah's burdens overwhelm him: he can escape neither his despair nor the desert sun'.[172] Elijah's ultimate return to stability is not found in running but

---

[165] Leithart, *1 and 2 Kings*, p. 136.

[166] Leithart, *1 and 2 Kings*, p. 136. This is the sheer gift that expresses God's loyal love.

[167] Brueggemann, *1 and 2 Kings*, p. 226.

[168] Brueggemann, *1 and 2 Kings*, p. 226. Brueggemann speaks here of vindication and credibility, respectively.

[169] The question of whether God instructed Elijah to slay the Baalist prophets invites a hermeneutic of suspicion. To contemporary readers, such action seems cruel and contrary to what is revealed of God in Christ. What can be said is that God works with and not apart from flawed human agency, even when that agency is divinely legitimized. Figuratively, Elijah punished all disobedience when the people's obedience was complete (2 Cor. 10.6).

[170] Brueggemann, *1 and 2 Kings*, p. 234.

[171] 'Depressive Disorder', *APA Dictionary of Psychology*, https://dictionary.apa.org/ major-depressive-disorder; *Depressive disorder* 'in DSM–IV–TR and DSM–5, [is] a mood disorder characterized by persistent sadness and other symptoms of a major depressive episode but without accompanying episodes of mania or hypomania or mixed episodes of depressive and manic or hypomanic symptoms'.

[172] Walsh, *1 Kings*, p. 267.

in becoming joined to Elisha, despite his own irascible and isolating nature (1 Kgs 19.20).[173]

2.4.1.3 Elijah from a Phenomenological Perspective

Elijah's arrival on the national scene and announcement of his participation in the heavenly council indicate that saturated phenomena are not unusual to him (1 Kgs 17.1; Jer. 23.18). He has previously experienced the numinous. Given his way of being, his apparent intimacy with the God of Israel, and his awareness of the unseen world (2 Kgs 2.10); he seemed to have 'possessed the characteristically mystical consciousness and passed through the normal stages of mystical growth'.[174] Elijah exhibits all the markers of someone with what Steinbock calls 'sensitivity to vertical givenness'.[175]

The *givenness* of an experience can be described as a saturated phenomenon that 'cannot be wholly contained within concepts that can be grasped by our understanding'.[176] It is 'the most basic ambition of phenomenology',[177] the way that phenomenologists understand how 'phenomena … are *given* to consciousness'.[178] Personal biases and subjectivity can alter how phenomena are experienced and described as being given. Caution and circumspection are warranted when articulating these phenomena. Most importantly (and considering the nature of deception, the lack of discernment, and the immature and incomplete awareness of how the spiritual senses function), it is

---

[173] For a more detailed study of Elijah's extreme psychological state following the Mount Carmel events and Jezebel's death threat, see Mark J. Chironna, 'What Does Psychology Have to Do with the Prophetic?', *Firebrand* (June 14, 2022), https://firebrandmag.com/articles/what-does-psychology-have-to-do-with-the-prophetic. There I cover the finer points of his anguish and its effects on his prophetic role.

[174] Evelyn Underhill, *The Mystic Way: A Psychological Study in Christian Origins* (London: J.M. Dent & Sons, 1913), p. viii.

[175] Anthony J. Steinbock, *Phenomenology and Mysticism: The Verticality of Religious Experience* (Bloomington, IN: Indiana University Press, 2007), p. 1.

[176] Shane Mackinlay, *Interpreting Excess: Jean-Luc Marion, Saturated Phenomena, and Hermeneutics* (New York: Fordham University Press, 2010), p. 1.

[177] Tarek R. Dika and W. Chris Hackett, *Quiet Powers of the Possible: Interviews in Contemporary French Phenomenology* (New York: Fordham University Press, 2016), intro.

[178] Dika and Hackett, *Quiet Powers*, intro (emphasis added).

essential to understand how religious phenomena present themselves and how their *givenness* is interpreted.[179]

For Underhill, the sharpening of discernment requires an 'organic growth'.[180] This involves having to 'pass through a series of profound psychic changes and readjustments' on the way to 'spiritual maturity'.[181] Due to Elijah's omitted prior history, we cannot see these processes. However, from his first appearance onward, we do see that whatever 'vertical evidence' has been given to him is working in him.[182] In his backstory, he has undergone a process of individuation toward spiritual maturity through a 'heightened correspondence with Reality'.[183] Via his prophetic expressions and the signs and wonders accompanying them, we witness that heightened correspondence. The phenomenological realities that served Elijah's individuation for prophetic legitimacy somewhat reveal his 'enhanced power of dealing with circumstances'.[184] Yet, in relation to expressing what has been shown him phenomenologically, areas of his personal and emotional self-regulation are somewhat fractured. They do not disrupt his discerning of the domains of consciousness and perception related to prophetic legitimacy, yet he needs a transitional season – his trek to Sinai – in which to face his fragmentation.

Elijah spends the night at the cave at Horeb. In the darkness, the 'word of the Lord came to him' (1 Kgs 19.9). This is a vertical experience, a moment of saturated phenomenon. By whatever means the word arrives, the saturation of Elijah's intuition is significant, so that

---

[179] Regarding religious phenomena and experience, such realities do not conform to the norms presupposed in relation to, say, the givenness of a chair or apple. Encounters with the angelic or the divine present in ways that transcend 'norms' within the 'space of rationality', Dika and Hackett, *Quiet Powers*, intro. Hence Marion argues regarding the saturation of the intuition (which for Steinbock is an aspect of verticality) that there is an 'excess of intuition' relating to 'what gives itself and what shows itself', Jean-Luc Marion, *In Excess: Studies of Saturated Phenomena*, Perspectives in Continental Philosophy (Fordham University Press, 2002), p. xxi. The phenomena encountered on the horizontal plane of human experience – object to object and person to person, within the visible and known domains of what is defined as reality – are not the same as encounters with reality on a vertical plane.

[180] Underhill, *Mystic Way*, p. viii.
[181] Underhill, *Mystic Way*, p. viii.
[182] Steinbock, *Phenomenology and Mysticism*, p. 1.
[183] Underhill, *Mystic Way*, p. viii.
[184] Underhill, *Mystic Way*, p. viii. The phenomenological realities that served Elijah's individuation did so through the shaping of his consciousness and perception.

he recognizes the divine and responds appropriately. Yet his response seems not to indicate an awareness that he is talking to God himself.

The word is interrogative: 'What are you doing here, Elijah?' This raises the question of who is behind Elijah's arrival at Horeb. Did God direct him there, or did God accommodate and condescend to Elijah's self-directed choice? Elijah knows the God of Israel and has experienced the verticality of saturated phenomena. Although he recognizes the encounter, he answers God as though not realizing that it is he. Why does Elijah address God in the third person, saying, 'I have been very zealous for the Lord, the God of hosts' (1 Kgs 19.10)? This seems suggestive of some dissociation, perhaps indicating that his spiritual senses have been impacted by his psychological despair. Thus, he finds himself not only isolated relationally and geographically but internally, from God. This condition did not begin at Horeb but was evident at the broom tree, where Elijah asked God to take his life. There, his despair was self-oriented, presenting a lack of consideration for the divine intent and the nation's needs.

Walsh recognizes Elijah's cognitive distortions, noting, 'He wants God to act here and now, not for God's own sake or for the people's, but simply for Elijah's: "I've had enough, and I want it to end. Now!"'[185] Elijah recognizes the Transcendent One's nature and power. Phenomenologically, however, he remains unmoved by anything he has experienced with God. His indifference is perplexing. The one asking to die presents a preexisting deadness in his innermost ways of relating to the God who is life. God responds not by taking his life but by supplying angelic support and sustenance. In this notably vertical religious experience, Elijah remains detached, ingesting small portions of the repast in an obligatory fashion. In refusing to finish it, he reverts to a sleep-in-hope-of-death state, only to be reawakened by the angel and made to finish the meal.

Despite Elijah's state, the word of the Lord comes. The text does not articulate the givenness of the moment. Is it an audition, a vision and an audition, or some sort of internal exchange? How the saturated phenomenon transpires is unknowable, but an exchange occurs in which God asks Elijah what he is doing in Horeb (1 Kgs 19.9). Walsh notes that 'Yahweh expects Elijah to be somewhere else'.[186]

---

[185] Walsh, *1 Kings*, p. 267.
[186] Walsh, *1 Kings*, p. 272.

The text itself implies that Elijah made this long trek on his own volition.

Elijah wants out. That he journeys to Horeb to voice his complaint is significant. He seems not only to know the location but to have frequented it. Had he previously experienced saturated phenomena at Horeb? The possibility exists. Yet, now, in response to the divine query, Elijah fully voices his 'hopelessness ... disillusion, and despair'.[187] He does this in a five-pronged response (1 Kgs 19.10). The first two of his five statements raise questions that cannot be answered clearly, but they relate to his psychological state:

- 'I have been very zealous for the Lord'. (Elijah speaks of God in the third person. Why?).
- 'The Israelites have forsaken your covenant'. (Elijah switches to the personal pronoun, *you*. Why the change?).
- They 'have thrown down your altars' (even though they have already repented).
- They 'have killed your prophets with the sword' (even though they have helped slay the prophets of Baal as a sign of renunciation).
- 'I alone am left' (even though the witnesses on the mountain expressed a willingness to return to Yahweh). 'They are seeking my life, to take it away' (not Israel but Jezebel).

Moses' encounter at Horeb comes to mind. Moses complains about what God requires of him (Exod. 33.12-13). There is some negotiating about to whom the people belong (Exod. 33.13-15). Walsh summarizes the exchange by saying that Moses 'gives God an ultimatum: either assure us of your presence or abandon us'.[188] While God promises Moses that he will see his glory, he summons Elijah to the mouth of the cave, after he responds to God's probing question. Specifically, God says, 'Go out and stand' (1 Kgs 19.11), calling Elijah to exit his hiding place. Is this a call to personal exodus? Is God calling Elijah from the pit of despair and distorted reality back to prophetic legitimacy? Walsh seems to imply as much, stating, 'Yahweh, then, is not calling Elijah merely to witness a theophany but to

---

[187] Walsh, *1 Kings*, p. 267.
[188] Walsh, *1 Kings*, p. 271.

witness it precisely as a faithful servant – in other words, to take up once again his prophetic ministry'.[189]

Elijah resists God's directive: he neither exits the cave nor stands on the mountain. Creation offers a symphonic prelude to the saturated phenomenon of theophany: a great wind comes, along with earthquake and fire. Creation's groanings herald the presence of the transcendent. Yet Elijah refuses to stand and witness the procession. None of these phenomena contain the givenness of a vertical religious experience. Elijah knows the difference. What he does not know is the givenness that will occur in the vertical moment ahead. A 'sound of sheer silence' arrests Elijah's attention, and he exits the cave and stands before the Lord (1 Kgs 19.12-13), albeit enveloping his face in his mantle. This parallels Moses' being hidden by God in the cleft of the rock (Exod. 33.21-22). The initiative in this case is Elijah's. God shields Moses from his blinding glory; Elijah shields himself from the sheer silence and its thunderous impact. In cloaking his face, he expresses the importance of hiddenness, even in the face of his imperfect obedience.

Perhaps what defies all rational categories of givenness is the transcendent's fundamental mystery. The numinous cannot be rationally categorized, being 'free, creative, impalpable'.[190] Elijah hears this impossible-to-hear yet audible silence, the paradox of which is irrefutable. Walsh explains, 'the numinous power of the image lies precisely in our inability to grasp it'.[191] He recognizes the verticality of the phenomenon by describing the sound of silence as numinous. Saturated phenomena cannot be grasped. Any approach to the Absolute is necessarily enshrouded in the mystery of absolute transcendence. Although mystery invites exploration, it defies the same.

As the sheer silence speaks to Elijah, God asks again: 'What are you doing here?' (1 Kgs 19.13). The text places Elijah at the mouth of the cave. His location has changed, but he is not yet standing on the mountain. God's repeated question may have a double meaning. Perhaps he is not merely asking why Elijah is in Horeb. Perhaps the question now asks, 'Having come to Horeb seeking an answer and hearing my instructions, why are you still at the cave's door?'

---

[189] Walsh, *1 Kings*, p. 274.
[190] Underhill, *Mystic Way*, p. 3.
[191] Walsh, *1 Kings*, p. 276.

Elijah reiterates verbatim what he has already said. Speaking to Elijah's core issues of resistance and reluctance, Walsh writes, 'Neither the divine commands nor the majesty and mystery of the divine self-revelation have had the slightest effect on his purposes'.[192] Regardless of what Elijah has ignored and the saturated phenomenon that drew him out of the cave, he will not be moved. He simply wants out. Yet, Yahweh will not allow him to abandon his calling. He also knows that Elijah will ultimately obey (to a degree) what is expected of him. He is to return to his duties as prophet ('Go, return on your way'), anoint two kings (Hazael and Jehu), and anoint Elisha as prophet in his place (1 Kgs 19.15-16).[193] Nothing can threaten Elijah's future, except perhaps Elijah.

Elijah completes only the anointing of Elisha. Yet, it will be a transcendent, numinous, saturated phenomenon, which will usher Elijah off the scene (2 Kgs 2.11).

2.4.2 Elisha: Carrying the Burden Forward

2.4.2.1 Elisha from a Theological Perspective

Leithart contends, 'Elijah is a new Moses, and Elisha his Joshua'.[194] As the successor raised up to move the community of the faithful toward the messianic expectation, Elisha ensures prophetic continuity. When he receives Elijah's mantle, other prophetic witnesses are present, and schools of the prophets exist in Gilgal, Bethel, and Jericho (2 Kgs 2.1-18).[195] If Leithart's Moses-Joshua parallel holds,

---

[192] Walsh, *1 Kings*, p. 277.

[193] Walsh, *1 Kings*, p. 277, notes, 'The Hebrew verb forms make it clear that though Yahweh expects Elijah to carry out all three commissions, they need not be carried out in the order listed'.

[194] Leithart, *1 and 2 Kings*, p. 172.

[195] The question is whether these guilds existed prior to the choosing of Elisha or whether (as Leithart, *1 and 2 Kings*, p. 173, asserts) they came into existence because of Elijah's fruitfulness, as a sign that he had become 'a potent father' after his dark season (2 Kgs 2.12). 'Yahweh promises at Sinai to preserve seven thousand that will not genuflect to Baal. But as Elijah prepares to leave, prophets pop up at various places' (p. 173). If the guilds existed prior and were among the seven thousand Yahweh mentioned to Elijah at Horeb (1 Kgs 19.18), Elijah's unawareness of them can have several causes, including the Omride Dynasty's persecution, Elijah's travels, and other factors, such as (1) the guilds having fallen into oblivion for reasons of persecution and execution by Jezebel, (2) Elijah's being distanced from firsthand knowledge of events due to his exile between being hidden by the Brook Cherith and his lengthy time with the widow of Zarephath (1 Kgs 17.3-24), (3)

Elijah's relationship with Elisha recovers Elijah's own potency. The existence of the schools as historic locations in the narrative could indicate that they had become marginalized due to Omride opposition. Because Elijah is said to restore the hearts of the fathers to the sons on the Day of the Lord (Mal. 4.5-6), there may be a veiled allusion with the sons of the prophets typifying that future day.[196]

The question is why God chose someone from outside the remainder of surviving prophets as Elijah's successor. The Elisha narrative reveals a lack of maturity among the sons of the prophets and the need to expand facilities due to the growth under Elisha's oversight (2 Kgs 4.38-41, 6.1-7). The lack of maturity seemingly stemmed from a lack of mentoring and was disqualifying of prophetic legitimacy, implying that what remained of Samuel's intent for the schools had been eroded and God chose Elisha to begin anew. Whatever the case, Elisha is God's choice to stand underneath and ultimately assume Elijah's place (1 Kgs 19.16).[197] Therefore, Elijah will transition and bequeath his role. Through him, and despite his despondency and loss of passion, Yahweh will leave a blessing behind in a difficult season (Joel 2.14).

As he is directed to do, Elijah finds Elisha, who is actively plowing with the twelfth of a dozen pair of oxen (1 Kgs 19.19).[198]

Elijah's potential lack of awareness of whatever prophets remained after the slaying of most by Jezebel (according to 1 Kgs 18.4, Obadiah preserved one hundred of their number in groups of fifty in caves; yet this rendered them effectively voiceless), or (4) Elijah sees Obadiah as an 'insider' whose service to Ahab renders his voice insignificant and/or illegitimate in Elijah's view.

[196] It can be argued that this would not have been possible apart from Elisha's influence on the one who claimed to be God's lone prophet (1 Kgs 19.14).

[197] William Lee Holladay (ed.), 'תַּחַת', *A Concise Hebrew and Aramaic Lexicon of the Old Testament* (Leiden: Brill, 2000),

I תַּחַת): 490(תַּחַת, sf. תַּחְתֵּיכֶם, תַּחְתֶּיהָ, תַּחְתָּיו, תַּחְתַּי, also 2 תַּחְתֵּנִי, תַּחְתָּם S 22:37, 40; 48, 1– תַּחְתֶּנָּה :. (as noun) what is underneath, below: taḥtennâ Gn 2:21, sugg. (closed) what was underneath ([with] flesh); taḥtāyw 2 S 2:23 Qr (and he died) where he stood; – 2. prep. under, beneath: taḥat hāʿēṣ Gn 18:4; – 3. in his place > instead of, for (the sake of): Gn 4:25; taḥat ʿênô (he shall let him go free) for (the sake of) his eye Ex 21:26; taḥat meh why? Je 5:19 (but ironic reversal of ʿal-meh?); – 4. ʾel-taḥat (to) under Je 3:6; – 5. taḥat-ʾašer inasmuch as Dt 28:47; – 6. taḥat kî inasmuch as Pr 1:29; – 7. taḥat le underneath (in relation to) Ez 10:2; – 8. mittaḥat (out) from under(neath): hôṣiʾ mittaḥat Ex 6:7;—9. mittaḥat adv. beneath Ex 20:4; – 10. mittaḥat le underneath (in relation to) Gn 1:7; – 11. = lemittaḥat le 1 K 7:32; – 12. ʿad-mittaḥat le as far as below 1 S 7:11.

[198] These details speak of diligence and industry; his plowing with the twelfth pair speaks to leadership, implying that he is overseeing the entire enterprise.

Brueggemann observes, '[Elijah] throws his mantle over him, the same mantle he used to protect himself from the theophany'.[199] Brueggemann offers the possibility of Elijah's incomplete obedience. The assumption is that the liturgical act of anointing requires oil (1 Sam. 16.1). Does Elijah ignore that detail? Or does he consider throwing his own coat over Elisha to suffice? Walsh contends, 'we have no evidence that anointing played a part in the commissioning of a prophet in Israel'.[200] What then of Elijah's action? Walsh leans toward Brueggemann's view, stating that Elijah is 'acting at odds with Yahweh's command by designating Elisha as prophet without anointing him'.[201] Can we know for certain? Does Elijah find it more difficult to obey God now than he did in his former seasons? Is this related to his disillusionment with himself (and perhaps God)? He clearly does not anoint the two kings he was instructed to anoint. Thus, his reluctance appears to be overarching. Is the throwing of the mantle an act of careless indifference? Or might it be a prophetic enactment – Elijah's way of communicating to Elisha a change of governance in Israel?[202]

Consider that the throwing of the mantle is a nonverbal prophetic enactment,[203] a *wordless word*, somewhat like the mysterious sound of sheer silence to which Elijah responded at Horeb (where he was instructed regarding Elisha). That experience occurred when the Lord was about to 'pass by' (1 Kgs 19.11).[204] Now, Elijah tosses the mantle as he 'passed by' Elisha (1 Kgs 19.19). This subtle connection is not

---

[199] Brueggemann, *1 and 2 Kings*, p. 238.
[200] Walsh, *1 Kings*, p. 278.
[201] Walsh, *1 Kings*, p. 278.
[202] Although Elijah does not know Elisha, Elisha's response suggests that Elijah's reputation has preceded him in Elisha's awareness.
[203] Brueggemann, *1 and 2 Kings*, 238.
[204] Wilhelm Gesenius and Samuel Prideaux Tregelles, *Gesenius' Hebrew and Chaldee Lexicon to the Old Testament Scriptures* (Bellingham, WA: Logos Bible Software, 2003),

> עָבַר fut. יַעֲבֹר. – (1) to pass over. (Arabic عبر to pass over, to cross a stream; also to go away, to depart, to die; عُبْر, عَبْر shore, bank of a stream, *Ufer*, غبر to go away, to depart … Prop. To pass over a stream, the sea, followed by an acc. Gen. 31:21; Josh. 4:22; 24:11; Deut. 3:27; 4:21; followed by בְּ Josh. 3:11; 2 Sa. 15:23; Zec. 10:11; בְּתוֹךְ Num. 33:8. Absol. *To pass over*, sc. A stream (*er setzte über*), Josh. 2:23, and followed by an acc. Of that *to* which we pass over, Jer. 2:10, כִּתִּיִּים אִיֵּי עִבְרוּ 'pass over (the sea) unto the shores of Chittim;' Am. 6:2; followed by אֶל Num. 32:7; 1 Sam. 14:1, 6 (where it means to pass over to an opposite place).

solitary. Just as God instructs Elijah to 'go, return' and fulfill his prophetic responsibilities (1 Kgs 19.15), Elijah also instructs Elisha to 'go back again' when Elisha requests to kiss his parents farewell (1 Kgs 19.20).[205] Is this intentional on Elijah's part? Or is Yahweh's hidden presence at work, foreknowing Elijah's despondency, yet engraving in his memory the actions taken to draw him back to his calling? Cannot both be true?

Upholding the free agency that he entrusts in our personal subjectivity and interpreting of the divine, Yahweh may be affording Elijah the freedom to determine how he fulfills his duties. In passing by and throwing the mantle, Elijah reenacts the Horeb experience. This is arguably incarnational, with Elijah embodying the way that God moves, acts, and directs. Thus, he releases to Elisha the means of learning God's ways. Elisha will learn intentionally and otherwise by being attentive to Elijah. He comprehends and apprehends what Elijah intends, which is essential to maturation and prophetic legitimacy. Now the divine initiative demands a response, a willingness to don the coat that will transform Elisha's trajectory. As such, the narrative and cloak are inseparable, with the cloak telling the entire story (2 Kgs 2.13-14).

This narrative shows the hidden work of the formative Spirit of Prophecy. The mantle touching and the passing by of Elijah (which prophetically foreshadows his eventual passing from the scene) bring to Elisha's consciousness the coming change and the knowledge of his being chosen to fill the gap. To that end, he now enters liminal space. The felt weight of the cloak is far greater than that of oil on the head. Because of Elijah's formidable and overshadowing influence, the garment becomes the definitive calling card of the prophet's office, even during the days of the Elijah-to-come (Mk 1.6).

In the overall narrative, the garment seems equivalent to oil. The relation between garments and consciousness is not new to Torah tradition; Jacob gives Joseph a garment, after which two dreams about calling rise from the depths of Joseph's consciousness (Gen. 37.3, 5, 9). The impact and heft of the cloak alert Elisha to the need for his current life chapter to close. To give himself fully to God's prophetic intent implies his seeking of such closure. He responds in the affirmative, comprehending what is required of him. The call-by-

---

[205] Elisha requests this to bring a terminus to his current season.

mantle suggests no manifestation of theophanic glory and no witness of the calling being legitimized before the heavenly council (Jer. 23.18). However, these experiences will attend Elijah's departure into heaven in a whirlwind (2 Kgs 2.10-14).

Despite the somewhat subdued nature of this prophetic enactment, something moves Elisha to respond affirmatively when the mantle falls on him. (It bears noting that the notion of impartation seen in the Elijah-Elisha narrative proved a significant doctrinal emphasis in Latter Rain Pentecostalism.)[206] The indication that Elisha accepted the wordless call intimates that God's Spirit had prepared him for this synchronous moment.[207] Considering the view this work holds that the coat is the means of impartation used by the Spirit in lieu of anointing oil, one could argue that, despite Elijah's internal struggles, he knows what will move (or deter) a potential prophetic agent's response. At a time when spiritual recovery is so urgently needed, who can communicate the weightiness of the prophetic mantle better than Elijah?

Some earlier details of the narrative have bearing here. God tells Elijah where to find God's chosen heir (1 Kgs 19.16): he is in Abel-meholah, in the northern territory of the tribe of Issachar (Josh. 17.11; 1 Kgs 4.12; Judg. 7.22). Elisha is from that tribe, which Jewish scholarship cites as being wise and possessing prophetic proclivities, consciousness, and perception.[208] Elisha's plowing with twelve yoke

---

[206] Violet Kiteley, 'Laying on of Hands – 1948 – Northern Canada', *Revival Doctrine Syllabus*, *Violet Kiteley Papers*, p. 1. Violet Kiteley, 'Elijah and Elisha: A Study of the Prophetic Ministry of Elijah and Elisha Taken from 1st and 2nd Kings', *Violet Kiteley Papers* (Shiloh Bible College, Oakland, CA). More will be considered regarding this in Chapter 4.

[207] How he was prepared is unspoken in the text but implied by his readiness to obey.

[208] J.D. Heck, 'Issachar', in T. Desmond Alexander and David W. Baker (eds.), *Dictionary of the Old Testament: Pentateuch* (Downers Grove, IL: InterVarsity Press, 2003), p. 459:

> Issachar in Jewish Scholarship—In Jewish scholarship, the proximity of Issachar to Zebulun in the last testament of Jacob (Gen 49:13–15) and the pairing of Issachar and Zebulun in the last testament of Moses (Deut 33:18–19) set up the two tribes as a paradigm for life. Zebulun was the merchant, while Issachar was the scholar who studied the Torah. Zebulun's livelihood made possible Issachar's important work of study, and, according to rabbinic exegesis, Issachar made a more worthy choice.

Issacharian leaders understand the times and have knowledge of how Israel must navigate them wisely (1 Chron. 12.32).

of oxen is significant.[209] In Boyer's view, this affirms Elisha's prophethood.[210] If Boyer is correct, the numerological emphasis signifies his prophetic legitimacy.[211] Elisha's request to kiss his parents farewell is not resistance but his way to 'set things right at home (19:20-21a)'.[212] This speaks to Elisha's ethical integrity and faithfulness to Torah observance (as in Exod. 20.12). Walsh recognizes that 'the destruction of beasts and their tackle represents a break with Elisha's past'.[213] His first prophetic enactment signifies the close of one chapter and the start of a new one. It affirms his acceptance of the mandate and of what has transpired. The preparing of a feast for

---

[209] David L. Jeffrey, 'Numerology', *A Dictionary of Biblical Tradition in English Literature* (Grand Rapids, MI: Eerdmans, 1992):

> Number symbolism has enjoyed a prominent role in the Judeo-Christian tradition, although its roots – whether primitive and elemental, astrological, Pythagorean, or Platonic – are essentially pagan. Its importance to the literary arts, especially in the medieval and Renaissance periods, is attributable to the Ptolemaic view of a symmetrical universe structured upon sympathetic correspondences syncretized with the Hebraic view that God created all things 'in measure, and number, and weight' (Wisd. 11:21).

[210] Mark G. Boyer, *From Contemplation to Action: The Spiritual Process of Divine Discernment Using Elijah and Elisha as Models* (Eugene, OR: Wipf & Stock, 2018), p. 22:

> The point of mentioning the twelve yoke of oxen is to note the sacred number twelve (three, the divine, plus four, the earth, plus five, the books of Torah, equal twelve), the mythological number of the tribes of Israel and Judah. In other words, like Elijah, Elisha is prophet for all God's people.

[211] Walter A. Elwell and Barry J. Beitzel, 'Numbers and Numerology', in Walter A. Elwell (ed.), *Baker Encyclopedia of the Bible* (Grand Rapids, MI: Baker Book House, 1988), p. 1562:

> Eleven appears to have no special biblical significance, but 12 certainly has. The clearest proof of this is the existence of the 12 tribes in Israel. In Revelation 7:4-8, where it is mathematically important that the number of tribes be limited to 12, the tribe of Dan is altogether omitted on account of Dan's sin of idolatry (Jgs 18:14-20). Some have compared the number 12 with the 12 months of the year, as symbolizing completion, but, if so, the Bible gives no hint of it. Ishmael's descendants were also divided into 12 clans (Gn 17:20), so that the number 12 was apparently significant outside Israel as well. In the NT Christ chose 12 apostles (Mt 10:1-4). The link with the number of tribes is made specific when Christ tells the apostles that they will sit on 12 thrones, judging the 12 tribes (Mt 19:28). However, it is interesting that, after the election and appointment of Matthias (Acts 1:26), the Christian church apparently made no subsequent efforts to maintain the number of apostles. Like 'seven times seven,' 'twelve times twelve' increases the force of the number. When this is further multiplied by a thousand, the figure becomes the 144,000 redeemed (Rv 7:4), who were sealed 'out of all the tribes of Israel'.

[212] Brueggemann, *1 and 2 Kings*, p. 239.
[213] Walsh, *1 Kings*, p. 279.

his parents and employees conveys the spreading of the communion table. His feeding them foreshadows his prophetic service to them and the nation,[214] and it exhibits his love of God and neighbor. In sacrificing his oxen, he relinquishes his rightful double-portion heritage (Deut. 21.17), solidifying his conscription and the closure of his former life. Elisha is now 'Elijah's recruit and, by implication, Yahweh's man'[215] – the guarantee that prophetic legitimacy will be maintained in Israel, and the word of the Lord will be with him (2 Kgs 3.11-12).

Elijah's successor faces a necessary period of acclimation and formation. The text reveals that he becomes Elijah's 'servant'.[216] This is later alluded to metaphorically as the pouring of water on Elijah's hands (2 Kgs 3.11). Walsh declares, 'Elisha's service is that of a chief assistant (the same word is used of Joshua's position in Moses' service; see Exod 33:11)'.[217] In his former chapter, Elisha has plowed the soil for its receptivity to seed. Now his willingness to be answerable and accountable to Elijah will contribute to the plowing of his own heart to receive the word of the Lord. At the final transition, the whirlwind will take Elijah to heaven (2 Kgs 2.1), a theophany solidifying Elisha's legitimate succession.[218] The narrative creates

---

[214] Walsh, *1 Kings*, pp. 279-80:

But two clues hidden in the Hebrew text reveal a deeper meaning of the meal. First, the verb *zbḥ.* (NRSV, 'slaughtered') generally means to kill an animal *as a sacrifice*. Second, the sentence about boiling the animal's flesh is oddly worded and strongly poetic in Hebrew; this calls attention to the phrase. One word in it is particularly unusual, *bšlm*, 'he boiled them'; the formation evokes the notion of a *šlm*, or communion sacrifice, in which a person offers an animal to Yahweh in thanksgiving for divine blessings and uses the sacrificial meat to host a meal for family and friends. Elisha's action, therefore, combines elements of separation from his old life, cultic thanksgiving upon undertaking the new, and ritual solidarity with 'the people' among whom he will pursue.

[215] Brueggemann, *1 and 2 Kings*, p. 239.

[216] K. Engelken, 'שרת', *TDOT*, XV, p. 503; regarding 'שרת' *šrt* – I - 1. *Meaning, Occurrences, Etymology*. The root *šrt* has the basic meaning 'serve'; often it has the more specific sense 'do cultic service, serve as a priest.' Westermann holds that the word denotes primarily service to a person; Sedlmeier² believes that a 'public' dimension is always present in the service performed'.

[217] Walsh, *1 Kings*, p. 280.

[218] Robert L. Cohn, *2 Kings* (Berit Olam Studies in Hebrew Narrative and Poetry; Collegeville, MN: Liturgical Press, 2000), p. 11. 'From the outset Yhwh is named as the subject of this marvelous occurrence and the *sĕʿārāh* ('storm, whirlwind', a term often associated with theophany [e.g. Job 38:1]) as the agent of Elijah's ascent to the sky'.

anticipation over the passing of the coat, which the fiery Tishbite wore day after day, to the shoulders of the one who groomed it when his master retired each night.[219]

It must be noted that Elijah thrice attempts to deter Elisha's pursuit of him (2 Kgs 2.2, 4, 6). Unlike the compliant servant who remained at Beer-sheba while Elijah went on alone (1 Kgs 19.3), Elisha invokes the name of Yahweh in the same way his master invokes it.[220] In Elisha, Elijah meets his respectful but persistent match. The protégé knows the mantle is his (1 Kgs 19.19), and Elijah's attempts to deter him raise questions regarding Elijah's reluctance to obey God fully. It is also possible that Gilgal, Bethel, and Jericho are testing points. Because of the weightiness of Elisha's new endeavor and his master's acute awareness of his own sufferings, Elijah seeks to solidify the younger man's sense of commitment (an area in which he himself has faltered). This reading is possible, because testing a person's faith in relation to what has been promised is not beyond the God of Abraham, Isaac, and Jacob (i.e. Gen. 22.2).

At Bethel, Gilgal, and Jericho, the two men encounter the 'company of the prophets' (2 Kgs 2.3, 5, 7),[221] which Wilson sees as 'peripheral' groups.[222] They lived at the margins of the social order, denoting resistance to the powers of the Baal cult and the Omride Dynasty. However, Leithart contends that they are 'faithful' prophets.[223] Williams argues that they 'were organized by, or *became organized* under, Elijah' but may have previously been an 'uncoordinated

---

[219] The transfer of power coincides with the power transfer to Jehoram following the death of Ahaz (2 Kgs 1.17-18, 3.10).

[220] Cohn, *2 Kings*, p. 11.

[221] The term is translated 'sons of the prophets' in some versions. The Hebrew reads '*bĕnê hannĕbî'îm*', Cohn, *2 Kings*, p. 12. Wilson, *Prophecy and Society*, p. 202:

> Seen from a sociological perspective, the sons of the prophets closely resemble members of a peripheral possession cult. Although there is no direct evidence on this point, members of the group were presumably peripheral individuals who had resisted the political and religious policies of the Ephraimite kings and who had therefore been forced out of the political and religious establishments. After having prophetic experiences these individuals joined the group, which was under the leadership of Elisha. In the group they found mutual support and were encouraged to use prophecy to bring about change in the social order.

[222] Wilson, *Prophecy and Society*, p. 202.

[223] Leithart, *1 and 2 Kings*, p. 173.

element'.[224] They move to 'a high influential status under Elisha',[225] the issue being the successful transfer of power from Elijah to Elisha, and Elisha's assumption of headship for the marginalized prophetic communities.[226]

The only conversations recorded in the text are between Elisha and the sons of the prophets. It seems that, true to his then-current posture, Elijah prophetically passes by these historic sites, intentionally retracing in reverse order Israel's entry into the Promised Land. He will be taken up in the wilderness east of the Jordan, much as Moses was removed prior to entering the Promised Land. Not unlike Jesus in Samaria en route to Jerusalem for his exodus, Elijah will 'set his face' to his point of departure (Lk. 9.51). These are lessons for Elisha and his protégés relating to covenant history and prophetic continuity.[227]

When the sons of the prophets see Elijah passing by, they ask a pointed rhetorical question: 'Do you know that today the Lord will take your master away from you?' (2 Kgs 2.3). They perceive Elijah's coming departure. Has Elijah communicated this or are they aware through their own prophetic inclinations? Assuming they are faithful prophets, they know by revelation that the event will transpire. In speaking of Elijah to Elisha as 'your master', they seem to distance

---

[224] J.G. Williams, 'The Prophetic "Father"', *Journal of Biblical Literature* 85 (1966), p. 345 (emphasis added).

[225] Williams, 'Prophetic "Father"', p. 345. Wesley J. Bergen, *Elisha and the End of Prophetism* (JSOTSup 286; Sheffield: Sheffield Academic Press, 1999), p. 13, holds an alternative and less than positive view of Elisha and the sons of the prophets. He writes,

> Elisha serves to undermine the rather grandiose picture of the prophet which might otherwise be produced by the narrative. The great prophets like Moses, Samuel and Elijah are mirrored by Elisha, who crosses the Jordan on dry ground (2 Kgs 2:14), acts as adviser to kings (3:16–20), heals and restores to life (4:35; 5:14). Yet he also causes suffering (2:24; 5:27), his aid in time of battle is finally insufficient (3:27; 6:23–24), his miracles unrequested (4:28) or pointless (6:6–7). The voice of Yhwh is never heard by the reader, and we have only Elisha's word that Yhwh has ever spoken. Thus readers are warned regarding the aggrandizement of the prophet. The prophet is powerful, but the power is not unambiguously good.

[226] If these companies of prophets were present as guilds or bands and Jezebel had them put to death in large numbers, then Williams' assertion needs to be seen as a valid consideration in contrast to Wilson and Leithart (1 Kgs 18.13).

[227] In this regard, Israel's formative narrative is foundational to prophetic legitimacy.

themselves from direct relations with the elder prophet, seeing Elisha as his particular and exclusive servant.[228]

Elisha indicates that he knows Elijah's departure is imminent. Such *knowing* would be common among faithful prophets at the sites Elijah and Elisha pass by, as they would share access to the revelatory dimension. Yet, Elisha requests that they 'keep silent' and 'be silent' about what they know (2 Kgs 2.3, 5). Given Elijah's ironic introversion and limited relational capacity, he likely kept his departure from Elisha. Thus, there is good reason for these prophetic ways of knowing to be discerned and then discussed communally, for the sake of evaluation.

Nevertheless, Elisha pushes against the sons of the prophets' inquiries. He is not muzzling their speech but perhaps inviting them to realize that they 'know only in part, and [they] prophesy only in part' (1 Cor. 13.9). The sons of the prophets realize that they are not the mantle's heirs. Elisha knows that he is. They do not know Elijah's ways as intimately as the one who calls Elijah his 'father' (2 Kgs 2.12).[229]

Elisha presses on, intending to receive and wear the mantle at the appropriate time. When he and Elijah arrive at the Jordan, 50 prophets bear witness to what will transpire after they cross over (2 Kgs 2.7). Elijah works one final miracle, rolling his mantle to mimic a rod or staff and striking the Jordan's waters so they part (2 Kgs 2.8). As Brueggemann says, 'Elijah, until the last, is capable of high drama in which he replicates the wonder of Moses'.[230] Despite Elijah's weaknesses and faults, his capacity to work signs and wonders has not abated. Regarding prophetic legitimacy, it is important not to reduce this act to a magic feat. The sign is significant, not only in recapitulating the Exodus and perhaps foretelling the Babylonian exile, but also in being sequential to the passing of the mantle, Elisha's

---

[228] The notion of 'your master away from you' is more accurately translated 'from upon your head', reinforcing the idea of headship within the master-servant relationship; Mordechai Cogan and Hayim Tadmor, *II Kings: A New Translation with Introduction and Commentary* (Anchor Yale Bible 11; New Haven, CT: Yale University Press, 2008), p. 32. This reinforces the idea of headship within the master-servant relationship.

[229] Elisha knows his master's ways intimately, despite Elijah's difficulty in relating to others. 'Father' is 'a leading prophet's honorific title', Williams, 'Prophetic "Father"', p. 344. In some sense, Elijah has become the adoptive father of the protégé who kissed his own father farewell.

[230] Brueggemann, *1 and 2 Kings*, p. 295.

necessary entry into liminal space, and his reentry as prophet-in-Elijah's-place.

As the two men cross onto dry ground, Elijah asks the essential question: 'Tell me what I may do for you, before I am taken from you' (2 Kgs 2.9). This question seems to quell all doubt as to Elijah's motives in testing Elisha until the Jordan crossing is complete. Elijah has failed to reenter the work of anointing kings in the Northern and Southern Kingdoms but has worked with Elisha adroitly, as will be seen in what transpires. I would argue that Elijah's question is tender. The irascible, reluctant, recalcitrant prophet is a father whose heart turns to his son, desiring to leave something for him and his protégés to grow on (Mal. 4.6). Elisha, having given up his 'double share' from his birth father (Deut. 21.17; 1 Sam. 1.5), now wants the right of the firstborn son from Elijah – the bequeathing of his father's spirit (*ruach*). This is a desire for investiture with power, so that Elisha might know and act in accordance with prophetic legitimacy. This requires nothing less than the work of the charismatic Spirit.

Brueggemann notes, 'Elijah's response to the request is less than reassuring. Apparently, he does not know whether his disciple's request can be honored, as he not able to assign *rûah* (see Mark 10:40).'[231] However, Elijah is perfectly clear in saying, 'You have asked a *hard thing*; yet, if you *see me as I am being taken* from you, it will be granted you; if not, it will not' (2 Kgs 2.10, emphasis added). These dual notifications indicate a key – not to refusal or uncertainty, but to assurance and guarantee. It is noteworthy that Elijah found Elisha 'plowing' with twelve yokes of oxen. The Hebrew word translated 'hard thing' is קָשָׁה which describes, among other things, the difficulty of bearing a yoke.[232] If anything, Elisha's hearing of Elijah's answer could have served as immediate confirmation that his prior chapter had prepared him for the difficult one ahead.

Elijah also tells Elisha that if he *sees*, his request will be granted.[233] This is tied to the expansion of Elijah's consciousness and spiritual

---

[231] Brueggemann, *1 and 2 Kings*, p. 295.
[232] M. Zipor, 'קָשָׁה', *TDOT*, XIII, p. 189. 'A "hard" (NRSV 'heavy') yoke can be a metaphor for heavy labor (1 K. 12:4 = 2 Ch. 10:4)'.
[233] H.F. Fuhs, 'רָאָה', *TDOT*, XIII, pp. 208-10.

The root *r'(y)* is attested most widely in the South Semitic languages: OSA *r'y*; Eth. *rĕ'ĕya*, 'see,' with the nominal derivatives *rĕ'ĕyat*, 'view, vision'; *ra'āy*, 'viewer,

perception by theophanic vision. The secret to Elijah's power is not in his natural abilities or dominating personality but a consciousness and perception long saturated by divine encounter. This is Elijah's promise to Elisha that these will be bequeathed to him, not by Elijah but by Yahweh. Thus, for the remainder of the journey, Elisha intensely focuses his attention and powers of observation on his master.

During their ensuing conversation, a theophany occurs. A 'chariot of fire and horses of fire' appear from an open heaven,[234] separating Elijah from Elisha (2 Kgs 2.11). The chariot-throne that Elisha sees what Ezekiel, Daniel, and perhaps all the prophets in the heavenly council saw (Ezek. 1.4-28, 10.1-5; Daniel 7; Jer. 23.18). Once Elisha sees, his perception is transformed, and *unseeing* becomes impossible (2 Kgs 6.17). This is the way of seeing and knowing by which Elijah has historically operated.[235] What seems somewhat unexpected is the grief that accompanies the vision. When Elisha sees the theophanic glory, he cries out at his father's departure and continues observing

---

observer'; *'ar'ayā*, 'image, form, example'; *nĕrĕay*, 'horizon'; Arab. *ra'ā*, 'see,' with the deverbal nouns *ra'y*, 'view, opinion'; *ru'ya*, 'seeing, viewing, inspection'; *ra'yā*, 'vision, dream'; *mar'an*, 'sight, vision, apparition'; *mir'āt*, 'mirror, reflection'; *ri'ā'/riyā'*, 'eye service, hypocrisy'; *rā'in*, 'viewer, observer.' Among the Canaanite languages, apart from Hebrew, *r'y* is found only in the closely related Moabite. Ugar. *r'ydn* is uncertain. Cassuto separates the text, reading *r'y dn*, which he translates as 'great to look upon'; Caquot sees a reference to the god Ra'idān. Aram. *rēw(ā)*, 'appearance,' is probably a Canaanite loanword. In these languages *r'y* constitutes the semic basis for sensory perception: 'see (with one's eyes).' From this basic meaning evolve all the other aspects of perception.

[234] James R. Davila, 'Merkavah Mysticism', in Katharine Doob Sakenfeld (ed.), *The New Interpreter's Dictionary of the Bible* (Nashville, TN: Abingdon Press, 2009), p. 50:

The rabbinic literature regarded the merkavah (מֶרְכָּבָה), the heavenly 'throne-chariot' of God described in Ezek 1 and 10, as a dangerous topic that could actually harm those who studied it. The Babylonian Talmud tells of four 2nd-cent. rabbis who entered 'paradise' (arguably the celestial Temple, site of the merkavah), where one died, one went mad, one became a heretic, and only Rabbi Akiva returned unharmed. The Hekhalot literature is a bizarre collection of Jewish mystical texts in Hebrew and Aramaic that forms the basis of 'merkavah mysticism'. It seems to have been composed from late antiquity to the early Middle Ages and the contents of the individual works often vary widely in the manuscripts.

[235] Adherents of the Latter Rain Movement emphasized the prophet as the one who does the 'seeing', Violet Kiteley, 'Five Spiritual Senses', *Violet Kiteley Papers*, p. 1.

the vision until 'he [can] no longer see' Elijah (2 Kgs 2.12).[236] In abject sorrow and grief, Elisha 'grasped his own clothes and tore them in two pieces' (2 Kgs 2.12). It is in this experience of loss that the transfer of power occurs.

Elisha now has but one option: with his own garment and his role as servant lost, the mantle becomes his new garment. First, however, he replicates Elijah's sign of making the mantle a rod, and he strikes the waters twice (2 Kgs 2.14). With the first strike, he inquires about the whereabouts of Elijah's God. The text suggests no response to this question but proceeds to Elisha's second strike and the parting of the waters. I would argue that to accept fully his prophetic legitimacy, Elisha transfers his confidence from the God of Elijah to the Lord God of Elisha and strikes the waters knowing that God is with him.[237]

Elisha takes his place as the prophetic mediatorial agent qualified by theophanic confirmation and possessing the expanded consciousness and perception that lead to legitimate prophetic enactment.[238] For God to manifest his intent through Elisha, Elisha needs to see

---

[236] David L. Jeffrey, 'Chariot of Fire', *A Dictionary of Biblical Tradition in English Literature* (Grand Rapids, MI: Eerdmans, 1992):

> In Christian exegetical tradition, as with talmudic commentary, the fiery chariot translation is associated with extreme piety and ascetical purity: St. Ambrose credits Elijah's virginity with his being 'carried by a chariot into heaven' (*De virginibus*, 1.3.12). St. Augustine sees Elijah's ascension in the fiery chariot as an apt prefigurement of things to come for the persevering elect (*De civ. Dei* 20.29). In later medieval typological tradition the *Biblia Pauperum* pictures the ascensions of Enoch, Elijah, and Christ together: Elijah in his fiery chariot is both antitype of Enoch and type of Christ (pl. 34).

[237] Asaph reflects on the Exodus event under Moses and records these words: 'When the waters saw you, O God, when the waters saw you, they were afraid; the very deep trembled' (Ps. 77.16). Creation saw God in the human agent, Moses, sent to deliver the sons of Israel at the Red Sea. Similarly, Paul contends that all Creation groans, waiting for the sons of God to be revealed in maturity (Rom. 8.19).

[238] Brueggemann's take (Brueggemann, *1 and 2 Kings*, pp. 297-98) is slightly different:

> He seeks after Yahweh whom he identifies as 'the God of Elijah'. His first utterance is an enquiry and a petition. For without Yahweh, he has no power and no authority. He receives no answer. But his third act is to strike the water of the Jordan. He strikes the water; and then strikes it again. The narrative detail suggests that unlike Elijah in v. 8, his first striking is not effective and he must do it twice. Thus his power may be less than that of Elijah. But it is adequate. He does part the waters of the Jordan, replicating Elijah who, as we have seen, replicated Moses. Elisha crosses back over the Jordan, now entering into the land ostensibly governed by the monarchy.

himself as he is seen. This confidence is essential for prophetic legitimacy.

2.4.2.2 Elisha from a Psychological Perspective

Elisha's behavior suggests an unyielding commitment to his call and his mentor. As previously mentioned, he does not comply with Elijah's attempts to separate from him. Butler contends, 'Elisha's response to the call of God was most exemplary ... zealous, courageous, sacrificial, total, public, and considerate'.[239] Psychologically, these descriptors reveal the earnestness of one who maintains deep and 'serious intentions' and embodies the trustworthiness, sincerity, and truthfulness worthy of respect in the community.[240] This trustworthiness is significant from a psychological perspective because Elijah has become Elisha's spiritual father. It is as though when the mantle hits Elisha's shoulders, God's Spirit so bonds the two men emotionally and rationally as to render them inseparable.

Elisha draws his strength from the despondent and dejected elder prophet whose emotional and psychological states neither deter the servant's trust and commitment, nor his perseverance, devotion, and love. Elisha voices this truth, saying, 'As the Lord lives, and as you yourself live, *I will not leave you*' (2 Kgs 2.2, 4, 6, emphasis added). This is more than Elisha's statement in a climactic moment. It confirms the radical commitment he made when he asked to kiss his parents farewell. Therefore, regarding Elisha's legitimacy as heir-apparent, the narrative's most significant psychological note is his level of devotion and love for Elijah, which he expresses as grief when Elijah departs (2 Kgs 2.12).

Psychologically, Elisha's gaining of the mantle requires him to lose Elijah. Although Elijah does not die, his departure is equivalent to death. 'Crying out' in his loss and 'under great distress' (2 Kgs 2.12),[241] Elisha bellows, 'My father, my father, the chariots of Israel and its

---

[239] John G. Butler, *Elisha: The Miracle Prophet* (Bible Biography Series 4; Clinton, IA: LBC Publications, 1994), p. 17.

[240] 'Importance of Being Earnest and What Is Being Earnest?', *Impoff* (April 22, 2021), https://impoff.com/importance-of-being-earnest/.

[241] John E. Hartley, '1947 צָעַק, in *TWOT*, p. 772; crying out, from

1947 צָעַק [meaning] *cry, cry for help, call* ... 1947a צְעָקָה (*sĕʿāqâ*) *cry, outcry* ... This root means to call out for help under great distress or to utter an exclamation in great excitement (cf. II Kgs 2:12) ... This word often refers to the cry of those plundered and ravaged in war (cf. Jer 49:21).

horsemen!' (2 Kgs 2.12). The fiery prophet is Elisha's father and God's means of moving Israel toward an alternative vision and consciousness unlike those of the Omride Dynasty. While Elisha is groomed for all that transpires, the loss that thrusts him into prominence also shocks his system with grief and ushers him into liminal space. Elisha's rite of passage into prophethood is inseparable from this dynamic. According to Levine, rites of passage 'let us know what we can handle'.[242] Elisha is faced with handling his grief; the question becomes whether he can transition from serving the chariot of Israel to becoming that chariot. As Van Gennep postulated, prior to the moment of Elijah's departure, Elisha was in the 'preliminal period' that separated him from his former familial chapter and placed him into apprenticeship with Elijah.[243] He enters liminal space when Elijah departs, at which point he experiences the 'rites of transition' to full prophethood and prophetic legitimacy.[244] He feels the loss of Elijah deeply and vocalizes his grief in a loud, acute, and personal cry. Through the grief and dread of Elijah's departure, Elisha learns to recognize his own apprentices' anguish in the days ahead (see 2 Kgs 4.1-7, 38-41; 6.5).[245] Absent this level of empathy, there can be no prophetic legitimacy. Elisha has to experience this ending.

The chariot of Israel embodied in Elijah has departed, and the social reality left behind is in flux. The experience is theophanic, tornadic, and earth-shaking. Elisha feels the weight of it, much as Jesus feels the loss of his cousin John (the Elijah to come). Like Elisha, Jesus will seek liminal space to process his grief and find it filled with the distressed and downcast (Mt. 14.13-14). For comfort to be given,

---

[242] Martha Peaslee Levine, 'Rites of Passage with Wisdom to Grow', *Psychology Today* (August 3, 2014), https://www.psychologytoday.com/us/blog/your-write-health/201408/rites-passage-wisdom-grow.

[243] Arnold Van Gennep, *The Rites of Passage* (Chicago, IL: University of Chicago Press, 2nd edn, 2019), ch. 2.

[244] Van Gennep, *Rites of Passage*, ch. 2.

[245] Respectively, these events are involved (1) the naïve prophet who, during a famine, mistakes a poison gourd for food and places it in a pot of stew and cries out, 'O man of God, there is death in the pot!', (2) the widow who cries out when her husband, a son of the prophets, dies unexpectedly leaving great debt behind, and (3) one of the sons of the prophets who lost an axe head and cries, 'Alas master! It was borrowed'. Brueggemann looks for the genuine prophetic voice that 'brings to public expression the dread of endings', Brueggemann, *Prophetic Imagination*, p. 46.

the prophet voices 'the language of grief' for the sake of those who mourn (Mt. 5.4).[246]

Whatever energetic movement Elijah carried by the Spirit into Israel's social system, it had become psychologically challenging and led to a certain exhaustion in Elijah that required renewal. Now, the great loss of his departure needed to be grieved over. Elisha enters the liminal ambiguity of that loss and allows his imagination to be energized. To paraphrase Brueggeman's thought on being and becoming a prophetic agent, renewal in Israel's social system can be implemented.[247] If as Brueggemann states, *'It is the task of prophetic ministry and imagination to bring people to engage their experiences of suffering to death'*,[248] there can be no 'numbness about death'.[249] Instead, Elisha's experience of loss becomes his entrée into prophethood. Upon being separated from even the sight of Elijah, Elisha will therefore 'face and embrace' this equivalent of death to move forward.[250]

Elisha's cry of grief and tearing of his garments resembles Jesus' weeping at Lazarus' tomb (Jn 11.35). Jesus weeps for far more than his friend's passing. Jesus knows he will raise Lazarus from death; yet the act will seal his own execution by disrupting the religious power arrangements of kings who need to experience the 'loss of thrones'.[251] Elisha's grief in liminal space is comparable to Jesus' weeping in anticipation of his own liminality and exodus, and each instance 'permits newness'.[252]

---

[246] Brueggemann, *Prophetic Imagination*, p. 46.
[247] Brueggemann, *Prophetic Imagination*, p. 40.
[248] Brueggemann, *Prophetic Imagination*, p. 41.
[249] Brueggemann, *Prophetic Imagination*, p. 42.
[250] Brueggemann, *Prophetic Imagination*, p. 42. This could be considered an aspect of the via negativa in the life of Elisha the heir of the birthright of Elijah. Ekman P.C. Tam, 'Silence of God and God of Silence', *Asia Journal of Theology* 16.1 (2002), pp. 152-63:

> In Christian tradition there are two related paths in a spiritual journey: Via Positiva (a speaking God) and Via Negativa (silent God). According to the spiritual masters, God leads the Christian into the Via Negativa by two ways. Considers the negative path and suffering, maturity, and letting go of 'Godly expectation', spiritual darkness, corporate experience of darkness, and entering into the silence of God.

[251] Brueggemann, *Prophetic Imagination*, p. 57.
[252] Brueggemann, *Prophetic Imagination*, p. 57.

Liminal space is the realm of ambiguity.[253] If, relative to Elijah's departure, we demarcate his liminal space as the distance between the wilderness east of the Jordan and the Promised Land west of it, Elisha's journey back marks the metaphoric and psychological distance in which he transitions from being the prophet's servant to being the prophet himself.

2.4.2.3 Elisha from a Phenomenological Perspective

Elisha's visionary, transcendent vertical experience of Elijah's departure is phenomenologically charged. In Elisha's words, Elijah's ascent to heaven occurred on a chariot and horses of fire. The presence of fire implies a connection to Moses' personal theophany at Horeb and to the later theophanic experience of Moses with the children of Israel present (Exod. 3.1-22; 19.1-24). Sweeney sees Elisha's visionary experience as replete with 'military imagery'.[254] One can assume that Sweeney refers to the construct of chariots of fire and horses of fire. However, he simultaneously contends that the heavenly vision evokes the Holy of Holies and the ark at its center.[255] Sweeney claims that Elijah's ascent brings to consciousness the notion of the earthly temple as the 'gateway' bridging the heavenly and the earthly.[256] If Sweeney is correct, then Elisha's encounter with theophany is also his point of access into the heavenly council that ratifies his prophetic legitimacy (Jer. 23.18).

The similarity to Ezekiel's vision of the mobile chariot throne of God is striking (Ezekiel 1; 3). All of this occurs swiftly, as Elisha *sees* the whirlwind usher Elijah into heaven (2 Kgs 2.10-11). The tornadic wind seems reminiscent of the storm cloud approaching Ezekiel at the River Chebar, where he sits among the exiles (Ezek. 1.4).[257] The text speaks briefly about what Elisha sees, yet a litany of metaphors regarding chariots already exists in Israel's collective consciousness:

- Clouds as chariots (Ps. 104.3)

---

[253] Timothy Carson, *Liminal Reality and Transformational Power: Transition, Renewal and Hope* (Cambridge: Lutterworth Press, rev. edn, 2016), p. 20.
[254] Sweeney, *Jewish Mysticism*, p. 123.
[255] Sweeney, *Jewish Mysticism*, p. 124.
[256] Sweeney, *Jewish Mysticism*, p. 124.
[257] The chariot as symbol is part of Jewish mysticism known as Merkabah mysticism. Derek R. Brown, Wendy Widder, and E. Tod Twist, '2 Co 12:2-5', in John D. Barry (ed.), *2 Corinthians* (Lexham Research Commentaries; Bellingham, WA: Lexham Press, 2013). *Merkabah* is the transliterated Hebrew word for chariot and represents God's mobile throne.

- Whirlwinds as chariots (Jer. 4.13; Isa. 66.15)
- Chariots of salvation involving the imagery of horses (Hab. 3.8)
- Chariots as living creatures (1 Chron. 28.18)
- Chariots of fire (2 Kgs 2.11; 6.17).

Such language is highly metaphoric, attempting to describe invisible realities using words the natural senses can perceive. Just as Elijah has parted the waters, there is the splitting asunder of the veil between heaven and earth, whereby Elisha accesses a genuine and awakened spiritual sight. A transitory moment of saturated phenomenon enlivens his spiritual senses, charismatically expands his consciousness and perception, and touches his intuition.

Assuming, as Sweeney does in relation to military imagery, that Elisha's visions are part of Jewish mysticism, they can be considered from the modern perspective of William James, who saw the 'religious attitude in the soul' as connected to the 'belief that there is an unseen order'.[258] This religious attitude involves aligning the soul to the harmony of that order.[259] James argues for a 'mystical state of consciousness' that lies in the domain of 'personal religious experience'.[260] While he does not personally attest to such experiences, he considers them real and supremely important in relation to their function.[261] James claims there are four marks of a mystical state, which he lays out in the following order:

1. Ineffability: James describes this as a negative mental state, not because it is deleterious but because it 'defies expression'.[262] While one might attempt to describe a mystical state, words are inadequate to do so.[263] For James, this is so because it is a direct experience.[264] By this he means that the person having the experience is fully engaged, not in a state of intellect but of feeling.[265] If with Sweeney we understand Elisha's visions at the Jordan as belonging to the realm of Jewish mystical experience, we need to admit that although Elisha had a

---

[258] James, *Varieties of Religious Experience*, p. 53.
[259] James, *Varieties of Religious Experience*, p. 53.
[260] James, *Varieties of Religious Experience*, p. 379.
[261] James, *Varieties of Religious Experience*, p. 379.
[262] James, *Varieties of Religious Experience*, p. 380.
[263] James, *Varieties of Religious Experience*, p. 380.
[264] James, *Varieties of Religious Experience*, p. 380.
[265] James, *Varieties of Religious Experience*, p. 380.

direct experience, the text describes his state of feeling with words. This violates James' mark of ineffability. Elisha conveys the feelings tied to the unseen reality, which phenomenologically, is a religious experience. I would argue with Sweeny that Elisha is (1) having a mystical experience, (2) it is a form of saturated phenomena, and (3) despite certain aspects of ineffability, he bears witness (well enough, under the circumstances) of that which he sees. Despite James' contention, what Elisha experienced directly was tied to mystical consciousness – indeed prophetic consciousness. He encountered an aspect of the mystery of God, which is inherently ineffable, God being enshrouded in mystery.

2. Noetic quality: James contends that a mystical experience has a 'noetic quality',[266] which implies mystical states as 'states of knowledge'.[267] Simply put, there is a state of insight that is unavailable to the distracted and wandering mind.[268] Therefore, a state of insight can be revelatory, illuminating, and weighty.[269] Once again for James, this mark seems inarticulate, perhaps being too broad and generalizing. Noting that the text shows Elisha's state of mind and consciousness to be clear, what he sees is insightful, revelatory, and weighty. Notwithstanding the limitations of human speech, Elisha articulates his experience. His vision is unquestionably noetic. Also, without question, people outside the experience can grasp its revelatory nature and truth, based on Elisha's apprehension, acceptance, and verbalization.

3. Transiency: This is the first of the two lesser marks of mystical states. It simply means that the state is brief and not sustained.[270] In Elisha's case, that is true. The event's brevity seems evident. However, Ezekiel had lengthy visionary experiences that are highly detailed and were sustained for longer periods. (For example, see Ezek. 1.1-28, 2.1-9, and 3.1-12.) Therefore, transiency might not apply to all mystical states.

4. Passivity: This implies that people who have mystical experiences do not control those experiences, their volition being

---

[266] James, *Varieties of Religious Experience*, p. 380.
[267] James, *Varieties of Religious Experience*, p. 380.
[268] James, *Varieties of Religious Experience*, p. 380.
[269] James, *Varieties of Religious Experience*, p. 380.
[270] James, *Varieties of Religious Experience*, p. 381.

suspended as they are 'grasped ... by a superior power'.[271] Elisha is certainly grasped by God's power; yet his volition is not suspended. This is not to say that this *cannot* happen in an ecstatic state. However, in this case, Elisha's will remains active. According to the standards of Jewish mysticism, his phenomenological encounter is valid. In relation to his phenomenological encounter with the numinous, his consciousness and perception are enlarged. Therefore, the encounter becomes the nexus of his prophetic legitimacy.

2.5 Conclusion

In this chapter, I have sought to present a realistic and biblically supported synopsis of prophetic function and legitimacy within the OT setting. I did this by presenting documented examples of four OT prophets who functioned mediatorially via the graces afforded them, and within the context of their humanity. As all prophets do, they contended with personal insufficiencies as their understanding of the divine will developed. Their callings, experiences, and ministry outcomes help us to trace the historical continuity of prophetic tradition, function, and legitimacy prior to the birth of Christ and of his church. I have shown these figures embodying the ideals of prophetic consciousness, perception, and enactment; I have also shown how examining the texts develops a deeper understanding of the prophetic legitimacy's foundations and continuities, leading us to the ultimate fulfillment in Jesus, the prophetic Messiah.

We now shift our focus to the Lukan narrative and its portrayal of the prophetic Messiah, which furthers our understanding of prophetic legitimacy within the Pentecostal movement. Luke's reliance on the Elijah-Elisha narratives in Luke-Acts offers us a framework to comprehend the prophetic dimensions of Jesus' ministry. As the culmination of prophetic legitimacy, Jesus embodies the consciousness, perception, and memory of ancient Israel's prophetic ideal. The chapter will also trace the prophetic record through the examples of John the Baptist, Agabus, and the apostle Paul.

---

[271] James, *Varieties of Religious Experience*, p. 381.

3

NEW TESTAMENT PROPHETIC LEGITIMACY

3.1 Introduction

Having considered prophetic legitimacy relative to the OT canon, we now view it within the NT context. The predominant texts under review include Luke-Acts, certain Pauline epistles, and the Gospel of John. Other synoptics are pertinent; however, Luke-Acts is the focus.

The Pentecostal's place at the theological and ecclesiological table comes 'at the beginning of the twentieth century'.[1] Thus, we need to reckon with the movement's proliferation, which exceeds all other movements currently in the global church. I would concur with Mittelstadt's view, 'through the first century of their existence, Pentecostals found their theological and practical identity through their reading Luke-Acts'.[2] If Mittelstadt is correct about the 'centrality of the Lukan narratives for Pentecostal theology and praxis',[3] then constructing a Pentecostal theology of prophetic legitimacy would rely on those narratives.

Perhaps the way we read the Luke-Acts texts determines our articulation of Pentecostal distinctives. Andrew Davies states, 'Pentecostal fires never burn more fervently than when they encounter the kindling of the biblical text'.[4] Davies asserts, 'we [Pentecostals] have

---

[1] Martin William Mittelstadt, *Reading Luke–Acts in the Pentecostal Tradition* (Cleveland, TN: CPT Press, 2010), intro.
[2] Mittelstadt, *Reading Luke–Acts in the Pentecostal Tradition*, intro.
[3] Mittelstadt, *Reading Luke–Acts in the Pentecostal Tradition*, intro.
[4] Andrew Davies, 'What Does it Mean to Read the Bible as A Pentecostal?', *Journal of Pentecostal Theology* 18.2 (2009), p. 217.

sought to identify our own experiences with those of the earliest church, described in detail in what we recognise as the historical narrative of the Acts of the Apostles'.[5] Pentecostals also tend to engage the Scriptures expressly to 'meet God in the text'.[6] The exuberance of prophetic agents within Pentecostalism's many forms has much to glean from the Lukan narrative. Therefore, the argument of this work also calls for a return to the Lukan text, which is a springboard for comprehending prophetic legitimacy from a NT perspective.

Even as a 'theological evolution' has transpired over the past century and beyond,[7] a parallel evolution within the context of prophetic expression, function, consciousness, perception, and enactment betides us. Although some of this evolution is admirable, some is nebulous and insubstantial, and some is illegitimate, unfaithful, and contrived. In recent decades, a keen interest has pursued Luke-Acts in relation to developing a Pentecostal pneumatology. Such a pneumatology bears profoundly on legitimate prophetic function and expression and requires an in-depth consideration of the same. This pneumatology should have a wholistic impact on prophetic legitimacy, which is never divorced from personal subjectivity. Davies argues for a 'distinctive appropriation of the text' and adds 'that our readings are worth hearing by others'.[8] This starkly contrasts the historical-grammatical approach to the reading of Scripture. I embrace Davies's contention that Pentecostals' engagement of the text has 'a specific and distinct purpose'.[9] As to what purpose that would be, Davies points to 'what encountering the divine in the text does in, through, for and to us'.[10]

Considering my interdisciplinary argumentation (theology, psychology, and phenomenology) and regarding prophetic legitimacy and personal subjectivity, the integrated order of 'in, through, for and to' is pertinent. In relation to prophetic consciousness, perception, and enactment, the order is the same. Consciousness is *in* and relates to interiority. Perception, which flows from consciousness, is *through* and leads to interpretive function that is always *for* a specific intent

---

[5] Davies, 'What Does it Mean', p. 218. That historical narrative is Luke the Physician's second volume, the first being his Gospel.
[6] Davies, 'What Does it Mean', p. 219.
[7] Mittelstadt, *Reading Luke–Acts in the Pentecostal Tradition*, intro.
[8] Davies, 'What Does it Mean', p. 222.
[9] Davies, 'What Does it Mean', p. 223.
[10] Davies, 'What Does it Mean', p. 223.

and purpose. Enactment is *to* the community in which the prophetic agent functions.

However, before approaching these issues in the Lukan account, we need to first consider the narrative's overall perspective. Regarding Luke-Acts, Amos Yong states that there is 'the experiential dimension of pentecostal theology' and 'the exegetical privileging of Luke-Acts in pentecostal hermeneutics'.[11] Those who counter this exegetical privileging and miss the prophetic include the well-known dispensationalist scholar Darrell Bock, who acknowledges the historical context of Luke-Acts but seems to gloss over the narrative in favor of his approach to 'God's plan'.[12] In addition, although F.F. Bruce is not a dispensationalist, neither does his commentary reflect a Pentecostal pneumatology.[13] Van Johnson notes the contention that Pentecostal reliance on eisegesis imposes questionable textual interpretations but claims, 'such a charge ignores its underlying cultural preferences' and counters newer approaches that 'incorporate the reader into the interpretive event'.[14]

---

[11] Amos Yong, *An Amos Yong Reader: The Pentecostal Spirit* (ed. Christopher A. Stephenson; Eugene, OR: Cascade Books, 2020), p. 199.

[12] Darrell L. Bock, *Luke* (Baker Exegetical Commentary on the New Testament; Grand Rapids, MI: Baker Academic, 1994), I, p. 49. Currently, this is a popular way of describing the whole of salvation history, even in relation to those passages recognizably involving prophetic expression. 'His account carefully builds on precedent and is grounded in a tradition from eyewitnesses. In addition, Luke has gone back through the events carefully and now sets about telling the story in a way that assures the reader about God's plan' (I, p. 4). Bock's references to anything prophetic within the Luke-Acts account recognize prophetic function and expression, yet without any sense of its experiential pneumatological implications.

> Prophecy 177, 1550, 1562, 1656, 1936; prophetic pronouncement 317, 557, 624–26; prophetic warning 300–301, 623–24, 1233–34, 1252–53, 1291–92, 1385–86, 1543–44, 1550, 1552, 1597, 1633, 1641, 1651, 1658, 1664, 1678; prophets 697, 823, 968, 981, 986, 1013, 1157, 1192, 1230, 1232, 1238–39, 1249, 1252, 1350–51, 1578, 1592, 1598, 1632, 1643, 1666, 1913, 1916, 1936–37 (II, p. 2036).

[13] F.F. Bruce, while more lenient in relation to theology and history, is also sparse on how he handles the issue of prophecy and the prophetic in the Lukan account. See the index listing, 'Prophecy, gift of, 52, 229, 314, 398, 400-1', in F.F. Bruce, *The Book of the Acts* (New International Commentary on the New Testament; Grand Rapids, MI: Eerdmans, rev. edn, 1988), p. 3.

[14] Van Johnson, 'Pentecostals and Luke-Acts: Reading St. Luke in the Pre- and Post-Stronstad Eras', in Riku P. Tuppurainen (ed.), *Reading St. Luke's Text and Theology: Pentecostal Voices; Essays in Honor of Professor Roger Stronstad* (Eugene, OR: Pickwick, 2019), ch. 5. Regarding a Pentecostal hermeneutic and particularly Luke-Acts,

Pentecostals found their pathway into NT Christianity via Luke-Acts, seeing these texts as one testimony to the work of the Spirit. For them, the selfsame Spirit that was present with and in Luke to shape the Lukan narrative (and all of Scripture) is present when the community reads the text. In part because Luke-Acts is a narrative, current Pentecostal academic scholars also affirm narrative as an especially appropriate genre for developing doctrinal thought and

---

Stronstad and Fee disagree about 'how Pentecostals do hermeneutics'. Roger Stronstad, 'Pentecostal Hermeneutics', *Pneuma* 15.2 (Fall 1993), p. 217. Pentecostals see the Luke-Acts narrative as their story in which the Spirit bears witness to his activity. They see themselves as walking interpretations of the story, while 'recognizing that Pentecostal tradition is only one of the various legitimate Christian traditions'. Kenneth J. Archer, 'Afterword: On the Future of Pentecostal Hermeneutics', in Kenneth J. Archer and L. W. Oliverio, Jr. (eds.), *Constructive Pneumatological Hermeneutics in Pentecostal Christianity* (New York: Palgrave Macmillan, 2016), p. 316. Systematic and dogmatic theologians find reason to relegate the Lukan text, as 'traditional theological approaches see theological doctrines as primary and the stories as derivative'. T.W. Tilley, 'Narrative Theology', in Joseph A. Komonchak, Mary Collins, and Dermot A. Lane (eds.), *The New Dictionary of Theology* (Collegeville, MN: Liturgical Press, 2000), p. 702. However, Tilley demonstrates that narrative theologies essentially precede 'doctrinal formulations or theological systematization … [and] could not make sense without a narrative context' (p. 702). Gordon D. Fee and Douglas Stuart, *How to Read the Bible for All Its Worth* (Grand Rapids, MI: Zondervan, 2014), ch. 5, herald this reasoning when they claim, 'Narratives are stories – purposeful stories retelling the *historical events* of the past that are intended to give meaning and direction for a given people *in the present*'. Fee and Stuart argue for a historical-grammatical methodology of interpretation.

Pentecostals indeed value narrative. They also value their encounters with the Spirit that come through a wide range of expressions for which they contend, based on what the narrative presents. However, not all Pentecostals agree with Fee and Stuart that reading the Bible for all its worth stems from the historical-grammatical approach. Nevertheless, Pentecostal history's approach to Luke-Acts affords Pentecostals a distinctive voice and place in the larger theological conversation from which they contend for the heritage they see in Luke-Act's claims. They find their Pentecostal identity in the record of how the Spirit has moved and the reality of how the Spirit is moving and will yet move. This does not preclude all concern within Pentecostal ranks regarding the ways in which some Pentecostals make claims. Looking at the Lukan writing and Acts in particular, Gordon D. Fee, *Gospel and Spirit: Issues in New Testament Hermeneutics* (Grand Rapids, MI: Baker, 1991), ch. 6, cautions that despite any theological content contained therein, 'it is *not* an epistle or a theological treatise'. Although Luke might be a theologian of sorts, Fee notes that the Lukan text is 'cast in the form of historical narrative' (ch. 6), and should, from a historical-grammatical perspective, be primarily understood as such. We can then consider its theological nature as being secondary. Not all of Fee's Pentecostal contemporaries share his view, particularly regarding its hermeneutical implications.

practice.[15] As Archer asserts: 'The Pentecostal story is the primary hermeneutical context for the reading of Scripture'.[16]

Insofar as literary-theological approaches can be considered to fit within the framework of narrative theology, this work is methodologically attentive to narrative. The intent is to integrate not only the scriptural and theological but also the psychological and phenomenological domains (namely personal consciousness, experience, and the interpretation of experience). Within the scope of the theological, psychological, and the storied nature of the community and its participants, the prophetic agent shares the narrative and is called to live it, presumably in a way that offers a kind of model from which others can glean.

Luke-Acts could be considered the *micro story* within the canon's *macro story*. The significance of the Luke-Acts narrative to pneumatology is applicable to the deep, widespread Pentecostal conviction that the Azusa outpouring was 'a fulfillment of prophecy'.[17] This has bearing on the prophetic legitimacy argument presented here. First-generation Pentecostals who held this conviction believed that Joel's utterance after the plague of locusts found its fulfillment in their lifetimes: 'O children of Zion, be glad and rejoice in the Lord your God; for he has given the early rain for your vindication, he has poured down for you abundant rain, the early and the later rain, as before' (Joel 2.23).[18]

Although some have accused Pentecostals of (1) imposing their personal experience with the Spirit on their interpretations of Scripture, (2) giving undue weight to scriptural narratives rather than

---

[15] See Kenneth J. Archer, 'Pentecostal Theology as Story: Participating in God's Mission', in Wolfgang Vondey (ed.), *The Routledge Handbook of Pentecostal Theology* (London: Routledge, 2020), ch. 4.

[16] Archer, *Pentecostal Hermeneutic*, p. 134.

[17] Amos Yong, *The Spirit Poured Out on All Flesh: Pentecostalism and the Possibility of Global Theology* (Grand Rapids, MI: Baker Academic, 2005), p. 83.

[18] Joel mentions two rains: (1) the early rain at the beginning of ancient Israel's harvest season, and (2) the light rain, also known as the latter rain, which ripened the growing grains at the end of harvest season. The term *latter rain*, although utilized by first-generation Pentecostals at the time of Azusa Street, would also come to designate the move of God that began in 1948 in North Battleford, Saskatchewan and brought a flourishing of the prophetic, as will be discussed in Chapter 4. Essentially, as Davies contends, this is not a 'neo-orthodox approach to the nature of the text', Davies, 'What Does it Mean', p. 224. Rather, it 'suggest[s] a more phenomenological approach' (p. 224). In relation to overall prophetic experience, I would argue that such an approach to the text is not optional but essential.

epistles and theological treatises, and (3) identifying unduly with the Luke-Acts micro story, sound arguments also refute these suppositions. First, a personal account by Agnes Ozman (which can similarly be claimed by countless others) shows that Scripture preceded the interpretation of her charismatic experience.[19] Second, multidisciplinary evidence supports the essential role of story in conveying truth to human beings who are 'hardwired' for story.[20] Third, Pentecostals identify with the Luke-Acts narrative because the early church's story confirms their own, with the Spirit bearing witness to his activity in the scriptural accounts.

With these things in mind, we now consider the scriptural narratives surrounding NT prophetic figures who serve as models of prophetic legitimacy from a Pentecostal perspective.

3.2 John the Baptist: Elijah's Expectation Fulfilled

3.2.1 John the Baptist from a Biblical and Theological Perspective

Before addressing John the Baptist, it should be noted that Zechariah, his father, initially resisted the message Gabriel delivered about John's coming birth. Zechariah's incredulity might serve as a negative example of one who was steeped in the priesthood and used prophetically yet found it difficult to embrace what came as good news.[21] Although his son John faced uncertainty in his own ministry, he was not shown in the text to resist divine direction.

Historically speaking, Luke recounts John's emergence by first articulating the fifteenth year in Tiberius' reign (Lk. 3.1),[22] naming Pilate

---

[19] Agnes N. Ozman, 'Personal Testimony of Being the First Person to Receive the Holy Ghost at "Stones Folly" in Topeka, Kansas (January 1, 1901)' *Apostolic Faith* (April – 1951); available in the Apostolic Archives International, Inc., https://www.apostolicarchives.com/articles/article/8801925/173171.htm.

[20] Lisa Cron, *Wired for Story: The Writer's Guide to Using Brain Science to Hook Readers from the Very First Sentence* (Berkeley, CA: Ten Speed Press, 2012).

[21] See Mark J. Chironna, 'Zechariah: The Incredulous Priest-Turned-Prophet: Biblical-Theological, Psychological, and Phenomenological Perspectives in Relation to Prophetic Legitimacy', https://www.markchironna.com/articles.

[22] This is concurrent with Pontius Pilate as prefect of Judea, Herod as tetrarch of Galilee, and Lysanias as tetrarch of Abilene. *GEL* p. 481, '37.79 τετρααρχέω: [meaning] to function as a tetrarch (see 37.78) – "to be a tetrarch, to be the governor of a region". τετρααρχοῦντος τῆς Γαλιλαίας Ηρώδου "Herod was tetrarch of Galilee" Lk 3:1.'

and others, and invoking Annas and Caiaphas, leaders of Israel's chief priesthood. Johnson expresses this simultaneity, stating, 'He begins with the empire, works through regional authorities and ends with the religious leadership'.[23] This is not for the sake of an exact chronology but for the narrative theology Luke is espousing.[24] Although Annas is not the high priest during John the Baptist's time, he exerts significant influence in all Gospel narratives, being the father-in-law of the ruling high priest, Caiaphas.[25] For Luke, it is essential to locate John's prophetic ministry amid the configuration of powers. Arterbury asserts, 'Luke aims to locate the events surrounding John's ministry, and, more important, Jesus' life in their proper historical setting'.[26] Precisely in this context, outside Jerusalem and the Promised Land's borders, Luke asserts John as being active in the desert, a wilderness detail reminiscent of Elijah's residency in the borderland east of the Jordan.[27]

Luke specifically places John at the Jordan's historic waters, preaching 'a penitential washing [i.e. baptism involving repentance] for the forgiveness of sins'.[28] Carroll notes, 'The desolate setting aptly symbolizes the separation from the previous way of life that John demands of his auditors, as he insists on *metanoia*, transformation of heart and mind'.[29] Also important is Luke's phraseology regarding John's prophetic call: 'the word of God came to John the son of

---

[23] Luke Timothy Johnson, *The Gospel of Luke* (Sacra Pagina 3; Collegeville, MN: Liturgical Press, 1991), p. 64.

[24] Johnson, *Gospel of Luke*, p. 64, 'As in the other instances, putting the chronological pieces together is difficult but ultimately irrelevant to Luke's *literary* purpose, which is to attach his story to the wider world culture'.

[25] Johnson, *Gospel of Luke*, p. 64:

The difficulty, reflected in the Greek, is that custom dictated only one chief priest at a time. Annas was chief priest from 6–15 C.E., and was eventually succeeded by his son-in-law Caiaphas (18–36 C.E. [cf. Josephus, *Antiquities of the Jews* 18:26; 35; 95]). Luke puts them together again in Acts 4:6. Matthew makes Caiaphas alone the high priest (26:3, 57), as does John (11:49; 18:13–28), but John also attests to Annas' continuing influence and importance (John 18:13, 24).

[26] Andrew E. Arterbury, *Reading Luke: A Literary and Theological Commentary* (Reading the New Testament; Macon, GA: Smyth & Helwys, 2019), p. 23.

[27] Christina Bosserman, 'Gilead', in John D. Barry, *et al.* (eds.), *The Lexham Bible Dictionary* (Bellingham, WA: Lexham Press, 2016), 'The term Gilead is used in the biblical texts to refer to both a broad and narrow region east of the Jordan River'.

[28] John T. Carroll, *Luke: A Commentary* (New Testament Library; Louisville, KY: Westminster John Knox Press, 2012), p. 91.

[29] Carroll, *Luke: A Commentary*, p. 91.

Zechariah in the wilderness' (Lk. 3.2). Luke has already informed Theophilus that he intends to hand down what was given by 'eyewitnesses and servants of the word' (Lk. 1.2). The significance from a Lukan perspective is the coming of 'the word of God' to John with 'the portrayal of prophets',[30] which affirms John's prophetic call.

Luke theologically places John's prophetic call outside the existing imperial and religious power arrangements, underscoring the contrast between the Messianic kingdom and all rival powers. This parallels the call to a fundamental transformation of mind, which is displayed publicly in the penitential cleansing in the Jordan,[31] away from the ceremonial baths outside of the Temple precincts. Regarding prophetic function in Israel's history, this is significant.

Considering John as prophet means remembering that he is foretold as 'the prophet of the Most High' and is linked to Elijah (Lk. 1.76, 17).[32] First, Luke recognizes John as a prophet from the womb, which recalls Jeremiah's story (Jer. 1.1-10). Second, Gabriel explains that he will come in 'the spirit and power of Elijah' (Lk. 1.17). This implies the community's familiarity with Elijah and his ultimate public challenge to Baal's prophets (1 Kgs 18.16-40; 17.1). Rutledge notes that when 'this strange figure from the desert suddenly exploded out of nowhere and dared to confront Ahab the king in his own council chamber, there was an inexplicable aura about him, as though he had

---

[30] Johnson, *Gospel of Luke*, p. 64, '*[W]ord of God*: Is thematic in Luke-Acts; see note on 1:1–4, and for the importance of 'word of God' for the portrayal of prophets, see introduction, pp. 17, 23'.

[31] Flavius Josephus, *The Works of Josephus: Complete and Unabridged* (ed. and trans. William Whiston; Peabody, MA: Hendrickson, 1987), p. 484,

> Now, some of the Jews thought that the destruction of Herod's army came from God, and that very justly, as a punishment of what he did against John, that was called the Baptist; (117) for Herod slew him, who was a good man, and commanded the Jews to exercise virtue, both as to righteousness towards one another, and piety towards God, and so to come to baptism; for that the washing [with water] would be acceptable to him, if they made use of it, not in order to the putting away [or the remission] of some sins [only], but for the purification of the body; supposing still that the soul was thoroughly purified beforehand by righteousness.

[32] Carroll, *Luke: A Commentary*, pp. 90-91:

> The angel's promise to Zechariah concerning the prophetic vocation of his son-to-be is now finding fulfillment. As with John's predecessors, the juxtaposition between prophet and powers anticipates coming conflict between agents of God's reign and Rome's, in both the Gospel and its sequel.

come from another world'.³³ Rutledge's 'inexplicable aura' is a dramatic term suggesting a presence not only commanding but mystical. By this, one might infer something related to Elijah's subjectivity in communion with the divine (and how it is perceived by those with whom he interacts). In addition, Symington states, 'Elijah represented the majesty and severity of divine law'.³⁴ Consider, therefore, how the OT narrative contrasts Elijah's representation with the wickedness of Ahab that Jezebel engenders (1 Kgs 21.25).

Much like Elijah's emergence from obscurity is John's period of solitude prior to his own appearance on the scene. This indicates his formal prophetic call and entrance into the fuller measure of prophetic consciousness and perception by which his enactment would be legitimized.³⁵ John's formation in the wilderness also suggests that of Moses, who was called and shaped for prophetic expression there (Exod. 3.1–4.17). Of course, Samuel came from a barren womb, as did Samson and John. These commonalities likely would have impacted John's consciousness and perception of his identity, the purpose of God, and John's unfolding personal narrative.³⁶

The text is silent as to when John's parents died. Stating that 'the child grew and became strong in spirit', Luke seems to suggest that his parents were present in his early years (Lk. 1.80).³⁷ Given what Luke reveals about Zechariah and Elizabeth being 'righteous' and 'living blamelessly according to all the commandments and regulations of the Lord' (Lk. 1.6), his early spiritual formation would have

---

³³ Fleming Rutledge, *And God Spoke to Abraham: Preaching from the Old Testament* (Grand Rapids, MI: Eerdmans, 2011), p. 131.

³⁴ Alexander Macleod Symington, *The Life and Ministry of John the Baptist* (Vox Clamantis; London: Religious Tract Society, n.d.), p. 8.

³⁵ Like Elijah in the court of Ahab and Jezebel (1 Kgs 17.1), John 'stood forth on the Lord's side', Symington, *John the Baptist*, p. 9. His warning in Luke of judgment and rebuke and his call to the crowds for repentance are also reminiscent of Elijah (Lk. 3.7). Johnson, *Gospel of Luke*, p. 33, states the affinity between Elijah's function and John's, writing, 'John plays the role assigned to Elijah of preparing the people (Sir 48:10; Mal 4:5)'.

³⁶ Wilderness imagery is pervasive in the Exodus narrative, making John's public appearance in the wilderness anticipatory of a new Exodus, via the cross. Luke affirms this at the Mount of Transfiguration, where desert travelers Moses and Elijah prepare Jesus for his exodus ('departure' in Lk. 9.31) and his preparing of humanity's exodus from fallenness. Liddell and Scott, 'ἔξοδο', *A Greek-English Lexicon* (Oxford: Clarendon Press, 1996), 'Departure' here is 'ἔξοδος (A), ἡ, *going out* ... **2.** *marching out, military expedition ... way out, outlet ... Entrances and exits*'.

³⁷ John's parents may have died long before he reached the age of thirty, however.

been thorough. Zechariah's priestly heritage included the narrative of the faith and the liturgical sensibilities involved with approaching and worshipping God.[38] John's parents would have embodied these values, thereby engraining them in his earliest consciousness and perception and informing his further maturation during his desert years.[39] Gabriel's instruction that John 'must never drink wine or strong drink' alludes to John being a Nazirite (Lk. 1.15),[40] which places him in the company of Samson and Samuel.[41]

Symington avers that Agag's demise would 'nurse' in John a 'severe regard to the will of God, preparing him to lay the axe to the root of the tree'.[42] John's preaching and terminology reflect this severity, as when he proclaims judgment on those who refuse to repent (Lk. 3.7, 9). John's aversion to such moral dereliction is also evident when he reproves Herod (Lk. 3.19). Consider John's knowledge of Samuel's narrative concerning Hophni, Phineas, and Eli and God's severe response to their abandoned righteousness (1 Sam. 2.12-17, 22-24, 27-36). John would have known of Samuel's calling to prepare Israel for the anointing of a king who foreshadowed the Messianic role (1 Sam. 8.1-22). In John's keeping of this tradition and

---

[38] See Chironna, 'Zechariah', https://www.markchironna.com/articles.

[39] Luke attests to John's spiritual formation (Lk. 1.80).

[40] Symington, *John the Baptist*, p. 39:

The law of the Nazarite will be found in Numbers 6:1-12, with Leviticus 10:8-11; 21:10-12, passages to which the reader may turn with advantage. The meaning of this singular character is well expressed in a single sentence, 'The Nazarite was a link of connexion between the priesthood of the Old Covenant and the priesthood of consecration to the will of God'. When a man assumed the vow, his doing so implied an unusual sense of the divine holiness, and a special willingness to serve God. And we may be sure John occupied the position of a Nazarite thus, although we know that he neither assumed it by his own choice in adult years, nor kept it for a fixed time, as others did.

[41] Symington, *John the Baptist*, pp. 39-40, 'Manoah's son and Hannah's, and Elisabeth's son would early hear from her the stories of Samson and Samuel'. Although Samson was consecrated as a child, he became compromised as an adult (Judges 14–16). Samuel was also consecrated as a child, but his sons became corrupt (1 Sam. 8.1-3). Noteworthy are questions about how John's youthful consciousness and perception reflect Samson's history against the Philistines and Samuel's encounter with the numinous from childhood onward. What also of the responsibilities that Samuel bore, first in being mentored by Eli the priest and then being a young prophet known from 'Dan to Beersheba?' (1 Sam. 3.20). Perhaps John found solace in Samuel's being distanced from his parents at an early age. Would that not shape his subjectivity and identity as surely as his father's Aaronic heritage would?

[42] Symington, *John the Baptist*, p. 40.

proclaiming the arrival of the Messiah, all the prophetic voices from Abraham to Malachi effectively converge (Lk. 1.68-79; 3.16; 7.28).[43]

John was immersed in the prophets' ways of seeing the divine intent worked out in human and salvation history (Lk. 3.4-17). Like Elijah, he is 'the voice of one crying out in the wilderness' (Lk. 3.4). There he addresses his hearers as a 'brood of vipers' (Lk. 3.7),[44] denoting not harmless snakes but untrustworthy and venomous ones.[45] His prophetic preaching in Luke addresses their delinquency and failure to produce 'fruits worthy of repentance' (Lk. 3.8). Luke brings John's preaching to a conclusion by speaking of the Messiah's 'winnowing fork' (Lk. 3.17), used in the threshing of grain.[46] The

---

[43] This convergence was contained in John's declaration of the might of the One who came after him and baptized 'with the Holy Spirit and fire' (Lk. 3.16). Luke's mention of John's wilderness proclamation of 'a baptism of repentance for the forgiveness of sins' has led some scholars (Lk. 3.3), including Joel Marcus, to connect John's message 'directly or indirectly with the Qumran sect' precisely because of the 1948 'discovery of the Scrolls' at Qumran. Joel Marcus, *John the Baptist in History and Theology* (Studies on Personalities of the New Testament; Columbia, SC: University of South Carolina Press, 2018), ch. 2. Marcus is persuaded, 'John started out as a member of the Qumran community' and acknowledges that it 'is a controversial assertion'. Luke Timothy Johnson, *Prophetic Jesus, Prophetic Church*, p. 132, notes, 'Luke reveals no knowledge of the Essenes'. Johnson enumerates his reasons, including three regarding: John's 'rite of immersion in water'; 'water rites practiced by the Baptist and by the Qumran sect [having] had a similar meaning, including their connection with repentance and forgiveness'; and 'the forgiveness spoken of in both cases ... [as] an *eschatological* remission of sins, directly linked with belief in an approaching crisis in world history, in which the wicked will be judged, the righteous vindicated, and the world transformed'. Marcus, *John the Baptist*, ch. 2. The debate will continue as to whether these reasons explain John's solitude and continuing spiritual formation in the wilderness. What can be presumed is that John knew his prophetic call from his earliest recollection and the rehearsing of his parents' narrative.

[44] The same appellation is recorded concerning the Pharisees and Sadducees in Mt. 3.7; 12.34; 23.33.

[45] 'Viper', https://www.dictionary.com/browse/viper, *Viper* refers to

any of several venomous Old World snakes of the genus *Vipera,* especially *V. berus,* a small snake common in northern Eurasia ... Any related snakes belonging to the family Viperidae, characterized by erectile, venom-conducting fangs ... any of various venomous or supposedly venomous snakes ... a malignant or spiteful person ... a false or treacherous person.

[46] Mark A. Hassler, 'Winnowing', in John D. Barry, *et al.* (eds.), *The Lexham Bible Dictionary* (Bellingham, WA: Lexham Press, 2016),

Winnowing (זָרָה, *zarah*). The use of a multi-prong wooden pitchfork (מִזְרֶה, *mizreh*; πτύον, *ptyon*) to toss threshed grain – usually wheat or barley – into the air so that the wind can separate the lighter straw from the heaver grain. When

metaphor was also 'used ... for judgment because of its inherent concept of separation'.[47] John prophetically addresses the fiery eschatological judgment that consumes the winnowed chaff, just as he earlier hinted at 'the wrath to come' (Lk. 3.7). John closes with expectation for the promised Messiah, but it is tied to the coming Messiah's impending judgment.

3.2.2 John the Baptist from a Psychological and Phenomenological Perspective

According to the message Gabriel delivered, John is filled with the Spirit in utero (Lk. 1.15). The Spirit continues empowering and maturing him, but not in the Temple precincts or the more traditional environs that formed his father. Nevertheless, John is a son of Israel with 'a knowledge of the Old Testament Scriptures'.[48] He saw Christ as the OT 'fulfillment in form and context' and was also chosen to be the Messiah's forerunner.[49] Yet, after asserting that Jesus was the coming One, he struggled psychically in his cognitions and perceptions with Jesus' identity (Lk. 7.18-22). Luke does not present John's struggle as unique but cites Cleopas and the unnamed disciple as 'slow of heart to believe all that the prophets have declared' (Lk. 24.25). For Luke, this slowness explains why 'their eyes were kept from recognizing [Jesus]' (Lk. 24.16), a failure that occurred at both affective and perceptual levels. John, the forerunner and proclaimer of Messiah, also struggles to recognize him, his offense at being imprisoned likely contributing to his doubts (Lk. 7.18-23).[50]

This raises the essential question of precisely what occurs when John is filled with the Spirit in utero. If he is truly filled, why does he waver about the 'more powerful' One whom he testified was coming? (Lk. 3.16). What discrepancy accommodates his question? Are such questions unnecessary, given that doubt is unavoidable in the human condition?

---

only the finer chaff remains, a winnowing shovel is used (רחת, *rachath*; Isa 30:24).

[47] Hassler, 'Winnowing'.

[48] Kenneth O. Gangel and Jim Wilhoit, *The Christian Educator's Handbook on Spiritual Formation* (Wheaton, IL: Victor Books, 1994), p. 21.

[49] Gangel and Wilhoit, *Christian Educator's Handbook*, p. 21.

[50] Regarding offense, Cleopas and the unnamed disciple were perhaps scandalized. Certainly, their hopes were shattered because they misinterpreted the crucifixion in relation to the Messianic role (Lk. 24.21).

> In therapeutic consciousness, we understand *doubt* as a
>
> lack of confidence or an uncertainty about something or someone, including the self. Doubt may center on everyday concerns (Can I accomplish this task?), issues of daily living (Can I change this ingrained habit?), or the very meaning of life itself. It is a perception, typically with a strong affective component, that is frequently a focus during psychotherapeutic intervention.[51]

John's being offended would seem connected to his uncertainty regarding Jesus. This is significant, because the prophet's rejection and suffering over Israel's reception of the prophetic message are essential aspects of prophetic legitimacy and the prophetic tradition, as Jesus attests (Lk. 13.33-34). Nevertheless, John is shaken, and his lack of confidence has a strong affective component. This can indicate a form of existential anxiety, 'a general sense of anguish or despair associated with an individual's recognition of the inevitability of death'.[52] Unquestionably, death looms over John, who would presumably be anguished. Can he reconcile that suffering as part of the prophetic tradition and calling? Or is he experiencing a deeper crisis relating to theodicy?[53]

John's ultimate existential crisis results from the message that was unwelcomed by Herod and resulted in John's imprisonment and beheading.[54] It recalls Elijah's existential crisis after he slayed Baal's prophets and Jezebel placed a bounty on his life (1 Kgs 19.4, 2). This perhaps suggests psychological consideration of Gabriel's statement that John would go in 'the spirit and power of Elijah' (Lk. 1.17). The word translated 'spirit' here is πνεῦμα; it describes 'an attitude or disposition reflecting the way in which a person thinks about or deals with some matter' and is akin to a 'way of thinking'.[55] It can be argued that spirit is deeply connected to temperament, 'the basic foundation

---

[51] 'Doubt', *APA Dictionary of Psychology*, https://dictionary.apa.org/doubt.

[52] 'Existential Anxiety', *APA Dictionary of Psychology*, https://dictionary.apa.org/existential-anxiety.

[53] James L. Crenshaw, 'Theodicy', in David Noel Freedman (ed.), *The Anchor Yale Bible Dictionary* (New York: Doubleday, 1992), pp. 445-47.

[54] 'Existential Crisis', *APA Dictionary of Psychology*, https://dictionary.apa.org/existential-crisis; an existential crisis is 'any psychological or moral crisis that causes an individual to ask fundamental questions about human existence'.

[55] *GEL*, p. 350.

of personality'.⁵⁶ The foundation of John's personality could have been fashioned much the way Elijah's was, thus lending itself to self-doubt and despair.⁵⁷ This seems plausible, considering the men's shared characteristics. Elijah was clinically depressed and wanted to die (1 Kgs 19.1-14).⁵⁸ While John was imprisoned, he might well have despaired of life and been scandalized by Jesus' choice not to personally visit him. These realities would have been difficult to process, both psychologically and spiritually. In such a state of mind, John would have struggled to assess objectively Jesus' response to John's messengers (Lk. 7.22-23). Might it not have seemed harsh and indifferent to him? Might he not have experienced a deep sense of 'unanticipated grief?'⁵⁹

The Johannine account might further identify the psychological and phenomenological realties John the Baptist faced. John 1.21 shows his quickness to deny aspects of his identity and calling and is remarkably like Elijah's post-Carmel self-appraisal, 'I am no better

---

⁵⁶ 'Temperament', *APA Dictionary of Psychology*, https://dictionary.apa.org/temperament.

⁵⁷ Chironna, 'What Does Psychology', *Firebrand Magazine* (June 14, 2022), https://firebrandmag.com/articles/what-does-psychology-have-to-do-with-the-prophetic.

⁵⁸ Michael J. Anthony, *et al.* (eds.), 'Depression', *Evangelical Dictionary of Christian Education* (Baker Reference Library; Grand Rapids, MI: Baker Academic, 2001):

> Depression is the most common emotional condition treated by psychiatrists, and some estimate that over half of all Americans will suffer from clinical depression at some point in their lives (Minirth and Meier, 1978). Though some identify depression with feeling a little 'down,' clinical or major depression describes a dramatically different condition than being a little blue. Signs of clinical depression include: 1. A despondent or empty feeling which lasts at least two weeks and may last months or years without relief 2. Loss of interest in normal activities such as work, relationships, children, sex, food, etc. 3. Sleep irregularities (normally insomnia but can be excessive sleep) 4. Complaints of low energy or fatigue 5. Thoughts of worthlessness, hopelessness, or guilt which consistently resist efforts at change 6. Lack of concentration and memory problems which may bring more discouragement as the person realizes how drastic these changes are 7. Thoughts about the futility of life and possibility of suicide.

Regarding Elijah's clinical depression, see Chironna, 'What Does Psychology', https://firebrandmag.com/articles/what-does-psychology-have-to-do-with-the-prophetic.

⁵⁹ The person experiencing unanticipated grief 'is so devastated by a sudden loss that he is unable to grasp the totality of what has happened. Mentally, he has difficulty accepting the loss because of its unexpectedness.' 'Insight for Living', *Counseling Insights: A Biblical Perspective on Caring for People* (Plano, TX: Insight for Living, 2007), p. 450.

than my ancestors' (1 Kgs 19.4). Such words disclose negation of family and personal history, which constitutes cognitive distortion.[60] Granted, when John was asked by the Jewish leaders whether he was the Messiah, he rightly confessed, 'I am not' (Jn 1.20). However, there is an 'I am not-ness' following every ensuing question. When asked if he was Elijah, John said 'No', when he could have legitimately answered that he was the one like Elijah.[61] When asked if he was 'the prophet' (Jn 1.21), he replied in the negative. Presuming that the question pointed to the prophetic messenger from Malachi, why would John negate what Jesus would affirm in Lk. 7.27?

John appropriates none of these realities, instead claiming only to be a voice. Given his reticence to embrace such self-identifications, the voice crying in the wilderness might be a dissociated one. Psychologically, 'I am a voice' could verbally define his prophetic call. It might also indicate that his ascetic disposition leans toward disclaiming aspects of his personhood.[62] In question here is asceticism's emphasis on the 'decentering of the self'.[63] If John was a member of

---

[60] Cognitive therapy,

as originally developed by Beck (1976, 1988) and by Ellis (1976) ... focuses on the way in which cognitive distortions produce emotional problems. Cognitive distortions refer to beliefs people hold about the meaning of events or communication. These beliefs or cognitions may distort what is actually said.

David C. Olsen, *Integrative Family Therapy* (Creative Pastoral Care and Counseling Series; Minneapolis, MN: Fortress Press, 1993), p. 27.

[61] Comparing this to what Jesus says on the Mount of Transfiguration, John is indeed the Elijah who was to come (Mt. 17.11-13).

[62] Prophets and ascetics are 'individuals associated with a religion that call people back to religious orthodoxy, represent extreme commitment to religious values, or ... foretell future events by divine communication'. David Witthoff (ed.), *The Lexham Cultural Ontology Glossary* (Bellingham, WA: Lexham Press, 2014). Did John's asceticism negatively impact his sense of personhood? Had his practices become too extreme? If so, can his experience inform contemporary prophetic formation and function?

[63] Lawrence M. Wills, 'Ascetic Theology Before Asceticism? Jewish Narratives and the Decentering of the Self', *Journal of the American Academy of Religion* 74.4 (December 2006), p. 902:

The study of early Christian asceticism, which formerly focused on ascetic practices, has been transformed in recent years. In addition to ascetic practices, scholars analyze the discourse of asceticism, which emphasizes the decentering of the self, the problematizing of the person's ability to govern the body and be considered righteous before God. Although this approach has pushed back the origins of ascetic discourses in Christianity, the decentering of the self can be observed in Qumran texts ... This ascetic discourse of the decentered self

the Qumran community whose formation was thus affected, the decentering process may have impacted him more radically than intended.[64] Consider Jesus' perspective: in his rebuke over the Pharisees' and lawyers false accusations (Jn 1.33-34), Jesus cites John's very different way of life. There is a distinction between Jesus' and John's approaches to the human experience that is both psychological and phenomenological: psychological because of its impact on John's cognitions, perceptions, and affections; phenomenological because of the structure of John's consciousness, which is based on his formation and its impact on his ontology (his way of being). At issue ontologically is not common human experience but John's personal ontological phenomenology and way of being human, including how he experienced life, defined his experience, and defined himself. If he is only a voice, what happened to the person? Has the person become so decentralized as to be effectively nonexistent? Is sublimation an issue?[65]

---

is traced in other pre-Christian Jewish texts and in an unexpected context – novelistic texts. This approach allows for an exploration of literary, ritual, and ascetic aspects of the texts, and some consideration is given to the social context of these important developments.

[64] Wills, 'Ascetic Theology', pp. 902-25.

[65] Vladislav Solc, 'Concept of Sublimation in Psychology of Sigmund Freud and Carl Gustav Jung', *Therapy Vlado*, https://therapyvlado.com/english/concept-of-sublimation-in-psychology-of-sigmund-freud-and-carl-gustav-jung/.notes Jung's approach to ego transformation via sublimation, as distinct from Freud's approach, stating,

transformation is the most important concept in Jungian psychology and is used to describe the *variety* of processes. (Stein, 1985) Jung said: 'Sublimation is not a voluntary and the forcible channeling of instinct into a spurious field of application' (…) '*Sublimatio* is a great mystery. Freud has appropriated this concept and usurped it for the sphere of the will, and the bourgeois, rationalistic *theos*'.

For Freud, sublimation was an egoic process involving the libido, whereas Jung said it was a mystery. 'Sublimation', *APA Dictionary of Psychology*, https://dictionary.apa.org/sublimation:

In classical psychoanalytic theory, [sublimation is] a defense mechanism in which unacceptable sexual or aggressive drives are unconsciously channeled into socially acceptable modes of expression and redirected into new, learned behaviors, which indirectly provide some satisfaction for the original drives. For example, an exhibitionistic impulse may gain a new outlet in choreography; a voyeuristic urge may lead to scientific research; and a dangerously aggressive drive may be expressed with impunity on the football field. As well as allowing

Would John's possibly extreme asceticism explain Mark's description of his dietary practices and dress (Mk 1.6)? All indications suggest that John was not only severe in his declarations but also in managing his personhood.[66] If he adhered to a form of extreme asceticism resulting in a radically decentralized sense of 'I', did it curtail his embrace of the 'I' who partook of God's love? Did this hinder the true internal cleansing (of all that is less than whole) that comes through Christ's baptism with the Spirit and fire? Does John's personhood expose a fundamental brokenness that negatively impacted but did not preclude him from fulfilling the prophetic call that served the community's ability to receive and act on his word?

'Yes' would seem the obvious answer. However, from a psychological and phenomenological perspective, John's experience invites us to acknowledge that prophetic legitimacy is not necessarily equated with the absence of fragmentation. An elemental brokenness seems present in John. In some ways, it can be traced through the entire Lukan narrative concerning him, seeming to contrast his intensity in prophetic function with his human frailty and fragility.

3.3 Agabus: Stewarding the Charismatic Expression of Prophecy

3.3.1 Agabus from a Biblical and Theological Perspective (The First Prophetic Example)

Although Agabus' appearances in Scripture are brief, they suggest significance and are pertinent to the matter of prophetic legitimacy. Whereas a company of traveling prophets came to Antioch from

---

for substitute satisfactions, such outlets are posited to protect individuals from the anxiety induced by the original drive.

C.G. Jung, *The Collected Works of C.G. Jung, Volume 7: Two Essays in Analytical Psychology* (ed. Herbert Read, *et al.*; Princeton, NJ: Princeton University Press, 1985), ch. 4, was interested in rites of passage in various religious and tribal traditions and 'transformation mysteries', which for him had 'the greatest spiritual significance'. Therefore, Jung states, 'Very often the initiands are subjected to excruciating treatment, and at the same time the tribal mysteries are imparted to them, the laws and hierarchy of the tribe in one hand, and on the other the cosmogonic and mythical doctrines' (ch. 4).

[66] Jung, *Two Essays*, ch. 4, claimed that all cultures have initiation rites, and many of them, even in his day, had 'survived among all cultures'. Among these rites are Christianity's rites of 'baptism, confirmation, and communion'. Jung claimed these rites were 'somewhat faded and degenerated'.

Jerusalem, Luke mentions Agabus by name (Acts 11.27-28). Johnson notes that despite Luke's use of distinctly prophetic terms to describe 'Jesus and the apostles',[67] his use of the title *prophētēs* is rare.[68] Johnson cites many passages where this is evident.[69] Yet, Luke uses the term in reference to Agabus and other 'charismatic figures' who noticeably 'lack entirely the kind of stereotypical "prophetic" coloration Luke gives to his major characters'.[70] Thus Johnson distinguishes these prophetic figures from Jesus, John the Baptist, and even the more ancient Israelite prophetic voices.[71] Observing the distinction, Luke depicts Agabus as operating more in the gift of 'prophecy as an important charism'.[72]

The company of prophets Luke mentions is obviously known by the Jerusalem church. As *prophētēs*, their legitimacy is understood, and there is some expectation that their inspired speech will be operative in their expressions and exhortations. Agabus indeed prophesies. Luke notes that he 'stood up', using a recurring term in Luke-Acts,[73] which 'assumes a meeting of the congregation in which he [Agabus] actively participated'.[74] By the Spirit, Agabus then asserts that famine

---

[67] Johnson, *Acts of the Apostles*, p. 205.
[68] Johnson, *Acts of the Apostles*, p. 205.
[69] Johnson, *Acts of the Apostles*, p. 205:

It is given directly or indirectly to Jesus only in Luke 4:24; 7:16, 39; 13:33-34; 24:19; Acts 3:22-23; 7:37), and the other 'men of the spirit' in Acts are not called by this title (but see 15:32). Luke's main use of the title is for the 'prophets of old' either as persons or as authors of prophecy (Luke 1:70; 3:4; 4:17, 27; 6:23; 9:8, 19; 10:24; 11:4, 47, 49, 50; 13:28; 16:16, 29, 31; 18:31; 24:25, 27, 44; Acts 2:16, 30; 3:18, 21, 24, etc.). He also applies it to John the Baptist (Luke 1:76; 7:26, 28; 20:6).

[70] Johnson, *Acts of the Apostles*, p. 205.
[71] Johnson, *Acts of the Apostles*, p. 205.
[72] Johnson, *Acts of the Apostles*, p. 205, 'Paul recognized such prophecy as an important charism (1 Cor 12:28-29; 14:29, 32, 37; Eph 2:20; 3:5; 4:11)'. Johnson finds similitude between Agabus and the 'wandering prophets', as evidenced in other literature he cites: 'We have evidence of wandering prophets (as well as the problems they presented) in *The Didache 11:3-12*; *Shepherd of Hermas*, Mand. 11:1-21'.

[73] Johnson, *Acts of the Apostles*, 205:

The phrase 'standing up' (*anastas*) is frequently used by Luke almost as a helping verb (Luke 1:39; 4:29; 6:8; 15:18, 20; 17:19; 23:1; Acts 5:6; 9:18, 39; 10:13). At other times, however, it has the specific sense of 'standing' in an assembly, and that is the meaning here (Luke 4:16; Acts 1:15; 5:17, 34).

[74] Eckhard J. Schnabel, *Acts* (Zondervan Exegetical Commentary on the New Testament; Grand Rapids, MI: Zondervan, exp. edn, 2012), p. 525.

is coming to the entire Roman Empire.[75] The Greek word, *esēmanen*, lends itself to semiotic expression and is both gestural and vocal.[76] Whether in the act of standing to speak or in making some movement to illustrate, Agabus discloses what the Spirit shows him.[77] The word σημαίνω also contains a predictive element, implying an ability to 'intimate something respecting the future'.[78]

Schnabel explains that Agabus' prophecy 'has two elements: (1) a future event: a famine (λιμός) that would be severe; (2) the place

---

[75] *GEL*, p. 406:

33.153 σημαίνω: to cause something to be both specific and clear – 'to indicate clearly, to make clear'. ἄλογον γάρ μοι δοκεῖ πέμποντα δέσμιον μὴ καὶ τὰς κατ' αὐτοῦ αἰτίας σημᾶναι 'for it seems unreasonable to me to send a prisoner without clearly indicating the charges against him' Ac 25:27.

Johnson, *Acts of the Apostles*, pp. 205-206:

For the translation of *oikoumenē* (literally, 'inhabited world') as 'empire,' see the notes on Luke 2:1 and 4:5. These passages and those in Acts 17:6 and 24:5 give a thoroughly 'political' nuance to the term. Compare Lucian of Samosata, *The Octogenarians* 7, and Josephus' use of *romaios oikoumenē* in *Jewish War* 3:29. The advantage of the rendering is that it not only conforms to Luke's usage elsewhere but saves him the embarrassment of claiming a 'world-wide' famine that by-passes Antioch! In fact there is good supporting evidence for extensive famine during the reign of the emperor Claudius, who ruled from 41–54 C.E.; see Suetonius, *Life of Claudius* 18; Tacitus, *Annals* 12:43. Josephus mentions a great famine in Palestine during the forties (*Antiquities* 20:101), and explicitly mentions a famine in Judea during the reign of Claudius (*Antiquities* 3:320–21).

[76] Spiros Zodhiates (ed.), 'σημαίνω *sēmaínō*', *The Complete Word Study Dictionary: New Testament* (Chattanooga, TN: AMG, 2000):

4591. σημαίνω *sēmaínō*; Fut. *sēmanó*, Aor. *esḗmana*, from *sḗma* (n.f., see *ásēmos* [767]), a mark, sign. To give a public sign or signal (Sept.: Num. 10:9). In the NT to signify, make known, declare (John 12:33; 18:32; 21:19; Acts 11:28; 25:27; Rev. 1:1; Sept.: Judg. 7:21; Esth. 2:22). Syn.: *dēlóō* (1213), to declare; *emphanízō* (1718), to manifest; *diaggéllō* (1229), to declare, announce; *gnōrízō* (1107), to make known.

[77] Might Agabus have been sent to deliver this message by the Jerusalem church? Considering the response following his declaration in Antioch, the possibility warrants consideration. Would that nullify the spontaneity of his exercise of the prophetic gift? I propose that it would not. The source of the message is the Spirit. Whether the Spirit showed this to Agabus during the gathering in Antioch or while he was in Jerusalem does not alter that fact.

[78] It is clear, therefore, that whatever Agabus has been shown about a coming famine will impact the saints in Jerusalem in a particularly severe way., 'σημαίνω', *BAGD*, p. 755, 'σημαίνω ... to intimate someth. respecting the future, *indicate, suggest, intimate* ... προσημαίνειν τὰ μέλλοντα of divine prediction of the future) ... Also of speech that simply offers a vague suggestion of what is to happen'.

where this event will take place: throughout the world'.[79] '"Throughout the world" (ἐφ' ὅλην τὴν οἰκουμένην) ... can refer to the entire inhabited world, to the Roman empire, a much larger area than a specific region, and to a particular region'.[80] This prophetic utterance speaks of an empire-wide occurrence that, in Schnabel's view, affects Egypt's grain production and bodes ill for the entire Roman Empire, which relies heavily on Egyptian grain.[81] Losses in Egypt would alter the balance between the overall supply of grain and the demand for it. Gapp notes, 'the cost of wheat at this time was more than twice as high as any other recorded price in the Roman period before the reign of Vespasian',[82] implying the threat of starvation and death for the most vulnerable.

The disciples sense a certain responsibility to their fellow saints in Jerusalem (Acts 2.44-45), where the greater danger would exist, partly due to the costs of transporting grain by land.[83] Therefore, they collect money in Antioch and send it to Jerusalem with Barnabas and Paul.[84] Because Antioch's believers apprehend and accept the word that Agabus first apprehends, accepts, and faithfully enacts, they seek to respond adequately. Therefore, Agabus' stewardship of the charismatic expression of prophecy has life-saving implications. If Schnabel is correct, the Jerusalem church received assistance 'at least a year earlier than [they] received aid through the action of Helena'.[85] Their preparedness when the crisis arrived also confirms that what Agabus prophesied was true and attests to the legitimacy of the genuine Spirit of Christ at work in the community, particularly in relation to the love of God and of neighbor.

3.3.2 Agabus from a Biblical and Theological Perspective (The Second Prophetic Example)

Agabus' reappearance in Acts 21 is proximate to the mention of Philip's 'four unmarried daughters' (Acts 21.9). Luke says, '*We* left and came ... [to] the house of Philip the evangelist ... and stayed

---

[79] Schnabel, *Acts*, p. 525.
[80] Schnabel, *Acts*, p. 525.
[81] Schnabel, *Acts*, p. 525.
[82] Kenneth Sperber Gapp, 'The Universal Famine Under Claudius', *Harvard Theological Review* 28.4 (October 1935), p. 259.
[83] Gapp, 'Universal Famine Under Claudius', p. 260.
[84] Gapp, 'Universal Famine Under Claudius', p. 260.
[85] Schnabel, *Acts*, p. 525.

with him … for several days' (Acts 21.8, 10, emphasis added).[86] Luke, an eyewitness of what transpired, apprises Theophilus of Philip's four unmarried, prophetically functioning daughters, having already informed Theophilus of 'prophecies of suffering accompanying Paul throughout his journey to Jerusalem' (Acts 20.23; 21.4).[87] Given what follows from Agabus, might Luke's mention of Philip's daughters suggest that they bore witness to the same crisis as Agabus did? Lawrence R. Farley notes, 'it is difficult to resist the conclusion that [they] had the same message'.[88] Either way, the women 'speak under the influence of divine inspiration'.[89] Their voice is recognized by the community, and in bringing them to Theophilus' attention, Luke legitimizes their speaking for the Spirit.[90]

Luke then reveals that while Paul and his apostolic company are at Philip's house, Agabus comes from Judea to speak to Paul (Acts 21.10-11). Luke introduces Agabus 'with no indication that the reader should remember him' from the earlier mention in Acts 11,[91] which seems to suggest that Luke forgot having previously named him.[92]

---

[86] Schnabel, *Acts*, p. 856:

Philip is identified (1) as the evangelist … which recalls his earlier missionary work in Samaria (8:4-9) and on the road to Gaza (8:25-40), and (2) as a member of the Seven … appointed by the Jerusalem church to organize the support ministry for the widows of the congregation. Luke had 'left' Philip in Caesarea in 8:40 …. Philip evidently had settled in Caesarea … and preached the gospel before Jews and, presumably, Gentiles in Caesarea and the surrounding areas— presumably after the events connected with the conversion of Cornelius through the ministry of Peter (10:1-48). Paul and his companions stayed (ἐμείναμεν) in the house of Philip, 'for several days' as it turns out (v. 10).

[87] Lawrence R. Farley, *The Acts of the Apostles: Spreading the Word* (Orthodox Bible Study Companion; Chesterton, IN: Ancient Faith, 2012), p. 252.

[88] Farley, *Acts of the Apostles*, p. 252.

[89] *GEL*, p. 440:

33.459 προφητεύω [means] to speak under the influence of divine inspiration, with or without reference to future events – 'to prophesy, to make inspired utterances'. προφήτευσον, τίς ἐστιν ὁ παίσας σε; 'prophesy, Who hit you?' Lk 22:64; ἐπροφήτευσεν ὅτι ἔμελλεν Ἰησοῦς ἀποθνῄσκειν 'he prophesied that Jesus was about to die' Jn 11:51.

[90] This reveals that regarding prophetic function that is immersed in the Pentecostal and charismatic Spirit, there is no respect of persons, male or female.

[91] Farley, *Acts of the Apostles*, p. 370.

[92] Is this an editorial mistake or is it intentional?

Agabus' second prophetic enactment is as semiotic as the first.[93] Having presumably positioned himself near Paul, he 'took Paul's belt'.[94] Johnson highlights the semiotic dimension, stating:

> Agabus seems to have specialized in prophecies that involved symbolic gestures. Thus in 11:28 he 'signed' (*esēmanen*) the coming famine, and here he uses Paul's belt/girdle (*zōnē*) to physically enact the import of his words.[95]

This evokes Ahijah's symbolic gesture of tearing his new garment into twelve pieces (1 Kgs 11.29-30). It is also suggestive of Jeremiah's uses of a new linen loincloth and an earthenware jar in illustrative prophetic decrees (Jer. 13.1-2; 19.1-2).

What transpired in the second vignette is what contemporary Pentecostal jargon labels a *personal word* or *personal prophecy*. It resembles Samuel's informing Saul about lost donkeys being found and about signs that would ensue following his departure from Samuel on the day he was anointed as king (1 Sam. 10.1-8). Contemporary leaders who embrace prophetic function see this as an important aspect of such function. Regarding personal prophetic words, Bill Hamon asserts, 'God still wants the revelation of His will to be vocalized' and uses such words to convey 'His personal will for [people's] lives'.[96] Hamon considers prophetic agents capable of offering 'specific instructions to individuals' about God's intent for their lives.[97]

The question becomes, 'What are the boundaries and parameters in which such enactment operates legitimately?' This is extremely important concerning Agabus and Paul, and it encourages the question of who is listening to the Spirit properly. If the prophetic voices are harmonized in warning Paul, and if Agabus seals the warning by (1) binding his own hands and feet with Paul's leather belt, and (2)

---

[93] 'Semiotic', *Online Etymology Dictionary*, https://www.etymonline.com/search?q=semiotic.

Semiotic (adj) 1620s, 'of symptoms, relating to signs of diseases', from Greek *semeiotikos* 'significant', also 'observant of signs', adjective form of *semeiosis* 'indication', from *semeioun* 'to signal, to interpret a sign', from *semeion* 'a sign, mark, token', from *sema* 'sign' (see semantic). Its use in psychology dates to 1923.

[94] This serves as a sign-act in relation to the prophetic utterance Agabus is about to give.

[95] Johnson, *Acts of the Apostles*, p. 370.

[96] Hamon, *Prophets and Personal Prophecy*, p. 33.

[97] Hamon, *Prophets and Personal Prophecy*, p. 33.

punctuating the act with an emphatic 'Thus says the Holy Spirit',[98] what is Paul's appropriate response?

Clearly, Luke sees Agabus' word as being legitimate. However, it is not an isolated word. Paul has already told the elders from Ephesus that he considers himself 'captive to the Spirit' to go to Jerusalem and even expresses uncertainty as to 'what will happen to [him] there' (Acts 20.22). Ironically, he adds, despite his uncertainty, that 'the Holy Spirit testifies to [him] in every city that imprisonment and persecutions are waiting for [him]' (Acts 20.23). Where then is the uncertainty?

Regardless of the prophetic witnesses and their warnings, Paul intentionally draws closer to Jerusalem.[99] Having been warned prior to Agabus' message, the man's prophetic act might perhaps persuade Paul to rethink his position. Is this the point – an ultimate graphic appeal for Paul to reconsider? Agabus claims sanction from the Spirit in his enactment, which raises a question about the subjectivity and intersubjectivity that transpire in prophetic function, even in personal prophecy. Agabus' declaration, 'Thus says the Holy Spirit', is reminiscent of many prophetic utterances among the ancient prophets.[100] However, Johnson notes its 'unparalleled' nature in the NT context.[101] If the formula is unparalleled, its significance is intended to stand out even more, so what is Luke inviting Theophilus to discern? Is Paul recalcitrant, as Zechariah was?[102] Or is the choir of prophetic voices that is resonating with Agabus undeserving of Paul's heed?

---

[98] This is redolent of the ancient Israelite prophets. '([S]ee Amos 3:11; 5:16; Nah 1:2; Haggai 1:6; Zech 1:16; Isa 3:16; Jer 2:31; Ezek 4:13)' (Johnson, *Acts of the Apostles*, p. 370).

[99] Luke bears personal witness that the Ephesian elders were 'grieving especially because of what he [Paul] had said, that they would not see him again' (Acts 20.38 NRSV). Is this grief attached to his departure from Ephesus or his imprisonment and eventual death (or both)?

[100] Exodus 4.22; 5.1; 7.17; 8.1, 20; 9.1, 13; 10.3; 11.4; 32.27; Josh. 7.13; 24.2; Judg. 6.8; 1 Sam. 10.16; 15.2; 2 Sam. 7.5, 8; 12.7, 11; 24.12; 1 Kgs 11.31; 12.24; 13.2, 21; 14.7; 17.14; 20.13, 14, 28, 42; 21.19; 22.11; 2 Kgs 1.4, 6, 16; 2.21; 3.16, 17; 4.43; 7.1; 9.3, 6, 12; 19.6, 20, 32; 20.1, 5; 21.12. There are many more examples from the Chronicles and from the Latter Prophets (Isaiah through Malachi).

[101] Johnson, *Acts of the Apostles*, p. 370, writes,

> The only other instance in the NT is found in the 'Spirit Letters' of the Book of Revelation, which probably derive at least in part from the oracles of Christian prophets (see Rev 2:1, 8, 12, 18; 3:1, 7, 14). The use of 'the Holy Spirit' with the formula is, so far as I can tell, unparalleled.

[102] See Chironna, 'Zechariah', https://www.markchironna.com/articles.

Paul is clear regarding Agabus' binding of hands and feet: the prophetic enactment is above question (Acts 20.23). When Paul enters the Temple in Jerusalem, the Asian Judaizers relentlessly pursuing him have now 'stirred up the whole crowd' (Acts 21.27), leading to Paul's nearly mortal beating and his placement in bonds based on false accusations (Acts 21.29-33).[103] Prior to these events, Paul was in Philip's house voicing his grief ahead of his coming departure (Acts 21.13). The violence just described was still ahead, yet Paul avowed that he was prepared to die for Jesus' name. Luke indicates that Paul did not fear such martyrdom but counted it an honor and 'would not be persuaded' to avoid the suffering ahead (Acts 20.13).[104] With resignation, Luke wrote, 'we [therefore] remained silent except to say, "The Lord's will be done"' (Acts 21.14). Those around Paul had been far from silent, as evidenced by their open grief. When their concerns failed to change Paul's posture, their only option was to adjust their own, which explains their 'state of silence'.[105]

3.3.3 Agabus from a Psychological and Phenomenological Perspective

Although they are concise, the Agabus narratives contain significant psychological and phenomenological insights that indicate prophetic legitimacy. Regarding prophetic enactment, Johnson writes,

> The prophet is led by the Holy Spirit not only to announce God's word – that is, God's vision for humanity – but also to *embody* that word in the prophet's own manner of life, and to seek to realize that word through action in the world.[106]

Luke presents Agabus as being Spirit-led, and his charismatically inspired speech and gestures indicate his declaring of something God has revealed. Psychologically and phenomenologically, Agabus' gestures imply his cognitive embodiment of the message. The Agabus

---

[103] The Jews will not bind Paul's hands. The Gentiles carry out that act. Johnson, *Acts of the Apostles*, p. 370, insightfully infers: 'The Gentiles (*ethnōn*) makes this prophecy echo the passion predictions of Jesus himself in Luke 9:44; 18:32'.

[104] Paul would not be persuaded or convinced, as in '33.301 πείθω*: to convince someone to believe something and to act on the basis of what is recommended – "to persuade, to convince"', *GEL*, p. 423.

[105] *GEL*, p. 402, '33.119 ἡσυχάζω^c; ἡσυχία^b, as *f* [means] to maintain a state of silence, with a possible focus upon the attitude involved – "to say nothing, to remain quiet"'.

[106] Johnson, *Prophetic Jesus, Prophetic Church*, p. 130 (emphasis added).

vignettes exemplify the prophetic temperament that intimates his pronouncement through his 'action in the world'.[107]

Agabus' cognitive embodiment, which is inseparable from his temperament, speaks to his manner of life.[108] Within the construct of temperament, psychologists recognize a 'shy-bold continuum'.[109] Agabus' temperament in Luke-Acts seems to favor the continuum's bolder side. Within the framework of what I am calling a *prophetic temperament*, there is no sense of self-will; nor is there a sense in which Agabus is attempting to make his actions original. It can be considered here that his formation in the tradition of the ancient Israelite prophets precedes his prophetic expressions.

Butler reminds us, 'first appearances in Scripture are often the key to what follows'.[110] Agabus was known in Christian communities yet perhaps unknown in Antioch, depending on one's reading of the narrative. He is 'characterized by abruptness, boldness, zealousness, and the dramatic',[111] making his appearances reminiscent of Elijah's as he emerged from obscurity to prophesy in Ahab's courts (1 Kings 17 and 18). Elijah announces a drought that will demand repentance from his audience. Similarly, Agabus foretells an empire-wide famine that demands a response of love from those who can help Jerusalem's most vulnerable – the poor.

Considering this guidance, the Agabus context ironically suggests a posture of partiality and ethnocentrism that delays the gospel's transmission 'to the ends of the earth' (Acts 1.8). The Jerusalem faith community's tardiness involves a protracted hesitation in obeying

---

[107] Johnson, *Prophetic Jesus, Prophetic Church*, p. 130.

[108] 'Temperament', *APA Dictionary of Psychology*, https://dictionary.apa.org/temperament: as 'the basic foundation of personality', temperament is 'usually assumed to be biologically determined and present early in life, including such characteristics as energy level, emotional responsiveness, demeanor, mood, response tempo, behavioral inhibition, and willingness to explore'.

[109] 'Shy-Bold Continuum', *APA Dictionary of Psychology*, https://dictionary.apa.org/shy-bold-continuum:

> The tendency of some individuals within a group to be fearful or cautious of new stimuli and of others to explore novel stimuli. The more fearful individuals are less likely to be preyed on but also less able to use new resources. A shy–bold continuum has been demonstrated in many species, from fish through human beings, and may be a universal dimension of behavioral variation.

[110] John G. Butler, *Elijah: The Prophet of Confrontation* (Bible Biography Series 3; Clinton, IA: LBC, 1994), p. 14.

[111] Butler, *Elijah*, p. 14.

Jesus' command.[112] The transition to a multiethnic community produces psychological shifts in consciousness, including changes in 'personal attitudes, laws, institutional policies, and informal practices that perpetuate race, ethnic and gender biases'.[113] The publicly and privately held attitudes and biases of the Jews toward Samaritans, for example, indicate the issues facing the Jewish community that embraced Christ's Lordship.[114] From the establishment of Samaria as the Northern Kingdom's capital, 'feelings, cognitions, and behavioral predispositions' between Jews and Samaritans deteriorated.[115] However, Luke-Acts makes the theological point that the Samaritans are not outsiders but part of Israel (Acts 1.8).[116]

---

[112] The details Luke provides cannot be ignored. The stoning of Stephen in CE 35 leads to the scattering of believers (except for the apostles) 'throughout the countryside of Judea and Samaria' (Acts 8.1), with some going as far as 'Phoenicia, Cyprus, and Antioch' (Acts 11.19). At Antioch, Barnabas witnesses God's grace among the Gentiles and becomes a strong encourager (Acts 11.23). Although ethnocentricity produced resistance, Barnabas embraced the Gentiles and sought to build bridges. Antioch became pivotal in that regard. Luke shows that while many of the saints were 'scattered because of the persecution that took place over Stephen' in approximately 35–36 CE (about six years after the Day of Pentecost), '*some … on coming to Antioch … spoke to the Hellenists*' (Acts 11.19-20). Their efforts were fruitful, as 'a great number became believers' (Acts 11.21). The mention about Greeks alerts us to a growing challenge as the gospel advanced into Gentile territory. Apart from persecution, the saints would not have dispersed for mission, and only some of them reached out to the Greeks. Barnabas was sent from Jerusalem because of his gracious and encouraging demeanor. Luke does not hide the earliest church's ethnocentrism, even disclosing Simon Peter's resistance toward an ecstatic vision (Acts 10.9-16). Simon Peter confesses before Cornelius and others his former tendency toward favoritism, partiality, and elitism that God rejects (Acts 10.34). He states, 'You yourselves know that it is unlawful for a Jew to associate with or to visit a Gentile; but God has shown me that I should not call anyone profane or unclean' (Acts 10.28).

[113] James M. Jones, John F. Davidio, and Deborah L. Vietze, *The Psychology of Diversity: Beyond Prejudice and Racism* (Chichester: Blackwell, 2014), ch. 2.

[114] See Jn 4.9. James and John wished to call down fire on the Samaritans, based on the presumed precedent of Elijah's act (Lk. 9.51-56; 2 Kgs 1:1-18). Acknowledging the split between the Northern and Southern Kingdoms after Solomon (as prophesied by Ahijah in 1 Kgs 11.31-35), Luke shows that the prophetic Messiah came to bring reconciliation. Since 740 BCE, Pul and Tiglath-pileser, kings of Assyria conquered the Northern Kingdom (1 Chron. 5.26) and brought in foreigners to comingle with the Israelites. Within two decades and after the siege, Samaria became the Northern Kingdom's capital (722 BCE, 2 Kgs 17.5-6).

[115] Jones, Davidio, and Vietze, *Psychology of Diversity*, ch. 2.

[116] According to James L. Jones, *et al.*, prejudice is a multifaceted attitude comprised *cognitively* of irrational beliefs about others, *affectively* of negative feelings toward them, and *behaviorally* of 'a tendency to avoid or harm the target group'. Jones,

Agabus' presence indicates that he was willing to forego the Jewish community's hesitancies.[117] Psychologically and phenomenologically, he presents as a bold and courageous figure.[118] Delivering his prophetic utterances required such characteristics, yet his careful and humble address of Paul reveals a sensitivity of prophetic temperament. First, Agabus defers to the Spirit. Second, he refers to Paul not by name but as 'the man who owns this belt' (Acts 21.11). This couching of words conveys respect and honor and seems to indicate a tempering through wisdom that guides Agabus' delivery before someone of Paul's stature. Also, his reference to Paul as 'the man'

Davidio, and Vietze, *Psychology of Diversity*, ch. 2. All three components were present in Jewish-Samaritan relations, the former contending against the latter. According to Gordon W. Allport, *The Nature of Prejudice* (New York: Perseus Books, 25th anniversary edn, 1979), p. 6, 'Ethnic prejudice is an antipathy based on a faulty and inflexible generalization' that targets groups or those who associate with them. For Agabus, therefore, the journey from Jerusalem to Antioch is more than physical; it also reveals a necessary transformation of consciousness that would allow the Messianic community to embrace the Gentiles. This need is expressed from a Lukan perspective. Agabus does not display any sort of 'negative attitude that is unfair and unjust and contributes to persistent disadvantage among peoples and groups', Jones, Davidio, and Vietze, *Psychology of Diversity*, ch. 2. By the time we see the prophets with Agabus in multiethnic Antioch, 'social and structural bias' is not present among the narrative's key players, Jones, Davidio, and Vietze, *Psychology of Diversity*, ch. 2.

[117] The Lukan account suggests that persecution triggered the gospel's spread outside Jerusalem. Had the apostles grown too comfortable where they once feared staying? Jesus made the mission clear; however, persecution brought its accomplishment. This poses questions about the resistance to building multiethnic communities of faith. Like Barnabas, Agabus seems to embrace the Gentiles. The promise that all nations would be blessed through the seed of Abraham (Gal. 3.8; Gen. 12.3), had not changed. Miroslav Volf, *Exclusion and Embrace: A Theological Exploration of Identity, Otherness, and Reconciliation* (Nashville, TN: Abingdon Press, 2019), ch. 1, reminds us that the blessing promised to Abraham was 'laying the foundations for a multi-ethnic community'. For Luke, those foundations include the narrative of the Temple, the legal tradition, and the prophetic tradition, plus the presence of an apostolic and prophetic company of figures (Acts 1.13-17; 9.1-9; 11.22, 27). In Eph. 2.20, Paul informs his churches that the New Covenant community is built upon this foundation.

[118] Stanley J. Grenz and Jay T. Smith, 'Courage', *Pocket Dictionary of Ethics* (IVP Pocket Reference Series; Downers Grove, IL: InterVarsity Press, 2003): Courage is defined as

> a virtue that entails the capability to endure, resist or alter adversity. Together with wisdom, justice and temperance, courage (or fortitude) – defined as the ability to act according to reason in the face of fear – is numbered among the four cardinal virtues of ancient Greek thought. The Bible enjoins a courage that goes beyond the mere managing of one's fears, for the exercise of this virtue arises out of confidence in God.

invokes Paul's humanness and Agabus' concerns for any corresponding susceptibilities. These choices reveal the prophetic temperament of a charismatic prophet who lived in the 'dance' between subjectivity and intersubjectivity.

The classical prophetism of ancient Israel would seem to have influenced Agabus' development.[119] From a psychological and phenomenological perspective, his behavior required a consciousness of divine calling. As Aune states, this consciousness 'is often thought to be integral to the prophetic role'.[120] Such an awareness seems evident in the Agabus accounts.

3.4 Paul: Apostle to the Gentiles Owing to Jeremiah's Prophetic Tradition

3.4.1 Paul from a Biblical and Theological Perspective

In developing the great mission of the gospel, Luke devotes the first

---

[119] As mentioned, Agabus' prophetic declaration regarding famine is suggestive of Elijah's proclamation of a drought (1 Kgs 17.1), and the taking of Paul's belt evokes Jeremiah's wearing of the linen loincloth (Jer. 13.1-11). All of Jeremiah's and Ezekiel's sign-acts were well-known in the early Christian community of Jewish believers, and Agabus would have been familiar with them. Kelvin G. Friebel, *Jeremiah's and Ezekiel's Sign-Acts* (JSOTSup 283; Sheffield: Sheffield Academic Press, 1999), pp. 14-15:

> The term 'sign-act' is applied to all the nonverbal behaviors (i.e. bodily movements, gestures and paralanguage) whose primary purpose was communicative and interactive: Jer. 13:1-11; 16:1-9; 19:1-13; chs. 27–28; 32:1-44; 35:1-19; 43:8-13; 51:59–64a; Ezek. 3:22-27 / 24:25-27 / 33:21-22; chs. 4–5; 6:11-12; 12:1-16; 12:17-20; 21:11-29; 24:15-24; 37:15-28. By the inclusion of such acts as the clapping in Ezek. 6:11-12 and the wailing in Ezek. 21:17-22, the category of 'sign-act' is broader than the traditional connotations of the appellation 'symbolic action' whose criteria for classification were frequently based not on the nonverbal function or purpose but on literary form. Thus if the account of a nonverbal behavior did not correspond to the form-critical structure, or if the behavior was viewed as being a stereotypical gesture ... the behavior was not classified as a 'symbolic action'. But such distinctions do not correspond with definitions and categories as employed within the studies of nonverbal communication where the communicative nature of a nonverbal action is not contingent on the form of its literary recounting, or on whether it is an idiosyncratic or stereotypical behavior, or on it having a specific type of conjunction with the verbal part of the message.

[120] Aune, *Prophecy in Early Christianity*, p. 97.

half of Acts to Peter, the apostle to the Jews.[121] The second half of Acts emphasizes Paul, the apostle to the Gentiles (Gal. 2.8).[122] In Acts 28, Luke depicts Paul in his rented quarters in Rome, awaiting his martyrdom and 'proclaiming the kingdom of God and teaching about the Lord Jesus Christ with all boldness and without hindrance' (v. 31).[123] Acts 28.26-27 records Paul's prophetic reiteration of Isaiah's reproof from Isa. 6.9-10. Paul closes, saying, 'Let it be known to you then that this salvation of God has been sent to the Gentiles; they will listen' (Acts 28.28).

Although the ancient prophets spoke of the 'sufferings destined for Christ' (1 Pet. 1.11), the 'subsequent glory' Peter names includes the fulfillment and results of the outpouring Joel promised (1 Pet. 1.11; Acts 2.14-36). Paramount is Saul's apprehension by the ascended Christ,[124] after which he confesses that he 'was violently persecuting the church of God and was trying to destroy it' (Gal. 1.13). While 'breathing threats and murder against the disciples of the Lord'

---

[121] 'σύ', *BAGD*, pp. 779-80, 'Peter is first to be given the "keys"' (Matthew 16:19) In the Greek here 'you' is not plural, but rather personal: σύ (Hom.+) personal pron. of the second pers. σοῦ (σου), σοί (σοι), σέ (σε); pl. ὑμεῖς, ὑμῶν, ὑμῖν, ὑμᾶς: *you*'. On the Day of Pentecost, therefore, it falls to Peter to open the gateway to the Jews and proclaim the fulfillment of what Joel prophesied (Acts 2.14-21). Because the mission to the Gentiles must also be opened (and Saul has not yet emerged from his formation), Peter opens it using the keys (Acts 10.44). The Spirit fills those who heard him, despite his reticence and wrestling with ethnic prejudice (Acts 10.28). In the vision to 'kill and eat' (Acts 10.13), *kill* was a metaphor related to his ethnic prejudice. The *eating* metaphorically indicated Peter's need to embrace the Gentiles' assimilation into Abraham's blessing.

[122] Luke traveled with Paul and joined his circle of intimates just prior to Paul's call to Macedonia (Acts 16.9-10).

[123] Johnson, *Acts of the Apostles*, p. 473, 'The conditions of Paul's Roman captivity are sufficiently lenient to allow visitors ... Such accessibility makes the practical directives issued by Paul's captivity letters appear more plausible (see Phil 2:19-30; 4:18; Col 4:7-17; 2 Tim 1:16-17; 4:9-13)'.

[124] Keener's insights into Luke's framing of this beg consideration, Craig S. Keener, *Acts: An Exegetical Commentary: Introduction and 1:1–14:28* (Grand Rapids, MI: Baker Academic, 2012), I, pp. 1597-98:

> Why does Luke place Paul's conversion at this point in his narrative? It appears here immediately after the first Gentile's conversion (8:26-40) but immediately before Peter's Judean mission (9:32-43), which leads to Cornelius' conversion, apparently more widely known in the early Christian movement (10:1–11:18). It holds a strategic position in the narrative's logic: the conversion of the apostle to the Gentiles. It thus stands as one of three almost consecutive conversion stories (minus the material in 9:32-43 that prepares for Peter's ministry to Cornelius): the African official, Paul, and Cornelius.

(Acts 9.1), Saul encountered the theophanic glory and was temporarily blinded by an open vision (Acts 9.8-9).[125] Johnson notes, 'the verb translated "flashed" (as lightning, *periastraptō*) is used only here, and forms another connection to the story in 4 Macc 4:10'.[126] The flash blinded and disoriented Paul,[127] yet his eyes remained opened.[128] The audition of Christ's voice indicated his active presence with his disciples. His words implied that he was united with his followers, so that Saul's persecution of them was persecution of him.[129] For Johnson, the voice amid the blinding light recalls 'the voice from the bush in Exod 3:3 ("Moses, Moses") and from Mt. Sinai (Exod 19:16-20)'.[130] Jesus calls Saul's name twice, a significant pattern that Paul would have associated with three figures denoted as prophets in the canonical record.[131] Therefore, although this theophany is widely referred to as Saul's conversion, it reflects the prophetic calls of ancient Israelite prophets, all of which were qualified by Yahweh's self-disclosure.[132]

Although Paul equates his calling from the womb with the prophet Jeremiah's testimony (Jer. 1.5; Gal. 1.15), it is Saul's vision of

---

[125] This was well established in the prophetic tradition: Exod. 19.16; 2 Sam. 22.15; Ps. 17.14; 77.17; 96.4; 143.6; Ezek. 1.4, 7, 13; Dan. 10.6.

[126] Johnson, *Acts of the Apostles*, p. 163, 'And while Apollonius was going up with his armed forces to seize the money, angels on horseback with lightning flashing from their weapons appeared from heaven, instilling in them great fear and trembling' (4 Macc. 4.10).

[127] Years later, Paul testified to King Agrippa that it was brighter than the sun, saying, 'When at midday along the road, Your Excellency, I saw a light from heaven, brighter than the sun, shining around me and my companions' (Acts 26.13).

[128] As it was with Apollonius in the Maccabean record (4 Macc. 4.10).

[129] This was the genesis of revelation regarding the church as Christ's body. Here, it was seeded and would take theological shape in Saul's consciousness and logic. See Rom. 12.5; 1 Cor. 12.12-27; Eph. 3.6, 4.15-16, 5.23; Col. 1.18, 24.

[130] Johnson, *Acts of the Apostles*, p. 163.

[131] 'Abraham, Abraham!' (Gen. 22.11-13); 'Jacob, Jacob' (Gen. 46.1-4); 'Moses, Moses!' (Exod. 3.1-10); 'Samuel, Samuel!' (1 Sam. 3.1-10). This also happens to two others: 'Martha, Martha' (Lk. 10.38-42); 'Simon, Simon' (Lk. 22.31-32). God calls Abraham a prophet (Gen. 20.7); Moses is called a prophet (Deut. 18.15-18); Samuel is called a prophet (1 Sam. 3.20).

[132] That tradition conforms to the plumb line of Jer. 23.18: 'For who has stood in the council of the LORD so as to see and to hear his word? Who has given heed to his word so as to proclaim it?' As to God's self-disclosure, Stephen stated, 'the God of glory appeared to our ancestor Abraham when he was in Mesopotamia' (Acts 7.2). Jesus declared that Abraham 'saw [my day]' (Jn 8.56). God said he spoke 'face to face' with Moses (Num. 12.8). Samuel's encounter with the Lord was both auditory and visual (the Lord 'stood there, calling' him in 1 Sam. 3.10).

the ascended Christ that confirms his calling.[133] Saul knows this is God. Yet he faces a quandary,[134] which Johnson confirms in Saul's question, 'Who are you, Lord?' (Acts 9.5). As Johnson explains,

> The title *kyrios* ('Lord') should be taken at full value. Saul does not yet know it is *Jesus* who is Lord, but he recognizes that he is involved in a theophany! Such dialogue within a revelatory experience clearly serves the literary function of making the import of the experience clear to the reader (see Gen 15:1-6; Exod 3:4-15; Judg 6:11-18; 13:8-20).[135]

Saul's question leads to the divine self-disclosure: 'I am Jesus, whom you are persecuting' (Acts 9.6). This is not a dead Nazarene speaking but the risen Messiah. Ralph C. Wood notes from an Orthodox perspective that Christ identified with the church, implying that 'to oppress the church is to oppress Christ'.[136] Because he emphasized this relational reality over his identification as the Messiah and Son of God,[137] the theophany's subjective impact would bear down on Paul's psyche, bringing into sharp relief his malignant behavior toward the disciples and its impact on the heavenly Man. There is no room for Saul to respond; the command to get up implies that no other

---

[133] It could be argued that Paul sees his calling as conforming to the prophetic tradition, with the apostolic calling emerging from the ancient and preceding prophetic tradition (1 Cor. 1.1).

[134] Thomas G. Weinandy, 'Response: Paul's Conversion in His Own Words', in Charles Raith (ed.), *The Book of Acts: Catholic, Orthodox, and Evangelical Readings* (Washington, DC: Catholic University of America Press, 2019), p. 180:

> Some translations here translate κύριε as 'sir' rather than 'Lord'. They do so thinking that, at this initial point in the conversation, Paul does not know that he is speaking to the Lord Jesus and so is merely responding to an anonymous person, whom he is respectfully addressing as 'sir'. However, I believe this is a false interpretative translation. Because of the heavenly brilliant light that surrounds him, Paul perceives that he is in the presence of God, the Lord, but he does not know who this God, the Lord, might be whom he is persecuting, for he, up until this point, firmly believes he is zealously doing the Lord God's will by persecuting Christians. Paul is mentally utterly disordered and emotionally wholly distraught! His question – 'Who are you, Lord?' – is his befuddled attempt to sort things out. Jesus replies: 'I am Jesus, whom you are persecuting; but rise and enter the city, and you will be told what you are to do' (Acts 9:5-6).

[135] Johnson, *Acts of the Apostles*, p. 163.

[136] Ralph C. Wood, 'Divine Action and Human Response: Four Theological and Visual Interpretations of Paul's Conversion in Acts 9', in Charles Raith (ed.), *The Book of Acts: Catholic, Orthodox, and Evangelical Readings* (Washington, DC: Catholic University of America Press, 2019), p. 139.

[137] Wood, 'Divine Action', p. 139.

questions remain.¹³⁸ What does remain is obedience: Paul has to be led by the hand into Damascus, his impairment producing a fresh awareness of the consequences ahead and the consciousness yet to be transformed.

Regarding those who attended to Paul, discrepancies exist about what they saw and heard.¹³⁹ Paul's blindness lasted three days,¹⁴⁰ during which he neither ate nor drank. Whether he lost his appetite or found it necessary to abstain (or both), Luke does not say. Johnson insists, 'Paul is going through a holy period of transition, a stage of liminality, whose end is shown by his resuming the taking of food in 9:19'.¹⁴¹ Assuming this characterization of the transition, Saul has entered a place of thought and prayer (Acts 9.11-12), where he awaits further instruction from Ananias. Having experienced his own 'vision', Ananias has received the Lord's instruction regarding Saul. Because Ananias fears Saul's reputation for persecuting believers, he initially resists the Lord's directions. However, in Acts 9.15-16, the Lord allays his fears and reveals that Saul

- is a chosen instrument;
- will bring the name of Jesus before the Gentiles and earthly rulers;
- will bring Jesus' name to Israel's people;

---

¹³⁸ *GEL*, p. 794:

89.125 ἀλλά ᵃ: a marker of more emphatic contrast (as compared with δέ ᶜ, 89.124) – 'but, instead, on the contrary.' οὐκ ἦλθον καταλῦσαι ἀλλὰ πληρῶσαι 'I have not come to do away (with them), but to give (their teachings) full sense' Mt 5:17; τὸ παιδίον οὐκ ἀπέθανεν ἀλλὰ καθεύδει 'the child is not dead but is sleeping' Mk 5:39.

¹³⁹ Johnson, *Acts of the Apostles*, p. 163:

He saw nothing: Some Latin *mss* add color to the account by having Paul say to his companions, 'raise me from the ground,' and when they raised him, he saw nothing. Other *mss* have 'no one' (*oudena*) rather than 'nothing' (*ouden*). Paul will later bring a similar blindness on his opponent, the magician Elymas, as a punishment (Acts 13:11).

Keener, *Acts*, p. 1600, 'Although the basic picture is secure, a comparison of the three accounts of Paul's conversion in Acts raises questions concerning some of the details: Who fell (Acts 26:14; 9:4, 7)? Did they all hear Jesus (9:7; 22:9)?'

¹⁴⁰ Given the emphasis on the third day in relation to Christ's passion and the gospel message, there may be a semiotic connection in Luke's detail regarding the number of days that Saul is without sight, bread, and beverage. As Christ rose from death on the third say, Saul undergoes a certain sharing in his death, burial, and resurrection. Consider Lk. 24.21, 46; 1 Cor. 15.4.

¹⁴¹ Johnson, *Acts of the Apostles*, p. 164.

- will suffer for Jesus' name.

When Ananias obeys God and reaches Saul, he lays hands and affirms his brotherhood with the person whose spiritual family now consists of those he once persecuted (Acts 9.17).[142] Ananias baptizes Saul. Saul eats and regains his strength and abides with the disciples in Damascus. He begins proclaiming the message, stirring no small commotion (Acts 9.18-22). A bounty is placed on his head, and he is lowered through a window in the city wall to escape certain death (Acts 9.23-25). Saul's sufferings for Christ have begun.

In Jerusalem, Barnabas meets Saul, provides him entrance into the community, and allays the church's fears about him (Acts 9.26-27). Saul's preaching stirs more commotion and a death threat by the Hellenists (Acts 9.28-29).[143] Later, when Barnabas witnesses God's grace in Antioch, he realizes that Saul is needed there. He searches for Saul in Tarsus and returns to Antioch with him (Acts 11.25-26). There the two men lead and teach for a year (Acts 11.26), during which the relief offering for Jerusalem is gathered and eventually delivered (Acts 11.29-30).[144]

3.4.1.1 Paul Among the Prophets and Teachers

In Acts 13, Luke focuses on Paul and 'the gospel['s] spread throughout the Mediterranean world'.[145] Preceding this spread is the

---

[142] The fact that something like scales fell from his eyes indicates that although this theophany was beyond physical (Acts 9.18), it affected Saul's physicality.

[143] The attempt was foiled by believers who discovered the Hellenists' intent. Saul was ushered to Caesarea and sent to Tarsus, his place of origin (Acts 9.30).

[144] The relief offering responds to the famine Agabus prophesied. In this same era, Herod puts James, the lead elder in Jerusalem, to death and imprisons Peter. Regarding Barnabas and Saul, Luke's careful telling of Barnabas' relationship to Jerusalem, Antioch, and Saul (and the interrelations among all four) highlights Saul's significance to the mission to the Gentiles and elucidates the logical shift toward Saul/Paul as the focus of apostolic mission for the remaining Acts narrative. According to Johnson, *Acts of the Apostles*, p. 225,

> the pattern is set in this first passage. By having Saul recruited by Barnabas to work in the Church at Antioch (11:25–26), Luke had signaled to the reader that Saul was acceptable to the Jerusalem leadership. Then by having him sent with Barnabas to deliver the collection to the needy Church in Jerusalem, he showed further how Saul symbolically demonstrated through the disposition of possessions his obedience to that leadership (11:27–30).

[145] Johnson, *Acts of the Apostles*, p. 225. Johnson and Schnabel offer insight in this regard. Per Johnson,

commissioning by a prophetic presbytery in Antioch consisting of five leadership figures labeled as 'prophets and teachers' (Acts 13.1). What does this dual appellation denote? Does the coordinating conjunction *and* imply that some are prophets and some teachers? Or are all five leaders functioning in both roles?[146]

Considering the five, Dunn suggests that Acts 13.1-3 demonstrates 'the more charismatic ordering of the churches which Paul founded'.[147] He notes that James led the Jerusalem church, but the church at Antioch was headed by 'a group of five "prophets and teachers"' who fasted, attended 'to the voice of the Spirit', and demonstrated 'a readiness to commission their own missionaries'.[148] In Dunn's estimation, the Antioch model framed Paul's concept and teaching regarding the building of church community.[149]

If more can be concluded, it is this: while the Jerusalem church was more of a gathering place for the apostles, Antioch moved toward a prophetic and didactic model. It could be argued that prior to the dispersion of the apostles from Jerusalem by persecution, there

---

Luke's stated goal, we remember, is to provide *asphaleia* ('security') to Gentile readers by showing how the promises first made to Israel have been extended faithfully to them as well. We do not find here, therefore, a renegade apostle who abandons Israel and delivers a suspect gospel to the Gentiles, but an apostle whose divine commission is confirmed by prophetic election and the charge of the Church, whose activities are not only filled with the prophetic spirit but also mirror those of Jesus and Peter before him, who remains in constant contact with Jerusalem, and who until the very end of the story tries to convert his fellow Jews (p. 225).

Per Schnabel, *Acts*, p. 547:

In this second half of Acts, Luke relates in four major sections the missionary work of Paul in the cities of Cyprus and southern Galatia (13:1–15:33), his work in Macedonia and Achaia (15:35–18:22), his work in Ephesus (18:23–20:38), and his imprisonment in Jerusalem, Caesarea, and Rome (21:17–28:31). The present text is the first of five episodes which comprise Period 7 of Paul's missionary work (see *In Depth: Paul's Missionary Work*): Paul and Barnabas proclaim the gospel in several cities on Cyprus, south Galatia, and Pamphylia (13:14–14:23) – in Salamis and Paphos (13:1-12), Pisidian Antioch (13:13-52), Iconium (14:1-7), Lystra (14:8-20), and in Derbe and Perge (14:21-28).

[146] When Paul instructs the church at Corinth, he indicates, 'God has appointed in the church first apostles, *second prophets, third teachers*; then deeds of power, then gifts of healing, forms of assistance, forms of leadership, various kinds of tongues' (1 Cor. 12.28, emphasis added).

[147] James D.G. Dunn, *Beginning from Jerusalem* (Christianity in the Making 2; Grand Rapids, MI: Eerdmans, 2009), pp. 319-20.

[148] Dunn, *Beginning from Jerusalem*, pp. 319-20.

[149] Dunn, *Beginning from Jerusalem*, pp. 319-20.

was a disproportionately large retinue of what, in the current vernacular, might be called 'senior leadership' – specifically, a raft of residing apostles. Antioch seems preparatory to the more charismatic ordering of the churches that Paul founded, as indicated by his placement of the prophetic and teaching functions in relation to the local assembly (1 Cor. 12.28).

Why does Luke only mention prophets and teachers? Dunn reminds us, 'this is the only place in Acts where "teachers" as such appear'.[150] Regarding the importance of the coordinating conjunction, I agree with Dunn's assertion,

> the two together imply a balance necessary to the life of any church – an openness to new insight and development inspired by the Spirit (the role of the prophet), balanced by a loyalty to the tradition taught and interpreted (the role of the teacher).[151]

Yet, is it not possible that prophets (who are open to new insights and development by the Spirit) are also apt to teach and capable of balancing that with loyalty to the Tradition? Schnabel infers that possibility and suggests that clear-cut 'roles and functions of apostles, prophets, and teachers' were not necessarily apparent in the nascent church.[152] He notes, 'Peter, Paul, and Barnabas seem to have been apostles, prophets, and teachers in one'.[153] Thus, the coordinating conjunction in 'prophets *and* teachers' can indicate that the five charismatic leaders were prophetic and didactic. Given that such gifting combinations exist in the contemporary global Pentecostal community (as Chapter 4 will show), it is reasonable to contend that both aspects of grace were operative in the leaders Luke mentions.[154] Regarding their ethnic blend, there is the appearance (however speculative) that the Antioch faith community was multiethnic,[155] quite

---

[150] Dunn, *Beginning from Jerusalem*, p. 320.
[151] Dunn, *Beginning from Jerusalem*, p. 320.
[152] Schnabel, *Acts*, pp. 547-54.
[153] Schnabel, *Acts*, pp. 547-54.
[154] In this portion of the narrative, Luke indicates that two of these five are recognized for apostolic commissioning.
[155] Dunn, *Beginning from Jerusalem*, pp. 320-21:

> The diversity of the leadership group is also noteworthy: Barnabas first mentioned (embodying the continuity with Jerusalem begun in 11:23-26); Simeon, possibly a black man (Niger = 'black'); Lucius from Cyrene, where there were strong Jewish colonies (cf. 2:10; 11:20); Manaen, a man who may have been

unlike that in Jerusalem. As Dunn quickly suggests, 'the establishment of a church at Antioch marked the most significant advance to date in the emergence of earliest Christianity'.[156]

Regarding the opening verses of Acts 13, the mentioned prophets and teachers are involved in some aspect of liturgical worship along with fasting and prayer.[157] The root word for worship is the plural, λειτουργέω, which involves the performance of 'religious rites as

---

brought up with Herod (Antipas) the tetrarch and/or had been his intimate friend *(syntrophos);* and Saul.[337] The Greek may imply that the first three were designated as the prophets and the last two as the teachers – if so, an interesting status for Saul/Paul in the light of his subsequent work (cf. Stephen and Philip in chs. 6–8). That none of the names match those in 6:5 need not count as evidence against the view that the Antioch church was founded by Hellenists; in a rapidly developing mission new leadership would continually emerge.

Schnabel, *Acts*, p. 554:

The diversity of the group of five 'prophets and teachers' is noteworthy. Barnabas (see on 4:36) was a Greek-speaking Jew from Cyprus who had lived in Jerusalem and who guaranteed the continuity of the growing church in Antioch with the church in Jerusalem. He is mentioned first because of his leading role in the church in Antioch (cf. 11:23-26), possibly also because of his age. Simeon (Συμεών) might have been a black man of African origin as his grecized Latin name 'Niger' (Νίγερ) suggests, a term that means 'dark-complexioned' or 'black.' Lucius (Λούκιος) originally came from Cyrene in North Africa.[15] He may have belonged to the synagogue of the Cyrenians in Jerusalem (6:9) but came to Antioch fleeing from Jerusalem after Stephen's execution. Manaen (Μαναήν, Hebrew מְנַחֵם, *Menachem*) had been 'brought up' (σύντροφος) with Herod Antipas, the son of Herod I, who was the tetrarch ruling over Galilee during the ministries of John the Baptist and Jesus (Luke 3:1). Some have linked Manaen with Chuza, a steward of Herod Antipas (perhaps a manager of one of his estates), whose wife Joanna was among the women who accompanied Jesus (Luke 8:3). This connection must remain hypothetical, however. Manaen evidently belonged to a noble Jewish family with connections to the court of Herod I in Jerusalem. Since Herod I made sure that his sons had a good Greek education, the same can be assumed for Manaen, who thus belonged to the lay aristocracy in Jerusalem or in Galilee. Since 'bought up' σύντροφος was used as a title, Manaen, before his conversion, could have held an influential position at the court of Herod Antipas. Saul (Σαῦλος; see on 9:1-2) was a diaspora Jew from Tarsus who had studied under Gamaliel in Jerusalem, was present when Stephen was executed, had persecuted the believers in Judea, and had been a missionary in Damascus, in Nabatea, and in Cilicia before coming to Antioch (cf. 7:58; 9:20-22, 30; 11:25-26).

[156] Dunn, *Beginning from Jerusalem* p. 321.
[157] Schnabel, *Acts,* p. 554. Johnson, *Acts of the Apostles*, 221, 'In *The Didache 15:1*, we find it used for the work of church ministers: the bishops and deacons "also minister to you *(leitourgousi)* the ministry *(leitourgia)* of prophets and teachers"' λειτουργούντων δὲ αὐτῶν τῷ κυρίῳ καὶ νηστευόντων εἶπεν τὸ πνεῦμα τὸ ἅγιον· ἀφορίσατε δή μοι τὸν Βαρναβᾶν καὶ Σαῦλον εἰς τὸ ἔργον ὃ προσκέκλημαι αὐτούς.

part of one's religious duties'.¹⁵⁸ Given Luke's use of the word *liturgy* and its use in describing religious rites, there is a seeming indication of prescribed recommendations for fasting, prayers, and the Eucharist.¹⁵⁹ The prophets appear to have had some leeway for prophetic utterance throughout the liturgy, including during the Eucharist.¹⁶⁰ Schnabel sums it up saying,

> The worship of the church in Antioch would have included prayers (v. 3) as well as teaching and the breaking of bread (2:42). It also included the practice of fasting (νηστευόντων; present participle), evidently a regular part of the devotional discipline of the congregation.¹⁶¹

Perhaps these prophetic teachers fasted during prayer expressly to gain guidance and insight,¹⁶² as Baruch did on behalf of the prophet Jeremiah.¹⁶³ Luke affirms that the Spirit spoke during their fasting and prayer. Did 'one of the leaders of the church [receive] a specific prophetic utterance?'¹⁶⁴ Possibly. However, a consensus of intimations from the Spirit may have existed. This would not be unusual, as Paul indicates a recurring reality of confirming words in the various places in which he ministers (Acts 20.23). He instructs the Corinthian

---

¹⁵⁸ *GEL*, p. 533:

53.13 λειτουργέω^b; λειτουργίας, ας *f*. to perform religious rites as part of one's religious duties or as the result of one's role – 'to perform religious duties, to carry out religious rites.' λειτουργέω b: πᾶς μὲν ἱερεὺς ἔστηκεν καθ' ἡ'μέραν λειτουργῶν 'every priest stands day by day performing his religious rites' He 10:11. λειτουργίας: ἐγένετο ὡς ἐπλήσθησαν αἱ ἡμέραι τῆς λειτουργίας αὐτοῦ ἀπῆλθεν εἰς τὸν οἶκον αὐτοῦ 'when his period to perform the religious rites (in the Temple) was over, he went back home' Lk 1:23.

¹⁵⁹ See the *Didache* 8.1–10.6. Thomas O'Loughlin, *The Didache: A Window on the Earliest Christians* (London: Baker Academic, 2010), pp. 166-68.

¹⁶⁰ See the *Didache* 10.7. O'Loughlin, *Didache*, pp. 166-68.

¹⁶¹ Schnabel, *Acts*, p. 554.

¹⁶² James H. Charlesworth (ed.), *The Old Testament Pseudepigrapha, Volumes 1: Apocalyptic Literature and Testaments* (New York: Yale University Press, 1983), p. 623. '2 Bar. 9:2 and we rent our garments, and wept and mourned, and fasted for seven days. **10:1** And it happened after seven days that the word of God came to me and said to me: **2** Tell Jeremiah to go away in order to support the captives unto Babylon.'

¹⁶³ Noteworthy is the fact that although Jeremiah is a prophet, his disciple and scribe can operate in inspired speech for Jeremiah's sake (an important indication of the limitations of knowing, even by the prophet). See Elisha's own admittance to Gehazi in 2 Kgs 4.36-37.

¹⁶⁴ Schnabel, *Acts*, p. 554.

company about prophetic operation (1 Cor. 14.29); given this and Luke's presented likelihood that all five leaders are prophetic, they may have reached a shared sense (possibly during fasting and prayer) that it was time to commission Saul and Barnabas. I would argue this seemingly small point as an important safeguard of prophetic legitimacy relating to answerability and accountability. Had a single voice spoken, scrutiny by the others would have involved deliberation, and consensus would be needed for prophetic enactment to occur. Apart from such a consensus, the conferring laying on of hands (and more than likely an accompanying prophetic exhortation) would not proceed (1 Cor. 14.29; 1 Tim. 4.14). Also note that *after* acknowledging that the Spirit had spoken, the leaders continued to fast and pray, desiring full assurance of the Spirit's witness.

Given their simultaneous presence in Antioch, it would seem that Saul and Barnabas' relationship was forged there. The later encounter does not issue from Agabus having no knowledge of the men but from a genuine familiarity. Contrary to the contemporary church's common expectation that charismatic prophets minister only to people whom they do not know, Paul (who was familiar with Timothy) and other presbyters laid hands on Timothy and prophesied.[165]

Saul was of Hebrew parentage, previously known as a Pharisee, and given a Hebrew name (Phil. 3.5). Yet, he was raised in Tarsus in a privileged family that obtained Roman citizenship (Acts 22.25-28).[166] Therefore, he would have had an equivalent Latin name, which was *Paul*. Luke notes that Saul begins using his Latin name in Acts 13.9, most likely to build a bridge with the Gentile community to which he and Barnabas are sent.

Interestingly, the text in which Paul reproves the false prophet Elymas reveals Paul's charismatic prophetic expression.

> Paul, filled with the Holy Spirit, looked intently at [Elymas] and said, 'You son of the devil, you enemy of all righteousness, full of all deceit and villainy, will you not stop making crooked the straight paths of the Lord?' (Acts 13.9-10).

---

[165] This pattern was reminiscent of what Paul experienced in Acts 13. Paul's familiarity with Timothy did not hinder divine insight and inspired speech. (I propose that it can, perhaps, enhance them).

[166] Paul used his Roman citizenship to his and the church's advantage in Philippi (Acts 16.37).

Luke characteristically describes Paul's being filled with the Holy Spirit, denoting 'Paul as a prophet just as he had with Peter in the face of the challenge with Ananias and Sapphira (Acts 5:1-11), and Simon Magus (8:20-24)'.[167] Paul's caustic use of 'son of the devil' associates Elymas with the powers of darkness. Being 'full of all deceit and villainy' implies 'as a moral quality ... fraud or treachery (see LXX Deut 27:24; Ps 23:4; Wis 5:5; and especially Sir 19:26 [*plērēs dolou*] and Sir 1:30 [*hē kardia sou plērēs dolou*])'.[168] Paul exposes the person's character as reprehensible, even calling him an 'enemy of all righteousness'.

For Johnson, this 'recalls the prophecy of Jesus that his followers would tread upon "all the power (*dynamis*) of the enemy (*echthrou*)", meaning the demonic opposition (Luke 10:19)'.[169] For Paul, the gospel's advancement would not come without resistance from the powers of darkness.[170] In linking Elymas with such resistance, Paul exposes him as 'making crooked' the ways of the Lord (Acts 13.10), 'attempting to manipulate the guidance of God, who is leading the Roman governor and other people in Paphos to faith in Jesus'.[171] Paul's pronounced judgment of Elymas is the only conceivable outcome. Chastisement comes as temporary blindness. This is similar, ironically, to Paul's experience on the Damascus Road, and it leads to Elymas' having to be led by the hand as Paul once was (Acts 13.11; 9.8). The blindness intended to change Elymas' ways affected the witnessing proconsul who was genuinely converted (Acts 13.12).

3.4.2 Paul from a Psychological and Phenomenological Perspective

3.4.2.1 Aspects of Saul's Conversion in Relation to Christophany

Saul's conversion in Acts 9 is an 'experience ... catalogued as "religious"'.[172] Whether Acts 9 describes his specific call to the Gentiles

---

[167] Johnson, *Acts of the Apostles*, pp. 223-24.
[168] Johnson, *Acts of the Apostles*, p. 224.
[169] Johnson, *Acts of the Apostles*, p. 224.
[170] This alludes to aspects of the suffering Jesus said Paul would face (Acts 9.16).
[171] Schnabel, *Acts*, pp. 558-60.
[172] Joel B. Green, *Conversion in Luke-Acts: Divine Action, Human Cognition, and the People of God* (Grand Rapids, MI: Baker Academic, 2015), p. 21. Green suggests, 'a religious experience is ... interpreted as religious within a certain community and in terms of its traditions' (p. 22). In the case of Saul, the 'certain community' existed in the Second Temple period of Israel's history (530 BCE–7 CE).

is a matter of dispute.¹⁷³ Nevertheless, his encounter on the road to Damascus is integral to his formation as a prophetic agent and his example of prophetic legitimacy.

Boccaccini, *et al.*, remind us, 'conversion as an experience of radical abandonment of one's religious and ethical identity was indeed known in antiquity'.¹⁷⁴ They part company with Schnabel and Green regarding the term *conversion*,¹⁷⁵ based on varied views of Paul's Judaism. One can argue that Saul does not radically abandon his religious or ethical identity; but is the Boccaccini view of conversion adequately ubiquitous? At the purely psychological level, and apart from any relationship to religious experience, *conversion* is an 'actual change in an individual's beliefs, attitudes, or behaviors' in response to 'social influence'.¹⁷⁶ It is not comparable to compliance, which is 'outward and temporary' but occurs when an 'individual is personally convinced by a persuasive message or internalizes and accepts as his or her own the beliefs expressed by other group members'.¹⁷⁷

The Luke-Acts account and the Pauline epistles reveal a radical change in Paul's beliefs about God's identity, intent, and call following the Damascus Road encounter. Luke's narrative reveals a reordering of Paul's beliefs, attitudes, and behaviors (Acts 9.19-22).¹⁷⁸ There is nothing temporary about his psychological transformation. Additional aspects of the psychological definition of *conversion* need to be

---

¹⁷³ Janet Meyer Everts, 'Conversion and Call of Paul', in Gerald F. Hawthorne, Ralph P. Martin, and Daniel G. Reid (eds.), *Dictionary of Paul and His Letters* (Downers Grove, IL: InterVarsity Press, 1993), p. 156.

¹⁷⁴ Gabriele Boccaccini, Albert I. Baumgarten, and Daniel Boyarin, 'Introduction: The Three Paths to Salvation of Paul the Jew', in Gabriele Boccaccini and Carlos A. Segovia (eds.), *Paul the Jew: Rereading the Apostle as a Figure of Second Temple Judaism* (Minneapolis, MN: Fortress Press, 2016), p. 4.

¹⁷⁵ Boccaccini, Baumgarten, and Boyarin, 'Three Paths', p. 5:

Paul, who was born and raised a Jew, remained such after his 'conversion'; nothing changed in his religious and ethical identity. What changed, however, was his view of Judaism. In describing his experience not as a 'prophetic call', but as a 'heavenly revelation', Paul himself indicated the radicalness of the event. Paul did not abandon Judaism, but 'converted' from one variety of Judaism to another.

¹⁷⁶ 'Conversion', *APA Dictionary of Psychology*, https://dictionary.apa.org/conversion.

¹⁷⁷ 'Conversion', *APA Dictionary of Psychology*, https://dictionary.apa.org/conversion.

¹⁷⁸ The issue of social influence includes Paul's encounter with Christ and his introduction to the Body of Christ through Ananias, who calls him 'brother Saul' (Acts 9.17).

considered in light of Boccaccini's definition. The *APA Dictionary of Psychology* defines *conversion* as

> the process by which a person comes to embrace a new religious faith (or, sometimes, a more intense version of his or her existing belief). For example, a nonbeliever who becomes Catholic has experienced a conversion, as has a member of a minority religion who adopts the beliefs of a more mainstream faith. In Protestant traditions, conversion is often seen as a sudden transformation in which a person apparently undergoes a dramatic change in his or her personality, values, and lifestyle.[179]

Psychologically speaking, conversion can produce 'a more intense version of [one's] existing belief'. Arguably, Saul's post-conversion religious beliefs about Torah, the Prophets, and the Wisdom Literature constitute a more intense version of his prior beliefs and qualify psychologically as a conversion.[180] Johnson labels Saul's conversion a 'paradigmatic expression of the ironic truth spoken by Gamaliel (5:38-39)'.[181] Johnson's choosing of the term 'paradigmatic expression' denotes the radicality of a 'paradigm shift',[182] which is recognized even within psychology as 'a substantial and fairly rapid change in the whole pattern of ideas and assumptions'.[183] On the Damascus

---

[179] 'Conversion', *APA Dictionary of Psychology*, https://dictionary.apa.org/conversion.

[180] In my opinion, Boccaccini's argument is not as persuasive as Schabel's and Johnson's, for example. Schnabel, *Acts*, p. 443, considers the Damascus Road encounter a conversion, stating, 'The conversion of Saul … is initiated by a vision'. Johnson, *Acts of the Apostles*, p. 166, also considers Paul's encounter experience a conversion, citing as evidence his change from 'Pharisaic persecutor' into 'apostle of the Gentiles'.

[181] Johnson, *Acts of the Apostles*, p. 166, adds, 'No one worked harder to extirpate the messianic movement than this agent (as Luke has it) of the chief priest'. Paul's being instead 'transformed into its boldest advocate' strikes Luke as proof (1) of Christ's Lordship, and (2) 'that their movement "was from God"' (p. 166).

[182] The term was coined by Thomas S. Kuhn in 1962. See Thomas S. Kuhn, *The Structure of Scientific Revolutions* (Chicago, IL: University of Chicago Press, 4th edn, 2012), xi.

[183] 'Paradigm Shift', *APA Dictionary of Psychology*, https://dictionary.apa.org/paradigm-shift. An *idea,* from the perspective of cognition and cognitive psychology, is 'a mental image or cognition that is ultimately derived from experience but … may occur without direct reference to perception or sensory processes'. 'Idea', *APA Dictionary of Psychology*, https://dictionary.apa.org/idea. Psychologically, an *assumption* is 'the premise or supposition that something is factual or true; that is, the act of taking something for granted'. 'Assumption', *APA Dictionary of Psychology*, https://dictionary.apa.org/assumption.

Road, Saul processes cognitively that which is experiential. The encounter's vivid mental image alters his perceptual and sensory processes and impacts his ideas and assumptions. This experience is first phenomenological, relating to Saul's consciousness. It is then psychological because it alters his perceptions and cognitions, leading to new interpretations of his reality.

As noted in Chapter 2, phenomenologists see givenness in relation to a saturated phenomenon that 'cannot be wholly contained within concepts that can be grasped by our understanding'.[184] Saul's Damascus Road experience is a Christophany, 'a showing or appearing of Christ … applied only to the appearings of our Lord *after His resurrection*'.[185] Van Winkle sees the Damascus Road event as a conversion. Saul has been persecuting the church and will be apprehended by Christ for a specific purpose. In exploring 'the beginning of a new Dispensation',[186] Van Winkle avows, 'the object of this appearing is the *conversion* of Saul and his call as minister of the dispensation of the grace of God, especially to the Gentiles'.[187] The risen Christ apprehends and commissions Saul to proclaim 'the mystery kept secret since the world began' (Rom. 16.25, NKJV). As Christ revealed first to Ananias and then to Saul, 'I myself will show him how much he must suffer for the sake of my name' (Acts 9.16). This suffering grounds Paul's theological understanding of cruciformity and suggests a commitment from Jesus' follower to grasp the theological narrative that is integrated psychologically and phenomenologically through the Spirit's work in the follower's life.[188]

The theological narrative also becomes the psychological narrative, which McAdams, *et al.*, propose as the previously mentioned *narrative identity*.[189] If we consider *self-as-story* in relation to Saul's dramatic conversion and his embrace of a cruciform identity (Gal. 2.20), the need 'to have a cohesive sense of self, to have insight, to be loved, to feel safe, to satisfy biological appetites, to resolve inner conflicts, to

---

[184] Mackinlay, *Interpreting Excess*, p. 1.
[185] P. Van Winkle, *The Christophanies* (Galaxie Software, 2005), p. 3. 'The word *Christophany* comes from two Greek words – *Christos*, Christ; and *phaino*, to show'.
[186] Van Winkle, *Christophanies*, p. 8.
[187] Van Winkle, *Christophanies*, p. 8 (emphasis added).
[188] Consider Paul's argument for the cruciform life in 1 Cor. 2.1-16, and its inseparability from maturity and divine wisdom, lived out in earthly existence with charismatic dimensions present (as in 1 Cor. 1.1-9 and 1 Corinthians 12–14).
[189] McAdams and McLean, 'Narrative Identity', pp. 233-38.

be accepted, to overcome adversity, to have purpose, to find meaning, and to accept our own mortality' is answered.[190] Paul will tell the Corinthians, 'Be imitators of me, as I am of Christ' (1 Cor. 11.1). Paul is a prototypical NT disciple of Jesus whose example shows that the cross, resurrection, ascension, and indwelling of the Spirit imply suffering and charismatic empowerment.[191] These elements, as conjoined in Christ, are essential for spiritual and psychological soundness, cruciformity, faithful embodiment of Jesus' life, and prophetic legitimacy.

3.4.2.2 The Psychological and Phenomenological Impact of the Heavenly Vision

Schnabel infers that Saul's interior psychological response results from his visionary encounter. He explains, 'Saul sees the "light from heaven"'.[192] Paul asserts in 1 Cor. 9.1 that he has 'seen' (ἑόρακα) the Lord in terms of 'a real, "objective" seeing of a supernatural reality in divine splendor of light, which makes itself known as the "Lord" and is recognized by him as such'.[193] For Schnabel, the givenness of the phenomenological dimension described in terms of the sudden, flashing light in Acts 9.3 involves seeing from a visionary perspective and a real, objective one. If the encounter is real, it is 'existing or occurring in the physical world; not imaginary, fictitious, or theoretical; actual'.[194] Thus, Saul is not delusional.[195] His vision of Christ so transforms his consciousness that he repeatedly refers to its impact

---

[190] Frank Tallis, *The Act of Living* (New York: Basic Books, 2020), intro.
[191] These are rooted in love of God and love of neighbor.
[192] Schnabel, *Acts*, p. 443.
[193] Schnabel, *Acts*, p. 443.
[194] 'Real', *Collins English Dictionary* (Glasgow: HarperCollins, 8th edn, 2006).
[195] 'Delusional Disorder', *APA Dictionary of Psychology*, https://dictionary.apa.org/delusional-disorder: *Delusional disorder*

> in *DSM–IV–TR*, [is] any one of a group of psychotic disorders with the essential feature of one or more nonbizarre delusions that persist for at least 1 month but are not due to schizophrenia. The delusions are nonbizarre in that they feature situations that could conceivably occur in real life (e.g., being followed, poisoned, infected, deceived by one's government). Diagnosis also requires that the effects of substances (e.g., cocaine) or a medical condition be ruled out as causes of the delusions ... Their potential presence as a result of an ingested substance, a medical condition, or another mental disorder sometimes associated with firmly held delusional beliefs (e.g., obsessive-compulsive disorder, body dysmorphic disorder) must be ruled out.

on his life and proclamations of the gospel (Gal. 1.12, 16; Acts 22.6-7; 26.13-14; 9.1).

Interesting about self-as-story is how Paul sees himself and the experience, after the fact: he writes, 'Last of all, as to one untimely born, he appeared also to me' (1 Cor. 15.8). Louw and Nida attribute to the phrase 'untimely born' (ἔκτρωμα) the idea of being born late in the process, 'at the wrong time' rather than 'too soon'.[196] Thistleton argues the opposite, questioning whether the term 'aborted foetus' refers to Paul or is used as an 'abusive insult'.[197] Either way, Thiselton sees Paul's opportunity to 'glor[y] in God's sheer goodness and grace' knowing that the 'skeletons' in his closet did not deter them or 'God's generosity'.[198]

Whichever approach one takes, embraced within Paul's presuppositions about cruciformity is his sense of self-as-story (Gal. 2.20; 1 Cor. 2.1-2). Through the work of the Spirit, he has integrated any lingering psychological effects of his conversion in a way that accepts his narrative identity. This could be tied psychologically to something Paul discloses to Agrippa: 'When we had all fallen to the ground, I heard a voice saying to me in the Hebrew language, "Saul, Saul, why are you persecuting me? *It hurts you to kick against the goads?*"' (Acts 26.14, emphasis added).[199] Johnson suggests, 'God has been pushing' against Paul's refusal 'to become a Messianist'. He contends, '*sklēron soi*' indicates Paul's resistance and recalls 'the theme of "hardness" (*sklēros*) in Torah (see Exod 6:9; Deut 15:18; 31:27; 1 Sam 25:3)'.[200]

Saul indeed resists God. Psychologically, he entertains no detectable sense of guilt, although he has threatened, imprisoned, and murdered members of Christ's body, and seems to have heartily approved Stephen's stoning (Acts 9.1; 7.58). The Lukan account does not show him actively or aggressively opposing Roman rule, but his aggression

---

[196] *GEL*, p. 257:

Here Paul refers to himself, but the event in question is the appearance of Jesus to Paul, evidently on the road to Damascus. The reference, therefore, would seem to be his being born as a Christian. This spiritual birth, however, would appear to be rather late in the process rather than premature.

[197] Anthony C. Thiselton, *First Corinthians: A Shorter Exegetical and Pastoral Commentary* (Grand Rapids, MI: Eerdmans, 2006), pp. 263-64.

[198] Thiselton, *First Corinthians*, pp. 263-64.

[199] Luke omits this in the original telling of the vision but recounts it here.

[200] Johnson, *Acts of the Apostles*, p. 435.

against Jesus' followers indicates his extremism.[201] Although there is no record that he is psychologically disturbed by his actions, the risen Christ speaks metaphorically of cattle prods impacting his consciousness, conscience, and psyche. This seems, at the very least, to imply the convicting work of Christ's Spirit, which precedes conversion. Christ takes Saul's aggressions as acts against himself, producing a convictional experience that imprints on Saul's consciousness the 'devastating social consequences' of his acts,[202] thus influencing his psychology and phenomenology.

Joel Green explains that even in encounters with the divine, a cognitive (psychological) component and a brain-based (neurological) component are present. He states: 'religious experience belongs to the category of all human experiences that are embodied and have a neural basis'.[203] This invites reconsideration of the perceived dichotomy between the sacred/spiritual and the secular/natural and constitutes what could be understood as a prophetic call within the ancient tradition.[204]

The radical alteration of consciousness within the process of Saul's conversion is also the call to speak for God. The call legitimizes what Saul incorporates into his self-as-story (his narrative identity), integrating in his psyche his call with that of Jeremiah (Gal. 1.15). Paul places himself squarely in the prophetic tradition. Hence in Acts 13, he is included and sees himself in the ranks of the prophets and teachers.

3.4.2.3 The Prophetic Witness of Agabus and Paul's Disagreement

The final psychological and phenomenological consideration regarding Paul is Agabus' prophecy, the climax among prophetic warnings concerning the 'imprisonment and persecutions' that await Paul in Jerusalem (Acts 20.23). Paul's words attest to his willingness to suffer martyrdom (Acts 20.24). It would not be difficult to surmise that in

---

[201] Zeal 'can be unreasonable and self-defeating', 'Zeal', *Psychology iResearchnet*, http://psychology.iresearchnet.com/social-psychology/control/zeal/.

[202] 'Zeal', *Psychology iResearchnet*, http://psychology.iresearchnet.com/social-psychology/control/zeal/.

[203] Green, *Conversion in Luke-Acts*, p. 22.

[204] Aune, *Prophecy in Early Christianity*, p. 97, asserts, 'the term *nabî*, normally translated "prophet", is widely thought to have originally meant "one called", and the *consciousness of having been divinely called* is often thought to be integral to the prophetic role' (emphasis added).

his initial meeting with Saul, Ananias mentioned that Saul would suffer many things for Christ's sake, possibly including death (Acts 9.16).

Saul's psychological preparation for death could have begun on the Damascus Road and in the initial days of his calling. Almost certainly, Ananias would have told him that he would stand before 'gentiles and kings' (Acts 9.15). Jesus made similar remarks to the twelve in relation to 'governors and kings' (Mt. 10.18). It would be difficult to presume that Paul was unaware of this. Cognitively then, pattern recognition would be present,[205] as it is in many human psychological functions.[206] From a purely cognitive perspective and given (1) what Paul has known since his conversion, (2) what he has experienced in relation to his promised sufferings, and (3) what he knows awaits him in Jerusalem, he is predisposed to embrace the likelihood of martyrdom.

Paul's seeming refusal to honor the desires of Agabus and other concerned prophetic voices can raise questions about the wisdom of not heeding their warnings. Agabus, a seasoned prophetic voice, embodies his warning in a way that drives home the situational gravity for both Paul and the onlookers. Whether Agabus was to be heeded or not, Paul's martyrdom bears witness before kings. Paul recognizes the cognitive function of his psyche via pattern recognition, intuition, reflection, and meaning making (among other functions). Therefore, he is psychologically prepared for his death and trusts the Spirit to grant him grace for it on a phenomenological level.

---

[205] 'Pattern Recognition', *APA Dictionary of Psychology*, https://dictionary.apa.org/pattern-recognition: Pattern recognition is

> the ability to recognize and identify a complex whole composed of, or embedded in, many separate elements. Pattern recognition is not only a visual ability; in audition, it refers to (a) the recognition of temporal patterns of sounds or (b) the recognition of patterns of excitation of the basilar membrane, such as that which occurs during the perception of vowels in speech.

[206] Pattern recognition involves mechanisms of the psyche including 'sense, memory, study, and thinking' and is a 'typical perception process which depends on knowledge and experience people already have'. Youguo Pi, *et al.*, 'Theory of Cognitive Pattern Recognition', in Peng-Yeng Yin (ed.), *Pattern Recognition Techniques, Technology and Applications* (Intech, 2008), pp. 433-62 (434), www.intechopen.com.

3.5 Jesus as Prophet

From the outset, Luke places his narrative within the flow of Israel's history, starting with the archangel Gabriel's prophetic proclamations concerning John the Baptist and Jesus (Lk. 1.8-17, 30-37). Luke's work is essential in developing a Pentecostal theology of prophetic legitimacy, which we explore now in relation to Jesus.

Generally, a Pentecostal reading in relation to the prophetic Spirit is Lukan. Luke presents Jesus as the preeminent prophet and the culmination of the prophetic tradition – not only the last in the line of prophets but the fullness of prophecy itself. This is how Latter Rain adherents read Jesus, as we will see in Chapter 4. Although Chapter 5 will detail Jesus' prophetic praxis, a brief overview of Jesus as Prophet is essential here.

3.5.1 Jesus from a Biblical and Theological Perspective

Because Luke's depiction of the Person and work of Jesus is inseparable from the Pentecostal tradition, no serious talk of prophetic legitimacy is possible apart from the Lukan record. This includes the angel Gabriel's utterances in Lk. 1.30-37, which precede Jesus' birth and establish his prophetic legitimacy. As Green purports, the events are linked to the history of God's salvific acts.[207] Luke's narrative of Jesus as Prophet doesn't happen in a vacuum but within the historic trajectory and fulfillment of the prophetic promises made to Abraham and expounded through the OT canon.

The entire canonical narrative is about the One who is coming, as Luke's account indicates (Lk. 24.25-27). By the time Gabriel announces the coming birth of the Messiah's prophetic forerunner (Lk. 1.12-17), messianic expectations coexist with prophetic fervor and *'eschatological anticipation* in its myriad forms'.[208] Gabriel prophesies to Mary that (1) her son will be named Jesus, and (2) he will be both human and divine, the Son of the Most High conceived through the Creator-Spirit's overshadowing of her virginal womb (Lk. 1.31, 35). This son will fulfill all messianic expectations as David's greater son (Lk. 1.31-32).

---

[207] Joel B. Green, *The Gospel of Luke* (New International Commentary on the New Testament; Grand Rapids, MI: Eerdmans, 1997), p. 52.
[208] Green, *Gospel of Luke*, p. 59.

Croatto declares, 'Very significant ... is Luke's construction of the figure of Jesus as a prophet'.[209] Once Jesus opens the scroll of Isaiah and affirms his identity as the 'spirit-filled anointed one' (Lk. 4.16-21),[210] he self-identifies as a prophet (Lk. 4.24). Judgmentalism within his hometown congregation over his ministry to perceived outsiders prompts him to cite an ancient proverb and fully identify with the prophetic ministries of Elijah and Elisha (Lk. 4.23-27).[211] Although the Elijah and Elisha narratives are replete with signs and wonders,[212]

---

[209] J. Severubi Croatto, 'Jesus, Prophet Like Elijah, and Prophet-Teacher Like Moses in Luke-Acts', *Journal of Biblical Literature* 124.3 (2005), p. 451.

[210] Johnson, *Prophetic Jesus, Prophetic Church*, p. 29.

[211] The congregation apparently took issue with Jesus' ministry to Gentiles in Capernaum. Johnson, *Gospel of Luke*, p. 82, suggests, 'he is not acceptable in his own country because his mission extends beyond his own country'.

[212] David Pyles, 'A Double Portion of Thy Spirit', http://www.bcbsr.com/survey/eli.html:

> Miracles in the Career of Elijah: 1) Causing the rain the cease f½3 1/2 years (1Ki 17:1) 2) Being fed by the ravens (1Ki 17:4) 3) Miracle of the barrel of meal and cruse of oil (1Ki 17:14) 4) Resurrection of the widow's son (1Ki 17:22) 5) Calling of fire from heaven on the altar (1Ki 18:38) 6) Causing it to rain (1Ki 18:45) 7) Prophecy that Ahab's sons would all be destroyed (1Ki 21:22) 8) Prophecy that Jezebel would be eaten by dogs (1Ki 21:23) 9) Prophecy that Ahaziah would die of his illness (2Ki 1:4) 10) Calling fire from heaven upon the first 50 soldiers (2Ki 1:10) 11) Calling fire from heaven upon the second 50 soldiers (2Ki 1:12) 12) Parting of the Jordan (2Ki 2:8) 13) Prophecy that Elisha should have a double portion of his spirit (2Ki 2:10) 14) Being caught up to heaven in a whirlwind (2Ki 2:11) Miracles in the Career of Elisha: 1) Parting of the Jordan (2Ki 2:14) 2) Healing of the waters (2Ki 2:21) 3) Curse of the she bears (2Ki 2:24) 4) Filling of the valley with water (2Ki 3:17) 5) Deception of the Moabites with the valley of blood (2Ki 3:22) 6) Miracle of the vessels of oil (2Ki 4:4) 7) Prophecy that the Shunammite woman would have a son (2Ki 4:16) 8) Resurrection of the Shunammite's son (2Ki 4:34) 9) Healing of the gourds (2Ki 4:41) 10) Miracle of the bread (2Ki 4:43) 11) Healing of Naaman (2Ki 5:14) 12) Perception of Gehazi's transgression (2Ki 5:26) 13) Cursing Gehazi with leprosy (2Ki 5:27) 14) Floating of the axe head (2Ki 6:6) 15) Prophecy of the Syrian battle plans (2Ki 6:9) 16) Vision of the chariots (2Ki 6:17) 17) Smiting the Syrian army with blindness (2Ki 6:18) 18) Restoring the sight of the Syrian army (2Ki 6:20) 19) Prophecy of the end of the great famine (2Ki 7:1) 20) Prophecy that the scoffing nobleman would see, but not partake of, the abundance (2Ki 7:2) 21) Deception of the Syrians with the sound of chariots (2Ki 7:6) 22) Prophecy of the seven-year famine (2Ki 8:1) 23) Prophecy of Benhadad's untimely death (2Ki 8:10) 24) Prophecy of Hazael's cruelty to Israel (2Ki 8:12) 25) Prophecy that Jehu would smite the house of Ahab (2Ki 9:7) 26) Prophecy that Joash would smite the Syrians at Aphek (2Ki 13:17) 27) Prophecy that Joash would smite Syria thrice but not consume it (2Ki 13:19) 28) Resurrection of the man touched by his bones (2Ki 13:21).

Jesus' reference enraged his hearers and blinded them to his stated identity (Lk. 4.28).

The resistance to statements of Jesus' identity did not abolish those statements. When he raised the widow's son in Nain, the villagers said, 'A great prophet has risen among us' (Lk. 7.16). When Jesus made plain his coming Passion, he again identified himself as a prophet, specifically, one who would be executed in the Holy City (Lk. 13.33).[213] Jesus' uncle, Cleopas, would also identify him as a prophet (Lk. 24.19).

In his Transfiguration account of Moses and Elijah speaking to Jesus' departure/exodus (Lk. 9.30-31), Luke replays the prophetic role of Moses as deliverer,[214] conveying the association between Moses and Elijah and their foreshadowing of Jesus as prophetic deliverer. Johnson summarizes these references, stating, 'Jesus embodies – "fulfills", if one desires – the qualities of a very specific sort of prophetic figure'.[215] Johnson suggests which figure is key, stating that 'Luke draws the strongest connection between Jesus, his followers, and the figure who was the first and greatest of the prophets of this type, Moses'.[216]

Prior to Jesus' baptism, Luke notes John the Baptist's claim that Jesus will 'baptize ... with the Holy Spirit and fire' (Lk. 3.16). Luke advances his view of this baptism's prophetic nature and states that after Jesus' resurrection, he continues to teach and lead his disciples in and by the power of the Spirit (Acts 1.2). This in no way indicates anything contrary to Jesus' legitimate prophetic operation but only his continued, post-resurrection functioning as the prophetic Messiah. 'All that Jesus did and taught from the beginning' (Acts 1.1, ISV), he continued to do in and through the Spirit.

In Acts 2, the One already filled with the Spirit and anointed for his work pours out the Spirit in fulfillment of Joel 2.28 (Acts 2.17), empowering others to speak beyond their natural capacity (Acts 2.4). The Joel text also promised portents, signs, and wonders on earth and in the heavens (Joel 2.30; Acts 2.19). The prophetic is rooted in

---

[213] This perhaps references Isaiah, who (according to tradition) was 'sawn in two' (Heb. 11.37).

[214] *GEL*, p. 188, 'ἔξοδος^b, ου f [is] ... a figurative extension of meaning of ἔξοδος^a "departure"'.

[215] Johnson, *Prophetic Jesus, Prophetic Church*, p. 31.

[216] Johnson, *Prophetic Jesus, Prophetic Church*, p. 31.

the Spirit's work after the outpouring on Pentecost. As Spirit-baptizer, Jesus imparts the ability for God's children to become prophetic witnesses. According to Peter, this confirms Christ's exaltation and supreme favor at the 'right hand of God' (Acts 2.33).

Luke notes that in his Day of Pentecost sermon, Peter identified Jesus as a prophet (Acts 2.22), with signs and wonders being part and parcel of his prophetic legitimacy. Additionally, Jesus is exclusively the 'prophet like [Moses]' who fulfilled the Mosaic prophecy (Acts 3.22; Deut. 18.15).[217] After the healing at the Corinthian Gate, Peter described believers in Jesus as 'descendants of the prophets' (Acts 3.25). Thus, they and we are heirs of prophetic legacy.

3.5.2 Jesus from a Psychological and Phenomenological Perspective

In arguing for a Pentecostal theology of prophetic legitimacy in relation to Jesus, this chapter's psychological and phenomenological considerations derive from Luke-Acts.[218] Viewing Jesus through a lens of

---

[217] The ancient text honors Moses by speaking of his knowing God 'face to face' and having no equal (until Jesus) in relation to 'signs and wonders' (Deut. 34.10-12).

[218] Regarding psychological and phenomenological perspectives, any confessionally Christian epistemological and ontological approaches to Jesus' prophetic consciousness, perception, and enactment begin with the presupposition that Jesus is fully divine and fully human. As to prophetic legitimacy, Jesus' self-consciousness proves challenging for naturalism as it relates to scientism. This work will not engage that debate. The Nicene Creed's second article states, 'he is the one who, because of us humans and because of our salvation, came down from heaven and was enfleshed from the Holy Spirit and Mary the Virgin and was made human'. Earle Treptow, "'For Us and for Our Salvation, ... He Became Truly Human'": The Translation of the Nicene Creed in Christian Worship', preliminary draft for an intended future article in *Wisconsin Lutheran Quarterly*, PDF, https://static1.squarespace.com/static/5c75c39016b6407f48ef57c1/t/5faf16fae44daa6be0182eb4/1605310202747/cw-nicene-creed.pdf.

Yet in being made human, Athanasius (*Athanasius: On the Incarnation of the Word of God* [trans. T. Herbert Bindley; London: Religious Tract Society, 2nd edn, 1903]), p. 28) indicates, 'the Word was not so circumscribed in the body as to be there only and nowhere else. He was still the energizing principle of all things as before. He was in everything, but not essentially identified with everything; being only entirely in the Father alone.' Not being limited in his God-hood to the body, but still being 'the energizing principle of all things' distinguishes Jesus from all other human beings (p. 28). Unlike them, he is fully human and fully divine. His 'being only entirely in the Father alone' demands our realizing that his psychological framework (which is rooted in his consciousness, i.e. phenomenology) utterly transcends our capacity to analyze or scrutinize (p. 28). As Athanasius explains, 'The human actions attributed to Him are those of the body of God the Word; they prove the

prophetic legitimacy therefore involves Luke's 'descriptions of Jesus',[219] which include his words and actions. Green states that in his preface (Lk. 1.1-4), '[Luke] himself categorizes his work as a "narrative" or "orderly account"'.[220] Mittelstadt states that narrative theology includes 'fresh opportunities to voice ideas previously out of bounds or otherwise difficult to convey'.[221] This is significant to psychology, and particularly to narrative identity, which McAdams postulates as one of the three layers of personality.[222] Greco alternatively refers to narrative identity as 'self as autobiographical social author'.[223] All of this is relevant to what can be gleaned from Jesus' 'behavioral outline' and self-disclosure in relation to his life events,[224] the context within which those events unfolded, and their chronological placement in history.

Regarding Jesus' baptism, Arterbury notes,

---

hypostatic union, and the reality of His body' (p. 28). He accomplished all word and deed as 'the Word in the body' (p. 28). The works Luke recorded that he did in the flesh 'prove him to be God'. Lk. 4.38-41; 5.1-11, 12–14, 17-26; 6.6-11; 7.1-10, 11–17; 8.22-25, 26-33 (p. 28). Among them is the stilling of the storm at sea, which Athanasius suggests 'prove Him to be the Lord of Nature' (p. 28).

Regarding phenomenology and consciousness, Roman Catholicism tells us that Jesus' life 'testifies to his consciousness of a filial relationship with the Father'. International Theological Commission of the Catholic Church, *The Consciousness of Christ Concerning Himself and His Mission* (Vatican City: Libreria Editrice Vaticana, 1985), Logos Bible Software 9. All he does as the 'perfect 'servant' attests to an authority 'belonging to God alone', exceeding that of other prophets, and issuing from his relationship with the one he calls 'my Father'. International Theological Commission of the Catholic Church, *Consciousness of Christ*, Logos Bible Software 9. Given the Nicene tradition, the Jesus in Luke's Gospel is truly and fully human, embodying a holistic awareness and living in a domain of consciousness uncontaminated by sin. His consciousness, observations, interpretations, cognitions, and perceptions can be observed, estimated, appreciated – and to the extent possible – evaluated and interpreted based on the same text.

[219] Matti Kankaanniemi, 'A Psychobiography of Jesus – Part 1: Personality Traits', *ABO Akademi Journal for Historical Jesus Research* 1 (2015), p. 9.

[220] Green, *Gospel of Luke*, p. 1.

[221] Martin William Mittelstadt, *Reading Luke-Acts in the Pentecostal Tradition* (Cleveland, TN: CPT Press, 2010), p. 82.

[222] Dan P. McAdams, *The Art and Science of Personality Development* (New York: Guilford Press, 2015), p. 5.

[223] Franco Greco, 'What Is Personality? It Is a Lot More Complicated Than Myers-Briggs', *Franco Greco Your Psychologist* (blog, January 31, 2021), https://www.yourpsychologist.net.au/what-is-personality-its-more-complicated-than-myers-briggs.

[224] Greco, 'What Is Personality', https://www.yourpsychologist.net.au/what-is-personality-its-more-complicated-than-myers-briggs.

Luke sets up a vivid contrast between Jesus as the Holy Spirit-empowered, beloved Son of God (3:22) and Adam as the son who failed to obey God's commands (3:38). God is 'well pleased' with Jesus, but God banished Adam from the garden (Gen 3:22-24).[225]

Psychologically, the gift of affirmation through the Father's words legitimizes sonship, prophethood, and the messianic role. There is also the gift of approbation through the filling of the Spirit; 'the implications of this anointing with the Spirit for Luke's understanding of messiahship ... unfold' within the narrative.[226]

Self-affirmation theory, as postulated within positive psychology, 'asserts that the overall goal of the self-system is to protect an image of its self-integrity, of its moral and adaptive adequacy'.[227] Any perceived destabilization of this image triggers attempts to 'restore self-worth'.[228] While this personal approach to affirmation protects self-integrity, the denial of affirmation could imply, 'the emotional life cannot unfold further'.[229] Luke reveals that under Mary and Joseph's oversight, Jesus 'increased in wisdom and in years, and in divine and human favor' (Lk. 2.52). This indicates a strong sense of well-being that contrasts with an outcome Baars and Terruwe describe: the withholding of a mother's love that dooms a 'baby's emotional life ... to retain a deep-seated dissatisfaction and unrest, a feeling of frustration and deprivation' involving the 'most primitive and fundamental striving'.[230] The Lukan account contraindicates such a scenario. Jesus' mother deeply and lovingly affirms him. Her distress over his extended absence during the Passover reveals her intimate relationship with him (Lk. 2.48).

The Child was raised in an approving atmosphere. Although Joseph was an affirming surrogate father, the affirmation Jesus needed to accomplish his role as prophetic Messiah necessarily came from his heavenly Father, at the Jordan. Phenomenologically, Jesus' baptismal encounter (the opening of the heavens, the descent and filling

---

[225] Arterbury, *Reading Luke*, p. 29.
[226] Johnson, *Gospel of Luke*, p. 69.
[227] David K. Sherman and Geoffrey L. Cohen, 'The Psychology of Self-Defense: Self-Affirmation Theory', *Advances in Experimental Social Psychology* 38 (2006), p. 185.
[228] Sherman and Cohen, 'Psychology of Self-Defense', p. 185.
[229] Baars and Terruwe, *Healing the Unaffirmed*, ch. 1.
[230] Baars and Terruwe, *Healing the Unaffirmed*, ch. 1.

of the Spirit, and the voice of the Father's affirmation recorded in Lk. 3.21-22) strengthens Jesus' core identity, worth, and self-integrity as the fully human and fully divine Son. Significantly, in his post-baptismal period, this strengthening will meet the inevitable encroachment against his sense of self. Beginning with his testing in the wilderness, the powers aim at his sense of self and his place in Israel's prophetic history. Thus, he fully identifies with Israel's testing in the wilderness (Deut. 8.2; 6.16; Exod. 16.1-12; 32.1-35), although his full surrender and obedience contrast Israel's resistance and disobedience.

The powers frame their psychological approach of veiled accusations in a primal linguistic style recalling the misrepresentation of God's words in Gen. 3.1-7. The conditional statement, 'If you are the Son of God', attempts to (1) unsettle Jesus' sense of the Father's affirmation, and (2) incite him to prove his legitimacy in ways inappropriate to his calling. Instead of resting in the Father's validation, he is provoked to ensure it. However, the affirmation that already strengthened his self-integrity now supports his resistance to temptation, and the approbation he received at his Jordan baptism supports his refusal to prove his legitimacy by working an illegitimate miracle.[231]

Luke places the call for Jesus to throw himself off the Temple's pinnacle third in the sequence of temptations. This perhaps foreshadows the hometown rejection of his Messianic role and is another temptation to self-qualify and thereby deny his established legitimacy (Lk. 4.28-30). Satan's repeating, 'If you are the Son of God' – a direct affront to Jesus' essential nature – phenomenologically denies the affirmation and urges a psychological aberration. However, each time Satan presents the conditional 'if', Jesus is resolute. The middle temptation, to worship Satan in exchange for all the world's kingdoms (Lk. 4.5-8), denies the need for suffering and cruciformity. It is the satanic attempt to separate Jesus from the work of the cross and delegitimize his prophetic and messianic mission.

Arterbury notes,

> where Israel failed, Jesus succeeds due to the presence and power of the Spirit. The devil desires to shape Jesus' *fundamental identity and use of power*, yet Jesus refuses to yield to the devil's direction.

---

[231] Such a performance would abuse the abilities Jesus indeed possesses.

Instead, the Spirit of God defines Jesus' role and directs his actions.[232]

Luke states, 'the devil had finished every test' and 'departed … until an opportune time' (Lk. 4.13). The statement's tenor and the extreme vulnerability of Jesus' wilderness period suggest that 'an opportune time' involves gaining advantage over consciousness and cognition during a more vulnerable season. Johnson notes, 'The term *kairos* has the sense of "particular season" … but in Acts 13:11, the exact same phrase means simply, "for a time"'.[233] He cautions against speculation regarding this kairotic period. Yet the opportune time could have been Christ's Passion, when (1) Satan enters Judas and demands permission to sift the twelve (Lk. 22.3, 31), (2) Jesus collapses in agony and extreme anxiety during prayer (Lk. 22.42-44), (3) Jesus hears the 'If you are … ' phrase from the soldiers (Lk. 23.36-37), and (4) one of the two bandits between whom he is crucified trifles with his legitimacy (Lk. 23.39).

Jesus emerges from the wilderness having conquered all that Israel lost during their testing season. He endures their affliction to provide for their ultimate salvation, in fulfillment of Isaiah's suffering Servant passages (Isa. 42.1-4, 49.1-6, 50.4-11, and 52.13–53.12). As Johnson states, 'Jesus is, in the heart, a truly obedient Son'.[234] Returning to Galilee in the 'power of the Spirit' (Lk. 4.14), his return from the wilderness is both psychologically and phenomenologically reminiscent of the hero's journey monomyth.[235] In that heroic return, legitimization resides in the consciousness and perception of the prophetic Messiah, leading to prophetic enactment, including the signs and wonders that verified his prophetic legitimacy (Lk. 4.14-15, 31-37, 38-41).

Throughout the OT, the prophet prays (Dan. 9.3-19; 1 Kgs 17.21; Jon. 2.1; Hab. 3.1; Jer. 32.16-25; Exod. 15.25). Likewise, Luke depicts Jesus' early missional life as being characterized by prayer (Lk. 3.21-22). Concerning prayer, the Transfiguration and the beginning of the

---

[232] Arterbury, *Reading Luke*, p. 31 (emphasis added).
[233] Johnson, *Gospel of Luke*, p. 75.
[234] Johnson, *Gospel of Luke*, p. 76.
[235] Amanda Penn, 'Mythology and Psychology: Myth Tells Us Who We Are', *Shortform* (blog, November 15, 2019), https://www.shortform.com/blog/mythology-and-psychology/: 'Myths are a society's *outward* manifestations of inner conflicts and desires – they represent the expression of *unconscious* fears and desires. Psychology exists within mythology'.

Passion provide psychological and phenomenological insight into the prophetic Messiah's experience (Lk. 9.28-36; 22.39-46).

In speaking of the phenomenology of prayer, Mooney asserts, 'prayer seems firmly centered in the heart, in those passions that infuse the center of the person, the center of the soul'.[236] Mooney seeks to legitimize passion as the core of prayer. Although Mooney's detractors would argue, 'passions ... *can* subvert a worthy life',[237] his concern is 'bringing passion back from disrepute'.[238] In the Lukan Transfiguration and the opening of the Passion accounts (Lk. 9.28-36; 22.39-46), Jesus' praying demonstrates 'a refinement of passion'.[239] The Transfiguration reveals a passionate love for the Father's reputation and majestic glory; the Passion reveals the sheer agony of what awaits Jesus. The events are related: During the prayer attending the Transfiguration, the prophetic figures of Moses and Elijah appear with Jesus in glory – according to Luke, to prepare him for the exodus he will accomplish at the cross. Mooney recalls Kierkegaard who 'confides that prayer, like possibility, is the break of spirit – and thus prayer makes space for life's necessary passions'.[240] These passions for the prophetic Messiah are tied to the *Missio Dei*, the purpose of the Incarnation, which finds its culmination in suffering, death, burial, resurrection, and ascension.[241]

'Husserl ... understood prayer in terms of the inward turn of his transcendental phenomenology'.[242] Wright refers to a letter from Husserl to Metzger that speaks of Husserl's experience of prayer as utterly transformational, and the reason he changed trajectories, from mathematics to phenomenology. Wright cites Husserl: 'My vocation ... may lie in overpowering religious experiences and complete

---

[236] Edward F. Mooney, 'Becoming What We Pray: Passion's Gentler Resolutions', in Bruce Ellis Benson and Norman Wirzba (eds.), *The Phenomenology of Prayer* (Perspectives in Continental Philosophy; New York: Fordham University Press, 2005), p. 51.

[237] Mooney, 'Becoming What We Pray', p. 51.

[238] Mooney, 'Becoming What We Pray', p. 51.

[239] Mooney, 'Becoming What We Pray', p. 51.

[240] Mooney, 'Becoming What We Pray', p. 52.

[241] All of this is precursor for the outpouring of the passionate prophetic Spirit on the Day of Pentecost.

[242] Terence C. Wright, 'Prayer and Interiority', in Bruce Ellis Benson and Norman Wirzba (eds.), *The Phenomenology of Prayer* (Perspectives in Continental Philosophy; New York: Fordham University Press, 2005), p. 134.

transformations'.²⁴³ In the Lukan account, Jesus is not overpowered by his praying; however, the Transfiguration is a transformative experience, his interior identity being unveiled to Peter, James, and John, who, being instructed to pray, are both overwhelmed and overtaken by the sight (2 Pet. 1.16).

Husserl calls the transcendent God's divine consciousness an 'Absolute' that is distinct 'from the Absolute of Consciousness' itself,²⁴⁴ being *'transcendent in a totally different sense'* as the Divine Transcendent.²⁴⁵ When experienced in consciousness, cognition, and perception, this Divine Transcendent can be referenced phenomenologically as the saturated phenomena mentioned earlier, which 'undergo saturation by the excess of intuition over the concept or signification in them'.²⁴⁶ It would seem impossible to describe Jesus' experience of the Transfiguration as a saturated phenomenon, given that he is fully divine, fully human, and lacking any sense of separation from the Father. For Peter, James, and John, however, witnessing the Transfiguration would be a saturated phenomenon. In their fragmented human state, each person's ego is constituted by the phenomenon 'to the extent that *ego* cannot comprehend the phenomenon'.²⁴⁷ Their sense of being overwhelmed at an egoic level indicates a saturated phenomenon of which Jesus was the absolute, transcendent source. That epiphany made Jesus manifest as the divine Son in human splendor. In that moment, the phenomenology of prayer in Jesus' passion presents a 'givenness of truth' through the God-Man,²⁴⁸ from the Father, to the disciples, and by the Spirit. This necessarily and simultaneously provides for the exchange with Moses and Elijah that prepares Jesus for his suffering and death.²⁴⁹

---

²⁴³ Wright, 'Prayer and Interiority', p. 134.
²⁴⁴ Edmund Husserl, *Ideas: General Introduction to Pure Phenomenology* (London: Routledge, 2013), ch. 4.
²⁴⁵ Husserl, *Ideas*, ch. 4.
²⁴⁶ Nesteruk, *Sense of the Universe*, p. 519.
²⁴⁷ Nesteruk, *Sense of the Universe*, p. 519.
²⁴⁸ Nesteruk, *Sense of the Universe*, p. 519.
²⁴⁹ This could be considered in light of a *communio sanctorum*: 'Basil, Isidore of Pelusium, Athanasius, and Pseudo-Basil, refer *communio sanctorum* to a communion *with* the saints, i.e., holy persons', Kenan B. Osborne, 'The Communion of the Saints', in Joseph A. Komonchak, Mary Collins, and Dermot A. Lane (eds.), *The New Dictionary of Theology* (Collegeville, MN: Liturgical Press, 2000), p. 214. This also presents a givenness of truth regarding the experiential nature of prayer and how, phenomenologically, it led to an exchange with two major but long-departed figures appearing alive on the mount.

At the Jordan, the Spirit anoints Jesus for his prophetic and messianic role (Lk. 3.22). Thus, all that Jesus does, he does by the breath of God. Phenomenologically for Jesus, breathing and being in the breath of God are inseparable. The mutual indwelling of the Spirit, Son, and Father cause the physiology of the God-Man to be wholly attuned to his spirit. Jesus' human existence involves a vital integrity; he also embodies a fullness of humanity. Therefore, the Transfiguration is a phenomenological display of perfect attunement between his physiology and psyche. From a prophetic perspective, what this might imply sets Jesus apart from all other prophetic agents, their attunement being imperfect. Even as a fully human being, Jesus is not at the mercy of any bodily dysfunction.

Whenever he prays, Jesus addresses his Father.[250] Bosworth states, 'attachment language' is studied in relation to 'attachment theory' and involves (1) an infant's forming of attachments with its caregivers, and (2) the 'reciprocal bonds' that caregivers form in return.[251] Children's ideas about 'attachment figures' reflect their personal experiences.[252] This would be true for Jesus, who reveals a profound awareness and attachment to 'abba' from his formative years (Lk. 2.49), and to his personal mission in that regard. Concerning prayer from a psychological perspective in the ancient world, Bosworth argues, 'deities served as attachment figures for the ancient Near Eastern peoples who prayed to them'.[253] Arguably, therefore, Jesus' use of 'attachment language' (*abba*) speaks to his sense of his Father,[254] who was invisible yet well-known in Jesus' interiority and continually 'elicit[ed] caring behaviors' that influenced Jesus' 'pattern of behaviors'.[255] Thus, all that Jesus does as prophetic Messiah emerges from his communion with his Father, by the Spirit. Much as humans who, from infancy, 'monitor themselves and their environment for signs of distress (hunger, the appearance of a stranger) and for the

---

[250] *GEL*, p. 140, 'πατήρ, πατρός *m*; αββα (a Greek transliteration of an Aramaic word meaning 'father'): (titles for God, literally 'father') one who combines aspects of supernatural authority and care for his people – "Father"'.

[251] David A. Bosworth, 'Ancient Prayers and the Psychology of Religion: Deities as Parental Figures', *Journal of Biblical Literature* 134.4 (2015), pp. 681-82.

[252] Bosworth, 'Ancient Prayers', p. 681.

[253] Bosworth, 'Ancient Prayers', p. 681.

[254] Bosworth, 'Ancient Prayers', p. 682.

[255] Bosworth, 'Ancient Prayers', p. 682.

availability of the attachment figure',[256] Jesus self-monitors within this communion.

From his earliest days of formation, Jesus concerns himself with his Father's affairs and his 'Father's house' (Lk. 2.49). The fact that Jesus 'increased in wisdom and in years' indicates psychologically his learning and mastery of 'social and cognitive skills' (Lk. 2.52).[257] These skills were not only formed and informed by his subjection to Joseph and Mary but also through his intuitions and interior knowing by the Spirit (Lk. 2.51). Already, he was highly 'socially integrated' with the adult world he would ultimately inhabit.[258]

Prayer, as revealed in Jesus' attachment language, was foundational to the forming of his consciousness, perceptions, cognitions, and eventual prophetic enactments. The profound attachment between the Son and the Father that is evidenced in Jesus' prayer life is precisely what the powers of darkness would seek to destroy, as the wilderness temptation shows (␣k. 4.1-12). His identity as the eternally beloved Son permeates his consciousness, cognitions, perceptions, imagination, intuitions, memories, and overall phenomenology (Lk. 3.22). His prophetic lament over Jerusalem – reminiscent of Jeremiah's weeping with its congruent, embodied, and attuned psychological and phenomenological exigencies (Lk. 19.41) – is followed by his enactment of the Temple cleansing. Taken together, this all stems from his intimate love of his Father and his view of his Father's house as 'a house of prayer' (Lk. 19.46).

All of this testifies to prophetic legitimacy. Consider Bosworth's view of the language of attachment reflecting God's provision of safety and security in religious structures such as temples:[259] Jesus cleanses his Father's house because it is no longer a haven for prayer. The sacred space of the Temple is the most appropriate place to utter attachment language, and prayer could be considered the most prophetic of all speech. Clearly, Luke has already established this in the Simeon and Anna narrative (Lk. 2.25-38).

In relation to his children's needs, Kaufmann sees God as the primary protective and caring One whose reliability and availability are

---

[256] Bosworth, 'Ancient Prayers', p. 682.
[257] Bosworth, 'Ancient Prayers', p. 682.
[258] Bosworth, 'Ancient Prayers', p. 682.
[259] Bosworth, 'Ancient Prayers', p. 686.

inexhaustible.²⁶⁰ From Gethsemane through the crucifixion, Jesus' Passion (psychologically and phenomenologically) involves extreme trauma. The pressure is so great that (even physiologically) he sweats great drops of blood, collapses from extreme anxiety, and requires angelic assistance (Lk. 22.43-44). Yet, he fully experiences and processes the trauma, by abiding in prayer (Lk. 22.39-46; 23.44-46). This ability resided in his eternal bond of love with his Father. This too, he maintained through the discipline of embodied prayer that is congruent with the suffering of what could be termed *prophetic intercession*.²⁶¹

This resonates powerfully with the Father as protector and intercessor.²⁶² Regardless of the extreme distress Jesus experiences at Gethsemane, his prayer betrays no sense whatsoever of 'the absence of the deity as the source of fear counted as separation anxiety'.²⁶³ Instead, he continues to speak to his Father as a present reality. That he addresses God as 'abba' indicates a 'desire for proximity',²⁶⁴ the antiwork of separation anxiety and witness of an acute awareness of Father-Son nearness and intimacy. This intimacy empowers the Son in his prophetic expressions to reveal the Father and speak what is transformative to the alienated who need reconciliation with his Father, as his words to Zacchaeus show (Lk. 19.9-10). This and other prophetic expressions are the highest form of forthtelling and are indicative of prophetism. They are borne of a consciousness and perception of unbroken communion with the Father. Such a phenomenological reality speaks ontologically of Jesus' way of being, which includes his prophetic expressions and emotive domain, including his feelings and moods, and how he embodies them.

---

²⁶⁰ Gordon Kaufman, *The Theological Imagination: Constructing the Concept of God* (Philadelphia, PA: Westminster, 1981), p. 67. Jesus affirms this in his way of being. Kaufmann contrasts flawed and failed human parents with the flawless divine Parent, citing several psalms that speak of God's various attributes as the Mighty Warrior, Sustaining Creator, Faithful, and forever Upright One (Ps. 24.7-8, 10; 95.3-7; 146.3-9).

²⁶¹ Consider the dialogue between God and Ezekiel as God looks for one to 'stand before me in the gap' (Ezek. 22.30, NIV). Jesus stands in the breach between fallen humanity and a loving God, which the Old Covenant represented as the land of Israel and God's people who inhabited it while desperately needing redemption and reconciliation.

²⁶² Bosworth, 'Ancient Prayers', p. 685.
²⁶³ Bosworth, 'Ancient Prayers', p. 686.
²⁶⁴ Bosworth, 'Ancient Prayers', p. 686.

When Jesus speaks to the daughters of Jerusalem about the city's impending destruction, his speech act reveals a temperament of classical prophetism and prophetic legitimacy (Lk. 23.28-31). Such lament over his people's ignorance leads him to beseech the Father to forgive them (Lk. 23.34). For Johnson, this plea 'fits within Luke's narrative schema: in the time of the prophet's first sending the people reject him because of their "ignorance" (Acts 3:17; 7:25; 13:27)'.[265] The people's ignorance does not deter Jesus' loyal love. His prophetic consciousness and perception fully embody that love through suffering, even during the most painful hour of his death. His martyrdom is the quintessential Spirit of Prophecy (Rev. 19.10).

Beginning with John the Baptist, this chapter has traced the heritage of prophetic legitimacy from OT prophetism to its ultimate expression in Jesus. As exemplars, John the Baptist, Agabus, and Paul reflected their canonical prophetic predecessors while attesting to the fulfillment their counterparts could only anticipate – the coming of the Christ. Chapter 4 will now trace the Tradition forward and consider an exemplar within somewhat contemporary Pentecostalism. Although she was not mentioned or widely noted in the historical literature, she can be viewed paradigmatically in relation to prophetic legitimacy and its related contingencies. Her name is Violet Kiteley.

---

[265] Johnson, *Gospel of Luke*, p. 376.

4

LATTER RAIN PARTICIPANT VIOLET KITELEY AS EXEMPLAR OF PROPHETIC LEGITIMACY

4.1 Introduction

In every movement's history, key figures provoke pivot points and shape future generations. Violet Kiteley is such a figure. Although scholars such as Bill Faupel and Mark Hutchinson have extensively documented Latter Rain history,[1] their accounts do not mention Violet Kiteley.[2] However, because of her presence and involvement with the key figures they mention,[3] she became a principal character in the story.

Kiteley was raised in the Classical Pentecostal tradition and later participated in the postwar Latter Rain movement.[4] Her leadership in the movement's early days had significant implications throughout

---

[1] D. William Faupel, 'The New Order of the Latter Rain: Restoration or Renewal?', in Michael Wilkinson and Peter Althouse (eds.), *Winds from the North: Canadian Contributions to the Pentecostal Movement* (Leiden: Brill, 2010), pp. 239-63.

[2] Faupel, 'New Order', pp. 239-63.

[3] These key figures include Ernie Hawtin, George Hawtin, Milford Kirkpatrick, Myrtle D. Beall, Raymond Hoekstra, Reg Layzell, and George Warnock.

[4] David Kiteley, 'Video Interview by Mark J. Chironna' (Orlando, FL, November 19, 2018). The late Pastor David Kiteley was in his seventies when interviewed and had served alongside his mother from the time he was a child. He believed he was the youngest person present during the initial historic event at North Battleford (he was approximately two and a half in February 1948). Prior to his passing in October 2021, he may well have been the event's last living eyewitness. His recollections were reconstructions based on his personal experiences and conversations with his mother and others. (For clarity, all shortened footnotes citing David Kiteley will contain his first and last name. Shortened footnotes citing his mother, Violet Kiteley, will not include her first name.)

her life and ministry. For the purposes of this work, Kiteley serves as an exemplar – a Latter Rain participant whose ministry continued into the twenty-first century and maintained standards of prophetic legitimacy and accountability that are often sacrificed in popular 'prophetic' circles.

Kiteley's story is revealed in handwritten and typewritten sermon and lecture notes and syllabi from her four-year Bible college curriculum.[5] From her extensive body of work, this chapter will focus on (1) her biographical history leading up to and including her experiences in North Battleford during the Latter Rain movement, (2) her resultant understanding of prophetic function in the NT, particularly regarding prophecy as a charismatic manifestation of inspired speech in the Christian communities and her understanding of Jesus as prophet within the Luke-Acts narrative, and (3) her collected papers and teachings centered on prophetic function and her prophetic perspective.[6]

Directly related to her body of work and understanding of prophetic function is Kiteley's perception of God's 'prophetic promise to restore'.[7] This perception is not necessarily new, as the restorational paradigm was already present in Pentecostalism.[8] Kiteley also found profound significance in the relationship between the laying on of hands and the accompanying prophetic expressions of the charismata. She saw these as essential to each member of Christ's body, as a means of finding 'his [and her] place in the great economy of God and the Body of Christ'.[9] These acts were performed by apostolic and prophetic presbyters who served in an authoritative way,

---

[5] Violet Kiteley's body of work contains no footnotes or citations of sources she used, although the language within certain portions suggests other sources.

[6] Kiteley taught a broad spectrum of biblical topics, but for the purpose of this work, the focus will be on collected materials that convey her sense and overall perspective of prophetic function.

[7] Violet Kiteley, 'Section III: The Church – Prophetic Promise to Restore', *Violet Kiteley Papers*, p. 14.

[8] G.T. Sheppard, 'Pentecostals and the Hermeneutics of Dispensationalism', *Pneuma* 6.2 (Fall 1984), p. 7, quoted in French L. Arrington, 'Dispensationalism', *NIDPCM*, p. 585; Kenneth J. Archer, 'Pentecostal Story: The Hermeneutical Filter for the Making of Meaning', *Pneuma* 26.1 (Spring 2004), pp. 45-54.

[9] Violet Kiteley, 'Lesson Two: Laying on of Hands', Shiloh Bible College, Oakland, CA, *Violet Kiteley Papers*, p. 2.

bringing confirmation to local churches and their members' functions.[10]

Often unbeknownst to charismatic and Third Wave movements, the current freedom and controversy surrounding apostolic and prophetic function could stem from the 1948 revival. Kiteley's work can therefore provide a historical perspective on prophetic and charismatic phenomena that would help today's communities evaluate present charismatic expressions. From Kiteley's teachings, such insights will be incorporated into a Pentecostal theology of prophetic legitimacy.

Before proceeding, it should be noted that although the whole of Latter Rain Pentecostalism might not refer to the creedal confessions, at minimum, they affirm the creeds' second article concerning Jesus being fully human and fully divine. As previously stated, Pentecostals generally and Latter Rain adherents particularly (with its strong emphasis on the prophetic Jesus), see Jesus as the very fullness of prophecy and the fulfillment of Moses' prophecy in Deut. 18.15. This is based on their approach to Luke-Acts and is evidenced in Violet Kiteley's work.[11]

Like all Pentecostals, Kiteley read Luke-Acts in relation to Jesus. Importantly, she identified with the Pentecostal tradition that was Trinitarian. As Warrington states, 'Pentecostals have traditionally identified themselves as Trinitarian and thus (often unknowingly) affirmed the classical creeds'.[12] The prophetic legitimacy argument under discussion requires a call to prophetic formation that grasps three creedal confessions: the Apostle's Creed, Nicene Creed, and Athanasian Creed, as well as the Definition of Chalcedon.[13] Like other Latter Rain adherents, Kiteley affirmed Jesus as being fully human and fully divine, per a Pentecostal reading of the Lukan text. Even if her archived notes don't go further than that, her understanding of the Godhead is clearly Trinitarian and creedal. For Kiteley, the testimony of Jesus *is* the Spirit of Prophecy (Rev. 19.10). Understood within the

---

[10] Amid today's proliferating expressions of the charismata, prophetic utterance is often directed to individuals rather than local assemblies.

[11] Violet Kiteley, 'Life of Christ' (Lecture Notes, 2011), *Violet Kiteley Papers*, p. 32.

[12] Keith Warrington, *Pentecostal Theology: A Theology of Encounter* (London: T&T Clark, 2008), p. 29.

[13] 'The Definition of the Council of Chalcedon (451 A.D.)', *Monergism*, https://www.monergism.com/definition-council-chalcedon-451-ad.

Latter Rain tradition therefore, Jesus is not only the One who was prophesied but the measure of prophetic truthfulness itself and the very goal of prophecy. The entire point is to have the experience of Jesus and to be made like him. This is what the early doctors of the church referred to as *theosis*.

4.2 Introducing Violet Kiteley to the Latter Rain Story

The following chronological account will focus on certain formative and otherwise consequential experiences that impacted Violet Kiteley's ministry, particularly as it relates to her understanding of prophetic function. This summary does not evaluate her theological presuppositions but does provide a framework for approaching the formation of her prophetic consciousness, which includes theological, psychological, and phenomenological views.

4.2.1 Kiteley's Family, Youth, and Baptismal Encounter

Violet Kiteley (1925–2015) was born to Albert and Mary Jane Whitney, in Vancouver, British Columbia.[14] Her father was a wealthy farmer who lost everything in the Great Depression,[15] a reversal that reduced the family to poverty and prompted their outreach to the disenfranchised in the city's poorest section.[16] The Whitneys' commitment to the marginalized remained with Kiteley and would be reflected in her eventual ministry.

The Whitney family was immersed in Vancouver's Classical Pentecostal tradition and aware of the larger Pentecostal movement. Smith Wigglesworth and Charles S. Price were personal friends of Violet Kiteley's parents and one or both men stayed in their home.[17] Both men 'prophesied' that 'God will move mightily again but we will

---

[14] Abraham Ruelas, *Women and the Landscape of American Higher Education: Wesleyan Holiness and Pentecostal Founders* (Eugene, OR: Pickwick, 2010), ch. 26.

[15] David Kiteley, video interview.

[16] Ruelas, *Women and the Landscape of American Higher Education*, ch. 26; David Kiteley, video interview.

[17] Violet Kiteley, 'An Unbroken Line: Latter Rain Movement/1948 Revival', *Violet Kiteley Papers*, p. 2; Kiteley, 'Violet Kiteley Account', p. 2. Violet Kiteley, 'Healing and Latter Rain Movements 1947–48: An Eyewitness Account; Interview with Dr. Violet Kiteley', interview by Abraham Ruelas and Alma Thomas, *Violet Kiteley Papers*, p. 7.

not see it. It will happen after we are gone'.[18] These words remained in Kiteley's memory and seemed to affirm her later Pentecostal experience.

Kiteley was raised in the Church of the Foursquare Gospel,[19] and her family was significantly influenced (albeit from a distance) by Aimee Semple McPherson. In 1937, McPherson became an immediate and seminal figure in Kiteley's life when she presided over a water baptismal service in which Kiteley was baptized.[20] In a recorded interview, Kiteley's only child, the late Pastor David Kiteley, reconstructed from memory the baptismal account that his mother and grandfather recounted to him over the years. He explained that as Violet emerged from the baptismal waters, Aimee 'reached over … and gave her … a prophetic word'.[21] In Violet Kiteley's own words, 'She [McPherson] put her hand on my head and said that the mantle of God was on [me] and I would minister around the world'.[22]

The local Pentecostal community was aware of Kiteley's baptismal encounter.[23] At fourteen, she began to preach and minister.[24] By the time she was seventeen, she and her parents attended Vancouver's Broadway Tabernacle, pastored by Walter McAlister.[25] Broadway Tabernacle had a Chinese outreach church whose pastor had been conscripted due to the Second World War, along with other men and

---

[18] Kiteley, 'Unbroken Line', p. 2. Kiteley added emphatic underlining to these words in her typewritten notes.

[19] David Kiteley, video interview; 'History', *The Foursquare Church*, https://www.foursquare.org/about/history/; David Kiteley, video interview, 'What the Foursquare Church Believes', *The Foursquare Church*, https://foursquare-org.s3.amazonaws.com/resources/Print_Brochure_What_Foursquare_Believes_English.pdf.

[20] David Kiteley, video interview; Ruelas, 'Mantle of God', ch. 26. The baptismal service was held at the Kingsway Foursquare Church.

[21] David Kiteley, video interview.

[22] Steven Lawson, 'Kiteley Family a Point of Light in Troubled Oakland', *Charisma* (December 31, 2002), https://www.charismamag.com/site-archives/154-peopleevents/people-and-events/817-kiteley-family-a-point-of-light-in-troubled-oakland.

[23] David Kiteley, video interview.

[24] Kiteley, 'Healing and Latter Rain', p. 5.

[25] Pastor Walter McAlister and his brother Jack were the sons of John McAlister. John McAlister and his uncle R.E. McAlister were PAOC pioneers. John McAlister became superintendent of the PAOC in late 1948 or early 1949. Jack McAlister pastored in Prince Albert. Both Walter and Jack McAlister were part of the PAOC.

male ministers in the community.²⁶ Although McAlister resisted the idea of women pastoring churches, he was aware of Kiteley's seminal experience with Aimee Semple McPherson and placed seventeen-year-old Kiteley as pastor over the Chinese congregation.²⁷ Kiteley's tenure was fruitful, and the church began to thrive. At that point, according to David Kiteley, McAlister and the board removed Kiteley as pastor, preferring a man to oversee the work.²⁸

4.2.2 Kiteley's Marriage and Widowhood, Prophecy from a Trans-Jordanian Prophet, and Healing from Paralysis

In 1944, at age nineteen,²⁹ Violet married Raymond Kiteley,³⁰ 'a soloist and worship leader at Reverend Ern Baxter's church [Evangelistic Tabernacle] in Vancouver'.³¹ The couple shared the call to ministry and planned to become missionaries to West Africa upon Raymond's return from war.³² Tragically, Raymond and several other airmen were killed in a 'fiery crash' in the Pacific on July 13, 1945.³³

Pregnant with her only child, Kiteley became a nineteen-year-old war widow. When her son David was born, the trauma left her paralyzed and bedridden. She later wrote:

> On October 13, 1945, just three days after my son's birth, I became a cripple. For thirteen months I didn't get any medical help ... poison went through my system, and I became paralyzed. It was a lack of proper care that caused my health problem.³⁴

Kiteley stated, 'many people were questioning why God allowed my husband to be killed and me to be ill for as long as I was'.³⁵ The implication, Kiteley believed, was that her hardship resulted from overstepping her bounds as a woman and assuming that she was called to preach. 'When she was paralyzed ... some in the church'

---

²⁶ David Kiteley, video interview.
²⁷ David Kiteley, video interview; Kiteley, 'Healing and Latter Rain', p. 5. David Kiteley, *I Didn't Mean to Cause Trouble: Supernatural Stories* (Orlando, FL: Kudu, 2017), ch. 1.
²⁸ David Kiteley, video interview.
²⁹ Kiteley, 'Healing and Latter Rain', p. 5.
³⁰ Ruelas, 'Mantle of God', ch. 26.
³¹ Ruelas, 'Mantle of God', ch. 26; Kiteley, 'Healing and Latter Rain', p. 5.
³² David Kiteley, video interview; Ruelas, 'Mantle of God', ch. 26.
³³ Kiteley, 'Unbroken Line', p. 2; Kiteley, 'Violet Kiteley Account', p. 2.
³⁴ Kiteley, 'Healing and Latter Rain', p. 6.
³⁵ Kiteley, 'Healing and Latter Rain', p. 6.

pressed beyond the rhetorical question and 'told her she was suffering God's punishment for breaching the pulpit'.[36]

Amid her grief, Kiteley found unexpected hope and later wrote, 'In November 1946, the voice of the Lord spoke into my spirit and told me that God was going to raise me up. A minister was going to come at 3 p.m. the next day, and I was going to walk.'[37] In fact, a Trans-Jordanian minister whom Kiteley later identified as 'Brother Smith' was heading to Vancouver at the time.[38] Smith was fluent in the charismatic expression of prophecy. As his flight approached Vancouver, he became aware (presumably by the Spirit) of a young woman's tragic state.[39] Although unaware of the details of airman Kiteley's death, Smith shared what he perceived with Pastor McAlister.[40] Recognizing that Smith was speaking of Violet Kiteley, McAlister escorted him to Kiteley's home. There, McAlister joined the 'missionary prophet' in praying for Kiteley and in the laying on of hands.[41] Thus, McAlister heard the prophetic word being delivered and became an eyewitness to Kiteley's being raised up.[42] Kiteley wrote of the visit, saying,

> The [prophetic] word that I got was that I was going to preach a new message. Brother Smith, the missionary from Trans-Jordan, was brought by Pastor Walter McAlister to pray for me. Brother Smith told Pastor McAlister that God had spoken to him, while coming over on the plane from Trans-Jordan, that a young lady was to be healed and raised up to preach a new message. Pastor McAlister was really touched by the fact that he saw me come out of the bed walking that day.[43]

Kiteley understood the moment to be freighted with significance for her future. It seemed clear to her that Smith's prophecy 'was highly unusual because first of all the ministry of Prophet was not

---

[36] Dennis Balcombe, *China's Opening Door: Incredible Stories of the Holy Spirit at Work in One of the Greatest Revivals in Christianity* (Lake Mary, FL: Charisma House, 2014), p. 44.
[37] Kiteley, 'Healing and Latter Rain', p. 6.
[38] Kiteley, 'Healing and Latter Rain', p. 6.
[39] Kiteley, 'Unbroken Line', p. 2.
[40] Kiteley, 'Healing and Latter Rain', p. 6.
[41] Kiteley, 'Unbroken Line', p. 2; Kiteley, 'Healing and Latter Rain', p. 6.
[42] Kiteley, 'Unbroken Line', p. 2; Kiteley, 'Healing and Latter Rain', p. 6; David Kiteley, video interview.
[43] Kiteley, 'Healing and Latter Rain', p. 6.

widely accepted at that time'.[44] David Kiteley added that personal prophecy was particularly rare and controversial when it involved the call of women to preaching ministry within mainline Pentecostal denominations.[45]

Immediately after the prophet's visit, Violet Kiteley reported, 'the Lord did raise [her] up'.[46] The miracle of her healing was enough for Walter McAlister to arrange an extensive itinerary within the Pentecostal Assemblies of Canada and other Pentecostal churches so that Kiteley might share her testimony.[47]

4.2.3 Kiteley's Itinerant Ministry and a Prophecy from a Retired Missionary

For the next year and a half, Kiteley traveled 'from church to church and province to province eastward',[48] bearing witness to her miracle healing, preaching the gospel, and praying for the sick.[49] In 'the fall of 1947',[50] Kiteley became 'aware' of a movement stirring in North Battleford.[51] She explained, 'because of the position [she] was in' (through her healing and her travels as sanctioned by the Pentecostal Assemblies of Canada),[52] she heard reports from various places. She also kept 'very close contact with Milford Kirkpatrick', a family friend who was in North Battleford.[53] Kiteley wrote, 'I had a good opportunity to know how God was moving progressively in their midst'.[54]

Kiteley understood that the Pentecostal Assemblies of Canada (or PAOC, in which the McAlisters were very influential)[55] strongly opposed the North Battleford movement. She recalled that the Hawtin Brothers, Milford Kirkpatrick, and local Bible school students involved in the outpouring 'were greatly persecuted for fasting and

---

[44] Kiteley, 'Unbroken Line', p. 2.
[45] David Kiteley, video interview. David Kiteley noted that Walter McAlister was uncomfortable with the notion of women in the pulpit.
[46] Kiteley, 'Unbroken Line', p. 2.
[47] David Kiteley, video interview. According to David Kiteley, Walter McAlister could not deny the Body of Christ's need to hear Violet Kiteley's healing testimony.
[48] Kiteley, 'Unbroken Line', pp. 2-3.
[49] David Kiteley, video interview.
[50] Kiteley, 'Healing and Latter Rain', p. 6.
[51] Kiteley, 'Healing and Latter Rain', p. 6.
[52] Kiteley, 'Healing and Latter Rain', p. 6.
[53] Kiteley, 'Healing and Latter Rain', p. 6. Kirkpatrick's sister was in the PAOC in Vancouver and attended Walter McAlister's church there.
[54] Kiteley, 'Healing and Latter Rain', p. 6.
[55] Kiteley, 'Healing and Latter Rain', pp. 6-7.

praying',[56] with most of the persecution coming from the denomination.

When Kiteley shared her testimony in Pastor Jack McAlister's church in Prince Albert,[57] Saskatchewan (just 'sixty miles northeast of North Battleford')[58] an elderly female retired missionary whom Kiteley 'had never met' approached her while Kiteley ministered at the altar.[59] The missionary urged her to go to North Battleford and said that 'a group of hungry Bible School students were fasting night and day for the birth of a fresh new move of God'.[60] The woman laid hands on Kiteley and prophesied that she would receive an impartation in North Battleford for a message she was called to preach to the nations.[61]

Yet again, the laying on of hands was followed by a prophetic word, and that message bore witness to previous prophecies received through Aimee Semple McPherson and Brother Smith. Kiteley approached Pastor Jack McAlister about it, knowing that he 'was already geared to be against' the events in North Battleford.[62] In fact, as Kiteley wrote, 'I had known about the move and was warned not to have anything to do with it'.[63]

4.2.4 Kiteley's Embrace of the North Battleford Movement

The elderly missionary's encouragement stirred something already present in Kiteley. Although she regarded the warnings from church leadership, Kiteley strongly felt that 'this [outpouring] could be that word God had spoken into [her] spirit in November of 1946',[64] the night before she met the Trans-Jordanian prophet. Clearly, because of her upbringing and life experience, she believed her intuitive sense of the Spirit's leading was pointing her toward a future that awaited her arrival.

---

[56] Kiteley, 'Healing and Latter Rain', p. 3.
[57] As previously mentioned, Jack McAlister was the brother of Walter McAlister.
[58] Kiteley, 'Healing and Latter Rain', p. 6.
[59] Kiteley, 'Unbroken Line', p. 3.
[60] Kiteley, 'Unbroken Line', p. 3.
[61] David Kiteley, video interview.
[62] Kiteley, 'Healing and Latter Rain', p. 6.
[63] Kiteley, 'Healing and Latter Rain', p. 6. Violet was warned in this instance by Pastor Jack McAlister.
[64] Kiteley, 'Healing and Latter Rain', p. 6.

Being far more aware of the North Battleford environment than she allowed Jack McAlister to know,[65] Kiteley announced her intention to attend 'the revival to see it for [herself]' and attested that 'Pastor Jack [McAlister] tried to talk [her] out of it'.[66] He explained the PAOC's reasoning. He and others who countered the movement told Kiteley, 'You're too young to understand'.[67] Exhibiting the resolve developed in her youth, she replied, 'You've got to get something better than that to reject the message'.[68] She pointed to her history and said, 'I've had a lot of life, and I've seen a lot; and I'm going to go there and see this for myself'.[69]

Both resolute and provoked by the resistance she met, Kiteley likened her determination to that of her mother, Mary Jane, writing,[70]

> My mother was really a praying person. My dad was, also – but my mother had known the Lord much longer, since 1906 in Belfast, Ireland. She had to stand alone in her family. She was a tiny woman, 4 feet 10 inches. She was with the Holiness Movement; and she often had a word of knowledge in prayer that was proven on many occasions.[71]

Kiteley's experiences at this time occurred within the context of a 'real spiritual dearth',[72] which she witnessed prior to the 1948 outpouring. She enumerated its causes: 'During the war years, 1939 to 1945, many were without money and without jobs'.[73] Canada was 'devastated so badly' that 'it was as if there was a deep depression of people's spirit'.[74] 'Canada was torn up financially [and] manpower was

---

[65] Kiteley, 'Healing and Latter Rain', p. 6; Kiteley explained, 'It was a very secret thing because of the pressure against it, and you were fearful of who you spoke to and what you might relate', not wanting 'anyone to be hurt'.
[66] Kiteley, 'Healing and Latter Rain', p. 6.
[67] Kiteley, 'Healing and Latter Rain', p. 7.
[68] Kiteley, 'Healing and Latter Rain', p. 7.
[69] Kiteley, 'Healing and Latter Rain', p. 7.
[70] Ruelas, 'Mantle of God', ch. 26.
[71] Kiteley, 'Healing and Latter Rain', p. 7.
[72] Kiteley, 'Restoration Basics', p. 1. Although 'Dec 3 /09' is jotted on this document, the typewritten portion of text appears to have been pasted for reuse, suggesting that the teaching was developed at some earlier time and perhaps taught repeatedly over the years.
[73] Kiteley, 'Restoration Basics', p. 1.
[74] Kiteley, 'Healing and Latter Rain', p. 6.

greatly depleted.'[75] Kiteley stated that in Nanaimo, British Columbia, where she was from, 'not one man returned from the war'.[76]

Within this 'dearth', Kiteley noted, 'for a person to receive the Holy Spirit was a time of long tarrying, sometimes for months'.[77] She wrote emphatically, *'People were hungry by 1947 for God, and were* crying out for God to do something fresh'.[78] She believed that the dearth drove the people's hunger. She also stated, 'in the late part of 1947, people were seeking God the same as they had done in 1906 in Azusa Street … They got hold of God in prayer.'[79]

Kiteley connected the Pentecostal community's condition and cry to God in 1947 with conditions that precipitated events on Azusa Street in 1906. Also significant in her mind was the fact that both Charles Price and Smith Wigglesworth passed in 1947. Based on the prophecies Kiteley had heard from them years earlier,[80] she equated their passing with the end of Pentecostalism's former era. For her, their words validated the 1948 outpouring, and she saw the new movement as their prophecies' fulfillment.

4.2.5 Kiteley Witnesses and Receives Prophetic Words in North Battleford

Kiteley's experiences and awareness contributed to her being in North Battleford as an eyewitness when Ernie Hawtin, one of the movement's leaders, 'received a prophetic utterance' regarding 1 Tim. 4.14.[81] Her eyewitness experience and her own encounter with the Spirit in North Battleford further affirmed events, which she recorded in this personal account:

> On February 13, 1948, after an all-night of praying and worship (I was there), one of the primary leaders of the movement (Ernie Hawtin), who had a very serious speech impediment, which made his speech barely understandable, received a prophetic utterance

---

[75] Kiteley, 'Healing and Latter Rain', p. 6.
[76] Kiteley, 'Healing and Latter Rain', p. 6.
[77] Kiteley, 'Restoration Basics', p. 1.
[78] Kiteley, 'Restoration Basics', p. 1; emphasis is Kiteley's.
[79] Kiteley, 'Restoration Basics', p. 3.
[80] Kiteley, 'Unbroken Line', p. 2.
[81] Kiteley, 'Unbroken Line', p. 3. Kiteley's two-and-a-half-year-old son David accompanied her on the journey and through her experiences at North Battleford. Kiteley, 'Healing and Latter Rain', p. 6. She noted, 'I was there shortly after the revival started, and I remained there five months continually – every day, every hour' (p. 7).

quickening regarding 1 Tim 4:14, and he spoke clearly without any difficulty of speech. Ernie Hawtin was totally delivered from his speech impediment that night ... This was the *birthing of the presbytery* as we know it.[82]

This perceived 'birthing of the presbytery' confirmed Kiteley's personal prophetic experiences since the age of twelve. She advanced this conviction and described the actions of the presbytery:

From time to time, the Lord would indicate certain candidates, which had a prepared heart and sacrificial willingness to serve the Body and ... they would be sent forth to the nations. In God's mercy alone, I was chosen as one among many of the candidates, as God knew my heart and that I could receive at that time.[83]

As the presbytery laid hands on Kiteley at North Battleford, their prophetic words seemed strikingly confirming of those she had heard from Aimee Semple McPherson, the prophet from Trans-Jordan, and the retired missionary at Prince Albert. The presbyters' words also struck a personal note. As Kiteley reported,

George Hawtin started to pray prophetically. He told me that I had lost my husband, and they never knew anything about me because I stayed in the background. I didn't want to talk to anyone about my life personally.[84]

---

[82] Kiteley, 'Unbroken Line', p. 3 (emphasis added).

[83] Kiteley, 'Unbroken Line', p. 5. All handwritten emphasis within Kiteley's document is her own. 'In God's mercy alone', is inserted by her hand into this typewritten document.

[84] Kiteley, 'Healing and Latter Rain', p. 7; Kiteley noted, '[The prophesying] took several hours, I was told. I was really lost in the Presence of the Lord'. Prophetic words from the presbytery in North Battleford also spoke to her family's future prophetic legacy, as Kiteley explained:

The prophecy ... my David who was only 3 years old when I received the word ... that 'out of my womb had come forth a prophet to the nations, and out of him was going to come forth another prophet'. My grandson Patrick wasn't born until 1973, but he had a prophetic word given to him in 1948 (p. 5).

The prophecy received in 1948 would prove essential decades later, when Kiteley's grandson Patrick was born two months premature and placed on life support on April 7, 1973. David Kiteley, *Didn't Mean*, ch. 5, David Kiteley wrote that Patrick was born with 'Hyaline Membrane Disease' and was given a '1 in 40 chance of living'. A pediatrician told David Kiteley that if his son 'made it, he would more than likely have some physical defects due to being on 100 percent oxygen for such

4.3 Latter Rain Restorationism

The restorationist aspects of Violet Kiteley's beliefs examined here will ultimately lead to the construction of a Pentecostal theology of prophetic consciousness, perception, and enactment.[85] It should be stated that prophecy is included in the praxis of many Christian traditions. Within all these contexts, eschatological views, and supporting presuppositions, prophetic legitimacy and integrity can be established or maintained. However, the eschatological framework from which one views the Scriptures and applies them to the times affects one's prophetic consciousness, perception, and enactment. Various traditions influence prophetic consciousness largely by how they relate to the wisdom of the larger Christian Tradition.[86] This relationship with the larger Tradition is an important aspect of understanding the role of the Latter Rain movement regarding prophetic legitimacy.

4.3.1 Latter Rain Restorationism and the 'Dark Ages'

Understanding the framework from which Latter Rain participant Violet Kiteley exercised prophetic function provides a window into her sense of urgency regarding what the church was called to be and become. She argued:

> The Dark Ages left the Church spiritually deaf and blind. The Church had lost touch with the Spirit of God. As a result, God's Spirit no longer led and directed this organization of man into all the truth. The religious leaders of this religious system were spiritually blind, and having eyes they could not see. This Church did not listen for the voice of the Spirit behind them directing their paths, but their ears were stopped by human traditions, having ears

---

a long period of time', David Kiteley, *Didn't Mean*, ch. 5. On his thirty-fifth birthday in 2008, Patrick was installed as the third pastor of the Oakland, California, church his grandmother founded. He succeeded his father, David, in that pastorate, inheriting it with the laying on of hands by a presbytery in fulfillment of the prophecy given by the North Battleford presbytery in North Battleford in 1948. Although he is not currently pastoring the Oakland congregation, Patrick Kiteley remains active in the ministry.

[85] For additional context on Latter Rain Restorationism and its place in the history of Restorationism overall, see Mark J. Chironna, 'Latter Rain Restorationism as Understood by Violet Kiteley and Other Latter Rain Adherents', https://www.markchironna.com/articles.

[86] Anti-traditionalism is justified in many Pentecostal circles by appeals to what Jesus said about 'the traditions of men' (see Mt. 15.1-9; Mk 7.1-9, 11-13).

they did not hear. The pity of it is that all the time the religious leaders and most of the people felt that they did see and did hear. They felt they were in the perfect way. The people of the Middle Ages were duped by the traditions of men.[87]

Here Kiteley asserts her ways of perceiving and understanding church history and her subjective evaluation of the saints' spiritual disposition during the Middle Ages. Because her assertions are not substantiated with historical references, it is difficult to evaluate the basis upon which they are founded. However, some clarity might emerge as her argumentation is considered within her personal and historical context.

Kiteley's cited remarks about the Middle Ages do not mention Aimee Semple McPherson. However, based on McPherson's seminal role in the Pentecostal movement and in Kiteley's personal life,[88] one might conjecture that McPherson's train of thought profoundly influenced Kiteley's. In a 1917 McPherson sermon entitled 'Lost and Restored', McPherson spoke from the 'Primitivism or Restorationism' that was present from the earliest days of the Classical Pentecostal movement.[89] At one point in McPherson's sermon, a connection with Kiteley's assertions about the Middle Ages seems apparent, with both women referring to the epoch as the *Dark Ages*. McPherson opined:

> No wonder they are called the Dark Ages. Ah! dark indeed is the night without Jesus ... Men and women groping in this darkness tried to win their way to Heaven by doing penance, by locking themselves up in dungeons, walking over red-hot plowshares in their bare feet, and inflicting unnamable tortures upon themselves and upon one another, blindly trying by some work or deed to pay the debt that had already been paid on Calvary's rugged cross.[90]

McPherson, who expired four years prior to the 1948 events in North Battleford, and Kiteley, a participant in those events, held

---

[87] Kiteley, 'Prophetic Promise to Restore', p. 14.
[88] McPherson was also influential in early Pentecostalism. See Chas. H. Barfoot, *Aimee Semple McPherson and the Making of Modern Pentecostalism* (London: Routledge, 2014); Ruelas, 'Mantle of God', ch. 26.
[89] Steven L. Ware, 'Restorationism in Classical Pentecostalism', *NIDPCM*, p. 1019.
[90] Ware, 'Restorationism', p. 1019.

similar views of medieval church history. Their metaphors differ slightly, however: for Kiteley, the medieval masses were spiritually deaf and blind.[91] For McPherson, they were 'groping in the darkness'.[92] Whereas Kiteley attributed the blindness of medieval religious leaders to their bondage by human traditions, McPherson highlighted extreme ascetic practices. Both points of view are reconcilable as approximately addressing the same issues and impacts on the collective consciousness of medieval saints.

4.3.2 The Schema of Latter Rain Restorationism: Roots, Metaphors, and Thought Systems

The Pentecostal movement's Restorationism echoes prominent Reformation voices and is largely rooted in disaffection, distrust, and disdain for the Rome papacy. What perhaps elucidates Kiteley's bias as a Latter Rain restorationist is her assertion that the medieval church was 'literally bound in chains of bondage to a Babylonian system … [and had] lost their Deliverer (Christ) and their hope'.[93] Kiteley's disdain is evident. As she quotes Isa. 42.18-22 (KJV), for example, she ends by saying, 'None saith, Restore' and attributes the failure to 'their ignorance'.[94]

With the prophetic cry for restoration absent, Kiteley believed the church was lost to Christ. From this viewpoint, Latter Rain Restorationism became an earmark of the movement that deepened and broadened her restorationist convictions. Kiteley believed it was imperative to recover 'the divine principles and truths that were known, believed, taught, and experienced by the Early Church',[95] and she cited numerous scriptures to express what was foundationally 'laid by the early apostles and prophets'.[96]

Notable is the consistent reliance on apostles and prophets to function prophetically within the church and trans-locally. The prophetic became an overshadowing of the entire Latter Rain Restorationist impulse, which involved 'a renewal of that spiritual life that is

---

[91] Kiteley, 'Prophetic Promise to Restore', p. 14.
[92] Ware, 'Restorationism', p. 1019.
[93] Kiteley, 'Prophetic Promise to Restore', p. 14.
[94] Kiteley, 'Prophetic Promise to Restore', p. 14. Kiteley refers to the Greek term ἀποκαταστάσεως (*apokatastaseos*), as meaning 'to restore'.
[95] Kiteley, 'Prophetic Promise to Restore', p. 15.
[96] Kiteley, 'Prophetic Promise to Restore', p. 15. See Eph. 2.20; 1 Cor. 3.10; 1 Tim. 4.6.

the result of the application' of the principles revealed in the cited scriptural texts.[97] Thus, the church could 'return to the pattern that God has set for it'.[98] With the pattern restored, Kiteley believed the church '[could not] help but experience that "breath of life" that God breathed into it on the Day of Pentecost'.[99]

Kiteley's primitivist framework is clear. Yet despite her somewhat veiled reference linking the Roman church to the Babylonian system, she did state that the Charismatic Movement 'from 1967 into the early '70s ... was prophesied at North Battleford in 1948'.[100] She noted that the promise of God within that prophetic utterance was 'to send revival to the Catholic denomination, bringing salvation and correcting mistakes in their doctrine'.[101] She stated, 'old-line Pentecost' rejected the Charismatic movement,[102] having 'been taught that there was no hope for the Catholic church, that it was "Babylon"'.[103] She added her own commentary, stating, 'Of course there is some Babylon in their teachings'.[104] Although she showed antipathy toward Catholics as a denomination, she claimed, 'Pentecost is an experience, not a denomination'.[105] Therefore, she was open to what transpired 'in 1967 ... at Notre Dame (a Roman Catholic university)',[106] stating that it 'was fulfillment of the 1948 prophecy'.[107]

Kiteley's terminology and references to Babylon bring to mind Martin Luther's 1520 Manifesto, 'The Babylonian Captivity of the Church'.[108] It is uncertain whether Kiteley was familiar with John Knox's characterization of the Roman Catholic church as the

---

[97] Kiteley, 'Prophetic Promise to Restore', p. 15.
[98] Kiteley, 'Prophetic Promise to Restore', p. 15.
[99] Kiteley, 'Prophetic Promise to Restore', p. 15.
[100] Kiteley, 'Healing and Latter Rain', p. 10.
[101] Kiteley, 'Healing and Latter Rain', p. 10.
[102] Kiteley, 'Healing and Latter Rain', p. 10.
[103] Kiteley, 'Healing and Latter Rain', p. 10.
[104] Kiteley, 'Healing and Latter Rain', p. 10.
[105] Kiteley, 'Healing and Latter Rain', p. 10.
[106] Kiteley, 'Healing and Latter Rain', p. 10.
[107] Kiteley, 'Healing and Latter Rain', p. 10.
[108] Martin Luther, 'The Babylonian Captivity of the Church 1520' (trans, A.T.W. Steinhauser; revised by Frederick C. Ahrens, and Abdel Ross Wentz), http://www.onthewing.org/user/Luther%20-%20Babylonian%20Captivity.pdf. Whereas Pentecostals seem to have broad-brushed their complaints and often dismissed the Roman church, Luther centered his argument on sacramentology and the Eucharist, even while reproaching the papacy.

fulfillment of the antichrist in the Book of Revelation.[109] This would not be uncommon among the Reformers, as Joachim and others also associated 'the antichrist with the papacy'.[110] In Pentecostalism, the persuasion is linked to an eschatological emphasis. French Arrington notes, 'pentecostals as a whole shared the premillennial vision of the future',[111] which would be true of Kiteley's view. Gerald T. Sheppard states, 'Pentecostals commonly thought of the twentieth-century outpouring of the Spirit as evidence of the "latter rain" or at least as a sign of a "last days" restoration of the Apostolic church prior to the return of Christ'.[112] The notion of the Pentecostal outpouring as the fulfillment of Joel's prophesied latter rain (which differs from Kiteley's position) was established in the collective consciousness of Pentecostals prior to 1948.

Within Pentecostalism and the Latter Rain movement, dispensational leanings are clear. Arrington claims that as a system of thought, dispensationalism 'provides a convenient method of organizing biblical history and teaches that it is possible to fit the full range of prophetic Scripture into something like a complicated puzzle'.[113] Although Latter Rain Restorationism is not necessarily fully dispensational, it does approach eschatology as a 'complicated puzzle' in which the dots between Latter Rain Restorationism and an eschatological interpretation of church history can be connected.

4.3.3 The Schema of Latter Rain Restoration: Kiteley's Interpretation of Scripture and Prophetic Motivation

The restorational schema determines how Kiteley and other Latter Rain principals interpret(ed) the prophets and the NT, and it explains their emphasis on the restoration of apostolic anointing and teaching.[114] Kiteley primarily based her readings of Joel, 1 Kings, Ezekiel 33–48, Psalms, Isaiah, Haggai, and Acts on their historical context; but from a restorational perspective, she applied the texts to the times in which the Latter Rain movement occurred.[115] She saw the fulfilled restoration of divine fellowship revealed in Amos 5.14 and the

---

[109] Richard Kyle, 'John Knox and Apocalyptic Thought', *The Sixteenth Century Journal* 15.4 (Winter 1984), p. 449.
[110] Kyle, 'John Knox', p. 452.
[111] Arrington, 'Dispensationalism', p. 585.
[112] Sheppard, 'Hermeneutics of Dispensationalism', p. 585.
[113] Arrington, 'Dispensationalism', p. 585.
[114] Kiteley, 'Prophetic Promise to Restore', p. 16.
[115] Kiteley, 'Prophetic Promise to Restore', p. 16.

awakening of the conscience as present realities.[116] Certainly, these passages can be preached prophetically and applied to the church's contemporary contexts. However, Kiteley and many of her peers found in these passages particular significance following the Pentecostal outpouring of the nascent twentieth century.

Regarding Acts 3.21 (KJV), Kiteley believed that the phrase 'times of restitution' implied that God was 'working on a timetable',[117] and she emphatically pointed to 'times when God [would] give to the Church that which was lost'.[118] Kiteley saw the times that Peter referenced not as generalities but as allusions to her own era. This is essential to understanding her sense of urgency regarding prophetic proclamation and her belief in the extreme significance of prophetic function in relationship to God's promises.

Within the Latter Rain movement, the prophetic seems to have played an almost primary role. Kiteley averred, 'The return of Christ cannot take place until all that the prophets spoke be fulfilled'.[119] Her concision persisted as she avouched, 'The language here seems to imply that this time [of restitution] will *immediately precede* the Second Coming of Christ'.[120] Regardless of whether the text implies this precise timing, Kiteley's assessment captures the sense among Latter Rain leaders that the church was approaching the final eschaton.

Kiteley added, 'whatever God's holy prophets have spoken will come to pass. This is one of the tests of a true prophet. The Church should be eagerly searching the prophetic Scriptures for clues to our position in God's timetable.'[121] Here Kiteley offered a double assertion. On the one hand, she spoke of 'God's holy prophets', meaning the canonical prophets. She asserted that because they were true prophets, their words would come to pass. This would occur according to an eschatological framework, presumably the one she inferred from the texts. At the same time, she expected the predictive utterances of contemporary prophets (whose authority is not commensurate with that of canonical prophets) to be judged by the same standard. Her expectation can be deduced from her literary way of

---

[116] Kiteley, 'Prophetic Promise to Restore', p. 16.
[117] Kiteley, 'Prophetic Promise to Restore', p. 17.
[118] Kiteley, 'Prophetic Promise to Restore', p. 17.
[119] Kiteley, 'Prophetic Promise to Restore', p. 17.
[120] Kiteley, 'Prophetic Promise to Restore', p. 17 (emphasis added).
[121] Kiteley, 'Prophetic Promise to Restore', p. 17.

invoking 'true prophet[s]'.[122] She could have framed her language to indicate the canonical prophets exclusively, but she did not. Instead, she seemed to presuppose that the 'holy' canonical prophets are, by definition, within the Tradition, which precludes any possibility that they would not be true prophets. It follows, therefore, that she mentions 'true prophets' to instruct her hearers as to those in the NT church (and particularly the contemporary church) who claim prophetic office. These prophets are subject to 'tests'.[123] Kiteley singled out for mention the test of the true prophet's words coming to pass.[124] This test has eschatological consequences. Clarifying the restorationist schema, Kiteley implied those consequences, saying,

> The return of Christ cannot take place until all that the prophets spoke be fulfilled. Many people think that Christ could come at any minute. He could come for them any minute, but He will not come for the Church until all be fulfilled. In fact, the heavens must retain Him against that time, for when He returns He is coming for *a full-restored Church* – a Church that is glorious, not having spot or wrinkle or any such thing (Ephesians 5:27).[125]

Here Kiteley seems not to hold to an imminent return of Christ, but to predicate the Parousia on the 'full-restored Church' that necessarily precedes it.[126] This speaks to Kiteley's prophetic consciousness and perception, and her approach to them for the sake of the church Paul described: 'a glorious church, not having spot, or wrinkle, or any such thing' (Eph. 5.27, KJV). For Kiteley, this is what motivates all that is said and done in the church.

4.3.4 Kiteley's View: Aspects of a Church Prepared for the Parousia

Kiteley stated, 'restoration involves many aspects in relation to the dealing of God with man'.[127] She added, 'restoration for the church involves at least three aspects' that signify a church that is ready for Christ's return:[128]

---

[122] Kiteley, 'Prophetic Promise to Restore', p. 17.
[123] Kiteley, 'Prophetic Promise to Restore', p. 17.
[124] Kiteley, 'Prophetic Promise to Restore', p. 17.
[125] Kiteley, 'Prophetic Promise to Restore', p. 17 (emphasis added).
[126] Kiteley, 'Prophetic Promise to Restore', p. 17.
[127] Kiteley, 'Prophetic Promise to Restore', p. 15.
[128] Kiteley, 'Prophetic Promise to Restore', p. 15.

1. 'The recovery of the divine principles and truths that were known, believed, taught, and experienced by the Early Church.'[129] This included what was lost through 'compromises made in the years of Church history'.[130] Kiteley argued that the recovery of divine principles requires a 'returning to the foundation which was laid by the early apostles and prophets. (See Ephesians 2:20; 1 Corinthians 3:10; 1 Timothy 4:6)'.[131]
2. The 'renewal of that spiritual life that is the result of the application' of the divine principles mentioned in the previous point.[132]
3. 'A completion of God's plan of the ages'.[133] Kiteley indicates that this is spoken of in Acts 3.21 and Rom. 16.26. She states, 'All that God has said, He will do. This, too, involves a restoration – a restoration that ends up at the Tree of Life'.[134]

Kiteley's writings show that her prophetic consciousness and perception (and therefore her enactment) were shaped within an eschatological framework of Latter Rain Restorationism. The purpose of this work is not to argue for the accuracy or inaccuracy of the schema. Rather, it is to provide a window into (1) the factors that molded Kiteley's view of the time and place she occupied in history, and (2) the way she stewarded what she believed was entrusted to her.

---

[129] Kiteley, 'Prophetic Promise to Restore', p. 15.
[130] Kiteley, 'Prophetic Promise to Restore', p. 15.
[131] Kiteley, 'Prophetic Promise to Restore', p. 15.
[132] Kiteley, 'Prophetic Promise to Restore', p. 15.
[133] Kiteley, 'Prophetic Promise to Restore', p. 15.
[134] Kiteley, 'Prophetic Promise to Restore', p. 15. Kiteley's statement resonates with Aimee Semple McPherson's 'Lost and Restored' sermon in which McPherson refers to 'the church as a tree and us[es] the prophetic images of agricultural blight and recovery in Joel 1–2'. Ware, 'Restorationism', p. 1019. Kiteley refers to 'the restoration period', which she clearly saw as having begun in 1948. What she believed would be evident in this period is the fulfillment of Jer. 33.11, when 'the voice of joy and the voice of gladness will be heard in the House of the Lord'. Kiteley, 'Prophetic Promise to Restore', p. 17. Per the same passage in Jeremiah, Kiteley wrote, 'the voice of the Bride will again be heard', and 'the voice of the Bridegroom will be heard among God's people'. Kiteley, 'Prophetic Promise to Restore', p. 17. The Jeremiah passage also involves restoring 'the spirit of praise', which Latter Rain adherents presumed was 'lost'. Kiteley, 'Prophetic Promise to Restore', p. 17. Its recovery would be intricately tied to the restoration of the 'tabernacle of David', resulting in 'a renewed understanding of spiritual worship'. Garry D. Nation, 'The Restoration Movement', *Christianity Today* (May 18, 1992), pp. 30-31; Kiteley, 'Prophetic Promise to Restore', p. 21.

4.3.4.1 Prepared for the Parousia: Restoration and the Five Spiritual Senses

A renewed spiritual life involves the spiritual senses. Aquino points out in Maximus' writings an 'epistemology of perception' related to spiritual perception and (particularly) the five spiritual senses.[135] Perfecting these senses is a developmental process leading to a way of knowing what the Spirit is saying, which is essential to prophetic expression.

Violet Kiteley acknowledged human subjectivity and the ongoing sanctification needed to temper it. She emphasized this dynamic and its role in perfecting the saints even within the Latter Rain context.[136] In relation to prophetic legitimacy, she aspired to realize her prophetic potential and all that the restorational paradigm promised for the Body of Christ.[137] Thus, she considered the economic Trinity as the relations between the Triune God and Christ's image-bearers, and she held to the ascension-gift ministries. In lectures, Kiteley utilized the language of 'five spiritual senses' in diagrammatic fashion (see Figures 1-3),[138] dealing with interrelated aspects of the divine nature, human nature, and the ascension-gift ministries (Eph. 4.11-16).

Kiteley's train of thought has bearing on prophetic legitimacy. Figure 1 denotes her Trinitarian perspective of the divine nature: the Father is the Source of the spiritual senses; the Spirit is the Substance of the spiritual senses; and the Son is depicted as the Outflow of these senses. Given what texts remain from Kiteley's teaching, it would be difficult to evaluate her reason for the Father-Spirit-Son order except to note that it shows the Spirit substantively as the connective reality between what comes from the Father as Source and what issues from the Son as Outflow. Thus, she sees in the Son the mature, perfected expression of the spiritual senses. One could therefore argue that any perfecting of the spiritual senses results from

---

[135] Frederick D. Aquino, 'Maximus the Confessor', in *The Spiritual Senses: Perceiving God in Western Christianity* (ed. Paul L. Gavrilyuk and Sarah Coakley; Cambridge: Cambridge University Press 2012), ch. 6.

[136] Kiteley, 'Prophetic Promise to Restore', p. 19. Kiteley talks about the restoration of Truth and its progressive work in conforming us to the image of Christ.

[137] Kiteley, 'Prophetic Promise to Restore', pp. 19-22.

[138] Figures 1 and 2 are replicated from Kiteley, 'Five Spiritual Senses', p. 1; Figure 3 is from Kiteley, 'Principles of Church Life Lesson 26 – Continued', *Violet Kiteley Papers*, p. 1.

what the Father reveals through the Spirit's substantial work in and through the Incarnate Son.

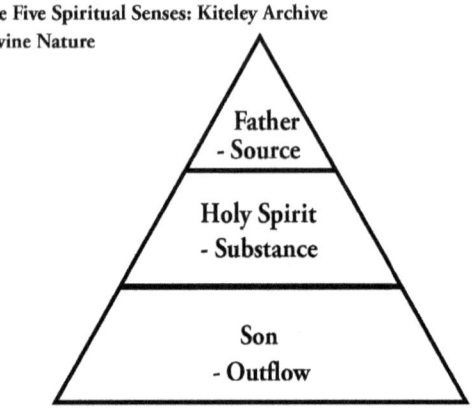

Figure 1: The Divine Nature

Regarding human nature and the spiritual senses, Kiteley considered (1) the human spirit, (2) the human personality, which she placed in the domain of the soul (the seat of the psychological life), and (3) the body as the physical life of personhood. In relation to ontology, she saw the spiritual life flowing from the human spirit as the junction of human-divine interaction. The soul, the seat of the personality, is where interaction with the self transpires. The body is the physiological domain in which contact with the outside world happens. Therefore, Kiteley saw the five spiritual senses and the natural senses overlapping, interacting, and finding expression in relation to God, self, and others.[139]

It appears that, for Kiteley, image and likeness were tripartite, related again to the spiritual, the psychological, and the physiological. Hence, the spiritual part would place the image-bearer in communion with the divine; the psychological would place the image-bearer in communion with self and others; and the physiological would embody the image-bearer in the world at large.

Kiteley also separated the five spiritual senses somewhat typologically in relation to apostolic, prophetic, evangelistic, didactic, and pastoral functions according to Eph. 4.11-13. Although I would argue that all five spiritual senses are essential to all five ascension-gift

---

[139] For all of this, Kiteley references Gen. 1.26-27.

expressions, it is important for the sake of Kiteley's viewpoint to see how she distinguished them in terms of how they are inclined to function (see Figure 2).

The Five Spiritual Senses: Kiteley Archive
Summary of the Five Spiritual Senses

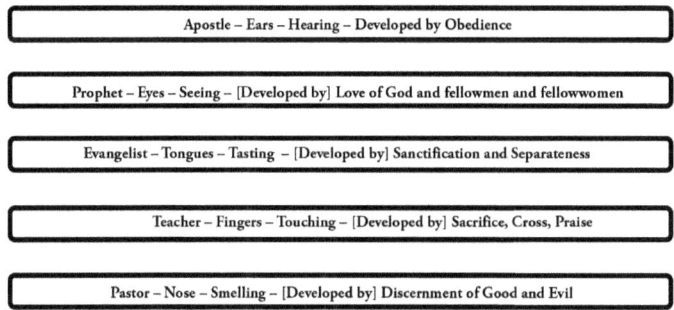

Figure 2: Summary of Spiritual Senses

In Kiteley's view, and in relation to the other four senses, the apostolic concerns the development of spiritual hearing that leads to obedience. She viewed the prophetic as operating in the 'seeing' function, which is essentially prophetic perception. (Kiteley linked this to the prophet's love of God and love of fellow human beings. This love must be developed so that prophetic vision is rooted in, developed in, and culminated in love). As is true of all the spiritual senses in all the ascension-gift functions, this seeing is developmental and progressive. Kiteley's perspective on the five gifts continues: The evangelistic involves spiritual 'tasting' resulting from the sanctifying work of the Spirit to make us separate from the world. The didactic concerns the development of spiritual 'touch', which is rooted in embracing the cross, the sacrificial life, and a life of praise. The pastoral requires the development of spiritual 'smelling', which involves discerning good and evil.

While Kiteley sees these functions typologically in relation to the five senses, it can be said that all five aspects work together to express the image and likeness of Christ. As will be shown in Chapter 5, the spiritual senses are essential for a Pentecostal theology of prophetic legitimacy.

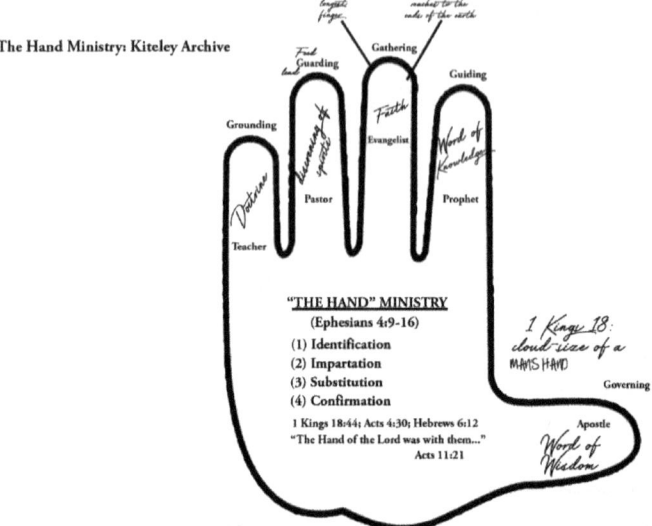

Figure 3: The Hand Ministry

Above is Kiteley's final diagram in this grouping. It is well-known in Latter Rain and Pentecostal history, with the image of the human hand being used to teach about the ascension-gift ministries (Eph. 4.9-16). From the Latter Rain perspective, the hand was significant, as impartation through the laying on of hands and the prophecy of the presbytery was an earmark of the 1948 revival.[140] This typological approach comes from a Pentecostal reading of 1 Kgs 18.44 where, for the seventh time, Elijah sends his servant to see whether his own intercession has stirred the elements by the sea. The servant reports seeing a cloud the size of a man's hand. According to this reading, a man's hand implied the fulfilling of the five ministries listed by Paul in Eph. 4.9-13. To Latter Rain adherents such as Kiteley, this was a last-days restoration of 'five-fold ministry' and the 'birthing [of] the rain' (*latter* being implied).[141] It refers to Joel 2.23-32 and a Pentecostal

---

[140] This earmark is perhaps the most celebrated within movement ranks and the most challenged outside of them.

[141] Kiteley, 'Prophetic Promise to Restore', p. 20; Violet Kiteley, 'Elijah Birthing the Rain', *Violet Kiteley Papers*, p. 1. In her notes, Kiteley, 'Elijah Birthing the Rain', p. 1, added, 'What has taken place is but a foretaste of what is to come ... We are going to experience the restoration of authentic New Test[ament] Christianity'.

view of former and latter rains being the 'historical gap between the first and twentieth centuries when signs and wonders were restored to the prodigal church'.[142] The primitive church experienced the former rain; the latter rain would complete the church's work and usher in Christ's return. Therefore, when Latter Rain adherents read the prayer of Peter, John, and other Jerusalem saints in Acts 4, they saw the stretching of God's hand for signs, wonders, and healing being fulfilled through his chosen ascension-gift ministries (Acts 4.30). Essential to their catechetical understanding was the foundational doctrine of the laying on of hands (Heb. 6.2).

Per Kiteley's diagram, the laying on of hands by seasoned presbyters was for identification with the Body of Christ and the missiological call; impartation of gifts and ministries, an aspect of Christ's substitutionary work on behalf of the presbytery candidates receiving prayer and prophecy; and confirmation of what God had already placed within those receiving prayer. The Pentecostal reading of 'the hand of the Lord' in Acts 11.21 was seen in the context of ascension-gift function and operations as expressions of Christ.

Within that framework, the individual fingers represent the ascension gifts. The thumb, able to touch all other fingers and function in all five expressions of Eph. 4.9-13, denotes the apostolic or governing gift that completes the hand's grasp. The overarching apostolic gifting is the *word of wisdom*, which could be considered with respect to Paul's self-reference as a 'wise master builder' (1 Cor. 3.10). The middle and longest figure represents the evangelist, who reaches 'to the ends of the earth' as a 'gather[er]' operating in the gift of faith for the harvest of converts.[143] The ring finger represents the pastoral gift used for 'guarding' the flock of God, being influenced by the 'discerning of spirits' to feed and lead them. The smallest finger speaks to the teaching gift – according to the Latter Rain view, the 'grounding' gift that makes doctrine known. I choose to address the pointing finger last, which is the prophetic gift. For Kiteley, the apostle grounded, while the prophet guided. With the apostle's gift of

---

[142] Allan Anderson, *To the Ends of the Earth: Pentecostalism and the Transformation of World Christianity* (Oxford Studies in World Christianity; Oxford: Oxford University Press 2013), p. 12.

[143] Kiteley, 'Principles of Church Life', p. 1.

spiritual hearing and the prophet's gift of spiritual sight in mind, this model makes logical sense.[144]

It is noteworthy that Latter Rain adherents considered Pentecostalism a sign of the last days. This influenced how the prophetic gifts *saw* the future. Because they considered the Lord's return to be imminent, the goal was to evangelize the globe. Thus, the Bride of Christ would be prepared for the marriage supper of the Lamb.[145] The prophetic gift is therefore motivational and based on an end-of-age harvest that Kiteley believed requires the saints to be equipped, through restoration's work, for the 'completion of God's plan for the ages'.[146]

It should also be noted that the prophetic speaks within the context from which it is framed. This does not imply that the prophetic cannot contain objective realities. However, it requires us to acknowledge that the doctrinal emphases shaping prophetic consciousness and perception also influence prophetic expression. While eschatological speculation often produces more challenges than solutions, it does not negate prophetic legitimacy. God will still speak through human agency to spur the church toward the fullness of Christ. Provided the prophetic agent voices God's ultimate intent, that prophetic function is legitimized.

4.4 Framing the Prophetic Presbytery

For Violet Kiteley, the prophetic presbytery was essential to the fulfillment of the divine intent, a view not limited to theory, theology, or doctrine. It was an important restoration that was profoundly ecclesial and deeply rooted in the experienced reality that shaped her life and sense of placement within the church. This experienced reality included the aforementioned 'spiritual dearth' and loss of jobs,[147] which contributed to World War II's effect on the churches:

---

[144] Prophetic sight (and perhaps foresight) becomes essential for the church to move into the future.

[145] Dale M. Coulter, 'The Spirit and the Bride Revisited: Pentecostalism, Renewal, and the Sense of History', *Journal of Pentecostal Theology* 21.2 (January 2012), pp. 303, 305-307, 309, 314-15.

[146] Kiteley, 'Prophetic Promise to Restore', p. 15. The belief was that what had been abandoned and aborted during the Dark and Middle Ages was being restored in the last days. Kiteley, 'Prophetic Promise to Restore', p. 14.

[147] Kiteley, 'Restoration Basics', p. 1.

The Second World War was over in the summer of 1945 and many of the churches and para-church ministries had lost a number of the cream of their crop in terms of young men and women and had been pretty devastated as they began the process of rebuilding their ministries.

There was a general discouragement and dearth dryness throughout the body of Christ and there was a general cry from intercessors throughout the nations for God to birth an Isaiah 43 Revival 'which was to be "a new thing" to cause rivers to once again flow in the desert'.[148]

Kiteley's impoverished history and early widowhood seemed to sensitize her to the economic and psychological conditions of the destitute. Her consciousness registered the devastating effects of postwar disillusionment, which also informed an eschatological urgency and need for the Latter Rain fervor.[149] As mentioned, Kiteley detected a hunger for God and for him 'to do something fresh'.[150] She asserted prophetically, 'millions would receive the Baptism of [the] Holy Spirit',[151] so that what began at Azusa would have further global ramifications.

---

[148] Kiteley, 'Unbroken Line', p. 1.

[149] Tim Mbiti, 'What Is Postwar Disillusionment?', *eNotes*, https://www.enotes.com/homework-help/what-postwar-disillusionment-375681:

> In the broadest of senses, postwar disillusionment refers to the pain of readjusting to life after war. This can be experienced in different lights. For example, after World War 1, significant elements of postwar disillusion can be seen in specific contexts. For Americans, this resulted in a complete isolationist viewpoint towards how Americans viewed Europe. There was a significant disillusion towards being able to assist Europeans and other nations in fighting off significant threats. At the same time, postwar disillusion in Europe resulted in a general rejection of the institutions and ideologies that plunged the continent into the worst of all wars. Faith in governments, religion, and society was reduced to the rubble that seemed to dominate the continent. Another example of postwar disillusion can be seen in the rise of an existential angst after the Second World War. Seeing the destruction brought about by the death camps of the Holocaust, the dropping of the atomic bomb in Japan, and the lack of any real and substantive justice against the Nazis, helped to develop a condition in which postwar disillusion was directed inwards at the individual sense of being as well as the idea that the individual was powerless in the face of wide ranging and such intense social conditions and realities. It is here where I think that postwar disillusion can be seen in different contexts after war has been raged and its damage felt.

[150] Kiteley, 'Restoration Basics', p. 1.
[151] Kiteley, 'Restoration Basics', p. 4.

Regarding prophetic consciousness, Kiteley's Latter Rain Restorationism was inseparable from her sense of God's timing.[152] She suggested that various truths need to be restored for the Lord's return to occur. Her diagram, entitled 'Revival in His Church after the Due Order',[153] pictures a circle with sixteen spokes representing specific understandings that were to be held in balance for the Latter Rain influence to be effectual. One spoke denotes 'Knowing God's Timeclock'.[154] This involves knowing what God was saying at any given time. Kiteley applied it in this case to the 1948 revival, which continued the 'restoration of truth' begun by Martin Luther in 1517.[155]

From a hermeneutical perspective, the Latter Rain doctrine contended, 'revival in God's church has to do with the restoration of truths that had been lost throughout the years (Joel 1)'.[156] One could infer that Kiteley and her peers theologically understood revival as the restoration of truth. In the schema of 'God's timeclock', the ticking stopped when the last apostle died, and it resumed in 1517.

4.4.1 The Presbytery, Impartation, and Placement in the Body of Christ

Kiteley and other Latter Rain principals believed that God 'restored the IMPARTATION OF GIFTS to the Church by the LAYING ON OF HANDS'.[157] Therefore, this act of impartation carried profound

---

[152] Restoration as a paradigm for correction was common within historical Christianity. Richard T. Hughes, 'Restoration, Historical Models Of', in Douglas A. Foster, *et al.*, *The Encyclopedia of the Stone-Campbell Movement* (Grand Rapids, MI: Eerdmans, 2004), p. 635, contends that as an ideal, it 'seeks to correct faults or deficiencies by appealing to the primitive church as normative model'. Hughes cites many examples, including Irenaeus' challenge to second-century Gnostics 'by appealing to the ancient Christian tradition and to bishops who received their offices in regular succession from the apostles'. See also, Irenaeus, *St. Irenaeus of Lyons: Against the Heresies* (3 vols.; trans. Dominic J. Unger; New York: Newman Press, 1992).

[153] Violet Kiteley, 'Revival in His Church After the Due Order', *Violet Kiteley Papers*, p. 1.

[154] Kiteley, 'Revival in His Church', p. 1. The timeclock metaphor provides insight into what Kenneth J. Archer, *Gospel Revisited*, p. 19, refers to as the 'hermeneuts and the methods', in respect to Latter Rain practitioners and their understanding of their times. Archer writes, 'Both the methods and the hermeneuts are socially, culturally, and theologically shaped entities that contribute to the making of meaning' (p. 19).

[155] Kiteley, 'Elijah and Elisha', p. 12.

[156] Kiteley, 'Elijah and Elisha', p. 12.

[157] Kiteley, '1948 – Northern Canada', p. 1.

weight. As Kiteley instructed, 'The present visitation of God has made a present reality of the ancient truth of "The Laying on of the Hands of the Presbytery". With this restored truth, comes a greater unfolding of God and His purposes.'[158]

The laying on of hands with prophetic utterance cannot be separated from the 'one body' metaphor and other Latter Rain implications about how unity would be attained. For Latter Rain practitioners, Christ's work on the cross made us one. Yet, they saw the body as divided, and Kiteley warned that 'a divided body cannot work properly'.[159] Pastorally, this was of utmost concern to her. She emphasized, 'God's purpose is to bring together this body by the LAYING ON OF HANDS and prophecy'.[160]

In Kiteley's theology, this idea was connected to Ezekiel 37 and the valley of dry bones – the reuniting of the bones speaking of 'Israel in the natural' and 'a life-giving work for the Body of Christ'.[161] To Kiteley, Ezekiel exemplified speaking via prophetic function when he was commanded to prophesy first to the bones and then to the wind.[162] In her view, the bones spoke of prophetic utterance influencing 'structure' (the context being ecclesial structure);[163] the wind involves 'breath[ing] upon the slain' (by implication, natural Israel and the Body of Christ).[164] Kiteley wrote, 'This is the purpose of the Holy Spirit now … to [revive] thy work (the wind of the Holy Spirit) in the midst of the years'.[165]

Regarding the bones coming together, Kiteley linked Ezekiel 37 to Psalm 133 and John 17.[166] As to the sense of bone to bone, she referenced 1 Cor. 12.18;[167] hence her emphasis on 'placement' in the body.[168] When conjoined with the laying on of hands, the prophetic

---

[158] Kiteley, 'Laying on of Hands', p. 2.
[159] Kiteley, '1948 – Northern Canada', p. 1.
[160] Kiteley, '1948 – Northern Canada', p. 1.
[161] Violet Kiteley, 'Ezekiel, Chapter 20' (Shiloh Bible College, Oakland, CA), *Violet Kiteley Papers*, p. 59.
[162] Kiteley, 'Ezekiel', p. 59.
[163] Kiteley, 'Ezekiel', p. 59.
[164] Kiteley, 'Ezekiel', p. 59.
[165] Kiteley, 'Ezekiel', p. 59 (emphasis added). 'In the midst of the years' refers to Hab. 3.2 and is applied to Kiteley's contemporary setting. Also, *revive* was incorrectly rendered 'receive' in the original. The word *work* is underlined in Kiteley's document.
[166] Kiteley, 'Ezekiel', p. 59.
[167] Kiteley, 'Ezekiel', p. 59.
[168] Kiteley, 'Unbroken Line', p. 5.

function was the 'creative word of the Lord'.[169] From this perspective, impartation is a creative function operating through the prophetic word and the laying on of hands. Therefore, in Kiteley's view, something akin to a prophetic magisterium is developed and incorporated into local church life. By it, recognized, seasoned prophetic voices administer the laying on of hands with prophetic utterance over each member of the local assembly. In the Latter Rain context, this was essential to the fulfillment of eschatological expectations as understood through the community's readings of the text. Kiteley adds: 'By the LAYING ON OF HANDS *each* member is given a gift of the Spirit or spiritual ministry (1 Cor. 12:7) and thereby placed in his or her proper place in the Body of Christ'.[170] This recalls the pivotal moment in North Battleford when events cemented the conviction that the Sovereign Spirit was effecting the divine will: specifically, the moment of Ernie Hawtin's healing from his speech impediment, which effectively launched the Latter Rain movement.

4.4.2 The 'Word of the Lord' and 'Birthing' of the Presbyter

Ernie Hawtin's experience and its effect were not significant purely because he 'spoke clearly without any difficulty'.[171] The significance derived largely from the content of his speaking: 'a prophetic utterance ... regarding 1 Tim. 4:14'.[172] Kiteley attested that Hawtin spoke 'the Word of the Lord',[173] a phrase commonly used by canonical prophets.[174] She then recorded Hawtin's unimpaired recitation of 1 Tim. 4.14-15: 'Do not neglect the gift that is in you which will be given to you by prophecy with the laying on of hands of the Presbytery. Meditate on these things; give yourself entirely to them that your progress may be evident to all'.[175] Hawtin continued with Paul's

---

[169] Kiteley, 'Ezekiel', p. 59.
[170] Kiteley, '1948 – Northern Canada', p. 1 (emphasis added).
[171] Kiteley, 'Violet Kiteley Account', p. 3.
[172] Kiteley, 'Violet Kiteley Account', p. 3.
[173] Kiteley, 'Violet Kiteley Account', p. 3.
[174] See Gen. 15.1, 4; 2 Sam. 7.4; 24.11; 1 Kgs 6.11; 13.20; 16.1; 17.2, 8; 18.1, 31; 19.9; 21.17, 28; 2 Kgs 20.4; 1 Chron. 22.8; 2 Chron. 11.2; 12.7; Jer. 1.2, 4, 11, 13; 2.1; 13.3, 8; 16.1; 18.5; 24.4; 28.12; 32.6, 23; 33.1, 19; 34.12; 36.27; 39.15; 42.7; Ezek. 1.3; 3.16; 6.1; 7.1; 11.14; 12.17, 21, 26; 13.1; 14.2, 12; 15.1; 16.1; 17.1, 11; 18.1; 20.45; 21.1, 8, 18; 22.1, 17, 23; 23.1; 24.1, 15, 20; 25.1; 26.1; 27.1; 28.1, 11, 20; 29.1, 17; 30.1, 20; 31.1; 32.1, 17; 33.1, 23; 34.1; 35.1; 36.16; 37.15; 38.1; Dan. 9.2; Jon. 1.1; 3.1; Hag. 2.20; Zech. 4.8; 6.9; 7.1, 8.
[175] Kiteley, 'Violet Kiteley Account', p. 3.

exhortation through 1 Tim. 4.16.[176] According to Kiteley, 'This was the *birthing of the presbytery* as we know it'.[177]

'Birthing' was significant for Kiteley, particularly regarding prayer. She noted that in 1 Kings 18, when Elijah intercedes for rain, the 'posture of Elijah [is] birthing the rain'.[178] Her train of thought suggests that the Latter Rain was likewise birthed in prayer, with multiple implications. She wrote, 'It was out of those humble, obscure beginnings, that God began to *rebirth* a number of the truths that we have today'.[179] This is the indicia of Kiteley's restorational interpretation of events.

Kiteley also used the birthing metaphor after describing how news of the revival spread: 'Some heard about [it] by word of mouth, but others received dreams, and visions, and some reported seeing the address in the sky'.[180] She and others apparently interpreted this as confirmation that something significant was occurring. She wrote, 'This was the birthing of the NT Apostles and prophets whom the denominational dispensationalists had stated were not for today'.[181] This portion of Kiteley's notes does not clarify the bridge between how word of the revival traveled and the birthing of apostles and prophets. However, it can be safely assumed that those who came (from various places in the Americas and elsewhere) by way of charismatic nudges and intuitions included a significant number who received the laying on of hands and had been commissioned apostolically and prophetically.

Functionally, Kiteley registered this in terms of ecclesial structure. She stated, 'the revelation of the Apostle and the Prophet was restored foundational ministry'.[182] However, she did not consider Hawtin's words to carry the same weight and authority as OT prophecy and prophets, as her words indicate:

---

[176] Kiteley, 'Violet Kiteley Account', p. 3.
[177] Kiteley, 'Violet Kiteley Account', p. 3 (emphasis added). Kiteley's understanding of 'the word of the Lord' warrants further explanation. In relation to Hawtin's utterance, what seems evident is (1) her sense of the inspiration required for Hawtin to utter the Pauline text, and (2) the import of carrying out Paul's exhortation in the immediate context of ministry.
[178] Kiteley, 'Unbroken Line', p. 5.
[179] Kiteley, 'Violet Kiteley Account', p. 4 (emphasis added).
[180] Kiteley, 'Unbroken Line', p. 4.
[181] Kiteley, 'Unbroken Line', p. 4.
[182] Kiteley, 'Unbroken Line', p. 4.

Prophetic ministry that was restored *at this time* was not the Old Testament prophetic ministry which prophesies over nations and international affairs, but it was a New Testament prophet which ministering over individuals in terms of *placement, or birthing a calling or mission*.[183]

The distinction 'at this time' is significant in Kiteley's developing restorational schema. She later added to this portion of her notes, drawing an arrow and hand-writing the words 'this could be restored now'.[184] This implied a next restorational step for the succeeding generation.

4.4.3 Rationale of the Restored Presbytery

The general reasoning for Restorationism is easily discerned: if the ancient faith has been corrupted, it must be restored. While mainline Protestantism was in no way identified with the Latter Rain, the movement's brand of Restorationism has a history within the Protestant Reformation. As Richard T. Hughes attests,

> We can identify four ways in which the restoration vision has been defined or put another way, four objectives that the restoration vision has sought to achieve. Those four are ecclesiastical primitivism, ethical primitivism, experiential primitivism, and gospel primitivism. It is important to recognize, however, that these four categories are not mutually exclusive, but intersect with one another in a variety of ways.[185]

In a broad overview, Hughes observes the presence of ecclesiastical, ethical, experiential, and gospel primitivism through various prominent Reformation voices. Clearly, experiential primitivism is an emphasis of the Pentecostal and Latter Rain movements.[186] Hughes

---

[183] Kiteley, 'Unbroken Line', p. 5 (emphasis added).
[184] Kiteley, 'Unbroken Line', p. 5.
[185] Hughes, 'Restoration', p. 635.
[186] Hughes, 'Restoration', p. 637:

> Experiential Primitivism locates the essence of the ancient Christian faith either in direct communication with God or in the work the Holy Spirit performs in the lives of believers. It is obvious from the preceding discussion of the Holiness movement that ethical Primitivism and experiential Primitivism often intersect. Yet, for some Christian movements, experiential Restorationism has been paramount.

considers all four emphases relative to Roman Catholicism, which for the Protestants

> had corrupted the ancient faith. They [restorationists] therefore sought to retrieve that faith and the practices it enjoined from the weight of corruption and tradition that – in their judgment – had accumulated for so many centuries. From this perspective, the restoration vision is central to the Protestant faith.[187]

For Kiteley, 'the emphasis is not on trying to maintain, keep alive or preserve some truths for a former age as admirable as that might be'.[188] Rather, 'there was still a great need for the restoration of the New Test[ament] pattern of the gifts and ministries of the Holy Spirit operating in the churches'.[189] Kiteley saw 'truths for a former age' within her framework of Heb. 6.1-3 and her understanding of the pivotal laying on of hands in 1948.[190] In seeing the key elements of the Hebrews text as foundational to restoration and fitting within its parameters, repentance from dead works was restored first; instruction about baptisms was restored next; the laying on of hands then followed.[191] Therefore, when Kiteley declared, 'all former revivals were preparing the members to receive LAYING ON OF HANDS',[192] she combined the Latter Rain reading of church history (based on its decline from the death of the apostles until the time of Martin Luther) with the order of Heb. 6.1-3.

---

[187] Hughes, 'Restoration', p. 635.
[188] Kiteley, 'Violet Kiteley Account', pp. 3-4; Kiteley, 'Unbroken Line', p. 3. Hughes notes the sense of Pentecost as an original state. Hughes, 'Restoration', p. 637.
[189] Kiteley, 'Violet Kiteley Account', p. 2.
[190] Kiteley, 'Laying on of Hands', p. 2.

> Therefore, let us go on toward perfection, leaving behind the basic teaching about Christ, and not laying again the foundation: repentance from dead works and faith toward God, instruction about baptisms, laying on of hands, resurrection of the dead, and eternal judgment. And we will do this, if God permits (Heb. 6.1-3).

[191] Kiteley, 'Elijah and Elisha', p. 12, lists the following 'markers': 'Martin Luther – Justification by faith' (1517); 'Anabaptists – Water Baptism' (1524); 'John and Charles Wesley – Holiness' (1700s); 'Missionary Alliance – Divine Healing in the Atonement' (1800s); 'Los Angeles [Azusa Street] and other places – Baptism of the Holy Spirit' (1906); 'North Battleford, Sask[atchewan] – Laying on of Hands (1948)'.
[192] Kiteley, '1948 – Northern Canada', p. 1.

As stated earlier, the prophetic presbytery was, in Kiteley's Latter Rain view, an authoritative way of confirming the vision and ministries within local churches, as well as the function of their members. She described it as operating through

> a group of two or more Presbyters (literally elders, or 'aged' men of the church, characterized by the maturity of their ministry), who are anointed of God with prophetic power to confirm and impart God's mind to the Body of Christ through the Laying on of Hands.[193]

Here we see the weight of responsibility Kiteley placed on the presbyters who had to be seasoned and recognized within their respective communities as being reputable and trustworthy, based on scriptural qualifications for elders. They also had to be graced and gifted with prophetic proclivities and the maturity to exercise them with integrity. They were seen as having the ability to both 'confirm and impart' the mind of God.[194]

As to whether prophetic presbyters are needed, Latter Rain principals would be expected to answer in the affirmative. For Kiteley, Acts 13.1-3 exemplified the presbytery's importance in church history.[195] Her theology of the presbytery was framed by the presence of prophets and teachers in Antioch, the discerning of the mind of the Spirit, the pursuit of consensus in relation to Saul and Barnabas, and the laying on of hands/commissioning that occurred in the original setting.

Doctrinally, Kiteley viewed the presbyters' shared practice as 'help[ing to] establish the will of God for the individual' by 'confirming the person's ministry in the Body of Christ'.[196] According to Kiteley, it confirms such a ministry to 'the candidate ... the pastor ... the congregation',[197] a threefold witness that became essential to prophetic validity and accountability. Therefore, the recipient needs to

---

[193] Violet Kiteley, 'Ministry of the Presbytery Seminar', *Violet Kiteley Papers*, p. 1. Ironically, Kiteley refers to 'men of the church', seemingly excluding herself and the many other women who functioned prophetically in the Latter Rain and were recognized as seasoned presbyters. Presumably, this is a grammatical form based on the gender language of the time and not an indication of any sense of inferiority on Kiteley's part.

[194] Kiteley, 'Ministry of the Presbytery', p. 1.
[195] Kiteley, 'Ministry of the Presbytery', p. 2.
[196] Kiteley, 'Ministry of the Presbytery', p. 2.
[197] Kiteley, 'Ministry of the Presbytery', p. 2.

sense that what is spoken confirms what the recipient already perceives. The pastoral oversight bears witness that what is spoken is evident in the person's life and calling. The congregation equally bears witness. This ensures a threefold witness that implies the Holy Spirit's approbation and affirmation.

Kiteley believed that via the presbytery, the recipient is 'strengthened by the impartation of spiritual gifts and graces' and is responsible to 'stir up [those] gifts'.[198] The local church benefits as the practice 'stimulates the whole church as they seek God through fasting and prayer'.[199] This ascetic approach recalls the renewal among the third-century desert fathers of Egypt. Interestingly, when Latter Rain adherents embrace this practice, they affirm the desert fathers' contribution to the tradition of fasting and prayer as practiced by John the Baptist.[200] Kiteley addressed the importance of these disciplines in relation to the prophetic presbytery, stating that fasting and prayer '[bring] dynamic results when done with the right motive'.[201] Although her notes do not elaborate, she clearly recognized that impure motives such as selfishness and self-aggrandizement would oppose the work of Christ's Spirit.

Because it serves to 'emphasize the various ministries and functions of the Body of Christ',[202] the prophetic presbytery influences the local assembly's health. Kiteley notably accentuated the wholeness of the body, writing that 'no one member has it all'.[203] The Latter Rain's deep commitments to the body's holistic function and unity hinge on all members finding their place. Additionally, the activity of the prophetic presbytery at set times for the stated purposes 'helps develop the enthusiasm of the whole church by their participating in the process of seeing individuals *placed* in their ministries in the local church'.[204]

Kiteley recognized the importance of the laying on of hands (Heb. 3.1-3) as a 'method of conferring divine blessings'.[205] Here

---

[198] Kiteley, 'Ministry of the Presbytery', p. 2.
[199] Kiteley, 'Ministry of the Presbytery', p. 4.
[200] Norman Russell (trans.), *The Lives of the Desert Fathers* (Collegeville, MN: Cistercian Publications, 1981).
[201] Kiteley, 'Ministry of the Presbytery', p. 4.
[202] Kiteley, 'Ministry of the Presbytery', p. 4.
[203] Kiteley, 'Ministry of the Presbytery', p. 4.
[204] Kiteley, 'Ministry of the Presbytery', 4 (emphasis added).
[205] Kiteley, 'Ministry of the Presbytery', p. 5.

again, the conferring exists within the construct of impartation. She elaborated on Aaron's high priestly ministry, citing Levitical passages and describing the laying on of hands as 'a means of identification with, or setting apart of someone or something for a purpose'.[206] She also supported the laying on of hands for impartation by citing the following: Gen. 48.14, when Jacob crossed his hands while praying for Joseph's sons;[207] Mt. 19.13, when Jesus laid his hands on children and blessed them;[208] and Num. 27.18-23 and Deut. 34.9, when Moses laid hands on Joshua before the priests and the congregation.[209] Additionally, Kiteley cited Lk. 24.50, where the ascending High Priest lifted his hands to impart a blessing to his disciples.[210] She then cited Acts 6 and 2 Timothy 1 where 'blessing, ordination and divine impartation' are conferred.[211] She also acknowledged that the laying on of hands 'is used for the healing of the sick' and for '[c]onferring the Holy Ghost'.[212]

4.4.4 The Centrality of Restoring the Presbytery and Laying on of Hands

Kiteley's commitment to the local church from her earliest years and in the Oakland, California work she ultimately pioneered contributed to her sense of pastoral vocation in relation to her prophetic consciousness and perception,[213] leading to the development of her pastoral theology within a Latter Rain context.[214] Within the schema she laid out, the equipping of ministers, clergy, and laity is essential and needs to be understood from her perspective within the movement. Her focus on equipping the saints was paramount, its urgency

---

[206] Kiteley, 'Ministry of the Presbytery', p. 5. Kiteley cites Lev. 8.14; 24.14; Num. 8.10.
[207] Kiteley, 'Ministry of the Presbytery', p. 6.
[208] Kiteley, 'Ministry of the Presbytery', p. 6.
[209] Kiteley, 'Ministry of the Presbytery', pp. 6-7.
[210] Kiteley, 'Ministry of the Presbytery', p. 7.
[211] Kiteley, 'Ministry of the Presbytery', p. 7. Kiteley cites Acts 6.6; 9.17; 2 Tim. 1.6, 14.
[212] Kiteley, 'Ministry of the Presbytery', pp. 7-8.
[213] Kiteley pioneered Shiloh Christian Fellowship, on School Street in Oakland.
[214] According to Thomas C. Oden, *John Wesley's Teachings, Volume 3: Pastoral Theology* (4 vols.; Grand Rapids, MI: Zondervan, 2012), III, p. 17, pastoral theology is 'the more down-to-earth part of theology, more pragmatic than speculative, and intended for the equipping of ministers, clergy and lay'.

attributable to the restorationist schema linking the kingdom's consummation with the fulfillment of certain events.[215]

Kiteley was persuaded that the Latter Rain Restorationist blueprint would empower contemporary movement leaders to *'replicate the exact forms of ministry*' present in the primitive church.[216] She believed that she lived in the times of the ultimate Latter Rain, which was sent in 1948 by divine appointment 'to finish the harvest'.[217] The laying on of hands was therefore considered to be *the* 'restored truth' of her epoch and 'God's special provision to the last-day Church'.[218] In fact, she articulated, 'all former revivals were preparing the members to receive the LAYING ON OF HANDS'.[219]

For Kiteley, the equipping of ministers, clergy, and lay people was essential in replicating the approach of the primitive church. She tied the practice to Christ's returning to fulfill that 'which God spoke by the mouth of His holy prophets' (Acts 3.21, NASB).[220] Hence, a sense of urgency attended the presbytery's prophetic function. The notion of '*each* Christian' finding his/her place is a vital Latter Rain emphasis'.[221] This is similar to Oden's evaluation of the laying on of hands and prophetic utterance in relation to Timothy, although Oden reserves this operation to those who are ordained to an office.[222] The

---

[215] Anthony C. Thiselton, *The Thiselton Companion to Christian Theology* (Grand Rapids, MI: Eerdmans, 2015), 'Restorationism'. Thiselton seeks to capture, from an observational perspective, the sense of what moves the restorational schema within the Pentecostal community: 'It describes a hermeneutic of the NT that aims *to replicate the exact forms* of ministry, the church, and experience of the Holy Spirit that characterized the church of the NT. This especially applies to the narrative of Acts, and to the expectation of Christ's imminent return. It often also applies to miraculous healings and speaking in tongues.' Thistleton's observation regarding 'the expectation of Christ's imminent return' is evident in Kiteley's beliefs.

[216] Thiselton, *Thiselton Companion*, 'Restorationism'.

[217] Thiselton, *Thiselton Companion*, 'Restorationism'; Violet Kiteley, 'Third Day People', *Violet Kiteley Papers*, p. 4.

[218] Kiteley, 'Laying on of Hands', p. 2.

[219] Kiteley, '1948 – Northern Canada', p. 1, emphasis is Kiteley's.

[220] Acts 3.19-23, spoke to Kiteley's overall restorational perspective.

[221] Kiteley, 'Laying on of Hands', p. 2 (emphasis added).

[222] Thomas C. Oden, *First and Second Timothy and Titus* (Interpretation: A Bible Commentary for Teaching and Preaching; Louisville, KY: John Knox Press, 1989), p. 125.

> The spiritual gift given to Timothy was intended to enable him to serve as preacher and teacher of the word. It had been accompanied by 'prophetic utterance' when the elders laid their hands upon him (v. 14; cf. I 1:18; Acts 6:6).

idea is rooted in the ancient Jewish traditions and was carried forward by first-century apostolic leaders after the ascension of Christ.[223]

For Kiteley as a Latter Rain adherent,

> the Laying on of Hands Revival was different, in that the main points or highlights of the revival leaned towards the unifying of the many members, making in Christ ONE BODY, which *together* will do exploits and overcome the last enemy which is death.[224]

Latter Rain participants saw all that happened previously as antecedent to what unfolded in 1948; thus, Kiteley's insistence, 'all former revivals were preparing the members to receive LAYING ON OF HANDS'.[225] What began as ordination for *some* through the laying on of hands has now been conjoined to the prophecy of the presbytery. Furthermore, such a sacred act is considered for *each* and for *all*, with a view toward unifying the many, 'making in Christ ONE BODY'.[226]

4.5 Kiteley's Hermeneutic as a Latter Rain Pentecostal

This brings us to the nature of Kiteley's hermeneutic as a Latter Rain Pentecostal. Ken Archer reminds us, 'the way in which Pentecostals or any community goes about doing "exegesis" and "theology"' correlates to 'their social location and theological formation'.[227] Kiteley was formed and raised in the Pentecostal heritage from humble beginnings, and her parents' understanding of the biblical narrative was decidedly Pentecostal. She saw the Azusa Street Revival as 'a "new" Pentecost'.[228] She noted, 'December 31, 1899 – gift of tongues restored to the Church, beginning in Topeka, Kansas',[229] referring to

---

He had been 'invested in the office of the ministry by the laying on of the hands of the presbytery' (Henry, p. 821) in a service anticipating later services of ordination, probably participated in by Paul and the elders of Derbe and Lystra. The laying on of hands was an outward sign of an inward gift for ministry.

[223] See Heb. 7.23; 2 Macc. 4.50; 13.3; Deut. 17.9; 19.17; 1 Macc. 11.63; Gen. 41.13; 1 Chron. 9.22; Acts 20.28; 1 Tim. 5.17.

[224] Kiteley, '1948 – Northern Canada', p. 1 (italics added). All other emphasis is Kiteley's.

[225] Kiteley, '1948 – Northern Canada', p. 1.

[226] Kiteley, '1948 – Northern Canada', p. 1.

[227] Archer, *Gospel Revisited*, p. 20.

[228] Kiteley, 'Restoration Basics', p. 1.

[229] Kiteley, 'Restoration Basics', p. 1.

Agnes Ozman's testimony as the first to receive the gift of tongues in Parham's school.[230]

Kiteley's use of the word *restored* is noteworthy: it indicates an interpretation of the text within the contemporary context that shaped her pre-adult consciousness, impacting her perceptions and, ultimately, her ways of prophetic enactment. For example, Kiteley was profoundly aware of the Azusa Street revival's important racial contributions to the Pentecostal movement and stated, 'We all owe a tremendous amount to the black people, who waited on God, and God used them to produce His move in Topeka'.[231] She added, 'Azusa Street was used to move out and touch the entire world'.[232] Her acknowledgment of the African-American community's influence on the Azusa outpouring would significantly affect her later transition from Vancouver to Oakland, California, where she established a local church in an African-American community. Kiteley sought to live according to the Pentecostal convictions shaped in her earliest days among the marginalized, and according to her perceptions about where and how God moves to restore.

Kiteley's statement also reveals the global reach of the Azusa movement and her global consciousness in relation to the Pentecostal message. Later referring to the 1967 Charismatic Renewal as 'neo Pentecost',[233] she inferred a continuum from what was prior, stating that this 'move of [the] Holy Spirit was not a new move, but a continuation of that move which sprung from 1906 on Azusa Street move of The Spirit [with Brother] Seymour'.[234] The notion of continuation became highly developed in Kiteley's understanding of how 'God's timing had come'.[235]

In considering Kiteley's ministry and hermeneutic as a Latter Rain participant, there is no question about her character or commitment to Christ. This is not a hagiographical defense. It is based on an understanding of prophetic legitimacy from Jesus' teachings in the Sermon on the Mount, which place Kiteley squarely in line with the faithful. If we can accept that (1) we know in part and prophesy in

---

[230] Ozman, 'Personal Testimony', https://www.apostolicarchives.com/articles/article/8801925/173171.htm.
[231] Kiteley, 'Restoration Basics', p. 1.
[232] Kiteley, 'Restoration Basics', p. 1.
[233] Kiteley, 'Restoration Basics', p. 1.
[234] Kiteley, 'Restoration Basics', p. 1.
[235] Kiteley, 'Restoration Basics', p. 1.

part, and (2) eschatological presuppositions at best have been contested since the church's inception, Kiteley's integrity is beyond question. The fruits of her labor have touched the nations in a significant way. Dennis Balcombe, who received from Kiteley the laying on of hands and was commissioned to accomplish his significant work in mainland China, attests to her involvement in China's underground church from the earliest days of her pioneering work in Oakland.[236] The issue of prophetic legitimacy in relation to the canon, the creed, and particularly the Sermon on the Mount will be considered in relation to consciousness, perception, and enactment in the final chapter of this work.

4.6 Risks and Problems within the Schema of Latter Rain Restorationism

Given the nature of personal subjectivity in relation to prophetic expression, it is essential to consider how consciousness, perception, and enactment were shaped not only by Kiteley's biblical hermeneutic and restorationist theology but also by her psychological and phenomenological realities. These domains overlap. Although they are not always considered together, they interact and are present, albeit in often hidden and less perceptible ways.

Given the nature of human subjectivity, it is essential to (1) acknowledge that Kiteley's subjectivity was rooted in her personal history and narrative identity, and (2) see any prophetic activity in light of her way of being as a prophetic agent. It can be argued therefore that prophetic consciousness plays itself out at three levels: the personal (which includes the deeply intertwined psychological and phenomenological), the theological, and the biblical. These three are the basis upon which the agent develops the internal construct needed to validate the means of discerning what the Spirit is saying. Therefore, this intersection between the activity of the indwelling Spirit and the function of the human psyche requires scrutiny. Ignoring the relations between theological presuppositions and psychological and phenomenological appraisals seems unwise. Kiteley's deeply held convictions, such as those shared with Pentecostal restorationist

---

[236] Dennis Balcombe, *One Journey One Nation: Autobiography of Dennis Balcombe Missionary to China* (Chambersburg, PA: eGenCo, 2011), p. 93.

communities, impacted her cognitions, perceptions, and judgments. They have bearing on the well-being of the community she shaped in Oakland and its adherence or contention within the Pentecostal tradition.

As daunting as the challenge might seem, the theological, psychological, and phenomenological dynamics of deeply held convictions warrant both understanding and exploration. How one arrives at theological conclusions is never independent of one's subjectivity, personal bias, and direct experience with the Spirit. Dissecting this reality need not be difficult; it simply requires attention and consideration to make possible an understanding of the domains' interworkings. In this case, we will apply that understanding to Kiteley's operative function as a prophetic agent within the Latter Rain tradition.

Without question, challenges exist within a Latter Rain restorationist paradigm, including exegetical fallacies common to the schema of Latter Rain Restorationism. However, this does not preclude the presence and power of the Spirit of Prophecy at work in Kiteley's life and ministry. For example, although Kiteley addressed concern over the church in the Dark Ages and seemed to dismiss all that preceded 1517, she nevertheless advocated much within her Latter Rain tradition that proved the very aspects of the larger Tradition she criticized. It could be argued that she arrived at the ancient Tradition obliquely, by way of resistance, even embodying many appropriate Tradition realities. In practice, therefore, she affirmed them.

This attests to the presence of the Spirit of Truth within the context of the church, despite the church's flaws, failings, idiosyncrasies, and suspect exegetical approaches. It also attests to the God who works with flawed human beings and through their subjectivity, proclivities, psychological makeup, and phenomenological frameworks. It seems important therefore, having considered the theological dynamics of the restorationist schema, to consider now the impact of bias on human consciousness and perception from a psychological and phenomenological perspective.

4.6.1 The Ubiquity of Biases

Within and without the church, resistance to evidence is largely attributable to biases that enforce recalcitrance. Among the most ubiquitous biases is confirmation bias, 'the tendency to gather evidence that confirms preexisting expectations, typically by emphasizing or pursuing supporting evidence while dismissing or failing to seek contradictory evidence'.²³⁷ Socially and collectively, when a community 'favor[s] information that confirms their beliefs or hypotheses and minimizes evidence to the contrary',²³⁸ it is difficult to dissuade the group or separate it from beliefs that are reinforced by mutual affirmation.

Implicit bias is also ubiquitous, its presence sometimes revealed when particular realities of consciousness affect mental function. For example, 'the human brain ... can process 11 million bits of information every second. But ... our conscious minds can handle only 40 to 50 bits of information a second'.²³⁹ Therefore, 'we sometimes take cognitive shortcuts ... that can lead to implicit bias, or as it's sometimes called *unconscious bias*'.²⁴⁰ This bias has 'serious consequences for how we perceive and act toward other people'.²⁴¹ Given the ubiquity of such biases, one can understand the ease with which some in the church have invalidated the pre-Reformation church. The devaluing and disdain of anything related to Roman Catholic and Eastern orthodoxy is a predictable by-product of these biases.

Additionally, psychological research reveals the construct of cognitive control, meaning 'the set of processes that organize, plan, and schedule mental operations'.²⁴² These processes are thoroughly intertwined with our mental functions, including our cognitions, perceptions, imaginations, intuitions, memories, and reflections. Because cognitive control mitigates toward a certain kind of organizing,

---

[237] 'Confirmation Bias', *APA Dictionary of Psychology*, https://dictionary.apa.org/ confirmation-bias.

[238] 'Examining Confirmation Bias', *Canvas*, https://lumen.instructure.com/courses/170090.

[239] Pragya Agarwal, interview by Emily Kwong, 'Understanding Unconscious Bias', NPR *Short Wave* (Podcast produced by Rebecca Ramirez; July 15, 2020), 00.05, https://www.npr.org/2020/07/14/891140598 /understanding-unconscious-bias.

[240] Agarwal, 'Understanding Unconscious Bias', 00.49.

[241] *Short Wave*, 'Understanding Unconscious Bias', NPR (July 15, 2020), https://www.npr.org/2020/07/14/891140598/understanding-unconscious-bias. Print article is based on podcast interview with Pragya Agarwal. Agarwal notes that cognitive shortcuts facilitate human function. Given that they are shortcuts, the tendency toward implicit bias is present, the nature of which, according to Brownstein, means 'people can act on the basis of prejudice and stereotypes without intending to do so'. Michael Brownstein, 'Implicit Bias', in Edward N. Zalta (ed.), *Stanford Encyclopedia of Philosophy* (Fall 2019), https://plato .stanford.edu/archives/fall2019/entries/implicit-bias/.

[242] 'Cognitive Control', *APA Dictionary of Psychology*, https://dictionary.apa.org/cognitive-control.

planning, and scheduling, timelines become ideal cognitive shortcuts for explaining the flow of church history. Therefore, it becomes essential to consider how such psychological realities interact with the theological dynamics of prophetic function.

4.6.2 Bias Exemplified and Extended through Scripture

Biases and methods of compensation are not unique to Latter Rain Restorationism. Consider the following conversation between the disciples and the risen Christ: 'So when they had come together, they asked him, "Lord, is this the time when you will restore the kingdom to Israel?" He replied, "It is not for you to know the times or periods that the Father has set by his own authority"' (Acts 1.6-7).[243]

The disciples' question exposes their unconscious and implicit biases and implies their political expectations. It is formed in the absence of the post-Pentecost understanding that the indwelling Spirit would supply. Notice that some consciousness of restoration is present in the question and is arguably reasonable, as Peter will affirm it in the healing of the crippled beggar at the Corinthian gate (Acts 3.21).

As variously noted, the touchstone of Latter Rain restoration theology is the belief in the 'restoration of all things, about which God spoke by the mouth of His holy prophets' (Acts 3.21, NASB). The lens through which Kiteley saw this paradigm influenced her way of interpreting the text. Her interpretive outcome is inseparable from how her theological presuppositions and her cognitive and perceptual constructs interacted. It is also indivisible from the biases these interactions may have produced.

It can be argued that certain psychological biases have infiltrated every theological framework in church history. Consider the early

---

[243] *GEL*, pp. 156-57; the Greek is

13.65 ἀποκαθίστημι; ἀποκατάστασις, εως f, ἐγείρω: to change to a previous good state – 'to restore, to cause again to be, restoration'/ ἀποκαθίστημι: ἐξέτεινεν, καὶ ἀπεκατεστάθη ἡ χεὶρ αὐτοῦ 'he stretched out his hand and it was restored' or ' ... it was healed' Mk 3:5. A rendering of ἀποκαθίστημι in Mk 3:5 as 'was healed' is justified on the basis that at a previous time the hand was crippled, but ἀποκαθίστημι in and of itself does not mean 'to be healed'. Note, however, a contrasting situation in ἰάομαι (13.66). ἀποκατάστασις: ἄχρι χρόνων ἀποκαταστάσεως πάντων ὧν ἐλάλησεν ὁ θεός 'till the times of restoring all things of which God spoke' or 'until the time of making all things new of which God spoke' Ac 3:21. ἐγείρω: καὶ ἐν τρισὶν ἡμέραις ἐγερῶ αὐτόν.

disciples of Jesus and their bias toward a certain kind of messiah. The problem plaguing them was Jesus' seeming failure to 'wrest the governance of Judea from the Romans during his earthly ministry'.[244] Prior to Pentecost, their logical deductions formed this question based on their biased preconceptions and cognitive shortcuts, namely, their interpretations of prophetic promises and their corresponding timelines.

Theologically, Fitzmyer asserts,

> the question formulates a hope for the restoration of an autonomous kingly rule for the Jews of Judea. Though the disciples who pose the question are Christians, they still speak as Judean Jews on behalf of 'Israel'. The ancient Jewish prayers, Šĕmônēh 'Eśrēh 14 and Qaddîš 2, called upon God for the restoration of the kingship to Israel and also of David's throne.[245]

These theological expectations were based in the ancient Israelite community's psychological framework and informed the disciples of Jesus who (phenomenologically) experienced oppression and marginalization and hoped for relief and freedom. This shaping of their psychological outlook inclined their way of being toward expecting a messianic figure who would conquer their physical enemies, as King David had done. Not surprisingly, the reality and ramifications of the suffering Messiah created an untenable psychological and phenomenological load. This bias therefore influenced their theological presuppositions.[246]

The promise was not the problem. God had indeed promised that none would be lacking to sit on David's throne. Yet from this, many Jews derived a distorted messianic hope. The identical challenge plagued Cleopas and the unnamed disciple on the road to Emmaus. When Jesus questioned them, they articulated their crushed expectations tied to the crucifixion and the perceived aborting of their messianic hopes. They said, 'We had hoped that he was the one to redeem Israel' (Lk. 24.21). Jesus' response is theologically, psychologically, and phenomenologically essential: 'Oh, how foolish you are, and how

---

[244] Joseph A. Fitzmyer, *The Acts of the Apostles: A New Translation with Introduction and Commentary* (Anchor Yale Bible 31; New Haven, CT: Yale University Press, 2008), p. 205.

[245] Fitzmyer, *Acts of the Apostles*, p. 205.

[246] Consider, upon his hearing that Messiah must be crucified, Peter's resistance to Jesus in Mt. 16.21-22.

slow of heart to believe all that the prophets have declared!' (Lk. 24.25).

This 'slowness of heart' reveals the presence of psychological and phenomenological realities that overlap their eschatological expectations. It could be argued that the theological dynamics relating to eschatological expectations are particularly significant from a psychological perspective, because expectation is 'a state of tense, emotional anticipation'.[247] Psychologist Jennifer Delgado describes expectations as 'personal beliefs about the events that may occur – or not'.[248] From a psychological perspective, assumptions about the future directly impact our psychological states and, therefore, our phenomenological responses. Delgado asserts that expectations 'are fundamentally fueled by our desires, illusions and beliefs'.[249] If these elements are interrelated, it seems evident that they are more likely tied to reality as one perceives it than to the reality that is.

Expectations 'have an automatic character',[250] implying that their psychological influence occurs below the level of immediate consciousness. Delgado avers, 'we feed them without being fully aware of their origin and without contrasting how realistic they are'.[251] This does not suggest that all expectations are illusory.[252] It is nevertheless impossible to divorce theological expectations from their psychological and phenomenological ramifications. Therefore, regarding how prophetic consciousness and perception lead to enactment, these dynamics are significant, even when they are not immediately evident.

Consider the fact that Violet Kiteley saw 1948 as a pivotal year in the church's timeline as she correlated February 14, 1948 (the Latter Rain onset), May 14, 1948 (the proclaiming of Israel as a state), and September 1948 (the formation of the United Nations and the World Council of Churches).[253] Believing 1948 'was an important year in

---

[247] 'Expectation,' *APA Dictionary of Psychology*, https://dictionary.apa.org/expectation.

[248] Jennifer Delgado, 'Expectations: The Silent Killer of Happiness', *Psychology Spot*, https://psychology-spot.com/expectation/.

[249] Delgado, 'Expectations', https://psychology-spot.com/expectation/.

[250] Delgado, 'Expectations', https://psychology-spot.com/expectation/.

[251] To approach things 'from a process of analysis of the different factors involved' can lend itself to a closer awareness of reality as it is. Delgado, 'Expectations', https://psychology-spot.com/expectation/.

[252] Delgado, 'Expectations', https://psychology-spot.com/expectation/.

[253] Violet Kiteley, 'The Great Restoration: The Dispensation of the Holy Spirit', *Violet Kiteley Papers*, p. 2.

three major ways',[254] she articulated three distinct *seeds* for the restoration of all things: the star seed, sand seed, and dust seed.[255] The star seed reveals Kiteley's expectation for the church. She tied it to Gen. 22.17 and interpreted it as the Latter Rain outpouring of February 14, 1948.[256] She also associated the sand seed with Gen. 22.17 and saw May 14, 1948, as the beginning of its fulfillment when 'natural Israel was a restored nation'.[257] Perhaps most interesting is the dust seed, which Kiteley connected to September 1948. In this regard, she described the demonic, cursed element of the dust as it relates to the 'United Nations [and] World Council of Churches [being] formed'.[258]

Kiteley's statement about the importance of 1948 was more than a theological assertion based in eschatological persuasions.[259] It was also a psychological and phenomenological determination. Her prophetic consciousness and perception, rooted in her theological persuasion, were not independent of her presuppositional expectations and their psychological and phenomenological effects. Therefore, it is necessary to consider that in relation to the 'desires, illusions and beliefs' that operate automatically and somewhat unconsciously,[260] the presence of cognitive distortions is all but inevitable.

4.6.3 Effect of Biases on the Human Heart

As mentioned in Chapter 1, cognitive distortion involves 'faulty or inaccurate thinking, perception, or belief'.[261] On the Emmaus Road, Jesus evaluates the heart condition of Cleopas and the unnamed disciple, as it relates to their foolishness and slowness of heart (Lk. 24.25). The foolishness to which Jesus refers pinpoints the danger posed by cognitive distortions and pertains to an 'unwillingness to

---

[254] Kiteley, 'Great Restoration', p. 2.
[255] Kiteley, 'Great Restoration', p. 2.
[256] Kiteley, 'Great Restoration', p. 2.
[257] Kiteley, 'Great Restoration', p. 2. Kiteley saw 'Israel itself [as] a signpost in God's calendar of end-time events'. Kiteley, 'Prophetic Promise to Restore', p. 18. Kiteley then articulated standard premillennial eschatological expectations. Therefore, the issue of Israel is not unique to Latter Rain Restorationism, as it was present in nineteenth-century Restorationism.
[258] Kiteley, 'Great Restoration', p. 2.
[259] Kiteley, 'Great Restoration', p. 2.
[260] Delgado, 'Expectations', https://psychology-spot.com/expectation/.
[261] 'Cognitive Distortion', *APA Dictionary of Psychology*, https://dictionary.apa.org/cognitive-distortion.

use one's mental faculties in order to understand'.²⁶² The text indicates some type of cognitive challenge, but the theological implications are not the immediate focus. In mentioning their slowness of heart, Jesus alludes 'to an extended period of time'.²⁶³ This is the experience of time itself, which for humans is framed by past, present, and future. The grieving disciples labor over timing issues, even while Jesus addresses timing in diagnosing their heart problem.

The *heart* refers to 'the causative source of a person's psychological life in its various aspects'.²⁶⁴ Therefore, the issues Jesus addresses on the road to Emmaus and with the disciples in Acts are not only theological but also psychological. In relation to kingdom restoration, Jesus does not appeal to their political expectations. At this point, they lack an understanding of any 'definitive form of the kingdom'.²⁶⁵ Through subsequent epochs of church history, Christ's adherents are equally challenged by their expectations. Because this is standard fare for the human psyche, ignoring the psychological and phenomenological realities would be to miss the undeniable where prophetic legitimacy is concerned: prophetic agents 'know only in part, and … prophesy only in part' (1 Cor. 13.9).

Time is involved in the final realization of the kingdom; however, the disciples' cognitions and perceptions are biased. It will take the Spirit to lead and guide them into all truth (Jn 16.13). Jesus had already explained on the Paschal eve that they were not yet capable of comprehending certain aspects of truth.²⁶⁶ It is evident, therefore, that their preconceptions and biases jaded their perceptions and

---

²⁶² *GEL*, pp. 386-87; the issue pinpointed by ἀνόητος is

the unwillingness to use one's mental faculties in order to understand – 'foolish, stupid, without understanding'. σοφοῖς τε καὶ ἀνοήτοις ὀφειλέτης εἰμί 'I am obligated to both wise and foolish men' Ro 1:14; ὦ ἀνόητοι Γαλάται 'oh, foolish Galatians' Ga 3:1. As in the case of ἀσύνετος (32.49), the meaning of ἀνόητος is that people presumably would not use their capacity for understanding and as a result, thought and behaved foolishly. ἀνόητος does not imply the mental state of being an idiot or imbecile.

²⁶³ *GEL*, p. 646.

²⁶⁴ *GEL*, p. 321; in reference to the heart, καρδία is a 'figurative extension of meaning of καρδία "heart", not occurring in the NT in its literal sense … the causative source of a person's psychological life in its various aspects, but with special emphasis upon thoughts – "heart, inner self, mind".'

²⁶⁵ Fitzmyer, *Acts of the Apostles*, p. 205.

²⁶⁶ 'I still have many things to say to you, but you cannot bear them now' (Jn 16.12).

therefore their interpretations of reality (here specifically, the unfolding of divine intent).

Returning to Kiteley's three seeds finding expression and taking root per the 1948 restorationist paradigm, we discover her theological assertion: 'We are living in the generation that God has chosen to make them whole (perfect)'.[267] Kiteley alludes to 1948 as a marker in the final countdown toward the eschatological Day of the Lord. She reinforces this allusion by citing 1 Thess. 5.23 and 1 Cor. 13.10.[268] This led her to believe that all would be consummated by 1988. Years later, when 1988 passed, her notes would reflect alterations of her early appraisal. In one case, she wrote '1948–1988?'[269] In another document, she adjusted the span, writing, '1948–2009'.[270]

4.6.4 Overgeneralization, Church History, and the Creeds

Regarding Violet Kiteley as an exemplar, my argument for prophetic legitimacy cannot ignore the realities impinging on theological, psychological, and phenomenological dynamics. The point is to recognize that all humans are susceptible to error and limitation. This, however, does not limit the working of the Spirit of Prophecy. The Spirit's transcendent nature enables prophetic processes to occur within a context of accountability by which checks and balances can be exercised.

Hence, amid Kiteley's restorational framework, the authority of the Scriptures, the local church eldership, the presbyters who are involved in the laying on of hands, and the members – all move toward the wholeness that comes as the Spirit moves us forward, leading and guiding us into all truth. This implies that we have not yet fully arrived. Therefore, it is necessary to understand the dynamics of the restorational schema that has been carried forward, not merely for the Latter Rain, but also for the contemporary church. This bears on how we navigate the church's movement (perhaps particularly that of the independent Pentecostal tribes) toward a greater sense of accountability, so that prophetic legitimacy can be maintained and preserved.

---

[267] Kiteley, 'Great Restoration', p. 2.
[268] Kiteley, 'Great Restoration', p. 2.
[269] Violet Kiteley, 'V. Kiteley Sermons', *Violet Kiteley Papers*, p. 20. This was Kiteley's belief, yet the question mark in this note demonstrates a measure of uncertainty.
[270] Violet Kiteley, 'Verses of Our End Time Revival', *Violet Kiteley Papers*, p. 3.

In this context, it seems paramount to understand that the current reality is a manifestation of the progression of church history. To understand the times (past, present, and future) and know what to do is to realize that the arc and trajectory of history are integral to any conclusions related to prophetic consciousness, perception, and enactment (1 Chron. 12.32). It is therefore essential to acknowledge that, within the restorational schema, church history is assessed largely based on perceptions (i.e. biases) that originated in prior centuries.

Looking back to the Great Reformation, 'the restoration vision emerged with extraordinary power'.[271] Strong opposition to corruption within Roman Catholic leadership laid the groundwork for the eventual Protestant bias against anything Rome-affiliated. The reformers painted with a broad brush for litigious or apologetic purposes, fostering their assessment that the church had at some point careened and now needed recovery (restoration). Although not all Protestant theology is restorational, it seems evident that all Restorationism is inescapably Protestant. As Hughes states, 'From this perspective, the restoration vision is central to the Protestant faith'.[272]

Because of its tendency to overgeneralize and dismiss any theological or ecclesial significance prior to 1517, Latter Rain Restorationism generates other challenges. It is not difficult to understand that prior to Pentecostalism, this disdain was so deeply ingrained within branches of the Protestant tree that its ability to value pre-1517 church history was compromised. One of Latter Rain Restorationism's greatest challenges is the stark bifurcation it instigates, pitting the restoration of unity against the generalized disqualifying of fourteen centuries of Christian witness. To claim that unity will be restored while divorcing the movement from its own Tradition is a form of cognitive dissonance that underwrites negative attitudes, skewed perceptions, and actions that fall short of loving God and loving others.

A second great problem develops when a slanted view of church history forces the church to deny the Spirit's witness through an extended period of that history. This view necessarily denies the Tradition that sustained the maligned period and emerged from it. Such

---

[271] Hughes, 'Restoration', p. 635.
[272] Hughes, 'Restoration', p. 635.

skepticism and disdain inadvertently yield the wholesale dismissal of second- and third-century apologists, the desert fathers and patristics through the seventh century, and the scholastics.

Third, if a swath of history is discarded, those who discard it will not be inclined to study it. Much is lost, particularly the understanding of how the apostolic faith and the *regula fidei* were preserved. If any in the group should choose to study the discarded period, its lessons will be extruded through the cognitive bias that discounted it, effectively filtering out the epoch's genuine contributions.

Consider, for example, the oxymoronic nature of the following conviction: 'The Churches of Christ began in the early nineteenth century as a quest for Christian unity – a unity based not on creeds but on the essential truths of Christianity as expressed in the New Testament'.[273] Although such sentiments can be found in many classical Pentecostal traditions, it is important to point out that the PAOC clearly embraced the creedal confessions of the ancient church.[274] Kiteley, having been raised within PAOC and Foursquare traditions would be familiar with the creeds. Questions remain as to whether the theological implications of the divine economy delineated in the creeds were thoroughly comprehended and understood to apply to the Spirit, the church, and its eschatological implications. Such inquiry would require further study. One could at least offer this possibility: had the divergent streams of Latter Rain Pentecostalism visited the faith that was (according to Jude 3) handed down from the early centuries of the church (without dismissing the early apologists and the patristics (based on negative perceptions of the Dark Ages), they might have reached a different conclusion. I therefore argue that engaging the creedal confessions can profoundly benefit, mature, and perfect prophetic legitimacy.

4.6.5 Restorational Bias and Nationalism

Finally, from the perspective of continuing restoration, there is the challenge of conflating nationalism with the proclamation of the Gospel, a risk that falls within the Latter Rain purview. Sustaining the notion of Christ's imminent return is difficult trans-generationally.

---

[273] Daniel G. Reid, *et al.*, 'Primitivism', *Dictionary of Christianity in America* (Downers Grove, IL: InterVarsity Press, 1990).

[274] Peter Althouse, 'The Ecumenical Significance of Canadian Pentecostalism', in Michael Wilkinson and Peter Althouse (eds.), *Winds from the North: Canadian Contributions to the Pentecostal Movement* (Leiden: Brill, 2010), p. 55.

Many historical and socio-cultural factors mitigate against such eschatological fervor. Yet within the tribes that embrace it, all history serves to confirm the schema.

Although the issue of exegetical fallacies can be considered in relation to the Latter Rain Restorationism already described, the prophetic impulse, which is never separate from personal subjectivity, can nourish cognitive biases.[275] Among these are the conflation of spiritual impulses with matters of political persuasion. As the restorationists' lodestar, the primitivist ideal is easily transposed, both cognitively and psychologically, onto a national yearning to rescue a parallel ideal. From the nationalist perspective, the endangered model must be restored in a culture that no longer seems to value it or understand its import.

As with Latter Rain Restorationism's erasure of a segment of church history, the nationalist schema rests largely on the belief that corruption, whether documented or merely perceived, has systemically dismantled the ideal. Therefore, the timeframe between the ideal and the present dystopia is invalid, and restoring the ideal is paramount. That the nationalist schema is flawed is secondary to the risk of its being conflated with the gospel of Jesus Christ.

4.6.6 The Risk of Perceived Immunity

It should be noted that 'harder' and 'softer' forms of Restorationism coexist. Suffice it to say that the restorationist schema is woven into sectors of the collective Protestant psyche and the highly developed Latter Rain architecture of belief. Therefore, certain issues are perceived as challenges to be ignored or compensated for as the movement proceeds in history. The danger for contemporary believers is in assuming that we have been liberated from such distortions. However, Restorationism itself is a shortcut designed to assuage the collective consciousness as adherents manage the uncertainty with which their minds must cope. Therefore, the preconceptions embedded within the restorationist mindset are so solidified that contrary claims cannot necessarily penetrate it.

4.6.7 Risks within the Rationale of the Restored Presbytery

Assuming that restoration was necessary, to look to the ancient church was to embrace an ideal, however nostalgic or romanticized,

---

[275] For example, the confirmation bias described earlier.

that ignores the challenges faced in the first-century apostolic age.[276] Nevertheless, 'the ideal looked backward to a golden age'.[277] Hughes contends, 'a backward glance is nothing more than that – a backward glance'.[278] If the glance is backward, the notion that it is 'nothing more' is debatable. If there is nothing from the past to restore, how can one reconcile a system of reintegrating the past and the scriptural account with the present? It could be suggested from a psychological perspective that aspects of Restorationism, including Latter Rain Restorationism, result from the human tendency toward projection.[279] Pentecostals would likely resist the notion, seeing the filling of the Spirit and the spontaneous expression of the charismata (including speaking in tongues) as authentication of what transpires.[280] However, considering the ubiquity of cognitive bias and psychological projection, it behooves the hermeneut to be vigilant in cultivating self-awareness where such tendencies are concerned.

One can argue the long and rich tradition of these practices dating back to the church's inception. Despite the restorationist obscuring

---

[276] Hughes, 'Restoration', p. 635.

[277] Hughes, 'Restoration', p. 635.

[278] Hughes, 'Restoration', p. 635.

[279] As shown in greater detail in Chapter 1, *projection* ('Projection', *APA Dictionary of Psychology*, https://dictionary.apa.org/projection) is 'the process by which one attributes one's own individual positive or negative characteristics, affects, and impulses to another person or group', often as 'a defense mechanism in which unpleasant or unacceptable impulses, stressors, ideas, affects, or responsibilities are attributed to others'.

[280] Hughes, 'Restoration', p. 637:

> Pentecostalism also emerges as a movement preoccupied with experiential. The very term 'pentecostalism' suggests the essence of this tradition: recovery of the supernatural gifts that the Holy Spirit showered on the earliest Christians on the day of Pentecost. In the Pentecostal world, the link between ethical primitivism and experiential primitivism is obvious. In fact, Pentecostalism grew from the womb of the Holiness movement. Holiness advocates sought to know whether their ethical behavior was truly the work of the Holy Spirit. If so, the early Pentecostals argued, then the Holy Spirit would authenticate that work by supernatural gifts such as speaking in tongues and healing. Perhaps no Pentecostal writer more fully captured the restorationist dimensions of the Pentecostal movement than B.F. Lawrence, who decried the leading denominations who could trace their histories to human founders. In his book *The Apostolic Faith Restored*, published in 1916, Lawrence proclaimed, 'The Pentecostal Movement has no such history; it leaps the intervening years crying, "*Back to Pentecost*". In the minds of these honest-hearted, thinking men and women, this work of God is immediately connected with the work of God in New Testament days'.

of some 1,400 years of church history, the practices 'restored' within the Latter Rain are traditional, a reemergence of the ancient wisdom, and a 'remembering' of what is in the mind of Christ. The Tradition that Latter Rain adherents rejected provided the basis for the tradition they embraced through their way of reading the text, helping to mitigate the problems created by the restorationist imagination, frame of reference, and habitual ways of thinking. What they perceived as being new and coming at the end of history was not new or indicative of history's close.

4.7 Violet Kiteley and Prophetic Legitimacy

Given the theological issues one could challenge in the restorational paradigm, prophetic legitimacy becomes an issue if Kiteley is to be considered an exemplar for prophetic function. This work supposes that the prophetic gift can be exercised in various contexts and from various frames of reference, including Latter Rain Restorationism. One of the markers of legitimacy is that the prophet confronts any aspects of the frame of reference that support cognitive biases, obscure the Scriptures, or make it difficult to discern the will of God. Prophetic legitimacy does not imply a standard of perfection in the sense of flawless exercise or enactment. Rather, it is tied to inward character and humility. To 'know only in part, and ... prophesy only in part' denies the possibility of one having all the answers or making claims beyond what the Spirit reveals to fallible and flawed human creatures (1 Cor. 13.9). Prophetic legitimacy simply involves a way of measuring the validity of the enactments and outcomes of prophetic expression and function.

In Matthew's Gospel, Jesus prophetically forecasts the issue of false prophets (Mt. 7.15-20; 24.11, 24). Concerning prophetic legitimacy, Jesus inextricably links discernment of the Spirit's work with the outcome of what is proclaimed by those who claim to speak for God. As Jesus asserted, 'You will know them by their fruits' (Mt. 7.16). The difficulty is that false prophets are numbered and credentialed among the faithful.[281] Therefore, they are difficult to distinguish, except for their fruits.

---

[281] David E. Garland, *Reading Matthew: A Literary and Theological Commentary on the First Gospel* (Reading the New Testament; Macon, GA: Smyth & Helwys, 2001), p. 88.

Regarding their fruits, Garland observes that they 'can be simulated and are the very garb that the wolves use to beguile the sheep. The metaphor of the good and evil tree makes it clear that bearing fruits is integrally related to one's inner existence'.[282] The inner life of the genuine prophetic agent is therefore to be rooted and grounded such that the good fruit Jesus mentions can issue from the agent's life.

The bearing of fruit is effortless, making Garland's view of simulation a stark insight into Jesus' warning. The implications of the metaphorical contrast between the outward appearance of sheep and the internal presence of ravenous wolves are far-reaching. Garland argues,

> these false prophets had all the credentials that are normally commended in the religious world, great deeds and orthodox confession; yet they still flunked the test. Bearing fruit has nothing to do with their confession of Lord, what signs and wonders they might pull off (see 24:24), or how successful they might appear [to be].[283]

The credentialed false prophets Garland describes are religious leaders who confess allegiance to orthodoxy and Yahweh's Lordship but produce incongruent deeds (Mt. 5.20). Jesus' words to such leaders are not sparing.[284] Therefore, both the stringency that prophetic legitimacy requires and the distinguishing of fruit begin with recognizing the difference between good trees and bad trees. Given that Scripture metaphorizes humans as trees (Judg. 9.12-15; Ps. 1.3; Isa. 60.21; 61.3), it is vital to examine what nourishes the tree. It falls to the discerning community to ascertain the root system – the inner existence that produces the tree's external outcomes (fruits). Jesus speaks of the zeal of the Pharisees and scribes and their self-righteous religious moralism indicating the nature of false prophethood (Mt. 5.20). The Pharisees claimed Yahweh as their Lord, yet Jesus renounced any such claim (Mt. 7.21), disqualifying it as evidence of sound rootedness and exposing the self-righteous soil that bears an evil harvest. The prerequisite for fruit-bearing is repentance (Mt. 3.8). Without it, any external display that suggests salvific inner transformation is false

---

[282] Garland, *Reading Matthew*, p. 88.
[283] Garland, *Reading Matthew*, 88.
[284] Consider the seven woes of judgment that Jesus prophetically pronounces on the scribes and Pharisees (Mt. 23.13-29).

and does not originate in the God and Spirit of truth (Isa. 65.16; Jn 16.13). Jesus warned the Pharisees, scribes, elders, and members of the high priestly line that they would lose the inheritance of the kingdom to those who produce kingdom fruits (Mt. 21.43). They would potentially be pruned as dead branches to be bound together and cast into the fire (Jn 15.6). Clearly, Jesus affirms that good fruit and its inward production are inseparable from genuine repentance (Mt. 3.8).

In being led progressively into truth by 'the Spirit of truth' (Jn 16.13), the prophetic agent can faithfully forthtell and reasonably forecast what is to come. This interior activity, which occurs at the intersection of the human psyche with the indwelling divine Spirit, bears the fruit of the cruciform life. Kiteley offered some tests for discerning authentic prophecy. Citing Rev. 5.6, she claimed that leaders 'need to have the Spirit of the Lamb'.[285] She averred that such leaders are 'like Jesus – gentle, defend less'.[286] She contended that King David foreshadows Jesus because 'David is placed among the sheep (lambs)'.[287] For Kiteley, this was essential preparation for kingship, which involves 'caring for sheep'.[288] As such, David as prophetic leader 'learned to talk to sheep' as 'he was, among the sheep'.[289]

With Jesus' stringent view of prophetic legitimacy in mind, one can argue that Violet Kiteley brought that legitimacy to bear on her ministry. Her sermons and teachings are Christo-centric,[290] and her notes make evident that her life was rooted and grounded in reverence and prayer.[291] Her focus on kingdom purposes was evident in her writings and conduct, as was her emphasis on the bearing of truthful witness. In their totality, they evidence her great care for the interior life of abiding.

In recounting Violet Kiteley's story, this chapter necessarily draws attention to the Latter Rain foundations of today's Independent

---

[285] Violet Kiteley, 'Leaders Who Need to Have the Spirit of the Lamb (Like Jesus)', *Violet Kiteley Papers*, p. 1.

[286] Kiteley, 'Spirit of the Lamb', p. 1. *Defenseless* was the intent, not 'defend less.'

[287] Kiteley, 'Spirit of the Lamb', p. 1.

[288] Kiteley, 'Spirit of the Lamb', p. 1.

[289] Kiteley, 'Spirit of the Lamb', p. 1.

[290] 'Christ suffered without the Gate to bring us within the gate Heb. 13:12'. Violet Kiteley, 'Deliverer Promised in Sermons Notebook', *Violet Kiteley Papers*, p. 16.

[291] Kiteley, 'Deliverer Promised', p. 16. Kiteley's admonitions from Scripture confirm her disposition.

Pentecostalism. Kiteley and her Latter Rain counterparts highly regarded the canonical prophets and particularly revered the first-century church. Their restorationist views, including those related to apostolic and prophetic function, were birthed from their sense of the early church as the model and their concern that the model had been corrupted. Kiteley's particular emphasis on prophetic legitimacy was not academic but evidenced in praxis and enduring integrity. Nevertheless, this chapter has also examined the inherent risks of the restorational schema. This is for the sake of the final task of this study: to construct a Pentecostal theology of prophetic legitimacy.

5

CONSTRUCTING A PENTECOSTAL THEOLOGY OF PROPHETIC LEGITIMACY

5.1 Introduction

Throughout Protestant history, restorationism has been a recurring theme. While its manifestations vary, the underlying focus is returning to the primitive church as the exemplar of God's intention, an emphasis that is prevalent in both denominational and Independent Pentecostal circles. The yearning for a return to the earliest practices was not and is not exclusive to Latter Rain Restorationism.

Eschatological urgency fuels Pentecostalism in all its forms, as the connection between protology and eschatology in the Pentecostal reading of the ancient text is evident in all Pentecostal expressions. The larger movement's vigorous view of the future shapes the prophetic urgency of present activity, with followers of the Latter Rain movement continuing in their Pentecostal forebears' yearning for a return to the primitive church, albeit in a far more robust way.

Despite differences in eschatological paradigms between myself and the original Latter Rain proponents, I recognize our shared roots and affirm the importance of Violet Kiteley's sense of urgency. However, I see it apart from the perspective of what remains to be fulfilled eschatologically in terms of timelines yet to be realized. I would argue that the urgency can be preserved yet disentangled from timeline paradigms that possibly engender conspiratorial thinking and conflate Christianity with nationalism. These mindsets are proving toxic and are undermining prophetic legitimacy, as mentioned in the first chapter.

It is important to remember, 'restorationism is a complex of ideas … implicit in and common to all of Protestantism'.[1] Although much of Restorationism has adopted conspiratorial and Christian Nationalist thinking, these issues were less pronounced in Kiteley's era. Hence, my choice to distance myself from the more extreme restorationist paradigm does not delegitimize Kiteley as an exemplar for prophetic legitimacy.

Why then my distancing from Restorationism? In its more pronounced forms, I contend that Restorationism has produced a false sense of urgency – a sense now rooted in the cognitive dissonance with which the conflation of nationalism with the Gospel is paired with conspiratorial thinking. These factors serve to taint prophetic articulations, and they were not Kiteley's approach. For her, urgency stemmed, in part, from her sense of 'a completion of God's plan for the ages';[2] 'a recovery of the divine principles and truths, that were known, taught, and experienced in the Early Church';[3] and 'the recovery of those elements that were lost to the Church by the compromises made in the years of Church history'.[4] While we can question the presuppositions about how 'God's plan for the ages' is to be comprehended eschatologically, the eschatological framework evident in Scripture has been embraced throughout the long Tradition of the church. Therefore, a certain respectful urgency can be present in prophetic function. In addition, while truth is never-changing, there is a long history of corrupt leaders deviating from 'the faith … once for all entrusted to the saints' and misleading the sheep (Jude 3). This reality does not preclude a legitimate sense of urgency that assures the honoring and effecting of sound truths.

Finally in this regard, renewal in truth is an ongoing work of the Spirit in all ages that allows for a legitimate sense of urgency apart from a timeline that misconstrues or distorts eternal realities. Kiteley's sense of urgency was not fully dependent on imminent eschatological factors alone.[5] Rather, her many decades of pastoral experience in providing soul care in her preaching, teaching, and counseling

---

[1] Ware, 'Restorationism', p. 1019.
[2] Kiteley, 'Prophetic Promise to Restore', p. 15.
[3] Kiteley, 'Prophetic Promise to Restore', p. 15.
[4] Kiteley, 'Prophetic Promise to Restore', p. 15.
[5] Meaning those factors tied to the imminent return of Christ at the end of the age, rooted in a sort of a timeline.

via local church oversight shaped her ecclesiology. Her ethics of pastoral and soul care and interpersonal relations were solidly grounded in orthodoxy, orthopraxy, and orthopathy. This, in my view, speaks to a profound sense of prophetic legitimacy.

Furthermore, Kiteley's life and ministry attest to the three dyads that will be presented in this chapter as being essential to prophetic legitimacy. As a Caucasian woman and prominent local pastor, her choice to march in the Civil Rights Movement with Dr. Martin Luther King Jr. attests to the first dyad: *love of God and love of neighbor.* Her conviction about orthodoxy, orthopraxy, and orthopathy speaks to the second dyad: *truth and falsehood.* As for the third dyad, Kiteley's strict standards for answerability and accountability in relation to the laying on of hands and the prophecy of the presbytery within a local church framework speak to the role of the community in *the apprehension and acceptance of prophetic intimations.*

Kiteley's keen awareness of the lived life of Pentecost was evident in her utter dependency on the indwelling Spirit; her ecclesiology; her broad, lived experience of Global Pentecostalism; and her history of local and global work, which testifies to sound leadership development based in the ethics and character of Jesus. These dispositions accompanied her embrace of Christ's preeminence (formed in her early Pentecostal heritage), an orthodox Trinitarian view of the Godhead, a eucharistic theology, and sound pastoral conduct. Thus, Kiteley built a solid and enduring local church and daughter churches that remain to this day. Through leadership development and the commissioning of missionaries by the prophetic presbytery and the laying on of hands, Kiteley developed a global reach with ongoing impact in Asia, Africa, and the Americas. Prophetically, ecclesiastically, and morally, she operated within a framework of bona fide prophetic consciousness, perception, and enactment. Pastorally and prophetically, she devotedly upheld prophetic orthodoxy, orthopraxy, and orthopathy.

Considering these facts, moving toward a Pentecostal theology of prophetic legitimacy that is grounded in a careful scrutiny of the canonical text, prophetic examples in the text, and Violet Kiteley as a recent exemplar of those examples bears in mind the interrelatedness of theology, psychology, and phenomenology in relation to the human condition. The human condition necessarily implies the same in human interactions with the divine – not only in the canonical examples but also in Kiteley as an exemplar.

The proposed Pentecostal theology of prophetic legitimacy builds on three elements: *prophetica discretio*, *prophetica conscientia*, and *prophetica praxis*. *Discretio* tempers the prophetic agent's carriage, encourages speech that is aligned with the testimony of Jesus, and withholds speech that is not. *Conscientia* involves not only the prophetic agent's subjective awareness but shared knowledge that exists in a collective sense, as within the body of Christ. *Praxis* speaks to the agent's range of practice, which includes prophetic enactments. Together, these three elements support the prophetic agent's discernment, undergird the agent's interaction and interconnectedness with those called to appraise his/her prophetic expression, and encourage the agent's appropriate practice of prophetic function.

The proposed theology also embodies the workings of the three dyads first mentioned in the Chapter 1: love of God and love of neighbor, truth and falsehood, and the apprehension and acceptance of prophetic intimations. I would note that in this concluding chapter, I will spend considerably less time on consciousness (*conscientia*) and perception (*discretio*) and a great deal of time on abiding as praxis. Because the work in prior chapters dealt extensively with consciousness and perception, they will be represented here only summarily. Additionally, this is not an exhaustive study on the issues of consciousness and perception, and I would argue that there is much work still needed in relation to the theological implications of these psychological and phenomenological realities. For the scope and purpose of this work, the work I have included on consciousness and perception seems both suitable and practicable.

Therefore, the focus on praxis and abiding as praxis is of the utmost importance to this final chapter. All the aspects of prophetic legitimacy are interwoven and result in outflows and inflows between one another. As such, it is difficult, in relation to prophetic enactment, to isolate prophetic consciousness, perception, and the internal praxis of abiding. In the agent's interiority, the interchange and movement among them is constant. For that reason, praxis has to be understood as a yieldedness that can resemble inaction but is never inactive. It is an expression resulting from the energetic graces of the indwelling Spirit of Prophecy in relation to prophetic legitimacy and proper prophetic and spiritual formation. If prophetic praxis is both faithful and consistent, there is an ongoing cleansing, purifying, and clarifying of prophetic consciousness and perception. Given the nature of intrapersonal subjectivity, the actions of faithful praxis will make evident the cruciformity of the testimony of Jesus and the Spirit of Prophecy.

In the same way, resistance to the dyads is made evident by the agent's way of doing what is compromised in the agent's way of knowing and way of seeing. The fruit an agent bears from their hidden intrapersonal subjectivity becomes evident by their praxis (Mt. 7.15-20). For that reason, this chapter will consider six aspects of prophetic praxis:
1. Prophetic perception as an essential posture,
2. Cleansing the doors of perception as process,
3. *Theoria* and meditation in relation to prophetic reading of Scripture as praxis,
4. Abiding in Christ as action,
5. The outworking of a praxis of abiding in Christ,
6. The nature of experiential immediacy.

5.1.1 Terms in Latin: The Reason
In their respective languages, certain terminologies can be constraining. Therefore, I am employing Latin terms that I believe will alleviate such limitations and better capture the breadth of meaning necessary to my closing argument. As Wittgenstein stated, 'The limits of language are the limits of my world'.[6] This certainly proved true of the English terms *consciousness* and *discernment*. As I now define the Latin terms I have chosen to use here, their expanses of meaning will make their usefulness evident.

The Latin terms used in this chapter resemble certain English terms used throughout this work. I reserved the Latin terms for my closing argument, for reasons I will now explain. *Prophetica discretio* is the first of three proposed elements of a healthy Pentecostal theology of prophetic legitimacy. In English, *discernment* essentially speaks to 'the quality of being able to grasp and comprehend what is obscure: skill in discerning'.[7] The term falls short of my intent in relation to its prophetic sense. The Latin *discretio* includes within

---

[6] 'What Did Wittgenstein Say?', *Philosophy*, https://philosophy-question.com/library/lecture/read/347674-what-did-wittgenstein-say#0.
[7] 'Discernment', *Merriam-Webster's Collegiate Dictionary* (11th edn).

discernment a discretionary, circumspect reserve in the way a prophetic agent carries herself. This circumspection can motivate the withholding of speech that is not in keeping with the testimony of Jesus (Rev. 20.19).[8]

The second proposed element is *prophetica conscientia*. A. Seth notes, 'the subjective nature of consciousness makes it difficult even to define'.[9] Therefore, I have chosen the Latin term *conscientia*, which includes subjective awareness but also the 'joint knowledge' that is shared with others in a collective sense.[10] We come closer to this concept in Jungian terminology in relation to the 'collective unconscious'.[11] *Conscientia* aids my way of using the term *prophetic consciousness* by including more than what the prophetic agent retains at a conscious level.

The third and final proposed element of a healthy Pentecostal theology of prophetic legitimacy is *prophetica praxis*. I use the term *praxis* throughout this work but perhaps in a more particular way in this chapter. I chose the term because it does not speak only of the skill or art of practice, but also the sense of 'practice[,] exercise[, and] action'.[12] From a Pentecostal perspective, this expanded understanding more aptly speaks to prophetic expression.

5.1.2 Three Dyads Further Explained

The three dyads introduced in Chapter 1 are integral to this chapter's proposed Pentecostal theology of prophetic legitimacy. Therefore, they now warrant further explanation.

---

[8] For example, the problems stated in Chapter 1 reveal a lack of *prophetica discretio* that resulted in speech not in keeping with the testimony of Jesus.

[9] Anil Seth, 'The Hard Problem of Consciousness Is Already Beginning to Dissolve', *New Scientist* (September 1, 2021), https://www.newscientist.com/article/mg25133501-500-the-hard-problem-of-consciousness-is-already-beginning-to-dissolve/#ixzz7WTrkMy4B.

[10] 'Conscientia', *Word Sense Dictionary*, https://www.wordsense.eu/conscientia/.

[11] C.J. Jung. *The Collected Works of C.G. Jung, Volume 8: Structure and Dynamic of the Psyche* (ed. Gerhard Adler and R.F.C. Hull; Princeton, NJ: Princeton University Press, 2nd end, 1969), p. 229.

[12] *Online Etymology Dictionary*, s.v. 'praxis,' accessed June 17, 2022, https://www.etymonline.com/word/praxis.

5.1.2.1 The First Dyad

The first dyad, *love of God and love of neighbor*,[13] operates within interpersonal and intrapersonal dynamics, particularly within (1) the prophet's relation to God, (2) the prophet's relation to self, and (3) the prophet's relation to the community.

It will become evident that interpersonal and intrapersonal dynamics are ever present in the proposed dyads and can be understood as 'directions and movements' that include both subjectivity and objectivity in relation to human experience. This is significant when considering the interpersonal and intrapersonal specifics related to the exchanges inherent in two relationships: the relationship between the prophet and God, and the relationship between the prophet and the community.

Both intersections suggest a necessary awareness of human fallibility in all its possible forms.[14] From a canonical perspective, one cannot divorce an anthropological view of the human condition from the reality of sin and evil present in human experience. While it is not the purpose of this work to focus on sin and evil in relation to a theodicy, it presupposes the biblical anthropological understanding of a fallen humanity. It also presupposes the progressive salvific process of making us human through the sanctifying work of the Holy Spirit. With these presuppositions in mind, it seems clear that even the worthiest attempts of prophets to speak on behalf of God do not bypass or preclude their human fallibilities.

At the same time, it is understood in the argument being presented that the first canonical mention of 'prophet' (*nabiy*) refers to Abraham as an intercessor (Gen. 20.7). Hence, underlying all prophetic function is a commitment to communion with God for the sake of the people, with the prophetic agent being called to a kenotic lifestyle.[15] In the communion accompanying this radical self-surrender and self-sacrifice, prophetic consciousness is formed, shaped, and sustained. Therefore, as it relates to prophetic legitimacy, I contend

---

[13] In both the OT and NT, this is the fulfillment of the law and the prophets according to Jesus; hence it provides a litmus test.

[14] This need is shared in both Eastern and Western traditions.

[15] *Kenosis*, meaning 'to empty'. Rick Brannan, 'κενόω', *Lexham Analytical Lexicon to the Greek New Testament* (Bellingham, WA: Logos Research Systems, rev. edn, 2013).

that genuine prophetic utterance is true to God, self, others, and the overall community entrusted with such expression.

5.1.2.2 The Second Dyad

Although the second dyad, *truth and falsehood*, would seem self-evident, it is essential to prophetic legitimacy. As to the relationship between truth and the Godself, the canon states that God is 'a God of truth and without injustice' (Deut. 32.4, NKJV). From a Christian perspective, any comprehension of truth can only be measured by the standard of the God who is truth. In the context of the triune God, truth is necessarily relational. Jesus states that he is the truth (Jn 14.6-7). Therefore, relating to the truth of God requires relationship with the God of truth. Jesus also refers to the Spirit as the Spirit of truth (Jn 15.26), the same Spirit who leads and guides the believer into all truth (Jn 16.12-14).

For God to communicate from his nature is to speak truth. In the prayer of Jesus, John notes that the Father's word is truth, and the disciples are therefore to be sanctified in truth (Jn 17.17). As the Father sent the Son to bear witness to the truth (Jn 18.37-38), the Son sends the disciples to do the same (Jn 17.18). Therefore, the Father sends both the Son and the Spirit to testify of the truth and cause it to be embodied within the community of faith. Implicit is the expectation that the community will continually be 'speaking the truth in love' (Eph. 4.15). The Greek word translated 'speaking' is ἀληθεύω, which implies 'being truthful and honest'.[16] The community of the faith is called to be 'truthful and honest', including in all prophetic articulation. Anything that is not truthful and honest is a falsehood, and its source cannot be the God of truth.

Regarding the community's responsibility to identify prophetic legitimacy or non-legitimacy, a vetting process based on established standards for judging is necessary in distinguishing truth from falsehood. Anything contradicting God's nature as revealed in canon and creed would be considered false. This litmus test is requisite in determining prophetic legitimacy. In addition, given the subjectivity of human experience, sound reasoning would need to be applied when weighing out these matters.

---

[16] *BAGD*, p. 36.

The fact that a particular error may be unintentional does not preclude the possibility that certain self-identified prophetic agents would speak falsely by intent. Prophetic falsehood is not necessarily deliberate and could well be a matter of ignorance or misunderstanding of the truth. Regardless of the intent, however, the message distorts the truth and is therefore a form of falsehood. Otherwise, the canon would not mention false prophets, and Jesus would not have warned of their existence and intent (Mt. 7.15-16). Jesus says that, inwardly, such figures are 'ravenous wolves' (Mt. 7.15). This indicates a predatory nature and a lack of character incompatible with truthfulness.

Jesus clearly and purposefully ascribes ulterior motives to these false agents. Likewise, it is essential for the community of faith to exercise discernment in the dyad of truth and falsehood in relation to prophetic legitimacy.

5.1.2.3 The Third Dyad

The third dyad, *apprehension and acceptance*, is the exchange through which God apprehends the potential prophetic agent who in turn accepts, understands, and surrenders to the apprehension. Through this dyad, indicators of acceptance become evident across a broad spectrum of OT and NT exemplars. Despite their unique personalities, the essential commonalities in their experiences describe a consistent thread of prophetic legitimacy, from beginning to end.

For example, if Moses and Amos are indeed prophets of God, the experience of the divine being's self-disclosure is necessarily consistent for both, regardless of the generations and dissimilar family and tribal dynamics that separate them. Their inclusion in the canon suggests that the God who reveals himself to Moses is the same God who reveals himself to Amos. The question then arises as to how divine self-disclosure constitutes the prophetic call, and how it is consistent within the canonical text. Also, what constitutes the agent's genuine understanding and acceptance of the divine apprehension? Finally, beginning with the initial encounter and continuing throughout the relationship by which the prophet participates in the work God has determined, what essential commonalities do prophetic agents across the spectrum share, and how might these commonalities ratify prophetic legitimacy?

The prophet's formation process is evident in the canonical literature already discussed. When it is not understood, illegitimate prophetic function and expression become more likely. In other words, prophetic agents become more susceptible to fallibility, in which case subjectivity and implicit bias can induce them to confuse their own voices with the voice of God. This work has considered this effect and examined Jungian psychological perspectives regarding projection and transference.

5.2 Advancing Themes toward a Pentecostal Theology of Prophetic Legitimacy

Inspired speech, as motivated by the Spirit of Prophecy and bearing witness to the testimony of Jesus (Rev. 19.10), is fruit borne of a more accurate way of observing and interpreting what unfolds and wants to unfold. The Spirit of truth leads and guides the prophetic agent into all truth (Jn 16.13).[17] Prophetic legitimacy is founded in the *prophetica conscientia* and perception that lead to prophetic enactment. As the dyads suggest, this legitimacy is grounded in the prophetic agent's choice to abide in the love of God and neighbor. It involves discriminating between the Spirit of truth and the spirit of falsehood, and it requires the capacity to apprehend and accept what is revealed. Thus, it can be shared through inspired prophetic expressions and be apprehended and accepted by the larger community, which also discerns between truth and falsehood and lives out the truth accordingly.

Contemporary prophetic praxis that is built on techniques is not the *prophetica praxis* under consideration in this chapter. Instead, it reduces the prophetic to utilitarian function. Spiritual discernment and the purifying of the spiritual senses are therefore inseparable from the renewal of an ethic supporting prophetic formation. This ethic is the ground from which the prophet's character can be cultivated. This cultivation occurs within a consciousness of the unseen kingdom, until the prophetic agent becomes as a child able to perceive it and embrace true greatness (Mt. 18.4). This outcome implies an essential receptivity that cannot be divorced from receptivity to the testimony of Jesus and, thus, the Spirit of Prophecy (Mt. 18.5). From a Pentecostal perspective, such childlikeness is nonnegotiable because

---

[17] The Spirit of truth is the Spirit of Prophecy (Rev. 19.10).

it postures the prophetic agent for answerability and accountability in relation to their subjective experience, not to a gathering of individuals but a community of persons.

For legitimate Pentecostal prophetism to be embodied and reveal the testimony of Jesus, pastoral love, compassion, and care are needed, beginning with a recovered awareness of theologically based personhood. This requires not merely a changing of terminology but a new consciousness that dismantles the consciousness of individualism and brings us, cruciformly, to a shared consciousness of 'it seemed good to the Holy Spirit and to us' (Acts 15.28). Thus, individualistic prophetic visions are replaced by a shared vision of shalom.[18] For Brueggemann, this speaks of Ezekiel's vision (Ezek. 34.25-29). However, the elect community's current reality more closely resembles the metaphoric valley of dry bones (Ezek. 37.1).

If Kiteley and the Latter Rain prophets envisioned Ezekiel's valley of dry bones becoming a mighty end-of-days army,[19] perhaps Pentecostals can reaffirm 'that the Holy Spirit is among us and within us'.[20] Prophet-priestly legitimacy is exercised, established, and endorsed by the Spirit of Prophecy in the agent's dedication to speaking mediatorially through prophetic expressions (to persons on behalf of God) and intercessory prophetic expressions (to God on behalf of persons).

5.2.1 The Prophetic Ethic

Central to prophetic legitimacy is the prophetic ethic that grounds all *prophetica conscientia*, perception, and enactment in the ways and mandates of the quintessential exemplar, Jesus. This requires trust, as Jesus implied in distinguishing 'the wise and the intelligent' from 'infants' and commending the 'infants' (Mt. 11.25-26).[21] This seems to suggest that childlike trust opens us to the revelatory awareness of

---

[18] Walter Brueggemann, *Living Toward a Vision: Biblical Reflections on Shalom* (New York: United Church Press, 1982), p. 16, sees this shalom as 'the substance of the biblical vision of one community embracing all creation'.

[19] Violet Kiteley, 'Price of Unity Seminar', *Violet Kiteley Papers* (Lecture Notes, Shiloh Christian Fellowship, Oakland, CA, March 1981), p. 2; Kiteley, 'Ezekiel', p. 59.

[20] Peterson, *Working the Angles*, p. 23.

[21] Dietrich Bonhoeffer, *Ethics* (ed. Clifford Green; trans. Reinhard Krauss, Charles C. West, and Douglas W. Stott; Dietrich Bonhoeffer Works Series 6; Minneapolis, MN: Fortress Press, 2005), p. 81, would find the former group 'in danger of missing the essential'.

what matters to the triune God (Mt. 11.27-30). To reduce us to trust, the Father will 'destroy the wisdom of the wise' and thwart 'the discernment of the discerning' (1 Cor. 1.19).[22] I contend that prophetic legitimacy requires prophetic agents to take the yoke of Jesus in gentleness, humility, childlike innocence, and purity, and thereby receive from the Spirit of Prophecy the requisite stillness for a more profound way of knowing the divine impetus (Ps. 46.10).

As Chapter 4 has shown in relation to Violet Kiteley, a Pentecostal reading of the Lukan text affirms Jesus as being fully human and fully divine, the very measure of prophetic truthfulness and the goal of prophecy. Thus, Jesus embodies and expresses the Spirit of Prophecy and is the exemplar of prophetic legitimacy. If, therefore, faithfulness to the testimony of Jesus determines a Pentecostal view of prophetic legitimacy, a constructive prophetic ethic begins with Jesus' life and teachings as revealed in Scripture. In Luke and Matthew, the Beatitudes and complete Sermon on the Mount/Sermon on the Plain are entwined with Jesus' claims about the kingdom of heaven. Matthew references the 'Son of David' who exemplifies God's reign through healing, deliverance, and liberation (Mt. 1.1; 9.27; 12.23; 15.22; 21.9; 21.15). Through this 'eschatological salvific power' dawns the ultimate conquest 'over cosmic powers and systemic evil'.[23]

When considering Jesus' prophetic ethic in the Beatitudes, the promise of blessedness is seen in the lifestyle of ruling one's spirit, under Jesus' oversight and by the Spirit's power. This explains Matthew's noting of Jesus' preamble, 'Repent, for the kingdom of heaven has come near' (Mt. 4.17).[24] An ontological shift is indicated when μετάνοιά – the changing of one's *way*[25] – occurs. The Matthean account suggests that Jesus intends his disciples to embody his

---

[22] If we ignore this effort, can anything labeled *prophetic* be legitimate?

[23] S. McKnight, 'Ethics of Jesus', in Joel B. Green, Jeannine K. Brown, and Nicholas Perrin (eds.), *Dictionary of Jesus and the Gospels* (Downers Grove, IL: IVP Academic, 2nd edn, 2013), p. 246. Issues of power and authoritarianism within contemporary prophetic expression often present a prophetic profile that is counter to the way of Jesus and congruent with systemic evil.

[24] Regarding repenting, *GEL*, p. 510, states,

41.52 μετανοέω; μετάνοια, ας *f*: [means] to change one's way of life as the result of a complete change of thought and attitude with regard to sin and righteousness – 'to repent, to change one's way, repentance. Though it would be possible to classify μετανοέω and μετάνοια in Domain 30 *Think,* the focal semantic feature of these terms is clearly behavioral rather than intellectual.

[25] *GEL*, p. 510.

kingdom rule in how they live amid his enemies.²⁶ How does Jesus' prophetic ethic work itself out? Can turning the other cheek be 'forced or compelled' as Craig Keen notes?²⁷ What kind of logic undergirds the blessed disciple's interiority?

A 'conduct that flows' from living out Jesus' prophetic ethic is prophetic because it witnesses to his sacrificial love for his enemies and peaceable kingdom, rather than a 'preoccupation with outward acts'.²⁸ The outward acts described in the Beatitudes flow from a 'corresponding inner loyalty to God' via the Spirit's inwrought work.²⁹ This work argues that a Pentecostal prophet is legitimate (truly called and anointed) only insofar as her conduct is cruciform, reflecting the anointed One she is called to serve.³⁰

If, as the Matthean Jesus taught, entrance into the kingdom requires a μετάνοιά (Mt. 4.17), a repentance that fundamentally shifts consciousness, perception, and ontology, it would follow that Jesus' ethic requires the rethinking of one's present reality. Thus, a legitimate and ethical prophetic witness lives in the nearness and *nowness* of the kingdom. If the Spirit who inspires such a witness is the 'pledge of our inheritance' (Eph. 1.14),³¹ then Jesus' prophetic ethic is rooted in the prophetic Spirit's presence and mission.³²

Understood this way, Jesus' call, promise, and ethic are related to what Keen calls 'the logic of crucifixion/resurrection'.³³ Keen argues that the logic of turning the other cheek requires 'thinking backwards from a redemptive future',³⁴ an *ethic from beyond*. The redemptive

---

²⁶ By following Jesus, his disciples share in the enmity against him.

²⁷ Craig Keen, *After Crucifixion: The Promise of Theology* (Eugene, OR: Cascade Books, 2013), p. 74.

²⁸ L.D. Hurst, 'Ethics of Jesus', in Joel B. Green, Scot McKnight, and I. Howard Marshall (eds.), *Dictionary of Jesus and the Gospels* (Downers Grove, IL: InterVarsity Press, 1992), p. 210.

²⁹ Hurst, 'Ethics of Jesus', p. 210.

³⁰ Regarding calling, anointing, and the anointed One, Pentecostals speak often of *calling* and *anointing*. As to personal conduct, Violet Kiteley argued, in keeping with the earliest Christians, that prophets should only be trusted to speak for Jesus if they live in ways that honor his name. See Kiteley, 'Spirit of the Lamb', p. 1; Kiteley, 'Ministry of the Presbytery', p. 1.

³¹ Pentecostals assume that the pledge witnesses to the ultimate, total redemption of all believers.

³² In McKnight's words, 'The future impinges on the present in such a way that a new day is already arriving in Jesus', McKnight, 'Ethics of Jesus', p. 246.

³³ Keen, *After Crucifixion*, p. 74.

³⁴ Keen, *After Crucifixion*, p. 74.

future enables true disciples to speak and act beyond the current reality. For Keen, thinking backward from a redemptive future 'open[s] the language of one's people to a sovereign love that comes as a gift'.[35] This sovereign love is congruent with the Spirit's enabling the disciples to speak beyond their own language and limitations on the Day of Pentecost (Acts 2.4).

5.2.1.1 Prophetic Ethic and *Prophetica Discretio*

Ethics are inseparable from discernment, as they address that which links one's knowing with one's doing.[36] Therefore, congruence between the two implies good discernment, which is essential to prophetic function and legitimacy. Lonergan claims that congruence is challenged by a duality that needs to be 'broken' down into 'knowing' and 'understanding' that leads to appropriate *doing*.[37] Thus, the prophetic agent necessarily begins from a place of God awareness that awakens self-awareness. Lonergan's point is more expansive than can be covered here, but if he is correct, our ethics are the result of the 'compound structure of one's knowing and doing'.[38] With that in mind, once the ethic of Jesus is established as foundational for a prophetic Pentecostal ethic,[39] it becomes necessary to form prophets in that ethic, which begins with developing the skills of discernment.[40]

Believers have historically sensed the need for discernment. Given Pentecostals' accentuated openness to charismatic manifestations

---

[35] Keen, *After Crucifixion*, p. 74.

[36] Georgia Harkness, 'Chapter 3: The Ethics of Jesus', *Religion Online*, https://www.religion-online.org/book-chapter/chapter-3-the-ethics-of-jesus/, makes it clear, 'Jesus taught an ethic completely integrated with his religion'. The reality of loving God is inextricably linked with the love of neighbor (Lev. 19.18). So, who is my neighbor? Jesus intimates that we treat many neighbors in less than neighborly ways based on our value judgments, prejudices, and personal preferences (Lk. 10.25-37). These present an ethical challenge. Can we be prophetic if we fail to discern our neighbors?

[37] Bernard Lonergan, *Insight: A Study of Human Understanding* (Collected Works of Bernard Lonergan 3:003; Toronto: University of Toronto Press, 1957), preface.

[38] Lonergan, *Insight*, preface.

[39] This ethic is enlivened and made livable by the presence of the Spirit.

[40] In Rom. 14.1; 1 Cor. 12.10, and Heb. 5.14, the Greek word from which we derive the English word *discernment* is used. It is διάκρισις, denoting a way of differentiating or making a distinction. '1247. διάκρισις *diakrisis* noun. Judicial differentiation, distinction. *Classical Greek* – The word *diakrisis* is a noun form of the verb *diakrinō* (1246) which means 'to differentiate, discern, and assess' in the sense of judgment or judging through with the goal of rendering an impartial decision.' Thoralf Gilbrant, 'Διάκρισις', *The New Testament Greek-English Dictionary* (Complete Biblical Library; WORDsearch, 1991).

and 'moves of the Spirit', they need to learn to distinguish truth, wisdom, and healthy praxis from their antitheses. This is best practiced communally, with leaders particularly taking responsibility. However, prophets need it, both in discerning their own thoughts and feelings and in serving/helping others to discern what is happening to or around them.[41]

Therefore, I offer a *prophetica discretio*, a prophetic theology of discernment that recognizes discernment's relevance to the totality of the disciple's life. Smith notes that discernment displays 'a wisdom evident in the quality of one's choices'.[42] This includes choices to utter what is asserted as truth and inspired speech. This discernment does not end with the speech act. The community needs to exercise the same, 'the ability to discern the voice of Jesus' being 'a critical spiritual skill'.[43]

Discernment is a discipline to be embraced and cultivated by the prophet-to-be. Noteworthy from a Pentecostal perspective is Aquino's consideration of three goals of spiritual formation.[44] A comprehensive list of requirements would exceed the breadth of this study, but I propose these as essential to a *prophetica discretio*:

1. 'The cultivation of a stable, tranquil, and properly disposed mind (e.g., purity of heart)'.[45]
2. 'The capacity to map aptly the practical and contemplative aspects of the spiritual life and thereby regulate the relevant practices and virtues toward their proper end (e.g., discernment)'.[46]
3. 'The acquisition of the ideal epistemic state of the spiritual life (e.g., the vision of God)'.[47]

---

[41] These needs are the reasons that 1 Corinthians 14 has been such a crucial text in the Pentecostal tradition.

[42] Gordon T. Smith, *The Voice of Jesus: Discernment, Prayer and the Witness of the Spirit* (Westmont, IL: IVP Books, 2015), intro.

[43] Smith, *Voice of Jesus*, intro. Nouwen similarly states, 'discernment is a spiritual understanding and an experiential knowledge of how God is active in daily life that is acquired through disciplined spiritual practice'. Henri Nouwen, *Discernment: Reading the Signs of Daily Life* (Oxford, England: SPCK, 2013), ch. 1.

[44] Frederick D. Aquino, 'Spiritual Formation, Authority, and Discernment', in William J. Abraham and Frederick D. Aquino (eds.), *The Oxford Handbook of the Epistemology of Theology* (Oxford: Oxford University Press, 2017), p. 157.

[45] Aquino, 'Spiritual Formation', p. 157.

[46] Aquino, 'Spiritual Formation', p. 157.

[47] Aquino, 'Spiritual Formation', p. 157.

Praxis involves process, but formation precedes praxis. Relevant *prophetica praxis* is inseparable from formation in discernment. As Macchia argues, affirming William Seymour's conviction, the Spirit empowers insofar as one 'bear[s] the divine Spirit'.[48] Formation then involves transformation.[49]

What is true for Christians generally is also true for Christian prophets. The lack of a robust *prophetica discretio* has bred problems in contemporary prophetic cultures.[50] Traditionally, Pentecostals have read Heb. 5.14 as a call to spiritual maturation and development, which tend to produce alertness rather than dullness of hearing.[51] For Attridge, this 'requires ... the effort of listening to "a lengthy and difficult discourse"'.[52] He claims the spiritual senses are to be matured and developed, theologically and philosophically – and I would add, psychologically – so that the phenomenology of prophecy can be tested with a high degree of soundness and scrutiny. If prophets and/or communities lack discernment, their actions lack soundness, and their methods are compromised, revealing a lack of prophetic formation that precedes all kinds of problems.[53]

---

[48] Frank Macchia, 'Finitum Capax Infiniti: A Pentecostal Distinctive?', *Pneuma* 29.2 (2007), p. 185.

[49] Macchia, 'Finitum Capax Infiniti', p. 186.

[50] Arguably, the nationalistic fervor seen in two of the first chapter's three exemplary accounts reveals an insufficient theological formation. The dearth of emphasis on Christ in the three accounts affirms Chrysostom's concerns that the hearing ear now moves randomly, instead of hearing the Spirit testify of Jesus (Rev. 19.10), which has been argued here as the foundation and cornerstone of prophetic legitimacy. John Chrysostom, 'Homily VIII', in *Saint Chrysostom: Homilies on the Gospel of St. John and Epistle to the Hebrews* (Select Library of the Nicene and Post-Nicene Fathers of the Christian Church; ed. Philip Schaff; trans. T. Keble and Frederic Gardiner; New York: Christian Literature Company, 1st ser., edn, 1889), XIV, p. 406.

[51] Isaiah 6.9-10 is often cited, arguably as a proof text.

[52] Harold W. Attridge, *The Epistle to the Hebrews: A Commentary on the Epistle to the Hebrews* (Hermeneia; Philadelphia, PA: Fortress Press, 1989), p. 162, holds that the spiritually immature are incapable of a discourse in ethical philosophy, which is foundational to discernment in and through the Spirit's power. Vondey, *Pentecostalism*, p. 136, notes something similar relating to formation that takes place within formal education. He asserts that historically, Pentecostals 'voiced a lack of patience at the prospect of forsaking or postponing the spread of the gospel as the result of the formal educational process'.

[53] Stephen J. Graham, 'Ten Prophetic Techniques to Amaze Your Friends', *stephenjgraham* (blog, September 8, 2017), https://stephenjgraham.wordpress.com/2017/09/08/ten-prophetic-techniques-to-amaze-your-friends/.

5.2.1.2 Prophetic Ethic and *Prophetic Conscientia*

To live and serve while being faithful to the ethic of Jesus and the Spirit of Prophecy, prophets also need to develop the *prophetica conscientia* that includes both consciousness and the conscience. Although Pentecostals would argue this to be the Spirit's work, it is not merely given but needs to be developed. As Fee explains, those who are empowered and indwelt by the Spirit live, walk, and are led by that same Spirit.[54] Thus they become habituated over the course of time and patience.

Theologically, the formation of consciousness is an aspect of theosis. All humans live, move, and have their being in God (Acts 17.28); however, being formed and shaped as Christ's image-bearers requires *learning* to live, walk, and be led by Christ's Spirit.[55] The progression that begins with calling and culminates in union with God, is what Nouwen describes as a 'movement of the spiritual life ... from a deaf, nonhearing life to a life of listening'.[56]

Kärkkäinen speaks in terms of 'Christification'.[57] There is a 'christological structure' to our humanness and the telos that awaits us in the consummation.[58] For Kärkkäinen, '*theosis* is the mystery of eternal life in communion with God in the divine Logos'.[59] This communion with the triune life, through the work of the Incarnate Son, by the Spirit, is the core of knowing and discerning. In Johannine terms, believers receive Christ's life as they 'abide' in him. The Pauline text promises that believers will reign with Christ, sharing in the spoils of his victory provided they suffer with him. In Lukan terms, this is the promise of being filled with the Spirit as one 'continue[s] performing Luke-Acts through their ongoing discernment of and response to what God continues to do through Christ's presence in the world'.[60]

---

[54] Fee, *God's Empowering Presence*, p. 898.

[55] *Theōsis* 'is a theological concept denoting the goal of salvation to be union with God made possible through a process of deification, or becoming like God or being made divine'. Wyndy Corbin Reuschling, 'The Means and End in 2 Peter 1:3-11: The Theological and Moral Significance of Theōsis', *Journal of Theological Interpretation* 8.2 (Fall 2014), p. 276.

[56] Nouwen, *Discernment*, ch. 1.

[57] Veli-Matti Kärkkäinen, *One with God: Salvation as Deification and Justification* (Collegeville, MN: Liturgical Press, 2004), p. 25.

[58] Kärkkäinen, *One with God*, p. 25.

[59] Reuschling, 'Moral Significance of Theōsis', p. 277.

[60] Joshua W. Jipp, 'The Beginnings of a Theology of Luke-Acts: Divine Activity and Human Response', *Journal of Theological Interpretation* 8.1 (2014), p. 33.

In other words, Luke uses narrative to form readers, tying them to God's continued work in the here and now.

This process is met with challenges that require the sanctifying work of the Spirit for Pentecostals who, like Seymour, believe, 'sanctification in the perfect love of God was necessary for Spirit baptism, essential to racial reconciliation and unity, and preparation for the return of Christ for a Bride [particularly for the sake of this argument] without "spot or wrinkle"'.[61] Love's process of purifying the saints for their partaking of the divine nature is the Pentecostal answer to 'the conflict between concupiscible and irascible passions'.[62]

---

[61] Steven J. Land, 'William J. Seymour: The Father of the Holiness-Pentecostal Movement', in Henry H. Knight III (ed.), *From Aldersgate to Azusa Street: Wesleyan, Holiness, and Pentecostal Visions of the New Creation* (Eugene, OR: Pickwick, 2010), p. 225.

[62] Nicholas E. Lombardo, *The Logic of Desire: Aquinas on Emotion* (Washington, DC: Catholic University of America Press, 2011), pp. 53-54:

> The technical Latin terms that Aquinas uses for the two powers of the sense appetite, *concupiscibilis* and *irascibilis*, are taken from William of Moerbeke's translation of Aristotle's *epithumetike* and *thumike*. These words have negative connotations in their etymological origins and associations that can obscure the meaning that Aquinas assigns them. *Concupiscentia*, the root of *concupiscibilis*, can signify lust as well as a general sort of desire. Furthermore, Augustine had coined a technical use of *concupiscentia* to describe the tendency toward sin and disordered pleasure caused by original sin, and Aquinas himself sometimes uses the word in this technical sense. Consequently, the category of *concupiscibilis* has negative associations with sinful desire that are not intended. Similarly, *ira*, the passion of anger and the root of *irascibilis*, also has misleading connotations. First, the passion of anger itself often has negative connotations of disorder and sin. Second, as was the norm, Aquinas uses *ira* to denote the vice of anger as well as the passion of anger. Since the passion of anger gives its name to the category of *irascibilis*, these negative associations can seem to carry over to the irascible passions. These negative connotations are clearly not intended by Aquinas. These terms and their negative associations are simply part of his inherited vocabulary. Aquinas unequivocally presents all of the elemental passions, including the passions of desire and anger, as ontologically good in themselves and capable of being shaped by virtue, even if they are all prone to disorder in our fallen condition. Similarly, Aquinas sometimes, but not always, uses *sensualitas* in a neutral sense, as a synonym for sense appetite, though the Latin word and its English cognate 'sensuality' are rife with negative connotations.

When the early doctors of the church speak of the 'concupiscible', they are speaking of that which '*desires* virtue and knowledge', Evagrius Ponticus, *Ad Monacho* (Ancient Christian Writers; ed. Dennis McManus; trans. Jeremy Driscoll; New York: Newman Press, 2003), LIX, pp. 10-11. The 'irascible' is that part which '*fights* ... evil thoughts'. The fighting is incensing and rooted in an anger that can work in the favor of the person. Therefore, there is a desiring part and an incensing or angering aspect.

Importantly, therefore, Yong espouses, 'the Spirit's sanctifying grace was intimately connected with the Spirit's empowering witness'.[63] This reinforces the significance of holiness as well as sanctification. As Yong states:

> Pentecostal formation – again: not that of the modern movement going by that label but of the normative Lukan vision – thus attends to our embodied physicality, but not in any reductive sense. Instead, human bodies are understood as intimately and intricately intertwined with human hearts (feelings), loves (devotion), and hopes (anticipations and purposes), and these fundamental elements are energetically harnessed by the Spirit to bear embodied witness, differentially and pluralistically, to the coming divine reign.[64]

Yong speaks to the awareness of the integration (theologically, psychologically, and phenomenologically) of how prophetic witness, prophetic expression, and prophetic legitimacy form a Pentecostal paradigm inseparable from proper orthodox prophetic formation.

Arguably, discernment is not only inseparable from the overshadowing presence of the Spirit but also (given the nature of human agency and personal subjectivity) from the working of the human mind. Munzinger notes that solving the dilemma requires an 'understanding of how mind and Spirit work together',[65] stressing that giving attention is 'fundamental for authentic discernment'.[66] As such, wisdom and knowledge from the Spirit provide discernment for 'holy living (Prov 28:7; Hos 14:9; 1 Cor 2:14; Phil 1:10)'.[67] Even God acts by the Spirit to discern the human heart (Ps. 139.3; Rom. 8.27). Therefore, spiritual discernment 'is only truly available through God'

---

[63] Amos Yong, *Spirit of Love: A Trinitarian Theology of Grace* (Waco, TX: Baylor University Press, 2012), p. 62.

[64] Amos Yong, *Renewing the Church by the Spirit: Theological Education after Pentecost* (ed. Ted A. Smith; Theological Education between the Times; Grand Rapids, MI: Eerdmans, 2020), p. 80.

[65] Andre Munzinger, *Discerning the Spirits: Theological and Ethical Hermeneutics in Paul* (Cambridge: Cambridge University Press, 2007), ch. 4. If we allow Luke's Gospel to show the way, we can conclude that disciples can be taught to discern the truth, provided their minds have been 'opened' to understand the Scriptures (Lk. 24.45; Acts 1.2-3).

[66] Munzinger, *Discerning the Spirits*, ch. 6.

[67] Leland Ryken, Jim Wilhoit, and Tremper Longman III (eds.), 'Discernment', *Dictionary of Biblical Imagery* (Downers Grove, IL: InterVarsity Press, 2000).

and requires God's Spirit (1 Cor. 2.14).[68] The Spirit's work in and through human agency is the basis of a *prophetica directionis*.

What then of the Spirit's work in relation to the mind? Munzinger acknowledges the Spirit's role as 'detective and judge' and the role of 'human mediation'.[69] He concludes that if the Spirit is detective and judge, the basis for judgment is a lifestyle of knowing 'Jesus Christ, and him crucified' (1 Cor. 2.2). Based on Jesus' ethic as stated thus far, I would argue that all genuine discernment stems from the cruciformity of one's life and the openness of mind it allows.[70]

Psychologically, consciousness is phenomenological, but has overarching influence over the psychic faculties that facilitate perception. Imagination and intuition influence perception in terms of an 'instantaneous apprehension or immediate knowing of something or someone without going through any conscious process of

---

[68] 'Discernment', *Dictionary of Biblical Imagery*.

[69] Munzinger, *Discerning the Spirits*, ch. 6.

[70] Human mediation in relation to the work of the Spirit is essential, simply because human beings receive no unmediated revelation. All such revelation is mediated in the human experience; therefore, it is understood via the psyche and its faculties (including the brokenness that is comingled with the beauty of the *imago Dei*) and the moving of the Spirit. Any approach to revelatory knowledge that dismisses human mediation will lead to erroneous thinking and acting, which can lead to deception and, in certain circumstances, delusion. Munzinger, *Discerning the Spirits*, ch. 6, therefore reminds the reader, 'Paul stands in a tradition in which revelation is not an objective entity external to any human participation'. There needs to be an understanding that 'human capacity *constitutes* revelation in actively receiving it'. If such understanding is needful, Munzinger seeks to clarify the Spirit's effects on understanding in the rational mind. He argues from an integrated perspective on what transpires in relation to understanding and states that Paul is not systematic but conceptual in his approach to the mind in relation to rationality. Munzinger notes 'that for Paul rationality, intentionality, volition and consciousness belong together' (ch. 6). At the juncture where these coalesce, Munzinger describes something being allowed, stating that the 'innate intuitive faculty *allows* us to apprehend and know God's basic moral demands' (ch. 2 (emphasis added)). Munzinger notes in relation to the renewal of the nous in Rom. 12.1-2, that grammatical imperatives in the Greek would be more accurately translated, 'Stop *allowing* yourselves to be conformed … let yourselves be transformed' (ch. 6, emphasis added). Letting oneself be transformed is synonymous with allowing oneself to be transformed. Something volitional transpires. Munzinger places this allowing in the domain of the intuitive, the concept of intuition implying 'to consider, to look at, to gaze at'. William H Shannon, 'Intuition', in Michael Downey (ed.), *The New Dictionary of Catholic Spirituality* (Collegeville, MN: Liturgical Press, 2000), p. 555. Thus, this is process-oriented. We will deal with this further in relation to prophetic praxis; for now, I note this as an aspect of the psyche with psychological and phenomenological implications.

reasoning'.[71] As already mentioned, and despite much popular understanding, the immediacy (or spontaneity) of certain occurrences in the consciousness does not imply or ensure divine inspiration. Technique-driven approaches are not grounded in sound spiritual formation and therefore become pseudo-prophetic works.

Prophetic discernment is impossible if prophetic agents are foundationally confused or misled about how the truth is known. Therefore, we need to attend to the theological, biblical, and psychological nuances involved. Brueggemann's critique of 'royal consciousness' illustrates ways in which a prophetic agent can be deceived.[72] Failure to discern the zeitgeist and its impact on imagination and intuition is a marker of failed discernment attributable to a lack of self-awareness. Failure to discern the Spirit's activity can lead one to impose on the Spirit the *prima materia* of one's own psyche, thereby misrepresenting human subjectivity as divine authority.

Munzinger's belief that the 'innate intuitive faculty *allows* us to apprehend and know God's basic moral demands' suggests volition and appeals to his sense that one cannot claim all prophetic function as the work of the Spirit.[73] In the Spirit's interaction with the human mind, the Spirit is not coercing, even when 'invasive (ecstatic) experiences' occur.[74] For those who discount any activity of the mind and will, Munzinger retorts that it 'reflects a false identification of spontaneity'.[75] Even more invasive ecstatic states require the mind to mediate in some way,[76] which can result from either 'highly charged emotional' or 'more subtle rational forms'.[77]

In the Pentecostal view, Elizabeth's exchange with Mary in Luke 1 is perhaps more 'highly charged' and is instructive in that it reveals a prophetic correspondence between the two women. Both are carrying children who are participants in the divine intent. It could be conjectured that the relations between Mary's 'Be it unto me … ' and Elizabeth's child share in a collective consciousness (Lk. 1.38, KJV).

---

[71] Shannon, 'Intuition', p. 555. Inasmuch as such activity can bypass conscious reasoning, the importance of discernment would seem almost self-evident.
[72] Brueggemann, *Prophetic Imagination*, p. 35.
[73] Munzinger, *Discerning the Spirits*, ch. 2; emphasis added.
[74] Munzinger, *Discerning the Spirits*, ch. 6.
[75] Munzinger, *Discerning the Spirits*, ch. 6.
[76] Munzinger, *Discerning the Spirits*, ch. 6, denotes a 'spectrum of experience' from the more 'invasive' to the more 'subtle'.
[77] Munzinger, *Discerning the Spirits*, ch. 6.

The leaping of the babe in Elizabeth's womb seems to serve as prophetic witness to Elizabeth that (1) the child's *raison d'etre* has drawn near in the womb of Mary, and (2) Mary's child is the One who baptizes in the prophetic Spirit. In the ebullient moment of Mary's greeting, Elizabeth cries aloud (Lk. 1.42). The impartation comes through the relational humanness of suffering in Jesus and is inseparable from the totality of the human experience and subjectivity.[78]

5.2.1.3 Prophetic Ethic and *Prophetica Praxis*

For the ancient fathers, '"spiritual" matters needed as much discernment as "material" matters'.[79] For this work, the spiritual matter of wise discernment shapes the prophetic agent's utterance, elucidates its intent, and therefore informs the fruit it produces. Dautzenberg refers to this charismatic gift as 'diakrisis pneumaton',[80] a way of interpreting that which is given charismatically by the Spirit.

Regarding spiritual matters, Rich claims that the 'danger [is] greater and more hidden'.[81] The discerning of spirits is paramount in prophetic agency and expression. According to Rich, the ancient believer's quest was not for a human teacher of wisdom but 'to become

---

[78] Popular prophetism prefers a more gnostic approach to revelation, and thus finds itself in question as to what it discerns as true. Munzinger's account allows us to see an interplay, a tandem work between the Spirit and the human mind that occurs in various ways. As Fee, *God's Empowering Presence*, p. 899, argues in his reading of 1 Corinthians 14, 'at the individual level the life of the Spirit includes "praying in the Spirit" as well as with the *mind*'. I agree, 'we cannot serve God truly if we do not understand his will and concur with it', Munzinger, *Discerning the Spirits*, chap. 6. For that reason, when contemporary didactic approaches to prophetic function fail to thoroughly address these issues of discernment, what can be seen is the lack of a sound *prophetica directionis*, to the detriment of the prophetic agents, the believing communities, and those they are called to serve.

[79] Anthony D. Rich, *Discernment in the Desert Fathers: Diakrisis in the Life and Thought of Early Egyptian Monasticism* (Carlisle: Paternoster Press, 2007), p. 12.

[80] Thomas W. Gillespie, *The First Theologians: A Study in Early Christian Prophecy* (Grand Rapids, MI: Eerdmans, 1994), pp. 29-30:

> This subsequent and necessary interpretation of prophecy, according to Dautzenberg, is provided by the discrete charisma of *diakrisis pneumatōn* (1 Cor. 12:10; cf. 14:29). In a novel (and dubious) translation, the phrase is rendered as 'interpretation of Spirit revelations' rather than the conventional 'discernment of spirits'. This charisma is then related to prophecy in the same way that the text correlates interpretation *(hermeneia)* with tongues. The phrase thus denotes a charismatic interpretation or explanation, but not a judgment or evaluation, of the prophetic oracle.

[81] Rich, *Discernment in Desert Fathers*, p. 12.

open to the only teacher of the Christian who is Christ'.[82] Matthew records Jesus' statement that learning from him requires taking on his yoke (Mt. 11.29). Rich warns, 'blinding pride and self-confidence [have] to be eliminated'.[83] The prophetic agent's subjectivity needs to be acknowledged.[84] Prophetic integrity and legitimacy require discernment to be influenced by the Spirit of truth. Therefore, self-awareness and self-reflection are to become inveterate.

The underlying intent of discernment, according to Rich, is 'to be free to hear the will of God'.[85] Discernment is 'changed both with the person learning it and with those receiving it',[86] essentially making it part of spiritual growth and maturity. The believer (here, the prophetic agent) matures when discernment is exercised. This requires a praxis of abiding, a way in which the prophetic agent intuits their own 'immersion into the paschal mystery'.[87] This abiding shapes *prophetica conscientia*, which is the consciousness of Christ himself (1 Cor. 2.16), 'with and in the Holy Spirit'.[88] The agency of the Spirit causes spiritual discernment and even wise natural discernment to function as they do. To abide in Christ as praxis is to share the life of 'this abiding Spirit dwelling in us'.[89]

Munzinger shares his conviction of a fourfold consideration where interaction between the Spirit and the human mind effect true discernment.[90] Regarding this interaction, he argues, 'four particular aspects' serve as connective tissue:[91]

- 'The role of choice.'[92]
- 'The question of direct guidance by the Spirit and the conscience.'[93]

---

[82] Rich, *Discernment in Desert Fathers*, p. 12.
[83] Rich, *Discernment in Desert Fathers*, p. 12.
[84] This includes the agent's biases, cognitive distortions, perceptions, and projections.
[85] Rich, *Discernment in Desert Fathers*, p. 12. Discerning areas in which the prophetic agent is not free to hear God's will is as important as being able to hear where they are free.
[86] Rich, *Discernment in Desert Fathers*, p. 12.
[87] Mary Margaret Funk, *Discernment Matters: Listening with the Ear of the Heart* (Collegeville, MN: Liturgical Press, 2013), p. 1.
[88] Funk, *Discernment Matters*, p. 1.
[89] Funk, *Discernment Matters*, p. 1.
[90] Munzinger, *Discerning the Spirits*, ch. 6.
[91] Munzinger, *Discerning the Spirits*, ch. 6.
[92] Munzinger, *Discerning the Spirits*, ch. 6.
[93] Munzinger, *Discerning the Spirits*, ch. 6.

- 'The interrelationship of rationality and revelation.'[94]
- 'Dispositional change.'[95]

What role does choice play in the Spirit-mind exchange? If, as Munzinger notes, 'human capacity *constitutes* revelation in actively receiving it',[96] the active receiving is volitional. Therefore, there is something synergistic between the revelation the Spirit gives and its reception, discernment, and delivery via human agency. The domain of 'human mediation' is involved and includes Munzinger's 'spectrum of experience' ranging from 'invasive experiences' to 'more subtle rational forms'.[97]

Moving temporarily to a Johannine perspective, the example of John and Andrew might provide additional insight into choice and desire. When John the Baptist is standing at the Jordan with John and Andrew (Jn 1.35-40), the Baptist tells them 'Look, here is the Lamb of God!' (Jn 1.36). He does not address the entire crowd but only John and Andrew. Sanford notes, 'Look' here 'refers to the act of seeing when the emphasis is on the impression of what is seen on the mind of the observer'.[98] John is speaking in the imperative mood,[99] desiring at some level for John and Andrew to experience an impact based on the impression Jesus makes on their consciousness as the Lamb of God. This implies eschatological expectations, with John attesting by the Spirit to Jesus' preexistence (Jn 1.15). Given the relationship between the Baptist and John and Andrew, John the Baptist's imperative carries weight and authority. It seems that, desiring the impression of the Lamb, John and Andrew then follow Jesus as Rabbi. They therefore leave the Baptist's tutelage to pursue Jesus, who turns and asks, 'What are you looking for?' (Jn 1.38).[100] He asks

---

[94] Munzinger, *Discerning the Spirits*, ch. 6.
[95] Munzinger, *Discerning the Spirits*, ch. 6.
[96] Munzinger, *Discerning the Spirits*, ch. 6 (emphasis added).
[97] Munzinger, *Discerning the Spirits*, ch. 6. 'Invasive experiences' seem to indicate a 'highly charged emotional state'.
[98] *GEL*, p. 815, '91.13 ἰδού; ἴδε; ἄγε: prompters of attention, which serve also to emphasize the following statement – "look, listen, pay attention, come now, then"'. John A. Sanford, *Mystical Christianity: A Psychological Commentary on the Gospel of John* (New York: Crossroad, 1993), p. 27.
[99] Sanford, *Mystical Christianity*, p. 27.
[100] *BAGD*, p. 339, 'ζητέω impf. ἐζήτουν; fut. ζητήσω; 1 aor. ἐζήτησα ... try to find someth., *seek, look for* in order to find (s. εὑρίσκω 1a)'.

them to clarify their desire, and they ask where he abides (Jn 1.38).[101] The issue of abiding touches more than a physical location. Bearing in mind the decades intervening between events and the Johannine record, the author writes from a retrospective vantage point influenced by his own praxis of abiding during the intervening period.

Responding to Jesus' question, John and Andrew convey their bondedness to him as teacher, calling him 'Rabbi' (Jn 1.38). This initial movement of their consciousness is not toward any rabbi that might be available but toward the One they perceive to be the eschatological Lamb. This movement is rooted in their commitment to him, their teacher. With respect to Pauline theology, Munzinger sees this as the interplay between 'God's sovereign act of election' and the power of 'human decision'.[102] Again, Munzinger warns about theological presuppositions of the irrelevance of human choice. Although God's Spirit is at work in the narrative, there is a 'call and response' involving both the divine Spirit and the human spirit.[103] Therefore, human volition is vital.

Munzinger describes an 'evaluative and interpretive process' working in John and Andrew relating to John the Baptist's prophetic imperative, which he puts forth as inspired speech.[104] In telling them to behold the Lamb, he calls them to prophetic perceptuality. Here too, they appraise their mentor's words as having sufficient weight to warrant their action, so they begin to follow Jesus, albeit, from behind. They cannot see him face to face at this point; yet his questioning demonstrates his awareness of their pursuit. Their question about his abode begs an answer. The dynamic for divine encounter is in play, however mysteriously. The Spirit is guiding, with a sense of his power lying hidden (Hab. 3.4). As to rationality and revelation, Jesus probes the desire that moves them toward him as the eschatological Lamb. The affective domain is as engaged here as the rational domain is. There is an 'active reception' and a 'receptive attitude' when Jesus

---

[101] This is a prime example of the double entendre that abounds in John's Gospel.
[102] Munzinger, *Discerning the Spirits*, ch. 6.
[103] Munzinger, *Discerning the Spirits*, ch. 6, contends that any human attempt to resolve the existing tension between these two domains is beyond the scope of what can be known. Suffice it to say that both play a part.
[104] Munzinger, *Discerning the Spirits*, ch. 6.

invites them to 'Come and see' where he abides, and they 'come and stay' with him.[105]

When considering rationality, revelation, and dispositional change in relation to this text and the hidden 'guidance of the Spirit',[106] the ongoing divine-human interaction shows the human agent allowing the Spirit to effect dispositional change. Both the guidance and dispositional change begin with John the Baptist's authoritative influence on John's and Andrew's consciousness and perception. They are standing by his side, under his tutelage; yet, as Jesus passes by, the Baptist unhesitatingly commands them to follow Jesus. Something has evidently transpired in the Baptist's consciousness and perception, as he 'allows' John and Andrew to decide whether they will embrace the eschatological Lamb's imprint on their consciousness and perception. Thus, their evaluative and interpretive faculties begin to discern Jesus, who already knows (without having to turn in their direction) that they are in pursuit. His question prompts their question about his abode. Ultimately, the text will reveal that Jesus abides in the consciousness and perception of his Father (Jn 5.19). Although they are not yet mature enough to grasp it fully, John and Andrew long to do the same. This desire will be fulfilled as they participate in the triune life.

This example can intimate a *prophetica praxis* of abiding. The Baptist 'sees' by prophetic inspiration, then urges John and Andrew to see the same. Is this an initiation into prophetic spiritual discernment and wisdom that leads to participation in the triune life? Ultimately, Jesus invites them to 'Come and see' where he lives (Jn 1.39). However, the text records no physical location, perhaps intending to reveal that Jesus abides in the Father and the Father abides in him (Jn 17.21). Nevertheless, the two disciples accept the invitation and remain/abide with him (Jn 1.39).

If, in the Johannine text, the Baptist is one who sees (as in a *seer* in the Israelite prophetic tradition), this can be considered a precursor to the praxis of abiding and *beholding* (to be considered separately), which results in legitimate prophetic fruit. The internal posture of abiding that is tied to beholding is not passive but active – an engaged

---

[105] Munzinger, *Discerning the Spirits*, ch. 6.
[106] Munzinger, *Discerning the Spirits*, ch. 6.

waiting that can suggest a 'braiding or twisting' (Isa. 40.31).[107] There is therefore a *binding fast* that strengthens one in the waiting, enabling one to endure and expect. This binding fast involves the Spirit's interior work in the prophetic agent's life. The Spirit binds the prophetic agent to the cruciform Lamb, which allows the agent's formation into the same image and likeness. This requires from the prophetic agent an 'allowing' or willingness to 'come' and 'see'. The *coming* is an intentional movement toward; the *seeing* is a perceptual process of beholding. The two are interrelated. The pursuit emerges from the core desire ('What are you looking for?') and expands into a way of knowing that becomes a way of seeing or perceiving (beholding). Therefore, both faith (a posture of receptivity and allowing) and hope (a willing forward inclination and movement) are operative in the binding fast.

5.2.1.3.1 Prophetic Perception as Essential Posture
Regarding the praxis of abiding and a Pentecostal theology of prophetic legitimacy, the phenomenology of perception places us in the theoretical domain. The spiritual senses involve perceptuality known only by the senses' effects within the invisible realm of the prophetic agent's cognitive, perceptual, intuitive, imaginal, reflective, and reasoning processes, as well as overall consciousness in relation to prophetic insight and awareness. It is necessary to grasp for language (as limiting as it is) in hopes of adequately explaining how the processes and faculties of spiritual sensibility are structured. The search is for a Gestalt of sorts.[108]

---

[107] Gesenius and Tregelles, *Gesenius' Hebrew Chaldee Lexicon*, 'קָוָה – (1) prop. like the Arab. قوى to twist, to bind; whence قُوَّة a rope, Hebr. קָו and תִּקְוָה'.

[108] It is essential here to state that humans are incapable of immaculate perception. The human condition requires grace to perceive 'the spiritual in the material', Robert J. Dean and Fleming Rutledge, *Leaps of Faith: Sermons from the Edge* (Eugene, OR: Resource Publications, 2017). This is about 'the relationship between perception and reality' because 'what we directly perceive is always an image or "representation" in our minds'. Michael Huemer, *Skepticism and the Veil of Perception* (Lanham, MD: Rowman & Littlefield, 2001), intro. The psyche has a systematic way of representing reality to the consciousness via our perceptual processes. Therefore, the development of an ideal epistemic state that requires a way of perceiving can be understood as an ongoing cleansing of the senses, which requires the sanctifying work of the Spirit. This in turn requires a robust pneumatology that can address the dynamics that coexist between the senses' natural and spiritual functioning.

The epistle to the Hebrews speaks of the faculties being trained to practice discernment (Heb. 5.14).[109] Balthasar notes, 'God's human and sensory appearance in Christ could be reciprocated only by a "*hidden perception and response* on the part of man"'.[110] This implies some interior aspect of the heart and psyche that requires *sense-perception*. Is there an overlap between sense-perception from a purely natural perspective and that from a spiritual perspective? For McInroy, 'the task of perceiving the absolute beauty of the divine form (Gestalt) through which God is revealed to human beings' is at the core of Balthasar's presuppositions about the spiritual senses.[111] Our human-being-ness automatically assumes our natural state and natural senses. Therefore, our perceiving is native to our human-being-ness; and perceiving the divine form within our consciousness is a profound thought bordering on mystery.

If the interior perceiving of the divine form's beauty is a prerequisite, it can involve some level of recognizing one's mystical union with the indwelling Christ. It would have to be possible to perceive spiritually and sense the indwelling of Christ's Spirit. Theologically, regarding prophetic perception from a Pentecostal perspective, this perceiving is essentially rooted in a 'Christocentric spirituality [that] clearly accentuates the work of the Holy Spirit as the most essential component of living a Christ-like life'.[112] The indwelling Christ is not a generalized sense of the presence of the holy. Rather, it is the *particular presence* of the Christ, in and by his indwelling Spirit. Perceiving this particular presence is at the root of all that can be termed *prophetic perception*.

---

[109] *GEL*, p. 384: the idea is conveyed by '32.28 αἰσθάνομαι; αἴσθησις, εως *f*; αἰσθητήριον, ου *n*: to have the capacity to perceive clearly and hence to understand the real nature of something – "to be able to perceive, to have the capacity to understand, understanding"'. *BAGD*, p. 275, 'ἕξις, εως, ἡ (… "physical/mental state, proficiency, skill") in the only place in which it is used in our lit. it refers to a state of maturity, *maturity* … "skill, proficiency"'.

[110] Hans Urs von Balthasar, *The Glory of the Lord: A Theological Aesthetics, Volume 1: Seeing the Form* (trans. Erasmo Leiva-Merikakis; San Francisco, CA: Ignatius Press, 2009), p. 356 (emphasis added).

[111] Mark Johnson McInroy, 'Perceiving Splendor: The "Doctrine of the Spiritual Senses" in Hans Urs von Balthasar's Theological Aesthetics' (PhD dissertation, Harvard Divinity School, 2009), p. iii.

[112] Wolfgang Vondey, *Pentecostal Theology: Living the Full Gospel* (Systematic Pentecostal and Charismatic Theology; London: Bloomsbury T&T Clark, 2017), p. 15.

In his sermon from the Day of Pentecost, Peter states, '*This* Jesus God raised up' (Acts 2.32, emphasis added). The emphasis on *this* suggests particularity and finds its telos in Peter's summary statement: 'Therefore let the entire house of Israel know with certainty that God has made him both Lord and Messiah, *this* Jesus whom you crucified' (Acts 2.36, emphasis added). Therefore, *this* Jesus has been made Lord and Christ (Messiah).[113] For the sake of the argument being made here, *this Jesus* is the '*Existentiell* Jesus', the term *existentiell* being borrowed from Heidegger,[114] who wrestles with the notion of *presence*.[115] *Existentiell* is tied to comprehending presence in a certain way relating to past, present, and future.[116] Heidegger chooses the term in contrast to *existential*, which implies 'relating to existence'.[117] It is a 'more general and academic term',[118] whereas *existentiell* 'relates to a particular individual here and now'.[119] For a Pentecostal theology of prophetic legitimacy, perceiving the indwelling Spirit of the Existentiell Christ in his immediacy and nearness affirms Vondey's assertion, 'Pentecostal doctrine always passes through a personal encounter

---

[113] This is Mary's boy, per the Nicene-Constantinople Creed. 'Nicene-Constantinople Creed', *MIT*, http://web.mit.edu/ocf/www/nicene_creed.html.

[114] Tobias Henschen, 'Heidedgger's Correction of the Divine Word', in William Sailer, David C. Greulich, and Harold P. Scanlin (eds.), *Religious and Theological Abstracts* (Myerstown, PA: Religious and Theological Abstracts, 2012):

> In a 1927 lecture, Martin Heidegger claims that philosophy 'corrects' basic theological concepts by reducing them to their purely rational content and by formally indicating the ontological conditions of this content. This principle of 'correction' can be specified by applying it to Thomas Aquinas' concept of the divine word. Heidegger can be presented as reducing this concept to a purely rational content that he identifies with a new practical or linguistic meaning invented by a Dasein using tools or language in a radically new way. He also holds that the ontological condition of this purely rational content lie in the Dasein's disclosedness. His correction of Aquinas' concept of the divine word reveals that a common understanding of Heidegger's concept of authenticity, which is of central importance to his philosophy in 'Being and Time', is misguided: authenticity is not a mode exhibited by someone with a philosophical insight into Dasein's existential structure, but the existentiell mode of the existence of a Dasein who has the existentiell possibilities to invent new meaning by introducing new ways of using tools of language. (German).

[115] Heidegger refers to the presence as 'Praesans', Daniel O. Dahlstrom, *et al.* (eds.), *Heidegger's Being and Time: Critical Essays* (Lanham, MD: Rowman & Littlefield, 2005), ch. 2.

[116] Dahlstrom, *et al.*, *Heidegger's Being and Time*, ch. 2.

[117] 'Existential', *Concise Oxford English Dictionary* (Oxford: Oxford University Press, 11th edn, 2004).

[118] Thiselton, *Thiselton Companion*, 'Existentiell'.

[119] Thiselton, *Thiselton Companion*, 'Existentiell'.

with Christ through the Holy Spirit'.[120] For a Pentecostal, personal perception of the Existentiell Christ from within is in itself revelatory. That revelation issues from *this* Jesus (emphasizing again his particularity) being made both Lord and Messiah (Christ). By way of the Spirit, the prophetic agent beholds this Existentiell Christ – who is the Prophetic Messiah, this Jesus of Nazareth, crucified, risen, ascended, and in session at 'the right hand of the Father'[121] – in her interiority.[122]

In a portion of his sermon on the Day of Pentecost (Acts 2.25-28), Peter draws on the insights of David, who received counsel and instruction in his heart because of his internal posture of setting the Lord always before himself (Ps. 16.7-8). Prophetically, Peter ultimately ascribes this internal posture to Christ and, by extension, to its fulfillment in the prophethood of all believers. As a focus and awareness, this posture is a praxis of sorts. Noting an internal contemplative posture, the text presents David as being able to perceive the interactions between the Lord and himself. This hints at communion and a praxis of the ever-present God-in-Christ in a very personal manner, with God's presence as a foregone conclusion.[123] The text presents it as being beyond mere imagination. It proposes an intuition of something/someone supremely real and seems to signify an awareness of how human subjectivity is involved.[124]

In the Lukan account, Peter notes David's prophetic mention of the relations between the Incarnate Son and the Father (Acts 2.25). For the Incarnate Son, this internal beholding is unbroken communion.[125] Because of sin's alienation and the resulting fragmentation of the human psyche, our beholding of the Lord's form requires

---

[120] Vondey, *Pentecostal Theology*, p. 15.
[121] 'Nicene-Constantinople Creed', *MIT*, http://web.mit.edu/ocf/www/nicene_creed.html.
[122] I will return to the term *existentiell* in relation to how the Existentiell Christ prophetically gives *existentiell* words to the various churches via prophetic agents. There is a particularization of what Christ speaks by the Spirit to the existentiell local expressions of the 'holy catholic and apostolic church', which is the result of his crucifixion, resurrection, and ascension. 'Nicene-Constantinople Creed', *MIT*, http://web.mit.edu/ocf/www/nicene_creed.html.
[123] These conditions are possible because of the crucifixion, resurrection, ascension, and Pentecost.
[124] David's own heart gives him counsel; yet his heart interacts with the divine in such a way that he discerns the divine influence at work.
[125] This communion is attested to by Jesus' own disclosure (Jn 5.19; 17.21).

perfecting by the indwelling Spirit's sanctifying work based on the Son's reconciling work.[126] Athanasius notes that in the original revolt against the Creator, 'men's intellect fell to things of sense'.[127] This falling doesn't imply the need for sense to be eliminated but for it to be reconciled to original intent. Inspired by the Spirit, Peter looks at Psalm 16, understanding that because the Son discerned the Father's form, he was not shaken or disturbed but tranquil, even in his descent into death and hell. His flesh would not endure corruption but be transformed as the first fruits of New Creation, making theosis possible for humanity.

Athanasius states that due to the Fall, 'the Word submitted to appear through a body'.[128] This Incarnational reality was essential in reconciling human sensibilities, so 'that He as man might transfer men to Himself and direct their *senses* towards Himself'.[129] Athanasius speaks of restoring the intended spiritual perceptuality. Therefore, maturing the perceptual processes begins with the Incarnation, Christ being the expression of what humanity is intended to be. Prophetic perception is an aspect of our human yearning and call 'to participate in, and to be (re)united with, God'.[130] That reuniting through Christ's death, burial, resurrection, and ascension enables the Spirit to impact human perception and its processes, creating a human way of knowing things divine.

The goal was and remains to discern Christ after the Spirit. Balthasar argues that discerning Christ in his personhood is the foundation for spiritual sensibility. McInroy agrees and insists that understanding the 'perceptual faculties' leads to 'seeing the form',[131] which allows what flows from the form to be discerned. In contemporary prophetism, the popular parlance denotes the prophet 'getting a word'.[132] 'Getting a word' opens the psyche, which then allows itself to be influenced. However, if the form of Christ is not first

---

[126] The Son restores us. Therefore, through his Spirit, we cry, 'Abba! Father' (Rom. 8.15; Gal. 4.6; Mk 14.36).

[127] Athanasius, *On the Incarnation*, p. 71.

[128] Athanasius, *On the Incarnation*, p. 71.

[129] Athanasius, *On the Incarnation*, p. 71 (emphasis added).

[130] Nevena Dimitrova, *Human Knowledge according to Saint Maximus the Confessor* (Eugene, OR: Resource Publications, 2016), ch. 2.

[131] McInroy, 'Perceiving Splendor', p. iii.

[132] Given the lack of critical thinking and the limits of language, it would seem reductionistic to believe that the prophetic is about 'getting a word'. This oversimplification leads to error and confusion in prophetic praxis and a lack of orthodoxy.

recognized, the source of the 'word' can be problematic, with many 'forms' potentially occupying the space from which perception is sourced.

Given that Paul addresses many ways in which knowing by the Spirit is abused, his pastoral theology can assist our prophetic perception and all that affects its function. There is a reason that 'the discernment of spirits' is understood as relating to the source from which the prophetic agent operates (1 Cor. 12.10). If the form is not the divine Spirit, the word that is gotten is not divinely inspired. The doors of perception are therefore tainted with undiscerned psychological projections and personal preferences that obscure their energizing source. The problems stated in the first chapter indicate a seeming failure to behold the form of the divine, allowing agents to speak from other, suspect sources.[133] For Paul, the human spirit alone knows its own thoughts and needs to bear the cruciformity of Jesus (1 Cor. 2.11, 2). Paul is consistent in this theme and reiterates elsewhere the foundation of 'being conformed' to Jesus' death (Phil. 3.10, NKJV). In this conformity, the Holy Spirit makes the human spirit alive so that living in and by the Spirit becomes possible (Gal. 5.16-17). This is where essential meekness manifests by the Spirit as love of God and love of neighbor (Gal. 5.14). This, again, is inseparable from cruciformity at the core of human-being-ness, meaning at the foundation level of the animating principle – the human spirit itself. Cruciformity flows from that center. Failure of the will to yield in any manner or moment shifts one from abiding to resisting. Phenomenologically, this renders the human spirit susceptible to errant influences. Living from the human core, by the Spirit (Gal. 5.25), results in the bearing of good fruit.[134] Therefore, to choose a praxis of not abiding is to revolt against the life of the Spirit and expose human subjectivity to that which opposes cruciformity's work. This produces an essential relinquishing of the egocentricity and self-

---

[133] McInroy states, 'the epistemologically central task' is 'seeing the form'. McInroy, 'Perceiving Splendor', p. iii. Given that words and the ways we use them matter, the language of 'seeing the form' points to prophetic agency that issues from abiding in the triune life and the fellowship of the Son. The term 'getting a word' omits any such language, by implication reducing prophetic agency to a technique-driven process. The language suggests no recognition that the spiritual senses require seeing the form.

[134] Miroslav Volf, *Free of Charge: Giving and Forgiving in a Culture Stripped of Grace* (Grand Rapids, MI: Zondervan, 2009), ch. 3.

centeredness that resist the kenosis that empties self into others for love's sake. It is a resistance to theosis and is anti-prophetic.

For Paul, Jesus embodied the kenotic life that is evidenced by humility of mind (Phil. 2.5-11). What Jesus embodied stemmed from what he embraced at the core of his being (Phil. 2.6). He did not grasp for power. One could postulate that his being the beloved Son who pleases the Father was and is uniquely tied to his profound humility and meekness (Phil. 2.7-8), his selflessness making him the true expression of the Father. The rejection of personal aggrandizement reveals kenosis. Jesus rejected and divested himself of the power differentials that contribute to our estrangement from God, thus revealing both his human and divine natures. He embodied a prophetic self-restraint rooted in the love of his Father and humanity.

This is what Green refers to when he explains that personhood is established in emptiness, the perichoretic life of God being kenotic.[135] It can therefore be said that there is no theosis in our lives without kenosis. When the constraining power of Christ's love is not evident, it indicates a partial breaking of communion with the Spirit. The self that refuses kenosis resists humility, obedience, and cruciformity (Phil. 2.8). The egocentricity demonstrated in the exemplary accounts cited in the first chapter typify a refusal of Jesus' kenotic life that leads to the abuse of the prophetic and failure to discern the Lord's form. Suffice it to say that discerning the Lord's form is inseparable from discerning it in a cruciform manner. This is not about seeing an image but perceiving a way of being, a consciousness that is indicative of prophetic integrity and legitimacy.

Let us consider again Luke's allusions to perceptual processes in relation to life in the Spirit. Christ's post-resurrection/pre-ascension appearances reveal the weaning-away process of transposing natural sensibilities to spiritual ones. From his resurrection forward, Jesus intentionally appears and vanishes from sight (as in Lk. 24.31). Luke records Jesus as saying that the cause of perceptual dullness in the disciples on the road to Emmaus is their slowness of heart (Lk. 24.16, 25).

---

[135] Chris E.W. Green, 'Self-Emptying, Self-Awareness, and the Sharing of the Spirit, Pt 3', *Speakeasy Theology* (May 30, 2022), https://cewgreen.substack.com/p/god-does-not-want-to-be-everything?s=r.

Balthasar states emphatically, 'the human act of encounter' is rooted in perception.[136] In the Incarnation, 'God appears to man right in the midst of worldly reality'.[137] The nexus of the encounter is 'where the profane human senses, making possible the act of faith, become "spiritual"'.[138] Notice Balthasar's emphasis on 'profane human senses' as the initial point at which faith raises the sensibilities, moving the psyche from the solely natural sense to the heightened spiritual sense. This requires an action originating not in self but in God. Blake famously said, 'If the doors of perception were cleansed, everything would appear to man as it is, Infinite'.[139] In its fallen state, humanity has no capacity to cleanse the doors of perceptual process. What exists is what Tillich calls 'separation, and estrangement'.[140] For him, the grace needed to reawaken the spiritual senses requires not only reconciliation to God but 'the *re*union of life with life'[141] – the life of God with that of humanity.

Yet Tillich says something more. We are also estranged from life within ourselves. The human condition involves an essential estrangement from the life humans are intended to live. Therefore, redemption includes 'the *re*conciliation of the self with itself'.[142] This has implications for how one perceives self and other, which in turn impacts prophetic function. Jesus' clarity of perception is evident, and how he sees the other reveals our need for self to be reconciled to itself. Therefore, the doors of Simon's perception first need cleansing through the Incarnate Son's reconciling work (Lk. 22.31-32). To perceive accurately the Existentiell Christ's form, this cleansing includes the senses being reconciled to their original capacities in seen *and* unseen realms.[143]

---

[136] Balthasar, *Glory of the Lord*, pp. 356-57.
[137] Balthasar, *Glory of the Lord*, p. 357.
[138] Balthasar, *Glory of the Lord*, p. 357.
[139] William Blake, *The Marriage of Heaven and Hell* (Oxford: Oxford University Press, 1975), p. xxii.
[140] Paul Tillich, *The Shaking of the Foundations* (Eugene, OR: Wipf & Stock, 2011), p. 156.
[141] Tillich, *The Shaking of the Foundations*, p. 156.
[142] Tillich, *The Shaking of the Foundations*, p. 156.
[143] This occurs relative to all faculties of the psyche, which equally suffer from estrangement. The internal struggle between 'sin and reunion' impacts even our perceptual faculties. Tillich, *The Shaking of the Foundations*, p. 156. In all the popular sources cited in this work, little if any emphasis is placed on these realities as being essential to understanding the process of prophetic formation. What is recognized regarding discernment is cursory, at best.

How are the perceptual processes healed, so that one can see the divine form and partake of the divine life? An act of faith in Christ, grounded in the resurrection act, is essential. Balthasar avers that in the act of resurrection there is 'the resurrection of all flesh'.[144] The human condition undergoes a radical shift at resurrection. It elevates cleansing and transformation – from the profane to the spiritual – through the indwelling Spirit's operation.[145] Healing transpires at the 'causal joint' of which Farrer speaks,[146] reconciling the distance between the divine and the human creature.[147] Through the causal joint restored by the resurrection act, the Spirit is poured out on *'all flesh'* (Acts 2.17; Joel 2.28, emphasis added).[148] The human animating principle (the human spirit) can be renewed by faith because the Spirit infuses it with himself and conjoins himself to the human creature.

Torrance argues that in the Jordan, the Incarnate One received the Spirit as us and for us,[149] therefore being able at Pentecost to give us the Spirit trans-generationally (Acts 2.39). For Torrance, the giving of the Spirit at Pentecost is of a piece with Jesus' receiving the Spirit at the Jordan (Lk. 3.21-22).[150] It seems to me that by the activity of the indwelling Spirit and through the act of faith, the profane is purged. In my view, therefore, this allows the organs of external and spiritual sense to interact in ways that see things in wholes and not fragments.[151] Amid holism, the natural and spiritual senses correspond, enabling the prophetic agent to discern and perceive more accurately and interpret what she sees.[152] As a practical matter, based

---

[144] Balthasar, *Glory of the Lord*, p. 357.

[145] Resurrection does this because the beginnings of New Creation lie within it. It is in Christ, in his being both human and divine, that the cross and resurrection reconcile the finite with the infinite, the seen with the unseen, the physical with the spiritual.

[146] Austin M. Farrer, *Faith and Speculation: An Essay in Philosophical Theology* (London: Adam & Charles Black, 1967), p. 170.

[147] This is cause for Pentecostals to claim their heritage in the Spirit.

[148] Thus, the Spirit can reveal the form of Christ and enable his follower to cooperate with the divine willing and doing (Phil. 2.13). The Spirit received by faith becomes operative in a renewing fashion (Gal. 3.2; Rom. 12.1-2; Eph. 4.23).

[149] James B. Torrance, *Worship, Community, and the Triune God of Grace* (Carlisle: Paternoster Press, 1996), p. 64.

[150] Torrance, *Worship, Community*, p. 20.

[151] A Pentecostal holism is considered in section 5.2.2.2.

[152] For example, I offer that the act of faith enables Elisha to cling to Elijah while crossing the threshold of the Jordan. This symbolizes the transition and

on my years of prophetic experience, expression, and function, accurate discernment and perception contribute to the accurate apprehension and acceptance of prophetic intimations, thereby contributing to prophetic legitimacy.

Faith names a posture that is elemental *with* and *to* love and hope, constituting the knowing of God through the spiritual senses. Volf contends that faith is a 'posture of receptivity'.[153] It is an availability and attending to Jesus (the author and finisher of all knowing) and an openness to receiving continually that which he gives by the Spirit. It is also an awareness, attentiveness, and apprehension through the indwelling and overshadowing Spirit. Hence, all human perceiving transpires within and under the mediation of the Spirit-saturated Christ, enthroned by the Father as Lord.

5.2.1.3.1.1 Cleansing the Doors of Perception as Process
The path to seeing the divine form accurately requires some recurring testimony to validate what is seen. The *cleansing* of perceptual doors is an essential process for those being formed for prophetic agency. The limits of this argument forbid an exhaustive treatment of this theme. Nevertheless, it needs to be emphasized by briefly considering three scriptural instances involving the development of spiritual sensibilities. All but the Isaiah encounter were previously discussed from biblical/theological, psychological, and phenomenological perspectives. Isaiah's example is fitting here, in relation to the doors of perception being cleansed:
1. Isaiah and his primary encounter with the numinous in Isaiah 6,
2. Elisha and his primary encounter with the same, as covered in Chapter 2,

---

transposition from death to life, opens spiritual sensibility, and allows a way of seeing that spiritually reinterprets what is phenomenologically *given* before the prophet's eyes. The givenness of natural phenomena leads to the givenness of spiritual phenomena. The former, presented on the horizontal plane is infused with a givenness from the vertical plane. (Consider again Marion's saturated phenomena in relation to intuition and imagination.) Now the invisible world determines the discerning of the infinite reality that can only be perceived when perception is cleansed. In Elisha's case, the fleshly perceptual lens is transformed in the baptismal transition through the Jordan, not by the removal or declension of natural sense but by the expanded recovery of the spiritual sense lost when humanity chose to know and grow independent of intimacy with the infinite God.

[153] Volf, *Free of Charge*, ch. 2.

3. The encounter of Cleopas and the unnamed disciple with the numinous that is present but not immediately discerned, as previously noted in Chapters 1 and 4.

The following commonalities present in these encounters speak to the cleansing of the doors of perception:

- A death or death-like separation takes place.
  o King Uzziah dies (Isa. 6.1).
  o Elisha is separated from Elijah in the crossing of the Jordan and a tempestuous whirlwind (2 Kgs 2.11-12).
  o The Messiah is crucified, and two grieving disciples need to be brought through a process until their eyes are opened and they recognize him (Lk. 24.13-32).
- A transitional liminal space is entered where loss is embraced, and grief is processed.
  o 'In the year king that Uzziah died' (Isa. 6.1): This indicates that Isaiah has processed the loss of a king who once was blessed but became prideful through his amassing of military strength and power. He then trespasses into priestly territory. When confronted, he responds in anger, continues his actions, and is ultimately exiled, excluded from the house of the Lord until his death (2 Chron. 26.16-21). Isaiah would have grieved the loss. He cries out during the Beatific Vision, profoundly aware of God's 'other-ness' and his own 'unclean' state, his sense of being destroyed and rendered silent and wordless,[154] and his need of purgation (the beginning of theosis).[155]
  o Elisha refuses to leave Elijah's side, knowing his departure is near (2 Kgs 2.1-12). As Elijah performs his last Moses-like miracle, he asks Elisha what he wants. Elisha wants the firstborn's double-portion right (an immaterial request for the animating spirit that moved Elijah to

---

[154] James Swanson, 'דָּמָה', *Dictionary of Biblical Languages with Semantic Domains: Hebrew (Old Testament)* (Oak Harbor: Logos Research Systems, 1997).

[155] Jürgen Moltmann, *The Crucified God: The Cross of Christ as the Foundation and Criticism of Christian Theology* (Minneapolis, MN: Fortress Press, 1993), p. 277:

> The human God who encounters man in the crucified Christ thus involves man in a realistic divinization (*theosis*). Therefore in communion with Christ it can truly be said that men live *in God* and *from God*, 'that they live, move and have their being in him' (Acts 17:28).

accomplish all his works) (Deut. 21.17). The request is not Elijah's to grant, but he admonishes Elisha that if he *sees* when the departure take place, he will know that he has received what he asked. The departure comes and Elisha *sees*, yet he experiences deep grief and tears his garment in two, while simultaneously and briefly encountering numinous.

o Cleopas and the unnamed disciple are grief-stricken over the perceived loss of the Nazarene prophet whom they hoped would redeem Israel (Lk. 24.13-23). They are in the liminal three-day window between the Day of Passover and the Feast of First Fruits, the culmination of the Paschal Feast. Jesus addresses their grief and slowness of heart to believe all the prophets foretold about a suffering Messiah. He takes them through a process of cleansing the doors of their perception, beginning from the grief to the place where their eyes will be opened to recognize him in the breaking of the bread (Lk. 24.24-31).

These commonalities present three realities:
1. A death occurs, creating concerns about continuity and the discontinuity that results from the death.
2. The loss and grief that accompany death and discontinuity create an entrance into a transitional liminal space.
3. An opening of spiritual eyesight and an encounter with the numinous assures continuity.

In all three realities, Jesus speaks of spiritual perception and 'see[ing] God' (Mt. 5.8).[156] In the sixth Beatitude, Jesus clearly states the prerequisite of this seeing: it is purity of heart. Such processes cleanse the doors of perception, and the heart becomes ritually pure.[157] The cleansing therefore has liturgical dimensions. In the Isaianic account of his Beatific Vision, the prophet witnesses the liturgy of heaven and is summoned to participate in the heavenly council. This comes by virtue of the coal that cleanses his heart and lips to worship faithfully, so that he can faithfully utter inspired speech to those to whom he is sent.

---

[156] *BAGD*, pp. 581-82, 'ὁράω A. trans ... to perceive by the eye, catch *sight of, notice*'.

[157] *GEL*, p. 536, '53.29 καθαρός^b, ά, όν: pertaining to being ritually clean or pure – "clean, pure"'.

5.2.1.3.2 Theoria and Meditation: Prophetic Reading of Scripture as Praxis
Here we will take a brief excursus from the Lukan work, look at the fathers, and then return to the Lukan work in culminating this section.

Rickie D. Moore describes early Christian disciples as being 'inspired, empowered, and ignited to become witnesses of Jesus to the ends of the earth'.[158] This inspiration was inseparable from the Tradition that emphasized the 'God-breathed' Jewish Scriptures (2 Tim. 3.16-17, ESV). Understanding the inseparability they recognized, we are provoked to 'grasp the notion of the divine inspiration of inscripturated, or written, words'.[159] However, their inspiration was also inseparable from their relationship with Jesus, who opened to them the book that was written about him (Lk. 4.17; Ps. 40.7; Heb. 10.7). Prior to Pentecost, his Spirit impacted them, being present and operative through and in him. When the Spirit came to abide within them, their witness became empowered and continues as a prophetic witness of Jesus, intricately cojoined to the Spirit of Prophecy (Rev. 19.10). Moore's comprehensive theological observation shows that the Scriptures, Jesus, and the Spirit work together to accomplish the formative and transformative processes within the disciples, and in relation to this work, within the prophetic agent.

The encounter on the road to Emmaus culminates in the Eucharistic moment that reveals Jesus to the two disciples. The event can be considered from the ancient praxis of both *theoria* and meditation because the Scriptures are so strategic in the narrative and in Jesus' consciousness as he guides them to the moment at the table. The Greek equivalent of the Latin word *contemplatio* is *theoria* (θεωρία).[160] 'The Greek Fathers adopted the ideal of the "contemplative life"',[161] embracing the notion of θεωρία from Aristotle and Plato and adapting it to the knowledge of God.[162] Thus, they considered its significance for '"study of the Scriptures" with particular emphasis on the spiritual sense' of the text,[163] which was based in the hidden

---

[158] Moore, 'Revelation', ch. 5.
[159] Rickie D. Moore and Brian Neil Peterson, *Voice, Word, and Spirit: A Pentecostal Old Testament Survey* (Nashville, TN: Abingdon Press, 2017), intro.
[160] 'Comtemplation', in F.L. Cross and E.A. Livingstone (eds.), *Oxford Dictionary Christian Church* (Oxford: Oxford University Press, 3rd, rev. edn, 2005), pp. 412-13.
[161] 'Comtemplation', *Oxford Dictionary Christian Church*, pp. 412-13.
[162] 'Comtemplation', *Oxford Dictionary Christian Church*, pp. 412-13.
[163] 'Comtemplation', *Oxford Dictionary Christian Church*, pp. 412-13.

meaning.¹⁶⁴ The contemplative life was immersed in the Scriptures and 'devoted exclusively to the love of God'.¹⁶⁵ As history moved forward, theology commingled 'notions of meditation, prayer and contemplation around the idea of an intense love of God, felt in the affections'.¹⁶⁶ All questions about prophetic legitimacy, meditation, prayer, contemplation, and the affections are interrelated and could be considered within the nature of praxis, the human agent's interior movement in relation to the Spirit's operations, and the agent's cooperation with the same. It could be said that the Spirit manifests in diverse ways as we cooperate with him, which implies that grace has to be appropriated. Meditation, prayer, and contemplation are critical to prophetic expression, being the means of this appropriation. Synergy is present among all three and human affection; but there is also synergy between these and the Spirit himself. Regarding prophetic legitimacy, human participation is inseparable from divine operation.

Thus, the commingling of meditation, prayer, and contemplation is significant to the Lukan text: if we approach the narrative from a praxis of contemplation and meditation, we have two disciples disheartened over the tragedy of Good Friday (Lk. 24.15-20). The resurrected Christ is himself (*autos*) present (Lk. 24.15, 36),¹⁶⁷ Luke using

---

¹⁶⁴ Kathleen E. McVey, 'Theoria', in Paul Corby Finney (ed.), *The Eerdmans Encyclopedia of Early Christian Art and Archaeology* (Grand Rapids, MI: Eerdmans, 2017), p. 595:

> In their adaptation of Greek philosophy in general and in its application to nonliteral reading of Scripture, Christians used *theoria* in several interrelated senses. In Origen, e.g., *theoria* connotes insight into truth (*C. Cels.* 4.17, 5.28, 8.21) or contemplation of higher meanings of Scripture, which lead to spiritual ascent (ibid. 6.23; *Comm. Jn.* 32.338-39). Antiochene exegetes contrasted the term with *allegoria* to stress the foundation of spiritual interpretation of Scripture in the literal sense, but they also used it to encompass multiple meanings in prophetic speech (Froehlich, 1984, 19-23, 87-103; Hidal, 1996, 546-50). Alexandrians and Cappadocians continued to use *theoria* more or less synonymously with *allegoria* and developed its connection to mystical vision and ascent, most notably in Gregory of Nyssa's *Life of Moses* and in the Pseudo-Dionysian corpus.

¹⁶⁵ 'Comtemplation', *Oxford Dictionary Christian Church*, pp. 412-13.
¹⁶⁶ 'Comtemplation', *Oxford Dictionary Christian Church*, pp. 412-13.
¹⁶⁷ Luke writes, 'Jesus himself' at the beginning of the encounter on the road to Emmaus (Lk. 24.15); he uses it again in the upper room, after Cleopas and the unnamed disciple realize that Jesus had indeed revealed himself to them. When they share their experiences, Luke uses 'himself' yet again (Lk. 24.36). The narrative use of the *inclusio* brackets the entire section to instruct the reader of the significance of what transpired.

autos for emphasis as an inclusio. The two disciples do not recognize Jesus (Lk. 24.16). Johnson avers, 'their eyes were held (*krateō*) in order that they might not recognize (*epiginōskō*) him'.[168] What is the reason for this blind spot?[169] Jesus says that they were 'slow of heart to believe all that the prophets [had] declared' (Lk. 24.25). Lacking awareness, they became blinded to the necessity of the Messianic Son's sufferings and their compatibility with the enthronement the prophets promised (Lk. 24.26). Slowness of heart produced the spiritual blindness that affected their interaction with the Scriptures.

The narrative contains theological, psychological, and phenomenological implications. Jesus leads the two disciples through the text, ultimately enabling them, by the Spirit, to discern him in it.[170] As it relates to *theoria* and meditation, what transpires in the disciples is contingent upon the triad of Scripture, Jesus, and the Spirit. Contemplation here is tied to the insights derived from the text while the disciples interact with the Spirit; meditation relates to the prayerful conversation in and around the text with Jesus.[171] In the disciples'

---

[168] Johnson, *Gospel of Luke*, p. 393.

[169] Worthy of consideration is the work of C. Otto Scharmer, Senior Lecturer at MIT Sloan School of Management, in his book, *Theory U: Leading from the Future as It Emerges; The Social Technology of Presencing* (Oakland, CA: Berrett-Koehler, 2nd edn, 2009). Scharmer addresses 'presencing', his cofounding of the Presencing Institute (https://www.presencing.org), and the issue of blind spots in our ways of seeing/observing. The blind spot is 'the inner place from which an action – what we do – originates … The blind spot concerns the (inner) source from which we operate when we do what we do – the quality of attention that we use to relate to the world'. Otto C. Scharmer, *Presencing: Illuminating the Blind Spot of Leadership* (Massachusetts Institute of Technology, January 2002), pp. 1-10, https://www.researchgate.net/publication/237631506_Presencing_Illuminating_the_Blind_Spot_of_Leadership.

[170] During the forty-day period between resurrection and ascension, Luke makes it clear that Jesus was giving instructions 'through the Holy Spirit' (Acts 1.1-2). Luke's trinitarian theology is laced throughout the narrative. It is clear that when Jesus is doing what the Father has him doing, the Spirit is effectually involved.

[171] Laurence Freeman, 'Meditation', in Michael Downey (ed.), *The New Dictionary of Catholic Spirituality* (Collegeville, MN: Liturgical Press, 2000), p. 648:

In the early monastic period (5th–12th century), meditation was organically connected with contemplation in a unified vision of prayer. This sense of prayer began with *lectio*, a reading aloud and memorizing of Scripture in a way that integrated body and mind at prayer, as in the Jewish practice. Meditation was a stage of resting on the words of the text that led beyond the imaginative and rationalizing levels of the mind through *oratio*, in which a personal appropriation of the meaning was made, to *contemplatio*, which was a nonconceptual, triadic interaction, prophetic insight occurs. Although Jesus was present throughout, their blind spot postponed their *seeing him in the text* as both suffering Servant and conquering King. This prevented them from *seeing him in the context* of their current reality.

To be discerned in the context of life's ordinariness, which is where prophetic agents are called to live, Christ needs to be faithfully discerned in the text. Otherwise, prophetic expression flows from a blind spot. Prophetic agents cannot speak inspired words by the Spirit when they fail to (1) discern the testimony of Jesus in the text, and (2) discern his hidden ways of presenting himself in their daily existence.

Even what occurs on the road to Emmaus, which culminates in the Eucharist, reveals the testimony of Jesus and the Spirit of Prophecy at work. An appropriation of grace sacramentally opens the two disciples' eyes and brings cohesion to all that has occurred internally. It is evident that sight and affectation are related. Faith here is tied to a kind of seeing that had been absent prior to the risen Christ's operations of grace.[172] Something in Cleopas and the unnamed disciple bids them to invite the seeming stranger in for the evening. They attest to the burning in their hearts, which implies that their affections were moving in a grace-driven direction. An awakened element of faith is intended to deepen their vision of what is transpiring *before* their eyes, based on what is happening *behind* their eyes (in their interiority).[173] The interior synergistic appropriations of grace by the two disciples correspond to the synergy of the Spirit of Prophecy in making them aware of the prophetic Messiah's presence.

Through clear markers, the Lukan account reveals the important process that needs to be seen as it unfolds. Found in various places, these markers imply a clear psychological and phenomenological progression:

---

thought-free state of being in God rather than talking to God or thinking about God. These aspects of prayer only later hardened into methods and stages, notably after the 14th century.

[172] Arguably, grace never comes all at once. However, it can be asserted that when it does come, cooperation with the Spirit is necessary.

[173] If faith is an aspect of the operating grace of the Spirit, what happens in the breaking of the bread is a deeper immersion into the mystery of communion with the triune God through the mediation of the visible-for-the-moment prophetic Messiah, the unseen influence and grace of the prophetic Spirit, and the unseen presence of the Father.

1. Jesus interprets the Scriptures to them (Lk. 24.27).[174]
2. Jesus opens the Scriptures (Lk. 24.32).[175]
3. Jesus opens their minds 'to understand the Scriptures' (Lk. 24.45).
4. Jesus opens their hearts, per the disciples on the Emmaus Road: 'Were not our hearts burning within us, while he was talking to us on the road?' (Lk. 24.32).
5. Jesus opens their eyes and vanishes from sight (Lk. 24.31).[176]

This process leads to an inspired prophetic expression in the Upper Room and results in Jesus' appearing and confirming their words (Lk. 24.36). The expression is prophetic in that it leads to Christ manifesting amid the disciples. This is the telos of the Spirit of Prophecy (Rev. 19.10). The insight's revelatory nature comes through the psychological issues presenting themselves in relation to the human subjectivity of Cleopas and the unnamed disciple. These are experientially and progressively handled on the walk from Jerusalem to Emmaus, until their hearts are burning with a passionate intention and love for God.

For Cleopas and the unnamed disciple, this passionate intention unfolds through a praxis of *theoria* and meditation guided by Christ and his Spirit's inwrought work. It is reminiscent of Henry's statement: 'Coming into the condition of experiencing oneself and of being revealed to oneself is accomplished in the self-revelation of absolute Life in the Word'.[177] Revealing of the self requires an

---

[174] Johnson, *Gospel of Luke*, p. 396:

Interpreted for them: The verb *diermēneuō*, like its cognate *hermēneuō* (which some mss have here) means 'to translate' (as in Acts 9:36) or 'interpret' (as in 1 Cor 12:30; 14:5, 13, 27). In this case, Jesus shows them 'the things concerning himself,' that is, how he 'brought to fulfillment' the meaning of Scripture (see 22:37: 'that which is about me has a fulfillment'). Luke shows the risen Jesus teaching the Church the proper way to read the texts of Torah, that is, messianically.

[175] Johnson, *Gospel of Luke*, p. 397:

As he opened the Scriptures to us: Luke uses the same word (*dianoigō*) for the opening' of the texts as for the 'opening' of their eyes in verse 31. As they perceived the true, messianic meaning of the Scripture, they were also able to 'see' Jesus in the breaking of the bread. Luke uses *graphē* here and in verse 27 for Scripture, otherwise using the term only in 4:27, and in the scene that follows this one, 24:45 (but see Acts 1:16; 8:32, 35; 17:2, 11; 18:24, 28).

[176] The implication is that by virtue of the Eucharist, he has become embodied in them, so that they can learn to know him by the Spirit.

[177] Michel Henry, *Words of Christ* (trans. Christina M. Gschwandtner; Grand Rapids, MI: Eerdmans, 2012), p. 104.

encounter with Christ, the Source of true selfhood. The two disciples are confronted with a Jesus they do not discern, being barred from seeing themselves clearly. The very life in the Word brings about self-realization, perfecting insight and permitting one to discern the objective presence of the Christ who is both hidden and revealed, again and again. This veiling and unveiling occurs in the praxis of both *theoria* and meditation, apart from which there can be no prophetic insight or prophetic legitimacy.

5.2.1.3.3 Abiding as Action

A Pentecostal praxis of abiding is a 'Spirit-centered spirituality' rooted in an emphatically 'Spirit-filled life' integrally identified with '*mystical* and pietistic traditions'.[178] The purpose is to cultivate the kind of spiritual discernment in wisdom that enables the prophetic agent. This phenomenological prophetic way of being is evident in Mary's Magnificat (Lk. 1.46-55), Hannah's song (1 Sam. 2.1-10), Simeon's utterance (Lk. 2.29-32, 34-35), and Agabus' enactment and utterance with Paul's belt (Acts 21.11). This does not imply that the ancient Scriptures (including Hannah's song and prophetic utterances of Messiah) were unknown to Mary or Simeon. Rather, it implies that when these prophetic enactments occurred, there was an immediacy of knowing that required no aforethought. The Scriptures may have been hidden in the hearts of these persons (Ps. 119.11); yet in the moments in which they offered inspired prophetic expressions, there was no premeditation.

As praxis, abiding includes 'action'.[179] In Johannine terms, 'knowing truth is contingent upon doing it' (Jn 3.21).[180] Jesus teaches an ethical process in relation to discernment and wisdom; as prophetic Messiah, he additionally offers a *prophetica praxis*. In doing what he teaches,[181] one confirms spiritual wisdom and discernment. Of utmost importance relative to *prophetica conscientia* and prophetic perception is the *how* of doing. When the how is embraced in the intrapersonal domain, the *what* of prophetic enactment automatically

---

[178] Vondey, *Pentecostalism*, pp. 33-34 (emphasis added).

[179] S. Escobar, 'Praxis and Orthopraxis', in Martin Davie, *et al.* (eds.), *New Dictionary of Theology: Historical and Systematic* (London; Downers Grove, IL: InterVarsity Press, 2016), p. 696.

[180] Escobar, 'Praxis and Orthopraxis', p. 696.

[181] For Jesus, 'doing' (*poiesis*) is praxis. '90.45 ποιέω: a marker of an agent relation with a numerable event – "to do, to perform, to practice, to make"', *GEL*, p. 804.

flows outward toward the interpersonal domain. Were we to encapsulate this approach to a Pentecostal theology of prophetic legitimacy, it would present as follows:

- *Prophetica conscientia* as a way of *knowing*.
- Prophetic perception as a way of *seeing*.
- Prophetic enactment as a way of *doing*.

Were we then to summarize these dynamics in a singular expression, we would ontologically express it as a *prophetic way of being*. Although all of this is conceptual and descriptive, and although it necessarily has theological underpinnings and psychological operations, its core is entirely experiential. Therefore, from a Pentecostal perspective, the theological and psychological constellate around the phenomenological. In this, a careful reading of biblical texts, beginning with Luke-Acts is essential.

However, what is needed is more than explaining the teachings of Scripture. Due to the immediacy of the internal revelatory experience involved in prophetic enactment, this kind of consciousness and perception needs to be understood within the province of the phenomenological. Hart astutely states, 'philosophers seek to fill the logical space of reasons while poets and painters populate the formal space of experience'.[182] There is a theological logic to the content of legitimate prophetic utterance. The human psyche in all its functions and reasonings is also involved. Yet, in the moment, prophetic expression is done from a fluid place of competence that does not wonder whether the precise flow of words will come. The moment is more one of artistry (a *poiesis*) than of filling the logical space of reasoning.

Therefore, constructing a Pentecostal theology of prophetic legitimacy based in a praxis of discernment requires understanding *prophetica conscientia* as a *way of knowing* and perception as a *way of seeing*. Just as the consciousness to be formed is 'the mind of Christ', Kärkkäinen notes, 'beholding the things divine' requires 'pneumatic eyes'.[183] From a Pentecostal vantage point, this is congruent with Violet Kiteley's notes accompanying a triangular diagram (Figure 4). She

---

[182] Kevin Hart, 'How Marion Gives Himself', in Rachel Bath, *et al.* (eds.), *Breached Horizons: The Philosophy of Jean-Luc Marion* (Lanham, MD: Rowman & Littlefield, 2017), ch. 1.

[183] Veli-Matti Kärkkäinen, *Pneumatology: The Holy Spirit in Ecumenical, International, and Contextual Perspective* (Grand Rapids, MI: Baker Academic, 2002), p. 176. The perception being formed is thus attuned pneumatically.

wrote the words 'prophet ... eyes ... seeing'.[184] Because prophetic agents claim to be moved by the Spirit of Christ and are to lead others in the work of discernment, training in a suitable praxis is necessary. Learning to 'abide' is the heart of such training. Pentecostals reading John through Luke-Acts could argue that this abiding is made possible by the Spirit of Pentecost that rests on the body of Jesus.[185] As the prophet abides, she becomes a mature, faithful witness who (1) honors the difference between her own mind and the mind of Christ, and (2) honors the difference between her own gifts and the needs of those around her. As the work of God who is the source, guide, and goal of life, abiding is the origin, condition, and evidence of life in the Spirit and, therefore, prophetic legitimacy. The prophet's life and the ways in which she delivers her messages would therefore reflect this abiding.

As shown in Chapter 4, Violet Kiteley believed posture and praxis issue from a life of prayer that is inseparable from abiding. This was evident even in her voluminous and evolving personal notes, where extemporaneous jottings added over time display her continuing reflection, communion, and consideration of trinitarian realities. Kiteley interlaced the Lukan and Johannine accounts in framing the 'levels of prayer' in Jesus' life (Lk. 3.21; 5.15-16; 6.12-13; 9.18, 28-29; 11.1; 22.31-32; Jn 11.41-42, focusing on the Father-Son relationship).[186] Seeing Jesus as exemplar, Kiteley tied his prayer life to the believer's life. Relating prayer with submission to God (per James 4, particularly 4.14) and noting the arrogance of presuming upon God's will,[187] she emphasized Jesus' life of prayer as 'an established personal habit (Luke 3:21)'.[188] Based on her extensive notes, she viewed this abiding communion via prayer as a nonnegotiable lifestyle from which the conversation between God and believer is a natural outgrowth and the path to answered prayer (Jn 15.7).[189]

---

[184] Kiteley, 'Five Spiritual Senses', p. 1.
[185] Eugene F. Rogers Jr. (ed.), *The Holy Spirit: Classic and Contemporary Readings* (Chichester: Wiley-Blackwell, 2009), intro.
[186] Violet Kiteley, 'Levels of Prayer in Jesus' Life', *Violet Kiteley Papers*, p. 1.
[187] Violet Kiteley, 'Prayer – Our Spiritual Armour, Cont.', *Violet Kiteley Papers*, p. 1.
[188] Kiteley, 'Levels of Prayer', p. 1.
[189] Violet Kiteley, 'Untitled Prayer Notes', *Violet Kiteley Papers*, p. 1.

5.2.1.3.4 Outworking of a Pentecostal Praxis of Abiding

Given the ethic of Jesus as being foundational to the Christian life and given that prophets are called to bring Christ's word to bear in the church and world, abiding in Christ should ensure that prophets and prophecies reflect the character the Beatitudes describe. Therefore, Pentecostals cannot afford to ignore the Beatitudes, and prophetic legitimacy hinges upon the character that the Beatitudes reveal.[190]

Bonhoeffer's reading is helpful in considering how the Beatitudes describe the praxis of abiding. For Bonhoeffer, poverty of spirit indicates being 'needy in every way'.[191] As Jesus states, 'Apart from me you can do nothing' (Jn 15.5). Therefore, a Pentecostal praxis of abiding begins with poverty of spirit. *Prophetica conscientia* and prophetic perception require the same. Any tendency toward the self-sufficiency that is based in individualism suggests the abandonment of this posture,[192] as seen in the first two exemplary accounts in Chapter 1.

Regarding Jesus' ethic, Bonhoeffer sees the frequently caricatured and scapegoated Pharisees as 'insiders' at odds with Jesus' wisdom. He argues that they 'intended to be doers of the law' and approached righteousness as 'literal obedience to what was commanded'.[193] As flawed humans, 'their righteousness always remained incomplete'.[194] Acknowledging contemporary challenges to Matthew's representation of the Pharisees, he arguably identifies the following indications of a mind set against Jesus' ethic:

---

[190] The litany of the Beatitudes concludes with 'Blessed are you when people revile you and persecute you and utter all kinds of evil against you falsely on my account. Rejoice and be glad, for your reward is great in heaven, for in the same way they persecuted the prophets who were before you' (Mt. 5.11-12). Jesus is addressing the disciples as the heirs of the prophetic tradition, causing them to embrace their role as the new prophetic community and witness of Jesus.

[191] Dietrich Bonhoeffer, *Discipleship* (trans. Barbara Green and Reinhard Krauss; Dietrich Bonhoeffer Works: Reader's Edition; Minneapolis, MN: Fortress Press, 2015), p. 71.

[192] Bonhoeffer brings a scathing reproof to the self-sufficient, describing them as 'the representatives and preachers of the *national religion*, those powerful, respected people, who stand firmly on the earth inseparably rooted in the national way of life, the spirit of the times, the popular piety', Bonhoeffer, *Discipleship*, p. 71 (emphasis added).

[193] Bonhoeffer, *Discipleship*, p. 88.

[194] Bonhoeffer, *Discipleship*, p. 88.

- the conflation of self-serving nationalism for power to 'sit on Moses' seat' (Mt. 23.2),
- the love of elitism and making the rules but not living by them (Mt. 23.4),
- the drive to be 'seen by others' (Mt. 23.5),
- the addiction to wanting the seat of honor, being enamored by the zeitgeist (Mt. 23.6),
- the demand for 'respect in the marketplace' of ideas (Mt. 23.7),
- the determination to maintain popularity, being known by all and called by an appropriate title (Mt. 23.7).

In Matthew's vision, these proclivities are antithetical to poverty of spirit and resistant to the Spirit through whom Jesus declares good news to the poor. In Pauline terms, poverty of spirit can be understood as an aspect of the kenotic 'mindset', a phronema of the prophetic Messiah (Phil. 2.6-8).[195] Jesus' mindset was one of having 'emptied himself' and not considering 'equality with God as something to be exploited' (Phil. 2.7, 6). Therefore, poverty of spirit is an essential and fundamental consciousness. It flows from an internal awareness derived from a praxis of abiding. Phenomenologically, the Spirit keeps the prophetic agent in such a place, with the agent *allowing* the Spirit to accomplish it in and through her.

Bonhoeffer stresses the agent's present-moment awareness that 'they also have neither spiritual power of their own, nor experience or knowledge they can refer to and which could comfort them'.[196] Such agents are yoked with Jesus and his meekness by the indwelling Spirit (Mt. 11.29; 5.5). They see themselves as 'servant[s]' of Christ and are 'gently subjected' to God's will.[197] Thus, the Spirit bestows, experientially, the power, graces, energies, knowledge, and wisdom

---

[195] 'φρόνημα, ατος, τό', *BAGD*, p. 874: the idea of mindset here is 'φρόνημα, ατος, τό (fr. φρήν via φρονέω; Aeschyl., Hdt. *et al.*; Vett. Val. 109, 2; 2 Macc 7:21; 13:9; Philo, Joseph.; Hippol., Ref. 1, 2, 1 [philosophical: "point of view"]) the faculty of fixing one's mind on someth., *way of thinking, mind(-set)*'. A mindset is 'a mental attitude or inclination … a fixed state of mind', 'Mindset', *Merriam-Webster.com Dictionary*, https://www.merriam-webster.com/dictionary/mindset.

[196] Bonhoeffer, *Discipleship*, p. 71.

[197] D.G. Burke, 'Meek Meekness', in Geoffrey W. Bromiley (ed.), *International Standard Bible Encyclopedia* (Grand Rapids, MI: Eerdmans, rev. edn, 1988), p. 307.

needed to embody this way of being. The legitimate prophetic agent is dependent on the Spirit, with no 'arrogant reliance on self'.[198]

In this regard, a phenomenological givenness comes by the Spirit. Bonhoeffer remarks that the kingdom of heaven 'is already *given* them in the complete poverty of the cross'.[199] The *prophetica conscientia* awakened by its intimacy with the poor and the God of the poor moves toward a hungering and thirsting for justice (Mt. 5.6). As Bonhoeffer discerns, those who hunger and thirst embody a praxis of poverty of spirit, mournfulness, and meekness. This hunger and thirst are inseparable from the now-and-not-yet-ness of 'the coming of God's eschatological rule'.[200]

Read along these lines, the first four Beatitudes mark the nature of *prophetica conscientia*. The three subsequent Beatitudes – being merciful, having pure hearts, and being peacemakers – result in persecution, the interpersonal marker of abiding (as praxis) and prophetic legitimacy. Bonhoeffer notes, 'Jesus Christ lived in the midst of his enemies' and came 'for the express purpose of bringing peace to the enemies of God'.[201] Bonhoeffer infers that we are unable to avoid the same and instead 'belong … in the midst of enemies',[202] which is where we 'find [our] mission'.[203] In abiding, the prophetic agent

---

[198] Burke, 'Meek Meekness', p. 307. The absence of such dependency indicates a lack of allegiance to the Spirit and is evidenced by the resulting fruit. Thus, the lack of allegiance implies a lack of legitimacy.

[199] Bonhoeffer, *Discipleship*, p. 72 (emphasis added). This givenness is also manifest in the 'mourning' that indicates what Brueggemann terms 'the ultimate form of criticism' regarding the 'apathy of official optimism' present in all illegitimate uses of power (Mt. 5.4). Brueggemann, *Prophetic Imagination*, p. 46. It announces 'the sure end of the whole royal arrangement' typified in the consciousness of Pharaoh's power in Egypt and its sharp contrast to the alternative Mosaic community and vision of shalom that are seen where prophetic consciousness and imagination are cultivated.

[200] Donald A. Hagner, *Matthew 1–13* (Word Biblical Commentary 33A; Dallas, TX: Word, 1993), p. 93. This runs counter to popular contemporary prophetism that has embraced a triumphalism stemming from an over-realized eschatology. The longing for God to act cannot be translated as political power that conflates nationalism with the Gospel.

[201] Dietrich Bonhoeffer, *Life Together and Prayerbook of the Bible* (ed. Geffrey B. Kelly; trans. Daniel W. Bloesch and James H. Burtness; Dietrich Bonhoeffer Works 5; Minneapolis, MN: Fortress Press, 1996), p. 27.

[202] Bonhoeffer, *Life Together*, p. 27.

[203] Bonhoeffer, *Life Together*, p. 27. This does not suggest an ease of mission but a willingness to endure amid interpersonal difficulty. Agents who abide in this way are true heirs and sons of the prophets (Acts 3.19-22).

embraces 'extraordinary love, self-denial, and espousal of nonviolence and forgiveness of enemies'.[204]

5.2.1.3.5 Experiential Immediacy

Assuming the immediacy of knowing something without conscious aforethought cannot be equated with revelation or an unmediated experience, the phenomenological, experiential immediacy that a praxis of abiding produces does not override human agency or subjectivity. As a competence and mastery, it more closely resembles the artistry of poets and painters than the work of philosophers and reasoners. In Lukan terms, 'All of them were filled with the Holy Spirit and began to speak in other tongues as the Spirit *enabled* them' (Acts 2.4, NIV, emphasis added). The human subjectivity of the prophetic expression is immersed in the Spirit's overshadowing influence and enablement, which operate in tandem.

The journey to competency can be described in four stages: first, one realizes that one does not know what one does not know; next, one moves to knowing that one does not know; third, one knows that one knows; and fourth, one knows without the need for conscious thought.[205] Thus, knowing becomes visceral and even tacit.[206] This is akin to Polanyi's notion of 'tacit knowledge' by which 'we know more than we can tell'.[207] Adapting this to a Pentecostal theology of prophetic legitimacy, we can say that tacit knowing is a phenomenological reality that transpires in present-moment awareness, with the immediacy of the moment giving 'place to intuition and hunches' that are (1) generated by the influence of the Spirit, and (2) processed through human subjectivity within the human consciousness.[208] In scriptural language, this response is characterized by poverty of spirit and self-emptying.

---

[204] Geffrey B. Kelly, 'Editor's Introduction to the Reader's Edition of Dietrich Bonhoeffer's *Discipleship*', in Dietrich Bonhoeffer, *Discipleship* (Minneapolis, MN: Fortress Press, 2015), p. xiii.

[205] 'You Don't Know What You Don't Know: The Four States of Competence', *Movementum*, https://movementum.co.uk/journal/competence.

[206] 'Four States of Competence', *Movementum*, https://movementum.co.uk/journal/competence.

[207] Michael Polanyi, *The Tacit Dimension* (Chicago, IL: University of Chicago Press, 1966), p. 4.

[208] 'Michael Polanyi and Tacit Knowledge', https://infed.org/mobi/michael-polanyi-and-tacit-knowledge/.

Certainly, 'discernment is no easy process'.[209] As Castelo argues, 'Illumination and hard work go hand in hand; one without the other is an impoverishment, not simply in terms of results but of process, method, and (most crucially) formation as well'.[210] The process of discernment needs to be meticulous, the method thorough, and the formation achieved through overarching cruciformity. Criteria for discernment are essential.[211] If the criteria do not consider phenomenology with theology and psychology, they will fall short of clarity.

Although Brueggemann focuses on the necessity of prophetic imagination, prophetic intuition also warrants consideration. At a level of the 'natural world',[212] the function of imagination 'fine tunes' our perception of the world as it is.[213] Prophetic imagination, infused by the prophetic Spirit, fine tunes our perception of the world as it is intended to be and become. Whatever 'irregularities' exist in perceptions in the natural or spiritual domains,[214] the perfecting of imagination clarifies what is imagined and perceived as being possible and real. However, what is needed at a prophetic level is more than the 'empirical' domain of investigation.[215] The intuitive domain is paramount. From the perspective of depth psychology, 'Jung favored intuitive perception and cognition',[216] with the phenomenology of intuition seeing things from *within* the experience. Therefore, consider again Elisha's grief over Elijah's departure: The text describes Elijah exiting as by 'a chariot of fire and horses of fire' that ascend in a 'whirlwind' (2 Kgs 2.11-12). A Pentecostal reading would seek to get inside that experience. This requires the intuitive function through which a certain kind of discernment occurs. Elisha's grief is expressed as emotional distress; it opens his capacity to perceive what is given phenomenologically as the way in which his seeing now changes. He will see Elijah no more but will see the unseen domain as no less real than the seen world (2 Kgs 2.11-12). This way of seeing

---

[209] Daniel Castelo, *Pneumatology: A Guide for the Perplexed* (Guides for the Perplexed; London: Bloomsbury T&T Clark, 2015), p. 120.
[210] Castelo, *Pneumatology*, p. 120.
[211] Castelo, *Pneumatology*, p. 121.
[212] Lois Iseman, *Understanding Intuition: A Journey In and Out of Science* (London: Academic Press, 2018), p. 139.
[213] Iseman, *Understanding Intuition*, p. 139.
[214] Iseman, *Understanding Intuition*, p. 139.
[215] Iseman, *Understanding Intuition*, p. 139.
[216] Iseman, *Understanding Intuition*, p. 139.

will remain (2 Kgs 6.15-17). What Elisha senses at a natural level and how his imagination interprets it are now transferred to what he intuits of the spiritual world. In his interiority, the sensate world is essentially eclipsed by the Spirit's work.

This coincides with Jung's coupling of the 'opposing ways of apprehending the external world',[217] as in the sensation/intuition pairing of psychological functions.[218] Within Elisha's internal encountering of the numinous, there is an 'integrating' of the seen and unseen.[219] One could say that prophetic imagination takes an intuitive turn to see the unseen and hear the unheard, so that speaking the unspoken becomes possible. All of this is to be infused and initiated by the indwelling and in-breathing of the Spirit. If we argue that Pentecostals prefer intuitive encounters with the Spirit, it follows that prophetic Pentecostals favor the same. Regarding intuition, 'most systematic theology has been reluctant to give an affirmative answer'.[220] As Pentecostals arguing for spiritual intuition from a theological perspective, we make way for intuition from a prophetic perspective. Given systematic theology's reluctance, ought we to resist this? Or should we embrace and perfect it?

I propose the latter as the Pentecostal answer. Therefore, it becomes necessary to understand what intuition is and how it operates. As mentioned, intuition is an 'instantaneous apprehension or immediate knowing of something or someone without going through any conscious process of reasoning'.[221] Because this apprehension is instantaneous, we need to understand the psyche's liminal space as a precarious one – both a place of possibility with promise and one of deception and error. At this precise joint of liminality in the psyche, the Spirit's discernment and grace are needed to infuse the prophetic agent with the truth as it is in Jesus (Eph. 4.21). Tsevat places this 'joint' in the domain of the anthropological and phenomenological, stating, 'here the object of knowledge, human conduct, is a *successive*

---

[217] Iseman, *Understanding Intuition*, p. 139.
[218] Iseman, *Understanding Intuition*, p. 139.
[219] Iseman, *Understanding Intuition*, p. 139. Pentecostals, however, stand in contrast to those who argue against intuition in relation to the immediacy of revelation.
[220] Shannon, 'Intuition', p. 555.
[221] Shannon, 'Intuition', p. 555.

phenomenon'.²²² Is the knowledge explicit or tacit? Or is it a combination of both?²²³

From a Pentecostal perspective, the narrative *in*-forms us of that which forms us. The reading, telling, and living of the story invite us into the formative journey. Because we experience things as creatures of time and space, we experience them sequentially. If we again consider 2 King's Elijah-Elisha narrative, Elisha's reception of Elijah's mantle reveals a sequential, unfolding process. When Elijah is about to depart by whirlwind, his directive – 'If you see me as I am being taken from you' (2 Kgs 2.10) – reinforces Elisha's already present quality of attention.²²⁴ Elijah admonishes Elisha to *see*. Psychologically and phenomenologically, we can understand this as perceptual. Theologically, we can understand it as visionary. We can presume that Elisha's attention is the watchful silence he prescribes for the sons of the prophets (2 Kgs 2.3, 5). He is highly intentional, riveted on the givenness of Elijah in his field of vision and imagination, and fully present to Elijah. Elijah fills his vision and sensate imagination. All else escapes him. The text shows the two men continuing to walk and talk (2 Kgs 2.11). There is movement and conversation. Although the narrative does not disclose the conversation's content, the transition's imminence suggests something far from trivial.²²⁵ The narrative builds suspense and creates within the reader Elisha's felt sense as Elijah's departure nears. When the divine action separates them, Elisha *sees* the unseen realm, and his shift from the sensate domain to the intuitive one occurs. It is visionary and imaginative, yet real.²²⁶

This shift appears to be pure prophetic intuition infused with inspired imagination. As the whirlwind begins and the chariot appears, something triggers in Elisha, virtually instantaneously: he realizes he has lost his mentor. This generates Elisha's grief and the tearing of his garment as a public act of mourning. Having seen that which he was intended to see, he can no longer see the one who instructed him

---

²²² M. Tsevat, 'חָקַר', *TDOT*, V, p. 149 (emphasis added).

²²³ If the knowledge is intuitive, it would be helpful to know. How can one comprehend the structure of that which is successive?

²²⁴ Per 2 Kgs 2.2, 4, 6, Elisha is already determined not to leave Elijah's side until God separates them.

²²⁵ A Pentecostal reading would argue that the conversation expands the admonition to see.

²²⁶ The text indicates that only Elijah and Elisha can see what transpires; the distant, observing sons of the prophets cannot.

to see it (2 Kgs 2.12). If one were to place oneself in the narrative empathetically, one might presume that Elisha had no thought of the consequences of tearing his garment and rendering it unwearable. Nor would one imagine his awareness that taking up Elisha's fallen coat was imperative to replacing what he had lost. Yet, the tearing and letting go of his own garment leads to the receiving and donning of Elijah's,[227] and his request for the double share of Elijah's spirit is fulfilled.[228] All that preceded by way of Elisha's posture and praxis was part of what could be described as the *successive* dynamics leading to the awakening of prophetic imagination and, more importantly, prophetic intuition (2 Kgs 2.11).[229]

Assuming we embrace intuition as 'instantaneous apprehension or immediate knowing' requiring no 'conscious process of reasoning',[230] it can offer a certain knowledge of God. Considering systematic theology's reluctance 'to give an affirmative answer' in this regard,[231] Pentecostals might pose the question differently, seeing questions such as 'What kind of knowledge is God-knowledge?' through a larger lens than systematic theology.[232] Castelo states that for a Pentecostal, 'the work of theological reflection' cannot be divorced from 'one's prayer life' or 'piety'.[233] As such, 'theological effort' cannot be exercised apart from being 'dependent upon something greater than intellectual prowess and creativity'.[234] Therefore, from a Pentecostal perspective and in relation to prophetic legitimacy, one cannot ignore the intuitive dimension of 'a person's Spirit-imbued power and anointing'.[235] Whatever Pentecostals offer theologically is based in

---

[227] Brueggemann, *1st and 2nd Kings*, p. 297, refers to Elisha's tearing of his own coat as 'a gesture of grief and loss'.

[228] The change of garments could be read phenomenologically and theologically as a change of consciousness and perception in relation to prophetic imagination and intuition. It could also be argued that such moments would not or could not occur apart from the praxis of abiding and its shaping of consciousness over time, which forms how the prophetic agent apprehends and accepts these moments.

[229] The allusion to the pouring of water on Elijah's hands as a praxis can be equated with the poverty of spirit essential to a prophetic ethic.

[230] Shannon, 'Intuition', p. 555.

[231] Shannon, 'Intuition', p. 555.

[232] Daniel Castelo, *Pentecostalism As a Christian Mystical Tradition* (Grand Rapids, MI: Eerdmans, 2017), p. 18.

[233] Castelo, *Pentecostalism*, p. 20.

[234] Castelo, *Pentecostalism*, p. 20.

[235] Castelo, *Pentecostalism*, p. 21.

their experience of the triune life. While Thomas Merton was not a Pentecostal, he captures the intent of the intuitive knowledge of God stating, 'In the depths of contemplative prayer there seems to be no division between subject and object and there is no reason to make any statement about God or about oneself. He IS and this reality absorbs everything else.'[236]

Perhaps this psychological definition offers a window of understanding:

> [Intuition is] immediate insight or perception, as contrasted with conscious reasoning or reflection. Intuitions have been characterized alternatively as quasi-mystical experiences or as the products of instinct, feeling, minimal sense impressions, or unconscious forces.[237]

The sense of immediacy characterizes the intuitive experience. Yet, the absence of 'conscious reasoning or reflective process' does not preclude the operation of unconscious processes. The psychological definition recognizes intuition's possible mystical aspect, as well as its instinctual and affective characteristics and its relation to sensate impressions. Therefore, it is difficult to reduce intuition to a singular unconscious process or domain.

The concern for this work is the intuiting of the divine. Violet Kiteley contended that listening for the voice of the Spirit, individually and communally, was paramount.[238] Such a listening, based on contemporary psychology's view of intuition, could be considered a form of listening for that which comes intuitively.[239]

---

[236] Thomas Merton, *New Seeds of Contemplation* (New York: New Directions, 2007), p. 267.

[237] 'Intuition', *APA Dictionary of Psychology*, https://dictionary.apa.org/intuition.

[238] As shown in Chapter 4, Kiteley's belief that the medieval church had not listened to the Spirit was a matter of grave concern to her. Kiteley, 'Prophetic Promise to Restore', p. 14.

[239] Regarding Otto's previously mentioned notion of the numinous, Albert Norton, *Intuition of Significance: Evidence against Materialism and for God* (Eugene, OR: Resource Publications, 2020), ch. 2, contends, 'perception of the numinous exists *as an intuition*' (emphasis added). Norton argues that children are naturally inclined toward intuitional receptivity. So, are we 'born with true intuition?' If so, we arrive with knowledge that is a given of sorts. If not, we arrive with no such 'informational content'. Which is it? Psychology offers no answer relating to Pentecostalism, psychology not being in the domain of the Spirit. Where then might we look? Norton brings attention to the philosophical speculation of 'a *sensus divinatus*, a felt

How might all this apply to prophetic function? For Yong and some other Pentecostals, 'the gift of the Spirit' is 'a baptism of love'.[240] Yong describes the charismata as 'specific expressions of the most fundamental gift of love' and manifestations of the Spirit of God 'who is love'.[241] Within the context of the baptism as empowerment for witness missiologically, the foundational motivation of love of God and love of neighbor is primary and essential for prophetic legitimacy. Yong asserts a possible 'positive correlation between congregational renewal or revitalization, religious/mystical experience, and social benevolence'.[242] If this correlation is accurate, then renewal, mystical experience, and intentional acts of love in the parish community and beyond are integral to the testimony of Jesus (Rev. 19.10), reflective of it, and able to yield fruit in keeping with it. If the intuitive, 'even mystical' sense of the divine is present in Pentecostal prophetism,[243] how these intuitions present themselves to the subjective psyche needs to be discerned and acted upon.

Yong views these intuitions as 'experiences of divine love, that are related to divine presence, prophecy, and healing'.[244] Embedded in a Pentecostal spirituality and theology, an apparent deep appreciation of the intuitive and revelatory domain of 'deeper, spiritual experiences' is made available through the Holy Spirit.[245] However, this does not dismiss the need to substantiate further how the intuitive is approached. Considering the problems enumerated in this work, the intuitive domain needs to be addressed, and scrutiny is always required. The discernment of spirits is an essential part of charismatic

---

sense of God's presence'. For Norton, this can apply to intuitive experience. How then is the felt sense of God's presence supported from an epistemological framework? Norton notes that Augustine, Calvin, and contemporary philosopher Alvin Plantinga 'regard intuition as basic in epistemology' (ch. 2). If it is one of the ways in which we know what we know, it is arguably as important as rational processes of knowing. Norton affirms Plantinga's belief, 'we can attach meaning to the sense of yearning we all feel for that which we can but dimly perceive'. This is congruent with 'we know only in part, and we prophesy only in part'. 1 Cor. 13.9. Also, this sense of yearning directs the heart and mind to the transcendent, and to the love of God (ch. 2).

[240] Yong, *Spirit of Love*, p. 115.
[241] Yong, *Spirit of Love*, p. 116.
[242] Yong, *Spirit of Love*, p. 50. According to Paul (1 Corinthians 13), the charismata are to be exercised in and through the Spirit of love.
[243] Yong, *Spirit of Love*, p. 50.
[244] Yong, *Spirit of Love*, p. 50.
[245] Vondey, *Pentecostalism*, p. 136.

community life and can provide and maintain prophetic legitimacy (1 Corinthians 12.10).

As the functions of intuition appear distinct from the operations of discernment, what is the relationship between abiding as discernment and the immediacy of intuition (specifically, spiritual intuition)? Are spiritual discernment and spiritual intuition related? If so, how does that relationship function relative to *prophetica conscientia* and prophetic perception? Functionally, spiritual discernment is at least somewhat different from the 'immediate insight or perception' of intuition.[246] Like discernment, which is used in spiritual and material matters, spiritual and material intuitions are presented through 'complicated interaction between the unconscious and conscious mind'.[247] The immediacy of intuition seems to present itself phenomenologically with a sense of significance and at times urgency. From a prophetic perspective, it can be seen in what could be called a 'dis-confirmation' – something withheld by the Spirit from the prophetic agent.

In Chapter 2 and in this chapter, I pointed to Elisha's perception and intuition as he and Elijah approached the moment of their separation. Elijah told his successor to 'see' what was about to happen, and Elisha *saw*. Consider a different kind of situation: the narrative of the Shunamite's son being raised from the dead (2 Kgs 4.18-37). When the distressed Shunamite reports the child's death to Elisha, Gehazi attempts pushing her away from the prophet, who prevents him, saying, 'The Lord has hidden [her son's death] from me and has not told me' (2 Kgs 4.27). Elisha intuits not his seeing (or knowing) but his lack of knowing the Shunamite's need. This dis-confirmation operates as 'the Lord has *hidden* it from me' (emphasis added). The interior intuition and discernment come as an interplay between immediacy and distinguishing – the overlapping of spiritual intuition and spiritual discernment. In this instance, Elisha has discerned that the Lord has intentionally hidden something.

Regarding this interplay, I would briefly argue that within the prophetic agent's interiority, where genuine intuition is followed by discernment, the intuitive awareness bears a sense of immediacy that appears to defy the mediation inherent in functions of intuition and

---

[246] 'Intuition', *APA Dictionary of Psychology*, https://dictionary.apa.org/intuition.
[247] Iseman, *Understanding Intuition*, p. xv.

cognition. This defiance is largely attributable to the seeming (or actual) unconscious working of the mediation process. Not surprisingly, the process can be assumed not to exist, thereby limiting the intent or capacity of novice or undisciplined prophetic agents to distinguish their projections and subjectivity from what is, in fact, divinely inspired. Instead of discernment, therefore, a presumptive posture moves these agents toward expression without evaluation, acting *as if* the Spirit has spoken infallibly through them. Recognizing one's subjectivity and inherent mediation is therefore critical to discernment and the realization of prophetic legitimacy.

I would add that intuition doesn't directly involve emotion. However, intuition can operate in the realm of feeling.[248] Emotions are tied to 'bodily reactions … activated through neurotransmitters and hormones released by the brain'.[249] Feelings (which can be involved in the intuitive impulse) are 'the conscious experiences of emotional reactions'.[250] How can we understand these conscious emotional reactions in intuitive moments? Consider the Shunamite: her protracted experience of being denied a child and the associated suppression of that desire influenced her emotional distress. The pain from her son's death exists because her request for a child was granted (2 Kgs 4.16). Reconciling her conflicted emotions over this theodicy is difficult. However, something intuitively impels her to seek the prophet. She originally perceived his prophethood without his disclosing it (2 Kgs 4.9); that perception seems to have come with

---

[248] 'Intuition', *APA Dictionary of Psychology*, https://dictionary.apa.org/intuition.

[249] Bryn Farnsworth, 'How to Measure Emotions and Feelings (And the Difference Between Them)', *Imotions* (blog, April 14, 2020), https://imotions.com/blog/difference-feelings-emotions/.

[250] Farnsworth, 'Emotions and Feelings', https://imotions.com/blog/difference-feelings-emotions/. Intuition is not emotion-based yet can come as feeling. The terms *emotion* and *feeling* are not synonymous. Researchers at Wake Forest University contend, 'a fundamental difference between feelings and emotions is that feelings are experienced consciously, while emotions manifest either consciously or subconsciously', 'The Difference Between Feelings and Emotions', *Counseling Blog* (Wake Forest University), https://counseling.online.wfu.edu/blog/difference-feelings-emotions/. Emotions therefore can only be 'felt'. To be understood, the underlying unconscious content that drives feelings and emotions needs to be explored, namely the 'associated thoughts, beliefs, desires, actions' that lie below the surface of conscious awareness, however deeply embedded they might be. Feelings are more readily available to our awareness, as they are conscious. So, when Norton speaks of the felt sense of intuiting the divine, it approximates the psychological notion of the experience from an intuitive perspective.

a felt sense phenomenologically. This intuitive moment led to the Shunamite discerning the numinous in Elisha and choosing to lodge and care for him (2 Kgs 4.10). This led to her desire for a child being fulfilled. Now, however, it results in death and triggers the distresses she originally feared. Although unable to discern what has happened and to shake her emotional conflict and affliction, a felt sense causes her to say, 'It will be all right' (2 Kgs 4.23).[251] It is a moment of clarity anchored in her long-standing intuition about what Elisha carries. She equates it with a sense of the holy, which she had to have known intimately herself. This is an archetypal spiritual intuition of the numinous that leads to spiritual perception and spiritual discernment.

Despite her distress, the Shunamite managed considerable emotion-regulation and maintained a sense of equilibrium and resolve. The text reveals no cognitive distortion amid her afflictions. She remains able to discern what she holds to be true. Because of her son's death, many factors could have interfered with her intuition and discernment. Yet, they were overridden by a felt sense of the divine, an archetypal intuition of divine assurance. Funk contends that certain 'factors prevent us from having a direct experience with the Holy Spirit'.[252] Much personal and social conflict comes from our internal afflictions and dysfunctions. Discernment distinguishes and evaluates the sources from which such issues arise. Thus, our internal equilibrium can be restored and 'the whole of our life' can be 'toward God'.[253]

Pentecostals often rely on the Elijah-Elisha narratives to explain their leadings, as did Violet Kiteley.[254] The fallibility of prophetic agents cannot be precluded, but a praxis of abiding as discernment provides a plumb line for testing the spirits. In all its expressions, abiding is both the foundation and outcome of prophetic integrity, and its practice sustains prophetic legitimacy.

---

[251] The Shunamite is not impaired by her resolute assurance that 'it will be all right'. Because of her intuitive discernment, she moves with the intention and determination that 'it will be all right'. Psychology does not bridge the gap between intuition and discernment; however, the Spirit can and does.

[252] Funk, *Discernment Matters*, p. 1. These include the 'afflictions' that diminish our ability to 'abide in peace'. Paul speaks in Col. 3.16 of allowing the peace of Christ to play the umpire in our hearts. This involves our intersubjectivity and social awareness.

[253] Funk, *Discernment Matters*, p. 1.

[254] See Kiteley, 'Elijah and Elisha'; Kiteley, 'Elijah Birthing the Rain'. Kiteley's teachings, including course materials from Shiloh Bible College, reflect as much.

5.2.2 Conclusory Thoughts Regarding the Three Elements of Prophetic Legitimacy

The exploration of *prophetica discretio*, *prophetica conscientia*, and *prophetica praxis* closes with two brief conclusory topics followed by final remarks.

5.2.2.1 Prophetic Orthodoxy, Orthopraxy, and Orthopathy

Both *prophetica conscientia* and prophetic perception require a particular way of engaging with the Scriptures. The literary-critical method employed here has facilitated a viewing of the text from theological, psychological, and phenomenological vantage points, while the Pentecostal influence has impacted the methodology. This has permitted the building of a bridge to hidden meanings, not unlike the tradition of the Alexandrian school of thought. Vondey rightly asserts that when Pentecostals engage Scripture, there is a 'link between the authority of spirituality and the authority of doctrine'.[255] Therefore, this work is attentive to 'the human response to God'.[256] As such, there is a certain camaraderie with the more ancient consideration of the text's hidden meaning.[257] The Alexandrian approach sought to capture the 'spiritual sense',[258] not unlike the ways in which Pentecostals read the text today. The spiritual sense borrows from Greek philosophy's notion of *theoria*,[259] which Origen adopted in relation to '*contemplation (a key component in this argument) of a higher meaning*'.[260] The Cappadocian fathers did likewise and conjoined *theoria* to 'mystical vision and ascent'.[261] Contemplation, mystical vision, and ascent can be considered ways of knowing and seeing that provide a renewed

---

[255] Vondey, *Pentecostalism*, p. 72.

[256] Vondey, *Pentecostalism*, p. 72.

[257] There is a certain camaraderie with the more ancient consideration of the text's hidden meaning. Contemporary 'Western consciousness' tends to prefer rationalistic ways of thinking and materialistic ways of being. Sanford, *Mystical Christianity*, p. 2. Since the days of Tom Wolfe and the 'Me' decade and generation, the tendency is more highly individualized and self-centered. See Tom Wolfe, 'The "Me" Decade and the Third Great Awakening,' *New York* (April 8, 2008), https://nymag.com/news/features/45938/.

[258] Sanford, *Mystical Christianity*, p. 2.

[259] 'In the 4th c. b.c., philosophers, notably Plato and Aristotle, adopted and adapted this term in order to ground their discipline fully in the social, political, and religious aspects of Greek culture; thenceforward the philosopher is understood to be one who 'sees' the truth (ibid.)'. McVey, 'Theoria', p. 595.

[260] McVey, 'Theoria', p. 595.

[261] McVey, 'Theoria', p. 595.

understanding of *prophetica conscientia* and perception that influences *prophetica praxis*.

Therefore, if one's consciousness and perception are theologically based in orthodoxy (as in the Person, work, and teachings of Jesus) one's actions will be embodied in orthopraxy. It must be noted that prophetic orthodoxy is honored in faithful catechesis and mystagogy. Finally, with a basis in orthodoxy and orthopraxy, one's heart causes one to embody an orthopathy phenomenologically.

- Prophetic orthodoxy is rooted in the revelation of the triune God in Christ.
- Prophetic orthopraxy is rooted in the life of God as grounded in the charismatic Spirit.
- Prophetic orthopathy reveals, in its charismatic outworking, an embodied love of God and love of neighbor.

Figure 4 (below) illustrates the interworkings of *prophetica conscientia*, *prophetica praxis*, and *prophetica discretio* with prophetic orthodoxy, prophetic orthopraxy, and prophetic orthopathy. The root and animating source in all cases is the prophetic ethic that originates in Christ.

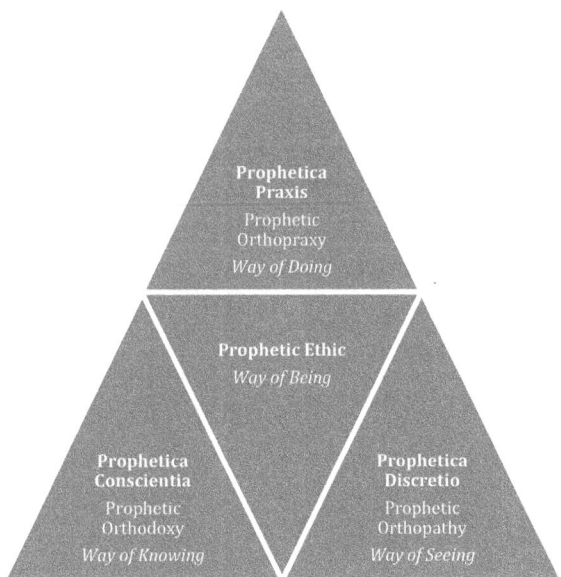

Figure 4: The Prophetic Ethic

5.2.2.2 Pentecostal Holism: Internal Integrity and External Integration

In 1985, Rev. Charles Simpson spoke from a largely philosophical perspective about the 'internal integrity and external integration of structures'.[262] The principle has innumerable applications, here serving the understanding of Pentecostal holism. Abiding as praxis, which is the origin, condition, and evidence of life in the Spirit, reveals a Pentecostal holism by which Pentecostals live out a 'holistic spirituality'.[263] Such holism is grounded in an *internal charismatic integrity* that results in the *external charismatic integration* of prophetic enactment.[264] In other words, to actualize the integrity and legitimacy of prophetic function, a Pentecostal praxis of abiding needs to be habituated. This requires, by way of embodied prophetic expression (Rev. 19.10), an internal posture that bears external witness to the truth that is in Jesus. The entire praxis subsumes the dyads of *love of God and love of neighbor, truth and falsehood*, and *apprehension and acceptance*. This movement from orthodoxy to orthopathy with abiding as praxis spans the theological, psychological, and phenomenological gamut as contained in the dynamics referenced. Much work in Pentecostal theology needs to be done here. For this work, sufficient is the recognition of its place in the interiority of the prophetic agent. This internal charismatic movement assimilates perceived ancient doctrinal realities so they might be embodied, fruit-bearing actualities.[265]

---

[262] Charles Simpson, 'Internal Integrity and External Integration of Structures by Charles Simpson 1985' (PDF transcript of sermon presented in 1985), p. 1.

[263] Vondey, *Pentecostalism*, p. 34.

[264] Prophetic enactments speak to the specific needs they are intended to meet. Internal charismatic integrity embraces a praxis of abiding that lends itself to the wisdom of spiritual discernment that shapes consciousness, cognitive processes and functions, emotions, feelings, and moods, as well as the domains of intuition and insight – all relative to the revelatory energies and influences of the charismatic Spirit.

[265] Not all Pentecostals are creedal. Yet, there has been maintained as much as possible a unity of the Spirit in the bond of peace. However, given the nature of the spread of global Pentecostalism and the proliferation of prophetic ways that are problematic in terms of doctrine and practice, reform is essential. One aspect of reform that can help greatly is to reconsider the importance of creedal confessions in the primitive church. Since primitivism is at the core of the Pentecostal conviction, what is tied to the primitive church needs to be considered and not summarily dismissed. This work proposes that while doctrinal differences on the trinity abound in Pentecostalism, a Pentecostal theology of prophetic legitimacy

5.3 Summary Remarks

Given the nature of the problem addressed in Chapter 1 and throughout this study, and given the greater Tradition of the church overall, I have argued for a Pentecostal theology of prophetic legitimacy that celebrates the genuine prophetic expression evident within the Pentecostal and Latter Rain Pentecostal tradition. To honor, sustain, and maintain the larger Tradition, I propose that a genuine Pentecostal prophetic ethic is essential in grounding all that flows from the exercise of prophetic expression. Within that ethic, *prophetica discretio*, *conscientia*, and *praxis* jointly ensure the integrity from which legitimacy is embodied and enacted. This requires a cruciformity that is evident in how the prophetic agent allows the doors of his or her perception to be continually sensitized by the sanctifying work of the Spirit. It is the outworking of that to which right believing (orthodoxy) leads – namely, right practice (orthopraxy) that is overshadowed by (to borrow the term from Jeremiah) the 'burden of the Lord' (orthopathy). This orthopathy grounds the prophetic agent in the love of God that demands the love of neighbor in all that is said and done.

Finally, the canon reiterates, 'the testimony of Jesus is the spirit of prophecy' (Rev. 19.10). To claim the Spirit of Prophecy but have nothing to do with the cruciform testimony of Jesus indicates illegitimacy. The Spirit testifies of the Incarnate Son in his person and work. The Son embodies the Spirit through whom the Father accomplishes all things in relation to his eternal purpose in sonship (theosis).

Therefore, we see in the ongoing incarnation of the Body of Christ the Mission of the Son (the testimony of Jesus), and the Mission of the Spirit (the Spirit of Prophecy), as part of the overall *Missio Trinitas*. As the Spirit of Prophecy, the Holy Spirit makes Jesus present to us as the Existentiell Christ. That the Spirit of Prophecy can speak to the entire church yet offer an existentiell word to each of the seven churches, implies that the outworking of the testimony of Jesus in each local setting requires particularity in terms of hearing

---

will benefit from a revisiting and renewing of the creedal tradition, namely both the Apostle's and the Nicene-Constantinople Creeds. Although biblicists might hold to a somewhat different view, my entire argument is made from the conviction that the creedal confessions of the historic church are vital.

what the Spirit is saying to each. At the same time, in holding to orthodoxy, orthopraxy, and orthopathy, such existentiell words will never contradict or conflict with what is true of the *Missio Trinitas*, the testimony of Jesus, or the Spirit of Prophecy, because all are enmeshed as deeply as the three-ness and the oneness of the Triune God are enmeshed.

If such a theology of prophetic legitimacy is embraced within the Pentecostal community at large, I am persuaded that the promise of genuine reform and restoration becomes possible, and renewal becomes evident in relation to overall prophetic expression for the building up of the Body of Christ.

APPENDIX: CITED VIOLET KITELEY PAPERS

Included for the reader's reference are direct images of cited document pages from the Violet Kiteley Papers collection. Many of the cited pages contain a combination of typed and handwritten text. In these cases, the handwritten notes are Mrs. Kiteley's jottings, added over time to lecture notes, sermon notes, diagrams, and other writings. Her jottings include asides, sidebars, underlining, asterisks, boxes, and other emphasizing features Mrs. Kiteley used to clarify her intended meaning and/or capture her thoughts as they developed through the years.

Appendix images are arranged alphabetically by the original documents' full titles, as first cited. Shortened titles used in subsequent citations are also provided. Fixed page numbers appearing in the original documents are typically cited. For original documents containing no fixed page numbers, numbering has been assigned based on the pagination of the digitized documents. Where the original page numbering is mixed or otherwise irregular (as in documents that were compiled by/for Mrs. Kiteley for various ministry applications), cited page numbering has been decided on a case-by-case basis. Pages from the collection not cited are not represented in the Appendix.

DELIVERER PROMISED, IN *UNTITLED SERMONS NOTEBOOK*, PAGE 16

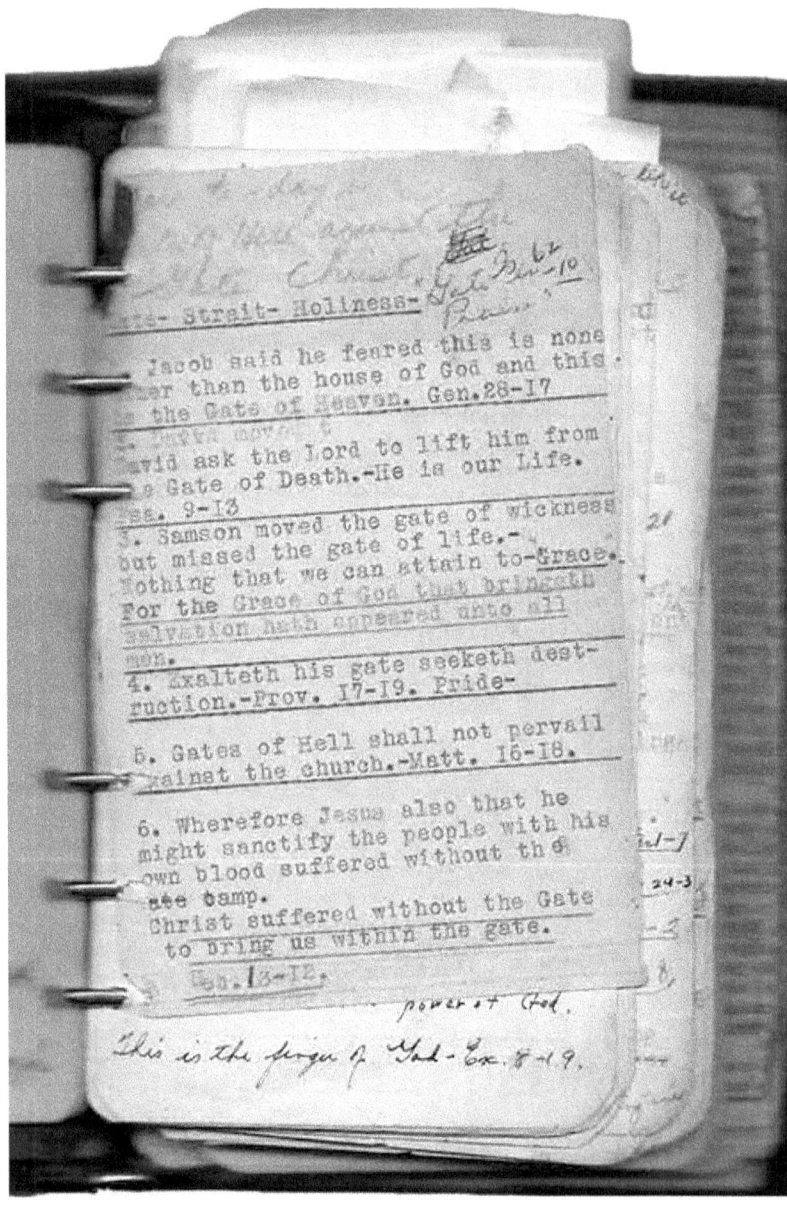

Elijah and Elisha: A Study of the Prophetic Ministry of Elijah and Elisha Taken from 1st and 2nd Kings

Shortened Title: Elijah and Elisha, Page 12

"REVIVAL IN THE CHURCH"

This is a very general statement which has many different meanings to different church groups.

WHAT DO WE AS NEW COVENANT CHURCHES MEAN BY "REVIVAL IN THE CHURCH"?

The word *revival* comes from the word *revive* which has to do with something that already existed and has died. Therefore, revival in God's church has to do with the restoration of truths that had been lost throughout the years (Joel 1).

RESTORATION OF TRUTH

1517	Martin Luther - *Justification by faith* (Romans 5:1)
1524	Anabaptists - *Water Baptism* (Matthew 3:15)
1700's	John and Charles Wesley - *Holiness* (Ephesians 4:24) Benefits: Created in Righteousness and Holiness
1800's	Missionary Alliance - *Divine Healing in the Atonement* (Isaiah 53:5) Benefits: Psalms 68:19, 103:52
1906	Los Angeles and other places - *Baptism of the Holy Spirit*
1948	North Battleford, Sask. - *Laying on of Hands to find placement in the Body of Christ* (1 Tim. 4-14) Benefits: Faith, Worship, Prayer • Coming together of the Body of Christ • Taking the world in One Generation • Praise, Worship, Joy, Gifts of the Spirit in operation

Revival New Covenant Churches - point of reference is the 1948 outpouring of the Spirit, as well as all of the above (Mat. 13:52, Lev. 26:10), "...*Bring forth old because of the new*."

Elijah Birthing the Rain, Page 1

> 1. ELIJAH – BIRTHING the RAIN
> WHAT HAS TAKEN PLACE IS BUT A
> FORETASTE OF WHAT IS TO COME.
>
> THE KINGDOM OF GOD IS ON THE
> THRESHOLD OF THE GREATEST
> REVIVAL IN HISTORY – IN 90'S
> (BECAUSE) WERE
> AS THE DAYS OF NOAH – THE GATES
> OF HELL MOVING UPON THE HUMAN
> FAMILY – TO DESTROY THEIR SOULS
> (REPEATED)
>
> WE ARE GOING TO EXPERIENCE
> THE RESTORATION OF AUTHENTIC
> NEW TEST. CHRISTIANITY – all over the world
>
> WHICH WILL GO AGAINST
> THE GATES HELL –
> AND OVERCOME THEM

Ezekiel, Chapter 20

Shortened Title: Ezekiel, Page 59

Page 59
Ezekiel
Shiloh Bible College

Chapter 37 - Ezekiel III (Cont'd)

Vs. 7
Noise

Shaking

Bones came together. Ps. 133, John 17

Bone to Bone 1 Corth. 12:18

Vs. 8 Though there was body formation, and it was in proper order yet there was no breath or Life in the body. Israel in the natural could be meet by God by having her land returned, a "formation" yet no spiritual breath or life in her. God is doing a life - giving work for the Body of Christ, putting his breath or life in them, not only a formation but it will be able to fully function in God's purposes.

Vs. 9 1 st PROPHESY WAS TO THE BONES
        2 nd PROPHESY WAS TO THE WIND
One to within the structure, "the bones", the other without "the Wind" "BREATHE UPON THE SLAIN." This is the purpose of the Holy Spirit now is to receive thy work (the wind of the Holy Spirit) in the midst of the years.

Vs. 10 The creative word of the Lord in prophesy produced breath or life to come into the structure of the body. As a result it stood up upon their feet (the last day company) an exceeding great army - like the floor being full of wheat. Joel 2:24.

Vs. 11 Explain who verse 1 and 2 really relate to.
"Whole house of Israel" - naturally and spiritually.
Their confession --
a. Our bones are dried

b. Our hope is lost

c. We are cut off from our parts

FIVE SPIRITUAL SENSES, PAGE 1

The 5 Spiritual Senses

1. Divine Nature — Human Nature

[Triangle diagram: Faith-Source / Holy Spirit-Substance / Son-Outflow]

[Triangle diagram: Nature/Spirit — Spiritual life contact God; Personality/Soul — Psychological life contact self; Person/Body — Physical life contact World]

Gen 1-26, 27.

Summary of the 5 spiritual Senses:

Office	Sense	Action	Result
Apostle	Ears	Hearing	Developed by obedience / Born by the love of God / of fellowman
Prophet	Eyes	Seeing	Sanctification, Spirit unto God
Evangelist	Tongues	Tasting	Sacrifice, cross, pure
Teacher	Fingers	Smelling	
Pastor	Nose	Smelling	Discernment of good & evil.

1. Hearing — Old Test to hear is to obey — also a thought in the new — John 10-27

2. Tasting — Matt 5-6 — be filled or satisfied
   1 Peter 2-2, 3. Ps. 119-103 John 13-17
   Eph 3-16, Ps 34-8
   Luke 11-9, 10 — Prayer develops our taste
   John 7-37 — if any man thirst — drink — filled with living waters.

3. Sight — Eph 1- 15-18; Prov 1-7, Prov 3-6-8
   Matt 5-8, Rev 4-23, John 8-12, 1 John 1-7
   1 John 3-2,3. John 3-3

THE GREAT RESTORATION: THE DISPENSATION OF THE HOLY SPIRIT

SHORTENED TITLE: GREAT RESTORATION, PAGE 2

1948 WAS AN IMPORTANT YEAR IN THREE MAJOR WAYS

STAR SEED
GEN. 22:17
Feb. 14, 1948 – God visited His church (the grace of God) with revival. Restored a truth – Laying On of Hands Gal. 6:16.

SAND SEED
GEN 22:17
May 14, 1948 – Natural Israel was a restored nation under her own rule, calling herself ISRAEL for the first time in history. Ps. 83:4-5. A sign.

" A sign always points to the product "   Rom. 9:4,6,7.

DUST SEED
GEN. 13:16
IS. 40:15
Sept. 1948 – ' United Nations ' & " World Council of Churches " formed.

We are living in the generation that God has chosen to make them whole (perfect). I Thess. 5:23. ". . . That which is in part shall be done away " I Cor. 13:10.

NOTES:

Healing and Latter Rain Movements 1947–48: An Eyewitness Account; Interview with Dr. Violet Kiteley

Shortened Title: Healing and Latter Rain, Page 3

These were the fundamentals of what happened. It was just a sovereign act of God. It was just like a manger experience where Jesus was born, in that every time God cradles something, it seems to be so uninviting in the natural. So the Spirit of God just moved; and every time I talk about it--anywhere, to any dimension at all--I say it was completely sovereign. It wasn't because of anybody . . . it wasn't that these men were so superspiritual, even though they did start waiting on God. And they did wait on God--not because they were pressured by anybody; in fact, the pressure was the opposite. They were greatly persecuted for fasting and praying.

So then did the Healing Movement go right into the Latter Rain Movement?

The healing ministry was already moving--for example, Sister McPherson was ministering through the teen's, into the 20's, into the 30's. Then God raised up Smith Wigglesworth--basically, he was at our house in 1926 when he went to Australia and New Zealand. In Australia and New Zealand, he introduced the message of the Baptism of the Holy Spirit. The brethren were concerned and interested and became very serious about it because God was working, especially in their spirits, that something was going to come out of the Branham ministry that was going to be very shortlived. Then God sovereignly, I believe, raised up Oral Roberts; he had tuberculosis when he was a child, and he was healed. He has Indian blood in him--he's part Native American, off the Indian reservation.

The Indians' religion, Shakers, is a cult. In 1953 I had a church in Bellingham, Washington; and I went and talked to Oral Roberts then. I asked him if he understood the Shakers, but he didn't know about it. I had studied it; I got onto the reservation by going through a hole in the fence. I got to talk to these Native Americans, and I was having classes and Bible studies with some of them in their homes. The healing was the thing that enticed them, so that was the reason they were coming to Oral Roberts' meetings. That was still 1953, and Oral Roberts had recently started having his tent ministry; he's in his late 80's now.

Although the movements are actually two separate things, the movement in North Battleford--to most people, even to this day--was small, insignificant; and it soon blew over. Of course, God allowed it to happen that way. It went all over the world, kind of under the blanket, as it were; but the healing was predominant and accepted greatly. Oral Roberts and T. L. Osborn were Pentecostal Church of God. These people were accepted because healing was accepted. Healing is a big thing. People will go to a healing meeting when they won't go to a prayer meeting. They want healing throughout the physical body, and that's understandable.

There is an absolute difference, in the sense that the North Battleford Movement was sovereignly ministering the fact that God was returning the gifts of the Spirit to the laity. It was a laity movement. People are talking now as if they've got some new truth. No--finding your place within the Body of Christ came with the North Battleford Movement. And it was not just for people who were ordained ministers--it was for every member of the Body of Christ that wanted it, that was hungry enough to pay the price to get it. God said He was going to raise up ministries. He was also going to have more of the Moses ministry, but that was not where His main mind was. He was going to have a Joshua ministry: Moses first and then Joshua--the priest carrying the ark of God through the waters. So that's the difference there.

Healing and Latter Rain Movements 1947–48: An Eyewitness Account; Interview with Dr. Violet Kiteley

Shortened Title: Healing and Latter Rain, Page 5

was going to eventually be saved) in his mind and his heart from his past. So he kind of muddied the waters later, but that's another story.

It was interesting too that around that very same time, God started to move in Belfast, Ireland and in Johannesburg, South Africa. The Holy Spirit spoke that God was going to bring a move into Canada in North Battleford. At the same time, down in the valley of Lafayette--in the next province, outside of Edmonton, Alberta which is principally comprised of black people--this visitation of God fell there.

Around February or March, the PAOC heard what was going on. They didn't agree with the revival; in fact, they didn't accept it at all--so they denounced it right away. Based on that, it went out from coast to coast that something foreign to God, foreign to the Holy Spirit, had come among these people. It was a warning not to have anything to do with it--don't touch it.

> Note: When I use names, I'm not trying to drop names. I do know these people, and my reason for knowing them is because of the position I was in. There were so few that stayed with the revival; and when things did go partially wrong, because of a very few people, everybody got tagged with that. I was young, but my life moved so quickly. I started ministering when I was 14, I pastored a church when I was 17, I was married when I was 19, my husband was killed just before my first wedding anniversary, and I was expecting my child. So by this time I'm just over 20 years of age, I'm a widow, I've got a child, and I've already pastored a church. So my life went fast; in wartime, your life goes fast. They conscripted my husband at 19 years of age, and all these things happened. It made life awfully different than it is right now. I was ministering all over, at 22 years of age, and I'd already had this much life.

There were two separate movements, that was the thing. The Healing Revival started but God also raised up Evangelists in a new way. In 1948, He raised up Billy Graham and restored the healing ministry in such men as Oral Roberts, T. L. Osborn, and many others.

I met William Branham because of Ernie Baxter, his campaign manager, who was a personal friend of the Hawtin's and of mine. Ernie had a church in Vancouver, British Columbia, called Evangelistic Tabernacle. My husband, Raymond Kiteley, was a soloist and a worship leader at Rev. Ern Baxter's church in Vancouver. Rev. Baxter was considered the "Spurgeon" of Canada. He was a tremendous orator--basically, in teaching. So of course people looked up to him; and if he said something, then it had to be true.

Richard Riss stated that in the 1948 Revival, Ernie Baxter was one of the men who was a historian and knew all about it; but Ern Baxter denounced the revival. He came to Shiloh before he died last year, and he told my son that he did denounce the revival. It wasn't until later, after William Branham fell off the wagon and got into error, that Ern Baxter started to find out what the revival was all about. He was so enamored with Branham, with the Healing Revival, he even went to India and saw 13 blind-from-birth people receive their sight--and that would enamor anybody.

Healing and Latter Rain Movements 1947–48: An Eyewitness Account; Interview with Dr. Violet Kiteley

Shortened Title: Healing and Latter Rain, Page 6

How long had the 1947-1948 Awakening been going on when you first became aware of it? What are the circumstances that brought it to your attention and how did you become involved with it?

I was aware of it in the fall of 1947, maybe October, because of the position I was in. The PAOC would send me from place to place to minister because of my testimony of healing. On October 13, 1945, just three days after my son's birth, I became a cripple. For thirteen months I didn't get any medical help; and that's why poison went through my system, and I became paralyzed. It was a lack of proper care that caused my health problem.

Then, in November 1946, the voice of the Lord spoke into my spirit and told me that God was going to raise me up. A minister was going to come at 3 p.m. the next day, and I was going to walk. The word that I got was that I was going to preach a new message. Brother Smith, the missionary from Trans-Jordan, was brought by Pastor Walter McAlister to pray for me. Brother Smith told Pastor McAlister that God had spoken to him, while coming over on the plane from Trans-Jordan, that a young lady was to be healed and raised up to preach a new message. Pastor McAlister was really touched by the fact that he saw me come out of the bed walking that day.

I came to Prince Albert, Saskatchewan (sixty miles northeast of North Battleford). I was ministering there for Rev. Jack McAlister whose father became the Assemblies of God superintendent from Canada in late 1948/early 1949; but Jack was already geared to be against the present revival. I had known about the move and was warned not to have anything to do with it. But I was stirred all the time when I heard they were against this; and I thought, "Well, this could be that word God had spoken into my spirit in November of 1946." And I had such a warning from the Lord not to question what God was doing, just as I had a warning when He took my husband. Many people were questioning why God allowed my husband to be killed and me to be ill for as long as I was.

Even though I had heard that the revival was not right, I was going to go there right away (in February); but then, of course, I was traveling. However, I was keeping very close contact with Milford Kirkpatrick who was in North Battleford because he was a personal friend of our family. His sister was in the Assemblies of God, PAOC, in Vancouver, B.C., where I was; so I had a good opportunity to know how God was moving progressively in their midst.

I was ministering in different places, and my testimony was a phenomenal thing which gave me many opportunities in various churches. Canada was devastated so badly because of the Second World War; it was as if there was a deep depression of people's spirit. Canada was really torn up financially. Manpower was greatly depleted in Nanimo, B.C.; not one man returned from the war.

When I was in Prince Albert, I told Pastor Jack that I was going to the revival to see it for myself. I had my son with me, and he was 2 1/2 years old. That was in the heart of winter, and it was cold--around 40 degrees below zero. Pastor Jack tried to talk me out of it; but I said, "No, I'm going to go and see; I need to see for myself." I knew a lot more than I was telling him, but I wasn't going to convey it to him. It was a very secret thing because of the pressure against it, and you were fearful of who you spoke to and what you might relate; you didn't want anyone to be hurt. The United States Assembly of God had a magazine called *The Evangel* which had articles against the revival, warning about the message that was being promulgated.

HEALING AND LATTER RAIN MOVEMENTS 1947–48: AN EYEWITNESS ACCOUNT; INTERVIEW WITH DR. VIOLET KITELEY

SHORTENED TITLE: HEALING AND LATTER RAIN, PAGE 7

The PAOC's indictment against the movement was that the people were fasting and praying for long periods of time. I told anyone I was talking to, especially Pastor Jack, "You've got to get something better than that to reject the message." And they said, "You're too young to understand." I said, "I've had a lot of life, and I've seen a lot; and I'm going to go there and see this for myself."

I remember what had been said over a period of many years. For example, when I was a child, Smith Wigglesworth was in our family home; and also, Dr. Charles Price was a close friend. So I knew they had said that God was going to move again and they were not going to be alive to see it; that was true of Sister McPherson, too.

What were your first impressions of the awakening?

My first impression was, "There can't be much wrong with extensive fasting and praying. I said that to all the critics who were approaching me. They were really afraid of my getting involved in it because they thought they were going to lose a good testimony.

My husband, Raymond, was fairly well known in the PAOC. He was an ordained minister and had attended a PAOC Bible college. But as the war became more severe, they started conscripting men from all walks of life. He was in the medical division of the Royal Canadian Air Force and was in an airplane that was shot down.

My mother was really a praying person. My dad was, also—but my mother had known the Lord much longer, since 1906 in Belfast, Ireland. She had to stand alone in her family. She was a tiny woman, 4 feet 10 inches. She was with the Holiness Movement; and she often had a word of knowledge in prayer that was proven on many occasions.

How long were you involved with the awakening? What are some of the experiences that left an indelible impression upon you?

I was there shortly after the revival started, and I remained there five months continually—every day, every hour. They prophesied over me three weeks after I got there. I had never seen anybody prophesied over—I was waiting to see it happen; but people were just starting to visit the meetings and learn to wait on the Lord. They were not really prepared for personal ministry.

When they prophesied over me, that was a phenomenal thing. It took several hours, I was told. I was really lost in the Presence of the Lord. They brought me forward on the cement floor, and the first thing was that George Hawtin started to pray prophetically. He told me that I had lost my husband, and they never knew anything about me because I stayed in the background. I didn't talk to anyone about my life personally. I was seriously waiting on the Lord because I wanted to see what God was going to do. My greatest impression was the Song of the Lord which started around 5 a.m. in the morning. They were singing unto God so sovereignly—singing whole passages of Scriptures.

The Hawtin brethren quoted I Timothy 4:14, "Neglect not the gift that is in thee, which was given thee by prophecy *[which is the word of knowledge in a*

Healing and Latter Rain Movements 1947–48: An Eyewitness Account; Interview with Dr. Violet Kiteley

Shortened Title: Healing and Latter Rain, Page 10

Colossians 3:16 and Ephesians 5:18 became alive when it says sing unto yourselves in psalms (*that was the Word, we were doing that*); hymns (*we already had them*); and then spiritual songs. We realized spiritual songs were prophetic songs--and that was the Song of the Lord. That was very predominant.

Azusa Street's message was strong on the coming together of the Body of Christ. It carried a lot of pressure because segregation was so bad. Brother Seymour, when he was in Kansas at a Bible college, wasn't allowed to sit inside the class because he was black. Later, Brother Seymour went to Los Angeles and started a church in a house on North Bonnie Brae Avenue. That was a marvelous thing because it was an interracial group of people. God was moving, and the fire of the Holy Spirit was upon the place continually. This was repeated--and more--at North Battleford in 1948. Like the Azusa Street Revival, the North Battleford Movement went worldwide without any advertisement or publicity except for a very meager paper put together called *Sharon Star*.

Pastor David was born in October 1945. Even to this day, when he goes some places to minister, some say negative statements against the 1948 Revival. It was wonderful that David was there because even though he was just a little child, he sovereignly received such an impression of what was going on, which is still a vital part of him. He picked up a tremendous amount. When I told him--at 2 1/2, 3 years of age--that when these people closed their eyes and spoke, that Jesus was speaking, he caught that because of God's grace. When he was 8 or 9 years of age, he could tell you the story of what God did because I told him. I repeated it many times. I explained it to him, and he could tell you when prophecy was operating. He knew when they were on target.

The previous movement of Azusa Street did influence the 1948 Revival; there was much correlation.

Subsequently, how did the 1947-1948 Awakening influence the Charismatic Movement of the late 1960's and early 1970's?

The Charismatic Movement was from 1967 into the early '70s. It was prophesied at North Battleford in 1948. God said He was going to send revival to the Catholic denomination, bringing salvation and correcting mistakes in their doctrine. The Charismatic Movement at first basically touched the Roman Catholics and later the Lutherans and the Episcopals. Pentecost is an experience, not a denomination.

The Charismatic Movement was prophesied, that God would take them out of these above denominations; and that's exactly what happened. This was a new thing altogether. It was not the old-line Pentecost because, again, they rejected that move, too. They had been taught that there was no hope for the Catholic church, that it was "Babylon." Of course, there is some Babylon in their teachings. God moved in sovereignly upon many and gave them a born-again experience and the Baptism of the Holy Spirit. In 1967 God poured out at Notre Dame (a Roman Catholic university) that was fulfillment of the 1948 prophecy.

The Charismatic Movement and the Jesus Movement came around the same time (late '60s into the early 70's). The Jesus Movement was separate, totally non-church people; and this was also prophesied in the 1948 Revival.

LAYING ON OF HANDS – 1948 – NORTHERN CANADA

SHORTENED TITLE: 1948 – NORTHERN CANADA, PAGE 1

10am 20 men

3rd Quarter
Lesson Two
Revival Doctrine

LAYING ON OF HANDS – 1948 – Northern Canada

A. History – a group of Christians in Northern Canada were fasting, waiting upon God. They too were wearied of the deadness of the ~~Pentecostal~~ Church, and earnestly desired God in their midst in an even more living way; literally to see the GLORY OF GOD revealed in their midst.
  - God began to deal with them about the ONENESS OF THE BODY.
  - God renewed to them a deep reverence for God, salvation, water baptism, refreshed them in healing, holiness and gave a fresh appreciation for the Baptism of the Holy Spirit.
  - He restored the IMPARTATION OF GIFTS to the Church by the LAYING ON OF HANDS.
  - Each year JOY has been increasing, evangelism, holiness and the expectation of the Return of Jesus.

B. Uniqueness –
  - All former revivals dealt chiefly with the relation of the individual to God, such as being saved, baptized, living a holy life, healed and being filled with the Holy Spirit.
  - The Laying on of Hands Revival was different, in that the main points or highlights of the revival leaned towards the unifying of the many members, making in Christ ONE BODY, which together will do exploits and overcome the last enemy which is death.
  - All former revivals were preparing the members to receive LAYING ON OF HANDS which brought them together....Ezek. 37:7 (Prophesy caused the bones to come together.)

DOCTRINES ACCOMPANYING THIS REVIVAL

A. Oneness of the Body of Christ–

  - A divided body cannot work properly. God's purpose is to bring together this body by the LAYING ON OF HANDS and prophecy.

  - By the LAYING ON OF HANDS each member is given a gift of the Spirit or a spiritual ministry (1 Cor. 12:7) and thereby placed in his or her proper place in the Body of Christ. All the gifts in operation will work effectively to bring the body together.
  - Neh. 4:15 and 19 related how each was in his own place doing his own work, thus getting the whole job done; not each trying to do the other's job, leaving his own position desolate and crowding the other's position. Is. 65:8 The NEW WINE is found in the cluster. There is a need for the whole body.

  - God has emphasized the gift of prophecy in this revial. All through scripture we find the "Blowing of Trumpets" is a type of prophesy. This was to call the people together.
    A. they blew the ram's horn – speaks of living word.
    B. 1 Cor. 14:8 – Trumpet shouldn't give uncertain sound.

LEADERS WHO NEED THE SPIRIT OF THE LAMB (LIKE JESUS)

SHORTENED TITLE: SPIRIT OF THE LAMB, PAGE 1

Rev. 5:6 – LEADERS – WHO NEED TO HAVE THE SPIRIT OF THE LAMB (LIKE JESUS) – Gentle, defendless

1. GOD KNEW THAT HE WAS GOING TO MAKE DAVID A KING – (LEADER)

SO DAVID IS PLACED AMONG THE SHEEP (LAMBS)

CARING FOR SHEEP IS KING'S SCHOOL

② DAVID LEARNED TO TALK TO SHEEP
* HE WAS, AMONG THE SHEEP

③ DAVID LEARNED TO BE ALONE WITH THE SHEEP – PRAYER
LEARNED TO TALK TO GOD HIS FATHER
LEARNED TO HEAR HIS VOICE
where the Sheep is, that is where the action is / KING'S School.

④ DAVID LEARNED RESPONSIBILTY AMONG THE SHEEP – ONLY CAN IMPART WHAT YOU HAVE LEARNED –

⑤ DAVID LEARNED WARFARE – IN WITH SPIRITUAL / PROTECTING THE SHEEP
ONCE CAME THE LION ANOTHER TIME THE BEAR –
LATER GOLAITH =

LESSON TWO: LAYING ON OF HANDS

SHORTENED TITLE: LAYING ON OF HANDS, PAGE 2

LESSON TWO

II. THE LAYING ON OF THE HANDS

Hebrews 6:2 - of the doctrine of baptisms, and OF LAYING ON OF HANDS, and of resurrection of the dead, and of eternal judgment.

The present visitation of God has made a present reality of the ancient truth of "The Laying on of the Hands of the Presbytery." With this restored truth, comes a greater unfolding of God and His purposes. This particular ministry is God's special provision to the last-day Church. By the laying on of the hands with prophetic utterance, each Christian can find his place in the great economy of God and the Body of Christ.

Before we explain this ministry in detail, we feel that it would be well to examine some general Bible references on the subject of "hands" - their significance and the important place they play in worship.

Typically speaking, hands speak of ministry. The HAND of the Church is the five ministries which are the gifts of Jesus on His Ascension -- ascension gifts of the Christ -- the nine gifts are the spiritual faculties of the Abiding Spirit which were given on the day of Pentecost and should be operative in the Spirit - controlled Church today. By the FRUIT, we FLOW, by the GIFTS we KNOW and by the MINISTRIES we ADMINISTRATE.

1. Here are some references on HANDS.

   II Kings 3:11 - Here is Elisha the son of Shaphat, which poured water on the HANDS of Elijah

   This was considered an action of servitude. This was an indication that here was a young man - a prophet in the making - who served the ministry - hands here typical of Elijah's ministry.

   Deuteronomy 21:6-7 - And all the elders of that city, that are next unto the slain man, shall WASH THEIR HANDS over the heifer that is beheaded in the valley; and they shall answer and say, Our hands have not shed this blood, neither have our eyes seen it.

   Here, we see the washing of hands to prove innocence. By washing hands, there was an open declaration of innocence of any involvement in whatever had transpired.

   Matthew 27:24 - When Pilate saw that he could prevail nothing, but that rather a tumult was made, he took water, and WASHED HIS HANDS BEFORE THE MULTITUDE, saying, I am innocent of the blood of this just person, see ye to it.

   This Scripture shows that Pilate had a knowledge of this custom, and by taking water and washing his hands he thought he could publicly declare himself innocent of the blood of the Son of God. From this custom comes the phrase which is used today: "I wash my hands of this or that matter."

   Genesis 14:22 - And Abram said to the King of Sodom, I have LIFT UP MINE HAND UNTO THE LORD, THE MOST HIGH GOD, the possessor of heaven and earth.

LEVELS OF PRAYER IN JESUS' LIFE

SHORTENED TITLE: LEVELS OF PRAYER, PAGE 1

Levels of Prayer in Jesus life:
1. Prayer as a planned or set time
   Matt. 14:22-23   Mark 6:46-48 — at temple gate
   Example in Peter & John's life   Acts 3

2. Prayer as a sacrificial choice — (Garden Principle)
   Mark 1:35 — Example Hannah's Prayer — 1 Samuel 1st chapter.

Prayer as an established personal habit
   Luke 3:21

Prayer in & during success — (This is the time of the greatest test.)
   Luke 5:15, 16

Prayer when making major decisions
   Luke 6:12, 13 Jesus prayed when He was choosing His 12 disciples

Prayer alone for renewal
   Luke 9:18

Corporate prayer partners (prayer of agreement)
   Luke 9:28, 29   (What Jesus was asking for in the garden of Geth.)

Prayer is contagious —
   Luke 11:1

Prayer for failing brothers { Luke 15 — Lost Sheep / Gal 6:1)
   Luke 22:31, 32 —   Heb 4:2 — Burnt Stones

Prayer of personal assurance — (guidance)
   John 11:41, #42 Jesus already knew what Father wanted to accomplish.

a. His approach was to Father — You have a Father - son relationship

1) "I thank thee" we are an unthankful people many times. The great prayers in the Bible do not say "Give me." They spent time exalting the omnipotent God.   Romans 1:19 to 21

LIFE OF CHRIST, PAGE 32

Life of Christ
Second Semester — 2011

Lecture Notes

Savior – Perhaps this is the title that best sums up the theme of Jesus' humanity and compassion. The word Savior occurs eight times in Luke, nine times in Acts, and nowhere else in the synoptic Gospels. A one verse summary of the entire Gospel is called a "*Kerygma*". Luke 19:10 is just such a verse. "For the son of man came to seek and to save that which was lost."

Prophet – Unique to Luke is his treatment of Christ as a prophet. He restores life to the widow of Nain's son as Elisha the prophet did to the Shunamite woman's son in 2 Kings 4:8-37. He recalls the crowd proclaiming Jesus a great prophet in Luke 7:16. Jesus refers to himself as a prophet in Luke 13:33. Luke's use of Old Testament scripture is used prophetically. All point to Jesus and must be fulfilled by him. In Luke 9:51-18:34 there are several parallels drawn between the role of a Prophet and Christ's role.

- Jesus is sent as God's messenger
- Jesus is sent to warn a stiff-necked generation
- Jesus is sent to warn of the coming destruction
- Jesus is rejected

Teacher of Parables – Twenty-eight of the forty passages most commonly classified as parables appear in Luke, fifteen of these are found only in Luke's gospel. Luke's parables seem to have a less symbolic and immediately apparent and practical meaning e.g. the good Samaritan (10:25-37), the rich fool (12:13-21), the Rich Man and Lazarus (16:19-31), and the Pharisee and the Publican (18:9-14).

The Resurrected and Exalted One, Benefactor – Luke focuses exclusively of the need for Christ's followers to imitate their master's servanthood. Christ's followers must not expect good in return for good (Luke 22:24-30). Christ's followers must trust in Jesus as their ultimate benefactor who will pay them back in the ways the people they help cannot.

MALACHI 3: GOD IS CALLING FOR REFORMATION

SHORTENED TITLE: CALLING FOR REFORMATION, PAGE 1

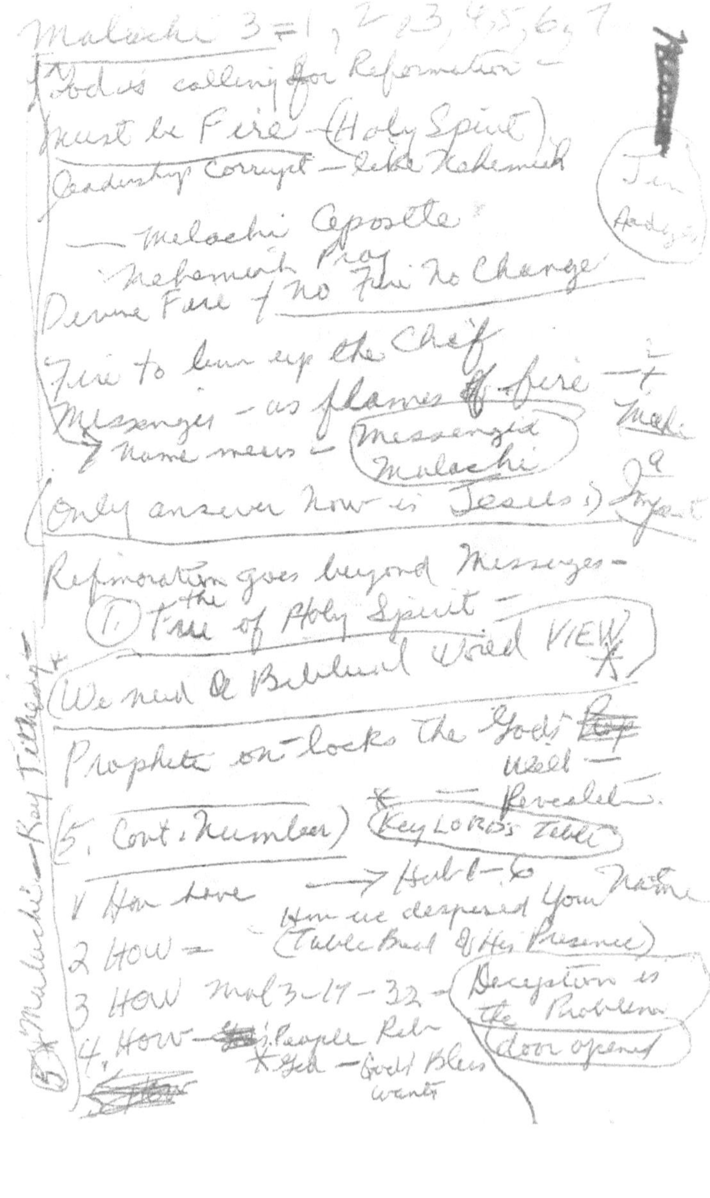

[Handwritten notes, partially legible:]

Malachi 3=1, 2, 3, 4, 5, 6, 7
God is calling for Reformation —
Must be Fire — (Holy Spirit)
Leadership Corrupt — like Nehemiah
— Malachi Apostle
Nehemiah Pray
Divine Fire / No Fire No Change
Fire to burn up the Chaff
Messenger — as flames of fire
Name means — Messenger
Malachi
(Only answer now is Jesus)
Reformation goes beyond Messages —
① Fire of Holy Spirit —
We need a Biblical World VIEW
Prophets un-locks the God's Will —
Revealed.
(5. Cont. Number) Key LORD's Table
1 How Love → Hurl — to You Name
How we despised You
2 HOW — (Table Bread & His Presence)
3 HOW Mal 3-17-32 — Deception is the Problem
4 HOW — People Rob door opened
God — God Bless
wants

[Margin: By Malachi — Roy Tilling???]

Ministry of the Presbytery Seminar

Shortened Title: Ministry of the Presbytery, Page 1

THE MINISTRY OF THE PRESBYTERY SEMINAR

What is a Presbytery?

A Presbytery is a group of two or more Presbyters (literally elders, or "aged" men of the church, characterized by the maturity of their ministry), who are anointed of God with prophetic power to confirm and impart God's mind to the Body of Christ through the Laying on of Hands.

What is the Purpose of the Presbytery Meeting?

The Ministry of the Presbytery is for the strengthening and equipping of the individual, sealing (in the presence of the pastor and congregation) the person to his or her ministry or placement in the Body, thus building up the Body of Christ and making us more fit for our ministry unto the world.

Ephesians 4:11 states that as Christ ascended, He "gave some to be apostles; some to be prophets; some to be evangelists; and some to be pastors and teachers...". Verses 12 and 13 give us the purpose of these ministries, which is "to prepare God's people for works of service, so that the body of Christ may be built up until we all reach unity in the faith and in the knowledge of the Son of God and become mature, attaining to the whole measure of the fullness of Christ." [NIV].

Through the Laying on of Hands, then, the Presbyters minister to individuals and couples. Through prophecy, visions, wisdom and other types of revelation, the Presbyters confirm God's will to each person, and also impart spiritual power for that person's ministry in the Body of Christ. The challenge and inspiration which is given to each person gives special significance to their place in the Church.

Ministry of the Presbytery Seminar

Shortened Title: Ministry of the Presbytery, Page 2

THE MINISTRY OF THE PRESBYTERY SEMINAR

When does a Presbytery meet?

When a need for prophetic guidance seems apparent, a Presbytery of suitable ministers should be summoned by the leadership of the local Church.

Acts 13:1-3 from the Amplified version says, "Now in the Church (assembly) at Antioch there were prophets - inspired of the will and purposes of God - and teachers, Barnabas, Simeon who was called Niger (black), Lucius of Cyrene, Manaen, member of the court of Herod the tetrarch, and Saul. While they were worshipping the Lord and fasting, the Holy Spirit said, Separate Me Barnabas and Saul for the work to which I have called them. Then after fasting and praying they put their hands on them and sent them away."

What are the Benefits of the Laying on of Hands and Prophecy by the Presbytery?

1. It helps establish the will of God for the individual by:

    Confirming the person's ministry in the Body of Christ
    —to the candidate
    —to the pastor
    —to the congregation

2. The individual is strengthened by the impartation of spiritual gifts and graces. [Regarding which, we have the responsibility to stir up the gifts which God is giving us!]

    In II Timothy 1:6 Paul says to Timothy, "Wherefore I put thee in remembrance that thou stir up the gift of God, which is in thee by the putting on of my hands."

    [That is why I would remind you to stir up - rekindle the embers, fan the flame and keep burning - the (gracious) gift of God, (the inner fire) that is in you by means of the laying on of my hands. - Amplified]

Ministry of the Presbytery Seminar

Shortened Title: Ministry of the Presbytery, Page 4

THE MINISTRY OF THE PRESBYTERY SEMINAR

<u>What are the Benefits of the Laying on of Hands and Prophecy by the Presbytery?</u>

9. It stimulates the whole church as they seek God through fasting and prayer (which brings dynamic results when done with the right motive).

10. It helps emphasize the various ministries and functions of the Body of Christ (no one member has it all!).

11. It helps develop the enthusiam of the whole church by their participating in the process of seeing individuals placed in their ministries in the local church. The entire Church thus becomes more effective in our ministry to God, to the Body and to the whole world.

<u>What is the Significance of Laying on of Hands?</u>

1. Scripture tells us that the Laying on of Hands is one of the doctrines of our faith.

   Hebrews 6:2 says to go on to maturity, and lists the foundations of our faith as being, "repentance from acts that lead to death, and of faith in God, instruction about baptisms, <u>the laying on of hands</u>, the resurrection of the dead, and eternal judgment." (NIV).

Ministry of the Presbytery Seminar

Shortened Title: Ministry of the Presbytery, Page 5

THE MINISTRY OF THE PRESBYTERY SEMINAR

2. The Laying on of Hands is a <u>method</u> of conferring divine blessings, or identification with by contact. Indeed, the very lifting up of the hands of the minister is used as a method of imparting divine blessing.

Leviticus 9:22 "Aaron lifted up his hands toward the people and blessed them..." There is a blessing in lifting up the hands of the ministry toward the people.

3. The Laying on of Hands is shown in scripture as a means of identification with, or setting apart of someone or something for a purpose (ie. for ministry, sacrifice, etc.), or for judgment.

Leviticus 8:14 "...and he brought for the sin offering; and Aaron and his sons laid their hands upon the head of the bullock for the sin offering." (Figuratively laying their sins, the sins of the people upon it, and setting it apart for the sacrifice.)

Leviticus 24:14 says to "bring forth him that hath cursed without the camp; and let all that heard him lay their hands upon his head, and let all the Congregation stone him.", and in Deuteronomy 17:7, "...the hands of the witnesses shall be first upon him to put him to death, and afterwards the hands of all the people. So thou shalt put the evil away from among you."

Numbers 8:10 tells Israel to "bring the Levites before the Lord, and the Israelites are to lay their hands on them."

Ministry of the Presbytery Seminar

Shortened Title: Ministry of the Presbytery, Page 6

THE MINISTRY OF THE PRESBYTERY SEMINAR

<u>How is the Laying on of Hands Used for Blessing and Prophetic Impartation?</u>

1. Many examples are given in Scripture of the Laying on of Hands being used for blessing, for ordination, and with prophetic impartation.

   In Genesis 48:14, when Israel (Jacob) was blessing his grandsons, we see a special significance given to the right hand, "...Israel stretched out his right hand and laid it upon Ephraim's head, who was the younger, and his left hand upon Manasseh's head, guiding his hand wittingly: for Manasseh was the firstborn."

   [...consciously directing his hands, although Manasseh was the first-born, according to the Berkeley Version.]

2. Jesus, Himself, used laying on of hands in the blessing of children.

   Matthew 19:13 "Then were brought unto Him little children, that He should put his hands on them and pray..."

   Mark 10:16 "And He took them up in His arms, put His hands upon them, and blessed them."

3. Laying on of Hands is shown in the Old Testament, for setting aside ministry, and imparting divine equipping for ministry. It was performed in the sight of the people, with the resulting benefit of gaining their obedience and cooperation with God-ordained leadership.

   Numbers 27:18-23 (vs 18) "...and the Lord said to Moses, Take thee Joshua the son of Nun, a man in whom is the Spirit, and lay thine hands upon him. And set him before Eleasar the priest, and before all the congregation; and give him a charge in their sight, And thou shalt put some of thine honour upon him, that all the congregation of the children of Israel may be obedient."

MINISTRY OF THE PRESBYTERY SEMINAR

SHORTENED TITLE: MINISTRY OF THE PRESBYTERY, PAGE 7

THE MINISTRY OF THE PRESBYTERY SEMINAR

Deuteronomy 34:9, "And Joshua the son of Nun was full of the spirit of wisdom; for Moses had laid his hands upon him: and the children of Israel harkened unto him, and did as the Lord commanded Moses."

4. Jesus, prior to His ascension into heaven, imparted a blessing to His followers.

Luke 24:50 "And He led them out as far as to Bethany, and He lifted up his hands, and blessed them..."

5. The New Testament also gives us examples of the Laying on of Hands for blessing, ordination and divine impartation.

Acts 6:6 "Whom they set before the apostles: and when they had prayed, they laid their hands upon them."

Acts 9:17 "And Ananias went his way, and entered into the house; and putting his hands on him said, Brother Saul, the Lord, even Jesus, that appeared unto thee in the way as thou camest, hath sent me, that thou mightest receive thy sight, and be filled with the Holy Ghost."

II Timothy 1;6,14 "...stir up the gift of God, which is in thee by the putting on of my hands. . . . That good thing which was committed unto thee keep by the Holy Ghost which dwelleth in us."
["...)the gracious) gift of God, (the inner fire) that is in you by means of the laying on of my hands (with those of the elders at your ordination)". Amplified]

What are Other Ways in Which the Laying on of Hands are Used?

1. Laying on of Hands is used for healing of the sick.

Note Matthew 8:3, Mark 1:41, Luke 5:13, Matthew 8:15, 9:29, 20:34, Luke 22:51, Luke 13:13, Acts 14:3, 19:11,28:8.

Mark 5:23 "My little daughter liest at the point of death: I pray Thee, come and lay thy hands on her, that she may be healed; and she shall live."

MINISTRY OF THE PRESBYTERY SEMINAR

SHORTENED TITLE: MINISTRY OF THE PRESBYTERY, PAGE 8

THE MINISTRY OF THE PRESBYTERY SEMINAR

Mark 6:5 "And He could there do not mighty work save that He laid his hands upon a few sick folk, and healed them."

Mark 16:18 "They shall take up serpents; and if they drink any deadly thing, it shall not hurt them; they shall lay hands on the sick and they shall recover."

Luke 4:40 "Now when the sun was setting, all they that had any sick with diverse diseases brought them unto him; and he laid his hands on every one of them, and healed them."

Acts 5:12 "And by the hands of the apostles were many signs and wonders wrought among the people; (and they were all with one accord in Solomon's porch.)"

2. Laying on of Hands was Used in Conferring the Holy Ghost.

Acts 8:18 says that when Simon saw that "through the laying on of the apostle's hands the Holy Ghost was given", he offered them money to impart that ability to himself.

see Acts 9:17, above.

Acts 19:6 "And when Paul laid his hands upon them, the Holy Ghost came upon them; and they spake with tongues and prophesied."

Prayer – Our Spiritual Armour, Cont., Page 1

Prayer – our spiritual Armour cont.
How should I pray?
With the Word of God – James 4:14
EXAMPLE – LUKE 1:46 to 55 – (Teach)
Mary the Mother of Jesus.

PRICE OF UNITY SEMINAR, PAGE 2

March 81 Seminar
Shiloh Christian Fellowship

PRICE OF UNITY Pg.2

G. Ezekiel 37:9 <u>Prophesy to the Wind</u>: "O breath, and breathe upon these slain, that they may live... Stood up upon their feet, an exceeding great army." Joel's army (fully restored to their strength and power).

This experience takes on its beginning with the baptism of the Holy Spirit, infilling of God in personality in order that mankind, through this force, might be moved by God. God lives in us, speaks through us from the impulse of the soul. God has His dwelling place in us.

To progress to be His great army, it requires a surrendered heart, a surrendered heart, a surrendered mind, a surrendered life. For it is God's intention through Jesus Christ that we should be a revelation of Jesus. God moving through us, using our hands, our feet, a mind in harmony with God, a soul in touch with Him, a spirit united in Jesus Christ.

Therefore, God is in the process of restoring all things to His church, as it was in the first church. Acts 3:21 says that Jesus is held in the heavens until the restitution (restoration) of all things. Jesus is held in the heavens for an example - Habakkuk 2:14 - is fulfilled. It says "For the earth shall be filled with the knowledge of the glory of the Lord, as the waters cover the sea".

This will come to pass when the restored Joel's army (the Bride of Christ) walks the earth in the fullness of His glory.

PRINCIPLES OF CHURCH LIFE LESSON 26 – CONTINUED

SHORTENED TITLE: PRINCIPLES OF CHURCH LIFE, PAGE 1

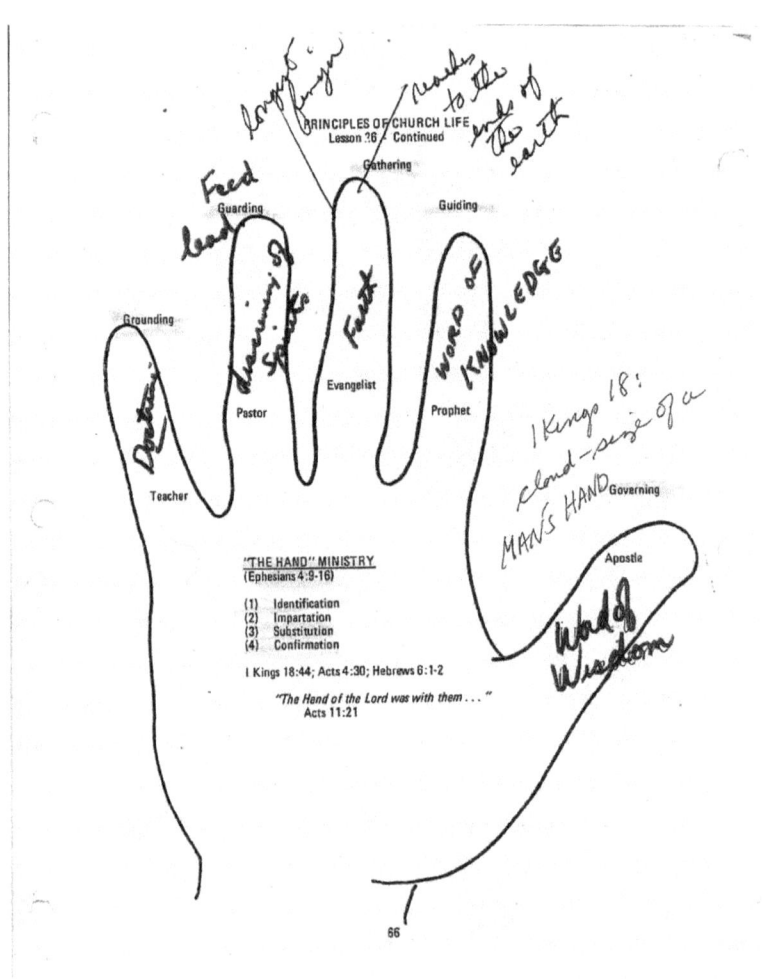

RESTORATION BASICS

SHORTENED TITLE: RESTORATION BASICS, PAGE 1

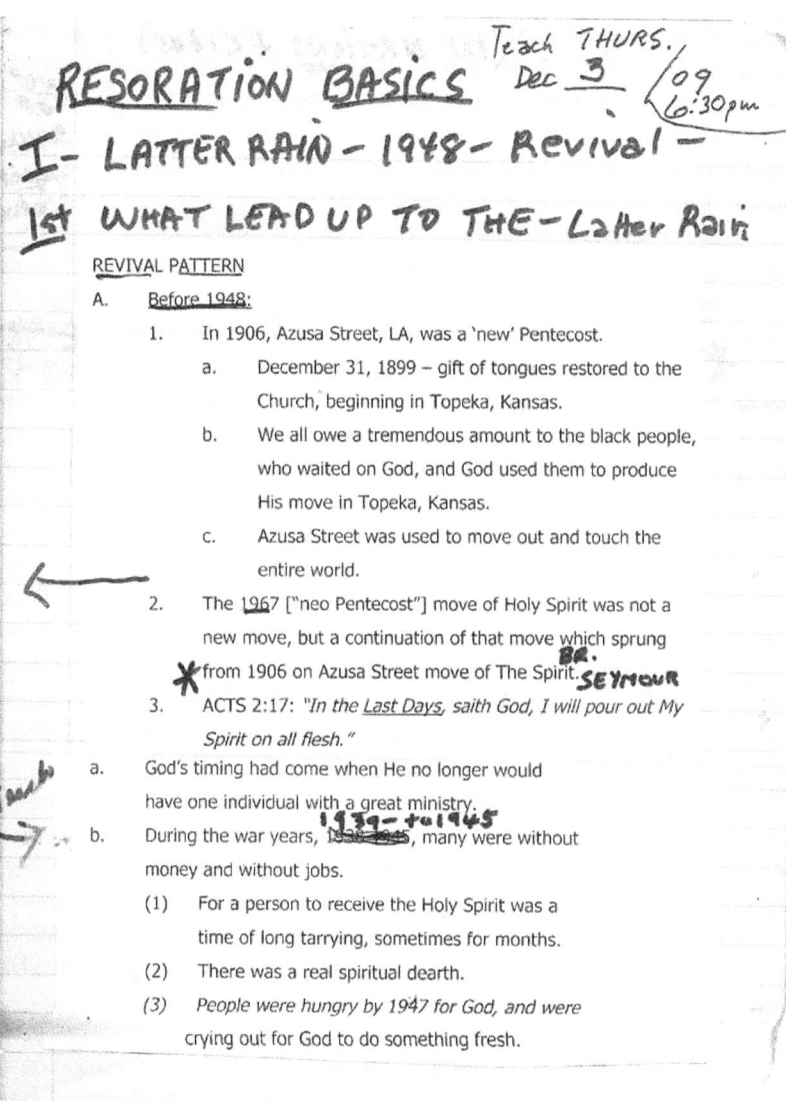

RESTORATION BASICS

SHORTENED TITLE: RESTORATION BASICS, PAGE 3

B. 1948 Renewal *(IN NATIONS & CITIES)* People saw the address in the coll[ing] of Nations Supernatural
   1. In the late part of 1947, people were seeking God the same as they had done in 1906 in Azusa Street.
      a. They got hold of God in prayer.

TELL ABOUT SMITH WIGGLESWORTH –

(HOW I GOT TO NORTH BATTLE– North Battleford – Person [to] Shiloh

   b. God moved in Saskatchewan, Canada.
   c. Fasting: ISAIAH 58 shows two kinds of fasting:
      (1) Fasting of "pointing the finger"
      (2) Fasting from "food"
          (a) Fasting is done for certain days
          (b) A true fast is "only water"
          (c) Prayer must accompany fasting.

   2. Important dates in 1948 Revival:
      a. The Church   February 15 1948
      b. Natural Israel   May 15, 1948
      c. World Council of Churches   September 1948
         and the United Nations
   3. ISAIAH 54:15: *"They are gathered together, but not by Me, saith the Lord."*

Appendix: Cited Violet Kiteley Papers 343

RESTORATION BASICS

SHORTENED TITLE: RESTORATION BASICS, PAGE 4

Prophecies of 1948: **(BEFORE)**
a. Holy Spirit would 'move' in years ahead of 1948.
<u>Greater move of The Spirit than the outpouring 1906.</u>
  (1) Millions would receive the Baptism of Holy Spirit. <u>1970?</u> tell the OAKLAND
  (2) <u>Move would touch the Catholic Church.</u> SHILOH STORY

— GIVE MY PERSONAL TESTAMONY OF HOW I
✝ GOT TO NORTH BATTLEFORD —

344 *Toward a Pentecostal Theology of Prophetic Legitimacy*

REVIVAL IN HIS CHURCH AFTER THE DUE ORDER

SHORTENED TITLE: REVIVAL IN HIS CHURCH, PAGE 1

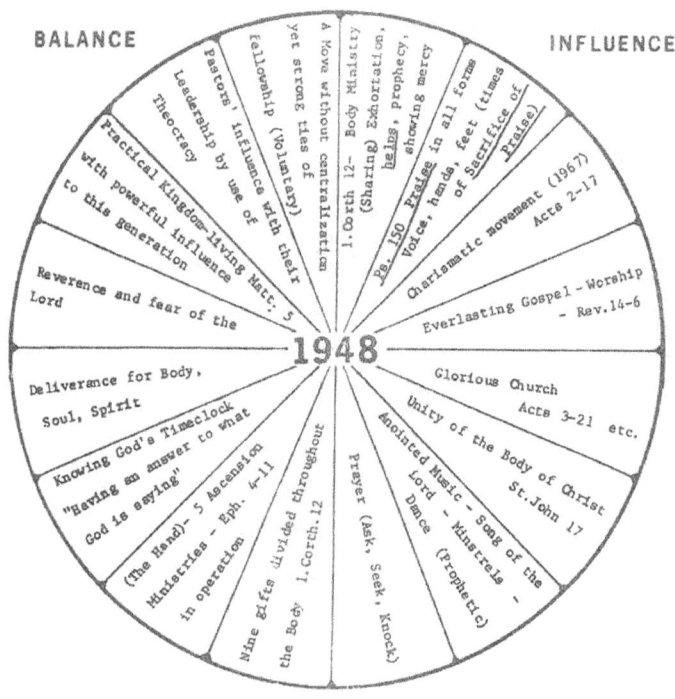

Section III: The Church – Prophetic Promise to Restore

Shortened Title: Prophetic Promise to Restore, Page 14

SECTION III

THE CHURCH – PROPHETIC PROMISE TO RESTORE

I A GOD OF RESTORATION

The Dark Ages left the Church spiritually deaf and blind. The Church had lost its touch with the Spirit of God. As a result, God's Spirit no longer led and directed this organization of man into all truth. The religious leaders of this religious system were spiritually blind, and having eyes they could not see. This Church did not listen for the voice of the Spirit behind them directing their paths, but their ears were stopped by human traditions, having ears they did not hear. The pity of it is that all the time the religious leaders and most of the people felt that they did see and did hear. They felt they were in the perfect way.

The people of the Middle Ages were duped by the traditions of men. They were a people robbed and spoiled of their spiritual heritage in Christ. They were snared by doctrines of men that made false demands upon them. They were literally bound in chains of bondage to a Babylonian system. Yet they didn't know it. They had lost their Deliverer (Christ) and their one hope, but because of their ignorance, none said, "Restore!"

> Hear, ye deaf; and look, ye blind, that ye may see. Who is blind, but my servant? or deaf, as my messenger that I sent? who is blind as he that is perfect, and blind as the Lord's servant? Seeing many things, but thou observest not; opening the ears, but he heareth not. The Lord is well pleased for his righteousness' sake; he will magnify the law, and make it honorable. But this is a people robbed and spoiled; they are all of them snared in holes, and they are hid in prison houses: they are for a prey, and none delivereth; for a spoil, and none saith, Restore (Isaiah 42:18-22).

But God is a God of faithfulness. God promised that He would restore the people of God. In this Section we would like to consider God's promise to restore His people and to set their feet on higher ground.

> And he shall send Jesus Christ, which before was preached unto you: Whom the heaven must receive until the times of restitution of all things, which God hath spoken by the mouth of all his holy prophets since the world began (Acts 3:20-21).

II DEFINITION OF "RESTORATION" OR "RESTITUTION"

In the New Testament the noun form of the Greek word "apokathistemi" (to restore) is used only once, in Acts 3:21. The word literally means to set something back again into its original order. This word was used in the secular Greek world to indicate the return of a possession of a piece of land to the rightful owner. The verb form of this word is found several times in the New Testament. It is most often used in connection with the miracles of Jesus when He healed various conditions. In these cases, the bodies of those healed were restored to their original state. (See Mark 3:5; 8:25; Matthew 12:13; Luke 6:10.)

Section III: The Church – Prophetic Promise to Restore

Shortened Title: Prophetic Promise to Restore, Page 15

The Hebrew words used throughout the Old Testament carry some of the following connotations: to be completed, to finish, to make prosper, to recompense, to rescue, to refresh, to set again, to retrieve, to cause to return or to renew. Restoration refers to the putting back into existence or use that which has been lost, misplaced or stolen.

III RESTORATION IN RELATION TO THE CHURCH

Because of the vastness of the definition of the word "restoration," it is clear that restoration involves many aspects in relation to the dealing of God with man. We saw that restoration means "finish" or "complete." This aspect of restoration has to do with the whole of redemptive history. Ever since the fall of man into sin, God has had a plan of restoration to restore man to the place where he can ultimately experience all that God has planned in the beginning. But the thought of restoration has a particular significance in relation to the Church, for it is by the Church that the manifold wisdom of God is shown forth. Restoration for the Church involves at least three aspects:

A. Restoration involves the recovery of the divine principles and truths that were known, believed, taught, and experienced by the Early Church. This would involve the recovery of those elements that were lost to the Church by the compromises made in the years of Church history. This aspect of restoration involves a returning to the foundation which was laid by the early apostles and prophets. (See Ephesians 2:20; I Corinthians 3:10; I Timothy 4:6.)

B. Restoration involves a renewal of that spiritual life that is the result of the application of the above principles (I Timothy 4:15-16). As the Church returns to the pattern that God has set for it, it cannot help but experience that "breath of life" that God breathed into it on the Day of Pentecost. The breath or Spirit of God brings with it that freshness and vitality that the Church of the former rain experienced.

C. Restoration also involves a completion of God's plan of the ages. It involves the bringing into existence of those things which were foretold by the prophets (Acts 3:21; Romans 16:26). All that God has said, He will do. This, too, involves restoration--a restoration that ends up at the Tree of Life (I Corinthians 15:26).

IV BIBLICAL TERMINOLOGY

The subject of restoration is woven all throughout Scripture. For the student who desires to search out this subject in a more complete way, there are certain key phrases that are repeated often in Scripture that are characteristic of this subject. They include the following:

1. "The times of restitution of all things" (Acts 3:20-21).
2. "Return of the captivity" (Jeremiah 33:7, 11, 26; 29:14; 30:3; Psalm 126:1; Zephaniah 3:20; Joel 3:1; Amos 9:14-15).
3. "As at the first" (Jeremiah 33:7, 11; Isaiah 1:26).
4. "Last days" (Joel 2:28-32).
5. "Last time" (I John 2:18; Jude 18).
6. "Last times" (I Peter 1:20).
7. "Time of the end" (Daniel 8:7; 12:9).
8. "Coming of the Lord" (I Thessalonians 5:23; 4:15).

Section III: The Church – Prophetic Promise to Restore

Shortened Title: Prophetic Promise to Restore, Page 16

9. "Day of the Lord's anger or "The day of the Lord" (Zephaniah 1:7, 14-18; 2:2-3; I Thessalonians 5:2; II Peter 3:10).
10. "Great and dreadful Day of the Lord" (Malachi 4:5).
11. "The day of vengeance of our God" (Isaiah 61:2; Luke 21:22).
12. "Times of the Gentiles be fulfilled" (Luke 21:24; Romans 11:25).
13. "The latter rain" (Joel 2:23-29; Hosea 6:1-3).

V RESTORATION IN SCRIPTURE

From cover to cover, the Bible is primarily a book of RESTORATION. In the book of Genesis, the book of beginnings, we have the origin of all things. Genesis is the seed-plot of the Bible. This book declares the purpose of God (Genesis 1:26) and the seed for every major Bible doctrine. Everything that begins in Genesis ends up in the book of Revelation. Revelation is the book of ultimates which tells us the final state of all things.

The Bible gives us the history of redemption. In Genesis we are told how man lost the image of God when he fell into sin and corrupted his way. We are told how man forfeited the Tree of Life and was expelled from the Garden. We are told how God sought to restore man and provide a covering by which he might again commune with God. In Revelation we see the work of redemption completed. We see man restored to the Tree of Life. Between Genesis 3:24 and Revelation 21:3-4 we see the panorama of restoration in its fullest sense (see Luke 15). On this basis we can expect to find this subject all throughout the Old and New Testaments.

A. Restoration was the theme of the Old Testament Prophets
The prophets were divinely inspired to warn God's people of their backsliding ways and idolatry. By proclaiming God's message, the prophet endeavored to awaken the conscience of the people and to RESTORE them to righteousness and divine fellowship (Amos 5:14).

1. The book of Joel is dedicated to the theme of restoration and shows how a backslidden nation brought God's judgment upon their heads. Then, thru repentance, they gained right standing, and God promised that He would "restore" (Joel 2:18-32).

2. Elijah is the classic example of a prophet who battled wickedness and idolatry. In I Kings 18:21 he forces a decision of the people. In his prayer (verse 37) he employs an expression referring to restoration. It should be noted that it is Elijah's ministry that is often connected with that which is to take place in the last days. (See Malachi 4:5-6; Luke 1:17; Mark 9:12; Matthew 17:11.)

3. Ezekiel depicts the message of restoration in fascinating visions (chapters 33-48). The resurrection (restoration) of the dry bones in chapter 37 pictures the theme of restoration in a most unforgettable manner.

4. Other Old Testament references to restoration include the following:
Psalm 23:3; 51:12; 69:4
Isaiah 1:26; 49:6; 57:15, 18-19; 58:12; 61:4-11
Jeremiah 30:17
Haggai 2:9

B. The New Testament emphasizes restoration
It would be well for us to examine what we are told in Acts 3:21 which says regarding Jesus, "Whom the heaven must receive until the times of restitution of all things, which God hath spoken by the mouth of all his holy prophets

SECTION III: THE CHURCH – PROPHETIC PROMISE TO RESTORE

SHORTENED TITLE: PROPHETIC PROMISE TO RESTORE, PAGE 17

since the world began."

1. We notice that there are "times of restitution." God is working on a timetable and has everything under control. These are times when God will give to the Church that which was lost. The language here seems to imply that this time will immediately precede the Second Coming of Christ.

2. We notice also that this verse doesn't tell us that all things are going to be restored. It goes on to qualify the "all things" to include only those things which are spoken of by the prophets. Whatever God's holy prophets have spoken will come to pass. This is one of the tests of a true prophet. The Church should be eagerly searching the prophetic Scriptures for clues to our position in God's timetable.

3. The return of Christ cannot take place until all that the prophets spoke be fulfilled. Many people think that Christ could come at any minute. He could come for them any minute, but He will not come for the Church until all be fulfilled. In fact, the heavens must retain Him against that time, for when He returns He is coming for a full-restored Church–a Church that is glorious, not having spot or wrinkle or any such thing (Ephesians 5:27).

VI SIGNS WHICH CHARACTERIZE THE RESTORATION PERIOD

All through Scripture God has given us glimpses of what this period of time will be like. It will indeed be a glorious time of expectation and excitement. Let's look at some of the language the Bible uses for this time:

A. The voice of joy and the voice of gladness will be heard in the House of the Lord (Jeremiah 33:11). In the period of the Dark Ages the Church was in a state of mourning. The music that comes to us from that age has a mournful sound. But God is restoring His House. The present songs of Zion are songs characterized by joy, gladness, shouting, and victory.

B. The voice of the Bride will again be heard (Jeremiah 33:11). The Church is to be God's mouthpiece to the world. For so many years the Church has let the world toss it to and fro. But once again the Church is arising and prophesying the Word of the Lord to the lost world. The law is going forth out of Zion.

C. The voice of the Bridegroom will be heard among God's people (Jeremiah 33:11). The Church lost that personal communion with the living Saviour when they stopped their ears to the voice of the Spirit. But Christ is coming a second time to the Church and the voice of prophecy is being heard today as never before (Revelation 19:10).

D. The voice of them that shall say "Praise the Lord" is another characteristic of restoration (Jeremiah 33:11). Over the years the Church lost the spirit of praise. They had to write down their liturgy because the song of praise was gone from their hearts. But God is raising up a generation that has a song of praise in their hearts which is finding expression on their lips (Psalm 102:13-18).

E. Restoration involves the return of ministries that will bring back the sacrifice of praise to the Church (Jeremiah 33:11). God is in the process of raising up ministries that are leading the Church to a renewed understanding of spiritual worship. Worship is not to be a mere form, but it is to be in spirit and in truth.

Appendix: Cited Violet Kiteley Papers

Section III: The Church—Prophetic Promise to Restore

Shortened Title: Prophetic Promise to Restore, Page 18

F. Restoration will also involve the return of true judges, counselors, and teachers to the Church (Isaiah 1:26; 30:8, 19-21). For many years the Church was run by hirelings who cared not for the flock but only for political position. In this day God is raising up men who love the Lord, have a knowledge of His Word, are in tune with the Holy Spirit, and are motivated by a genuine desire to serve the people of God.

G. We can expect restoration to be a growing from faith to faith and glory to glory (Romans 1:17; II Corinthians 2:17-18). God works in response to faith. Days of tremendous power must be days of tremendous faith. God's method of growth is line upon line, here a little, there a little (Isaiah 28:11). As the present-day Church is obedient to the Word of the Lord, we can expect that God will increase our faith.

H. As the Church is being restored we can expect that the powers of darkness will become more pronounced. Satan doesn't have to do much against a weak and powerless Church. But when the Church becomes strong and he sees it as a real threat to his kingdom, he must work overtime. Therefore we can expect an overt manifestation of the anti-christ system in these days (Revelation 13:1-8).

I. Restoration also has something to do with natural Israel. Although ultimate restoration for the Jew will come only as he receives Christ (Romans 11), we have to believe that Israel itself is a signpost in God's calendar of end-time events. (See Isaiah 11:12; Ezekiel 11:17; 28:25; 36:24; Amos 9:14-15; Luke 21:24.)

J. Restoration will be a time of deliverance and release from spiritual bondage. (See Galatians 4:22-31; Jeremiah 33:7, 11; Galatians 5:1; Psalm 126.) The Church has been in bondage to traditions of men. A great release in the Spirit is coming to the Church today as it applies the New Testament principles of discipline and life.

K. Restoration is a time in which we can expect the Gospel to be preached to all the world (Matthew 24:14). *MISSONS*

L. During the time of restoration we can expect that there will be a lukewarmness on the part of many to this endtime message (Revelation 3:15-17).

M. This lukewarmness will precipitate a great falling away in times of great pressure (II Thessalonians 2:3). This certainly does not mean that only a faithful few will remain to meet the Lord, but it does mean that the time is coming when those who are "riding the fence" in their spiritual commitment will be forced to make a decision one way or another. Many will go the way of the world, but many will come into a deeper life of complete consecration.

N. Restoration will be characterized by the continual recovery of lost truth (Acts 3:20-21). The Church will once again experience portions of the inheritance that was lost to it through unbelief, until the entire inheritance be possessed.

O. As true ministries arise in this time, we can also expect false ministries to arise. These false ministries will be empowered by Satan to do many mighty things (II Peter 2:1-3; Matthew 24:11, 24), and will be the ambassadors of strong delusion that will come in the last days. Whatever God is doing, Satan will attempt to counterfeit. For this reason, the people of God need to have spiritual discernment that they might try the spirits.

P. In the last time there will be signs in the heavens and earth (Matthew 24:29-30). The earth is waxing old like a garment. The natural signs of this old age will be manifested during the culmination of history.

Section III: The Church – Prophetic Promise to Restore

Shortened Title: Prophetic Promise to Restore, Page 19

VII   AREAS WHICH WILL BE RESTORED

Ezekiel tells us the condition of God's people and their need for restoration. The Scripture refers to at least seven areas in which we can expect God to move in restoration.

A. TRUTH

If God is going to fully restore His Church, then there is going to have to be an exposure to truth in a way that we have never experienced before. <u>Truth is the means God uses to change us.</u> As we look upon THE TRUTH we are changed from glory to glory (II Corinthians 3:18). All throughout Scripture truth is related to the concept of light. God's Word is the Word of Truth. (See Psalm 119:43; II Corinthians 6:7; Ephesians 1:13; Colossians 1:15; II Timothy 2:15; James 1:18.) "Thy word is a lamp unto my feet, and a light unto my path" (Psalm 119:105). It is exposure to the Word that brings us into the place of light (Psalm 119:130).

God is wanting to do a tremendous work in His Church today. (See Ephesians 3:10-11; 4.11-16; Acts 3:21, Revelation 7.1-4). However, it is important for us to see that when God works, He always works in the atmosphere of light--Truth (Genesis 1:3). It is the ministry of the Holy Spirit, the Spirit of Truth (see John 14:17; 15:26; 16:13; I John 4:6) to create the atmosphere for the reception of truth. In the first restoration we find a condition of darkness interrupted by the Spirit brooding or hovering over the face of the deep. "And God said, Let there be light: and there was light," Genesis 1:3. In the same way, the Holy Spirit can be seen in relation to the Candlestick in the Tabernacle of Moses. He is the oil from which that light is brought forth. The Holy Spirit has this ministry in the life of the believer also. He is the One who prepares the ground upon which that seed of truth, that seed of the Word (compare Luke 8:11 and John 17:17) may fall (I Corinthians 12:3).

If the endtime Church is going to experience something that no other generation of believers has experienced, it must experience the light of God to open its eyes. We must experience more light than any other generation. The Holy Spirit, the Revealer of Truth, is our Teacher who will lead us line upon line, precept upon precept (Isaiah 28:11) until we are changed into the image of Christ (Ephesians 4:13). This is God's method of teaching. It is always progressive.

There needs to be a restoration of truth to the Church. One doesn't have to read the New Testament too many times to know that we have lost something of the revelation and power of the Early Church. We stand with the Hebrew Christians in their need to be grounded firmly in the first principles of the doctrine of Christ (Hebrews 6:1-3). But beyond that we need to have an ear to hear that particular thing that God wants to do in regard to the Church of the last days. There are many truths that have never been made manifest throughout all history because they are reserved for this Church of the end time. We need to have an ear to hear what the Spirit is saying in this day. "Who are kept by the power of God through faith unto salvation ready to be revealed in the last time," I Peter 1:5.

Jesus said in John 14:6, "I am the way, the truth, and the life: no man cometh unto the Father, but by me." Jesus is the Way, the only Way to salvation and eternal life. He is actually the Way to a three-fold salvation of spirit, soul, and body (I Thessalonians 5:23). When we come to know the Lord and our spirit is born anew, we find Jesus as THE WAY. Jesus fulfills this role as the Lamb slain from the foundation of the world (Revelation 13:8).

But Jesus is also the Truth. He is renewing our souls daily after the image of the Creator (Colossians 3:10; Romans 12:2). This work of redemption has to do with the mind, the will and the emotions or, we could say, the soul

19

Section III: The Church – Prophetic Promise to Restore

Shortened Title: Prophetic Promise to Restore, Page 20

of man (Ephesians 4:23; II Corinthians 4:16). As we submit to this renewing process, we experience Jesus as THE TRUTH. Jesus fulfills this role as our Baptizer with the Holy Ghost and fire (Matthew 3:11-12).

Jesus also told us that He is the life. This has to do with the aspect of salvation that is waiting to be revealed in the last days (I Peter 1:5). This has to do with an experience of the life of God (I Corinthians 15:51-58). This has to do with the revelation of the life of Christ flowing to the Church and supplying that resurrection life and translation power to the people of God. When this becomes a part of the Christian experience, we will experience Jesus as THE LIFE. Jesus fulfills this role in His ministry as our great High Priest (Hebrews 7:15-16).

"I have no greater joy than to hear that my children walk in truth," III John 4.

B. MINISTRIES

When God restores a truth He will always have prepared true ministries to administer that truth. If a truth does not come under proper guidance and ministry, it can be dangerous. All one has to do is see how some of the modern-day movements have perverted a genuine Bible truth to the exclusion of the natural checks and balances in the rest of the Scripture to see the importance of God-directed ministries. There is a tremendous need for skilled workmen to rightly divide the Word of Truth. God is restoring the five-fold ministry of apostles, prophets, evangelists, pastors, and teachers for the perfecting of the saints, until we all come to the unity of the faith (Ephesians 4:11-16). The Church cannot be perfected without the five gifted or ascension gift ministries. They are God's gift to the Church.

As God works in restoration, we can expect that God will be preparing the proper leadership before hand, so that there will be skilled workmen to lead the people in. There will be a restoration of the husbandmen (Jeremiah 31:14, 24-26) who have received from the Lord and are, consequently, able to cause the flock to lie down (Jeremiah 33:12-13). From this type of ministry, there will be growth because the flocks will be fed and satisfied. Jesus is the Great Shepherd (John 10:1) who sets the pattern for all true shepherds of the sheepfold, the Church.

God is at the present time raising up these ministries and Isaiah 30:20-21 is being fulfilled.

> And though the Lord give you the bread of adversity, and the water of affliction, yet shall not thy teachers be removed into a corner any more, but thine eyes shall see thy teachers: And thine ears shall hear a word behind thee, saying, This is the way, walk ye in it, when ye turn to the right hand, and when ye turn to the left (Isaiah 30:20-21).

C. PEOPLE

During the Dark Ages and in any captivity, natural or spiritual, God's people are in a condition of being robbed and spoiled. Their bones are picked clean by the birds of the air and there is the smell of death and defeat. But God promises that as His people look to Him He will build them up (Jeremiah 31:4). There was a plucking up, a pulling down, and a destruction that came to the Church in the Dark Ages, but God promises that the nation that repents and turns from their evil He will again build and plant in a watered place (Jeremiah 19:6-9).

The Church was like those dry bones in Ezekiel 37 that had been picked clean by the theological buzzards of the day. They had the theological framework, but there was no life on the bones. As God visits His people, these bones have the potential of becoming the restored Body of Christ. God promises to make the bones of His people fat once again (Isaiah 58:11), they shall be like a watered garden, and they shall "flourish like an herb" (Isaiah 66.14). The people of God are now being restored. God is restoring our soul and leading us beside still waters. He is preparing a table before us wherein is life and health, both naturally and spiritually (Psalm 23).

D. WORSHIP

True worship in spirit and truth can only come from the lips of a people who have experienced the two witnesses of the Spirit and the Truth (John 4:23-24). This is the natural expression on the lips of a people who have been restored and who are walking in the light of His Presence wherein is fulness of joy (Jeremiah 31:12). The voice of the endtime Church will be saying, "Praise the Lord of Hosts" (Jeremiah 33:11), because it consists of a people who know the importance of bringing their spiritual sacrifices of praise into the House of the Lord (Hebrews 13.15).

The Church of God is to be His habitation by the Spirit (Ephesians 2:21-22), and we know that God inhabits the praises of His people (Psalm 22:3). It is clear that a restoration of true worship to the Church implies a restoration of the presence of the Lord to His House. God is building up Zion, the Church of the firstborn (Hebrews 12:22-23). Zion is where the Tabernacle of David was established which was the place of audible praise. It is this generation that shall break the appointment with death (Psalm 102:16-20).

> Therefore they shall come and sing in the height of Zion, and shall flow together to the goodness of the Lord, for wheat, and for wine, and for oil, and for the young of the flock and of the herd: and their soul shall be as a watered garden; and they shall not sorrow any more at all. Then shall the virgin rejoice in the dance, both young men and old men together: for I will turn their mourning into joy, and will comfort them, and make them rejoice from their sorrow (Jeremiah 31:12-13).

E. PATHS TO DWELL IN

God promises to restore the paths in which to dwell. This message of restoration leads to a deeper life in our daily experience. God is restoring practical principles to the individual, to the family, and, to the Church, for the cry is going out, "Get your house in order!" As we begin to apply God's principles to our everyday life, we will see a restoration of personal relationships and life experiences that we never dreamed possible. "And they that shall be of thee shall build the old waste places: thou shalt raise up the foundations of many generations; and thou shalt be called, The repairer of the breach, The restorer of paths to dwell in," Isaiah 58:12.

The decline of the Church began as a gap began to form between doctrine and experience. Many of the doctrines of the Church remained scriptural, but there was no corresponding experience in the life of the average believer. It was as if they were burning incense to vanity (worshipping useless things), because they stumbled from the path of truth (Jeremiah 18:15). As time went on in this subnormal level, even some of the great landmarks of doctrine were erased to measure up with the experience of the average person (Job 24:2-4). In so doing they rebelled against the light and were brought further out of the path (Job 24:13).

Section III: The Church – Prophetic Promise to Restore

Shortened Title: Prophetic Promise to Restore, Page 22

God has promised to restore these pathways and re-establish the landmarks (Jeremiah 31:21). He is doing this in His Church, the place of safety, the sheepfold. The Church should be the center of all the activity of the Church flock, spiritually and naturally. All recreation, fun and fellowship for young and old should come from the Church under the canopy of God's glory and the Shepherd's rod. God is revealing this as the way, and He is instructing us to "walk in it" (Isaiah 30:21).

F. YEARS

As the Church went into decline, we see that many years of history have been eaten up by backsliding and lack of progress. There are many individual Christians who have had similar experiences on a personal level. There are many ministers of the Gospel who know that for many years they were functioning in partial light. But God has promised to restore the years that were lost (Joel 2:25). He promises that the glory of the latter House will be greater than the glory of the former House (Haggai 2:9). He promises that the end of a thing is better than the beginning (Ecclesiastes 7:8). He gives us the picture of Samson, who did more in his last exploit than he did in all his other exploits put together (Judges 16:30).

G. KINGDOM

We can expect these last days of restoration will prepare the way for the Kingdom to come (Matthew 6:10). It will come as the laws of the Kingdom begin to be put into practice by the people of God. Jesus taught His disciples principles for Kingdom living (Matthew 5-7). As the Church learns to live in those things involved in the restoration of truth, ministries, people, paths, worship, and years, we will see a full restoration of God's Kingdom in the earth. The fulness of all these is yet to come, but we can be instrumental in bringing that Kingdom by praying for it and doing what we can to get our lives in order. "For the kingdom of God is not meat and drink; but righteousness, and peace, and joy in the Holy Ghost," Romans 14:17.

This Kingdom will be victorious over all other spiritual or earthly kingdoms and will ultimately be delivered to the Father (I Corinthians 15:24). It is an eternal Kingdom that God is restoring.

THIRD DAY PEOPLE, PAGE 4

Hosea 6:3 - Then shall we know. If we follow on to know the Lord, His going forth is prepared as the morning; and Jesus shall come unto us as the rain.

RAIN MEANS — FORMER — & LATTER
1. TO FINISH THE HARVEST (GLORY)
2. FULL MANIFESTATION OF HAND — Fold
   ELIJAH'S DAY

GOD IS NOW RAISING UP A Generation (3rd DAY PEOPLE) WHO KNOW HOW TO GET GOD'S ATTENTION.

"SET TIME HAS COME FOR ZION"

(END)

An Unbroken Line: Latter Rain Movement/1948 Revival

Shortened Title: Unbroken Line, Page 1

An ~~Unbroken~~ Unbroken Line

Latter Rain Movement/1948 Revival

AT MFI IS

The theme this year is "*An Unbroken Line*" which simply means that each generation is not starting Christianity over but that we learn from the preceding generation and we who are in leadership now prepare the younger leadership to take our place so that we have a great future so we keep overlapping the generations.

all people love it

So looking back to what God has done, one of these examples is The history related to the Latter Rain Movement

I would LIKE TO SHARE WAS

Spiritual Climate AT THAT TIME!
The Second World War was over in the summer of 1945 and many of the churches and Para-church ministries had lost a number of the cream of their crop in terms of young men and women and had been pretty devastated as they began the process of rebuilding their ministries.

There was a general discouragement and dearth dryness throughout the body of Christ and there was a general cry from intercessors throughout the nations for God to birth and Isaiah 43 Revival, "which was to be a new thing to cause rivers to once again flow in the desert." *WE NEED NOW AGAIN*

of all Nations
The Azusa Street Revival of 1906 had restored the baptism of the Holy Spirit and literally blanketed the world with the outpouring of the Holy Spirit, which celebrated the 100th anniversary last year.

But there was still a great need for the restoration of the New Testament Pattern of the Gifts and ministries of the Holy Spirit operating in the churches. *everywhere.*

1

An Unbroken Line: Latter Rain Movement/1948 Revival

Shortened Title: Unbroken Line, Page 2

Dr. Charles Price, a convert of Amy Simple McPherson and Smith Wigglesworth (a close friend of my mother, stayed in my parents home in Canada) prophesied that God will move mightily again but we will not see it. (It will happen after we are gone.)

Joel 2:23 "Be glad then, ye children of Zion and to rejoice in the Lord your God: for he hath given you the former rain moderately and He will cause to come down for you the rain, the Former Rain and the Latter Rain in the 1st month. (I will share my testimony as to how this verse affected my life personally).

On July 13, 1945, the death of my husband in a fiery air crash the Northern end of Vancouver Island.

After the fiery crash and death, and I was pregnant with our child and became paralyzed for a number of months. A missionary prophet from Transjordan was flying into Vancouver, Canada to minister in a conference at a church. While he was in the process of his plane landing in Vancouver, B.C., the Lord spoke to him that he was to go to a young woman's home and pray for her as she was paralyzed as a result of being traumatized due to a recent tragic bereavement.

When he came to my home, his word was that God was going to raise me up and I was going to preach a brand new message. This was highly unusual because first of all the ministry of Prophet was not widely accepted at that time.

Needless to say the Lord raised me up and The church that I was part of at the time sent me out to travel from church to church and

… *Appendix: Cited Violet Kiteley Papers* 357

AN UNBROKEN LINE: LATTER RAIN MOVEMENT/1948 REVIVAL

SHORTENED TITLE: UNBROKEN LINE, PAGE 3

province to province eastward, give the testimony of my miracle healing.

where I was in Prince Albert, Saskatchewan Canada, a lady whom I had never met came up to me and said that I needed to go to North Battleford where she just heard that a group of hungry Bible School students were fasting night and day for the birth of a fresh new move of God in an old abandoned Air force Barracks with very poor quality heating in the midst of a Canadian winter, which often went down to well below zero.

WHAT HAPPENED!

what miracle & Timing On February 13, 1948, after an all night of praying and worship, (I was there) one of the primary leaders of the movement (Ernie Hawtin) who had a very serious speech impediment, which made his speech barely understandable, received a prophetic utterance with a quickening regarding 1 Tim 4:14, and he spoke clearly without any difficulty of speech. Ernie Hawtin was totally delivered from his speech impediment that night.

The Word of the Lord saying, "Do not neglect the gift that is in you which will be given to you by prophecy with the laying on of hands of the Presbytery. Meditate on these things; give yourselves entirely to them that your progress may be evident to all.

Take heed to yourself and to the doctrine. Continue in them for in doing this, you will save both yourself and those that hear you.

This was the of birthing of the presbytery as we know it and I want to say that the emphasis is not on trying to maintain, keep alive or preserve some truths for a former age as admirable as that might be, but everything about God is increase, enlargement and multiplication in this *"Unbroken Line"*.

Into I LATER TRAVELED WITH THE HAWTIN PARTY TO MANY PLACES, CANADA USA ETC. IN PRESBERYS

3

An Unbroken Line: Latter Rain Movement/1948 Revival

Shortened Title: Unbroken Line, Page 4

There is a great emphasis on producing an atmosphere that was conducive to setting the stage for miracles. As we stated, North Battleford, Saskatchewan was a very remote unknown place even to most Canadians.

In 1948 it was totally unknown except for the military barracks that God saw fit to birth something there, which continues to be a point of reference for many of the foundational truths that we are enjoying today in what we call "*The Restoration Movement*".

It was out of those humble obscure beginnings that God began to bring a rebirth to a number of the truths that we have today.

It is noteworthy that people supernaturally came to that location from all over the world. They came from South Africa, Southern India, the Scandinavian countries, China, which wasn't closed until 1949, and from many parts of the United States and Canada.

Some heard about the revival by word of mouth, but others received dreams, and visions. And some reported seeing the address in the sky. Air travel was not very sophisticated; the primary travel would be by train etc.

This was the birthing of the New Testament Apostle and prophets whom the denominational dispensationalist had stated were not for today.

The revelation of the Apostle and the Prophet was restored as foundational ministry.

An Unbroken Line: Latter Rain Movement/1948 Revival,

Shortened title: Unbroken Line, Page 5

In my Father's House many places/mansions (John 14/1,2)

(this could be restored NOW)

They seemed comfortable using the word Prophet, but the word Apostle was a title they strayed away from at that time.

Prophetic ministry that was restored at this time was not the Old Testament prophetic ministry which prophesies over nations and international affairs, but it was a New Testament prophet which ministering over individuals in terms of placement, or birthing a calling and mission. But we should use it freely – we should not neglect use of the term Apostle as it is a part of our heritage (NOW.)
—(NOT A TITLE – ITS A SPIRITUAL OFFICE)

I Kings 18: "Posture of Elijah, birthing the rain."

The prophetic utterance and presbytery given during the Latter Rain Movement was that they were not to lay hands on anyone suddenly. It should never be done outside *"an atmosphere of extended fasting and prayer."* ("if possible") (some exception)

However, from time to time, the Lord would indicate certain candidates, which had a prepared heart and sacrificial willingness to serve the Body and Acts 13 model for the presbytery they would be sent forth to the nations. (READ v. Lit) *Opening now* *Ethiopian eunuch example now* *Hindu students to the Muslim World*
※ IN GOD'S MERCY ALONE
I was chosen as one of the candidates, as God knew my heart and that I could receive at that time.

The Prophecy I received – *Would* with m¹ son was (*My David was only 3 years old when I received the word:*) would come
"That out of my womb ~~was going~~ forth a prophet to the nations and out of him was going to come forth another prophet." My grandson Patrick wasn't born until 1973, but he had a prophetic word given to him in 1948.

→ "THIS IS AN SMALL EXAMPLE OF THE UNBROKEN LINE

UNTITLED PRAYER NOTES, PAGE 1

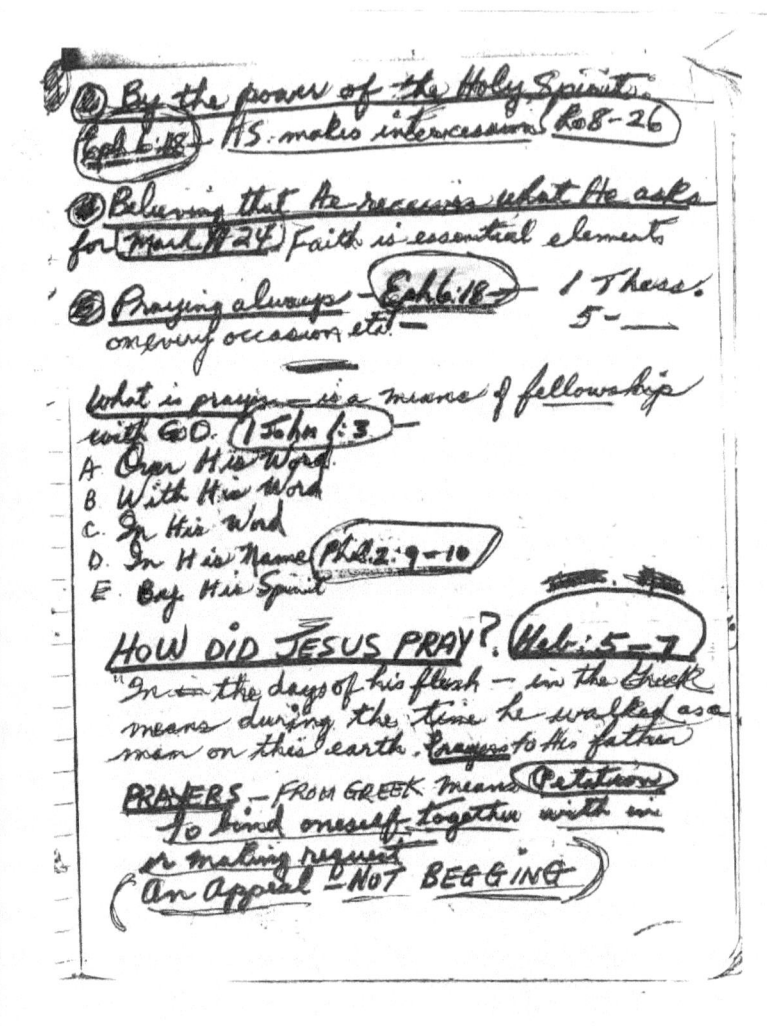

(Untitled) Violet Kiteley Personal and Latter Rain Account

Shortened Title: Violet Kiteley Account, Page 2

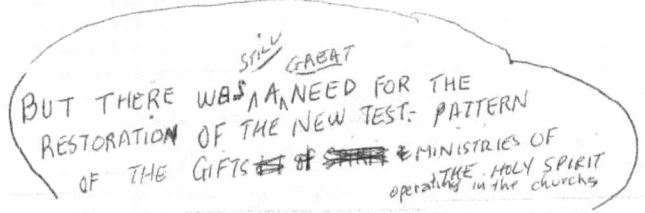

But there was still a great need for the restoration of the New Test. pattern of the gifts & ministries of the Holy Spirit operating in the churches

Dr. Charles Price, a convert of Amy Simple McPherson and Smith Wigglesworth (a close friend of my mother, stayed in my parents home in Canada) prophesied that God will move mightily again, but we will not see it. It will happen after we are gone.

Joel 2:23 "Be glad then, ye children of Zion and to rejoice in the Lord your God: for he hath given you the former rain moderately and he will cause to come down for you the rain, the Former Rain, and the Latter Rain in the 1st month. (I will share my testimony as to how this verse affected my life personally).

On July 13, 1945, the death of my husband in a fiery air crash off the Northern end of Vancouver Island – the wreckage was found 38 years later and they built a monument to the downed airmen.

After the fiery crash and death, I was pregnant with our child and became paralyzed for a number of months. A missionary prophet from Transjordan was flying into Vancouver, Canada to minister in a conference at a church. While he was in the process of his plane landing in Vancouver, B.C., the Lord spoke to him that he was to go to a young woman's home and pray for her as she was paralyzed as a result of being traumatized due to a recent tragic bereavement.

When he came to my home, his word was that God was going to raise me up and I was going to preach a brand new message. This was highly unusual because first of all the ministry of Prophet was not widely accepted at that time.

(Untitled) Violet Kiteley Personal and Latter Rain Account

Shortened Title: Violet Kiteley Account, Page 3

Needless to say the Lord raised me up and the church that I was part of at the time sent me out to travel from church to church and province to province eastward to give the testimony of my miracle healing.

I was in Prince Albert, Saskatchewan Canada, a lady whom I had never met came up to me and said that I needed to go to North Battleford where she just heard that a group of hungry Bible School students were fasting night and day for the birth of a fresh new move of God in an old abandoned Air force Barracks with very poor quality heating in the midst of a Canadian winter, which often went down to well below zero.

WHAT HAPPENED!

On February 13, 1948, after an all night of praying and worship, ("I WAS THERE") one of the primary leaders of the movement (Ernie Hawtin) who had a very serious speech impediment, which made his speech barely understandable, received a prophetic utterance quickening regarding 1 Tim 4:14, and he spoke clearly without any difficulty of speech. Ernie Hawtin was totally delivered from his speech impediment that night.

The Word of the Lord saying, "Do not neglect the gift that is in you which will be given to you by prophecy with the laying on of hands of the Presbytery. Meditate on these things; give yourselves entirely to them that your progress may be evident to all.

Take heed to yourself and to the doctrine. Continue in them for in doing this, you will save both yourself and those that hear you.

This was the of birthing of the presbytery as we know it and I want to say that the emphasis is not on trying to maintain, keep alive or preserve some truths for a former age as admirable as that might

(Untitled) Violet Kiteley Personal and Latter Rain Account

Shortened Title: Violet Kiteley Account, Page 4

be, but everything about God is increase, enlargement and multiplication in this *"Unbroken Line"*.

There is a great emphasis on producing an atmosphere that was conducive to setting the stage for miracles. As we stated, North Battleford, Saskatchewan was a very remote unknown place even to most Canadians.

It certainly was not one of the main transportation hubs or communication centers in Canada even to this day. You never heard of anyone going there for a vacation.

In 1948 it was totally unknown except for the military barracks that God saw fit to birth something there, which continues to be a point of reference for many of the foundational truths that we are enjoying today in what we call *"The Restoration Movement"*.

It was out of those humble obscure beginnings that God began to bring a rebirth to a number of the truths that we have today.

It is noteworthy that people supernaturally came to that location from all over the world. They came from South Africa, Southern India, the Scandinavian countries, China, which wasn't closed until 1949, and from many parts of the United States and Canada.

Some heard about the revival by word of mouth, but others received dreams, and visions. And some reported seeing the address in the sky. And this was without any emails, fax machines, or websites, all they had were Western Union Telegrams. Air travel was not very sophisticated; the primary travel would be by train (& boat).

This was the birthing of the New Testament Apostle and prophets whom the denominational dispensationalist had stated were not for today.

VERSES OF OUR END TIME REVIVAL, PAGE 3

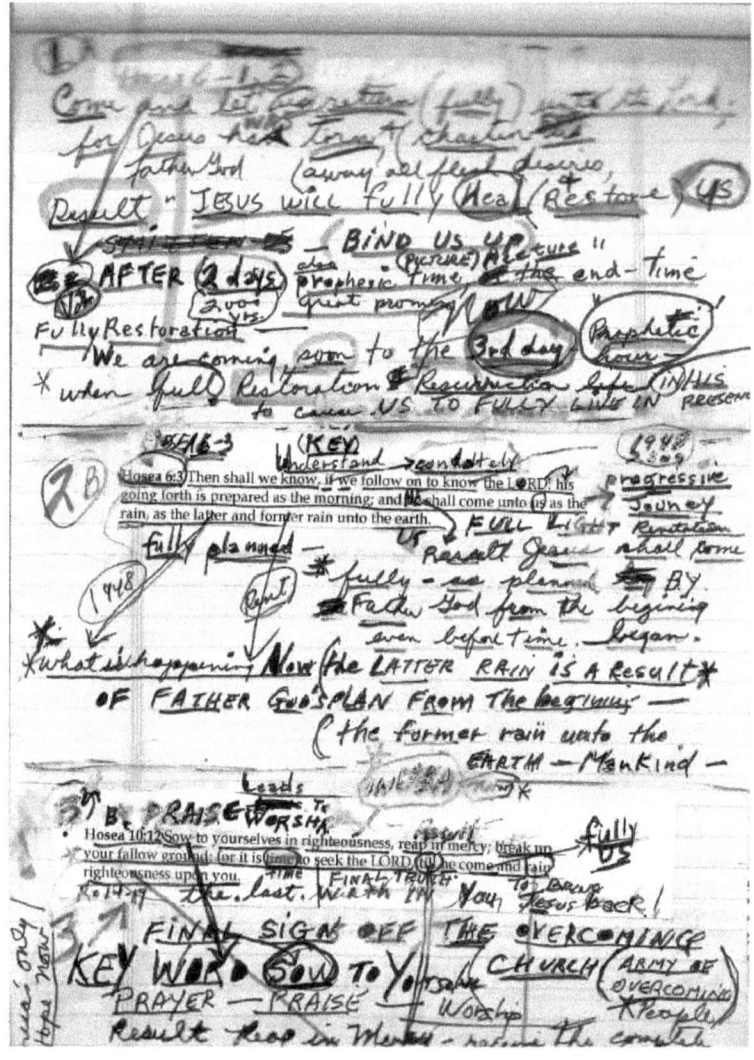

V. KITELEY SERMONS, PAGE 20

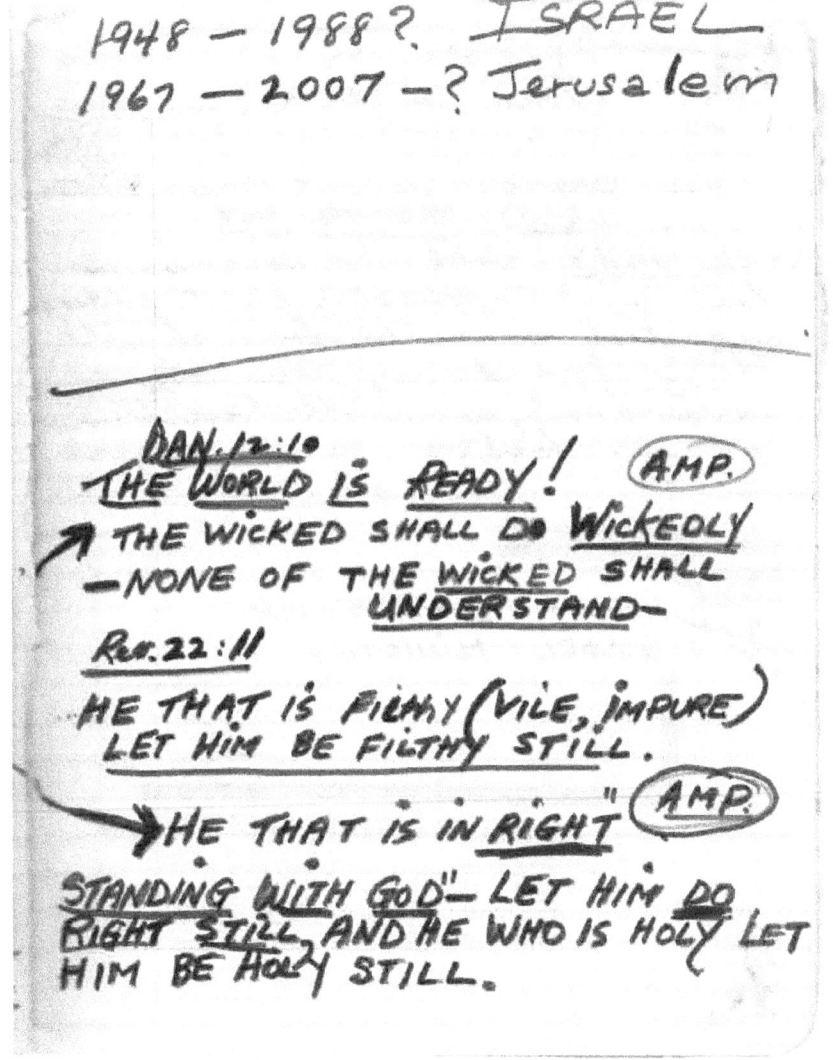

Bibliography

Documents from Violent Kiteley Papers (Private Collection)

Kiteley, Violet, 'Deliverer Promised', in *Sermons Notebook*.
—*Elijah and Elisha: A Study of the Prophetic Ministry of Elijah and Elisha Taken from 1st and 2nd Kings* (Shiloh Bible College. Oakland, CA).
—'Elijah Birthing the Rain'.
—'Ezekiel, Chapter 20' (Shiloh Bible College. Oakland, CA).
—'Five Spiritual Senses'.
—'The Great Restoration: The Dispensation of the Holy Spirit'.
—'Healing and Latter Rain Movements 1947–48: An Eyewitness Account; Interview with Dr. Violet Kiteley' (Interview by Abraham Ruelas and Alma Thomas).
—'Laying on of Hands – 1948 – Northern Canada', *Revival Doctrine Syllabus*.
—'Leaders Who Need to Have the Spirit of the Lamb (Like Jesus)'.
—'Lesson Two: Laying on of Hands' (Shiloh Bible College. Oakland, CA).
—'Levels of Prayer in Jesus' Life'.
—'Life of Christ', (Lecture Notes, 2011).
—'Malachi 3: God Is Calling for Reformation'.
—'Ministry of the Presbytery Seminar'.
—'Prayer – Our Spiritual Armour, Cont'.
—'Price of Unity Seminar' (Lecture Notes; Shiloh Christian Fellowship, Oakland, CA, March 1981).
—'Principles of Church Life Lesson 26 – Continued'.
—'Restoration Basics' (Lecture Notes; December 3, 2009).
—'Revival in His Church After the Due Order'.
—'Section III: The Church – Prophetic Promise to Restore'.
—'Third Day People'.
—'An Unbroken Line: Latter Rain Movement/1948 Revival'.
—'Untitled Prayer Notes'.
—'(Untitled) Violet Kiteley Personal and Latter Rain Account'.
—'Verses of Our End Time Revival'.
—*V. Kiteley Sermons*.

Other Works Cited

Agarwal, Pragya, 'Understanding Unconscious Bias', interview by Emily Kwong, *NPR Short Wave* (Podcast produced by Rebecca Ramirez; July 15, 2020), https://www.npr.org/2020/07/14/891140598/understanding-unconscious-bias.

Allport, Gordon W., *The Nature of Prejudice* (New York: Perseus Books, 25th anniversary edn, 1979).

Althouse, Peter, 'The Ecumenical Significance of Canadian Pentecostalism', in Michael Wilkinson and Peter Althouse (eds), *Winds from the North: Canadian Contributions to the Pentecostal Movement* (Leiden: Brill, 2010.), pp. 55-78.

Anderson, Allan Heaton, *To the Ends of the Earth: Pentecostalism and the Transformation of World Christianity* (Oxford: Oxford University Press, 2013).

Anthony, Michael J., Daryl Eldridge, Julie Gorman, and Warren S. Benson, (eds.), *Evangelical Dictionary of Christian Education* (Baker Reference Library; Grand Rapids, MI: Baker Academic, 200).

APA Dictionary of Psychology, https://dictionary.apa.org.

Aquinas, Thomas, *Summa Theologica* (trans. Fathers of the English Dominican Province; London: Burns Oates & Washbourne, n.d.).

Aquino, Frederick D., 'Maximus the Confessor', in Paul L. Gavrilyuk and Sarah Coakley (eds.), *The Spiritual Senses: Perceiving God in Western Christianity* (Cambridge: Cambridge University Press, kindle edn, 2012), ch. 6.

—'Spiritual Formation, Authority, and Discernment', in William J. Abraham and Frederick D. Aquino (eds.), *The Oxford Handbook of the Epistemology of Theology* (Oxford: Oxford University Press, 2017).

Archer, Kenneth J., 'Afterword: On the Future of Pentecostal Hermeneutics', in Kenneth J. Archer and L.W. Oliverio, Jr. (eds.), *Pneumatological Hermeneutics in Pentecostal Christianity* (New York: Palgrave Macmillan, 2016), pp. 315-28.

—*The Gospel Revisited: Towards a Pentecostal Theology of Worship and Witness* (Eugene, OR: Pickwick, 2011).

—*A Pentecostal Hermeneutic: Spirit, Scripture and Community* (Cleveland, TN: CPT Press, 2009).

—'Pentecostal Story: The Hermeneutical Filter for the Making of Meaning', *Pneuma: The Journal of the Society of Pentecostal Studies* 26.1 (Spring 2004), pp. 36-59.

—'Pentecostal Theology as Story: Participating in God's Mission', in Wolfgang Vondey (ed.), *The Routledge Handbook of Pentecostal Theology* (London: Routledge, Kindle edn, 2020), ch. 4.

Arndt, William, Frederick W. Danker, and Walter Bauer, *A Greek-English Lexicon of the New Testament and Other Early Christian Literature* (Chicago, IL: University of Chicago Press, 2000).

Arnold, Clinton E., 'Syncretism', in Ralph P. Martin and Peter H. Davids (eds.), *Dictionary of the Later New Testament and Its Developments* (Downers Grove, IL: InterVarsity Press, 1997), p. 1146.

Arrington, French L., 'Dispensationalism', *NIDPCM*, p. 585.

Arterbury, Andrew E., *Reading Luke: A Literary and Theological Commentary* (Reading the New Testament; Macon, GA: Smyth & Helwys, 2nd ser., 2019).

Ashbrook, James B., 'From Biogenetic Structuralism to Mature Contemplation to Prophetic Consciousness', *Zygon: Journal of Religion & Science* 28.2 (June 1993), pp. 231-50.

Ashby, G.W., *Go out and Meet God: A Commentary on the Book of Exodus* (International Theological Commentary; Grand Rapids, MI: Eerdmans, 1998).

Athanasius, *Athanasius: On the Incarnation of the Word of God* (trans. T. Herbert Bindley; London: Religious Tract Society, 2nd edn, 1903).

Attridge, Harold W., *The Epistle to the Hebrews: A Commentary on the Epistle to the Hebrews* (Hermeneia; Philadelphia, PA: Fortress Press, 1989).

Augustine, Daniela C., *Pentecost, Hospitality, and Transfiguration: Toward a Spirit-inspired Vision of Social Transformation* (Cleveland, TN: CPT Press, 2012).

Aune, David E., *Prophecy in Early Christianity and the Ancient Mediterranean World* (Grand Rapids, MI: Eerdmans, 1991).

Baars, Conrad W., and Anna A. Terruwe, *Healing the Unaffirmed: Recognizing Emotional Deprivation Disorder* (Staten Island, NY: Fathers and Brothers of The Society of St. Paul, Kindle edn, 2002).

Balcombe, Dennis, *China's Opening Door: Incredible Stories of the Holy Spirit at Work in One of the Greatest Revivals in Christianity* (Lake Mary, FL: Charisma House, 2014).

—*One Journey One Nation: Autobiography of Dennis Balcombe Missionary to China* (Chambersburg, PA: eGenCo, 2011).

Baldwin, Joyce G., *1 and 2 Samuel: An Introduction and Commentary* (Tyndale Old Testament Commentaries 8; Downers Grove, IL: InterVarsity Press, 1988).

Barfoot, Chas. H., *Aimee Semple McPherson and the Making of Modern Pentecostalism* (London: Routledge, 2014).

Barker, Kit, 'Speech Act Theory, Dual Authorship, and Canonical Hermeneutics: Making Sense of Sensus Plenior', *Journal of Theological Interpretation* 3.1–2 (2009), pp. 227-39.

Barry, John D., David Bomar, Derek R. Brown, Rachel Klippenstein, Douglas Mangum, Carrie Sinclair Wolcott, and Lazarus Wentz (eds.), *The Lexham Bible Dictionary* (Bellingham, WA: Lexham Press, 2016).

—'Tetragrammaton', in John D. Barry, *et al.* (eds), *The Lexham Bible Dictionary* (Bellingham, WA: Lexham Press, 2016).

Beacham, Doug, *Rediscovering the Role of Apostles and Prophets* (Franklin Springs, GA: LifeSprings, 2003).

Benner, David G., *Care of Souls: Revisioning Christian Nurture and Counsel* (Grand Rapids, MI: Baker Books 1998).

Benson, Bruce Ellis, and Norman Wirzba (eds.), *The Phenomenology of Prayer* (Perspectives in Continental Philosophy; New York: Fordham University Press, 2005).

Bergen, Robert D., *1, 2 Samuel* (New American Commentary 7; Nashville, TN: Broadman & Holman, 1996).

Bergen, Wesley J., *Elisha and the End of Prophetism* (JSOTSup 286. Sheffield: Sheffield Academic Press, 1999).

Black, Jonathan, 'Pentecostals and the Creed', *Apostolic Theology* (November 21, 2017), https://www.apostolictheology.org/2017/11/pentecostals-and-creed.html.

Blake, William, *The Marriage of Heaven and Hell* (Oxford: Oxford University Press, 1975).

Boccaccini, Gabriele, Albert I. Baumgarten, and Daniel Boyarin, 'Introduction: The Three Paths to Salvation of Paul the Jew', in Gabriele Boccaccini and Carlos A. Segovia (eds.), *Paul the Jew: Rereading the Apostle as a Figure of Second Temple Judaism* (Minneapolis, MN: Fortress Press, 2016), pp. 4-27.

Bock, Darrell L., *Luke* (2 vols.; Baker Exegetical Commentary on the New Testament; Grand Rapids, MI: Baker Academic, 1994–1996).

Bonhoeffer, Dietrich, *Discipleship* (trans. Barbara Green and Reinhard Krauss; Dietrich Bonhoeffer Works: Reader's Edition; Minneapolis, MN: Fortress Press, 2015).

—*Ethics* (ed. Clifford Green; trans. Reinhard Krauss, Charles C. West, and Douglas W. Stott; Dietrich Bonhoeffer Works Series 6; Minneapolis, MN: Fortress Press, 2005).

—*Life Together and Prayerbook of the Bible* (ed. Geffrey B. Kelly; trans. Daniel W. Bloesch and James H. Burtness; Dietrich Bonhoeffer Works 5; Minneapolis, MN: Fortress Press, 1996).

Bosserman, Christina, 'Gilead', in John D. Barry, *et al.* (eds), *The Lexham Bible Dictionary* (Bellingham, WA: Lexham Press, 2016).

Bosworth, David A., 'Ancient Prayers and the Psychology of Religion: Deities as Parental Figures', *Journal of Biblical Literature* 134.4 (2015), pp. 681-700.

Boyer, Mark G., *From Contemplation to Action: The Spiritual Process of Divine Discernment Using Elijah and Elisha as Models* (Eugene, OR: Wipf & Stock, 2018).

Branham, William, 'Church Ages', https://william-branham.org/site/topics/church_ages.

Brannan, Rick, *Lexham Analytical Lexicon to the Greek New Testament* (Bellingham, WA: Logos Research Systems, rev. edn, 2013).

—*Lexical Commentary on the Pastoral Epistles: First Timothy* (Bellingham, WA: Appian Way Press, 2016).

Bridges Johns, Cheryl, 'Grieving, Brooding, and Transforming: The Spirit, the Bible, and Gender', *Journal of Pentecostal Theology* 23.2 (2014), pp. 141-53.

Brown, Derek R., Wendy Widder, and E. Tod Twist, *2 Corinthians* (ed. John D. Barry; Lexham Research Commentaries; Bellingham, WA: Lexham Press, 2013.

Brown, Francis, Samuel Rolles Driver, and Charles Augustus Briggs, *Enhanced Brown-Driver-Briggs Hebrew and English Lexicon* (Oxford: Clarendon Press, 1977).

Brownstein, Michael, 'Implicit Bias', in Edward N. Zalta (ed.), *Stanford Encyclopedia of Philosophy*. https://plato.stanford.edu/entries /implicit-bias/.

Bruce, F.F., *The Book of the Acts* (New International Commentary on the New Testament; Grand Rapids, MI: Eerdmans, rev. edn, 1988).

Brueggemann, Walter, *The Creative Word: Canon as a Model for Biblical Education* (Philadelphia, PA: Fortress Press, 1982).

—*1 and 2 Kings* (Smyth and Helwys Bible Commentary; Macon, GA: Smyth & Helwys, 2000).

—*First and Second Samuel* (Interpretation: A Bible Commentary for Teaching and Preaching; Louisville, KY: John Knox Press, 1990).

—*Living Toward a Vision: Biblical Reflections on Shalom* (New York: United Church Press, 1982).

—*The Prophetic Imagination* (Minneapolis, MN: Fortress Press, 2001).

—*Testimony to Otherwise: The Witness of Elijah and Elisha* (St. Louis, MO: Chalice Press 2001).

—*Theology of the Old Testament: Testimony, Dispute, Advocacy* (Minneapolis, MN: Fortress Press, 2005).

BSSM School Planting, 'Activating Students in the Prophetic with Ben Armstrong', https://bssm.net/schoolplanting/2016/10/25/activating-students-in-the-prophetic-with-ben-armstrong/.

Burke, D.G., 'Meek Meekness', in Geoffrey W. Bromiley (ed.), *International Standard Bible Encyclopedia* (Grand Rapids, MI: Eerdmans, rev. edn, 1988), p. 307.

Butler, John G., *Elijah: The Prophet of Confrontation* (Bible Biography Series 3; Clinton, IA: LBC, 1994).

—*Elisha: The Miracle Prophet* (Bible Biography Series 4; Clinton, IA: LBC Publications, 1994).

Carpenter, Eugene, 'Exodus', in H. Wayne House and William D. Barrick (eds.), *Evangelical Exegetical Commentary* (Bellingham, WA: Lexham Press, 2012).

Carroll, John T., *Luke: A Commentary* (New Testament Library; Louisville, KY: Westminster John Knox Press, 2012).

Carson, Timothy, *Liminal Reality and Transformational Power: Transition, Renewal and Hope* (Cambridge: Lutterworth Press, rev. edn, 2016).

Carter, Howard, *Questions and Answers on Spiritual Gifts* (Tulsa, OK: Harrison House, 1976).

Casement, Ann, 'Persona', in David A. Leeming (ed.), *Encyclopedia of Psychology and Religion* (Boston, MA: Springer, 2014).

Castelo, Daniel, *Pentecostalism As a Christian Mystical Tradition* (Grand Rapids, MI: Eerdmans, 2017).

—*Pneumatology: A Guide for the Perplexed*. Guides for the Perplexed. London: Bloomsbury T&T Clark, 2015).

Charlesworth, James H. (ed.), *The Old Testament Pseudepigrapha, Volume 1: Apocalyptic Literature and Testaments* (New York: Yale University Press, 1983).

Cherry, Kendra, 'The Practice of Transpersonal Psychology: History, Popularity, and Research Areas', https://www.verywellmind.com/what-is-transpersonal-psychology-2795971.

Childs, Brevard S., *The Book of Exodus: A Critical, Theological Commentary* (Old Testament Library; Louisville, KY: Westminster John Knox Press, 2004).

Chironna, Mark J., 'Latter Rain Restorationism as Understood by Violet Kiteley and Other Latter Rain Adherents', https://www.markchironna.com/articles.

—'What Does Psychology Have to Do with the Prophetic?', *Firebrand* (June 14, 2022), https://firebrandmag.com/articles/what-does-psychology-have-to-do-with-the-prophetic.

—'Zechariah: The Incredulous Priest-Turned-Prophet: Biblical-Theological, Psychological, and Phenomenological Perspectives in Relation to Prophetic Legitimacy', https://www.markchironna.com/articles.

Chrysostom, John, 'Homily VIII', in *Saint Chrysostom: Homilies on the Gospel of St. John and Epistle to the Hebrews* (ed. by Philip Schaff; trans. T. Keble and Frederic Gardiner; Select Library of the Nicene and Post-Nicene Fathers of the Christian Church; New York: Christian Literature Company, 1st ser., 1889), XIV, pp. 403-408.

Clarkson, Frederick, and André Gagné, 'New Apostolic Reformation Faces Profound Rift Due to Trump Prophecies and "Spiritual Manipulation of the Prophetic Gift"', *Religion Dispatches* (August 9, 2022), https://religiondispatches.org/new-apostolic-reformation-faces-profound-rift-due-to-trump-prophecies-and-spiritual-manipulation-of-the-prophetic-gift/.

Cocksworth, Ashley, *Karl Barth on Prayer* (T&T Clark Studies in Systematic Theology 26; London: Bloomsbury T&T Clark, 2015).

Cogan, Mordechai, and Hayim Tadmor, *II Kings: A New Translation with Introduction and Commentary* (Anchor Yale Bible 11; New Haven, CT: Yale University Press, 2008).

Cohn, Robert L., 'The Literary Logic of 1 Kings 17–19', *Journal of Biblical Literature* 101.3 (1982), pp. 333-50.

—*2 Kings* (Berit Olam Studies in Hebrew Narrative and Poetry; Collegeville, MN: Liturgical Press, 2000).

Collins English Dictionary (Glasgow: HarperCollins, 8th edn, 2006).

Cornwall, Robert, 'Primitivism and the Redefinition of Dispensationalism in the Theology of Aimee Semple McPherson', *Pneuma: The Journal of the Society of Pentecostal Studies* 14.1 (January 1992), pp. 23-42.

Coulter, Dale M., 'The Spirit and the Bride Revisited: Pentecostalism, Renewal, and the Sense of History', *Journal of Pentecostal Theology* 21.2 (January 2012), pp. 298-319.

Craigie, Peter C., *The Book of Deuteronomy* (New International Commentary on the Old Testament; Grand Rapids, MI: Eerdmans, 1976).

Crenshaw, James L., 'Theodicy', in David Noel Freedman (ed.), *Anchor Yale Bible Dictionary* (New York: Doubleday, 1992), pp. 445-47.

Croatto, J. Severubi, 'Jesus, Prophet Like Elijah, and Prophet-Teacher Like Moses in Luke-Acts', *Journal of Biblical Literature* 124.3 (2005), pp. 451-65.

Cron, Lisa, *Wired for Story: The Writer's Guide to Using Brain Science to Hook Readers from the Very First Sentence* (Berkeley, CA: Ten Speed Press, 2012).

Culver, Robert D., '2095 רָאָה', in R. Laird Harris, Gleason L. Archer Jr., and Bruce K. Waltke (eds.), *Theological Wordbook of the Old Testament* (Chicago, IL: Moody Press, 1999), p. 823.

Dahlstrom, Daniel O., Graeme Nicholson, Richard Polt, and Günter Figal, *Heidegger's Being and Time: Critical Essays* (Lanham, MD: Rowman & Littlefield, 2005).

Davies, Andrew, 'What Does it Mean to Read the Bible as A Pentecostal?', *Journal of Pentecostal Theology* 18.2 (2009), pp. 216-29.

Davila, James R., 'Merkavah Mysticism', in Katharine Doob Sakenfeld (ed.), *The New Interpreter's Dictionary of the Bible* (Nashville, TN: Abingdon Press, 2009), p. 50.

Dean, Robert J., and Fleming Rutledge, *Leaps of Faith: Sermons from the Edge* (Eugene, OR: Resource Publications, 2017).

DeCarvalho, Roy José, 'A History of the "Third Force" in Psychology', *Journal of Humanistic Psychology* 30.4 (Fall 1990), pp. 22-44.

'The Definition of the Council of Chalcedon (451 A.D.)', *Monergism*, https://www.monergism.com/definition-council-chalcedon-451-ad.

DeGroat, Chuck, *When Narcissism Comes to Church: Healing Your Community from Emotional and Spiritual Abuse* (Downers Grove, IL: InterVarsity Press 2020).

Delgado, Jennifer, 'Expectations: The Silent Killer of Happiness', *Psychology Spot*, https://psychology-spot.com/expectation/.

Dictionary.com, https://www.dictionary.com.

'The Difference Between Feelings and Emotions', *Counseling Blog* (Wake Forest University), https://counseling.online.wfu.edu/blog/difference-feelings-emotions/.

Dika, Tarek R., and W. Chris Hackett, *Quiet Powers of the Possible: Interviews in Contemporary French Phenomenology* (New York: Fordham University Press, Kindle edn, 2016).

Dille, Sarah J., *Mixing Metaphors: God as Mother and Father in Deutero-Isaiah* (London: T&T Clark, 2004).

Dimitrova, Nevena, *Human Knowledge according to Saint Maximus the Confessor* (Eugene, OR: Resource Publications, Kindle edn, 2016).

Dunn, James D.G., *Beginning from Jerusalem* (Christianity in the Making 2; Grand Rapids, MI: Eerdmans, 2009).

Durham, John I., *Exodus* (Word Biblical Commentary 3; Dallas, TX: Word, 1987).

Eckhardt, John, *Prophetic Activation: Break Your Limitations to Release Prophetic Influence* (Lake Mary, FL: Charisma House, Kindle edn, 2016).

—*The Prophet's Manual: A Guide to Sustaining Your Prophetic Gift* (Lake Mary, FL: Charisma House, 2017).

Edwards, D. Miall, 'Mediation, Mediator', in James Orr *et al.* (eds.), *International Standard Bible Encyclopaedia* (Chicago, IL: Howard-Severance, 1915), p. 2018.

Elwell, Walter A., and Barry J. Beitzel, 'Numbers and Numerology', in Walter A. Elwell (ed.), *Baker Encyclopedia of the Bible* (Grand Rapids, MI: Baker Book House, 1988), p. 1562.

Engelken, K., 'שרת', *TDOT*, XV, p. 503.

Escobar, S., 'Praxis and Orthopraxis', in Martin Davie, Tim Grass, Stephen R. Holmes, John McDowell, and Thomas A. Noble (eds.), *New Dictionary of Theology: Historical and Systematic* (Downers Grove, IL: Inter-Varsity Press, 2016), p. 696.

Estes, Douglas, 'Introduction: The Literary Approach to the Bible', in Douglas Mangum and Douglas Estes (eds.), *Literary Approaches to the Bible* (Lexham Methods Series 4; Bellingham, WA: Lexham Press, 2016), pp. 9-39.

'Examining Confirmation Bias', *Canvas*, https://lumen.instructure.com/courses/170090.

Farley, Lawrence R., *The Acts of the Apostles: Spreading the Word* (Orthodox Bible Study Companion; Chesterton, IN: Ancient Faith, 2012).

Farnsworth, Bryn, 'How to Measure Emotions and Feelings (And the Difference Between Them)', *Imotions* (blog, April 14, 2020), https://imotions.com/blog/difference-feelings-emotions/.

Farrer, Austin M., *Faith and Speculation: An Essay in Philosophical Theology* (London: Adam & Charles Black, 1967).

Faupel, D. William, 'The New Order of the Latter Rain: Restoration or Renewal?', in Michael Wilkinson and Peter Althouse (eds), *Winds from the North: Canadian Contributions to the Pentecostal Movement* (Leiden: Brill, 2010.), pp. 239-63.

Fee, Gordon D., *The First Epistle to the Corinthians* (New International Commentary on the New Testament; Grand Rapids, MI: Eerdmans, rev. edn, 2014).

—*God's Empowering Presence: The Holy Spirit in the Letters of Paul* (Grand Rapids, MI: Baker Academic, 2011).

—*Gospel and Spirit: Issues in New Testament Hermeneutics* (Grand Rapids, MI: Baker, Kindle edn, 1991).

Fee, Gordon D., and Douglas Stuart, *How to Read the Bible for All Its Worth* (Grand Rapids, MI: Zondervan, Kindle edn, 2014).

Fitzmyer, Joseph A., *The Acts of the Apostles: A New Translation with Introduction and Commentary* (Anchor Yale Bible 31; New Haven, CT: Yale University Press, 2008).

Fraser-Thill, Rebecca, 'What Is Individuation?', https://www.verywellmind.com/individuation-3288007.

Freedman, David Noel, Allen C. Myers, and Astrid B. Beck (eds.), 'Seer', *Eerdmans Dictionary of the Bible* (Grand Rapids, MI: Eerdmans, 2000), p. 1179.

Freeman, Laurence, 'Meditation', in Michael Downey (ed.), *The New Dictionary of Catholic Spirituality* (Collegeville, MN: Liturgical Press, 2000), pp. 648-51.

Fretheim, Terence E., *Exodus* (Interpretation: A Bible Commentary for Teaching and Preaching; Louisville, KY: John Knox Press, 1991).

—*First and Second Kings* (Westminster Bible Companion; Louisville, KY: Westminster John Knox Press, 1999).

Friebel, Kelvin G., *Jeremiah's and Ezekiel's Sign-Acts* (JSOTSup 283; Sheffield: Sheffield Academic Press, 1999).

Fuhs, H.F., 'רָאָה', *TDOT*, XIII, pp. 208-10.

Fuller, Pamela, Mark Murphy, and Anne Chow, *The Leader's Guide to Unconscious Bias: How to Reframe Bias, Cultivate Connection, and Create High-Performing Teams* (New York: Simon & Schuster, 2020).

Funk, Mary Margaret, *Discernment Matters: Listening with the Ear of the Heart* (Collegeville, MN: Liturgical Press, 2013).

Gabriel, Andrew K., 'Three Ways People Misunderstand Tongues as "Initial Evidence" of Spirit Baptism', *Exploring Theology, Scripture, and Ministry*, https://www.andrewkgabriel.com/2017/01/24/misunderstanding-tongues-as-initial-evidence-of-spirit-baptism/.

Gangel, Kenneth O., and Jim Wilhoit, *The Christian Educator's Handbook on Spiritual Formation* (Wheaton, IL: Victor Books, 1994).

Gapp, Kenneth Sperber, 'The Universal Famine Under Claudius', *Harvard Theological Review* 28.4 (October 1935), pp. 258-65.

Garland, David E., *Reading Matthew: A Literary and Theological Commentary on the First Gospel* (Reading the New Testament; Macon, GA: Smyth & Helwys, 2001).

Gennaro, Rocco J., 'Consciousness', in James Fieser and Bradley Dowden (eds.), *Internet Encyclopedia of Philosophy*, https://iep.utm.edu/freud/#SH7d.

Gesenius, Wilhelm, and Samuel Prideaux Tregelles, *Gesenius' Hebrew and Chaldee Lexicon to the Old Testament Scriptures* (Bellingham, WA: Logos Bible Software, 2003).

Gilbrant, Thoralf, *The New Testament Greek-English Dictionary* (Complete Biblical Library; WORDsearch, 1991).

Gill, Kenneth, 'Dividing Over Oneness: The Oneness Movement Pushed Pentecostals to Organize', *Christianity Today*, https://www.christianitytoday.com/history/issues/issue-58/dividing-over-oneness.html.

Gillespie, Thomas W., *The First Theologians: A Study in Early Christian Prophecy* (Grand Rapids, MI: Eerdmans, 1994).

Gordon, V.R., 'Sign', in Geoffrey W. Bromiley (ed.), *International Standard Bible Encyclopedia* (Grand Rapids, MI: Eerdmans, rev. edn, 1988), p. 506.

Gowan, Donald E., *Theology in Exodus: Biblical Theology in the Form of a Commentary* (Louisville, KY: Westminster John Knox Press, 1994).

Graham, Stephen J., 'Ten Prophetic Techniques to Amaze Your Friends', *Stephenjgraham* (blog, September 8, 2017), https://stephenjgraham.wordpress.com/2017/09/08/ten-prophetic-techniques-to-amaze-your-friends/.

Greco, Franco, 'What Is Personality? It Is a Lot More Complicated Than Myers-Briggs', *Franco Greco Your Psychologist* (blog, January 31, 2021), https://www.yourpsychologist.net.au/what-is-personality-its-more-complicated-than-myers-briggs.

Green, Chris E.W., *Sanctifying Interpretation: Vocation, Holiness, and Scripture* (Cleveland, TN: CPT Press, 2nd edn, 2020).

—'Self-Emptying, Self-Awareness, and the Sharing of the Spirit, Pt 3', *Speakeasy Theology* (May 30, 2022), https://cewgreen.substack.com/p/god-does-not-want-to-be-everything?s=r.

—'"We Have Come to Fullness": Toward a Pentecostal Catholicity', *Journal of Biblical and Theological Studies* 5.2 (2020), pp. 357-67.

Green, Joel B., *Conversion in Luke-Acts: Divine Action, Human Cognition, and the People of God* (Grand Rapids, MI: Baker Academic, 2015).

—*The Gospel of Luke* (New International Commentary on the New Testament; Grand Rapids, MI: Eerdmans, 1997).

Grenz, Stanley J., and Jay T. Smith, *Pocket Dictionary of Ethics* (IVP Pocket Reference Series; Downers Grove, IL: InterVarsity Press, 2003).

Guzik, David, *Deuteronomy* (David Guzik's Commentaries on the Bible; Santa Barbara, CA: David Guzik, 2004).

Hagner, Donald A., *Matthew 1–13* (Word Biblical Commentary 33A; Dallas, TX: Word, 1993).

Hamon, Bill, *Apostles Prophets and the Coming Moves of God: God's End-Time Plans for His Church and Planet Earth* (Santa Rosa Beach, FL: Christian International, 1997).

—*Prophets and Personal Prophecy: God's Prophetic Voice Today* (Shippensburg, PA: Destiny Image, 1987).

—*Prophets Pitfalls and Principles: God's Prophetic People Today* (Shippensburg, PA: Destiny Image, 1990).

Harkness, Georgia, 'Chapter 3: The Ethics of Jesus', *Religion Online*, https://www.religion-online.org/book-chapter/chapter-3-the-ethics-of-jesus/.

Harrison, R.K., 'Nazirite', in Geoffrey W. Bromiley (ed.), *International Standard Bible Encyclopedia* (Grand Rapids, MI: Eerdmans, rev. edn, 1988), p. 501.

Hart, Kevin, 'How Marion Gives Himself', in Rachel Bath, Antonio Calcagno, Kathryn Lawson, and Steve G. Lofts (eds.), *Breached Horizons: The Philosophy of Jean-Luc Marion* (Lanham, MD: Rowman & Littlefield, Kindle edn, 2017), ch. 1.

Hartley, John E., '905 יָקַר', in R. Laird Harris, Gleason L. Archer Jr., and Bruce K. Waltke (eds.), *Theological Wordbook of the Old Testament* (2 vols.; Chicago, IL: Moody Press, 1999), p. 398.

—'1947 צָעַק', in R. Laird Harris, Gleason L. Archer Jr., and Bruce K. Waltke (eds.), *Theological Wordbook of the Old Testament* (2 vols.; Chicago, IL: Moody Press, 1999), p. 772.

Hartog, Paul A., 'Conscience', in John D. Barry, *et al.* (eds.), *The Lexham Bible Dictionary*, (Bellingham, WA: Lexham Press, 2016).

Hasel, G., 'זָעַק', *TDOT*, IV, pp. 112-13.

Hassler, Mark A., 'Winnowing', in John D. Barry, *et al.* (eds.), *The Lexham Bible Dictionary* (Bellingham, WA: Lexham Press, 2016).

Hauser, Alan J., 'Yahweh Versus Death – The Real Struggle in 1 Kings 17–19', in Alan J. Hauser and Russell Gregory, *From Carmel to Horeb: Elijah in Crisis* (Sheffield: Almond Press, 1990).

Heck, J.D., 'Issachar', in T. Desmond Alexander and David W. Baker (eds.), *Dictionary of the Old Testament: Pentateuch* (Downers Grove, IL: InterVarsity Press, 2003).

Henriques, Gregg, 'Self-Reflective Awareness: A Crucial Life Skill', *Psychology Today* (September 10, 2016), https://www.psychologytoday.com/us/blog/theory-knowledge/201609/self-reflective-awareness-crucial-life-skill.

Henry, Michel, *Words of Christ* (trans. Christina M. Gschwandtner; Grand Rapids, MI: Eerdmans, 2012).

Henschen, Tobias, 'Heidedgger's Correction of the Divine Word', in William Sailer, David C. Greulich, and Harold P. Scanlin (eds.), *Religious and Theological Abstracts* (Myerstown, PA: Religious and Theological Abstracts, 2012).

Heschel, Abraham Joshua, *The Prophets* (Peabody, MA: Hendrickson, 2010).

Hiller, Doris, 'Faith, Experience and the Concept of Prayer: Some Reflections on Theological Epistemology', *Neue Zeitschrift für Systematische Theologie und Religionsphilosophie* 42.3 (Jan 1, 2000), pp. 316–29.

'History', *The Foursquare Church*, https://www.foursquare.org/about/history/.

Hocken, Peter, 'Charismatic Movement', *NIDPCM* (Grand Rapids, MI: Zondervan, rev edn, 2002), p. 517.

Holladay, William Lee (ed.), *A Concise Hebrew and Aramaic Lexicon of the Old Testament* (Leiden: Brill, 2000).

Huemer, Michael, *Skepticism and the Veil of Perception* (Lanham, MD: Rowman & Littlefield, Kindle edn, 2001).

Hughes, Richard T., 'Restoration, Historical Models Of', in Douglas A. Foster, *et al.*, *The Encyclopedia of the Stone-Campbell Movement* (Grand Rapids, MI: Eerdmans, 2004).

Hurst, L.D., 'Ethics of Jesus', in Joel B. Green, Scot McKnight, and I. Howard Marshall (eds.), *Dictionary of Jesus and the Gospels* (Downers Grove, IL: InterVarsity Press, 1992).

Husserl, Edmund, *Ideas: General Introduction to Pure Phenomenology* (London: Routledge, Kindle edn, 2013).

'Importance of Being Earnest and What Is Being Earnest?', *Impoff* (April 22, 2021), https://impoff.com/importance-of-being-earnest/.

'Insight for Living', *Counseling Insights: A Biblical Perspective on Caring for People* (Plano, TX: Insight for Living, 2007).

'International Theological Commission of the Catholic Church', *The Consciousness of Christ Concerning Himself and His Mission* (Vatican City: Libreria Editrice Vaticana, 1985).

'Interview: Rowan Williams' (Goldsmiths, University of London), https://www.gold.ac.uk/faithsunit/current-projects/reimaginingreligion/landmark-interviews/rowan-williams/.

Irenaeus, *St. Irenaeus of Lyons: Against the Heresies* (Vols. 1-3; trans. Dominic J. Unger; New York: Newman Press, 1992).

Isacco, Anthony *et al.*, 'How Religious Beliefs and Practices Influence the Psychological Health of Catholic Priests', *American Journal of Men's Health* 10.4 (July 2016), pp. 325-37.

Iseman, Lois, *Understanding Intuition: A Journey In and Out of Science* (London: Academic Press, 2018).

James, William, 'The Stream of Consciousness', *Classics in the History of Psychology*, https://psychclassics.yorku.ca/James/jimmy11.htm.

—*The Varieties of Religious Experience: A Study in Human Nature* (New York: Longmans, Green, 1902).

Jeffrey, David L., *A Dictionary of Biblical Tradition in English Literature* (Grand Rapids, MI: Eerdmans, 1992).

Jipp, Joshua W., 'The Beginnings of a Theology of Luke-Acts: Divine Activity and Human Response', *Journal of Theological Interpretation* 8.1 (2014), pp. 23-43.

Johnson, Luke Timothy, *The Acts of the Apostles* (Sacra Pagina 5; Collegeville, MN: The Liturgical Press, 1992).

—*The Gospel of Luke* (Sacra Pagina 3; Collegeville, MN: Liturgical Press, 1991).

—*Prophetic Jesus, Prophetic Church: The Challenge of Luke-Acts to Contemporary Christians* (Grand Rapids, MI: Eerdmans, 2011).

Johnson, Todd M., 'The Global Demographics of the Pentecostal and Charismatic Renewal', *Society* 46.6 (November 2009), pp. 479-83.

Johnson, Van, 'Pentecostals and Luke-Acts: Reading St. Luke in the Pre- and Post-Stronstad Eras', in Riku P. Tuppurainen (ed.), *Reading St. Luke's Text and Theology: Pentecostal Voices; Essays in Honor of Professor Roger Stronstad* (Eugene, OR: Pickwick, Kindle edn, 2019), ch. 5.

Jones, James M., John F. Davidio, and Deborah L. Vietze, *The Psychology of Diversity: Beyond Prejudice and Racism* (Chichester: Blackwell, Kindle edn, 2014).

Josephus, Flavius, *The Works of Josephus: Complete and Unabridged* (ed. and trans. William Whiston; Peabody, MA: Hendrickson, 1987).

Jung, C.G., *The Collected Works of C.G. Jung, Volume 8: Structure and Dynamic of the Psyche* (ed. and trans. Gerhard Adler and R.F.C. Hull; Princeton, NJ: Princeton University Press, Kindle 2nd edn, 1969).

—*The Collected Works of C.G. Jung, Volume 7: Two Essays in Analytical Psychology* (ed. Herbert Read, Michael Fordham, Gerhard Adler, William McGuire; trans. R.F.C. Hull; Princeton, NJ: Princeton University Press, Kindle edn, 1985).

Kankaanniemi, Matti, 'A Psychobiography of Jesus – Part 1: Personality Traits', *ABO Akademi Journal for Historical Jesus Research* 1 (2015), pp. 5-11.

Kärkkäinen, Veli-Matti, *One with God: Salvation as Deification and Justification* (Collegeville, MN: Liturgical Press, 2004).

—*Pneumatology: The Holy Spirit in Ecumenical, International, and Contextual Perspective* (Grand Rapids, MI: Baker Academic, 2002).

Kaufman, Gordon, *The Theological Imagination: Constructing the Concept of God* (Philadelphia, PA: Westminster, 1981).

Keen, Craig, *After Crucifixion: The Promise of Theology* (Eugene, OR: Cascade Books, Kindle edn, 2013).

Keener, Craig S., *Acts: An Exegetical Commentary, Volume 1: Introduction and 1:1–14:28* (Grand Rapids, MI: Baker Academic, 2012).

Kellermann, Diether, 'עָמַי', *TDOT*, V, pp. 342-43.

Kelly, Geffrey B., 'Editor's Introduction to the Reader's Edition of Dietrich Bonhoeffer's *Discipleship*', in Dietrich Bonhoeffer, *Discipleship* (Minneapolis, MN: Fortress Press, 2015), pp. vii–xx.

Kgatle, Mookgo S., 'Spirit Baptism and the Doctrine of Initial Evidence in African Pentecostal Christianity: A Critical Analysis', *HTS Theological Studies* 76.1 (March 2020), https://hts.org.za/index.php/hts/article/view/5796.

King, Patricia, 'Prophetic Activation: Discerning the Times', *Patricia King YouTube Channel* (February 15, 2020), https://www.youtube.com/watch?v=37ZFmC0vMG0.

Kirkpatrick, Robert W., *The Creative Delivery of Sermons* (New York: MacMillan, 1944).

Kiteley, David, *I Didn't Mean to Cause Trouble: Supernatural Stories* (Orlando, FL: Kudu, Kindle edn, 2017).

—'Video Interview by Mark J. Chironna' (Orlando, FL, November 19, 2018).

Koehler, Ludwig, Walter Baumgartner, and Johann Jakob Stamm, *The Hebrew and Aramaic Lexicon of the Old Testament* (Leiden: Brill, 2000).

Komonchak, Joseph A., Mary Collins, and Dermot A. Lane (eds.), *The New Dictionary of Theology* (Collegeville, MN: Liturgical Press, 2000).

Konkel, August H., *1 and 2 Kings* (NIV Application Commentary; Grand Rapids, MI: Zondervan, 2006).

Kuhn, Thomas S., *The Structure of Scientific Revolutions* (Chicago, IL: University of Chicago Press, 4th edn, 2012).

Kydd, R.A.N., 'Healing in the Christian Church', *NIDPCM*, pp. 708-709.
Kyle, Richard, 'John Knox and Apocalyptic Thought', *The Sixteenth Century Journal* 15.4 (Winter 1984), pp. 449-69.
Lakoff, George, and Mark Johnson, *Metaphors We Live By* (Chicago, IL: University of Chicago Press, 1980).
Land, Steven Jack, *Pentecostal Spirituality: A Passion for the Kingdom* (Cleveland, TN: CPT Press 2010).
—'William J. Seymour: The Father of the Holiness-Pentecostal Movement', in Henry H. Knight III (ed.), *From Aldersgate to Azusa Street: Wesleyan, Holiness, and Pentecostal Visions of the New Creation* (Eugene, OR: Pickwick, 2010).
Lasch, Christopher, *The Culture of Narcissism: American Life in an Age of Diminishing Expectations* (New York: W.W. Norton, 1979).
Lawrence, B.F., 'Back to Pentecost', *The Weekly Evangel* (May 1916).
Lawson, Steven, 'Kiteley Family a Point of Light in Troubled Oakland', *Charisma* (December 31, 2002), https://www.charismamag.com/site-archives/154-peopleevents/people-and-events/817-kiteley-family-a-point-of-light-in-troubled-oakland.
Leithart, Peter J., *1 and 2 Kings* (Brazos Theological Commentary on the Bible; Grand Rapids, MI: Brazos Press, 2006).
—*A Son to Me: An Exposition of 1 and 2 Samuel* (Moscow, ID: Canon Press, 2003).
Levine, Martha Peaslee, 'Rites of Passage with Wisdom to Grow', *Psychology Today* (August 3, 2014), https://www.psychologytoday.com/us/blog/your-write-health/201408/rites-passage-wisdom-grow.
Liddell, Henry George, R. Scott, and Henry Stuart Jones (eds.), *A Greek-English Lexicon* (Oxford: Clarendon Press, 1996).
Lindbeck, George A., *The Nature of Doctrine: Religion and Theology in a Postliberal Age* (Louisville, KY: Westminster John Knox Press, Kindle 25th anniversary edn, 2009).
Lombardo, Nicholas E., *The Logic of Desire: Aquinas on Emotion* (Washington, DC: Catholic University of America Press, 2011).
Lonergan, Bernard, *Insight: A Study of Human Understanding* (Collected Works of Bernard Lonergan 3:003; Toronto: University of Toronto Press, Kindle edn, 1957).
Louw, Johannes P., and Eugene Albert Nida (eds), *Greek-English Lexicon of the New Testament Based on Semantic Domains* (New York: United Bible Societies, 1996).
Luther, Martin, 'The Babylonian Captivity of the Church, 1520', (trans. A.T W. Steinhauser; rev. Frederick C. Ahrens and Abdel Ross Wentz), http://www.onthewing.org/user/Luther%20-%20Babylonian%20Captivity.pdf.

Macchia, Frank D., *Baptized in the Spirit: A Global Pentecostal Theology* (Grand Rapids, MI: Zondervan, 2006).

—'Finitum Capax Infiniti: A Pentecostal Distinctive?', *Pneuma: The Journal of the Society of Pentecostal Studies* 29.2 (2007), pp. 185-87.

Mackinlay, Shane, *Interpreting Excess: Jean-Luc Marion, Saturated Phenomena, and Hermeneutics* (New York: Fordham University Press, 2010).

Mangum, Douglas, and Josh Westbury (eds.), *Linguistics and Biblical Exegesis* (Lexham Methods Series 2; Bellingham, WA: Lexham Press, 2016).

Mangum, Douglas, and Wendy Widder, 'Speech-Act Theory', in John D. Barry, *et al.* (eds.), *The Lexham Bible Dictionary*, (Bellingham, WA: Lexham Press, 2016).

Marcus, Joel, *John the Baptist in History and Theology* (Studies on Personalities of the New Testament; Columbia, SC: University of South Carolina Press, Kindle edn, 2018).

Martin, Lee Roy (ed.), *Pentecostal Hermeneutics: A Reader* (Leiden: Brill, 2013).

Maslow, Abraham H., *Toward a Psychology of Being* (Floyd, VA: Sublime Books, 2014).

Mather, Hannah R.K., *The Interpreting Spirit: Spirit, Scripture, and Interpretation in the Renewal Tradition* (Eugene: OR: Pickwick Publications, Kindle edn, 2020.

Mbiti, Tim, 'What Is Postwar Disillusionment?', *eNotes*, https://www.enotes.com/homework-help/what-postwar-disillusionment-375681.

McAdams, Dan P., *The Art and Science of Personality Development* (New York: Guilford Press, 2015).

—*The Person: An Introduction to the Science of Personality Psychology* (Hoboken, NJ: John Wiley & Sons, 5th edn, 2009).

McAdams, Dan P., and Kate C. McLean, 'Narrative Identity', *Current Directions in Psychological Science* 22.3 (June 2013), pp. 233-38.

McCollam, Dan, *Basic Training for Prophetic Activation* (Vacaville, CA: iWar, 2012).

McInroy, Mark Johnson, 'Perceiving Splendor: The "Doctrine of the Spiritual Senses" in Hans Urs von Balthasar's Theological Aesthetics' (PhD Dissertation, Harvard Divinity School, 2009).

McKay, John W., 'When the Veil Is Taken Away: The Impact of Prophetic Experience on Biblical Interpretation', in Lee Roy Martin (ed.), *Pentecostal Hermeneutics: A Reader* (Leiden: Brill, 2013), p. 61.

McKnight, S., 'Ethics of Jesus', in Joel B. Green, Jeannine K. Brown, and Nicholas Perrin (eds.), *Dictionary of Jesus and the Gospels* (Downers Grove, IL: IVP Academic, 2nd edn, 2013), p. 246.

McVey, Kathleen E., 'Theoria', in Paul Corby Finney (ed.), *The Eerdmans Encyclopedia of Early Christian Art and Archaeology* (Grand Rapids, MI: Eerdmans, 2017), p. 595.

Meier, Samuel A., *Themes and Transformations in Old Testament Prophecy* (Downers Grove, IL: IVP Academic, 2009).
Merriam-Webster.com Dictionary, https://www.merriam-webster.com.
Merton, Thomas, *New Seeds of Contemplation* (New York: New Directions, 2007).
Meyer Everts, Janet, 'Conversion and Call of Paul', in Gerald F. Hawthorne, Ralph P. Martin, and Daniel G. Reid (eds.), *Dictionary of Paul and His Letters* (Downers Grove, IL: InterVarsity Press, 1993), p. 156.
'Michael Polanyi and Tacit Knowledge', https://infed.org/mobi/michael-polanyi-and-tacit-knowledge/.
Mittelstadt, Martin William, *Reading Luke–Acts in the Pentecostal Tradition* (Cleveland, TN: CPT Press, Kindle edn, 2010).
Moes, Paul, and Donald J. Tellinghuisen, *Exploring Psychology and Christian Faith: An Introductory Guide* (Grand Rapids, MI: Baker Academic, 2014).
Moltmann, Jürgen, *The Crucified God: The Cross of Christ as the Foundation and Criticism of Christian Theology* (Minneapolis, MN: Fortress Press, 1993).
Mooney, Edward F., in Bruce Ellis Benson and Norman Wirzba (eds.), *The Phenomenology of Prayer* (Perspectives in Continental Philosophy; New York: Fordham University Press, 2005), pp. 50-62.
Moore, Rickie D., 'Revelation: The Light and Fire of Pentecost', in Wolfgang Vondey (ed.), *The Routledge Handbook of Pentecostal Theology* (London: Routledge, Kindle edn, 2020), ch. 5.
—*The Spirit of the Old Testament* (JPTSup 35; Blandford Forum: Deo, 2011).
Moore, Rickie D., and Brian Neil Peterson, *Voice, Word, and Spirit: A Pentecostal Old Testament Survey* (Nashville, TN: Abingdon Press, Kindle edn, 2017).
Moran, Dermot, and Joseph Cohen, *The Husserl Dictionary* (London: Continuum, 2012).
Moreau, A. Scott, Harold Netland, and Charles van Engen, *Evangelical Dictionary of World Missions* (Baker Reference Library; Grand Rapids, MI: Baker Books, 2000).
Munzinger, Andre, *Discerning the Spirits: Theological and Ethical Hermeneutics in Paul* (Cambridge: Cambridge University Press, Kindle edn, 2007).
Nagel, Thomas, 'What Is It Like to Be a Bat?', *Philosophical Review* 83.4 (Oct. 1974), pp. 435-50.
Nation, Garry D., 'The Restoration Movement', *Christianity Today* (May 18, 1992).
Nesteruk, Alexei V., *The Sense of the Universe: Philosophical Explication of Theological Commitment in Modern Cosmology* (Minneapolis, MN: Fortress Press, 2015).
'Nicene-Constantinople Creed', *MIT*, http://web.mit.edu/ocf/www/nicene_creed.html.

Nissinen, Martti, *Prophets and Prophecy in the Ancient Near East* (ed. Peter Machinist; Writings from the Ancient World; Atlanta, GA: Society of Biblical Literature, 2003).

Norton, Albert, *Intuition of Significance: Evidence against Materialism and for God* (Eugene, OR: Resource Publications, digital edn, 2020).

Nouwen, Henri, *Discernment: Reading the Signs of Daily Life* (Oxford: SPCK, Kindle edn, 2013).

Oden, Thomas C., *First and Second Timothy and Titus* (Interpretation: A Bible Commentary for Teaching and Preaching; Louisville, KY: John Knox Press, 1989).

—*John Wesley's Teachings, Volume 3, Pastoral Theology* (Grand Rapids, MI: Zondervan, 2012).

O'Loughlin, Thomas, *The Didache: A Window on the Earliest Christians* (London: Baker Academic, 2010).

Olsen, David C., *Integrative Family Therapy* (Creative Pastoral Care and Counseling Series; Minneapolis, MN: Fortress Press, 1993).

Online Etymology Dictionary, https://www.etymonline.com.

Osborne, Kenan B., 'The Communion of the Saints', in Joseph A. Komonchak, Mary Collins, and Dermot A. Lane (eds.), *The New Dictionary of Theology* (Collegeville, MN: Liturgical Press, 2000), p. 214.

Ozman, Agnes, 'Personal Testimony of Being the First Person to Receive the Holy Ghost at "Stones Folly" in Topeka Kansas (January 1, 1901)', *Apostolic Archives International*, https://www.apostolicarchives.com/articles/article/8801925/173171.htm.

Pelikan, Jaroslav, *Acts* (Brazos Theological Commentary on the Bible; Grand Rapids, MI: Brazos Press, 2005).

Penn, Amanda, 'Mythology and Psychology: Myth Tells Us Who We Are', *Shortform* (blog, November 15, 2019), https://www.shortform.com/blog/mythology-and-psychology/.

Peterson, Eugene H., *Working the Angles: The Shape of Pastoral Integrity* (Grand Rapids, MI: Eerdmans, 1987).

Philemon, Leulseged, *Pneumatic Hermeneutics: The Role of the Holy Spirit in the Theological Interpretation of Scripture* (Cleveland, TN: CPT Press, 2019).

Pi, Youguo, *et al.*, 'Theory of Cognitive Pattern Recognition', in Peng-Yeng Yin (ed.), *Pattern Recognition Techniques, Technology and Applications* (Intech, 2008), pp. 433-62.

Polanyi, Michael, *The Tacit Dimension* (Chicago, IL: University of Chicago Press, 1966).

Ponticus, Evagrius, *Ad Monacho* (Ancient Christian Writers; ed. Dennis McManus; trans. Jeremy Driscoll; New York: Newman Press, 2003), LIX.

Preuss, Horst Dietrich, 'יָצָא', *TDOT*, IV, pp. 225-26.

Prevot, Andrew, 'Reversèd Thunder: The Significance of Prayer for Political Theology', *The Other Journal: An Intersection of Theology and Culture* (September 17, 2012), https://theotherjournal.com/2012/09/17/reversed-thunder-the-significance-of-prayer-for-political-theology/.

Price, Ira M., 'The Schools of the Sons of the Prophets', *Old Testament Student* 8.7 (March 1889), pp. 244-49.

Psychology iResearchnet, http://psychology.iresearchnet.com.

Pyles, David, 'A Double Portion of Thy Spirit', http://www.bcbsr.com/survey/eli.html.

Raith II, Charles (ed.), *The Book of Acts: Catholic, Orthodox, and Evangelical Readings* (Washington, DC: Catholic University of America Press, 2019).

Reid, Daniel G., *et al.* (eds.), *Dictionary of Christianity in America* (Downers Grove, IL: InterVarsity Press, 1990).

Reuschling, Wyndy Corbin, 'The Means and End in 2 Peter 1:3–11: The Theological and Moral Significance of Theōsis', *Journal of Theological Interpretation* 8.2 (Fall 2014), pp. 275-86.

Rich, Anthony D., *Discernment in the Desert Fathers: Diakrisis in the Life and Thought of Early Egyptian Monasticism* (Carlisle: Paternoster Press, 2007).

Ridley, D. Scott, 'Reflective Self-Awareness: A Basic Motivational Process', *Journal of Experimental Education* 60.1 (Fall 1991), pp. 31-48.

Roberts-Miller, Patricia, *Rhetoric and Demagoguery* (Carbondale, IL: Southern Illinois University Press, 2019).

Rogers, Eugene F. Jr, *The Holy Spirit: Classic and Contemporary Readings* (Chichester: Wiley-Blackwell, Kindle edn, 2009).

Roszia, Sharon K., and Allison D. Maxon, *Seven Core Issues in Adoption and Permanency: A Comprehensive Guide to Promoting Understanding and Healing in Adoption, Foster Care, Kinship Families and Third Party Reproduction* (London: Jessica Kingsley, Kindle edn, 2019).

Rotenstreich, Nathan, 'On Prophetic Consciousness', *Journal of Religion* 54.3 (July 1974), pp. 185-98.

Ruelas, Abraham, *Women and the Landscape of American Higher Education: Wesleyan Holiness and Pentecostal Founders* (Eugene, OR: Pickwick, Kindle edn, 2010).

Russell, Norman (trans.), *The Lives of the Desert Fathers* (Collegeville, MN: Cistercian Publications, 1981).

Rutledge, Fleming, *And God Spoke to Abraham: Preaching from the Old Testament* (Grand Rapids, MI: Eerdmans, 2011).

Ryken, Leland, Jim Wilhoit, and Tremper Longman III (eds.), *Dictionary of Biblical Imagery* (Downers Grove, IL: InterVarsity Press, 2000).

Sanford, John A., *Mystical Christianity: A Psychological Commentary on the Gospel of John* (New York: Crossroad, 1993).

Sarna, Nahum M., *Exodus* (JPS Torah Commentary; Philadelphia, PA: Jewish Publication Society, 1991).

Scharmer, C. Otto, *Presencing: Illuminating the Blind Spot of Leadership* (Massachusetts Institute of Technology, January 2002).
—*Theory U: Leading from the Future as It Emerges; The Social Technology of Presencing* (Oakland, CA: Berrett-Koehler, 2nd edn, 2009).
Schlamm, Leon, 'Individuation', David A. Leeming (ed.), *Encyclopedia of Psychology and Religion* (Boston, MA: Springer, 2014).
—'Inflation', in David A. Leeming (ed.), *Encyclopedia of Psychology and Religion* (Boston, MA: Springer, 2014).
Schnabel, Eckhard J., *Acts* (Zondervan Exegetical Commentary on the New Testament; Grand Rapids, MI: Zondervan, expanded edn, 2012).
Schneiders, Sandra Marie, *New Wineskins: Re-Imagining Religious Life Today* (New York: Paulist Press, 1986).
Scholer, Abigail A., *et al.*, 'New Directions in Self-Regulation: The Role of Metamotivational Beliefs', *Current Directions in Psychological Science* 27.6 (2018), pp. 437-42.
Sean and Christa Smith Ministries, *Prophetic Activation Series*, https://seansmithministries.com/product/the-prophetic-activation-series/.
'The Serpent's Seed', *Voice of God Recordings*, https://branham.org/en/biblestudy/TheSerpentSeed.
Seymour, William J., 'Questions Answered', *Apostolic Faith* (June–September 1907).
Shannon, William H., 'Intuition', in Michael Downey (ed.), *The New Dictionary of Catholic Spirituality* (Collegeville, MN: Liturgical Press, 2000), p. 555.
Sheppard, G.T., 'Pentecostals and the Hermeneutics of Dispensationalism', *Pneuma: The Journal of the Society of Pentecostal Studies* 6.2 (Fall 1984), pp. 5-33.
Sherman, David K., and Geoffrey L. Cohen, 'The Psychology of Self-Defense: Self-Affirmation Theory', *Advances in Experimental Social Psychology* 38 (2006), pp. 183-242.
Short Wave, 'Understanding Unconscious Bias', *NPR* (July 15, 2020), https://www.npr.org/2020/07/14/891140598/understanding-unconscious-bias.
Sieler, Alan, *Coaching to the Human Soul: Ontological Coaching and Deep Change. Volume 1, Linguistic Basics of Ontological Coaching* (Australia: Victoria Newfield, 2005).
Simpson, Charles, 'Internal Integrity and External Integration of Structures by Charles Simpson 1985' (PDF transcript of sermon presented in 1985).
Slager, Donald, Preface to Roger A. Bullard and Howard A. Hatton, *A Handbook on Sirach* (United Bible Societies' Handbooks; New York: United Bible Societies, 2008).

Smith, Gordon T., *The Voice of Jesus: Discernment, Prayer and the Witness of the Spirit* (Westmont, IL: IVP Books, Kindle edn, 2015).

Smith, James K.A., *Thinking in Tongues: Pentecostal Contributions to Christian Philosophy* (Grand Rapids, MI: Eerdmans, 2010).

Soanes, Catherine, and Angus Stevenson (eds.), *Concise Oxford English Dictionary* (Oxford: Oxford University Press, 2004).

Sokolowski, Robert, *Introduction to Phenomenology* (Cambridge: Cambridge University Press, 2000).

Solc, Vladislav, 'Concept of Sublimation in Psychology of Sigmund Freud and Carl Gustav Jung', *Therapy Vlado*, https://therapyvlado.com/english /concept-of-sublimation-in-psychology-of-sigmund-freud-and-carl-gustav-jung/.

Soulen, R. Kendall, *Distinguishing the Voices. Volume 1: The Divine Name(s) and the Holy Trinity* (Louisville, KY: Westminster John Knox Press, 2011).

Steinbock, Anthony J., *Phenomenology and Mysticism: The Verticality of Religious Experience* (Bloomington, IN: Indiana University Press, 2007).

Stronstad, Roger, 'Pentecostal Hermeneutics', *Pneuma* 15.2 (Fall 1993), pp. 215-22.

Swanson, James, *Dictionary of Biblical Languages with Semantic Domains: Hebrew (Old Testament)* (Oak Harbor: Logos Research Systems, 1997).

Swearingen, Chet, and Phyllis Swearingen, '1948 Latter Rain Revival', https://romans1015.com/latter-rain/.

Sweeney, Marvin A., *Jewish Mysticism: From Ancient Times through Today* (Grand Rapids, MI: Eerdmans, 2020).

Symington, Alexander Macleod, *The Life and Ministry of John the Baptist* (Vox Clamantis London: Religious Tract Society, n.d.).

Tallis, Frank, *The Act of Living* (New York: Basic Books, Kindle edn, 2020).

Tam, Ekman P.C., 'Silence of God and God of Silence', *Asia Journal of Theology* 16.1 (2002), pp. 152-63.

Taylor and Francis Group, 'Earliest Memories Can Start from the Age of Two-and-a-Half: New Study and a Review of Decades of Data Pushes the Memory Clock Back Over a Year, but the Study Confirms Everyone Is Different', *ScienceDaily* (June 14, 2021), www.sciencedaily.com/releases/2021/06/210614110824.htm.

Thiselton, Anthony C., *First Corinthians: A Shorter Exegetical and Pastoral Commentary* (Grand Rapids, MI: Eerdmans, 2006).

—*The First Epistle to the Corinthians: A Commentary on the Greek Text* (New International Greek Testament Commentary; Grand Rapids, MI: Eerdmans, 2000).

—*The Thiselton Companion to Christian Theology* (Grand Rapids, MI: Eerdmans, 2015).

Thomas, John Christopher, 'Pentecostal Biblical Interpretation', in Steven L. McKenzie (ed.), *Oxford Encyclopedia of Biblical Interpretation* (Oxford: Oxford University Press, 2013), II, pp. 89-97.

—'Pentecostal Theology in the Twenty-First Century', *Pneuma: The Journal of the Society of Pentecostal Studies* 20.1 (Spring 1998), pp. 3-19.

Thornton, Stephen P., 'Sigmund Freud (1856–1939)', in James Fieser and Bradley Dowden (eds.), *Internet Encyclopedia of Philosophy*, https://iep.utm.edu/freud/#SH7d.

Tilley, T.W., 'Narrative Theology', in Joseph A. Komonchak, Mary Collins, and Dermot A. Lane (eds.), *The New Dictionary of Theology* (Collegeville, MN: Liturgical Press, 2000), pp. 702-703.

Tillich, Paul, *The Shaking of the Foundations* (Eugene, OR: Wipf & Stock, 2011).

Torrance, James B., *Worship, Community, and the Triune God of Grace* (Carlisle: Paternoster Press, 1996).

Treptow, Earle, '"For Us and for Our Salvation … He Became Truly Human": The Translation of the Nicene Creed in Christian Worship', Preliminary draft for an intended future article in *Wisconsin Lutheran Quarterly*, https:/static1.squarespace.com/static/5c75c39016b6407f48ef57c1/t/5faf16fae44daa6be0182eb4/1605310202747/cw-nicene-creed.pdf.

Tsevat, M., 'חָקַר', *TDOT*, V, pp. 148-49.

Tsumura, David Toshio, *The First Book of Samuel* (New International Commentary on the Old Testament; Grand Rapids, MI: Eerdmans, 2007).

Underhill, Evelyn, *The Mystic Way: A Psychological Study in Christian Origins* (London: J. M. Dent & Sons, 1913).

van Gennep, Arnold, *The Rites of Passage* (Chicago, IL: University of Chicago Press, Kindle 2nd edn, 2019).

van Wijk-Bos, Johanna W.H., *Reading Samuel: A Literary and Theological Commentary* (Reading the Old Testament Series; Macon: Smyth & Helwys, 2011).

van Winkle, P., *The Christophanies* (Galaxie Software, 2005).

Volf, Miroslav, *Exclusion and Embrace: A Theological Exploration of Identity, Otherness, and Reconciliation* (Nashville, TN: Abingdon Press, Kindle edn, 2019).

—*Free of Charge: Giving and Forgiving in a Culture Stripped of Grace* (Grand Rapids, MI: Zondervan, digital edn, 2009).

von Balthasar, Hans Urs, *The Glory of the Lord: A Theological Aesthetics, Volume 1, Seeing the Form* (trans. Erasmo Leiva-Merikakis; San Francisco, CA: Ignatius Press, 2009).

Vondey, Wolfgang, *Pentecostalism: A Guide for the Perplexed* (London: Bloomsbury T&T Clark, 2013).

—*Pentecostal Theology: Living the Full Gospel* (Systematic Pentecostal and Charismatic Theology; London: Bloomsbury T&T Clark, 2017).

Wallace, Daniel B., *The Basics of New Testament Syntax: An Intermediate Greek Grammar* (Grand Rapids, MI: Zondervan, 2000).

Walsh, Jerome T., *1 Kings* (Berit Olam Studies in Hebrew Narrative and Poetry; Collegeville, MN: Liturgical Press, 1996).

Ware, Steven L., 'Restorationism in Classical Pentecostalism', *NIDPCM*, p. 1019.

Warrington, Keith, *Pentecostal Theology: A Theology of Encounter* (London: T&T Clark, 2008).

Weinandy, Thomas G., 'Response: Paul's Conversion in His Own Words', in Charles Raith (ed.), *The Book of Acts: Catholic, Orthodox, and Evangelical Readings* (Washington, DC: Catholic University of America Press, 2019), p. 180.

Wenk, Matthias, 'What is Prophetic about Prophecies: Inspiration or Critical Memory? A Fresh Look at Prophets and Prophecy in the New Testament and Contemporary Pentecostalism', *Journal of Pentecostal Theology* 26.2 (September 2017), pp. 178-95.

Wesley, John, *Explanatory Notes upon the New Testament* (New York: J. Soule and T. Mason, 4th edn, 1818).

—*The Works of John Wesley* (London: Wesleyan Methodist Book Room, 3rd edn, 1872).

'What Did Wittgenstein Say?', *Philosophy*, https://philosophy-question.com/library/lecture/read/347674-what-did-wittgenstein-say#0.

'What the Foursquare Church Believes', *The Foursquare Church*, https://foursquare-org.s3.amazonaws.com/resources/Print_Brochure_What_Foursquare_Believes_English.pdf.

Wierwille, Jerry, 'An Overview of Exegetical Fallacies', *Study Driven Faith* (December 15, 2016), http://studydrivenfaith.org/2016/12/an-overview-of-exegetical-fallacies/.

Wilhite, Shawn J., 'Thirty-Five Years Later: A Summary of *Didache* Scholarship Since 1983', *Currents in Biblical Research* 17.3 (2019), pp. 266-305.

Williams, J.G., 'The Prophetic "Father"', *Journal of Biblical Literature* 85 (1966), pp. 344-48.

Williams, Rowan, *Christ the Heart of Creation* (London: Bloomsbury Continuum, 2018).

—'Overcoming Political Tribalism', *ABC Religion and Ethics* (October 2, 2019), https://www.abc.net.au/religion/rowan-williams-overcoming-political-tribalism/11566242.

—*The Way of St. Benedict* (London: Bloomsbury Continuum, 2020).

Wills, Lawrence M., 'Ascetic Theology Before Asceticism? Jewish Narratives and the Decentering of the Self', *Journal of the American Academy of Religion* 74.4 (December 2006), pp. 902-25.

Wilson, Robert R., *Prophecy and Society in Ancient Israel* (Philadelphia, PA: Fortress Press 1980).

Witthoff, David (ed.), *The Lexham Cultural Ontology Glossary* (Bellingham, WA: Lexham Press, 2014).

Wolfe, Tom, 'The "Me" Decade and the Third Great Awakening', *New York* (April 8, 2008), https://nymag.com/news/features/45938/.

Wood, Ralph C., 'Divine Action and Human Response: Four Theological and Visual Interpretations of Paul's Conversion in Acts 9', in Charles Raith (ed.), *The Book of Acts: Catholic, Orthodox, and Evangelical Readings* (Washington, DC: Catholic University of America Press, 2019), p. 139.

Word Sense Dictionary, https://www.wordsense.eu/.

Wright, Terence C., 'Prayer and Interiority', in Bruce Ellis Benson and Norman Wirzba (eds.), *The Phenomenology of Prayer* (Perspectives in Continental Philosophy; New York: Fordham University Press, 2005), pp. 134-41.

Yong, Amos, *An Amos Yong Reader: The Pentecostal Spirit* (ed. Christopher A. Stephenson; Eugene, OR: Cascade Books, 2020).

—*Renewing the Church by the Spirit: Theological Education after Pentecost.* (Theological Education between the Times; Grand Rapids, MI: Eerdmans, 2020).

—*Spirit of Love: A Trinitarian Theology of Grace* (Waco, TX: Baylor University Press, 2012).

—*The Spirit Poured Out on All Flesh: Pentecostalism and the Possibility of Global Theology* (Grand Rapids, MI: Baker Academic, 2005).

—*Spirit-Word-Community: Theological Hermeneutics in Trinitarian Perspective* (Eugene, OR: Wipf & Stock, 2002).

—'What Spirit(s), Which Public(s)?: The Pneumatologies of Global Pentecostal-Charismatic Christianity', *International Journal of Public Theology* 7.3 (January 2013), pp. 241-59.

'You Don't Know What You Don't Know: The Four States of Competence', *Movementum*, https://movementum.co.uk/journal/competence.

Zipor, M., 'קָשָׁה', *TDOT*, XIII, pp. 189-92.

Zodhiates, Spiros, *The Complete Word Study Dictionary: New Testament* (Chattanooga, TN: AMG, 2000).

Zornberg, Avivah Gottlieb, *Moses: A Human Life* (New Haven, CT: Yale University Press, Kindle edn, 2016).

Index of Biblical (and Other Ancient) References

Genesis		3.14	79	21.10-12	142
1.26-27	214	3.14-15	80	21.18	102
3.1-7	185	4.1	87		
3.17	84	4.6-7	87	Numbers	
3.22-24	184	4.14	78	6	95
12.3	159	4.18	77	6.1-12	142
15.1-6	163	4.22	155	10.29	77
20.7	162, 255	5.1	100, 155	12.8	162
22.2	119	6.9	176	26.59	73
22.11-13	162	6.20	73	27.18-23	228
22.17	238	7.3	99		
37.3	115	7.5	105	Deuteronomy	
37.5	115	7.17	155	4.34	99
37.9	115	8.1	155	6.4	103
41.13	230	8.20	155	6.14	100
46.1-4	162	9.1	155	6.16	185
48.14	228	9.13	155	7.1-7	101
49.13-15	116	10.3	155	8.2	185
		11.4	155	11.12	101
Exodus		15.25	186	11.14	101
1.15	73	16.1-12	185	15.18	176
1.22	73	19.1-24	128	17.9	230
2.1	73	19.1-20.20	80	17.14-20	89
2.2	73	19.16	162	18.15	72, 82, 88,
2.11	83, 85	19.16-20	162		182, 195
2.15	77	20.12	117	18.15-18	162
2.16-17	77	24.1-11	80	18.18	88
2.19	77	28.4	96	19.17	230
2.23-25	74	32.1-35	185	21.17	118, 122, 286
3.1	77, 85-86	32.27	155	26.1-11	93
3.1-10	162	33.11	118	27.24	171
3.1-22	128	33.12-13	110	31.27	176
3.1–4.17	80, 141	33.13-15	110	32.4	68, 256
3.3	162	33.21-22	111	33.18-19	116
3.4	78	Leviticus		34.9	228
3.4-15	163	4.7	105	34.10-12	182
3.6	84	10.8-11	142		
3.11	84	13.45	87	Joshua	
3.12	78	13.46	87	4.2-3	105
3.13	78	19.18	262	7.13	155

Index of Biblical (and Other Ancient) References 391

17.11	116	9.9	72, 89	17.1	100, 107, 140, 160
24.2	155	9.16	89		
		10	98	17.1-2	100
Judges		10.1-8	154	17.2	222
4.11	77	10.2	98	17.3-24	112
6.8	155	10.2-5	93	17.8	222
6.11-18	163	10.2-7	89	17.14	155
7.22	116	10.2-8	98	17.21	186
9.12-15	246	10.5	2	18	216, 223
13.8-20	163	10.5-6	98	18.1	222
14–16	142	10.9-13	90	18.4	113
21.25	89	10.10	2, 98	18.13	120
		10.16	155	18.15-17	100
1 Samuel		15.1	88	18.16-40	140
1.5	122	15.2	155	18.17	100
1.6-11	94	15.27	96	18.18	100
1.10-11	95	16.1	114	18.21	101, 102, 103
1.12-14	94	19.18-22	96	18.22	101, 103
1.17	94-95	19.18-24	2, 93	18.24	103
1.20	95	19.20	93, 94	18.25	102
1.20-28	96	25.3	176	18.26	104
2	91			18.31	222
2.1-10	292	2 Samuel		18.36-37	105
2.12-17	89, 91, 95, 142	7.4	222	18.37	106
		7.5	155	18.41	98
2.19	96	7.8	155	18.44	216
2.22-24	142	12	89	19.1-2	106
2.22-25	89	12.7	155	19.1-14	146
2.27-34	89	12.11	155	19.2	145
2.27-36	142	22.15	162	19.3	119
3.1	90, 92, 98	24.11	222	19.4	145, 147
3.1-10	162	24.12	155	19.4-10	106
3.2	91			19.9	108, 109, 222
3.3	91	1 Kings		19.10	109, 110
3.4-9	92	4.12	116	19.11	110, 114
3.5-7	91	6.11	222	19.12-13	111
3.9	91, 92	11.29-30	154	19.13	111
3.10	92, 162	11.31	155	19.14	113
3.19	92	11.31-35	158	19.15	115
3.20	89, 90, 142, 162	12.24	155	19.15-16	112
		13.2	155	19.16	113, 116
3.21	92	13.20	222	19.18	112
8.1-3	142	13.21	155	19.19	113, 114, 119
8.1-6	95	14.7	155	19.20	107, 115
8.1-22	142	16.1	222	19.20-21	117
8.4	96	16.31-33	100	20.13	155
9.8	90	17–18	157	20.14	155

20.28	155	4.16	306	23.4	171
20.42	155	4.18-37	305	24.7-8	191
21.17	222	4.23	307	24.10	191
21.19	155	4.27	305	31.5	68
21.25	141	4.36-37	169	40.7	287
21.28	222	4.38-41	113, 126	46.10	260
22.11	155	4.43	155	77.17	162
		6.1-7	113	95.3-7	191
2 Kings		6.15-17	300	96.4	162
1.1-18	158	6.17	123, 129	104.3	128
1.4	155	7.1	155	119.11	292
1.6	155	9.3	155	133	221
1.16	155	9.6	155	139.3	267
1.17-18	119	9.12	155	143.6	162
2.1	118	19.6	155	146.3-9	191
2.1-7	2	19.20	155		
2.1-12	285	19.32	155	Proverbs	
2.1-18	89, 112	20.1	155	28.8	267
2.2	119, 125, 300	20.4	222		
2.3	119, 120, 121, 300	20.5	155	Isaiah	
		21.12	155	2.1	97, 98
2.4	119, 125, 300			3.16	155
2.5	119, 121, 300	1 Chronicles		6	284
2.6	119, 125, 300	5.26	158	6.1	285
2.7	119, 121	6.22-30	90	6.9-10	161, 264
2.8	121	9.22	90, 230	40.31	275
2.9	122	12.32	116, 241	42.1-4	186
2.10	107, 122, 301	22.8	222	42.18-22	207
2.10-11	128	23.12-14	73	49.1-6	186
2.10-14	116	26.28	90	50.4-11	186
2.11	112, 123, 129, 300, 302	28.18	129	52–53	186
		29.29	90	60.21	246
2.11-12	285, 299			61.3	246
2.12	112, 121, 125, 126, 302	2 Chronicles		65.16	46, 68, 80, 129, 247
		11.2	222		
		12.7	222		
2.13-14	115	26.16-21	285	Jeremiah	
2.14	124			1.1-10	140
2.15	2	Job		1.2	222
2.21	155	4.13	102	1.4	222
3.10	119	29.18	81	1.5	75, 162
3.11	118			1.11	63, 222
3.11-12	118	Psalms		1.11-12	97
3.16	155	1.3	246	1.11-13	64
3.17	155	16	279	1.12	64, 65
4.1-7	126	16.7-8	278	1.13	222
4.9	306	17.14	162	2.1	222
4.10	307				

Index of Biblical (and Other Ancient) References   393

2.31	155	14.2	222	10.6	162
4.13	129	14.12	222		
13.1-2	154	15.1	222	Hosea	
13.1-11	160	16.1	222	14.9	267
13.3	222	17.1	222		
13.8	222	17.11	222	Joel	
16.1	222	18.1	222	1	220
18.5	222	20.45	222	1–2	212
19.1-2	154	21.1	222	2.14	113
23.18	100, 107,	21.8	222	2.23	137
	116, 123,	21.18	222	2.23-32	216
	128, 162	22.1	222	2.28	181, 283
23.18-20	78	22.17	222	2.28-29	50
24.4	222	22.23	222	2.30	181
26.15	21	22.30	191		
28.12	222	23.1	222	Amos	
32.6	222	24.1	222	1.1	98
32.16-25	186	24.15	222	3.7	94
32.23	222	24.20	222	3.11	155
33	25	25.1	222	5.14	209
33.1	222	26.1	222	5.16	155
33.11	212	27.1	222		
33.19	222	28.1	222	Jonah	
34.12	222	28.11	222	1.1	222
36.27	222	28.20	222	2.1	186
39.15	222	29.1	222	3.1	222
42.7	222	29.17	222		
		30.1	222	Micah	
Ezekiel		30.20	222	1.1	98
1.1-28	130	31.1	222		
1.3	128, 222	32.1	222	Nahum	
1.4	128, 162	32.17	222	1.2	155
1.4-28	123	33.1	222		
1.7	162	33.23	222	Habakkuk	
1.13	162	34.1	222	2.2	98
2.1-9	130	34.25-29	259	3.1	186
3.1-12	130	35.1	222	3.2	221
3.16	222	36.16	222	3.4	74, 273
4.13	155	37	221	3.8	129
6.1	222	37.1	259		
7.1	222	37.15	222	Haggai	
10.1-5	123	38.1	222	1.6	155
11.14	222			2.20	222
12.17	222	Daniel			
12.21	222	7	123	Zechariah	
12.26	222	9.2	222	1.16	155
13.1	222	9.3-19	186	4.8	222

6.9	222	23.6	296	3.16	143, 144, 181
7.1	222	23.7	296	3.17	143
7.8	222	23.13-29	246	3.19	142
		23.33	143	3.21	294
Malachi		24.11	245	3.21-22	185, 186, 283
3	45	24.24	245	3.22	184, 189, 190
4.5	141			3.38	184
4.5-6	72, 113	Mark		4.1-12	190
4.6	122	1.6	115, 149	4.5-8	185
		10.40	122	4.13	186
Matthew		14.36	279	4.14	76, 186
1.1	260			4.14-15	186
3.7	143	Luke		4.16-21	180
3.8	247	1	269	4.17	150, 287
4.13-14	126	1.1-4	183	4.23-27	180
4.17	260, 261	1.2	140	4.24	150, 180
5–7	25	1.6	141	4.27	150
5.4	127, 297	1.8-17	179	4.28	181
5.5	296	1.12-17	179	4.28-30	185
5.6	297	1.15	142, 144	4.31-37	186
5.11-12	295	1.17	140, 145	4.38-41	183, 186
5.8	286	1.30-37	179	5.1-11	183
5.20	246	1.31	179	5.12-14	183
7.15	257	1.31-32	179	5.15-16	294
7.15-16	257	1.35	179	5.17-26	183
7.15-20	245, 253	1.38	269	6.6-11	183
7.16	245	1.42	279	6.23	150
7.21	246	1.46-55	292	7.1-10	183
9.27	260	1.68-79	143	7.11-17	183
10.18	178	1.70	150	7.12-13	294
11.25-26	259	1.76	140, 150	7.16	150, 181
11.27-30	260	1.80	141, 142	7.18-22	144
11.29	271, 296	2.25-38	190	7.18-23	144
12.23	260	2.29-32	292	7.22-23	146
12.34	143	2.48	184	7.26	150
15.22	260	2.49	189, 190	7.27	147
16.21-22	236	2.51	190	7.28	143, 150
17.11-13	147	2.52	184, 190	7.39	150
18.4	258	3.1	138	8.22-25	183
18.5	258	3.2	140	8.26-33	183
19.13	228	3.3	143	9.8	150
21.9	260	3.4	143, 150	9.18	294
21.15	260	3.4-17	143	9.19	150
21.43	247	3.7	141, 142, 143, 144	9.28-29	294
23.2	296			9.28-36	187
23.4	296	3.8	143	9.30-31	181
23.5	296	3.9	142	9.31	141

Index of Biblical (and Other Ancient) References 395

9.44	156	24.25-27	179	Acts	
9.51	120	24.26	289	1.1	181
9.51-56	158	24.27	150, 291	1.1-2	289
10.19	171	24.31	281, 291	1.2	181
10.24	150	24.32	291	1.2-3	267
10.25-37	262	24.36	288, 291	1.6-7	235
10.38-42	162	24.44	150	1.8	157, 158
11.1	294	24.45	267, 291	1.13-17	159
11.4	150	24.46	164	2	181
11.47	150	24.50	228	2.4	181, 262, 298
11.49	150			2.14-21	50, 161
11.50	150	John		2.14-36	161
13.28	150	1.15	272	2.16	150
13.33	181	1.17	80	2.17	181, 283
13.33-34	145, 150	1.20	147	2.19	181
16.16	150	1.21	146, 147	2.22	182
16.29	150	1.33-34	148	2.25	278
16.31	150	1.35-40	272	2.25-28	278
18.31	150	1.36	272	2.30	150
18.32	156	1.38	272, 273	2.32	277
19.9-10	191	1.39	274	2.33	182
19.41	190	3.16	104	2.36	277
19.46	190	3.21	292	2.39	283
20.6	150	4.9	158	2.42	23
22.3	186	5.19	274, 278	2.44-45	152
22.31	186	8.56	162	3.17	192
22.31-32	162, 282, 294	11.35	127	3.17-26	88
22.39-46	187, 191	11.41-42	294	3.18	150
22.42-44	186	14.6	46	3.19-22	297
22.43-44	191	14.6-7	256	3.21	150, 210, 212, 229, 235
23.28-31	192	14.17	68	3.22	72, 182
23.34	192	15.5	295	3.22-23	150
23.36-37	186	15.6	247	3.24	88, 150
23.39	186	15.7	294	3.25	2
23.44-46	191	15.26	68, 256	4.30	217
24.13-23	286	16.12	239	5.1-11	171
24.13-32	285	16.12-14	256	5.38-39	173
24.13-48	18	16.13	20, 46, 67, 68, 239, 247, 258	6	228
24.15	288			7.2	162
24.15-20	288	17	221	7.25	192
24.16	144, 281, 289	17.17	256	7.37	150
24.19	150, 181	17.18	256	7.58	176
24.21	144, 164, 236	17.21	278	8.1	158
24.24-31	286	18.37	20	8.20-24	171
24.25	20, 144, 150, 237, 238, 281, 289	18.37-38	256	9	171
				9.1	162, 176

9.1-9	159	15.28	24, 259	2.2	268, 280	
9.3	175	15.32	150	2.10	305	
9.5	163	16.9-10	161	2.11	280	
9.6	163	16.37	170	2.14	267, 268	
9.8	171	17.28	37, 265, 285	2.16	271	
9.8-9	162	20.13	156	3.10	212, 217	
9.11-12	164	20.22	155	9.1	175	
9.15	178	20.23	153, 155,	11.1	175	
9.15-16	164		156, 169, 177	12–14	174	
9.16	174, 178	20.24	177	12.7	222	
9.17	165, 172	20.28	230	12.10	262, 280	
9.18	165	20.38	155	12.12-27	162	
9.18-22	165	21	152	12.18	221	
9.19-22	172	21.4	153	12.28	166, 167	
9.23-25	165	21.8-10	153	13.8	21	
9.26-27	165	21.9	152	13.9	121, 239,	
9.28-29	165	21.10-11	54, 153		245, 304	
9.30	165	21.11	159, 292	13.10	240	
10.9-16	158	21.13	156	14	270	
10.13	161	21.14	156	14.1	41	
10.28	158, 161	21.27	156	14.3	42	
10.34	158	21.29-33	156	14.29	170	
10.44	161	22.6-7	176	14.32	11	
11	153	22.25-28	170	15.1	222	
11.9	158	26.13	162	15.4	164, 222	
11.19-20	158	26.13-14	176	15.8	176	
11.21	158, 216, 217	26.14	176			
11.23	158	28	161	2 Corinthians		
11.25-26	165	28.26-27	161	3.6	57	
11.26	165	28.28	161	3.16-17	57	
11.27-28	150	28.31	161	3.17	39, 57	
11.28	154			10.6	106	
11.29-30	165	Romans				
13	170, 177	7.19-25	18	Galatians		
13.1	166	8.15	279	1.12	176	
13.1-3	166, 226	8.27	267	1.13	161	
13.9	170	12.1-2	268, 283	1.15	75, 162, 177	
13.9-10	170	12.5	162	1.16	176	
13.10	171	14.1	262	2.8	161	
13.11	171, 186	16.25	174	2.20	13, 16, 174,	
13.12	171	16.26	212		176	
13.27	192			3.2	283	
14.23	21	1 Corinthians		3.8	159	
15	24, 28	1.1	163	4.6	279	
15.7	24	1.9	3, 260	5.14	280	
15.22	24	2.1-2	176	5.16-17	280	
15.22-28	24	2.1-16	174	5.25	280	

Index of Biblical (and Other Ancient) References

Ephesians		3.16	20	1 John	
1.10	13	3.17	20	4.1	33
1.14	261	4.6	212		
2.20	159, 212	4.14	170, 204, 222	Jude	
3.6	162	4.14-15	222	3	242, 250
3.15	84	4.16	223		
4.9-13	216, 217	5.17	230	Revelation	
4.9-16	216			1.2	25
4.11	20, 21	2 Timothy		1.9	25
4.11-13	214	1	228	2.29	25
4.11-16	213	3.16-17	57, 287	3.22	25
4.13	12			5.6	247
4.15	256	Titus		12.17	25
4.15-16	162	1.5	21	19.10	13, 22, 25,
4.21	300				39, 60, 192,
4.23	283	Hebrews			195, 258,
5.23	162	1.2	23		291, 304,
5.27	211	2.17	82		310, 311
		3.1-3	227	20.19	254
Philippians		4.15	83		
1.10	267	5.14	262, 264, 276	Apocrypha	
2.5-11	281	6.1-3	225	Wisdom of Solomon	
2.6	281, 296	6.2	217	5.5	171
2.6-8	296	6.12	216		
2.7 2	96	7.23	230	Sirach	
2.7-8	281	9.12	104	1.30	171
2.8	281	10.7	287	19.26	171
2.13	283	11.24	82, 83	48.1	100
3.5	170	11.37	181	48.10	141
3.10	280	13.12	247		
				1 Maccabees	
Colossians		James		11.63	230
1.18	162	4	294		
1.24	162	4.14	294	2 Maccabees	
2.15	76	5.17	100	4.50	230
3.16	307			13.3	230
1 Thessalonians		1 Peter			
5.23	240	1.11	161	4 Maccabees	
				4.10	162
1 Timothy		2 Peter			
3.15	19, 21	1.16	188		

Index of Authors

Agarwal, P.   234
Allport, G.W.   17, 159
Althouse, P.   2, 242
Anderson, A.H.   44, 217
Anthony, M.J.   146
Aquinas, T.   20, 21-22
Aquino, F.D.   213, 263
Archer, K.J.   25, 27-28, 29, 30, 136, 137, 194, 220, 230
Arnold, C.E.   103
Arrington, F.L.   194, 209
Arterbury, A.E.   139, 184, 185-186
Ashbrook, J.B.   66
Ashby, G.W.   76
Athanasius   182, 279
Attridge, H.W.   264
Augustine, D.   41, 42
Aune, D.E.   33, 34, 46, 47, 48, 49, 59, 97, 160, 177
Austin, J.L.   61

Baars, C.W.   82, 83, 184
Balcombe, D.   199, 232
Baldwin, J.G.   89
Barfoot, C.H.   206
Barker, K.   61
Barry, J.D.   79
Baumgarten, A.I.   172
Baumgartner, W.   104
Beitzel, B.J.   117
Benner, D.G.   38
Bergen, R.D.   95
Black, J.   45
Blake, W.   282
Boccaccini, G.   172, 173
Bock, D.L.   135
Bonhoeffer, D.   259, 295, 296, 297
Bosserman, C.   139
Bosworth, D.A.   189, 190, 191
Boyarin, D.   172
Boyer, M.G.   117
Branham, W.M.   54

Brannan, R.   20, 255
Brown, D.R.   128
Brownstein, M.   234
Bruce, F.F.   135
Brueggemann, W.   66-67, 71, 74, 76, 77, 86-87, 93, 94, 98, 99, 100, 101, 106, 114, 117, 118, 121, 122, 124, 126, 127, 259, 269, 297, 302
Bullard, R.A.   100
Burke, D.G.   296, 297
Butler, J.G.,   125, 157

Carpenter, E.   73
Carroll, J.T.   139, 140
Carson, T.   128
Carter, H.   53
Casement, A.   19
Castelo, D.   299, 302
Charlesworth, J.H.   169
Cherry, K.   65
Childs, B.S.   78
Chironna, M.J.   107, 138, 142, 146, 155, 205
Chow, A.   6, 7
Chrysostom, J.   264
Cocksworth, A.   79
Cogan, M.   121
Cohen, G.L.   184
Cohen, J.   64
Cohn, R.L.   101, 118
Cornwall, R.   45
Coulter, D.M.   218
Crenshaw, J.L.   145
Croatto, J.S.   180
Cron, L.   138
Culver, R.D.   86

Davidio, J.F.   158-159
Davies, A.   25, 133, 134, 137
Davila, J.R.   123
Dean, R.J.   275
DeCarvalho, R.J.   15

Index of Authors

DeGroat, C.   18
Delgado, J.   237, 238
Dika, T.R.   107, 108
Dille, S.J.   81
Dimitrova, N.   279
Dunn, J.D.G.   166, 167, 168
Durham, J.I.   75, 77, 78, 80, 83

Eckhardt, J.   34, 52
Edwards, D.M.   71
Ellington, S.A.   25
Elwell, W.A.   117
Engelken, K.   118
Ervin, H.M.   27, 29
Escobar, S.   292
Estes, D.   26
Everts, J.M.   172
Ewart, F.J. 40-41

Farley, L.R.   153
Farnsworth, B.   306
Farrer, A.M.   283
Faupel, D.W.   2, 193
Fee, G.D.   27, 35, 53, 136, 265, 270
Fitzmyer, J.A.   236, 239
Fraser-Thill, R.   81
Freeman, L.   289
Fretheim, T.E.   73, 75, 76, 80, 86, 100
Friebel, K.G.   160
Fuhs, H.F.   122
Fuller, P.   6, 7
Funk, M.M.   271, 307

Gabriel, A.K.   52
Gangel, K.O.   144
Gapp, K.S.   152
Garland, D.E.   245, 246
Gennaro, R.J.   62
Gesenius, W.   114, 275
Gilbrant, T.   262
Gill, K.   40, 41
Gillespie, T.W.   270
Gordon, V.R.   99
Gowan, D.E.   73
Graham, S.J.   264
Greco, F.   183

Green, C.E.W.   29, 30, 50, 281
Green, J.B.   171, 172, 177, 179, 183
Gregory of Nyssa   288
Grenz, S.J.   159
Guzik, D.   31

Hackett, W.C.   107, 108
Hagner, D.A.   297
Hamilton, V.P.   96
Hamon, B.   154
Harkness, G.   262
Harrison, R.K.   95
Hart, K.   293
Hartley, J.E.   91, 125
Hartog, P.A.   19
Hasel, G.   74
Hassler, M.A.   143, 144
Hatton, H.A. 100
Hauser, I.J.   99
Heck, J.D.   116
Heidegger, M.   277
Henriques, G.   11
Henry, M.   291
Henschen, T.   277
Heschel, A.J.   66
Hiller, D.   79
Hocken, P.   9
Holladay, W.L.   113
Hollenweger, W.   42
Huemer, M.   275
Hughes, R.T.   220, 224, 225, 241, 244
Hurst, L.D.   261
Husserl, E.   188
Hutchinson, M.   193

Irenaeus   220
Isacco, A.   95
Iseman, L.   299, 300, 305

James, W.   7, 17, 62, 65, 65-66, 129, 130-131
Jacobsen, D.   43
Jeffrey, D.L.   117, 124
Jipp, J.W.   265
Johns, C.B.   25, 30, 31
Johns, J.D.   28

Johnson, L.T. 16, 59, 139, 140, 143, 150, 151, 154, 155, 156, 157, 161, 162, 163, 164, 165, 171, 173, 176, 180, 181, 184, 186, 192, 289, 291
Johnson, M. 84
Johnson, T.M. 42, 44
Johnson, V. 135
Jones, J.M. 158-159
Josephus, F. 140
Jung, C.G. 17, 18, 19, 62, 82, 148, 149, 254

Kalland, E.S. 92
Kankaanniemi, M. 183
Kärkkäinen, V. 265, 293
Kaufman, G. 191
Keen, C. 261, 262
Keener, C.S. 161, 164
Kellermann, D. 75
Kelly, G.B. 298
Kgatle, M.S. 52-53
King, P. 34
Kirkpatrick, R. 89, 90
Kiteley, D. 193, 196, 197, 198, 199, 200, 201, 204, 205
Kiteley, V. 45, 46, 56, 98, 116, 194, 195, 196, 197, 198, 199, 200, 201, 202, 203, 204, 205-206, 207, 208, 209, 210, 211, 212, 213, 214, 215, 216, 217, 218, 219, 220, 221, 222, 223, 224, 225, 226, 227, 228, 229, 230, 231, 237, 238, 240, 247, 250, 259, 261, 294, 303, 307
Koehler, L. 104
Kohut, H. 17-18
Konkel, A.H. 99, 100, 101
Kuhn, T.S. 173
Kydd, R.A.N. 54-55
Kyle, R. 209

Lackoff, G. 84
Land, S.J. 27, 39, 266
Lasch, C. 15, 18
Lawrence, B.F. 49
Lawson, S. 197
Leithart, P.J. 90, 96, 100, 106, 112, 119, 120

Levine, M.P. 126
Liddell, H.G. 141
Lindbeck, G.A. 31, 32, 53
Lombardo, N.E. 266
Lonergan, B. 262
Longman, T., III 267
Luther, M. 208

Macchia, F.D. 52, 264
Mackinlay, S. 107, 174
Mangum, D. 60-61, 61-62
Marcus, J. 143
Marion, J. 108
Martin, L.R. 29
Martin, P. 18
Maslow, A.H. 12, 15, 16
Mather, H.R.K. 27, 28, 30
Maxon, A.D. 94
Mbiti, T. 219
McAdams, D.P. 44, 81, 82, 85, 174, 183
McCollam, D. 34
McInroy, M.J. 276, 279, 289
McKay, J.W. 25, 29, 56, 57, 58
McKnight, S. 260, 261
McLean, K.C. 44, 85, 174
McLean, M.D. 29
McQueen, L.R. 29
McVey, K.E. 288, 308
Meier, S.A. 88
Menzies, W. 27
Merton, T. 303
Mittelstadt, M.W. 133, 134, 183
Moes, P. 64
Moltmann, J. 285
Mooney, E.F. 187
Moore, R.D. 25, 29, 56, 57, 58, 287
Moran, D. 64
Moreau, A.S. 77
Munzinger, A. 267, 268, 269, 270, 271, 272, 273, 274
Murphy, M. 6, 7

Nagel, T. 62, 63
Nation, G.D. 212
Nesteruk, A.V. 87, 188
Nissinen, M. 38

Index of Authors

Norton, A.   303-304
Nouwen, H.   263, 265

Oden, T.C.   228, 229-230
Oliverio, L.W.   136
O'Loughlin, T.   169
Olsen, D.C.   147
Osborne, G.R.   61
Osborne, K.B.   188
Otto, R.   37
Ozman, A.   138, 231

Pelikan, J.   23, 24
Penn, A.   186
Peterson, B.N.   287
Peterson, E.   92, 259
Philemon, L.   26
Pi, Youguo   178
Polanyi, M.   298
Ponticus, E.   266
Pratt, M.L.   62
Preuss, H.D.   75
Prevot, A.   79
Price, I.M.   88, 89, 93
Pyles, D.   180

Reid, D.G.   242
Reuschling, W.C.   265
Rich, A.D.   270, 271
Ridley, D.S.   14
Roberts-Miller, P.   7
Rogers, E.F.   294
Roszia, S.K.   94
Rotenstreich, N.   66
Ruelas, A.   196, 197, 198, 202, 206
Russell, N.   227
Rutledge, F.   140-141, 275
Ryken, L.   267

Sanford, J.A.   272, 308
Sarna, N.M.   77
Scharmer, O.C.   289
Schlamm, L.   18, 19, 82
Schnabel, E.J.   150, 151, 152, 153, 166, 167, 168, 169, 171, 172, 173, 175
Schneiders, S.M.   66

Scholer, A.A.   14
Scott, R.   141
Seth, A.   254
Shannon, W.H.   268, 269, 300, 302
Sheppard, G.T.   29, 194, 209
Sherman, D.K.   184
Sieler, A.   38
Simpson, C.   310
Slager, D.   100
Smith, C.   34
Smith, G.T.   263
Smith, J.K.A.   43
Smith, J.T.   159
Smith. S.   34
Sokolowski, F.   86
Solc, V.   148
Soulen, R.K.   79
Spittler, R.P.   29
Stamm, J.J.   104
Steinbock, A.J.   107, 108
Stronstad, R.   27, 136
Stuart, D.   136
Swanson, J.   102, 285
Swearingen, D.   55, 56
Swearingen, P.   55, 56
Sweeney, M.A.   101, 104, 105, 128, 129, 130
Symington, A.M.   141, 142

Tadmor, H.   121
Tallis, F.   175
Tam, E.P.C.   127
Taylor and Francis Group   85
Tellinghuisen, D.J.   64
Terruwe, A.A.   82, 83, 184
Thiselton, A.C.   11, 13, 14, 15, 176, 229, 277
Thomas, A.   196
Thomas, J.C.   25, 27, 28, 29
Thornton, S.P.   17
Tilley, T.W.   136
Tillich, P.   282
Torrance, J.B.   283
Tregelles, S.P.   114, 275
Treptow, E.   182
Tsevat, M.   301
Tsumura, D.T.   98

Twist, E.T.   128

Underhill, E.   107, 108, 111

Van Gennep, A.   126
Van Wijk-Bos, J.W.H.   91, 92
Van Winkle, P.   174
Vietz, D.L.   158-159
Volf, M.   159, 280, 284
Von Balthasar, H.U. (Balthasar)   28, 276, 282, 283
Vondey, Wolfgang   43, 264, 276, 278, 292, 304, 308, 310

Waddell, R.   29
Wallace, D.B.   23
Walsh, J.T.   100, 102, 103, 104, 106, 109, 110, 111, 112, 114, 117, 118
Ware, S.L.   206, 207, 250
Warrington, K.   195
Weinandy, T.G.   163

Wenk, M.   80, 81
Wesley, J.   11-12, 33
Widder, W.   60-61, 61-62, 128
Wierwille, J.   7-8
Wilhite, S.J.   40
Wilhoit, J.   144, 267
Williams, J.G.   120, 121
Williams, R.   22, 23, 25, 58
Wills, L.M.   147, 148
Wilson, R.R.   39, 90, 97, 119, 120
Witthof, D.   147
Wolfe, T.   308
Wood, R.C.   163
Wright, T.C.   187, 188

Yong, A.   8, 30, 34, 135, 137, 267, 304

Zipor, M.   122
Zodhiates, S.   151

www.ingramcontent.com/pod-product-compliance
Lightning Source LLC
Chambersburg PA
CBHW071234160426
43196CB00009B/1059